Shiprock At Dawn (5/1972), New Mexico
Photographer: Terry Eiler (1944-)
Compliments National Archives (544392)

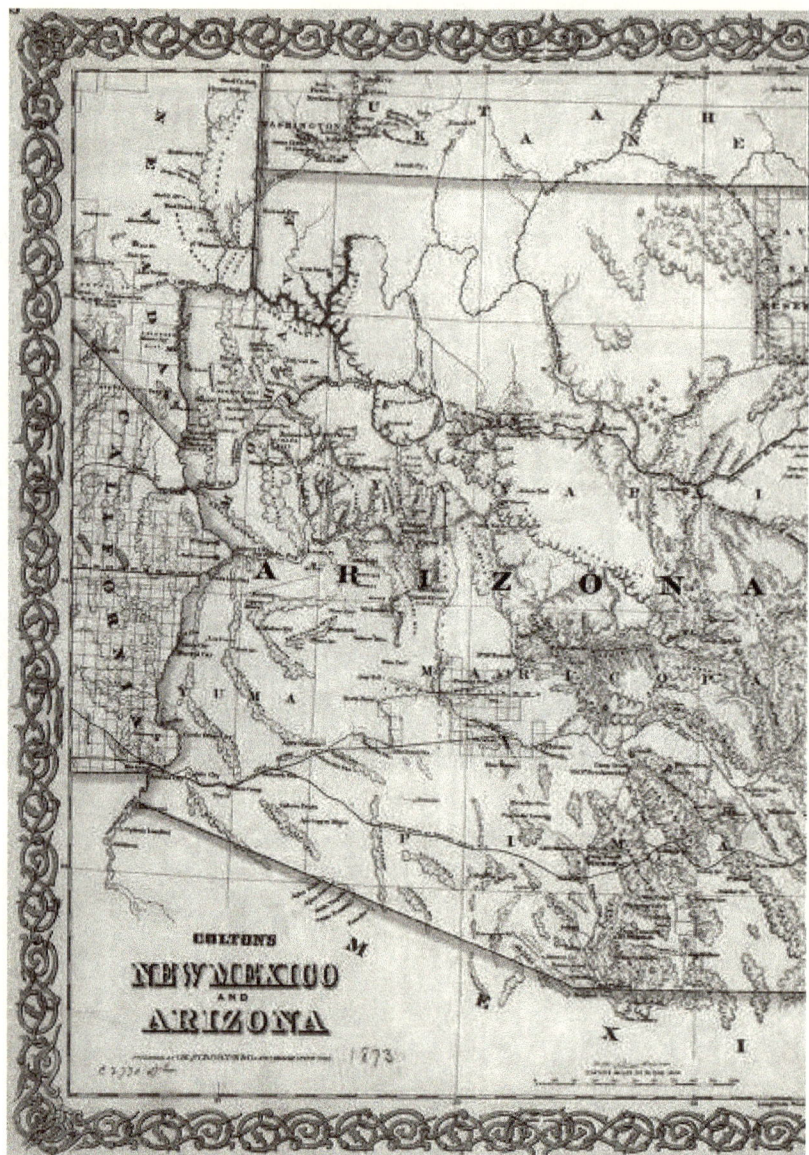

Map of Arizona
S. Augustus Mitchell
Compliments of the

# Other Books and Series by Jeff Bowen

*Compilation of History of the Cherokee Indians and Early History of the Cherokees by Emmet Starr with Combined Full Name Index* (Hardbound & Softbound)

*1901-1907 Native American Census Seneca, Eastern Shawnee, Miami, Modoc, Ottawa, Peoria, Quapaw, and Wyandotte Indians (Under Seneca School, Indian Territory)*

*1932 Census of The Standing Rock Sioux Reservation with Births and Deaths 1924-1932*

*Kiowa, Comanche, Apache, Fort Sill Apache, Wichita, Caddo and Delaware Indians Birth and Death Rolls 1924-1932*

*Census of The Blackfeet, Montana, 1897- 1901 Expanded Edition*

*Eastern Cherokee by Blood, 1906-1910, Volumes I* thru *XIII*

*Choctaw of Mississippi Indian Census 1929-1932 with Births and Deaths 1924-1931 Volume I*
*Choctaw of Mississippi Indian Census 1933, 1934 & 1937, Supplemental Rolls to 1934 & 1935 with Births and Deaths 1932-1938, and Marriages 1936-1938 Volume II*

*Eastern Cherokee Census Cherokee, North Carolina 1930-1939 Census 1930-1931 with Births And Deaths 1924-1931 Taken By Agent L. W. Page Volume I*
*Eastern Cherokee Census Cherokee, North Carolina 1930-1939 Census 1932-1933 with Births And Deaths 1930-1932 Taken By Agent R. L. Spalsbury Volume II*
*Eastern Cherokee Census Cherokee, North Carolina 1930-1939 Census 1934-1937 with Births and Deaths 1925-1938 and Marriages 1936 & 1938 Taken by Agents R. L. Spalsbury And Harold W. Foght Volume III*

*Seminole of Florida Indian Census, 1930-1940 with Birth and Death Records, 1930-1938*

*Texas Cherokees 1820-1839 A Document For Litigation 1921*

*Starr Roll 1894 (Cherokee Payment Rolls) Districts: Canadian, Cooweescoowee, and Delaware Volume One*
*Starr Roll 1894 (Cherokee Payment Rolls) Districts: Flint, Going Snake, and Illinois Volume Two*
*Starr Roll 1894 (Cherokee Payment Rolls) Districts: Saline, Sequoyah, and Tahlequah; Including Orphan Roll Volume Three*

*Cherokee Intruder Cases Dockets of Hearings 1901-1909 Volumes I & II*

*Indian Wills, 1911-1921 Records of the Bureau of Indian Affairs Books One* thru *Seven*
*Native American Wills & Probate Records 1911-1921*

# Other Books and Series by Jeff Bowen

*Turtle Mountain Reservation Chippewa Indians 1932 Census with Births & Deaths, 1924-1932*

*Chickasaw By Blood Enrollment Cards 1898-1914 Volume I thru V*

*Cherokee Descendants East An Index to the Guion Miller Applications Volume I*
*Cherokee Descendants West An Index to the Guion Miller Applications Volume II (A-M)*
*Cherokee Descendants West An Index to the Guion Miller Applications Volume III (N-Z)*

*Applications for Enrollment of Seminole Newborn Freedmen, Act of 1905*

*Eastern Cherokee Census, Cherokee, North Carolina, 1915-1922, Taken by Agent James E. Henderson*      *Volume I (1915-1916)*
                                   *Volume II (1917-1918)*
                                   *Volume III (1919-1920)*
                                   *Volume IV (1921-1922)*

*Eastern Cherokee Census, Cherokee, North Carolina, 1923-1929, Taken by Agent James E. Henderson*      *Volume I (1923-1924)*
                                   *Volume II (1925-1926)*
                                   *Volume III (1927-1929)*

*Complete Delaware Roll of 1898*

*Applications for Enrollment of Seminole Newborn Act of 1905 Volumes I & II*

*North Carolina Eastern Cherokee Indian Census 1898-1899, 1904, 1906, 1909-1912, 1914 Revised and Expanded Edition*

*1932 Hopi and Navajo Native American Census with Birth & Death Rolls (1925-1931) Volume 1 - Hopi*
*1932 Hopi and Navajo Native American Census with Birth & Death Rolls (1930-1932) Volume 2 - Navajo*

*Western Navajo Reservation Navajo, Hopi and Paiute 1933 Census with Birth & Death Rolls 1925-1933*

*Cherokee Citizenship Commission Dockets 1880-1884 and 1887-1889 Volumes I thru V*

*Applications for Enrollment of Chickasaw Newborn Act of 1905 Volumes I thru VII*
*Cherokee Intermarried White 1906 Volume I thru X*

*Applications for Enrollment of Creek Newborn Act of 1905 Volumes I thru XIV*

# Other Books and Series by Jeff Bowen

*Applications for Enrollment of Choctaw Newborn Act of 1905  Volumes I thru XX*

*Choctaw By Blood Enrollment Cards 1898-1914 Volumes I thru XX*

*Oglala Sioux Indians Pine Ridge Reservation 1932 Census  Book I*
*Oglala Sioux Indians Pine Ridge Reservation Birth and Death Rolls 1924-1932*
*Book II*

*Census of the Sioux and Cheyenne Indians of Pine Ridge Agency*
*1896 - 1897  Book I*
*Census of the Sioux and Cheyenne Indians of Pine Ridge Agency*
*1898 - 1899  Book II*

*Northern Cheyenne Tongue River, Montana 1904 - 1932 Census*
*1904-1916 Volume I*
*Northern Cheyenne Tongue River, Montana 1904 - 1932 Census*
*1917-1926 Volume II*
*Northern Cheyenne Tongue River, Montana 1904 - 1932 Census*
*1927-1932 Volume III*

*Sac & Fox - Shawnee Estates 1885-1910 (Under Sac & Fox Agency)*
*Volumes I-VIII*
*Sac & Fox - Shawnee Estates 1920-1924 (Under The Sac & Fox Agency,*
*Oklahoma) & Wills 1889-1924 Volume IX*
*Sac & Fox - Shawnee Deaths, Cemetery, Births, & Marriage Cards (Under The Sac*
*& Fox Agency, Oklahoma) 1853-1933 Volume X*
*Sac & Fox - Shawnee Marriages, Divorces, Estates Log Books Volumes 1 & 2, Log*
*Book Births & Deaths (Under Sac & Fox Agency, Oklahoma)1846-1924 Volume XI*
*Sac & Fox - Shawnee Guardianships Part 1 (Under Sac & Fox Agency, Oklahoma)*
*1892-1909 Volume XII*
*Sac & Fox - Shawnee Guardianships, Part 2 (Under The Sac & Fox Agency,*
*Oklahoma) 1902-1910 Volume XIII*
*Sac & Fox - Shawnee Guardianships, Part 3 (Under The Sac & Fox Agency,*
*Oklahoma) 1906-1914 Volume XIV*

*Census of the Pima, Tohono O'odham (Papago), and Maricopa Indians of the Gila*
*River, Ak Chin & Gila Bend Reservations 1932 with Birth and Death Rolls 1924-*
*1932*

*Identified Mississippi Choctaw Enrollment Cards 1902-1909  Volumes I, II, III*
*Identified Mississippi Choctaw Enrollment Cards' Dawes Packets  1902-1909*
*Volumes IV, V & VI*

*Census of the Northern Navajo, Navajo Reservation, New Mexico, 1930  Volume I*

Visit our website at **www.nativestudy.com** to learn more about these
other books and series by Jeff Bowen

and New Mexico, 1867
(Samuel Augustus). 1792-1868
Library of Congress (G4330 1867 .M5 TIL)

# Census of the Northern Navajo Navajo Reservation, New Mexico, 1931 Volume II

Transcribed By
## Jeff Bowen

NATIVE STUDY
Gallipolis, Ohio
USA

Native Study LLC
Gallipolis, OH
*www.nativestudy.com*




Library of Congress Control Number:   2022919212

ISBN:   978-1-64968-169-0

Bookcover:  Print of Pinion trees in New Mexico,
by George Elbert (1859-1939). Library of Congress
(#2014649341)

Title Page:   Photo of Navajo church near Fort
Wingate, New Mexico, 1873, by John K. Hillers
[1843-1925].  Library of Congress (#2018662099)




*Made in the United States of America.*

This series is dedicated to
Kevin Watson
who would dig to the depths
to investigate a situation.

Conversation with General William Sherman and Samuel Tappan, May 28, 1868

"It was told to us by our forefathers, that we were never to move east of the Rio Grande or west of the San Juan rivers and I think that our coming here has been the cause of so much death among us and our animals."

"I hope to God you will not ask me to go to any other country except my own."

Barboncito,

*The Long Walk The Forced Navajo Exile* by Jennifer Denetdale

v

Navajo girl (circa) 1904

Photographer:  Edward S. Curtis, 1868-1952
Library of Congress (#2006690072)

A typical Navajo Hogan
National Archives (#7003404)

[Copy of the Original Treaty]

# Ratified Indian Treaty 372:
# Navaho (Navajo) - Fort Sumner,
# New Mexico Territory, June 1, 1868

Andrew Johnson,

President of the United States of America,

To all and singular to whom these presents shall come, greeting:

Whereas a Treaty was made and concluded at Fort Sumner, in the Territory of New-Mexico, on the first day of June, in the year of our Lord one thousand eight hundred and sixty-eight, by and between Lieutenant-General W. T. Sherman, and Samuel F. Tappan, commissioners, on the part of the United States, and Barboncito, Armijo, and other Chiefs and Headmen of the Navajo tribe of Indians, on the part of said Indians, and duly authorized thereto by them, which Treaty is in the words and figures following, to wit:

#372

Articles of a Treaty and Agreement made and entered into at Fort Sumner New Mexico on the first day of June 1868, by and between the United States represented by its Commissioners Lieutenant General W. S. Sherman and Colonel Samuel F. Tappan of the one part, and the Navajo Nation or tribe of Indians represented by their Chiefs and Head men duly authorized and empowered to act for the whole people of said Nation or tribe (the names of said chiefs and Head men being hereto subscribed) of the other part, witness:-

## Article. 1

From this day forward all war between the parties to this agreement shall for ever cease. The Government of the United States desires peace, and its honor is hereby pledged to keep it. The Indians desire peace and they now pledge their honor to keep it.

If bad men among the whites or among other people, subject to the authority of the United States, shall commit any wrong upon the person or property of the Indians, the United States will upon proof made to the Agent and forwarded to the Commissioner of Indian Affairs at Washington City proceed at once to cause the offender to be arrested and punished according to the laws of the United States, and also to re-imburse the injured persons for the loss sustained.

If bad men among the Indians shall commit a wrong or depredation upon the person or property of any one, white, black or Indian subject to the authority of the United States and at peace therewith, the Navajo tribe agree that they will on proof made to their Agent, and on notice by him, deliver up the wrong-doer to the United States to be tried and punished according to its laws: and in case they willfully refuse so to do, the person injured shall be reimbursed for his loss from the annuities or other moneys, due or to become due to them under this Treaty, or any others that may be made with the United States. And the President may prescribe such Rules and Regulations for ascertaining damages under this Article as in his judgment may be proper; but no such damage

shall be adjusted and paid until
examined and passed upon by the
Commissioner of Indian Affairs, and
no one sustaining loss whilst violating
or because of his violating the provisions
of this Treaty, or the Laws of the United
States shall be reimbursed therefor.

## Article II

The United States agrees that the
following District of Country to wit—
Bounded on the North by the 37° degree
of North Latitude, south by an east and
west line passing through the site of Old
Fort Defiance in Cañon Bonito, east
by the parallel of longitude which if
prolonged south would pass through
old Fort Lyon, or the Ojo-de-oso, Bear
Spring, and west by a parallel of longitude
about 109° 30' west of Greenwich provided
it embraces the outlet of the Cañon-
de-Chilly, which cañon is to be all
included in this Reservation, shall be, and
the same is hereby set apart for the use

and occupation of the navajo tribe of Indians, And for such other friendly tribes or individual Indians as from time to time they may be willing with the consent of the United States to admit among them; And the United States agrees that no persons except those herein so authorized to do, And except such Officers, soldiers agents, And employés of the Government or of the Indians as may be authorized to enter upon Indian Reservations in discharge of duties imposed by law, or the orders of the President, shall ever be permitted to pass over; settle upon, or reside in the Territory described in this Article.

### Article. III

The United States, agrees to cause to be built at some point within said reservation where timber and water may be convenient the following buildings: a ware-house to cost not exceeding twenty five hundred dollars, an agency building for the residence of the Agent not to cost exceeding three thousand dollars, a.

carpenter shop, and blacksmiths shop not to cost exceeding one thousand dollars each; and a school house and chapel, so soon as a sufficient number of children can be induced to attend school, which shall not cost to exceed five thousand dollars.

## Article IV

The United States agrees, that the agent for the Navajos shall make his home at the agency building, that he shall reside among them and shall keep an office open at all times for the purpose of prompt and diligent inquiry into such matters of complaint by or against the Indians as may be presented for investigation, as also for the faithful discharge of other duties enjoined by law. In all cases of depredation on person or property he shall cause the evidence to be taken in writing and forwarded together with his finding to the Commissioner of Indian affairs

whose decision shall be binding
on the parties to this Treaty.

## Article V

If any individual belonging to said
tribe or legally incorporated with it, being
the head of a family shall desire to
commence farming he shall have the
privilege to select in the presence and with
the assistance of the agent then in
charge a tract of land within said
reservation not exceeding one hundred
and sixty acres in extent, which tract
when so selected, certified and recorded
in the "Land Book" as herein described,
shall cease to be held in common, but
the same may be occupied and held in
the exclusive possession of the person selecting
it, and of his family, so long as he or
they may continue to cultivate it.

Any person over eighteen years of
age, not being the head of a family,
may in like manner, select and cause to
be certified to, him or her for purposes
of cultivation, a quantity of land not

exceeding eighty acres in extent, and
thereupon be entitled to the exclusive
possession of the same as above directed.

For each tract of land so selected
a certificate containing a description
thereof and the name of the person
selecting it, with a certificate endorsed
thereon that the same has been recorded
shall be delivered to the party entitled
to it, by the agent, after the same
shall have been recorded by him,
in a book to be kept in his office,
subject to inspection, which said
book shall be known as the "Navajo
Land Books".

The President may at any time,
order a survey of the reservation, and
when so surveyed, Congress shall
provide for protecting the rights of
said settlers in their improvements,
and may fix the character of the
title held by each. The United States
may pass such laws on the subject
of alienation and descent of property
between the Indians and their descendants
as may be thought proper.

# Article VI

In order to insure the civilization of the Indians entering into this treaty, the necessity of education is admitted, especially of such of them as may be settled on said agricultural parts of this reservation, and they therefore pledge themselves to compel their children male and female between the ages of six and sixteen years, to attend school, and it is hereby made the duty of the agent for said Indians, to see that this stipulation is strictly complied with and the United States agrees that for every thirty children between said ages who can be induced or compelled to attend school a house shall be provided, and a teacher competent to teach the elementary branches of an english education; shall be furnished who will reside among said Indians and faithfully discharge his or her duties as a teacher,

The provisions of this Article to continue for not less than ten years

Struck out
June 2nd

## Article. VII

When the head of a family shall have selected lands and received his certificate as above directed and the agent shall be satisfied that he intends in good faith to commence cultivating the soil for a living, he shall be entitled to receive seeds and agricultural implements for the first year not exceeding in value one hundred dollars, and for each succeeding year he shall continue to farm, for a period of two years, he shall be entitled to receive seeds and implements to the value of twenty five dollars.

# Article. VIII

In lieu of all sums of money or other annuities provided to be paid to the Indians herein named under any treaty or treaties heretofore made, the United States agrees to deliver at the agency house on the reservation herein named on the first day of September of each year for ten years the following articles to wit:

Such articles of clothing — goods — or raw material, in lieu thereof, as the agent may make his estimate for, — not exceeding in value five dollars per Indian — each Indian being encouraged to manufacture their own clothing, blankets &c.; to be furnished with no article which they can manufacture themselves. And, in order that the Commissioner of Indian Affairs may be able to estimate properly for the articles herein named, it shall be the duty of the Agent each year, to forward to him a full and exact census of the Indians, on which the estimate from year to year can be based.

And in addition to the articles herein named, the sum of ten dollars for each person entitled to the beneficial

effects of this treaty, shall be annually
appropriated for a period of ten years
for each person who engages in farming
or mechanical pursuits to be used by
the Commissioner of Indian Affairs in
the purchase of such articles as from
time to time the condition and necessities
of the Indians may indicate to be proper.
And if within the ten years at any time,
it shall appear that the amount of
money needed for clothing, under the article
can be appropriated to better uses for
the Indians named herein. The Commissioner of Indian Affairs may change
the appropriation to other purposes, but
in no event shall the amount of this
appropriation be withdrawn or discontinued
for the period named provided they
remain at peace. And the President
shall annually detail an officer of
the army to be present and attest the
delivery of all the goods herein named
to the Indians, and he shall inspect and
report on the quantity and quality of
the goods and the manner of their delivery

# Article IX

In consideration of the advantages and benefits conferred by this Treaty, and the many pledges of friendship by the United States, the tribes who are parties to this agreement, hereby stipulate that they will relinquish all right to occupy any Territory outside their reservation, as herein defined, but retain the right to hunt on any unoccupied lands contiguous to their reservation, so long as the large game may range thereon in such numbers as to justify the chase, and they the said Indians further expressly agree:

1st That they will make no opposition to the construction of rail-roads now being built or hereafter to be built across the continent

2nd. That they will not interfere with the peaceful construction of any railroad, not passing over their reservation as herein defined

3rd. That they will not attack any persons at home or travelling, nor molest or disturb any wagon trains, coaches, mules or cattle belonging to the people of the United States, or to persons friendly therewith

4th That they will never capture, or
carry off from the settlements women or
children

5th They will never kill or scalp white
men nor attempt to do them harm

6th They will not in future oppose
the construction of rail-roads, wagon
roads, mail stations or other works of
utility or necessity which may be ordered
or permitted by the laws of the united
States; But should such roads or other
works be constructed on the lands
of their reservation the government will
pay the tribe whatever amount of damage
may be assessed by three disinterested
Commissioners to be appointed by the
President for that purpose, one of said
Commissioners to be a Chief or Head
man of the tribe

7th They will make no opposition
to the military posts or roads now
established, or that may be established
not in violation of treaties heretofore
made or hereafter to be made with
any of the Indian tribes

## Article X

No future treaty for the cession of any portion or part of the reservation herein described, which may be held in common, shall be of any validity or force against said Indians, unless agreed to and executed by at least three-fourths of all the adult male Indians occupying or interested in the same; and no cession by the tribe shall be understood or construed in such manner as to deprive without his consent any individual member of the tribe of his rights to any tract of land selected by him as provided in Article ____ of this treaty.

## Article XI

The Navajos also hereby agree that at any time after the signing of these presents they will proceed in such manner as may be required of them by the agent, or by the officer charged with their removal to the reservation herein

provided for, the United States paying for
their subsistence en-route, and providing
a reasonable amount of transportation
for the sick and feeble

## Article XII

It is further agreed by and between
the parties to this agreement; that the
sum of one hundred and fifty thousand
dollars appropriated or to be appropriated
shall be disbursed as follows, subject
to any conditions provided in the law
to wit:

1st The actual cost of the removal
of the tribe from the Bosque Redondo
Reservation to the reservation say Fifty
thousand dollars

2nd: The purchase of fifteen thousand
sheep and goats at a cost not to exceed
Thirty thousand dollars

3rd: The purchase of five hundred
beef cattle and a million pounds of
corn, to be collected and held at the
military post nearest the reservation.
subject to the orders of the Agent for

the relief of the needy during the coming winter

4th. The balance if any of the appropriation to be invested for the maintenance of the Indians pending their removal in such manner as the Agent who is with them may determine.

5th The removal of this tribe to be made under the supreme control and direction of the military Commander of the Territory of New Mexico, And when completed the management of the tribe to revert to the proper agent.

## Article XVIII

The tribes herein named by their representatives, parties to this Treaty agree to make the reservation herein described their permanent home, and they will not as a tribe make any permanent settlement elsewhere — reserving the right to hunt on

the lands adjoining the said reservation
formerly called theirs - subject to the
modifications named in this treaty and
the orders of the Commander of the
Department in which said reservation
may be for the time being And it is
further agreed and understood by the
parties to this treaty that if any Navajo
Indian or Indians shall leave the
reservation herein described to settle
elsewhere he or they shall forfeit all
the rights privileges and annuities
conferred by the terms of this treaty
And it is further agreed by the parties
to this treaty - that they will do all
they can to induce Indians now away
from reservations set apart for the
exclusive use and occupation of the
Indians - leading a nomadic life -
or engaged in war against the people
of the United States - to abandon such
a life and settle permanently in one
of the territorial reservations set apart
for the exclusive use and occupation of
the Indians.

In testimony of all which the
said parties have hereunto on this
the first day of June eighteen hundred
and sixty eight at Fort Sumner in

the Territory of New Mexico set their
hands and seals.


W. T. Sherman
St Gen.
                    Indian Peace Commissioner
S. F. Tappan
                    Indian Peace Commissioner




Barboncito    Chief        his X mark
Delgadito                  his X mark
Armijo                     his X mark
    Delgado
Manuelito                  his X mark
Largo                      his X mark
Herrero                    his X mark
Chiqueto                   his X mark
Muerto de Hombre           his X mark
Hombro                     his X mark
Narbono                    his X mark
Narbono  segundo           his X mark
Ganado  Mucho              his X mark
                    Council

| | |
|---|---|
| Riguo | his X mark |
| Juan Martin | his X mark |
| Jurginto | his X mark |
| Grande | his X mark |
| Incetinito | his X mark |
| Muchachos Mucho | his X mark |
| Chiqueto Segundo | his X mark |
| Cabello Amarillo | his X mark |
| Francisco | his X mark |
| Toririo | his X mark |
| Desdendado | his X mark |
| Juan | his X mark |
| Guero | his X mark |
| Gugadones | his X mark |
| Cabason | his X mark |
| Barbon Segundo | his X mark |
| Cabares Colorados | his X mark |

Attest:

Geo. W. Getty
Col 37th Infy
Bt Maj Genl. U.S.A.

B. S. Roberts
Bt Brig Genl USA
& Col 3d Cavy

Morris McKee
Bt Lt Colo. Surgeon U.S.A.

Theo. H. Dodd
U.S. Indian agt for Navajos

Chas. McClure
Bt. Maj. & C S. U.S.A.

James F. Weeds
Bvt Maj & Asst Surg U.S.A.

P. C. Sutherland
Interpreter
William Vaux,
Chaplain U.S.A.

xxxi

And whereas, the said Treaty
having been submitted to the
Senate of the United States for
its Constitutional action thereon,
the Senate did, on the twenty-
fifth day of July, one thousand
eight hundred and sixty-eight,
advise and consent to the
ratification of the same, by a
resolution in the words and
figures following, to wit:

Now, therefore, be it known that I, Andrew Johnson, President of the United States of America, do, in pursuance of the advice and consent of the Senate, as expressed in its resolution of the twenty-fifth of July, one thousand eight hundred and sixty-eight, accept, ratify, and confirm the said Treaty.

In testimony whereof I have hereto signed my name, and caused the seal of the United States to be affixed.

Done at the City of Washington this twelfth day of August, in the year of our Lord one thousand eight hundred and sixty-eight, and of the Independence of the United States of America the ninety-third.

Andrew Johnson

By the President:
W. Hunter.
Acting Secretary of State.

[Transcription of the Original Treaty]

Ratified Indian Treaty 372:
Navaho (Navajo) - Fort Sumner,
New Mexico Territory, June 1, 1868

Andrew Johnson,

President of the United States of America,

To all and singular to whom these presents shall come, greeting:

Whereas a Treaty was mad and concluded at Fort Sumner, in the Territory of New Mexico, on the first day of June, in the year of our Lord one thousand eight hundred and sixty-eight, by and between Lieutenant General W. T. Sherman, and Samuel F. Tappan, Commissioner, on the part of the United States, and Barboncito, Armijo, and other Chiefs and Headmen of the Navajo tribe of Indians, on the part of said Indians, and duly authorized thereto by them, which Treaty is in the words and figures following, to wit:

Articles of a Treaty and Agreement made and entered into at Fort Sumner New Mexico on the first day of June 1868, by and between the United States represented by its Commissioners Lieutenant General W. T. Sherman and Colonel Samuel F. Tappan of the one part, and the Navajo Nation or tribe of Indians represented by their Chiefs and Head men duly authorized and empowered to act for the whole people of said Nation or tribe (the names of said Chiefs and Head men being hereto subscribed) on the other part, witness:-

Article I

From this day forward all war between the parties to the agreement shall for ever cease. The Government of the United States desires peace, and its honor is hereby pledged to keep it. The Indians desire peace and they now pledge their honor to keep it.

If bad men among the whites or among other people, subject to the authority of the United States shall commit any wrong upon the person or property of the Indians, the United States will upon proof made to the Agent and forwarded to the Commissioner of Indian Affairs at Washington City proceed at once to cause the offender to be arrested and punished according to the laws of the United States, and also to re-imburse the injured persons for the loss sustained.

If bad men among the Indians shall commit a wrong or depredation upon the person or property of any one, white, black or Indian subject to the authority of the United States and at peace therewith, the Navajo tribe agree that they will on proof made to their agent, and on notice by him, deliver up the wrong-doer to the United States to be tried and punished according to its laws: and in case they willfully refuse so to do, the person injured shall be reimbursed for his loss from the annuities or other moneys, due or to become due to them under this Treaty, or any others that may be made with the United States. And the President may prescribe such Rules and Regulations for ascertaining damages under this Article as in his judgment may be proper; but no such damage shall be adjusted and paid until examined and passed upon by the Commissioner of Indian Affairs, and no one sustaining loss whilst violating or because of his violating the provisions of this Treaty, or the Laws of the United States shall be reimbursed therefor.

### Article II

The United States agrees that the following District of Country to wit-

Bounded on the north by the 37 degree of North Latitude, south by an east and west line passing through the site of Old Fort Defiance in Canon[sic] Bonito, east by the parallel of longitude which if prolonged south would pass through old Fort Lyon, or the Ojo-de-oso, Bear Spring, and west by a parallel of longitude about 109 degree 30' west of Greenwich provided it embraces the outlet of the Canon-de-chilly, which canon is to be all included in this Reservation, shall be, and the same is hereby set apart for the use and occupation of the Navajo tribe of Indians, and for such other friendly tribes or individual Indians as from time to time they may be willing with the consent of the United States to admit among them; and the United States agrees that no persons except those herein so authorized to do, and except such officers, soldiers agents, and employe's[sic] of the Government or of the Indians as may be authorized to enter upon Indian Reservations in discharge of duties imposed by law, or the orders of the President, shall ever be permitted to pass over; settle upon, or reside in the Territory described in this Article.

### Article III

The United States, agrees to cause to be built at some point within said reservation where timber and water may be convenient the following buildings: a ware-house to cost not exceeding twenty five hundred dollars, and agency building for the residence of the Agent not to cost exceeding three thousand dollars, a carpenter shop, and blacksmith shop not to cost exceeding one thousand dollars each; and a school house and chapel, so soon as a sufficient number of children can be induced to attend school, which shall not cost to exceed five thousand dollars.

## Article IV

The United States agrees, that the Agent for the Navajos shall make his home at the Agency building, that he shall reside among them and shall keep an office open at all times for the purpose of prompt and diligent inquiry into such matters of complaint by or against the Indians as may be presented for investigation, as also for the faithful discharge of other duties enjoined by law. In all cases of depredation on person or property he shall cause the evidence to be taken in writing and forwarded together with his finding to the Commissioner of Indian Affairs whose decision shall be binding on the parties to this Treaty.

## Article V

If any individual belonging to said tribe or legally incorporated with it, being the head of a family shall desire to commence farming he shall have the privilege to select in the presence and with the assistance of the agent then in charge a tract of land within said reservation not exceeding one hundred and sixty acres in extent, which tract when so selected, certified and recorded in the "Land Book" as herein described, shall cease to be held in common, but the same may be occupied and held in the exclusive possession of the person selecting it, and of his family, so long as he or they may continue to cultivate it.

Any person over eighteen years of age, not being the head of a family, may in like manner, select and cause to be certified to, him or her, for purposes of cultivation, a quantity of land not exceeding eighty acres in extent, and thereupon be entitled to the exclusive possession of the same as above directed.

For each tract of land so selected a certificate containing a description thereof and the name of the person selecting it, with a certificate endorsed thereon that the same has been recorded shall be delivered to the party entitled to it, by the agent, after the same shall have been recorded by him, in a book to be kept in his office, subject to inspection, which said book shall be known as the "Navajo Land Book".

The President may at any time, order a survey of the reservation, and, when so surveyed, Congress shall provide for protecting the rights of said settlers in their improvements, and may fit the character of the title held by each. The United States may pass such laws on the subject of alienation and descent of property between the Indians and their descendants as may be thought proper.

## Article VI

In order to insure the civilization of the Indians entering into this treaty, the necessity of education is admitted, especially of such of them as may be settled on said agricultural parts of this reservation, and they therefore pledge themselves to compel their children male and female between the ages of six and sixteen years, to attend school, and it is hereby made the duty of the agent for said Indians, to see that this stipulation is strictly complied with and the United States agrees that for every thirty children between said ages who can be induced or compelled to attend school a house shall be provided, and a teacher competent to teach the elementary branches of an english[sic] education, shall be furnished who will reside among said Indians and faithfully discharge his or her duties as a teacher.

The provisions of this article to continue for not less than ten years.

## Article VII

When the head of a family shall have selected lands and received his certificate as above directed and the agent shall be satisfied that he intends in good faith to commence cultivating the soil for a living, he shall be entitled to receive seeds and agricultural implements for the first year not exceeding in value one hundred dollars, and for each succeeding year he shall continue to farm, for a period of two years, he shall be entitled to receive seeds and implements to the value of twenty five dollars.

## Article VIII

In lieu of all sums of money or other annuities provided to be paid to the Indians herein named under any treaty or treaties heretofore made, the United States agrees to deliver at the agency house on the reservation herein named on the first day of September of each year for ten years the following articles to wit:

Such articles of clothing - goods - or raw material in lieu thereof as the agent may make his estimate for, - not exceeding in value five dollars per Indian - each Indian being encouraged to manufacture their own clothing, blankets &c; to be furnished with no article which they can manufacture themselves. And, in order that the Commissioner of Indian Affairs may be able to estimate properly for the articles herein named, it shall be the duty of the Agent each year, to forward to him a full and exact census of the Indians, on which the estimate from year to year can be based.

And in addition to the articles herein named, the sum of ten dollars for each person entitled to the beneficial effects of this treaty, shall be annually appropriated for a period of ten years for each person who engages in farming or mechanical pursuits to be used by the Commissioner of Indian Affairs in the purchase of such articles as from time to time the condition and necessities of the Indians may indicate to be proper, and if within the ten years at any time, it shall appear that the amount of money needed for clothing, under the article can be appropriated to better uses for the Indians named herein. The Commissioner of Indian Affairs may change the appropriation to other purposes, but in no event shall the amount of this appropriation be withdrawn or discontinued for the period named provided they remain at peace. And the President shall annually detail an officer of the Army to be present and attest the delivery of all the goods herein named to the Indians, and he shall inspect and report on the quantity and quality of the goods and the manner of their delivery.

Article IX

In consideration of the advantages and benefits conferred by this Treaty, and the many pledges of friendship by the United States, the tribes who are parties to this agreement, hereby stipulate that they will relinquish all right to occupy any Territory outside their reservation, as herein defined, but retain the right to hunt on any unoccupied lands contiguous to their reservation, so long as the large game may range thereon in such numbers as to justify the chase, and they the said Indians further expressly agree:

1st. That they will make no opposition to the construction of rail-roads now being built or hereafter to be built across the continent.

2nd. That they will not interfere with the peaceful construction of any rail-road, not passing over their reservation as herein defined.

3rd. That they will not attack any persons at home or travelling, nor molest or disturb any wagon trains, coaches, mules or cattle belonging to the people of the United States, or to persons friendly therewith.

4th. That they will never capture, or carry off from the settlements women or children.

5th. They will never kill or scalp white men nor attempt to do them harm.

6th. They will not in future oppose the construction of rail-roads, wagon roads, mail stations or other works of utility or necessity which may be ordered or permitted by the laws of the United States; But should such roads or other works be constructed on the lands of their reservation the government will pay the tribe whatever amount of damage may be assessed by three disinterested Commissioners to be appointed by the President for that purpose, one of said Commissioners to be a Chief or Head man of the tribe.

7th. They will make no opposition to the military posts or roads now established, or that may be established not in violation of treaties heretofore made or hereafter to be made with any of the Indian tribes.


## Article X

No future treaty for the cession of any portion or part of the reservation herein described, which may be held in common, shall be of any validity or force against said Indians, unless agreed to any executed by at least three-fourths of all the adult male Indians occupying or interested in the same, and no cession by the tribe shall be understood or construed in such manner as to deprive without his consent any individual member of the tribe of his rights to any tract of land selected by him as provided in Article       of this treaty.

## Article XI

The Navajos also hereby agree that at any time after the signing of these presents they will proceed in such manner as may be required of them by the agent, or by the officer charged with their removal to the reservation herein.

## Article XII

It is further agreed by and between the parties to this agreement, that the sum of one hundred and fifty thousand dollars appropriated or to be appropriated shall be disbursed as follows, subject to any conditions provided in the law to wit:

1st. The actual cost of the removal of the tribe from the Bosque Redondo Reservation to the reservation say Fifty thousand dollars.

2nd. The purchase of fifteen thousand sheep and goats at a cost not to exceed Thirty thousand dollars.

3rd. The purchase of five hundred beef cattle and a million pounds of corn, to be collected and held at the military post nearest the reservation, subject to the orders of the Agent for the relief of the needy during the coming winter.

4th. The balance of any of the appropriation to be invested for the maintenance of the Indians pending their removal in such manner as the Agent who is with them may determine.

5th. The removal of this tribe to be made under the supreme control and direction of the Military Commander of the Territory of New Mexico, and when completed the management of the tribe to revert to the proper agent.

## Article XIII

The tribes herein named by their representatives, parties to this Treaty agree to make the reservation herein described their permanent home, and they will not as a tribe make any permanent settlement elsewhere - reserving the right to hunt on the lands adjoining the said reservation formerly called theirs - subject to the modifications named in this treaty and the orders of the Commander of the Department in which said reservation may be for the time being and it is further agreed and understood by the parties to this treaty that if any Navajo Indian or Indians shall leave the reservation herein described to settle elsewhere he or they shall forfeit all the rights privileges and annuities conferred by the terms of this treaty and it is further agreed by the parties of this treaty - that they will do all they can to induce Indians now away from reservations set apart for the exclusive use and occupation of the Indians - leading a nomadic life - or engaged in war against the people of the United States - to abandon such a life and settle permanently in one of the territorial reservations set apart for the exclusive use and occupation of the Indians.

In testimony of all which the said parties have hereunto on this the first day of June eighteen hundred and sixty eight at Fort Sumner in the Territory of New Mexico set their hands and seals.

> W.T. Sherman
> Lt. Genl.
>    Indian Peace Commissioner
> S.F. Tappan
>    Indian Peace Commissioner

| | |
|---|---|
| Barboncito   Chief | his x mark |
| ~~Delgadito~~ | ~~his x mark~~ |
| Armijo | his x mark |
| Delgado | |
| Manuelito | his x mark |
| Largo | his x mark |
| Herrero | his x mark |
| Chiqueto | his x mark |
| Muerto de Hombre | his x mark |
| Hombro | his x mark |
| Narbono | his x mark |
| Narbono Segundo | his x mark |
| Ganado Mucho | his x mark |
|    Council | |
| | |
| Riquo | his x mark |
| Juan Martin | his x mark |
| Serginto | his x mark |
| Grande | his x mark |
| Inoetenito | his x mark |
| Muchachos Mucho | his x mark |
| Chiqueto Segundo | his x mark |
| Cabello Amarillo | his x mark |

| Francisco | his x mark |
| Torivio | his x mark |
| Desdendado | his x mark |
| Juan | his x mark |
| Guero | his x mark |
| Gugadore | his x mark |
| Cabason | his x mark |
| Barbon Segundo | his x mark |
| Cabares Colorados | his x mark |

Attest:

Geo. W. Getty
    Col. 37th Infy
        Bt. Maj. Genl. U.S.A.
B. S. Roberts,
    Bt. Brg. Genl U.S.A.
        Lt. Col. 3rd Cavy.
J. Cooper McKee,
    Bt. Lt. Col. Surgeon U.S.A.
Theo. H. Dodd,
    U. S. Indian Agt for Navajos.
Chas. McClure,
    Bt. Maj. & C.S. U.S.A.
James F. Weeds,
    Bt. Maj. & Asst. Surg. U.S.A.
J. C. Sutherland,
    Interpreter.
William Vaux,
    Chaplain U.S.A.


And whereas, the said Treaty having been submitted to the Senate of the United States for its Constitutional action thereon, the Senate did, on the twenty-fifth day of July, one thousand eight hundred and sixty-eight, advise and consent to the ratification of the same, by a resolution in the words and figures following, to wit:


In Executive Session,

Senate of the United States

July 25, 1868.

Resolved, two thirds of the Senators present concurring, that the Senate advise and consent to the ratification of the Treaty between the United States and the Navajo Indians, concluded at Fort Sumner, New Mexico, on the first day of June, 1868.

Attest:

Geo. C. Gorham
Secretary
by   W. J. McDonald
Chief Clerk

Now, therefore, be it known that I, Andrew Johnson, President of the United States of America, do, in pursuance of the advice and consent of the Senate, as expressed in its resolution of the twenty-fifth of July, one thousand eight hundred and sixty-eight, accept, ratify, and confirm the said Treaty.

In testimony whereof I have hereto signed my name, and caused the seal of the United States to be affixed.

Done at the City of Washington this twelfth day of August, in the year of our Lord one thousand eight hundred and sixty-eight, and of the Independence of the United States of America the ninety-third.

Andrew Johnson

By the President:

W Hunter
Acting Secretary of State.

DEPARTMENT OF THE INTERIOR,

Washington, August 4" 1868.

Dear Sir,

Has the treaty concluded with the Navajoe[sic] Indians, by Lt. Genl. Sherman and Sam$^l$ F. Tappan Commissioners, reached the State Dept.  If so when can it be proclaimed?

Yours very truly

A S H White

Actg Chf Clk


R. S. Chew Esq

Chf Clk

Dept of State.

#372.

Rec 18. Aug.

## DEPARTMENT OF THE INTERIOR.
### Office of
### Indian Affairs.
Washington, D. C.  Aug. 18<sup>th</sup> 1868.

Sir

    Will you please furnish for the use of this office, six copies of each of the following named treaties, ratified at the last session of the Senate, if the same have been printed.

| | |
|---|---|
| Pottowatomie[sic] | Feb. 27" 1867 #362 |
| Cheyenne & Arapahoe | Oct. 28"  "  #366 |
| Kiowa Comanche & Apache | "  21"  "  #365 |
| Kiowa & Comanche | "  24"  "  #364 |
| Crows | May  7" 1868 #370 |
| Northern Cheyenne and) Arapahoes  ) | "  10"  "  #371 |
| Navajoes | June 20"  "  #372 |

Very respectfully
Your Obd't. Serv't.
A. G. Taylor
Commissioner

Hon W<sup>m</sup> Hunter
    Asst. Sec'y. of State.

#372.

Department of State,

Washington  September 3. 1868.

Hon Orville H Browning

     Secretary of the Interior.

Sir:

I have the honor to transmit, herewith, for the use of the Department of the Interior, 250 copies of each of the following named Treaties with Indians, to wit:

Treaty with the Crows of May 7. 1868.  #379

    "    "    "  Navajos of June 1. 1868.  #372

    "    "    "  Cheyennes & Arapahoes of October 28. 1867  #366

    Be pleased to acknowledge their receipt

I am your obedient servant

William H Seward

#372.

# INTRODUCTION
## "The Long Walk"

Historian Hampton Sides worded it the best in describing what the government, General Carleton and Kit Carson had done to the Navajo in putting them on a path to their own, Trail of Tears and many separate forced marches to Bosque Redondo. On page 495 of *Blood and Thunder*, he quotes General William Tecumseh Sherman who was someone that had seen every misery available to humankind after living through the American Civil War, "Sherman was no softhearted advocate for the Indians, but he could see that the reservation was an abject failure, that the Navajos were despondent and the farms fallow. "I found the Bosque a mere spot of grass in the midst of a wild desert," He later wrote, "and that the Navajos had sunk into a condition of absolute poverty and despair."

Most people think about the Navajo as a friendly people who have lived peacefully their whole lives through with close-knit families and wonderful cultural tradition and that they have always made every attempt to live peacefully as well as productively among the mountains of the Southwest for as long as one can remember. During the middle of the 19th century the Navajo had already been in the Southwest for at least 400 years. During the 16th century as the Spanish began making contact with them they found that the Navajo were both hunters and noted agriculturalists.

Thus the Navajo name and connotation, people with planted fields; from Webster literally, "arroyo with planted fields". They became a people that lived a stable life with a seminomadic background through hunting, farming, and raising livestock. But it seems these intelligent diverse people would many times over fall victim to those that felt they deserved their share of someone else's hard work. A big part of this introduction bears witness to the suffering of a people; the Navajo, but first understand they had happy productive lives before Bosque Redondo and after Bosque Redondo. Two books written by Walter Dyk, first; *Son of Old Man Hat A Navaho Autobiography* (1938), republished in 1966, [Lefthanded], an ethological study and story personally told to Dyk and transcribed by him about the very detailed life of a Navajo man from childhood to adulthood; then second in book two, *Left Handed A Navajo Autobiography* (1980) *Sequel to the Anthropological Study, Son of Old Man Hat*, by Walter and Ruth Dyk. From the blurb on the back of the first book Dyk describes it the best. "ANTHROPOLOGY *Son Of Old Man Hat* is the autobiography of a Navaho Indian from childhood to maturity. With a simplicity as disarming as it is frank, it tells of his birth in the spring "when the cottonwood leaves were about the size of my thumbnail," of how he first shared family tasks by guarding the sheep near the hogan, of his sexual awakening. As he grows older, into the story come accounts of life in the open, of nomadic cattle-raising, farming, trading, communal enterprises, tribal dances and ceremonies, love-making and marriage.

Free though it is, it is a life founded upon principal: as Son Of Old Man Hat grows in understanding as well as in stature, the accumulated wisdom of his race is made known to him. He learns the necessity of honesty, foresightedness, self-discipline."

You actually, by reading both books, feel the Navajo culture and who they were before and after, The Long Walk. Almost reasoning in your own heart they would have been just fine if only left alone. The researcher of their Navajo roots needs to understand the responsibility to themselves they need to fulfill by reading these two books that hold their very Navajo being and culture so they can feel who they are rather than just search out a name within these pages. This introduction isn't only about the negative impact the white- Europeans made upon a Native people but it is a recommendation of pages that can be read to discover who you are....

The basis of real trouble began with the Spanish then the Mexicans and eventually the arrival of the U.S. Military and afterward gathering a volunteer army of Mexicans, or then known as New Mexicans, the Navajo's original nemesis. This quote seems to point out a consistent historical approval of legalized and accepted robbery and victimization of the Navajo people making it open season on their women, children and livestock and very lives in general, "By 1720 the Spaniards managed to arrange an uneasy peace with the Navajos. By this time the Indians had acquired livestock to supplement their farming endeavors, and could subsist reasonably well without raiding. Moreover, the Spaniards had conducted several punitive expeditions during which they captured Navajo women and children whom they took back to the Rio Grande villages. Here the captives served as laborers or household servants. The peace, however, did not last.
In the 1750's the Spanish settlers received land grants and began invading Navajo country in northwestern New Mexico. The Indians, in turn, started stealing livestock, and another series of military expeditions followed. Navajo raids and depredations increased, and many settlers abandoned their isolated ranches. In 1786 Governor Juan Bautista de Anza of New Mexico reached an agreement with the Navajos. Indian farmlands in the disputed region would be protected, provided that the Navajos did not molest Spanish livestock. In general, both parties observed the treaty, and within a decade the New Mexicans regarded the Navajos as wealthy settled people. The Indians raised extensive crops of corn and wheat, and possessed enormous flocks of sheep, as well as herds of cattle and horses.
After 1800, New Mexicans again attempted to extend their holdings into Navajoland – and again the Indians retaliated. Spanish troops took the field, and in January of 1805 Antonio Narbona's soldiers inflicted a defeat on the Navajos in Canyon de Chelly. Although a paper peace followed, lasting nearly twenty years, the Navajos increasingly placed a greater importance on raiding and warfare in their culture. Repeatedly they seized Mexican women and children, and a pattern of Navajo—New Mexican intermarriage developed. By the 1820's the Navajos were the

most feared Indians of the Southwest. Warfare and raiding now had evolved into a way of life.

The Mexican government, which came into power in 1821, continued the old Spanish treaty system with the Navajos. The Indians, however, were aware of the military weakness of the frontier governors. Whenever a Mexican army campaigned against the Indians, they quickly pleaded for peace, and the Mexicans would accept. Treaty followed treaty, with no enduring peace. Then, suddenly, the Mexicans departed, and a new type of white man came on the scene.

In 1846 an American army under Brigadier General Stephen W. Kearny took control in New Mexico. The new conquerors adopted the old Spanish Mexican policies of expeditions and treaties, and, like their predecessors, had no success in securing peace."[1]

The quotes above only show the Navajos as prosperous for centuries as farmers and entrepreneurs till another culture appears to rob the prosperous and make them defend themselves. The only trouble with this is practically nobody knows about the enormous suffering the Navajo endured for no reason at all during earlier periods then into the late 1860's. The day that the American military got out of the Native American business was a blessing.

Think about those last few words. American military-Native American. Isn't it interesting that the American government would ride down on an AMERICAN Indian tribe to teach them to do what they were already doing. Expose them to their natural enemies, then in the name of all things good destroy their way of life until they couldn't feed themselves or live peacefully. Despite others that thought they knew better the Navajo endured.

Again the military would be responsible for the death of many which is an understatement considering the sufferings the Navajo as well as other surrounding tribes would go through because of two main characters in this awful story. Colonel Christopher "Kit" Carson and Major General James H. Carleton and their creation of a nightmare called Bosque Redondo and the Long Walk. There will be no attempt to position this article or introduction with exact chronological order while mentioning incidental circumstances but the attempt will be made to layout the cause behind the actions involved during this Navajo history.

Carleton would assume his new assignment in the New Mexico Territory with zeal and cruelty unbeknownst to him during the fall of 1862. He may have thought he was on the right side of history but he wasn't. This isn't to say the Navajo didn't have other tribal conflicts or trouble with their young men or not have to fight for what they felt were encroachments within their borders, by many. But by nature they were a pastoral people, herdsmen, farmers, hunters, gatherers and yet warriors. They seemed to be learned from their very beginnings, wise and extremely adaptive....

---

[1] The Army and the Navajo; Pg. 3-4; Para. 3-8.

They had no choice but to follow the warrior mentality with the Spanish first, then the New Mexican or Mexican government in Mexico City. The U.S. Military circa: 1846 again had walked into a 50-year war between the Navajo and New Mexicans. The Americans seemed more concerned with conquering an Indian tribe by treaty and being told by the New Mexicans that the Navajo were the problem rather than notice it was the Navajo who were being violated. The Navajo like anyone would fight if their woman and children daily were being kidnapped and put into slavery; their animals stolen and slaughtered. If common sense were used at the time, anyone could see the Navajo were extremely productive people. They owned hundreds of thousands of animals; sheep, horses, cattle, goats. They were a pastoral people, as well as agricultural geniuses with thousands of acres of wheat, corn, beans, pumpkins, melons and huge lush peach orchards that showered the human eye with the beauty of Mother Nature at every turn. Hardly the activity of raiders and killers. But soon the oppressed.

Even clear into 1861 twelve years later with the Civil War in the East and soldiers choosing their allegiances the Texans were moving on New Mexico with the desire of defeating the Union forces. The Navajo again being thrust to the back of the line, while being blamed for any negative act by the very same instigators and con-artists with premeditation and evil in their hearts. Caught between many fires and the greed of so many. Burned at every turn by those wanting power, land and money. They were caught in the deceptive practices of varying whites seeing dollar signs; government, Mormons, crooked traders, misplaced loyalties and relentless thieves and murderers.

Except for one man in 1861 left with the responsibility of trying to understand what the Navajo were enduring, "Colonel Edward R.S. Canby, Commander of the Department of New Mexico. A veteran officer stationed in the West since 1857, Canby had commanded the most recent punitive expedition against the Navajos during the fall and winter of 1860-61. In February, 1861, he succeeded in obtaining the promises of twenty-four Navajo headmen to control their lawless members and to confine the movements of all their people to an area far to the west of white settlement. Then from Santa Fe came a directive ordering the abandonment of his post in the Navajo country and the transfer of most of his men to other duty in the East. As the secession crisis deepened his southern colleagues one by one resigned and defected to the Confederacy, and Canby soon found himself the senior officer in the Department. On June 11, 1861, Colonel W.W. Loring, who had assumed command of the Department only the previous March, departed for Texas leaving the command in Canby's hands. At the time Canby took command, the Mesilla Valley in southern New Mexico was occupied by the Confederate force from Texas. Most of his attention was necessarily directed to this menace, but he did not ignore the signs of growing Indian restlessness in the frontier areas. Throughout the summer of 1861

Canby addressed numerous requests to the Territorial Governor urging him to raise volunteer companies for service against both the Texans and the Indians. At the same time he cautioned that unless the natives were restrained from raiding the Navajo settlements in violation of the peace he had concluded in 1861, new depredations could be expected. In November, as the Texans began to advance northward from Mesilla, Canby resolved to separate the "friendly Navajos" from their more bellicose countrymen and to remove them to a reservation where they could be isolated, and at the same time protected from the New Mexicans. In December, he advised Washington that recent conflicts in the Navajo country "have so demoralized and broken up that nation, that there is now no choice between their absolute extermination or their removal and colonization at points so remote from the settlements as to isolate them entirely from the inhabitants of the territory." In concert with the Superintendent of Indian Affairs, he decided to "establish such of the Navajos as have heretofore acted in good faith in communities, where they can be isolated and protected until some permanent arrangements can be made by the government." Before this decision could be implemented, however, Canby had to face the Texans who were threatening to overrun the entire Territory. Canby formed a low opinion of the New Mexican volunteer regiments at the battle of Valverde in February, 1862, when many of the volunteers broke and ran during a Texan charge, and later deserted."[2]

Canby was right in thinking the Navajos were being decimated in every way by the New Mexicans as well as being manipulated by so many others, they had been for years, but at the same time everything was in a state of confusion and every military man that came along always thought a reservation was the answer. He was thinking with the correct measures in protecting the Navajo or possibly using that as an excuse was still following the concept of taking the land. Every thought applied to the Native American was always the same no matter where it was taking place from the East Coast to the West, they were here first so we need to be rid of them. Set aside the Indian problem move on with Manifest Destiny; but Canby whether right or wrong, approximately seven months later would be sent back east and replaced by James Henry Carleton along with every bad decision he would make and the Navajo personally paying for it....

Here is one of the first quoted letters from Carleton to Kit Carson just to show what the Navajo were up against. This instruction initially was for the Mescalero Apaches but soon would also apply to the Navajo people.

---

[2] Navajo Roundup; Pg. 1-2; Para. 3-4.

"Head Quarters, Department of
New Mexico Santa Fe, N.M.
October 12th, 1862.

"Confidential"

Colonel Christopher Carson
  1st New Mexican Volunteers,
  En route to Fort Stanton, N.M.

Colonel:

\*          \*          \*          \*          \*

All Indian men of that tribe are to be killed whenever and wherever you can find them: the women and children will not be harmed, but you will take them prisoners and feed them at Fort Stanton until you receive other instructions about them. If the Indians send in a flag and desire to treat for peace, say to the bearer that when the people of New Mexico were attacked by the Texans, the Mescaleros broke their treaty of peace, and murdered innocent people, and ran off their stock: that now, our hands are untied and you have been sent to punish them for their treachery and their crimes: That you have no power to make peace; that you are there to kill them wherever you can find them; that if they beg for peace, their Chiefs and twenty of their principal men must come to Santa Fe to have a talk here; but tell them fairly and frankly that you will keep after their people and slay them until you receive orders to desist from these Head Quarters; that this making of treaties for *them* to break whenever they have an interest in breaking it, will not be done any more; that that time has passed by; that we have no faith in their promises; that we believe if we kill some of their men in fair open war, they will be apt to remember that it will be better for them to remain at peace, than to be at war. I trust that this severity in the long run will be the most humane course that could be pursued toward these Indians.

You observe that there is a large force helping you, I do not wish to tie your hands by instructions: the whole duty can be summed up in a few words: the Indians are to be soundly whipped without parleys or councils except as above.

\*          \*          \*          \*          \*

I am, Colonel,
Respectfully,
Your friend,
James H. Carleton
Brig General,
Com'd."[3]

The constant pattern of those in power like Carleton and those wanting to satisfy their superiors were narcissists (or with no conscience or remorse) as quoted in the letter above to another narcissist, Carson. Then the Navajo's would eventually pay the full price.

---

[3] Navajo Roundup; Pg. 11-12; Para. 4.

As repeatedly stated by several historians different opinions of Carleton were thought of in terms of energy, perseverance, integrity, stern, unbending and zealous.

But yet just think of stern, unbending and zealous under the wrong circumstances or psyche. Sabin in his *Kit Carson Days 1809-1868 Volume 1* on page 481 shows the nature of someone with a lack of conscience. Fremont during 1846 while waiting for a reason to insert himself into the fight for California and whom Carson admired greatly is told to do his duty. Fremont had heard about a couple Americans that were brutally executed by the Mexicans. The timing as such turns out that Carson and his men captured three Mexicans off a ship taking them prisoner. Carson goes to Fremont for advice, asking what he should do with these men, Fremont says he is not interested in prisoners. "Do your duty." Carson himself admitted to shooting them without question. It is known that at some point Fremont had saved Carson's life and vice versa. But more than once during his career when he felt he owed a superior, he didn't seem capable of right or wrong. He seemed cold to the point of total loss of conscience or outright depravity built within his personality which the Navajo would later find out.

It was bad enough and well known that Carson's degenerative notions placed the Native people in constant danger but also he had no control over his men. Kelly mentions on page 15 of his thorough study in *Navajo Roundup*, that Carleton constantly had to lecture Carson about his men and their "Murder, alcoholism, embezzlement, sexual deviation, desertion, and incompetence...." showing his reluctance to do what's right as well as the type of personnel he allowed himself to be surrounded by.

On top of that Carson had no sooner begun his campaign against the Navajo reporting on July 24, 1863 by letter of his first progress against small numbers, those who were busy herding sheep and tending to family chores that his Ute's had killed several; (approx. 12) and of how his Ute's of which he was once an Indian agent for and his Ute's the mortal enemies of the Navajo now had possession of eleven captives, (women and children). Carson then proceeded by private letter to write Carleton to request hiring more Utes because they were doing such a great job and as reward for their hard work be given the women and children as slaves. Let the letter below be shown as proof from *Navajo Roundup*, page 30. He had already sent an official communication or letter with the very same date but kept the letter below separate so it wouldn't be seen in any official capacity obviously because of the treacherous nature of what he was requesting.

"Camp at Pueblo Colorado N. Mex.
July 24th 1863.

Dear General,
    I send by Captain Cutler the Official report of the operations of my Command since leaving Los Lunas, but in it have made no mention of the Women and children captured by the Utes (four Women & seventeen children.) It is expected by the Utes, and has, I believe, been customary to allow them to keep the Women & children, and the property captured by them, for their own use and benefit; and as there is no way to sufficiently recompense these Indians for their invaluable services, and as a means of insuring their continued zeal and activity; I ask it as a favor that they be permitted to retain all that they may capture. I make this request the more readily as I am satisfied

that the future of the captives disposed of in this manner would be much better than if sent even to the Bosque Redondo. As a general thing, the Utes dispose of their captives to Mexican families, where they are fed and taken care of and thus cease to require any further attention on the part of the government. Besides this, their being distributed as Servants thro' the Territory causes them to loose[sic] that collectiveness of interest as a tribe, which they will retain if kept together at any one place.

Will you please let me know your views on this matter as soon as possible that I may govern my conduct accordingly.

The Utes *more* than come up to the expectations I had formed of their efficiency as spies, nor can any small straggling parties of Navajoes hope to escape them. I trust you will grant me permission to send Capt. Pfeiffer to their Villages to employ some more of them. I am very badly off for Guides, and intend to employ some Zuni Indians as such in a few days, when I shall visit their Village.

The Navajoes have planted a large quantity of grain this year. Their Wheat is as good as I have ever seen.—Corn is rather backward and not so plentiful I have directed Major Cummings to send out a party tomorrow to bring in all the grain on this creek which will amount to over seventy five thousand pounds of wheat, and a large amount of corn....

Respectfully yours,<br>
C Carson<br>
Col 1 N.M. Vols.

To
   Brig: Genl: J.H. Carleton.
      Comdg Dept of N. Mex:
         Santa Fe"[4]

There is no need to finish this particular transcription, Carson had to have known what would happen to the women and children, thankfully Carleton didn't go along with the request. But interestingly enough Carson refers to the Bosque and these captives being better off as slaves rather than being sent to Carleton's visionary reservation. He had to have known the ground and early on what the Navajo's would be facing since Carleton's own staff rejected the place and project. Takes you back to Carleton being "Stern and Unbending." But Carson was willing to slaughter those that raised the finest grain he had ever seen then steal it, then make off with their women and children after killing those herding their animals. How many times had the government wanted other tribes to civilize and do exactly what the Navajos were already doing?

The Navajo tried peace like other tribes before them. They believed in those that uttered false promises while carrying felonious motives within their very souls. These so called government representatives from Washington all overwhelmingly proclaimed warm sincerity with cold hearts that was difficult to reveal because the very people they were pandering to would never dream of treating another human being in the same manner.

Indian agent John Ward to General Edward R.S. Canby as Commander to the Department of New Mexico, while still in charge, had communicated thru a letter

---

[4] Navajo Roundup; Pg. 30-31; Para. 1-4.

of August 22, 1862 noting; "no complaints had been received either "from citizens or pueblo Indians" about the conduct of these Navajos, but that they had been continually subjected to punitive raids by Mexicans and whites who had plundered them and stolen their children." From *Navajo Roundup*, page 17; footnote (*ibid.,* W-99-1862).

The first telling example can be told of an old headman from an earlier time; Narbona a man that had worked to build his outfit up in early days, sometimes he had to fight for his people but held peace in his heart with the hope they could carry on with their lives and support his relatives. He wanted to teach others the culture he had grown up with. Singing the songs of his people so they could flourish. Watching their animals multiply, while tasting the nectar from their peach orchards and yet casting an eye on green fields of corn as far as the eye could see. All he had known his life through was his life's blood, family, friends; Navajo country.

From approximately 1819 Narbona had to leave his home ground because of really harsh drought conditions never seen before. Driving them west into Arizona and into Hopi lands to the base of the most Western Navajo territorial mountains that they called, "Light Always Glitters on Top. It was another of the four sacred mountains, this one anchoring the southwestern corner of the Navajo lands (the mountain is now known as the San Francisco Peaks, which rise to an elevation of more than twelve thousand feet near present-day Flagstaff, Arizona)."[5]

As time passed Narbona had heard the drought had broken and they could go home only to find that his homeland had been heavily raided by their enemies; hundreds of their women and children had been taken and enslaved, causing the Navajo the necessity to fight back or be destroyed once more.

Finally coming home Narbona was in his sixties, returning after hearing the great drought has dissipated but the treachery hadn't. The Mexican government had called the Navajo's into a council while Narbona was still away from his country. This council ended as a plot to harm the Navajo's where the Mexican's slaughtered over twenty of their headmen. In hopes of peace he found that the Mexican government was just as bad and as vicious as the Spanish. He still tried to advance peace realizing that fighting was a worthless bloody task especially when counseling with devils.

Then it was the Americans turn only this time near 30 years later he would lose his life over a horse. Narbona was at least ninety years of age, his health poor, yet approached by Indian Affairs agent John Calhoun and Colonel Washington; Calhoun told him the Navajo were now within U.S. jurisdiction and it needed to be obeyed. Being informed that Calhoun and Washington intended to hold a large

---

[5] Blood and Thunder; Pg. 82 Para. 4

council at Canyon de Chelly with the whole of the Navajo Nation they insisted he come along but Narbona refused being he didn't feel he was representative of all Navajo as well as not feeling up to the trip. Washington kept insisting, finally Narbona agreed but only with the assistance of two younger headmen. "The council broke up to everyone's apparent satisfaction, and for a moment matters between the Navajos and the United States of America seemed hopeful. But then one of the New Mexican militiamen spotted a horse among the Navajo warriors that, he insisted, was his. The militiaman was sure of it, he said. The natives had stolen his horse a few months ago, and now he demanded it back. The Navajos did not dispute that the horse had been stolen, but they indicated that it had passed through so many different hands that it was impossible to ascertain the true owner now—and that, in any case, something like a statute of limitations had taken effect. There was a brief scuffle, and charges were shouted back and forth. When Colonel Washington got wind of what was happening, he sided with the New Mexican's version of events. The colonel demanded that the Navajo hand over the horse. At this the Navajos "demurred," as Simpson described it. Tempers were flaring all around. After all the abstractions lofted by Colonel Washington, negotiations had finally reached a concrete topic that the Navajos understood with clarity and passion: *a horse.* The situation had become a tense standoff. "Unless the horse is restored," Washington threatened through an interpreter, "you will be fired upon!" By this point the accused horse thief had taken off for the hills—riding, of course, the very mount at issue. Not knowing what to do, Washington then told the officer of the guard, a Lieutenant Torrez, to seize another horse in reprisal, any horse he fancied. When Torrez moved toward the throng of mounted Navajos to pick out a horse, the Indians sensed immediately what was happening. In a flash they wheeled about and galloped away—"scampering off," Simpson wrote, "at the top of their speed." At this, Colonel Washington ordered, *"Fire!"* Shots ripped through the crowd, as army marksmen posted around the perimeter of the council site fired their muzzle-loading rifles. Artillerymen, meanwhile, turned the enormous bronze barrel of the six-pound field gun—the thunderwagon—and in a close triad of concussions, they blasted the field. Then Washington ordered mounted soldiers to pursue the retreating Navajos, but it was impossible to catch them, for they scattered in all directions and disappeared into a distant ravine. When the dust settled, Colonel Washington found that none of his own men had been hurt, although Simpson noted with much regret that a few mules had been lost in the "hurry-skurry." The field was now empty but for seven Navajo bodies. Some of them were wounded, some of them apparently lifeless. Upon closer inspection, Washington learned that one of the writhing forms in the grass was none other than Narbona. The great patriarch was sprawled in a pool of blood. Shrapnel from the thunderwagon had apparently sliced into him, and now he had four or five gaping wounds ranging over his crippled body. A few minutes later, Narbona lay still. If their leader's death was not insult enough to the Navajos, then what happened next proved to be the final indignity. A New Mexican souvenir hunter walked up to the old man's corpse, leaned down, and raked a sharp knife across his forehead."[6]

The task of the army through Carleton's guidance and Carson's abundant brutality was to force the Navajo to the Bosque; clearly a prosecution of destructive hate though they may have called it duty. Their communication clearly points out the unwarranted attacks and senseless bloodletting on farmers, herdsmen and innocent Navajo families. For the theft of the land they provide a trail of their dark intentions.

It's almost too easy when reading what they wrote during their so-called endeavors, almost deserving of a posthumous loss of rank and service time. If a metal was won for this campaign each and every one should be lost or taken from congressional record with such open proof of malice and premeditation. Below you will find the header for the letter received from Headquarters, Navajoe Expedition addressed to Captain B.C. Cutler. Approximately 29 lines down within the text it mentions the productivity of the Navajo skills while during this campaign making every effort to enforce a governmental will on a simple people who were to be forced into starvation because a greater power thought they should live where they were told. Again Bosque Redondo which would turn into another failure by those who thought they knew better. In this partial transcription you'll read about a people's success and what may sound like some kind of dictator's delusional image of what somebody else should do with their life while not even knowing how to manage their own. This note is part of the beginnings of driving thousands on foot over approx. 400 miles to a place that would do nothing but reap cruelty and death with every step.

"Head quarters, Navajoe Expedition
Fort Canby, N.M. August 31st 1863.

To
    Capt. B.C. Cutler
      A.A. Gen'l
        HdQrs Dept of N.M.
          Santa Fe N.M.

Captain.
    ....About 10 A.M., the command arrived at a large bottom containing not less than one hundred acres of as fine corn as I have ever seen. Here I determined to encamp that I might have it destroyed. Just as the advance guard reached the corn field, they discovered a Navajo whom they pursued and killed. He slightly wounded one horse with an arrow in the neck. Lieut Fitch was in charge of the guard. At 8 A.M. on the 23d arrived at the west opening of Cañon de Chelly, but could find no water. About twelve miles farther found abundance of running water and good grass and encamped. I made a careful examination of the country on this day's march particularly in the immediate neighborhood of Cañon de Chelly, and am satisfied that

---

[6] Blood and Thunder; Pg. 273-275 Para. 4-10

there are very few Indians in the Cañon, and these of the very poorest. They have no stock and were depending entirely for subsistence on the corn destroyed by my command on the precious day—the loss of which will cause actual starvation, and oblige them either to come in and accept emigration to the Bosque Redondo, or to fly south to Red River to join the wealthy bands now there. I am inclined to think they will adopt the first of these courses. On the 24th I encamped on a bottom of very fine grass, which my animals were very much in need of. My guide informed me that General Canby encamped here with his command for several days when on his campaign of 1860...."

Carson makes this last point in the final paragraph of this letter.

"....In summing up the results of the last month's scout, I congratulate myself on having gained one very important point Viz: a knowledge of where the Navajos have fled with their stock, and where I am certain to find them. I have also gained an accurate knowledge of a great portion of the country, which will be of incalculable benefit in our future operations. I have ascertained that a large party of Navajos are on Salt River near the San Francisco Mts among the Apaches, and within easy striking distance of the Pima villages. I would respectfully suggest that a force operating against them from that point, would greatly facilitate the entire subjugation of the Navajo Nation....

Very Respectfully<br>
Your Obt Serv't<br>
C. Carson<br>
Col. 1st N.M. Vol's.<br>
Commanding"[7]

During Carleton's massive push to capture the Navajo they were severely punished; countless men, women and children. U.S Troops many Mexican or New Mexican; natural enemies of these herders and farmers who tried to defend their own were repeatedly pursued in the worst of conditions. Under Carson as another example from Canyon de Chelly he found as stated in *Navajo Roundup* on page 72; "in January, he found several hundred numbed and starving Navajos sheltered in the Canyon." This was January 1864.

Just between Chinle, New Mexico (Canyon de Chelly) and Fort Sumner, New Mexico the walk is close to 400 miles alone, some say 300 miles. The army then and present at that time was totally dysfunctional, they were corrupt, cruel, murderous and self-serving, drunk, stealing from each other with constant perverted behavior while constant streams of arrests and Court Martials took place within their ranks, all this can be found within official records, National Archival Rolls M-427, Record Group 393, letters sent, etc. Sweltering excuses for human beings under malicious direction and greed were sent after someone that just wanted to live in peace.

---

[7] Navajo Roundup; Pg. 41-44; Para. 1-5.

Imagine the Navajo in the hands of people like these during the worst weather ever. It can't even be described. The men leading the patrols in official letters to their commander's repeatedly describe they shot one, two, three Navajo's and captured their herds, harvested (stole) their crops and punished these Indians for their own deceptive crimes, each time it must have been a formidable struggle for the Bluecoats to snipe out someone tending his sheep or picking his corn.

It was felt that a series of certain lines from the actual military communications containing the date, location, party written to and received by through quotes and in proper sequence could fully describe the actual intent and attitude as well as the character of some individuals from the private to commanding general could prove the radical thought process as well as actionable cruelty the Navajo people of New Mexico faced. It was also felt that a great deal of the reader's time would be wasted by transcribing complete letters thereby showing poor justifications rather than just coming to the point of what actually took place through actions and mental attitudes toward the Navajo.

These quoted lines are limited to the proof of damage wrought upon an innocent people that were only defending their homes, family and way of life. These sources came from actual documented materials found in the Old Military Records division of the National Archives. The files in the Department of New Mexico, Record Group 393, Records of the U.S. Army Continental Commands, 1821-1920, contain original letters received from Christopher Carson's command as well as the copybooks of letters sent by Carleton to Carson and to Washington, D.C. There is an index of the persons or commands to which the letters are addressed. Letters received are filed by a letter, a number code according to surname for every person sending the letter with year and sequence received. Also under Record Group 94 materials can be found through microfilms such as M-619, Records of the Adjutant General's Office, Letters Received, 1861-1870. Other documentation can be searched by reading materials within microfilm M-427, containing Records of Volunteer Union Soldiers Who Served in Organizations from the Territory of New Mexico. Feel free to look up these reference materials for full documentation for each communication quoted below.

"Head Quarters, Navajo Expedition
Fort Canby, N.M. Jany 3rd 1864.

Captain Ben: C. Cutler,
    Asst: Adjt: General
Head Quarters Dept: of N. Mex
        Santa Fé, N.M.

Captain:
    ....Judging from the appearance of these captives, the generality of the Navajos are completely destitute. They are almost entirely naked, and had it not been for the unusual growth of the Piñon-berry this year, they must have been without any description of food. This is owing to the destruction of their grain amounting to about two Millions of Pounds by my command on its first arrival in this country, and which they depended on for their Winter's Sustenance. The dread of being discovered by my Scouting parties which are continually in the field, prevents them building fires for

warmth, and this adds greatly to the horrors of their Situation, when all the severity of the winter in their Mountains must be borne by them without protection.

There can be no doubt whatever but that by prosecuting the campaign with the vigor which has heretofore characterized it, during the next spring and Summer—so as to prevent them from planting their grain, that actual Starvation will compel any who may hold out that long to come in and avail themselves of the means offered them of sharing in the plenty enjoyed by those of their people now on Reservations....

Very respectfully<br>
Yr: Obt.Servt:<br>
C. Carson<br>
Colo. 1 Cav. N.M. Vols<br>
Comdg:"

This first communication points out the needless destruction of the Navajos' self-sustaining abilities to live and take care of themselves and were destroyed by an aggressor with a premeditated cause to take what wasn't theirs under the guise of helping the savage become civilized. The next communication points out the waste as well as the admiration of what the Navajo had and what this General commanding really felt and points out their real intentions.

"Head-Quarters, Department of New Mexico,<br>
Santa Fe, N.M.  March 12, 1864.

To
Brig. General Lorenzo Thomas,
    Adjutant General U.S. Army,
        Washington, D.C.

General,

....You have from time to time been informed of every step which I have taken with reference to operations against Indians in this country.  I multiplied as much as possible the points of contact between our forces and themselves; and, although no great battle has been fought, still the persistent efforts of small parties acting simultaneously over a large extent of country, has destroyed a great many, and harrassed[sic] the survivors until they have become thoroughly subdued.  Now, when they have surrendered and are at our mercy, they must be taken care of; must be fed, clothed and instructed.  This admits neither of discussion nor delay.  These six thousand mouths must eat; and these six thousand bodies must be clothed.  When it is considered what a magnificent pastoral and mineral country they have surrendered to us—a country whose value can hardly be estimated—the mere pittance in comparison which must at once be given to support them, sinks into insignificance as a price for their natural heritage.

They *must* have two millions of pounds of breadstuffs sent from the states.  This can be done by installments; the first installment to be started *at once*; say, five hundred thousand pounds of flour and corn in equal parts.  The next installment to reach the Bosque Redondo in August next; and *all* to be delivered by the middle of next November.  This amount will last them, with what we can buy here, until the crop comes off in 1865; when, from that time forward, so far as food may go, they will, in my opinion, be self-sustaining....

....But unless you make in the law all the arrangements here contemplated, you will find this interesting and intelligent race of Indians will fast diminish in numbers, until, within a few years only, not one of those who boasted in the proud name of Navajoe will be left to upbraid us for having taken their birthright and then left them to perish....

....The Exodus of this whole people from the land of their fathers, is not only an interesting but a touching sight. They have fought us gallantly for years on years. They have defended their mountains and their stupendous *cañons* with a heroism which any people might be proud to emulate. But, when at length they found it was *their* destiny, too, as it had been that of their bretheren[sic], tribe after tribe, away back towards the rising of the sun, to give way to the insatiable progress of our race, they threw down their arms, and, as brave men entitled to our admiration and respect, have come to us with confidence in our magnanimity, and feeling that we are too powerful and too just a people to repay that confidence with meanness or neglect. Feeling, that, for having sacrificed to us their beautiful country, their homes, the association of their lives, the scenes rendered classic in their traditions,– we will not dole out to them a miser's pittance in return *for what they know to be* and what we know to be, a princely realm....

I am, General,
Very respectfully,
Your ob't servant,
James H. Carleton,
Brig. General, Comd'g."

Just with these two communications it can be understood the aggressive vileness portrayed upon these people. Carleton openly brags to his superior in Washington about how their land was magnificent, a pastoral and a mineral country (Carleton and his cronies as well as the government knew that it was rumored that there was gold in New Mexico as there had been in California), he called it "a princely realm", their depravity had no bounds. He knew that his troops had destroyed the food the Navajos had intended on using for the winter. He called these people intelligent, interesting; yet, according to him, they needed his help to be civilized and were being forced into starvation and nakedness during the winter months. Many were found frozen and the ones that lived were captured and held just to be thrown on a reservation that in the end would not sustain their lives. They would be again starved with their rations cut time and again. They were promised life-supporting supplies only to be denied these necessities due to government agents defrauding the Navajo by manipulating the money that was originally provided to purchase these needs.

These next quotations will show the conditions and the depredations that were put on these, "pastoral people" as Carleton himself called them.

"Head Quarters, "Navajo Expedition,"
Fort Canby, N.M. Jan. 24d 1864.

Capt. Ben: C. Cutler,
    A.A. General
Head Qrs Department of New Mexico,
    Santa Fé, N.M.

Captain:
....He killed three Indians (two men) and brought in nineteen prisoners, women and children. He found two bodies of Indians frozen to death in the Cañon. I respectfully enclose his Report (marked "A"), which is very interesting. While *en route* on my return to Camp I was joined by three Indians with a flag of truce, requesting

lxv

permission to come in with their people and submit. I told them through my Interpreter that they and their people might come unmolested to my camp up to ten o'clock A.M. next day, but that after that time if they did not come, my Soldiers would hunt them up and the work of destruction recommence....

I am, Captain, very respectfully,
Your most obt Sevt
C. Carson
Colonel 1st Cav. N. M. Vols.
Comd'g."

From a footnote on page 99 of *Navajo Roundup*, to show the destructiveness of Carson's orders just to upset the very order of Navajo life is mentioned one of the most hated actions he had ever ordered; "Because Carson specifically ordered Carey to destroy the Navajo peach orchards and because the orchards were subsequently destroyed, nearly every account of this phase of the expedition which I have encountered has assumed that Carey destroyed them at this time. However, Carey makes no mention of the orchards in his report, which is otherwise very full. An entry in the muster rolls of Company K for July-August, 1864, states that the trees (5,000 in number) were actually destroyed by Captain Thompson in early August, 1864, after most of the Navajos had been transported to the Bosque Redondo. See Microcopy M-427, Roll 1 (Company K Muster Roll)."

"Fort Sumner N. Mexico
May 12th, 1864

Sir
....The main body of the Indians travelled between the advance Guard and the train, and in advance of my company, and I gave orders that a strict watch should be kept on their movements. On the second days march a very severe snow storm set in which lasted for four days with unusual severity, and occassioned great suffering amongst the indians, many of whom were nearly naked and of course unable to withstand such a storm....

very Respectfully
Your Obt. Svt
Francis McCabe
Capt 1st NM Cav
Comdg.

The A A Genl.
    HdQrs Dept N.M.
        Santa Fe N.M."

---

"Head Quarters, Navajo Expedition
Fort Canby, N.M. April 10, 1864

Genl. J.H. Carleton,
    Comd'g: Dept. of New Mexico,
        Santa Fé., New Mexico.

General:

....I have the honor to enclose a list of the Navajo Chiefs who signed the last Treaty of Peace made with them by General Canby; with such remarks opposite each as I have been enabled to collect. It is probable that "Herrera Grande" may be able to tell you the number of each Chief's followers, and so arrive at an approximation of their strength.

The wisdom of removing the Navajoes from this country cannot be to highly appreciated, nor do I think that any other or better location could be found for them than their present Reservation. Aside from the fact that there is no one place in this country sufficiently large, combining all the requisites of Water, Fuel, and Productiveness of soil for a Reservation, the permitting them to remain in their own country would have the same effect as a Treaty of Peace; and the experience of the last one hundred and eighty (180) years has proven the worthlessness of such Treaties, and what little attention has been paid to them by these savages.

I am, General, very respectfully,
Your most obt servant
C. Carson.
Col. 1st Cav. N.M. Vols. Comd'g."

The author of *Navajo Roundup*, on pages 90-91, vividly points out the hopelessness that was put upon the Navajo by Carson. "Despite these many problems, the preparation for the exploration of Canyon de Chelly continued. On December 21, 1863, Carson sent Captains Thompson and Berney to the Mesa de la Vaca, far to the west of the Canyon de Chelly and just north of the Hopi villages, where he believed a large group of Navajos were hiding. This "scout" was hampered by a heavy fall of snow and, although thirteen prisoners were taken and several Navajos were killed, the majority of the Indians scattered and fled. Carson's summary report on this engagement contains the first indication that the crop destruction of the previous fall was beginning to take effect. The pitiful condition of the captives brought a plea for blankets and also an optimistic prediction: the campaign would be over by the summer. It is obvious, however, that the Colonel had no premonition of the large-scale surrenders which were to follow his penetration of the Canyon de Chelly."

Then again on page 114, he states, "On March 13, Berney arrived at Fort Sumner with 1,430 Navajos; his casualties along the way were ten who had perished from the cold, three who were stolen, and two who had strayed away."

On page 121, "In early March the second large convoy, the first from Fort Canby, was dispatched to the Bosque. During the time the Navajos were waiting for transportation, over 2,500 of them had congregated at the fort. Of these, 126 died there and another 197 would die before the march to the Bosque was completed. Some of them died from the extreme cold; others perished from dysentery "occasioned by eating too heartily of half-cooked bread made of our flour to which they were not accustomed." Although this was the largest group of Navajos to be moved at one time, Captain Thompson's report on the journey is disappointingly brief and lacking in detail."

On page 133, "The march from Fort Canby to Fort Wingate took place during a "severe snowstorm," and at least forty Navajos died on this portion of the trip. Even more slipped away and returned to their homes. Those who survived learned upon their arrival at the fort that the food supply there was not sufficient for the journey to Los Pinos. This resulted in half rations for the next seven days and some anxious moments for McCabe who feared trouble as a result."

The dedication and intense study that the author of *Navajo Roundup*, the book is to be thankfully and highly commended for every second that he spent studying about the great loss that the Navajo had to endure. The justice and honesty that he exhibited within every page of his work could never be fully appreciated.

It was felt through official communications that more proof had to be shown as to what the Navajo went through on the way to the Bosque as transcribed below as well as the mention in many of these communications the deaths of so many innocent people:

"Santa Fé N.M.
April 7th 1864.

To the
    Asst. Adjt. General
        Hd Qrs Dept. of New Mexico
            Santa Fé N.M.

Sir:
....One chief told me that the Ute Indians had taken seventeen thousand sheep from him alone. I arrived at Fort Sumner Bosque Redondo on the 12th of March, where I turned over fourteen hundred and thirty (1430) Indians to Major H.D. Wallen Post Commander. I lost fifteen Indians on the road, principally boys, three of which were stolen, two strayed from my camp on the Rio Pecos, and ten died from the effects of the cold &c....

I am, Sir, Very Respectfully
Your obt Servt.
Joseph Berney
Capt. 1st Cav. N.M. vols."

---

"Head Quarters, Návajoe Expedition,
Fort Canby, N.M. March 6th 1864.

Captain Ben. C. Cutler,
    A.A. General Dept. N.M.
        Santa Fé, N.M.

Captain:
....Since the 20th of last month 126 Indians have *died* at this post making with those just sent to the Bosque a reduction of 2,263, Navajoes from the population of this country. This I am satisfied is a larger number than could have been subdued and forced to give themselves up had a vigorous war been continued. The truce which I extended to them expired on the first of this month, and Capt McCabe was in the field to convince them of the fact....

I am, Sir,
Very respectfully
Your Obdt Servt
A.B. Carey
Capt. 13th Infty Commanding."

---

"Fort Sumner New Mexico,
April 15th, 1864.

Captain

I have the honor to report my arrival at this Post on the 13th inst. with 2400 Navajo Indians. I left Fort Canby, N.M on the 4th of March 1864—with 2170 Indians Received at Bear Springs N M 97 more, and arrived at Los Pinos N. M. on the 19th and left on the 21st of March. I received at Los Pinos 360 but had to send back 300 from Bairds Ranch after being two days out for want of transportation. I received at San Jose one (1) and at Bernal Springs N M twenty four (24) I have lost since I left Canby 197 by deaths and gained on the trip 245, which gain was made on the road between Fort Canby and Los Pinos N M by Indians coming in from the mountains. The Indians have lost 50 head of horses and mules which were stolen by Mexican thieves—the Inf under my command captured six head of the stolen animals at San Antonita N M and for the want of mounted men to follow up the Robbers the balance were lost.

Respectfully
Submitted
J. Thompson
Capt 1st Cavly N.M.Vols.

Capt B.C Cutler
A.A. General
Santa Fe
N M"

---

"Head Quarters, Navajoe Expedition
Fort Canby, N.M. March 13th, 1864.

Captain:

....The results of the operations of this party since January 1st, the Capt informed me was 26 Indians killed, 4 taken prisoners which were turned over here, and 5 Horses captured.

I am, Capt.
Very Respectfully
Your Obd't Servt
A.B. Carey
Capt 13th Infty.
Comd'g Nav. Expedition

Capt. B. C. Cutler,
A.A. General
Dept N.M.
Santa Fé, N.M.

---

"Fort Sumner N. Mexico
May 12th, 1864

Sir
....I had them march into the Fort and seated in lines to be counted, and the Officer of the day counted 788 indians. I left Fort Canby with 800 and Received 146 en Route to Fort Sumner making about 946 in all. Of this number about 110 died, and twenty five were enticed away by Pino Baca & the remainder I think returned to Canby or Ft. Wingate on account of inclement weather; but I am satisfied that not a warrior left with hostile intentions.

very Respectfully
Your Obt. Svt
Francis McCabe
Capt 1st NM Cav
Comdg.

The A A Genl. HdQrs Dept N.M.
Santa Fe N.M."

These military communications during the time of the Long Walk in New Mexico create a strong case against those that said they cared but by personal actions exhibited no human feeling in any form or manner from the soldier on the field to the very top in Washington.

It needs to be pointed out also the conditions under which the Navajo were forced to work in while attending Carleton's dream of making the Bosque happen. The circumstances for the Navajo on this reservation were as murderous as the Long Walk was. They were forced to plow fields in freezing weather as well as deadly conditions during February 1865. "Despite the cold weather, Captain Calloway kept the Navajos busy in the fields during his last days as Superintendent of Indian Labor. The plowing progressed fairly well, but in February heavy snowstorms stalled the work. Labadie reported that over one hundred Indians died from exposure and other effects of the cold. On February 23 another violent blizzard struck. While Navajo families struggled vainly to keep warm in their hogans, the military forced others to continue plowing."[8] It wasn't long after that Calloway would be discovered stealing and selling supplies and farming implements to Indian Agent Labadie; purchased by the government for the Navajo Farm. At least he was dismissed from the army but no jail time was mentioned when there should have been.

The final reveal or seal of fate that killed Carleton's experiment on the Pecos River came from his own tongue. A Congressional group investigating Indian policy in the West called the Doolittle Committee headed by a Senator Doolittle from Wisconsin would reach New Mexico in late June 1865 where during the 25th of the month they would visit the Bosque Redondo Reservation. They asked for testimony from Carleton to privates to Natives. Naturally the stories were all over the map. But the

---

[8] The Army And The Navajo; Pg. 76; Para. 2.

reveal that changed everything though slowly and the "March Home" not till June of 1868; would help Doolittle understand what eventually needed to be done and eventually send the Navajo back to their homes. "Doolittle then asked Carleton if he thought Indians were industrious. He responded by describing the young Navajos at the Bosque as being both docile and industrious. In contrast, the grown men seemed lazy and could not be prevented from "their savage desire to roam about and lead a life of idleness." The older Navajos must die off, Carleton observed, and the younger ones take their places before any marked improvement could be observed in the tribe.

Should reservations be established by treaties? The reservation system was necessary, Carleton said, for all wild tribes, and should be set aside by law and enforced by arms. He did not believe, however, in treaties. It was beneath the dignity of the United States to sign a treaty when the other party was not a legal nation. The government would have its own way, regardless of the Indians' desire, and to go through the form of making a treaty was theatrical. "*We can do right*," he wrote "without resorting to any theatricals simply for effect." On this note the questions ended. Carleton's answers were indeed revealing of the motivations for his policies at the Bosque Redondo."[9]

This series is for the Northern Navajo but in order for there to be a complete understanding of the Navajo Nation of today it has to include an explanation that contains the huge land base called the Four Corners and the modern day Navajo Nation. If there is any redundancy of factual matters within this introduction it is because of the importance of the subjects and the quotations used within the sources referenced. The Navajo Nation has become the largest Indian Nation in the United States, "The Navajo Nation (Navajo: *Naabeehó Diné Biyaad*), also known as Navajoland, is a Native American reservation in the United States. It occupies portions of northeastern Arizona, northwestern New Mexico, and southeastern Utah; at roughly 17,544,500 acres (71,000 km$^2$; 27,413 sq mi), the Navajo Nation is the largest land area held by a Native American tribe in the U.S., exceeding ten U.S. states. In 2010, the reservation was home to 173,667 out of 332,129 Navajo tribal members; the remaining 158,462 tribal members lived outside the reservation, in urban areas (26 percent), border towns (10 percent), and elsewhere in the U.S. (17 percent). The seat of government is located in Window Rock, Arizona.

Reservation and expansion: In the mid-19th century, primarily in the 1860s, most of the Navajo were forced to abandon their homes due to a series of military campaigns by the U.S. Army conducted with a scorched-earth policy and sanctioned by the U.S. government. The Army burned their homes and agricultural fields, and stole or killed livestock, to weaken and starve the Navajo into submission. In 1864, the main body of Navajo, numbering 8,000 adults and children, were marched 300 miles on the Long Walk to imprisonment in Bosque Redondo. The Treaty of 1868 established the "Navajo Indian Reservation" and the Navajo people left Bosque Redondo for this territory.

---

[9] The Army And The Navajo; Pg. 91; Para. 4-5.

The borders were defined as the 37th parallel in the north; the southern border as a line running through Fort Defiance; the eastern border as a line running through Fort Lyon; and in the west as longitude 109°30′.

As drafted in 1868, the boundaries were defined as: the following district of country, to wit: bounded on the north by the 37th degree of north latitude, south by an east and west line passing through the site of old Fort Defiance, in Canon Bonito, east by the parallel of longitude which, if prolonged south, would pass through old Fort Lyon, or the Ojo-de-oso, Bear Spring, and west by a parallel of longitude about 109° 30′ west of Greenwich, provided it embraces the outlet of the Canon-de-Chilly [Canyon de Chelly], which canyon is to be all included in this reservation, shall be, and the same hereby, set apart for the use and occupation of the Navajo tribe of Indians, and for such other friendly tribes or individual Indians as from time to time they may be willing, with the consent of the United States, to admit among them; and the United States agrees that no persons except those herein so authorized to do, and except such officers, soldiers agents, and employees of the Government, or of the Indians, as may be authorized to enter upon Indian reservations in discharge of duties imposed by law, or the orders of the President, shall ever be permitted to pass over, settle upon, or reside in, the territory described in this article. Though the treaty had provided for one hundred miles by one hundred miles in the New Mexico Territory, the size of the territory was 3,328,302 acres (13,470 km$^2$; 5,200 sq mi) slightly more than half. This initial piece of land is represented in the design of the Navajo Nation's flag by a dark-brown rectangle. As no physical boundaries or signposts were set in place, many Navajo ignored these formal boundaries and returned to where they had been living prior to US occupation. A significant number of Navajo had never lived in the Hwéeldi (near Fort Sumner). They remained or moved near the Little Colorado and Colorado rivers, on *Naatsis'áán* (Navajo Mountain), and some lived with Apache bands.

The first expansion of the territory occurred on October 28, 1878, when President Rutherford Hayes signed an executive order pushing the reservation boundary 20 miles to the west. Further additions followed throughout the late 19th and early 20th century (see map). Most of these additions were achieved through executive orders, some of which were confirmed by acts of Congress. For example, President Theodore Roosevelt's executive order to add the region around Aneth, Utah in 1905 was confirmed by Congress in 1933.

The eastern border was shaped primarily as a result of allotments of land to individual Navajo households under the Dawes Act of 1887. This experiment was designed to assimilate Native Americans to mainstream American culture. The federal government proposed to divide communal lands into plots assignable to heads of household – tribal members – for their subsistence farming, in the pattern of small family farms common among Americans. This was intended to extinguish tribal land claims for such territory. The land allocated to these Navajo heads of household was initially not considered part of the reservation. Further, the federal government determined that land "left over" after all members had received allotments was to be considered "surplus" and available for sale to non-Native Americans. The allotment program continued until 1934. Today, this patchwork of reservation and nonreservation land is called the "checkerboard area". It resulted in the loss of much Navajo land.

In the southeastern area of the reservation, the Navajo Nation has purchased some ranches, which it refers to as its *Nahata Dził*, or New Lands. These lands are leased to Navajo individuals, livestock companies, and grazing associations.

Administrative divisions; Agencies and chapters: The Navajo Nation is divided into five agencies. The seat of government is located at the Navajo Governmental Campus in Window Rock/*Tségháhoodzání*. These agencies are composed of several chapters each, and reflect the five Bureau of Indian Affairs (BIA) agencies created in the early formation of the Navajo Nation.

The five agencies within the Navajo Nation are Chinle Agency in Chinle, Arizona; Eastern Navajo Agency in Crownpoint, New Mexico; Western Navajo Agency in Tuba City, Arizona; Fort Defiance Agency in Fort Defiance, Arizona; and Shiprock Agency in Shiprock, New Mexico. The BIA agencies provide various technical services under direction of the BIA's Navajo Area Office at Gallup, New Mexico.

Agencies are divided into chapters as the smallest political unit, similar to municipalities or small U.S. counties. The Navajo capital city of Window Rock is located in the chapter of St. Michaels, Arizona.

The Navajo Nation also operates executive offices in Washington, DC to facilitate government-to-government relations and for lobbying services and congressional relations.

Adjacent to or near the Navajo Nation are the Southern Ute of Colorado, and the Ute Mountain Ute Tribe of Colorado, Utah, and New Mexico, both along the northern borders; the Jicarilla Apache Tribe to the east; the Zuni Pueblo and White Mountain Apache to the south; and the Hualapai Bands in the west. The Navajo Nation's territory fully surrounds the Hopi Indian Reservation.

In the 1980s, a conflict over shared lands peaked when the Department of the Interior attempted to relocate Navajo residents living in what is still referred to as the Navajo–Hopi Joint Use Area. The litigious and social conflict between the two tribes and neighboring communities ended with "The Bennett Freeze" Agreement, completed in July 2009 by President Barack Obama. The agreement lessened the contentious land disagreement by providing a 75-year lease to Navajo who had land claims dating to before the US occupation of the territory.

Geography: The land area of the Navajo Nation is over 27,000 square miles (70,000 km$^2$), making it the largest Indian reservation in the United States; it is approximately 8,000 km$^2$ larger than the state of West Virginia.

Situated on the Navajo Nation are Canyon de Chelly National Monument, Monument Valley, Rainbow Bridge National Monument, the Shiprock monadnock, and the eastern portion of the Grand Canyon. Navajo Territory in New Mexico is popularly referred as the "Checkerboard" area because it is interrupted by Navajo and non-Native fee ownership of numerous plots of land. In this area, Navajo lands are intermingled with fee lands, owned by both Navajo and non-Navajo, and federal and state lands under various jurisdictions. Three large noncontiguous sections located in New Mexico are also under Navajo jurisdiction: these are the Ramah Navajo Indian Reservation, the Alamo Navajo Indian Reservation, and the Tohajiilee Indian Reservation near Albuquerque."[10]

The resource materials for the censuses within this series and each volume has been transcribed from National Archives Film, Indian Census Rolls 1885-1940; M-595 Rolls 303-307. It is with full respect of the Navajo people both past and present that this work and history has been studied and made available. Also it is realized that without the study, hard work and dedication of the authors from even decades ago the references inside these pages couldn't have been fulfilled without a proper history or understanding of the truth and what took place. This effort hopefully can be an encouragement for the Navajo of today or for others to be interested in Navajo history and understand the great injustice so many fell victim to.

Jeff Bowen
Gallipolis, Ohio
*NativeStudy.com*

---

[10] Navajo Nation; Wikipedia

# INSTRUCTIONS

(A) A separate roll is to be made of each reservation; also, of each *rancheria* or reserve, and a separate roll of Indians allotted on the public domain or homesteading. The roll is to be based on enrollment and not on residence.

(B) Persons are to be listed by families alphabetically; that is, not only by the first letter of the surname, but also by the second and subsequent letters, when the first letter or letters are the same. For example: Abalon, Abbott, Abcon, Abend, Abiet; Ball, Bell, Bill, Boll, Bull; Carley, Carmen, Carton, etc. Families having the same surname are also to be listed in this way, e. g.: Brown, *Anson*; Brown, *Bill*; Brown, *Charles*; Brown, *David*. In the case of English translations of Indian names, such as John *Flying-Elk*, Flying-Elk is the surname and is to be listed under F. In such cases the first word of the translated Indian name determines the alphabetical position. The best way to accomplish this will be to write the names of each family group on a separate card; then, arrange the cards alphabetically and type the names therefrom onto the census roll.

Members of a family are to be listed in the following order: Head, first; wife second; then children, whether sons or daughters, *in the order of their ages*; and lastly, all other relatives and persons living with the family who do not constitute another family group.

Annuity and per capita payment rolls are also to be prepared in the same manner.

(C) A family is composed of the following members:

1. Both parents and their unmarried children, if any, living with them; all other relatives and persons living with the family who do not constitute another family group.

2. Either parent and the unmarried children, if the other parent is dead; all other relatives and persons living with the family who do not constitute another family group.

3. A single person over 21 years of age, not living with a relative.

(D) For each person the following information is to be furnished:

1. NUMBER.—A number is to be assigned in serial order. Thus, the first person listed is to be numbered as "1," the second, as "2," and so on until the census is completed.

2. NAME.—If there are both an Indian and an English name, the allotment or annuity roll name is to be given. First, the last or surname; then, the given name in full. Ditto marks are to be used under the surname of the head for the surnames of the other members of one family.

3. SEX.—"M," for male; "F," for female.

4. AGE AT LAST BIRTHDAY.—Age in completed years at last birthday is to be shown. For infants under 1 year, age in completed months, expressed as twelfths of a year. Thus, 3 months is $\frac{3}{12}$ yr.

5. TRIBE.—Care is to be taken that tribe, not band or local name, is given. Thus, Ute tribe, not Pahvant, which is a band of Ute. Likewise, Hupa tribe, not Bear River, which is a local name for the members of the Hupa tribe living near Bear River.

6. DEGREE OF BLOOD.—"F," for full blood; "¼+," for one-fourth or more Indian blood; "—¼," for less than one-fourth Indian blood.

7. MARITAL STATUS.—"S," for a single or unmarried person; "M," for a married person; and "Wd," for widowed of either sex.

8. RELATIONSHIP TO HEAD OF FAMILY.—The head, whether husband or father, widow or unmarried person of either sex, is to be designated as such. For the other members, the appropriate term which designates the particular relationship the person bears to the head is to be used.

9. RESIDENCE.—

(a) At *jurisdiction* where enrolled: Yes or no. The term jurisdiction includes all reservations and public domain allotments under the agency.

(b) Or at another jurisdiction. The name of the jurisdiction is to be given.

(c) Or elsewhere:

1. Post office: Both the proper name of the post office and the class by which it is known (city, town, village, etc.) are to be given. Thus, Lewiston, city.

2. County.

3. State.

10. WARD.—Yes or no. Wardship depends primarily upon the ownership of individual property held in trust or upon membership in a tribe living on a Federal reservation. See Circular 2145.

11. ALLOTMENT, ANNUITY, AND IDENTIFICATION NUMBERS.—"Al," for allotment; "An," for annuity; and "Id," for identification, before the appropriate number or numbers. All numbers are to be shown.

(E) Rolls not prepared in strict conformity with the above instructions will be returned for correction.

# CENSUS OF THE

# NORTHERN NAVAJO

# NAVAJO RESERVATION

# NEW MEXICO

as of April 1, 1931,

Taken by Ernest H. Hammond, District Superintendent in Charge.

NOTE: In this census the birth year is marked out but coincides with each individual's age. The census taker placed a handwritten age above the marked out year. For sake of clarity both are being transcribed.

NOTE 2: In many instances the census taker or a secondary party would take a full page and put an "X" over the Post Office, County, and State entries wiping out complete information for where a party may have lived and it was felt that this information should be completely transcribed for the sake of full disclosure. It seems that each individual that touched the information in the census would make changes or put markings the way they felt they wanted it and sometimes causing a loss of full information. So during the transcription if the information appeared solid and complete it was felt that it should not be left out.

1

Census of the **Northern Navajo** reservation of the **Northern Navajo** jurisdiction, as of **April 1**, 1931, taken by **Ernest H. Hammond, District**, Superintendent. **in Charge**

**Key:** Number; NAME: Surname, Given; Sex; Birth Year (if given), Age At Last Birthday; Tribe; Degree of Blood; Marital Status; Relationship To Head of Family; Last Census Roll Number; At Jurisdiction Where Enrolled (Yes or No); At Another Jurisdiction; ELSEWHERE: Post office, County, State; Ward (Yes or No); Allotment, Annuity, and Identification Numbers.

1; Aaron; M; Unk; Navajo; F; M; Head; 1; Yes; Yes; 23600
2; Aaron's wife; F; 51; Navajo; F; M; Wife; 2; Yes; Yes; 23601
3; Elmer; M; 23; Navajo; F; S; Son; 3; Yes; Yes; 23602
4; McKinley; M; 18; F; S; Son; 4; Yes; Yes; 23603
5; Al-kih-haz-bah; F; 15; F; S; Daughter; 5; Yes; Yes; 23604
6; Ned; M; 11; Navajo; F; S; Son; 6; Yes; Yes; 23605
7; Dah-hih-bah; F; 9; Navajo; F; S; Daughter; 7; Yes; Yes; 23606
8; Dah-hih-bah; F; 6; Navajo; F; S; Daughter; 8; Yes; Yes; 23607
9; Doh-naz-bah; F; 12; Navajo; F; S; Grand-daughter; 9; Yes; Yes; 12608
10; Wilson; M; Unk; Navajo; F; S; Son; 10; Yes; Yes; 23919

11; Bega, Aaron; M; Unk; Navajo; F; M; Head; 11; Yes; Yes; 23787
12; Yah-nih-hah; F; 20; Navajo; F; M; Wife; 12; Yes; Yes; 23788

13; Bega, Aaron; M; 21; Navajo; F; M; Head; 13; Yes; Yes; 23609
14; Keh-yil-nih-bah; F; 25; Navajo; F; M; Wife; 14; Yes; Yes; 23424

15; Abraham; M; 35; Navajo; F; M; Head; 15; Yes; Yes; 19316
16; Bontoni-yazzie-bitsih; F; 28; Navajo; F; M; Wife; 16; Yes; Yes; 19317
18; Atate-yazzie; F; 11; Navajo; F; S; Step-daughter; 18; Yes; Yes; 19318
18; Kee-soh; M; 9; Navajo; F; S; Son; 18; Yes; Yes; 19319
20; Yah-des-bah; F; 7; Navajo; F; S; Daughter; 20; Yes; Yes; 19320
20; Natah-yil-ciz-zih; M; 1927, 4; Navajo; F; S; Son; 20; Yes; Yes; 19321
21; Na-tah-ye-hah-wudt; M; 2; Navajo; F; S; Son; 21; Yes; Yes; 19514

22; Adki-nez; M; 1877, 54; Navajo; F; M; Head; 22; Yes; Yes; 19455
23; Hosteen-bih-nah-atinih-bitsih; F; 63; Navajo; F; M; Wife; 23; Yes; Yes; 19456
24; Jay; M; 26; Navajo; F; S; Son; 24; Yes; Yes; 19457
25; Has-Wudt; M; 24; Navajo; F; S; Son; 25; Yes; Yes; 19458
26; Zohe-nih-adake, Flora; F; 21; Navajo; F; S; Daughter; 26; Yes; Yes; 19459
27; Yazzie; F; 20; Navajo; F; S; Daughter; 27; Yes; Yes; 19460
28; Atate-te-yaz; F; 9; Navajo; F; S; Grand-daughter; 28; Yes; Yes; 19461

29; Adzan-hasbidih-toh; M; 44; Navajo; F; Wd; Head; 29; Yes; Yes; 17982
30; Hoschie; M; 38; Navajo; F; S; Son[sic]; 30; Yes; Yes; 17983
31; Descheeny-bega; M; 28; Navajo; F S; Son[sic]; 31; Yes; Yes; 17984
32; Natoni-bega; M; 26; Navajo; F; S; Son; 32; Yes; Yes; 17985
33; Gee-kee; M; 7; Navajo; F; S; Grand-Son; 33; Yes; Yes; 17986
34; Has-goh-ad-; M; 3; Navajo; F; S; Son; 34; Yes; Yes; 17987
[Note: Nos. 29-33 The above ages do not coincide, the children could have been the wife's offspring since he's a widower.]

35; Adzan-top-ah-hah; F; 78; Navajo; F; Wd; Head; 35; Yes; Yes; 21305

3

Census of the **Northern Navajo** reservation of the **Northern Navajo** jurisdiction, as of **April 1**, 19**31**, taken by **Ernest H. Hammond, District**, Superintendent. **in Charge**

**Key:** Number; NAME: Surname, Given; Sex; Birth Year (if given), Age At Last Birthday; Tribe; Degree of Blood; Marital Status; Relationship To Head of Family; Last Census Roll Number; At Jurisdiction Where Enrolled (Yes or No); At Another Jurisdiction; ELSEWHERE: Post office, County, State; Ward (Yes or No); Allotment, Annuity, and Identification Numbers.

36; Top-ah-hah-bih-che; F; 39; Navajo; F; Wd; Daughter; 36; Yes; Yes; 21306
37; Dah-nih-bah; F; 11; Navajo; F; S; Grand Daughter; 37; Yes; Yes; 21307
38; Tahn-hah-bah; F; 9; Navajo; F; S; Grand Daughter; 38; Yes; Yes; 21308
39; Adzan-suen; F; 5; Navajo; F; S; Grand Daughter; 39; Yes; Yes; 21309
40; Kee; M; 18; Navajo; F; S; Grand-Son; 40; Yes; Yes; 21310

41; Adzan-hah-tahly; M; 59; Navajo; F; Wd; Head; 41; Yes; Yes; 24986
42; McDonald, Harry; M; 23; Navajo; F; S; Nephew; 42; Yes; Yes; 24987
43; June; F; 21; Navajo; F; S; Daughter; 43; Yes; Yes; 24988
44; Harley; M; 26; Navajo; F; S; Son; 44; Yes; Yes; 24989
45; Abbie; F; 20; Navajo; F; S; Daughter; 45; Yes; Yes; 24990
46; Yee-nih-bah; F; 18; Navajo; F; S; Daughter; 46; Yes; Yes; 24991
47; Jenny; F; 18; Navajo; F; S; Grand Daughter; 47; Yes; Yes; 24992
48; Bil-kih-ziz-bah; F; 93; Navajo; F; Wd; Mother; 48; Yes; Yes; 24993
49; Ben; M; 9; Navajo; F; S; Nephew; 49; Yes; Yes; 24994

50; Adzan-sen-chil-sah-kadih; F; 64; Navajo; F; Wd; Head; 50; Yes; Yes; 24701
51; Bahih; M; 20; Navajo; F; S; Son; 51; Yes; Yes; 24702
52; Edna; F; 21; Navajo; F; S; Daughter; 52; Yes; Yes; 24703
53; Dinay-I-bahih, Edward; M; 26; Navajo; F; S; Son; 53; Yes; Yes; 24704
54; Chih-bah; F; 9; Navajo; F; S; Grand-daughter; 54; Yes; Yes; 24705

55; Adzan-Toh-dih-cheeny-bitsoih; M; 43; Navajo; F Wd; Head; 55; Yes; Yes; 22358
56; Rose; F; 13; Navajo; F; S; Daughter; 56; Yes; Yes; 22359

57; Adzan-toh-das-anih; F; 78; Navajo; F; Wd; Head; 57; Yes; Yes; 22342
58; Atate; F; 13; Navajo; F; S; Grand-daughter; 58; Yes; Yes; 22343

59; Adzan-bisah-ahlani; F; 78; Navajo; F; Wd; Head; 59; Yes; Yes; 20941
60; Nocki-Dinay-Nez, Mabel; F; 15; Navajo; F; S; Grand Daughter; 60; Yes; Yes; 20942
61; Bin-ziz-bah; F; 60; Navajo; F; Wd; Daughter; 61; Yes; Yes; 20943
62; Nah-glih-ee-bah; F; 4; Navajo; F; S; Grand Daughter; 62; Yes; Yes; 20944

63; Azan-l-bahih; F; 33; Navajo; F; Wd; Head; 63; Yes; Yes; 21326
64; Eskee-l-chee; M; 15; Navajo; F; S; Son; 64; Yes; Yes; 21327
65; Nah-tah-yil-has-wudt-ih; M; 9; Navajo; F; S; Son; 65; Yes; Yes; 21328
66; See-bahih; M; 7; Navajo; F; S; Son; 66; Yes; Yes; 21329
67; Yee-nil-wudt; M; 25; Navajo; F; S; Brother; 67; Yes; Yes; 21330

68; Adaki-soh-bega; M; 31; Navajo; F; M; Head; 68; Yes; Yes; 19980
69; Adaki-soh-bega's wife; F; 38; Navajo; F; M; Wife; 69; Yes; Yes; 19981

Census of the **Northern Navajo** reservation of the **Northern Navajo** jurisdiction, as of **April 1**, 1931, taken by **Ernest H. Hammond, District**, Superintendent. **in Charge**

**Key:** Number; NAME: Surname, Given; Sex; Birth Year (if given), Age At Last Birthday; Tribe; Degree of Blood; Marital Status; Relationship To Head of Family; Last Census Roll Number; At Jurisdiction Where Enrolled (Yes or No); At Another Jurisdiction; ELSEWHERE: Post office, County, State; Ward (Yes or No); Allotment, Annuity, and Identification Numbers.

70; Yathe, Geraldine; F; 21; Navajo; F; S; Step-daughter; 70; Yes; Yes; 19982
71; Chee-yazzie; M; 16; Navajo; F; S; Step-son; 71; Yes; Yes; 19984
72; Yath; F; 18; Navajo; F; S; Daughter; 72; Yes; Yes; 19983
73; Hoska-chee-des-wudt; M; 5; Navajo; F; S; Son; 73; Yes; Yes; 19985

74; Adaki-soh-bega; M; 24; Navajo; F; M; Head; 74; Yes; Yes; 19978
75; Kes-bah; F; 20; Navajo; F; M; Wife; 75; Yes; Yes; 19979

76; Adaki, Francis; M; 42; Navajo; F; M; Head; 76; Yes; Yes; 19204
77; Adaki, Bessie; F; 20; Navajo; F; M; Wife; 77; Yes; Yes; 19205
78; Baby; M; 2; Navajo; F; S; Son; 78; Yes; Yes; 19503

79; Adaki-soh; M; 62; Navajo; F; M; Head; 79; Yes; Yes; 28495
80; Bah; F; 61; Navajo; F; M; 1st. wife; 80; Yes; Yes; 28496
81; Charley; M; 28; Navajo; F; S; Son; 81; Yes; Yes; 28497
82; Alvin; M; 16; Navajo; F; S; Grand-Son; 82; Yes; Yes; 28498
83; Bih-hek-dinnih-bitsih; F; 48; Navajo; F; M; 2nd. wife; 82-a; Yes; Yes; 28499
84; Valentine, Gray; M; 27; Navajo; F; S; Son; 83; Yes; Yes; 28500
85; Zah-bah; F; 18; Navajo; F; S; Daughter; 84; Yes; Yes; 28501
86; Yee-chih-haz-bah; F; 15; Navajo; F; S; Daughter; 85; Yes; Yes; 28502
87; Nah-glih-yee-naz-bah; F; 10; Navajo; F; S; Daughter; 86; Yes; Yes; 28503
88; Haska-yee-kih-des-wudt; M; 7; Navajo; F; S; Son; 87; Yes; Yes; 28504

89; Adazanih-soh; F; 81; Navajo; F; Wd; Head; 88; Yes; Yes; 26959
90; Hah-bah; F; 50; Navajo; F; Wd; Daughter; 89; Yes; Yes; 26960
91; Gleesah, Fritz; M; 23; Navajo; F; S; Grand-Son; 90; Yes; Yes; 26961
92; Gleesah, Binton; M; 18; Navajo; F; S; Grand-Son; 91; Yes; Yes; 26962
93; Kes-wudt; M; 11; Navajo; F; S; Grand-Son; 92; Yes; Yes; 26963

94; Adobe-bega; M; 46; Navajo; F; M; Head; 93; Yes; Yes; 26887
95; Tah-dez-bah; F; 51; Navajo; F; M; Wife; 94; Yes; Yes; 26888
96; Comelia; F; Unk; Navajo; F; S; Daughter; 95; Yes; Yes; 26890
97; Haska-yee-dah-hah-ah; M; Unk; Navajo; F; S; Son; 96; Yes; Yes; 26891
98; Bil-nih-ziz; F; 10; Navajo; F; S; Step-Grand-daughter; 97; Yes; Yes; 26892

99; Adaki, Little John; M; 45; Navajo; F; M; Head; 98; Yes; Yes; 18178
100; Bontoni-yan-bitsih; F; 45; Navajo; F; M; Wife; 99; Yes; Yes; 18179
101; Yazzie, John; M; 20; Navajo; F; S; Son; 100; Yes; Yes; 18180
102; Nih-jih-bah; F; 18; Navajo; F; S; Daughter; 101; Yes; Yes; 18181
103; Yaz; F; 12; Navajo; F; S; Daughter; 102; Yes; Yes; 18182
104; Bontoni-yen-bitsih; F; 43; F; M; 2nd wife; 103; Yes; Yes; 18183
105; Eskee-nanl-cadih; M; 15; Navajo; F; S; Son; 104; Yes; Yes; 18184
106; Dah-yis-bah; F; 9; Navajo; F; S; Daughter; 105; Yes; Yes; 18185

Census of the __Northern Navajo__ reservation of the __Northern Navajo__ jurisdiction, as of __April 1__, 19**31,** taken by __Ernest H. Hammond, District__, Superintendent. **in Charge**

**Key:** Number; NAME: Surname, Given; Sex; Birth Year (if given), Age At Last Birthday; Tribe; Degree of Blood; Marital Status; Relationship To Head of Family; Last Census Roll Number; At Jurisdiction Where Enrolled (Yes or No); At Another Jurisdiction; ELSEWHERE: Post office, County, State; Ward (Yes or No); Allotment, Annuity, and Identification Numbers.

107; Adxan-bah-hah-zohnih[sic]; F; 7; F; S; Daughter; 106; Yes; Yes; 18186
[Name should be Adzan-bah-hah-zohnih]
108; Adzanih-bellee-thlani; F; 23; Navajo; F; Wd; Daughter; 107; Yes; Yes; 18187
109; Kee-sihih; M; 13; Navajo; F; S; Grand-Son; 108; Yes; Yes; 18188

110; Adzanih-bitsee-Citsoih-Bihyaz; M; 24; Navajo; F; M; Head; 109; Yes; Yes; 17010
111; Sinn-sah-cadnih-cho-bega's Daughter; F; 22; Navajo; F; M; Wife; 110; Yes; Yes; 17011

112; Adzan-nanl-cadih-bigsoih; M; 62; Navajo; F; M; Head; 111; Yes; Yes; 32462
113; Dinay-chilli-bitsih, Maud; F; 37; Navajo; F; M; Wife; 112; Yes; Yes; 32463
114; Maudie; F; 15; Navajo; F; S; Daughter; 113; Yes; Yes; 32464
115; Jack; M; 12; Navajo; F; S; Son; 114; Yes; Yes; 32465
116; Keh-yee-nah-bah; F; 7; Navajo; F; S; Daughter; 115; Yes; Yes; 32466

117; Adzan-deel; F; Unk; Navajo; F; Wd; Head; 116; Yes; Yes; 28538
118; Hosteen-taih-benally; M; 24; Navajo; F; S; Son; 117; Yes; Yes; 28539
119; Phillip Oliver; M; 23; Navajo; F; S; Son; 118; Yes; Yes; 28540
120; Saul; M; 22; Navajo; F; S; Son; 119; Yes; Yes; 28541
121; Mike; M; 10; Navajo; F; S; Son; 120; Yes; Yes; 28542

122; Adaki-sosie; M; 62; Navajo; F; M; Head; 121; Yes; Yes; 28412
123; Hosteen-tah-hih-bitsih; F; 53; Navajo; F; M; Wife; 122; Yes; Yes; 28413
124; Eskee-nilih; M; 36; Navajo; F; S; Son; 123; Yes; Yes; 28414
125; Atate-nih-yazzie; F; 12; Navajo; F; S; Daughter; 124; Yes; Yes; 28415

126; Adzanih-soh-bhi-che[sic]; F; 45; Navajo; F; Wd; Head; 125; Yes; Yes; 26964
[Name could be Adzanih-soh-bih-che]
127; Evan; M; 23; Navajo; F; S; Son; 126; Yes; Yes; 26965
128; Keh-yil-nih-nih-bah; F; 8; Navajo; F; S; Daughter; 127; Yes; Yes; 26966

129; Adzan-tah-cheenih; F; 78; Navajo; F; Wd; Head; 128; Yes; Yes; 23586
130; Bah; F; 23; Navajo; F; S; Grand-daughter; 129; Yes; Yes; 23587
131; James Henderson; M; 25; Navajo; F; S; Grand-Son; 130; Yes; Yes; 23588
132; Edith; F; 15; Navajo; F; S; Grand-daughter; 131; Yes; Yes; 23589

133; Adzaniho-bih-kinn; F; 73; Navajo; F; Wd; Head; 132; Yes; Yes; 18206
134; Adzanih-nah-lozih; F; 13; Navajo; F; S; Grand-daughter; 133; Yes; Yes; 18207
135; Banh-yih-bah, Billy; M; 9; Navajo; F; S; Grand-Son; 134; Yes; Yes; 18208
136; Adzan-suen; F; 7; Navajo; F; S; Grand-daughter; 135; Yes; Yes; 18209

Census of the **Northern Navajo** reservation of the **Northern Navajo** jurisdiction, as of **April 1**, 19**31,** taken by **Ernest H. Hammond, District**, Superintendent. **in Charge**

**Key:** Number; NAME: Surname, Given; Sex; Birth Year (if given), Age At Last Birthday; Tribe; Degree of Blood; Marital Status; Relationship To Head of Family; Last Census Roll Number; At Jurisdiction Where Enrolled (Yes or No); At Another Jurisdiction; ELSEWHERE: Post office, County, State; Ward (Yes or No); Allotment, Annuity, and Identification Numbers.

137; Adzanih-zolie; F; 61; Navajo; F; Wd; Head; 136; Yes; Yes; 18079

138; Adaki-bega; M; 29; Navajo; F; M; Head; 137; Yes; Yes; 17911
139; Ah-ha-nih-bah; F; 31; Navajo; F; M; Wife; 138; Yes; 17912
140; Hoska-yah-ye-gahl; M; 6; Navajo; F; S; Son; 139; Yes; Yes; 17913

141; Adzanih-lapahih; F; 54; Navajo; F; Div.; Head; 140; Yes; Yes; 17316
142; Kin-nopbah; F; 18; Navajo; F; S; Grand-daughter; 141; Yes; Yes; 17317
143; Glih-obah; F; 15; Navajo; F; S; Grand-daughter; 142; Yes; Yes; 17318

144; Adaki-soh-bega; M; Unk; Navajo; F; M; Head; 143; Yes; Yes; 17261
145; Dohi-bega-bitsih; F; 26; Navajo; F; M; Wife; 144; Yes; Yes; 17262
146; Adaki-soh, Emma; F; 5; Navajo; F; S; Daughter; 145; Yes; Yes; 17263
147; Adaki-soh, Jerry; M; 7; Navajo; F; S; Son; 146; Yes; Yes; 17264
148; Askee-Yazzie; M; 3; Navajo; F; S; Son; 147; Yes; Yes; 20438

149; Adzanih-bitsee-lahpaih; M; 63; Navajo; F; Wd; Head; 148; Yes; Yes; 17169
150; Toh-hosebah; F; 15; Navajo; F; S; Grand-daughter; 149; Yes; Yes; 17170

151; Adzan-l-suen; F; 99; Navajo; F; Wd; Head; 150; Yes; Yes; 23270
152; Dagaihih, Calvin; M; 21; Navajo; F; S; Grand-Son; 151; Yes; Yes; 23271
153; Longfellow; M; 23; Navajo; F; S; Grand-Son; 152; Yes; Yes; 23272
154; James; M; Unk; Navajo; F; S; Grand-Son; 153; Yes; Yes; 23273

155; Adzan-Batoni; F; 71; Navajo; F; Wd; Head; 154; Yes; Yes; 23383
156; Willie; M; 22; Navajo; F; S; Son; 155; Yes; Yes; 23384
157; Toh-des-bah; F; 33; Navajo; F; Wd; Daughter; 156; Yes; Yes; 23385
158; Keh-yil-chin-bah; F; 4; Navajo; F; S; Grand-daughter; 157; Yes; Yes; 23386
159; Al-keh-hah-bah; F; 4; Navajo; F; S; Grand-daughter; 158; Yes; Yes; 23387

160; Adaki-soh-bitah; M; Unk; Navajo; F; M; Head; 159; Yes; Yes; Yes; 29176
161; Biz-ess-bah; F; 28; Navajo; F; M; Wife; 160; Yes; Yes; 29177
162; Doh-bah; F; 5; Navajo; F; S; Daughter; 161; Yes; Yes; 29178
163; Seeih; F; 4; Navajo; F; S; Daughter; 162; Yes; Yes; 29179
164; Tah-deyah; M; 4; Navajo; F; S; Son; 163; Yes; Yes; 29180

165; Adzan-Ah-tlohi-benally; M; 24; Navajo; F; M; Head; 164; Yes; Yes; 32289
166; Salou-l-sosie-benally; F; 21; Navajo; F; M; Wife; 165; Yes; Yes; 32290
167; Bih-kih-zoz-bah; F; 3; Navajo; F; S; Daughter; 166; Yes; Yes; 32291

168; Adzanih-bitsee-lagaih; M; 74; Navajo; F; Wd; Head; 167; Yes; Yes; 31084
169; Nah-tah-hoh-lel; M; 10; Navajo; F; S; Son; 168; Yes; Yes; 31085

Census of the **Northern Navajo** reservation of the **Northern Navajo** jurisdiction, as of **April 1** , 1931, taken by **Ernest H. Hammond, District** , Superintendent. **in Charge**

**Key:** Number; NAME: Surname, Given; Sex; Birth Year (if given), Age At Last Birthday; Tribe; Degree of Blood; Marital Status; Relationship To Head of Family; Last Census Roll Number; At Jurisdiction Where Enrolled (Yes or No); At Another Jurisdiction; ELSEWHERE: Post office, County, State; Ward (Yes or No); Allotment, Annuity, and Identification Numbers.

170; Adzan-soh-zilth-nih-bih-yaz; M; 37; Navajo; F; M; Head; 169; Yes; Yes; 29873

171; Ah-nah-gahnih-sosie-bysih; F; 21; Navajo; F; M; Wife; 170; Yes; Yes; 29874

172; Adzan-ach-zilth-nih; F; 78; Navajo; F; Wd; Mother; 171; Yes; Yes; 29875

173; Adzanih-toh-dih-koze; F; 64; Navajo; F; Wd; Head; 172; Yes; Yes; 32914

174; Raymond; M; 32; Navajo; F; S; Son; 173; Yes; Yes; 32915

175; Keh-yah-nih-bah; F; 16; Navajo; F; S; Grand-daughter; 174; Yes; Yes; 32916

176; Adzan-hahtahly-bega; M; 37; Navajo; F; M; Head; 175; Yes; Yes; 19841

177; Klee-nanl-cadih-bitsih; F; 32; Navajo; F; M; Wife; 176; Yes; Yes; 19842

178; Katie; F; 11; Navajo; F; S; Daughter; 177; Yes; Yes; 19843

179; Ah-keh-nal-wudt; M; 6; Navajo; F; S; Daughter[sic]; 178; Yes; Yes; 19844

180; Shorty-yazzie; M; 3; Navajo; F; S; Son; 179; Yes; Yes; 19845

181; Ahtcity-bega; M; 43; Navajo; F; M; Head; 180; Yes; Yes; 17072

182; Hosteen-deel-benally; F; 38; Navajo; F; M; Wife; 181; Yes; Yes; 17073

183; Adzanih-obah; F; 27; Navajo; F; S; Daughter; 182; Yes; Yes; 17074

184; Ahtcity, Jeff; M; 20; Navajo; F; M; Son; 183; Yes; Yes; 17075

185; Ahtcity, Martha; F; 18; Navajo; F; S; Daughter; 184; Yes; Yes; 17076

186; Ahtcity-kay-desbah; F; 16; Navajo; F; S; Daughter; 185; Yes; Yes; 17077

187; Adzanih-chee; F; 14; Navajo; F; S; Daughter; 186; Yes; Yes; 17078

188; Ahtcity-tah-despas; F; 9; F; S; Daughter; 187; Yes; Yes; 17079

189; Ahtcity-shi-nanobah; F; 8; Navajo; F; S; Daughter; 188; Yes; Yes; 17080

190; Ahtcity-Alchahobah; F; 5; Navajo; F; S; Daughter; 189; Yes; Yes; 17081

191; Big Ezy-rah; M; 1; Navajo; F; S; Son; [Blank]; Yes; Yes; 17417

192; Kito-wood; F; 2; Navajo; F; S; Grand-daughter; [Blank]; Yes; Yes; 17416

193; Ahnahgahl-yazzie; M; 53; Navajo; F; M; Head; 190; Yes; Yes; 17270

194; Descheeny-ahtcity-bitsih; F; Unk; Navajo; F; M; Wife; 191; Yes; Yes; 17271

195; Ahnahgahi-yazzie-denay-tohl; M; 18; Navajo; F; S; Son; 192; Yes; Yes; 17272

196; Denah Tuli; M; 13; Navajo; F; S; Son; [Blank]; Yes; Yes; 17415

197; Ahtcitty-yen-bennally; M; 25; Navajo; F; M; Head; 193; Yes; Yes; 21446

198; Thelma; F; 26; Navajo; F; M; Wife; 194; Yes; Yes; 21447

199; Al-kih-nih-bah; F; 3; Navajo; F; S; Daughter; 195; Yes; Yes; 21448

200; Ah-jehih-benally; M; 27; Navajo; F; M; Head; 196; Yes; Yes; 22416

201; Tahn-nan-bah; F; 23; Navajo; F; M; Wife; 197; Yes; Yes; 22417

202; Nah-tah-yil-kee-wudt; M; 4; Navajo; F; S; Son; 198; Yes; Yes; 22418

203; Ah-jeh-ih-bega; M; 61; Navajo; F; M; Head; 199; Yes; Yes; 22386

204; Dil-awashih-bega-bitsih; F; 51; Navajo; F; M; Wife; 200; Yes; Yes; 22387

Census of the **Northern Navajo** reservation of the **Northern Navajo** jurisdiction, as of **April 1**, 19**31**, taken by **Ernest H. Hammond, District**, Superintendent. **in Charge**

**Key:** Number; NAME: Surname, Given; Sex; Birth Year (if given), Age At Last Birthday; Tribe; Degree of Blood; Marital Status; Relationship To Head of Family; Last Census Roll Number; At Jurisdiction Where Enrolled (Yes or No); At Another Jurisdiction; ELSEWHERE: Post office, County, State; Ward (Yes or No); Allotment, Annuity, and Identification Numbers.

205; Kin-nih-bah; F; 23; Navajo; F; S; Daughter; 201; Yes; Yes; 22388
206; Estelle; F; 21; Navajo; F; S; Daughter; 202; Yes; Yes; 22389
207; Hoska-yil-cheh-l-wudt; M; 20; Navajo; F; S; Son; 203; Yes; Yes; 22390
208; Yee-kaz-wudt; M; 14; Navajo; F; S; Son; 204; Yes; Yes; 22391
209; Yil-yee-gahl; M; 10; Navajo; F; S; Son; 205; Yes; Yes; 22392

210; Ahtcitty-benally; M; 23; Navajo; F; M; Head; 206; Yes; Yes; 22554
211; Zaz-bah; F; 20; Navajo; F; M; Wife; 207; Yes; Yes; 22555
212; Hoska-yee-tah-nal-wuhl; M; 3; Navajo; F; S; Son; 208; Yes; Yes; 22556

213; Ahtcitty, Jim; M; 22; Navajo; F; M; Head; 209; Yes; Yes; 22654
214; Dale-Stephen's Dau.; F; 20; Navajo; F; M; Wife; 210; Yes; Yes; 22655

215; Aht-sosie-bega; M; 45; Navajo; F; M; Head; 211; Yes; Yes; 19816
216; Hoska-yen-benally; F; 42; Navajo; F; M; Wife; 212; Yes; Yes; 19817
217; Bah-hah-zoh; M; 16; Navajo; F; S; Son; 213; Yes; Yes; 19818
218; Ahtsosie, Luke; M; 13; Navajo; F; S; Son; 214; Yes; Yes; 19819
219; Nan-nih-bah; F; 8; Navajo; F; S; Daughter; 215; Yes; Yes; 19821
220; Nah-tahe; M; 6; Navajo; F; S; Son; 216; Yes; Yes; 19822
221; Hoska-ye-tah-des-wudt; M; 4; Navajo; F; S; Son; 217; Yes; Yes; 19823

222; Ah-han-bah; F; 29; Navajo; F; Wd; Head; 218; Yes; Yes; 22450
223; Nah-tah-yil-ni-dee-zah; M; 4; Navajo; F; S; Son; 219; Yes; Yes; 22451

224; Ahtcitty-yen-bega, Joe; M; 39; Navajo; F; M; Head; 220; Yes; Yes; 22452
225; Hosteen-gonih-bega; F; 33; Navajo; F; M; Wife; 221; Yes; Yes; 22453
226; Hoska-yil-yeel-wohl; M; 14; Navajo; F; S; Son; 222; Yes; Yes; 22454
227; John Joe; M; 12; Navajo; F; S; Son; 223; Yes; Yes; 22455
228; Hoska-yil[sic]; M; 9; Navajo; F; S; Son; 224; Yes; Yes; 22456
[Name in 1930 Census was Hoska-yil-hah-yah]
229; Nah-glih-has-bah; F; 5; Navajo; F; S; Daughter; 225; Yes; Yes; 22457
230; Luke; M; 3; Navajo; F; S; Son; 226; Yes; Yes; 22458

231; Aht-citty-yen-bitah; M; 51; Navajo; F; M; Head; 227-A; Yes; Yes; 21442
232; Gilbert; M; 18; Navajo; F; S; Son; 227; Yes; Yes; 21443
233; Hoska-yee-chih-has-wudt; M; 13; Navajo; F; S; Son; 228; Yes; Yes; 21444

234; Aht-citty-bega; M; 42; Navajo; F; M; Head; 229; Yes; Yes; 21214
235; Beleen-lizin-bih-chek; F; 48; Navajo; F; M; Wife; 230; Yes; Yes; 21215
236; Des-woody; M; 18; Navajo; F; S; Son; 231; Yes; Yes; 21216
237; Adzan-suen; F; 15; Navajo; F; S; Daughter; 232; Yes; Yes; 21217
238; Aht-citty, Byron; M; 13; Navajo; F; S; Daughter[sic]; 233; Yes; Yes; 21218
239; Natoni; M; 10; Navajo; F; S; Son; 234; Yes; Yes; 21219

Census of the __Northern Navajo__ reservation of the __Northern Navajo__ jurisdiction, as of __April 1__ , 1931, taken by __Ernest H. Hammond, District__, Superintendent. __in Charge__

**Key:** Number; NAME: Surname, Given; Sex; Birth Year (if given), Age At Last Birthday; Tribe; Degree of Blood; Marital Status; Relationship To Head of Family; Last Census Roll Number; At Jurisdiction Where Enrolled (Yes or No); At Another Jurisdiction; ELSEWHERE: Post office, County, State; Ward (Yes or No); Allotment, Annuity, and Identification Numbers.

240;  Glih-des-bah; F; 8; Navajo; F; S; Daughter; 235; Yes; Yes; 21220
241;  Nah-tahl-bahih; M; 6; Navajo; F; S; Son; 236; Yes; Yes; 21221

242;  Aht-citty-yen-bih-adzan; F; 63; Navajo; F; Wd; Head; 237; Yes; Yes; 21230
243;  Doh-yazzie; M; 16; Navajo; F; S; Son; 238; Yes; Yes; 21231

244;  Lily; F; 12; Navajo; F; S; Head (Daughter); 239; Yes; Yes; 21455
245;  Kay-yil-nah-nih-bah; F; 7; F; S; Daughter; 240; Yes; Yes; 21456
246;  Kee-deyah; M; 4; Navajo; F; S; Son; 241; Yes; Yes; 21457
247;  Lena; F; 13; Navajo; F; S; Niece; 242; Yes; Yes; 21458

248;  Aht-citty-yen-bega; M; 43; Navajo; F; M; Head; 243; Yes; Yes; 21507
249;  Bah; F; 36; Navajo; F; M; Wife; 244; Yes; Yes; 21508

250;  Aht-citty, Ned; M; 27; Navajo; F; M; Head; 245; Yes; Yes; 21515
251;  Hosteen-Gah-bitsoih; F; 25; Navajo; F; M; Wife; 246; Yes; Yes; 21516
252;  Doh-yah; M; 6; Navajo; F; S; Son; 247; Yes; Yes; 21517
253;  Kin-dah-yis-bah; F; 4; Navajo; F; S; Daughter; 248; Yes; Yes; 21518

254;  Atsosie; M; 39; Navajo; F; M; Head; 249; Yes; Yes; 19393
255;  Bitsih, Sam; F; 38; Navajo; F; M; Wife; 250; Yes; Yes; 19394
256;  Yee-che-desbah; F; 16; Navajo; F; S; Daughter; 251; Yes; Yes; 19395
257;  Capitan-bega; F; 15; Navajo; F; S; Daughter; 252; Yes; Yes; 19396
258;  Doh-des-bah; F; 14; Navajo; F; S; Daughter; 253; Yes; Yes; 19397
259;  Shin-deh-tih; F; 13; Navajo; F; S; Daughter; 254; Yes; Yes; 19398
260;  Aht-sosie, Caleb; M; 11; Navajo; F; S; Son; 255; Yes; Yes; 19399
261;  Adzan-suen; F; 10; Navajo; F; S; Daughter; 256; Yes; Yes; 19400
262;  Shih-kolie; M; 8; Navajo; F; S; Son; 257; Yes; Yes; 19401
263;  Diney-yis-yunih; M; 6; Navajo; F; S; Son; 258; Yes; Yes; 19402
264;  Diney-clitsoihgi; M; 5; Navajo; F; S; Son; 259; Yes; Yes; 19403
265;  Diney-bih-skay; M; 3; Navajo; F; S; Son; 260; Yes; Yes; 19404

266;  Aht-citty-neg-bega[sic]; M; Unk; Navajo; F; M; Head; 261; Yes; Yes; 23677
       [Name is probably Aht-citty-nez-bega]
267;  Yahn-naz-bah; F; 23; Navajo; F; M; Wife; 262; Yes; Yes; 23678
268;  Haska-yee-nan-tah; M; 5; Navajo; F; S; Son; 263; Yes; Yes; 23679
269;  Haska-yil-ee-del; M; 4; Navajo; F; S; Son; 264; Yes; Yes; 23680
270;  Haska-yil-nil-wudt; M; 18; Navajo; F; S; Son; 265; Yes; Yes; 23682
271;  Keh-yil-haz-bah; F; 16; Navajo; F; S; Daughter; 266; Yes; Yes; 23683
272;  Shelly; F; 2; Navajo; F; S; Daughter; 266-A; Yes; Yes; 23929

273;  Aht-citty; M; 57; Navajo; F; M; Head; 267; Yes; Yes; 26020
274;  Glih-yee-ah-dez-bah; F; 35; Navajo; F; M; Wife; 268; Yes; Yes; 26021

10

Census of the **Northern Navajo** reservation of the **Northern Navajo** jurisdiction, as of **April 1**, 19**31**, taken by **Ernest H. Hammond, District**, Superintendent. **in Charge**

**Key:** Number; NAME: Surname, Given; Sex; Birth Year (if given), Age At Last Birthday; Tribe; Degree of Blood; Marital Status; Relationship To Head of Family; Last Census Roll Number; At Jurisdiction Where Enrolled (Yes or No); At Another Jurisdiction; ELSEWHERE: Post office, County, State; Ward (Yes or No); Allotment, Annuity, and Identification Numbers.

275; Amelia; F; 16; Navajo; F; S; Daughter; 269; Yes; Yes; 26022
276; Frank; M; 14; Navajo; F; S; Son; 270; Yes; Yes; 26023
277; Fred; M; 13; Navajo; F; S; Son; 271; Yes; Yes; 26024
278; Arlene; F; 11; Navajo; F; S; Daughter; 272; Yes; Yes; 26025
279; Nah-tah-yee-kih-dahyis-wudt; M; 9; Navajo; F; S; Son; 273; Yes; Yes; 26026
280; Al-kih-dah-yiz-bah; F; 8; Navajo; F; S; Daughter; 274; Yes; Yes; 26027
281; Nah-tahl-bahih; M; 6; Navajo; F; S; Son; 275; Yes; Yes; 26028
282; Hah-tah-yee-kih-dil-ez; M; 21; Navajo; F; S; Son; 277; Yes; Yes; 26030
283; Nah-tah-yazzie; M; 20; Navajo; F; S; Son; 278; Yes; Yes; 26031
284; Yah-nih-bah; F; 18; Navajo; F; S; Daughter; 279; Yes; Yes; 26032

285; Ahtsoni-benally; M; 49; Navajo; F; M; Head; 280; Yes; Yes; 17145
286; Bitsee-pahih-bega-bitsih; F; 33; Navajo; F; M; Wife; 281; Yes; Yes; 17146
287; Ahtsoni-benally-clee-ahnopbah; F; 18; Navajo; F; S; Daughter; 282; Yes; Yes; 17147
288; Ahtsoni-benally-keetsoh; M; 18; Navajo; F; S; Son; 283; Yes; Yes; 17148
289; Ahtsoni-benally-Ese-bah; F; 10; Navajo; F; S; Daughter; 284; Yes; Yes; 17149
290; Ahtsoni-benally; M; 3; Navajo; F; S; Son; 285; Yes; Yes; 17150

291; Aht-citty-nez-badoni; M; 56; Navajo; F; M; Head; 286; Yes; Yes; 23713
292; Aht-citty-nez-bitsih; F; 53; Navajo; F; M; Wife; 287; Yes; Yes; 23714
293; Anderson Bert; M; 30; Navajo; F; S; Son; 288; Yes; Yes; 23715
294; Tom Lee; M; 23; Navajo; F; S; Son; 289; Yes; Yes; 23716
295; Al-nan-nih-bah; F; 20; Navajo; F; S; Daughter; 290; Yes; Yes; 23717
296; Al-Keh-yil-nih-nih-bah; F; 11; Navajo; F; S; Daughter; 291; Yes; Yes; 23718
297; Nah-tah-yee-tah-gah; M; 7; Navajo; F; S; Son; 292; Yes; Yes; 23719
298; Chee-ih; M; 8; Navajo; F; S; Grand-Son; 293; Yes; Yes; 23720
299; Nez, Dempsey; M; 21; Navajo; F; S; Son; 294; Yes; Yes; 23721

300; Ahtsani-bega; M; Unk; Navajo; F; M; Head; 295; Yes; Yes; 17179
301; Ahtsani-bis-yahad; F; 65; Navajo; F; M; Wife; 296; Yes; Yes; 17180
302; Chinn-opbah; F; 20; Navajo; F; S; Daughter; 297; Yes; Yes; 17181
303; Hoska-bades-wudt; M; 15; Navajo; F; S; Grand-Son; 298; Yes; Yes; 17182

304; Aht-citty-yazzie; M; 44; Navajo; F; M; Head; 299; Yes; Yes; 24878
305; Aht-citty-yazzie's wife; F; 53; Navajo; F; M; Wife; 300; Yes; Yes; 24879
306; Dah-naz-bah; F; 20; Navajo; F; S; Step-daughter; 301; Yes; Yes; 24880
307; Rosie; F; 22; Navajo; F; S; Step-daughter; 302; Yes; Yes; 24881
308; Wilson; M; 18; Navajo; F; S; Step-son; 303; Yes; Yes; 24882
309; Zoh, Aaron; M; 16; Navajo; F; S; Step-son; 304; Yes; Yes; 24883
310; Keh-ah-bah; F; 11; Navajo; F; S; Step-daughter; 305; Yes; Yes; 24884
311; Gey-bah, Manuelito; F; 25; Navajo; F; S; Step-daughter; 306; Yes; Yes; 24885
312; Manuelito, Peter; M; 4; Navajo; F; S; Step-Grand-son; 307; Yes; Yes; 24886

11

Census of the **Northern Navajo** reservation of the **Northern Navajo** jurisdiction, as of **April 1**, 19**31**, taken by **Ernest H. Hammond, District**, Superintendent. **in Charge**

**Key:** Number; NAME: Surname, Given; Sex; Birth Year (if given), Age At Last Birthday; Tribe; Degree of Blood; Marital Status; Relationship To Head of Family; Last Census Roll Number; At Jurisdiction Where Enrolled (Yes or No); At Another Jurisdiction; ELSEWHERE: Post office, County, State; Ward (Yes or No); Allotment, Annuity, and Identification Numbers.

313; Ah-hehihi-yen-bega; M; 63; Navajo; F; M; Head; 308; Yes; Yes; 23526
314; Bah; F; 61; Navajo; F; M; Wife; 309; Yes; Yes; 23527
315; Lewis, Rita Betty; F; 22; Navajo; F; S; Daughter; 310; Yes; Yes; 23528
316; Nez, Arthur; M; 20; Navajo; F; S; Grand-Son; 311; Yes; Yes; 23529

317; Aht-citty-badoni, Charley; M; 40; Navajo; F; M; Head; 312; Yes; Yes; 24860
318; Yahn-nah-bah; F; 43; Navajo; F; M; Wife; 313; Yes; Yes; 24861
319; Haska-yil-hal-wudt; M; 18; Navajo; F; S; Son; 314; Yes; Yes; 24862
320; Ben; M; 16; Navajo; F; S; Son; 315; Yes; Yes; 24863
321; Edward; M; 22; Navajo; F; S; Son; 316; Yes; Yes; 24864
322; Nah-tah-yee-nas-wudt; M; 10; Navajo; F; S; Son; 317; Yes; Yes; 24865
323; Al-keh-nah-bah; F; 4; Navajo; F; S; Daughter; 318; Yes; Yes; 24866

324; Ahtcity-bega; M; 43; Navajo; F; M; Head; 319; Yes; Yes; 17294
325; Hosteen-l-suen-yazzie-bega-bitsih; F; 39; Navajo; F; M; Wife; 320; Yes; Yes; 17295
326; Ahtcity-benally; M; 20; Navajo; F; S; Son; 321; Yes; Yes; 17296
327; Ahtcity-bega, Dempsey; M; 18; Navajo; F; S; Son; 322; Yes; Yes; 17297
328; Ahtcity-bega-Dinay-pahih; M; 15; Navajo; F; S; Son; 323; Yes; Yes; 17298
329; Ahtcity-bega-dinay-chee; M; 11; Navajo; F; S; Son; 324; Yes; Yes; 17299
330; Ahtcity-bega-cheeih; M; 7; Navajo; F; S; Son; 325; Yes; Yes; 17300
331; Ahtcity-bega-dinay-suie; M; 6; Navajo; F; S; Son; 326; Yes; Yes; 17301
332; Ahtcity-bega-hoska-yazzie; M; 3; Navajo; F; S; Son; 327; Yes; Yes; 17302
333; Ahtcity-bega-nah-asynn; M; 13; Navajo; F; S; Son; 328; Yes; Yes; 17303
334; Ahtcity-bega-chink-despa; M; 1-3/12; Navajo; F; S; Son; 329; Yes; Yes; 18267

335; Aht-sosiebega, Harvey, Jean; M; 40; Navajo; F; M; Head; 330; Yes; Yes; 19201
336; Nocki-bitsih, Harvey, Louise; F; 38; Navajo; F; M; Wife; 331; Yes; Yes; 19202
337; Kee-pahih, Henry; M; 10; Navajo; F; S; Son; 332; Yes; Yes; 19203
338; Haska-ye-chi-wudt; M; 2; Navajo; F; S; Son; 333; Yes; Yes; 19502

339; Aht-citty-bitsoih; M; 35; Navajo; F; M; Head; 334; Yes; Yes; 28806
340; Nocki-nez-deyih; F; 42; Navajo; F; M; Wife; 335; Yes; Yes; 28807
341; Mazih; M; 15; Navajo; F; S; Son; 336; Yes; Yes; 28808
342; Joely; F; 8; Navajo; F; S; Daughter; 337; Yes; Yes; 28809
343; Woody; M; 16; Navajo; F; S; Nephew-in-law; 338; Yes; Yes; 28810
344; Bah-ah-yazzie; F; 12; Navajo; F; S; Niece-in-law; 339; Yes; Yes; 28811
345; Isobel; F; 20; Navajo; F; S; Niece-in-law; 340; Yes; Yes; 28812
346; Adzan-nanl-cadih; F; 38; Navajo; F; S; Sister-in-law; 341; Yes; Yes; 28813

Census of the **Northern Navajo** reservation of the **Northern Navajo** jurisdiction, as of **April 1**, 19**31,** taken by **Ernest H. Hammond, District**, Superintendent. **in Charge**

**Key:** Number; NAME: Surname, Given; Sex; Birth Year (if given), Age At Last Birthday; Tribe; Degree of Blood; Marital Status; Relationship To Head of Family; Last Census Roll Number; At Jurisdiction Where Enrolled (Yes or No); At Another Jurisdiction; ELSEWHERE: Post office, County, State; Ward (Yes or No); Allotment, Annuity, and Identification Numbers.

347; Ahtcitty-nez; M; 77; Navajo; F; M; Head; 342; Yes; Yes; 23530
348; Keh-yah-nih-nih-bah; F; 41; Navajo; F; M; Wife; 343; Yes; Yes; 23531
349; Grace; F; 15; Navajo; F; S; Daughter; 344; Yes; Yes; 23532
350; Glih-bah-yaz; F; 14; Navajo; F; S; Daughter; 345; Yes; Yes; 23533
351; Yee-hih-bah; F; 12; Navajo; F; S; Daughter; 346; Yes; Yes; 23534
352; Glih-siz-bah; F; 8; Navajo; F; S; Daughter; 347; Yes; Yes; 23535
353; Tah-zoz-bah; F; 6; Navajo; F; S; Daughter; 348; Yes; Yes; 23536
354; Nah-nih-bah; F; 4; Navajo; F; S; Daughter; 349; Yes; Yes; 23537
355; Arthur; M; 18; Navajo; F; S; Son; 350; Yes; Yes; 23916
356; Nocki-yay-kothl; M; 1- 4/12; Navajo; F; S; Son; 351; Yes; Yes; 23917

357; Ah-nah-glohih-bega; M; 32; Navajo; F; M; Head; 352; Yes; Yes; 26845
358; Chih-naz-bah; F; 23; Navajo; F; M; Wife; 353; Yes; Yes; 26846
359; Haska-yee-chih-has-wude[sic]; M; 13; Navajo; F; S; Son; 354; Yes; Yes; 26847
[Name is probably Haska-yee-chih-has-wudt, as in 1930 Census]
360; Haska-yee-nel-wudt; M; 12; Navajo; F; S; Son; 355; Yes; Yes; 26848
361; Haska-yee-neh-yah; M; 10; Navajo; F; S; Son; 356; Yes; Yes; 26849
362; Keh-hee-bah; F; 9; Navajo; F; S; Daughter; 357; Yes; Yes; 26850
363; Chih-des-wudt; M; 7; Navajo; F; S; Son; 358; Yes; Yes; 26851
364; Foster; M; Unk; Navajo; F; S; Nephew-in-law; 359; Yes; Yes; 26852
365; Foster, Eunice; F; 21; Navajo; F; S; Niece-in-law; 360; Yes; Yes; 26853
366; Adzan-bih-naz-bah; F; 74; Navajo; F; Wd; Grand-mother-in-law; 361; Yes; Yes; 26854

367; Aht-citty-yen-bega; M; 24; Navajo; F; M; Head; 362; Yes; Yes; 28818
368; Long, John Bitsih; F; 34; Navajo; F; M; Wife; 363; Yes; Yes; 28819
369; Tah-nih-bah; F; 13; Navajo; F; S; Daughter; 364; Yes; Yes; 28820
370; Louise; F; 10; Navajo; F; S; Daughter; 365; Yes; Yes; 28821
371; Batoni-nez; M; 9; Navajo; F; S; Son; 366; Yes; Yes; 28822
372; Bih-kah-ziz-bah; F; 7; Navajo; F; S; Daughter; 367; Yes; Yes; 28823
373; Nah-glih-yil-ee-bah; F; 4; Navajo; F; S; Daughter; 368; Yes; Yes; 28824
374; Aht-citty-yen-bih-adzen[sic]; F; 72; Navajo; F; Wd; Mother; 369; Yes; Yes; 28825 [Name should be Aht-citty-yen-bih-adzan]
375; Aht-citty-yen-bihtih; F; 62; Navajo; F; Wd; Sister; 370; Yes; Yes; 28826
376; Bih-kah-ziz-bah; F; 4; Navajo; F; S; Niece; 371; Yes; Yes; 28827

377; Ahtcitty-sosie-bega; M; 30; Navajo; F; M; Head; 372; Yes; Yes; 28846
378; Aht-citty-yeh-benally; F; 32; Navajo; F; M; Wife; 373; Yes; Yes; 28847
379; Baz-nih-bah; F; 7; Navajo; F; S; Daughter; 374; Yes; Yes; 28848
380; Yee-kis-was-wudt; M; 5; Navajo; F; S; Son; 375; Yes; Yes; 28849
381; Nah-glih-naz-bah; F; 4; Navajo; F; S; Daughter; 376; Yes; Yes; 28850
382; Nah-hazne-lah; F; 2; Navajo; F; S; Daughter; 377; Yes; Yes; 28554

Census of the **Northern Navajo** reservation of the **Northern Navajo** jurisdiction, as of **April 1** , 19**31,** taken by **Ernest H. Hammond, District**, Superintendent. **in Charge**

383; Ah-glain-bega, Stradavanus[sic]; M; 30; Navajo; F; S; Head; 378; Yes; Yes; 19909 [Name is probably Ah-glain-bega, Stradavarus]

384; Aht-benally-aholtahi; M; 35; Navajo; F; M; Head; 379; Yes; Yes; 17171
385; Neeth-dih-thlohi-bitsih; F; 42; Navajo; F; M; Wife; 380; Yes; Yes; 17172
386; Tohsani, Edward; M; 20; Navajo; F; S; Step-son; 381; Yes; Yes; 17173
387; Toh-sani-bega; M; 23; Navajo; F; S; Step-son; 382; Yes; Yes; 17174
388; Tohsani, Anita; F; Unk; Navajo; F; S; Step-daughter; 383; Yes; Yes; 17175
389; Tohsani, Iris; F; Unk; Navajo; F; S; Step-daughter; 384; Yes; Yes; 17176
390; Ahtsani-benally-ganah-chee; M; 9; Navajo; F; S; Son; 385; Yes; Yes; 17177
391; Hoska-yi-yilih-wudt; M; 3; Navajo; F; S; Son; 386; Yes; Yes; 17178

392; Antonig, Willie; M; 34; Navajo; F; M; Head; 387; Yes; Yes; 27515
393; Nah-glih-yil-dez-bah; F; 29; Navajo; F; M; Wife; 388; Yes; Yes; 27516
394; Jeo[sic]; M; 11; Navajo; F; S; Son; 389; Yes; Yes; 27517
     [Name is probably Joe]
395; Tom; M; 9; Navajo; F; S; Son; 390; Yes; Yes; 27518
396; Haska-yi;-nih-nih-yah[sic]; M; 6; Navajo; F; S; Son; 391; Yes; Yes; 27519
     [Name is probably Haska-yil-nih-nih-yah]
397; Paul; M; 4; Navajo; F; S; Son; 392; Yes; Yes; 27520
398; Taylor; M; 18; Navajo; F; S; Brother; 393; Yes; Yes; 27521
399; Harry; M; 16; Navajo; F; S; Brother; 394; Yes; Yes; 27522

400; Ahtl-ohi; M; 56; Navajo; F; M; Head; 395; Yes; Yes; 17914
401; Ahtl-ohi's wife; F; 33; Navajo; F; M; Wife; 396; Yes; Yes; 17915
402; Ah-thlohi, William; M; 18; Navajo; F; S; Son; 397; Yes; Yes; 17916
403; Ah-thlohi, Beth; F; 13; Navajo; F; S; Daughter; 398; Yes; Yes; 17917
404; Al-has-hah-bah; F; 11; Navajo; F; S; Daughter; 399; Yes; Yes; 17918
405; Tah-yil-wudt; M; 7; Navajo; F; S; Son; 400; Yes; Yes; 17919
406; Keh-hah-nih-bah; F; 3; Navajo; F; S; Daughter; 401; Yes; Yes; 17920
407; Zannie; F; 12; Navajo; F; S; Niece; 402; Yes; Yes; 17922

408; Ah-nah-gahnih, Business; M; 48; Navajo; F; M; Head; 403; Yes; Yes; 28441
409; Yabney-bitsih; F; 43; Navajo; F; M; Wife; 404; Yes; Yes; 28442
410; Kehn; F; 23; Navajo; F; S; Daughter; 405; Yes; Yes; 28443
411; Elmer; M; 12; Navajo; F; S; Grand-son; 406; Yes; Yes; 28444

412; Aht-citty-dil-kah-benally, John; M; 44; Navajo; F; M; Head; 407; Yes; Yes; 25236
413; Yil-hah-naz-bah; F; 35; Navajo; F; M; Wife; 408; Yes; Yes; 25237
414; Yee-nah-bah; F; 6; Navajo; F; S; Daughter; 409; Yes; Yes; 25238
415; Keh-hah-bah; F; 4; Navajo; F; S; Daughter; 410; Yes; Yes; 25239

Census of the **Northern Navajo** reservation of the **Northern Navajo** jurisdiction, as of **April 1**, 19**31**, taken by **Ernest H. Hammond, District**, Superintendent. **in Charge**

**Key:** Number; NAME: Surname, Given; Sex; Birth Year (if given), Age At Last Birthday; Tribe; Degree of Blood; Marital Status; Relationship To Head of Family; Last Census Roll Number; At Jurisdiction Where Enrolled (Yes or No); At Another Jurisdiction; ELSEWHERE: Post office, County, State; Ward (Yes or No); Allotment, Annuity, and Identification Numbers.

416; Aht-citty-bega; M; 34; Navajo; F; M; Head; 411; Yes; Yes; 25939
417; Kih-ziz-bah; F; 27; Navajo; F; M; Wife; 412; Yes; Yes; 25940
418; Nah-tah-yah; M; 6; Navajo; F; S; Son; 413; Yes; Yes; 25941
419; Nah-tah-yazzie; M; 4; Navajo; F; S; Son; 414; Yes; Yes; 25942

420; Aht-citty; M; Unk; Navajo; F; M; Head; 415; Yes; Yes; 26386
421; Beh-hah-kih-ges-bah; F; 61; Navajo; F; M; Wife; 416; Yes; Yes; 26387
422; Hah-siz-bah; F; 18; Navajo; F; S; Daughter; 417; Yes; Yes; 26388

423; Aht-citty-sisie[sic]; M; 34; Navajo; F; M; Head; 418; Yes; Yes; 26667
       [Name should be Aht-citty-sosie]
424; Al-hih-daz-bah; F; 32; Navajo; F; M; Wife; 419; Yes; Yes; 26668
425; Bih-nih-ziz-bah; F; 11; Navajo; F; S; Daughter; 420; Yes; Yes; 26669
426; Bih-nih-ziz-bah; F; 7; Navajo; F; S; Daughter; 421; Yes; Yes; 26670
427; Chih-des-wudt; M; 5; Navajo; F; S; Son; 422; Yes; Yes; 26671

428; Aht-citty-nez-bega; M; 23; Navajo; F; M; Head; 423; Yes; Yes; 23616
429; Han-bah; F; 22; Navajo; F; M; Wife; 424; Yes; Yes; 23617
430; Unk.; M; 4; Navajo; F; S; Son; 425; Yes; Yes; 23618

431; Aht-citty-bitsoih, Friday; M; 24; Navajo; F; M; Head; 426; Yes; Yes; 18883
432; Nocki-yazzie-bega-bitsih; F; 21; Navajo; F; M; Wife; 427; Yes; Yes; 18884
433; Tah-nih-bah; F; 4; Navajo; F; S; Daughter; 428; Yes; Yes; 18885

434; Aht-citty-yen-bitsoih; M; 34; Navajo; F; M; Head; 429; Yes; Yes; 18195
435; Aht-citty-yen-bitsoih's wife; F; 33; Navajo; F; M; Wife; 430; Yes; Yes; 18196
436; Ah-kee; M; 10; Navajo; F; S; Son; 431; Yes; Yes; 18197

437; Ah-deet-sahigi-Hosteen; M; Unk; Navajo; F; M; Head; 432; Yes; Yes; 17367
438; Ah-deet-sahigi-Hosteen's wife; F; 65; Navajo; F; M; Wife; 433; Yes; Yes; 17368

439; Ahtsani-benally; M; 30; Navajo; F; M; Head; 434; Yes; Yes; 17061
440; Des-cheeny-bitsih; F; 23; Navajo; F; M; Wife; 435; Yes; Yes; 17062
441; Ahtsani-chinabah-yazzie; F; 7; Navajo; F; S; Daughter; 436; Yes; Yes; 17063
442; Ahtsani-chee; F; 5; Navajo; F; S; Daughter; 437; Yes; Yes; 17064
443; Ahtsani-yeetsah-napah; F; 3; Navajo; F; S; Daughter; 438; Yes; Yes; 17065

444; Aht-citty-sosie; M; 50; Navajo; F; M; Head; 439; Yes; Yes; 28833
445; Aht-citty-yen-bitsoih; F; 33; Navajo; F; M; Wife; 440; Yes; Yes; 28834
446; Beleen-lagaih-yazzie; M; 12; Navajo; F; S; Son; 441; Yes; Yes; 28835
447; Naz-dee-bah; F; 10; Navajo; F; S; Daughter; 442; Yes; Yes; 28836
448; Batoni-l-gaith; M; 56; Navajo; F; S; Son; 443; Yes; Yes; 28837

15

Census of the **Northern Navajo** reservation of the **Northern Navajo** jurisdiction, as of **April 1**, 19**31,** taken by **Ernest H. Hammond, District**, Superintendent. **in Charge**

Key: Number; NAME: Surname, Given; Sex; Birth Year (if given), Age At Last Birthday; Tribe; Degree of Blood; Marital Status; Relationship To Head of Family; Last Census Roll Number; At Jurisdiction Where Enrolled (Yes or No); At Another Jurisdiction; ELSEWHERE: Post office, County, State; Ward (Yes or No); Allotment, Annuity, and Identification Numbers.

449; Askan-deel, Roma; F; 21; Navajo; F; S; Sister-in-law; 444; Yes; Yes; 28838

450; Ah-dest-sahigih (Taylor), Frank[sic]; M; Unk; Navajo; F; M; Head; 445; Yes; Yes; 20230 [Name is probably Ah-deet-sahigih (Taylor), Frank]
451; Ah-seet-sahigih's wife[sic]; F; 40; Navajo; F; M; Wife; 446; Yes; Yes; 20231 [Name is probably Ah-deet-sahigih's wife]
452; Ah-deet-sahigih, Esther; F; 16; Navajo; F; S; Daughter; 447; Yes; Yes; 20232
453; Wudt; M; 10; Navajo; F; S; Son; 448; Yes; Yes; 20233
454; Hoska-yil-hah-yah; M; 10; Navajo; F; S; Son; 449; Yes; Yes; 20234
455; Hoska-yil-hah-yah; M; 8; Navajo; F; S; Son; 450; Yes; Yes; 20235
456; Nan-i-pah; F; 2; Navajo; F; S; Daughter; 451; Yes; Yes; 20236

457; Aht-citty-benally; M; 36; Navajo; F; M; Head; 452; Yes; Yes; 29810
458; See-chosie-bitsih; F; 23; Navajo; F; M; Wife; 453; Yes; Yes; 29811
459; Nah-glih-hah-bah; F; 9; Navajo; F; S; Niece; 454; Yes; Yes; 29812

460; Aht-citty-bega, John Paul; M; 34; Navajo; F; M; Head; 455; Yes; Yes; 29813
461; Yil-naz-bah; F; 22; Navajo; F; M; Wife; 456; Yes; Yes; 29814
462; Haska-yil-nil-wudt; M; 6; Navajo; F; S; Son; 457; Yes; Yes; 29815
463; Al-kih-yil-naz-bah; F; 4; Navajo; F; S; Daughter; 458; Yes; Yes; 29816

464; Aht-citty-yen-bitsoih; F; 33; Navajo; F; Div.; Head; 459; Yes; Yes; 29835
465; Pete; M; 20; Navajo; F; S; Son; 460; Yes; Yes; 29836

466; Aht-citty, Archie; M; 39; Navajo; F; M; Head; 461; Yes; Yes; 29796
467; Elizabeth; F; 38; Navajo; F; M; Wife; 462; Yes; Yes; 29797
468; Ida; F; 12; Navajo; F; S; Daughter; 463; Yes; Yes; 29798
469; Pearl; F; 5; Navajo; F; S; Daughter; 464; Yes; Yes; 29800
470; Frank; M; 20; Navajo; F; S; Brother; 465; Yes; Yes; 29802

471; Aht-citty, Henry; M; 30; Navajo; F; M; Head; 466; Yes; Yes; 29803
472; Bernice; F; 23; Navajo; F; M; Wife; 467; Yes; Yes; 29804
473; Nahn-nih-bah; F; 3; Navajo; F; S; Daughter; 468; Yes; Yes; 29805

474; Aht-citty-benally, Charley; M; 39; Navajo; F; M; Head; 469; Yes; Yes; 29781
475; Ah-hih-dee-bah; F; 21; Navajo; F; M; Wife; 470; Yes; Yes; 29782
476; Yee-kih-haz-bah; F; 4; Navajo; F; S; Daughter; 471; Yes; Yes; 29783

477; Aht-citty-bega-bihnih; M; 65; Navajo; F; M; Head; 472; Yes; Yes; 29784
478; Topah-ah-nez-bitsih; F; 63; Navajo; F; M; Wife; 473; Yes; Yes; 29785
479; Yes-hah-bah; F; 18; Navajo; F; S; Daughter; 474; Yes; Yes; 29786

480; Ahtcitty-benally; M; 26; Navajo; F; M; Head; 475; Yes; Yes; 29787

Census of the **Northern Navajo** reservation of the **Northern Navajo** jurisdiction, as of **April 1**, 19**31**, taken by **Ernest H. Hammond, District**, Superintendent. **in Charge**

**Key:** Number; NAME: Surname, Given; Sex; Birth Year (if given), Age At Last Birthday; Tribe; Degree of Blood; Marital Status; Relationship To Head of Family; Last Census Roll Number; At Jurisdiction Where Enrolled (Yes or No); At Another Jurisdiction; ELSEWHERE: Post office, County, State; Ward (Yes or No); Allotment, Annuity, and Identification Numbers.

481; Kiz-bah; F; Unk; Navajo; F; M; Wife; 476; Yes; Yes; 29788
482; Bih-gee-bah; F; 4; Navajo; F; S; Daughter; 477; Yes; Yes; 29789

483; Aht-citty-bega, John; M; Unk; Navajo; F; M; Head; 478; Yes; Yes; 29728
484; Glih-nez-bah; F; 22; Navajo; F; M; Wife; 479; Yes; Yes; 29729
485; Christine; F; 20; Navajo; F; S; Daughter; 480; Yes; Yes; 29730
486; Dah-yiz-wudt; M; 8; Navajo; F; S; Son; 481; Yes; Yes; 29731
487; Haska-yee-dah-yil-wudt; M; 6; Navajo; F; S; Son; 482; Yes; Yes; 29732
488; Nah-glih-yee-kih-nih-bah; F; 3; Navajo; F; S; Daughter; 483; Yes; Yes; 29733

489; Ah-banih-badoni; M; 42; Navajo; F; M; Head; 484; Yes; Yes; 30385
490; Ah-banih-bitsih; F; 32; Navajo; F; M; Wife; 485; Yes; Yes; 30386

491; Ah-keah, Sam; M; 35; Navajo; F; M; Head; 486; Yes; Yes; 30262
492; Frances; F; 29; Navajo; F; M; Wife; 487; Yes; Yes; 30263
493; Eleanor; F; 4; Navajo; F; S; Daughter; 488; Yes; Yes; 30265
494; Robert; M; 2; Navajo; F; S; Son; 489; Yes; Yes; 30266

495; Ah-nah-gahnih-sosie-bega; M; 36; Navajo; F; M; Head; 490; Yes; Yes; 29867
496; Neskahi-yazzie-bitsih; F; 25; Navajo; F; M; Wife; 491; Yes; Yes; 29868
497; Gil-woody; M; 8; Navajo; F; S; Son; 492; Yes; Yes; 29869
498; Haska-yee-tas-wudt; M; 6; Navajo; F; S; Son; 493; Yes; Yes; 29870
499; Nah-ziz-bah; F; 4; Navajo; F; S; Daughter; 494; Yes; Yes; 29871
500; Yee-nas-wudt; M; 12; Navajo; F; S; Nephew; 495; Yes; Yes; 29872

501; Ah-nah-thichin-bega; M; 27; Navajo; F; M; Head; 496; Yes; Yes; 30938
502; Aht-citty-nez-bennally; F; 22; Navajo; F; M; Wife; 497; Yes; Yes; 30939
503; Nah-tah-yil-nih-nih-yah; M; 2; Navajo; F; S; Son; 498; Yes; Yes; 30940
504; Aht-citty-nez-benally, Allen; M; 20; Navajo; F; S; Brother-in-law; 499; Yes; Yes; 30941

505; Ah-nah-tlohi-bih-yaz, Mike; M; 45; Navajo; F; M; Head; 500; Yes; Yes; 32282
506; Blue Eye's daughter; F; 44; Navajo; F; M; Wife; 501; Yes; Yes; 32283
507; Charley; M; 26; Navajo; F; S; Son; 502; Yes; Yes; 32284
508; Nas-wudt; M; 22; Navajo; F; S; Son; 503; Yes; Yes; 32285
509; Ah-hiln-bah; F; 14; Navajo; F; S; Daughter; 504; Yes; Yes; 32286
510; Yee-nel-wudt; M; 10; Navajo; F; S; Son; 505; Yes; Yes; 32287
511; Bil-hah-ziz-bah; F; 6; Navajo; F; S; Daughter; 506; Yes; Yes; 32288

512; Ah-nah-tlohi-bitah; M; Unk; Navajo; F; M; Head; 507; Yes; Yes; 32315
513; Bih-nah-atin-bitsih, Jim; F; 31; Navajo; F; M; Wife; 508; Yes; Yes; 32316
514; Willis; M; 11; Navajo; F; S; Son; 509; Yes; Yes; 32317

17

Census of the **Northern Navajo** reservation of the **Northern Navajo**
jurisdiction, as of **April 1**, 19**31,** taken by **Ernest H. Hammond, District**,
Superintendent. **in Charge**

**Key:** Number; NAME: Surname, Given; Sex; Birth Year (if given), Age At Last Birthday; Tribe; Degree of
Blood; Marital Status; Relationship To Head of Family; Last Census Roll Number; At Jurisdiction Where
Enrolled (Yes or No); At Another Jurisdiction; ELSEWHERE: Post office, County, State; Ward (Yes or No);
Allotment, Annuity, and Identification Numbers.

515; Biz-des-bah; F; 10; Navajo; F; S; Daughter; 510; Yes; Yes; 32318
516; Nah-tah-yil-des-wudt; M; 5; Navajo; F; S; Son; 511; Yes; Yes; 32319
517; Nah-tah-yee-tah-des-wudt; M; 2; Navajo; F; S; Son; 512; Yes; Yes; 32320

518; Aht-citty-bega; M; 60; Navajo; F; M; Head; 513; Yes; Yes; 30670
519; Topah-ah-nez-bitsih; F; 41; Navajo; F; M; Wife; 514; Yes; Yes; 30671
520; Ernest; M; 10; Navajo; F; Son; 515; Yes; Yes; 30674
521; Al-chih-dez-bah; F; 5; Navajo; F; S; Daughter; 516; Yes; Yes; 30675
522; Paul; M; 1 5/12; Navajo; F; S; Son; 517; Yes; Yes; 31258

523; Aht-citty-bega; M; 49; Navajo; F; M; Head; 518; Yes; Yes; 30408
524; Dah-nih-bah; F; 22; Navajo; F; M; Wife; 519; Yes; Yes; 30410

525; Aht-citty-bega-; M; 61; Navajo; F; M; Head; 520; Yes; Yes; 30276
526; Kesh-colih-bitsih; F; 57; Navajo; F; M; Wife; 521; Yes; Yes; 30277
527; Elmer; M; 22; Navajo; F; S; Son; 522; Yes; Yes; 30278
528; Seese; F; 18; Navajo; F; S; Daughter; 523; Yes; Yes; 30279
529; Ah-keah, William; M; 14; Navajo; F; S; Son; 524; Yes; Yes; 30280
530; Hi-del-een; M; 1921; Navajo; F; S; Son; 525; Yes; Yes; 30281

531; Aht-citty-bega, Froggy; M; 57; Navajo; F; M; Head; 526; Yes; Yes; 29876
532; Boh-woh-atin-bitsih; F; 46; Navajo; F; M; Wife; 527; Yes; Yes; 29877
533; John; M; 23; Navajo; F; S; Son; 528; Yes; Yes; 29878
534; Uienth-nez; M; 21; Navajo; F; S; Son; 529; Yes; Yes; 29879
535; Russell; M; 20; Navajo; F; S; Son; 530; Yes; Yes; 29880
536; Kee-yazzie; M; 15; Navajo; F; S; Son; 531; Yes; Yes; 29881
537; Bah-yazzie; F; 11; Navajo; F; S; Daughter; 532; Yes; Yes; 29882
538; Haska-yee-has-wudt; M; 8; Navajo; F; S; Son; 533; Yes; Yes; 29883
539; Boh-woh-atin-bih-adzan; F; 76; Navajo; F; Wd; Mother-in-law; 534; Yes;
Yes; 29884

540; Aht-citty-bega, Sam; M; 57; Navajo; F; M; Head; 535; Yes; Yes; 30507
541; Yee-chih-haz-bah; F; 20; Navajo; F; S; Daughter; 536; Yes; Yes; 30508
542; Haska-yah-nah-zah; M; 18; Navajo; F; S; Son; 537; Yes; Yes; 30509
543; Haska-yee-tah-nih-yah; M; 14; Navajo; F; S; Son; 538; Yes; Yes; 30510
544; Haska-yee-tas-wudt; M; 9; Navajo; F; S; Son; 539; Yes; Yes; 30511
545; Tah-nahn-bah; F; 7; Navajo; F; S; Daughter; 540; Yes; Yes; 30512

546; Aht-citty-benally, Charley; M; 31; Navajo; F; M; Head; 541; Yes; Yes; 30656
547; Neski-benally; F; 26; Navajo; F; M; Wife; 542; Yes; Yes; 30657
548; Keh-ah-dez-bah; F; 10; Navajo; F; S; Daughter; 543; Yes; Yes; 30658
549; Keh-hahn-nih-bah; F; 8; Navajo; F; S; Daughter; 544; Yes; Yes; 30659
550; Edison; M; 6; Navajo; F; S; Son; 545; Yes; Yes; 30660

Census of the **Northern Navajo** reservation of the **Northern Navajo** jurisdiction, as of **April 1** , 1931, taken by **Ernest H. Hammond, District**, Superintendent. **in Charge**

**Key:** Number; NAME: Surname, Given; Sex; Birth Year (if given), Age At Last Birthday; Tribe; Degree of Blood; Marital Status; Relationship To Head of Family; Last Census Roll Number; At Jurisdiction Where Enrolled (Yes or No); At Another Jurisdiction; ELSEWHERE: Post office, County, State; Ward (Yes or No); Allotment, Annuity, and Identification Numbers.

551; Lopan, Ellis; F; 2; Navajo; F; S; Daughter; 546; Yes; Yes; 30661
552; Abbie Jane; F; 18; Navajo; F; S; Sister-in-law; 547; Yes; Yes; 30662

553; Aht-citty, Fred; M; 35; Navajo; F; M; Head; 548; Yes; Yes; 30282
554; Clah-zinih-benally; F; 32; Navajo; F; M; Wife; 549; Yes; Yes; 30283
555; Zan-nih-bah; F; 10; Navajo; F; S; Daughter; 550; Yes; Yes; 30284
556; Ah-keh-yee-nih-bah; F; 8; Navajo; F; S; Daughter; 551; Yes; Yes; 30285
557; Gis-wudt; M; 4; Navajo; F; S; Son; 552; Yes; Yes; 30286

558; Aht-citty-benally, James; M; 26; Navajo; F; M; Head; 553; Yes; Yes; 30676

559; Aht-citty-benally; M; 31; Navajo; F; M; Head; 555; Yes; Yes; 30909
560; Minnie; F; 19; Navajo; F; M; Wife; 556; Yes; Yes; 30910
561; Salou-clah-bih-adzan; F; Unk; Navajo; F; Wd; Mother-in-law; 557; Yes; Yes; 30912

562; Aht-citty-benally; M; 30; Navajo; F; M; Head; 558; Yes; Yes; 32324
563; Bih-nah-atin-bitaih, Jim; F; 23; Navajo; F; M; Wife; 559B; Yes; Yes; 32325
564; Nah-tah-has-wudt; M; 7; Navajo; F; S; Son; 560; Yes; Yes; 32326
565; Nah-tah-yee-nil-wudt; M; 6; Navajo; F; S; Son; 561; Yes; Yes; 32327

566; Aht-citty-nez-bitsoih; M; 31; Navajo; F; M; Head; 562; Yes; Yes; 30687
567; Neskahi-benally; F; 29; Navajo; F; M; Wife; 563; Yes; Yes; 30688
568; Tah-dez-bah; F; 11; Navajo; F; S; Daughter; 564; Yes; Yes; 30690
569; Dah-nih-bah; F; 10; Navajo; F; S; Daughter; 565; Yes; Yes; 30691
570; Gonna-nez-bitah; M; 30; Navajo; F; S; Brother-in-law; 566; Yes; Yes; 30693

571; Aht-citty, Robert; M; 44; Navajo; F; M; Head; 567; Yes; Yes; 30287
572; Yil-ee-bah; F; 40; Navajo; F; M; Wife; 568; Yes; Yes; 30288
573; Lloyd; M; 27; Navajo; F; S; Son; 569; Yes; Yes; 30289
574; Ned; M; 22; Navajo; F; S; Son; 570; Yes; Yes; 30290
575; Nah-tah-yil-hal-wudt; M; 20; Navajo; F; S; Son; 571; Yes; Yes; 30291
576; Tah-nih-bah; F; 7; Navajo; F; S; Daughter; 572; Yes; Yes; 30292
577; Haska-yil-nah-yah; M; 7; Navajo; F; S; Son; 573; Yes; Yes; 30293
578; Gih-nih-bah; F; 3; Navajo; F; S; Daughter; 574; Yes; Yes; 30294

579; Aht-citty-yen-bega; M; 55; Navajo; F; M; Head; 575; Yes; Yes; 30963
580; Frank Dale's daughter; F; 21; Navajo; F; M; Wife; 576; Yes; Yes; 30964
581; Al-keh-hah-bah; F; 4; Navajo; F; S; Daughter; 577; Yes; Yes; 30965
582; Foster, Henry; M; 23; Navajo; F; S; Brother-in-law; 578; Yes; Yes; 30966
583; Sophia; F; 19; Navajo; F; S; Sister-in-law; 579; Yes; Yes; 30967
584; Nih-gee-wudt; M; 17; Navajo; F; S; Brother-in-law; 580; Yes; Yes; 30968

Census of the **Northern Navajo** reservation of the **Northern Navajo** jurisdiction, as of **April 1**, 19**31,** taken by **Ernest H. Hammond, District**, Superintendent. **in Charge**

**Key:** Number; NAME: Surname, Given; Sex; Birth Year (if given), Age At Last Birthday; Tribe; Degree of Blood; Marital Status; Relationship To Head of Family; Last Census Roll Number; At Jurisdiction Where Enrolled (Yes or No); At Another Jurisdiction; ELSEWHERE: Post office, County, State; Ward (Yes or No); Allotment, Annuity, and Identification Numbers.

585; Aht-soh, Dick; M; 34; Navajo; F; M; Head; 581; Yes; Yes; 31011
586; Aht-soh, Wilma; F; 30; Navajo; F; M; Wife; 582; Yes; Yes; 31012
587; Marjory; F; 14; Navajo; F; S; Daughter; 583; Yes; Yes; 31013
588; Rosalie; F; 2; Navajo; F; S; Daughter; 584; Yes; Yes; 31014
589; Richard, Jr.; M; 1-3/22; Navajo; F; S; Son; 585; Yes; Yes; 31210

590; Ah-doleh-bih-adzan; F; 77; Navajo; F; Wd; Head; 586; Yes; Yes; 32969

591; Ah-nah-gah-nih, Leroy; M; 26; Navajo; F; M; Head; 587; Yes; Yes; 32996
592; Betty Jean; F; 2; Navajo; 1/4; S; Daughter; 588; Yes; Yes; 32997

593; Ah-nah-tlohi-bih-adzan; F; 42; Navajo; F; Wd; Head; 589; Yes; Yes; 32881
594; Molly; F; 18; Navajo; F; S; Daughter; 590; Yes; Yes; 32882
595; Nah-tahyih-nayah[sic]; M; 6; Navajo; F; S; Son; 591; Yes; Yes; 32883
[Name should be Nah-tah-yih-nayah]
596; Nah-tah-yil-des-wudt; M; 6; Navajo; F; S; Son; 592; Yes; Yes; 32884

597; Aht-citty-nez-bega; M; 45; Navajo; F; M; Head; 593; Yes; Yes; 31146
598; Hosteen-sinnih-bitsih; F; 44; Navajo; F; M; Wife; 594; Yes; Yes; 31147
599; Nez; M; 16; Navajo; F; S; Son; 595; Yes; Yes; 31148
600; Hahn-ziz-bah; F; 10; Navajo; F; S; Daughter; 596; Yes; Yes; 31149

601; Clah, Albert; M; 30; Navajo; F; M; Head; 597; Yes; Yes; 24851
602; Hah-ah-sidih-benally; F; 33; Navajo; F; M; Wife; 598; Yes; Yes; 24852
603; Alice; F; 15; Navajo; F; S; Daughter; 599; Yes; Yes; 24853
604; Adele; F; 12; Navajo; F; S; Daughter; 600; Yes; Yes; 24854
605; Tah-deyah; M; 7; Navajo; F; S; Son; 601; Yes; Yes; 24855
606; Chih-hah-bah; F; 4; Navajo; F; S; Daughter; 602; Yes; Yes; 24856

607; Allen, George; M; 38; Navajo; F; M; Head; 603; Yes; Yes; 21078
608; Hosteen-nez-bitsih; F; 24; Navajo; F; M; Wife; 604; Yes; Yes; 21079
609; John; M; 6; Navajo; F; S; Son; 605; Yes; Yes; 21080
610; William; M; 4; Navajo; F; S; Son; 606; Yes; Yes; 21081
611; Hoska-yee-kay-lahl; M; 19; Navajo; F; S; Brother-in-law; 607; Yes; Yes; 21082
612; Toh-nas-bah; F; 16; Navajo; F; S; Sister-in-law; 608; Yes; Yes; 21083
613; Kee; M; 12; Navajo; F; S; Brother-in-law; 609; Yes; Yes; 21084
614; Hosteen-nez-bitsih; F; 14; Navajo; F; S; Sister-in-law; 610; Yes; Yes; 21085

615; Al-soh-ee-bah; F; 78; Navajo; F; Wd; Head; 611; Yes; Yes; 21519
616; Hoska-yil-nee-gahl; M; 21; Navajo; F; S; Grand-Son; 612; Yes; Yes; 21520

617; Allen, Charley; M; 30; Navajo; F; M; Head; 613; Yes; Yes; 30576

Census of the **Northern Navajo** reservation of the **Northern Navajo** jurisdiction, as of **April 1**, 19**31**, taken by **Ernest H. Hammond, District**, Superintendent. **in Charge**

**Key:** Number; NAME: Surname, Given; Sex; Birth Year (if given), Age At Last Birthday; Tribe; Degree of Blood; Marital Status; Relationship To Head of Family; Last Census Roll Number; At Jurisdiction Where Enrolled (Yes or No); At Another Jurisdiction; ELSEWHERE: Post office, County, State; Ward (Yes or No); Allotment, Annuity, and Identification Numbers.

618;  Doh-hal-tahih-bitsih; F; 30; Navajo; F; M; Wife; 614; Yes; Yes; 30577
619;  Yee-naz-bah; F; 7; Navajo; F; S; Daughter; 615; Yes; Yes; 30578
620;  Yazzie, Charley; M; 3; Navajo; F; S; Son; 616; Yes; Yes; 30579

621;  Apboy-ken-benally, Little Jim; M; 47; Navajo; M; Head; 617; Yes; Yes; 21239
622;  Doh-haih-ih-bitsih; F; 39; Navajo; F; M; Wife; 618; Yes; Yes; 21240
623;  Benally, Allen; M; 16; Navajo; F; S; Son; 619; Yes; Yes; 21241
624;  Kee; M; 6; Navajo; F; S; Son; 620; Yes; Yes; 21242
625;  Haska-yazzie; M; 4; Navajo; F; S; Grand-Son; 621; Yes; Yes; 21709
626;  Biz-des-bah; F; 20; Navajo; F; S; Daughter; 622; Yes; Yes; 21710

627;  Apboy-yen-benally, Jelly; M; 43; Navajo; F; M; Head; 623; Yes; Yes; 18904
628;  Belenn-legaih-bitsih[sic]; F; 35; Navajo; F; M; Wife; 624; Yes; Yes; 18905
[Name is probably Beleen-lagaih-bitsih]
629;  Yilth-has-bah; F; 20; Navajo; F; S; Daughter; 625; Yes; Yes; 18906
630;  Joe; M; 16; Navajo; F; S; Son; 626; Yes; Yes; 18907
631;  Jelly, Hugh; M; 14; Navajo; F; S; Son; 627; Yes; Yes; 18908
632;  Dinay-sohih; M; 11; Navajo; F; S; Son; 628; Yes; Yes; 18909
633;  Hoska-yen-tah-yil-wudt; M; 6; Navajo; F; S; Son; 629; Yes; Yes; 18910
634;  Yee-has-wudt; M; 4; Navajo; F; S; Son; 630; Yes; Yes; 18911

635;  Apboy-in-benally; M; Unk; Navajo; F; M; Head; 631; Yes; Yes; 17092
636;  Ahtcity-in-bitsih; F; 60; Navajo; F; M; Wife; 632; Yes; Yes; 17093
637;  Natah-chee, Clyde; M; 26; Navajo; F; S; Nephew; 633; Yes; Yes; 17094

638;  Apboy-yen-benally; M; 45; Navajo; F; M; Head; 634; Yes; Yes; 20030
639;  Hoska-yen-benally, Hazel; F; 44; Navajo; F; M; Wife; 635; Yes; Yes; 20031
640;  Ganih-nez, Anna; F; 9; Navajo; F; S; Daughter; 636; Yes; Yes; 20032

641;  Antonio-bega, Jim Johnson; M; 29; Navajo; F; M; Head; 637; Yes; Yes; 32970
642;  Natele-bikis-bitsih; F; 25; Navajo; F; M; Wife; 638; Yes; Yes; 32971
643;  Haska-chih-hahyah; M; 5; Navajo; F; S; Son; 639; Yes; Yes; 32972
644;  Haska-nih-deel-wudt; M; 2; Navajo; F; S; Son; 640; Yes; Yes; 32973

645;  Arthur, Ruth; F; 21; Navajo; F; S; Head; [Blank]; Yes; Yes; 26338
646;  Kah-yah-nih-bah; F; 10; Navajo; F; S; Niece; [Blank]; Yes; Yes; 26336

647;  Ashinh-ih-nez, Rufus; M; 30; Navajo; F; M; Head; 641; Yes; Yes; 21207
648;  Hah-tahly-sosie-bitsih; F;  28; Navajo; F; M; Wife; 642; Yes; Yes; 21208
649;  Ah-dih-lah-ih; M; 8; Navajo; F; S; Son; 643; Yes; Yes; 21209
650;  Al-han-bah; F; 5; Navajo; F; S; Daughter; 644; Yes; Yes; 21210
651;  Kee-kah-nas-bah; F; 4; Navajo; F; S; Daughter; 645; Yes; Yes; 21211

Census of the **Northern Navajo** reservation of the **Northern Navajo** jurisdiction, as of **April 1**, 1931, taken by **Ernest H. Hammond, District**, Superintendent. **in Charge**

**Key:** Number; NAME: Surname, Given; Sex; Birth Year (if given), Age At Last Birthday; Tribe; Degree of Blood; Marital Status; Relationship To Head of Family; Last Census Roll Number; At Jurisdiction Where Enrolled (Yes or No); At Another Jurisdiction; ELSEWHERE: Post office, County, State; Ward (Yes or No); Allotment, Annuity, and Identification Numbers.

652; Askink-ih-nez-bitsih; F; 2; Navajo; F; S; Daughter; 646; Yes; Yes; 21707

653; Askan-sosie-bega; M; 31; Navajo; F; M; Head; 647; Yes; Yes; 21285
654; Toh-sonih-bitsoih; F; 26; Navajo; F; M; Wife; 648; Yes; Yes; 21286
655; Bah-nih-bah; F; 11; Navajo; F; S; Daughter; 649; Yes; Yes; 21287
656; Haska-yil-jil-wudt; M; 9; Navajo; F; S; Son; 650; Yes; Yes; 21288
657; Dah-des-bah; F; 6; Navajo; F; S; Daughter; 651; Yes; Yes; 21289
658; Al-kih-has-bah; F; 3; Navajo; F; S; Daughter; 652; Yes; Yes; 21290

659; Ashini-ih-nez-bikis; M; 24; Navajo; F; M; Head; 653; Yes; Yes; 21212
660; Awa-yazzie; F; 24; Navajo; F; M; Wife; 654; Yes; Yes; 21213
661; Ah-nah-gee-bah; F; 3; Navajo; F; S; Daughter; 655; Yes; Yes; 21703
662; Haska-yil-kee-see-cin; M; 1- 4/12; Navajo; F; S; Son; 656; Yes; Yes; 21704

663; Askan-deel; M; Unk; Navajo; F; M; Head; 657; Yes; Yes; 28801
664; Aht-citty-yen-bitsih; F; 45; Navajo; F; M; Wife; 658; Yes; Yes; 28802
665; Leanord[sic]; M; 23; Navajo; F; S; Son; 659; Yes; Yes; 28803
[Name should be Leonard]
666; Adzan-seeih; F; 23; Navajo; F; S; Step-daughter; 660; Yes; Yes; 28804
667; Tohly; M; 15; Navajo; F; S; Grand-Son; 661; Yes; Yes; 28805

668; Askan-yazzie-bega (Wool Boy); M; 49; Navajo; F; M; Head; 662; Yes; Yes; 18047
669; Askan-yazzie-bega's wife (Wool Boy); F; 40; Navajo; F; M; Wife; 663; Yes; Yes; 18048
670; Adzanih-tahn; F; 20; Navajo; F; S; Daughter; 664; Yes; Yes; 18049
671; Haska-yil-yee-gath; M; 18; Navajo; F; S; Son; 665; Yes; Yes; 18050
672; Askan-yazzie, Luke; M; 16; Navajo; F; S; Son; 666; Yes; Yes; 18051
673; Atate-l-bahih; F; 14; Navajo; F; S; Daughter; 667; Yes; Yes; 18052
674; Askan-yazzie, Andy; M; 11; Navajo; F; S; Son; 668; Yes; Yes; 18053
675; Descheeny-yazzie; M; 7; Navajo; F; S; Son; 669; Yes; Yes; 18054
676; Bah; F; 5; Navajo; F; S; Daughter; 670; Yes; Yes; 18055
677; Askan-yazzie-bega, Bertha; F; 4; Navajo; F; S; Daughter; 671; Yes; Yes; 18270

678; Askan-stseesih-bega[sic]; M; 37; Navajo; F M; Head; 672; Yes; Yes; 17369
[Name should be Askan-etseesih-bega]
679; Ah-destsahigi-bitsih; F; 33; Navajo; F; M; Wife; 673; Yes; Yes; 17370
680; Askan-Etseesih-chin-ohbah; F; 17; Navajo; F; S; Daughter; 674; Yes; Yes; 17371
681; Askan-etseesih-ath-nahah-bah; F; 13; Navajo; F; S; Daughter; 675; Yes; Yes; 17372

Census of the **Northern Navajo** reservation of the **Northern Navajo** jurisdiction, as of **April 1**, 19**31**, taken by **Ernest H. Hammond, District**, Superintendent.                                                          **in Charge**

**Key:** Number; NAME: Surname, Given; Sex; Birth Year (if given), Age At Last Birthday; Tribe; Degree of Blood; Marital Status; Relationship To Head of Family; Last Census Roll Number; At Jurisdiction Where Enrolled (Yes or No); At Another Jurisdiction; ELSEWHERE: Post office, County, State; Ward (Yes or No); Allotment, Annuity, and Identification Numbers.

682; Askan-etseeshi-hosswoody[sic]; M; 10; Navajo; F; S; Son; 676; Yes; Yes; 17373    [Name should be Askan-etseesih-hosswoody]
683; Askan-et-seesih-eskes-suih[sic]; M; 9; Navajo; F; S; Son; 677; Yes; Yes; 17374    [Name should be Askan-etseesih-eskes-suih]
684; Askan-etseesih-dinay-suih; M; 7; Navajo; F; S; Son; 678; Yes; Yes; 17375
685; Askan-etseesih-yih-nelwudt; M; 16; Navajo; F; S; Adopted Son; 679; Yes; Yes; 17376

686; Askan-nez-blah, David; M; 34; Navajo; F; M; Head; 680; Yes; Yes; 28436
687; Uienth-nezzih-bitsih; F; 36; Navajo; F; M; Wife; 681; Yes; Yes; 28437
688; Wayih; M; 16; Navajo; F; S; Step-son; 681[sic]; Yes; Yes; 28438
                              [Previous ID No. was 681-A]
689; Kehn; F; 9; Navajo; F; S; Step-daughter; 682; Yes; Yes; 28439
690; Ah-kee; M; 6; Navajo; F; S; Step-son; 683; Yes; Yes; 28440

691; Askan-sohoh; M; 61; Navajo; F; M; Head; 684; Yes; Yes; 28000
692; Seginih-bitsih; F; 41; Navajo; F; M; Wife; 685; Yes; Yes; 28001
693; Carson; M; 15; Navajo; F; S; Son; 686; Yes; Yes; 28002
694; Percy; M; 12; Navajo; F; S; Son; 687; Yes; Yes; 28003
695; Nah-tah-yazzie; M; 9; Navajo; F; S; Son; 688; Yes; Yes; 28004
696; Harvey; M; 2; Navajo; F; S; Son; 689; Yes; Yes; 28100

697; Askan-sohoh-bega; M; 25; Navajo; F; M; Head; 690; Yes; Yes; 28008
698; Toh-dil-yil-bitsih; F; 32; Navajo; F; M; Wife; 691; Yes; Yes; 28009
699; Grover; M; Unk; Navajo; F; S; Step-son; 692; Yes; Yes; 28010
700; Nah-tah-yil-yel-wohl; M; 8; Navajo; F; S; Son; 693; Yes; Yes; 28011
701; Dinay-nih-zo; M; 6; Navajo; F; S; Son; 694; Yes; Yes; 28012
702; Nah-tah-yil-has-le; M; 21; Navajo; F; S; Nephew; 695; Yes; Yes; 28014

703; Ashihi-nez; M; 25; Navajo; F; M; Head; 696; Yes; Yes; 18925
704; Clinton's daughter Jones; F; 23; Navajo; F; M; Wife; 697; Yes; Yes; 18926
705; Bha-jih-bah; F; 7; Navajo; F; S; Daughter; 698; Yes; Yes; 18927
706; Maxey; M; 5; Navajo; F; S; Son; 699; Yes; Yes; 18928
707; McCracken; M; 3; Navajo; F; S; Son; 700; Yes; Yes; 18929

708; Askan-estseesih-bitsih; F; 49; Navajo; F; Wd; Head; 701; Yes; Yes; 17381
709; Yah-ah-mo-bah; F; 24; Navajo; F; S; Daughter; 702; Yes; Yes; 17383
710; Dinay-suih; M; 15; Navajo; F; S; Son; 703; Yes; Yes; 17384

711; Askan-yazzie-bitsih; F; 43; Navajo; F; Wd; Head; 704; Yes; Yes; 17124
712; Adzanih-yazzie; F; 23; Navajo; F; S; Daughter; 705; Yes; Yes; 17125
713; Beleen, Elizabeth; F; 17; Navajo; F; S; Daughter; 706; Yes; Yes; 17126

Census of the __Northern Navajo__ reservation of the __Northern Navajo__ jurisdiction, as of __April 1__, 19**31,** taken by __Ernest H. Hammond, District__, Superintendent. __in Charge__

Key: Number; NAME: Surname, Given; Sex; Birth Year (if given), Age At Last Birthday; Tribe; Degree of Blood; Marital Status; Relationship To Head of Family; Last Census Roll Number; At Jurisdiction Where Enrolled (Yes or No); At Another Jurisdiction; ELSEWHERE: Post office, County, State; Ward (Yes or No); Allotment, Annuity, and Identification Numbers.

714; Dinay-estsosie[sic]; M; 12; Navajo; F; S; Son; 707; Yes; Yes; 17127
[Name is probably Dinay-etsosie]

715; Askan-etsosiesiligi-bitah; M; 36; Navajo; F; M; Head; 708; Yes; Yes; 17095
716; Tah-dih-cheeny-etsosie-bitah; F; 31; Navajo; F; M; Wife; 709; Yes; Yes; 17096
717; Nahtah-askan-etseeiligi-bitah; M; 11; Navajo; F; S; Son; 710; Yes; Yes; 17097
718; Askan-etseesiligi-bitah[sic], Charley; M; 5; Navajo; F; S; Son; 711; Yes; Yes; 17098 [Name could be Askan-etseeiligi-bitah, Charley]

719; Askawahsohoh-etseesihigi; M; 66; Navajo; F; M; Head; 712; Yes; Yes; 17070
720; Askawahsohoh-etseeshigi's[sic] wife; F; 60; Navajo; F; M; Wife; 713; Yes; Yes; 17071 [Name could be Askawahsohoh-etseesihigi's wife]

721; Askan-soh-et-seesih-bega; M; 28; Navajo; F; M; Head; 714; Yes; Yes; 17043
722; Hosteen-sain-benally; F; 28; Navajo; F; M; Wife; 715; Yes; Yes; 17044
723; Yah-nas-pah; F; 10; Navajo; F; S; Daughter; 716; Yes; Yes; Yes; 17045
724; Alchinn-despah; F; 8; Navajo; F; S; Daughter; 717; Yes; Yes; 17046
725; Dah-yil-wudt; M; 6; Navajo; F; S; Son; 718; Yes; Yes; 17047
726; Baby; M; 3; Navajo; F; S; Son; 719; Yes; Yes; 17048

727; Askan-yazzie-bega; M; 40; Navajo; F; M; Head; 720; Yes; Yes; 20060
728; Kin-seely-bitsih; F; 28; Navajo; F; M; Wife; 721; Yes; Yes; Yes; 20061
729; Eskee-l-bahih; M; 10; Navajo; F; S; Son; 722; Yes; Yes; 20062
730; Chin-bah-ih; F; 7; Navajo; F; S; Daughter; 723; Yes; Yes; 20063
731; Taos-bah; F; 4; Navajo; F; S; Daughter; 724; Yes; Yes; 20064

732; Askan-etseeih-bega; M; 25; Navajo; F; M; Head; 725; Yes; Yes; 20324
733; Adzan-L-chee; F; 22; Navajo; F; M; Wife; 726; Yes; Yes; 20325
734; Yi-ka-des-bah; F; 2; Navajo; F; S; Daughter; 727; Yes; Yes; 20418

735; Askan-shish-yah-ih; M; Unk; Navajo; F; M; Head; 728; Yes; Yes; 28881
736; Wudt; M; 19; Navajo; F; S; Son; 729; Yes; Yes; 28883
737; Nina; F; 13; Navajo; F; S; Daughter; 730; Yes; Yes; 28884
738; Nah-tah-yazzie; M; 7; Navajo; F; S; Son; 731; Yes; Yes; 28885
739; Haska-yazzie; M; 5; Navajo; F; S; Son; 732; Yes; Yes; 28886

740; Ashihih-nez-bega; M; Unk; Navajo; F; M; Head; 733; Yes; Yes; 23151
741; Yah-nah-nih-bahih; F; Unk; Navajo; F; M; Wife; 734; Yes; Yes; 23152

742; Bih-jah-atin-biteih; F; 21; Navajo; F; Wd; Head; 735; Yes; Yes; 29115

743; Ashinh-bega, John; M; 27; Navajo; F; M; Head; 736; Yes; Yes; 30559

Census of the **Northern Navajo** reservation of the **Northern Navajo** jurisdiction, as of **April 1**, 19**31,** taken by **Ernest H. Hammond, District**, Superintendent. **in Charge**

**Key:** Number; NAME: Surname, Given; Sex; Birth Year (if given), Age At Last Birthday; Tribe; Degree of Blood; Marital Status; Relationship To Head of Family; Last Census Roll Number; At Jurisdiction Where Enrolled (Yes or No); At Another Jurisdiction; ELSEWHERE: Post office, County, State; Ward (Yes or No); Allotment, Annuity, and Identification Numbers.

744; Aht-citty-benally; F; 20; Navajo; F; M; Wife; 737; Yes; Yes; 30560

745; Ashinh-clah-bega; M; 44; Navajo; F; M; Head; 738; Yes; Yes; 20253
746; Dinay-sosie-bitsih; F; 33; Navajo; F; M; Wife; 739; Yes; Yes; 20254
747; Nil-wudt; M; 18; Navajo; F; S; Son; 740; Yes; Yes; 20255
748; Hol-wudt; M; 17; Navajo; F; S; Son; 741; Yes; Yes; 20256
749; Moses; M; 11; Navajo; F; S; Son; 742; Yes; Yes; 20257
750; Atate; F; 14; Navajo; F; S; Daughter; 743; Yes; Yes; 20258
751; Gee-ih; F; 8; Navajo; F; S; Daughter; 744; Yes; Yes; 20259
752; Chih-nih-bah; F; 3; Navajo; F; S; Daughter; 745; Yes; Yes; 20260

753; Ashinh-clah; M; 64; Navajo; F; M; Head; 746; Yes; Yes; 29108
754; Ashinh-clah's wife; F; 61; Navajo; F; M; Wife; 747; Yes; Yes; 29109
755; Eva; F; 19; Navajo; F; S; Daughter; 748; Yes; Yes; 29110
756; Adzanih-bahih; F; 22; Navajo; F; S; Niece-in-law; 749; Yes; Yes; 29111
757; Yee-tah-nih-bah; F; 7; Navajo; F; S; Grand-daughter; 750; Yes; Yes; 29112
758; Yazzie-dah-sis; F; 9; Navajo; F; S; Grand-daughter; 751; Yes; Yes; 29113

759; Aspaas, Hans; M; 41; Navajo; F; M; Head; 752; Yes; Yes; 30426
760; Anne; F; 38; Navajo; F; M; Wife; 753; Yes; Yes; 30427
761; Frank; M; 16; Navajo; F; S; Son; 754; Yes; Yes; 30428
762; Daisy; F; 12; Navajo; F; S; Daughter; 755; Yes; Yes; 30429
763; Stella; F; 10; Navajo; F; S; Daughter; 756; Yes; Yes; 30430

764; Askan-deel, Joe; M; 31; Navajo; F; M; Head; 757; Yes; Yes; 31136
765; Dinay-yazzie-bitsih; F; 30; Navajo; F; M; Wife; 758; Yes; Yes; 31137
766; Haz-des-bah; F; 11; Navajo; F; S; Daughter; 759; Yes; Yes; 31138
767; Joe; M; 4; Navajo; F; S; Son; 760; Yes; Yes; 31139
768; Bessie; F; 2; Navajo; F; S; Daughter; 761; Yes; Yes; 31140

769; Benally, Charley; M; Unk; Navajo; F; M; Head; 762; Yes; Yes; 26929
770; Tah-hah-bah; F; 31; Navajo; F; M; Wife; 763; Yes; Yes; 26930
771; Haska-yil-deyah; M; 10; Navajo; F; S; Son; 764; Yes; Yes; 26931
772; Yil-haz-bah; F; 6; Navajo; F; S; Daughter; 765; Yes; Yes; 26932
773; Haska-yee-tah-hah-lel; M; 5; Navajo; F; S; Son; 766; Yes; Yes; 26933

774; Bega, Charley; M; 42; Navajo; F; M; Head; 767; Yes; Yes; 26804
775; Sih-bah; F; 42; Navajo; F; M; Wife; 768; Yes; Yes; 26805
776; Bih-nih-ziz-bah; F; 9; Navajo; F; S; Niece; 769; Yes; Yes; 26806

777; Bitsoih-yazzie; M; 52; Navajo; F; M; Head; 775; Yes; Yes; Yes; 20178
778; Bitsoih-yazzie's wife; F; 51; Navajo; F; M; Wife; 776; Yes; Yes; Yes; 20179

Census of the **Northern Navajo** reservation of the **Northern Navajo** jurisdiction, as of **April 1**, 1931, taken by **Ernest H. Hammond, District**, Superintendent. **in Charge**

**Key:** Number; NAME: Surname, Given; Sex; Birth Year (if given), Age At Last Birthday; Tribe; Degree of Blood; Marital Status; Relationship To Head of Family; Last Census Roll Number; At Jurisdiction Where Enrolled (Yes or No); At Another Jurisdiction; ELSEWHERE: Post office, County, State; Ward (Yes or No); Allotment, Annuity, and Identification Numbers.

779;  Bitsoih-yazzie, Theodore; M; 20; Navajo; F; S; Son; 777; Yes; Yes; Yes; 20180
780;  Al-tah-nas-bah; F; 16; Navajo; F; S; Daughter; 778; Yes; Yes; 20181
781;  Bitsoih-yazzie, Tuly; M; 13; Navajo; F; S; Son; 779; Yes; Yes; 20182
782;  Nas-wudt; M; 11; Navajo; F; S; Son; 780; Yes; Yes; 20183
783;  Kee-bahih; M; 9; Navajo; F; S; Son; 781; Yes; Yes; 20184
784;  Nah-tahl-suen; M; 5; Navajo; F; S; Son; 782; Yes; Yes; 20185

785;  Bah-dagah-legaih-bega, Bigmouth; M; 54; Navajo; F; M; Head; 783; Yes; Yes; 19422
786;  Clah-hazah-bitsih; F; 44; Navajo; F; M; Wife; 784; Yes; Yes; 19423
787;  Bigmouth, Willie; M; 22; Navajo; F; S; Son; 785; Yes; Yes; 19424
788;  Bigmouth, Vida; F; 20; Navajo; F; S; Daughter; 786; Yes; Yes; 19425
789;  Bah's nez[sic]; F; 11; Navajo; F; S; Daughter; 787; Yes; Yes; 19426
        [Name could be Bah nez]
790;  Bigmouth, Tony; M; 10; Navajo; F; S; Son; 788; Yes; Yes; 19427
791;  Kee-l-bahih; M; 6; Navajo; F; S; Son; 789; Yes; Yes; 19428
792;  Bigmouth, Joe; M; 3; Navajo; F; S; Son; 790; Yes; Yes; 19429
793;  Clah-hazohgah; M; 74; Navajo; F; Wd; Father-in-law; 791; Yes; Yes; 19430

794;  Beleen-lagaih-bitah-bega; M; 24; Navajo; F; M; Head; 792; Yes; Yes; 19419
795;  Bigmouth, bitsih; F; 22; Navajo; F; M; Wife; 793; Yes; Yes; 19420
796;  Bigmouth, bitsoih; M; 3; Navajo; F; S; Son; 794; Yes; Yes; 19421

797;  Beleen-lagaih-bitah, Sam; M; 58; Navajo; F; M; Head; 795; Yes; Yes; 19322
798;  Tah-des-bah; F; 51; Navajo; F; M; Wife; 796; Yes; Yes; 19323
799;  Capitan-bega, Sam; M; 24; Navajo; F; S; Son; 797; Yes; Yes; 19324
800;  Capitan-bega, Fannie; F; 15; Navajo; F; S; Daughter; 798; Yes; Yes; 19325
801;  Capitan-bega, Annie; F; 13; Navajo; F; S; Daughter; 799; Yes; Yes; 19326
802;  Nocki-deetsah-natoni; M; 11; Navajo; F; S; Grand-son; 800; Yes; Yes; 19327

803;  Bitsee-pahih-benally; M; 31; Navajo; F; M; Head; 801; Yes; Yes; 17151
804;  Descheeny-yazzie-bitsih; F; 24; Navajo; F; M; Wife; 802; Yes; Yes; 17152
805;  Neel-iwudt; M; 7; Navajo; F; S; Son; 803; Yes; Yes; 17153

806;  Bih-nath-lagaih-bega; M; 29; Navajo; F; M; Head; 804; Yes; Yes; 17054
807;  Askan-absohoh-bitsih; F; 23; Navajo; F; M; Wife; 805; Yes; Yes; 17055
808;  Baby; [M]; 1-3/12; Navajo; F; S; [Son]; 806; Yes; Yes; 17409
        [Baby is a male]

809;  Bitsee-pahih-bega; M; 44; Navajo; F; Wd; Head; 807; Yes; Yes; 17141
810;  Bitsee-pahih-bega, Francis; M; 24; Navajo; F; S; Son; 808; Yes; Yes; 17142
811;  Bitsee-pahih-bega, John; M; 19; Navajo; F; S; Son; 809; Yes; Yes; 17143

Census of the **Northern Navajo** reservation of the **Northern Navajo** jurisdiction, as of **April 1**, 19**31**, taken by **Ernest H. Hammond, District**, Superintendent. **in Charge**

**Key:** Number; NAME: Surname, Given; Sex; Birth Year (if given), Age At Last Birthday; Tribe; Degree of Blood; Marital Status; Relationship To Head of Family; Last Census Roll Number; At Jurisdiction Where Enrolled (Yes or No); At Another Jurisdiction; ELSEWHERE: Post office, County, State; Ward (Yes or No); Allotment, Annuity, and Identification Numbers.

812; Glin-bah-bitsee-pahih-bega; F; 18; Navajo; F; S; Daughter; 810; Yes; Yes; 17144

813; Batonih-yazzie; M; 79; Navajo; F; Wd; Head; 811; Yes; Yes; 19206

814; Bih-bayse-yen-bega; M; 51; Navajo; F; M; Head; 812; Yes; Yes; 20155
815; Nah-glih-l-bahih; F; 26; Navajo; F; M; Wife; 813; Yes; Yes; 20156
816; Nas-bahih; F; 5; Navajo; F; S; Daughter; 814; Yes; Yes; 20157
817; Ace; M; 3; Navajo; F; S; Son; 815; Yes; Yes; 20158

818; Bih-nee-dih-tlohi; M; 46; Navajo; F; M; Head; 816; Yes; Yes; 20351
819; Hah-tah-ly-sosie-bih-che-K; F; 32; Navajo; F; M; Wife; 817; Yes; Yes; 20352
820; Eskee-l-suen; M; 17; Navajo; F; S; Son; 818; Yes; Yes; 20353
821; Eskee-yazzie; M; 9; Navajo; F; S; Grandson; 819; Yes; Yes; 20354
822; Adzan-etseeihgi; F; 83; Navajo; F; Wd; Mother; 820; Yes; Yes; 20355

823; Bitah, Billy; M; Unk; Navajo; F; M; Head; 821; Yes; Yes; 23101
824; Bitah-bih-adzan, Billy; F; 57; Navajo; F; M; Wife; 822; Yes; Yes; 23102

825; Bontoni-yazzie-bih-azan; F; 63; Navajo; F; Wd; Head; 823; Yes; Yes; 19365
826; Dah-yiz-bah; F; 10; Navajo; F; S; Grand-daughter; 824; Yes; Yes; 19366

827; Beelen-lagaih-bega[sic], Slim; M; 30; Navajo; F; M; Head; 825; Yes; Yes; 18887  [Name could be Beleen-lagaih-bega, Slim]
828; Bitsih, Thomas; F; 30; Navajo; F; M; Wife; 826; Yes; Yes; 18888
829; White Horse, Felix; M; 11; Navajo; F; S; Step-son; 827; Yes; Yes; 18889
830; Kee-l-Chee; M; 10; Navajo; F; S; Son; 828; Yes; Yes; 18890
831; Zannie; F; 8; Navajo; F; S; Daughter; 829; Yes; Yes; 18891
832; Yee-kas-bah; F; 6; Navajo; F; S; Daughter; 830; Yes; Yes; 18892
833; Haska-yee-chah-neel-wudt; M; 3; Navajo; F; S; Son; 831; Yes; Yes; 18893

834; Beleen-clit-soih-bega; M; 30; Navajo; F; M; Head; 832; Yes; Yes; 20197
835; Adzan-deel; F; 24; Navajo; F; M; Wife; 833; Yes; Yes; 20198

836; Beleen-lagaih; M; 59; Navajo; F; M; Head; 834; Yes; Yes; 18894
837; Beleen-lagaih's wife; F; 46; Navajo; F; M; Wife; 835; Yes; Yes; 18895
838; Dah, Sadie; F; 23; Navajo; F; S; Daughter; 836; Yes; Yes; 18896
839; Beleen-lagih-bega[sic], Charley; M; 19; Navajo; F; S; Son; 837; Yes; Yes; 18897  [Name could be Beleen-lagaih-bega, Charley]
840; White horse[sic], Billy; M; 17; Navajo; F; S; Son; 838; Yes; Yes; 18898
841; White Horse, Wanda; F; 15; Navajo; F; S; Daughter; 839; Yes; Yes; 18899
842; White Horse, Ben; M; 10; Navajo; F; S; Son; 841; Yes; Yes; 18900
843; Al-l-nah-bah, Betty; F; 6; Navajo; F; S; Daughter; 840; Yes; Yes; 18901

Census of the **Northern Navajo** reservation of the **Northern Navajo** jurisdiction, as of **April 1**, 1931, taken by **Ernest H. Hammond, District**, Superintendent. **in Charge**

**Key:** Number; NAME: Surname, Given; Sex; Birth Year (if given), Age At Last Birthday; Tribe; Degree of Blood; Marital Status; Relationship To Head of Family; Last Census Roll Number; At Jurisdiction Where Enrolled (Yes or No); At Another Jurisdiction; ELSEWHERE: Post office, County, State; Ward (Yes or No); Allotment, Annuity, and Identification Numbers.

844; Bih-bayse-yen-bega-bitsih; F; 19; Navajo; F; M; Head; 842; Yes; Yes; 20288
845; Yil-des-bah; F; 6; Navajo; F; S; Daughter; 843; Yes; Yes; 20289
846; Dinay-Yazzie; M; 5; Navajo; F; S; Son; 844; Yes; Yes; 20290
847; Hosteen-yazzie-benally; M; 1-3/12; Navajo; F; S; Son; 845; Yes; Yes; 20409

848; Bega, John; M; 35; Navajo; F; M; Head; 846; Yes; Yes; 23103
849; Benally, Billy; F; 26; Navajo; F; M; Wife; 847; Yes; Yes; 23104
850; Bahih; M; 9; Navajo; F; S; Son; 848; Yes; Yes; 23105
851; Hah-yah; M; 7; Navajo; F; S; Son; 849; Yes; Yes; 23106

852; Beleen-lizin; F; 59; Navajo; F; Wd; Head; 850; Yes; Yes; 24931
853; Chih-dez-hah; F; 17; Navajo; F; S; Daughter; 851; Yes; Yes; 24932
854; Adzan-toh-ih; F; 72; Navajo; F; Wd; Mother; 852; Yes; Yes; 24933

855; Bayse-toh-nih; M; 51; Navajo; F; M; Head; 853; Yes; Yes; 20267
856; Baysee-toh-nih's[sic] wife; F; 53; Navajo; F; M; Wife; 854; Yes; Yes; 20268
[Name is probably Bayse-toh-nih's wife]
857; Hoska-yee-nay-yah; M; 19; Navajo; F; S; Son; 855; Yes; Yes; 20269
858; Nah-tah-seesih; M; 10; Navajo; F; S; Son; 856; Yes; Yes; 20270

859; Bay-gashih-benally; M; 31; Navajo; F; M; Head; 857; Yes; Yes; 20263
860; Yil-nih-bah; F; 27; Navajo; F; M; Wife; 858; Yes; Yes; 20264
861; Hoska-yil-nas-wudt; M; 7; Navajo; F; S; Son; 859; Yes; Yes; 20265
862; Adzanih; F; 5; Navajo; F; S; Daughter; 860; Yes; Yes; 20266
863; Ated-latsee-lapaih or Yi-tah-dez-bah; F; 2; Navajo; F; S; Daughter; 861; Yes; Yes; 20422

864; Bah-al-chinih-naki, Franklin; M; 49; Navajo; F; M; Head; 862; Yes; Yes; 20186
865; Bitsee-bizi-bitsih; F; 51; Navajo; F; M; Wife; 863; Yes; Yes; 20187
866; Hanley, Max; M; 31; Navajo; F; S; Son; 864; Yes; Yes; 20188
867; Hanley, Thomas; M; 23; Navajo; F; S; Son; 865; Yes; Yes; 20189
868; Hanley, John; M; 23; Navajo; F; S; Son; 866; Yes; Yes; 20190
869; Hanley, Ned (Thomas' Son); M; 2; Navajo; F; S; Grand-Son; 867; Yes; Yes; 20419
870; Adzanih-gaih; F; 21; Navajo; F; S; Daughter; 868; Yes; Yes; 20191
871; Hanley, Carrie; F; 17; Navajo; F; S; Daughter; 869; Yes; Yes; 20192
872; Adzan, Ruth; F; 13; Navajo; F; S; Daughter; 870; Yes; Yes; 20193
873; Adzan-bah; F; 7; Navajo; F; S; Daughter; 871; Yes; Yes; 20194

874; Bay-gashih-yen-bega; M; 58; Navajo; F; M; Head; 872; Yes; Yes; 20253
875; Kinih-bah; F; 34; Navajo; F; M; Wife; 873; Yes; Yes; 20254
876; Nah-tah-yil-nas-wudt; M; 10; Navajo; F; S; Son; 874; Yes; Yes; 20255

Census of the **Northern Navajo** reservation of the **Northern Navajo** jurisdiction, as of **April 1**, 1931, taken by **Ernest H. Hammond, District**, Superintendent. **in Charge**

**Key:** Number; NAME: Surname, Given; Sex; Birth Year (if given), Age At Last Birthday; Tribe; Degree of Blood; Marital Status; Relationship To Head of Family; Last Census Roll Number; At Jurisdiction Where Enrolled (Yes or No); At Another Jurisdiction; ELSEWHERE: Post office, County, State; Ward (Yes or No); Allotment, Annuity, and Identification Numbers.

877; Atate-seesih; F; 3; Navajo; F; S; Daughter; 875; Yes; Yes; 20256

878; Adzanih-yazzie; F; 26; Navajo; F; Wd; Head; 876; Yes; Yes; 26696
879; Nah-glih-yah-nih-bah; F; 8; Navajo; F; S; Daughter; 877; Yes; Yes; 26697
880; Haska-yee-tah-hoh-lel; M; 6; Navajo; F; S; Son; 878; Yes; Yes; 26698
881; Nah-tah-yil-nah-dahl; M; 4; Navajo; F; S; Son; 879; Yes; Yes; 26699

882; Beleen-li-chee-bega; M; 33; Navajo; F; M; Head; 880; Yes; Yes; 26777
883; Kih-haz-bah; F; 25; Navajo; F; M; Wife; 881; Yes; Yes; 26778
884; Chih-hoh-lel; M; 7; Navajo; F; S; Son; 882; Yes; Yes; 26779
885; Yil-haz-bah; F; 6; Navajo; F; S; Daughter; 883; Yes; Yes; 26780
886; Yil-hah-bah; F; 4; Navajo; F; S; Daughter; 884; Yes; Yes; 26781
887; Nah-tah-yeeth-nee-yah; M; 2; Navajo; F; S; Son; 885; Yes; Yes; 27089

888; Bitsee-bahih-benally; M; 23; Navajo; F; M; Head; 886; Yes; Yes; 20257
889; Ah-hah-dee-bah; F; 24; Navajo; F; M; Wife; 887; Yes; Yes; 20258

890; Benally-bega (Silas) Johnny Boo; M; 21; Navajo; F; M; Head; 888; Yes; Yes; 19360
891; Batoni-yazzie-bitsih; F; 21; Navajo; F; M; Wife; 889; Yes; Yes; 19361
892; Glin-he-bah; F; 2; Navajo; F; S; Daughter; 890; Yes; Yes; 19519

893; Bih-bayse-yen-bega-yazzie, John; M; 52; Navajo; F; M; Head; 891; Yes; Yes; 20346
894; Dagah-yen-bitsoih; F; Unk; Navajo; F; M; Wife; 892; Yes; Yes; 20347

895; Bih-chan-tailly-bega; M; 41; Navajo; F; M; Head; 893; Yes; Yes; 20051
896; Klizie-lizin-bitah; F; 29; Navajo; F; M; Wife; 894; Yes; Yes; 20052
897; Bih-chan-tailly, Dora; F; 12; Navajo; F; S; Daughter; 895; Yes; Yes; 20053
898; Yih-chee; M; 9; Navajo; F; S; Son; 896; Yes; Yes; 20054
899; Des-wudt; M; 7; Navajo; F; S; Son; 897; Yes; Yes; 20055
900; Chis-chilli, Sadie; F; 17; Navajo; F; S; Sister-in-law; 899; Yes; Yes; 20057
901; Ah-codih, Asa; M; 20; Navajo; F; S; Brother-in-law; 900; Yes; Yes; 20058
902; Kee-chee; M; 24; Navajo; F; S; Brother-in-law; 901; Yes; Yes; 20059
903; Zan-bah; F; 2; Navajo; F; S; Daughter; 902; Yes; Yes; 20432

904; Bitsih, Barber; F; 53; Navajo; F; Wd; Head; 903; Yes; Yes; 27631
905; John Barber; M; 27; Navajo; F; S; Son; 904; Yes; Yes; 27632
906; Bitcilli Barber John, Roy; M; 20; Navajo; F; S; Son; 905; Yes; Yes; 27633

907; Beeleen-dih-jadih[sic]; M; 52; Navajo; F; M; Head; 906; Yes; Yes; 19207
[Name is probably Beeleen-dih-jadih]
908; Gadt-ee-eyih-bitsih; F; 43; Navajo; F; M; Wife; 907; Yes; Yes; 19208

Census of the **Northern Navajo** reservation of the **Northern Navajo** jurisdiction, as of **April 1**, 19**31,** taken by **Ernest H. Hammond, District**, Superintendent. **in Charge**

**Key:** Number; NAME: Surname, Given; Sex; Birth Year (if given), Age At Last Birthday; Tribe; Degree of Blood; Marital Status; Relationship To Head of Family; Last Census Roll Number; At Jurisdiction Where Enrolled (Yes or No); At Another Jurisdiction; ELSEWHERE: Post office, County, State; Ward (Yes or No); Allotment, Annuity, and Identification Numbers.

909;  Beleen-dih-jadih, Ruth; F; 21; Navajo; F; S; Daughter; 908; Yes; Yes; 19209
910;  Bitsee-ba, Tom; M; 19; Navajo; F; S; Son; 909; Yes; Yes; 19210
911;  Beleen-dih-jadih, Jane; F; 15; Navajo; F; S; Daughter; 910; Yes; Yes; 19211
912;  Hah-des-bah; F; 12; Navajo; F; S; Daughter; 911; Yes; Yes; 19212
913;  Yee-nih-bah; F; 9; Navajo; F; S; Daughter; 912; Yes; Yes; 19213
914;  Dah-nih-bah; F; 6; Navajo; F; S; Daughter; 913; Yes; Yes; 19214
915;  Edward; M; 3; Navajo; F; S; Son; 914; Yes; Yes; 19215

916;  Bowen, John; M; 63; Navajo; F; M; Head; 915; Yes; Yes; 27650
917;  Yahn-dez-bah; F; 32; Navajo; F; M; Wife; 916; Yes; Yes; 27651
918;  Wilson; F[sic]; 18; Navajo; F; S; Brother-in-law; 917; Yes; Yes; 27652
      [Should be male.]

919;  Bay-gashih-lagaih-bega; M; 39; Navajo; F; M; Head; 918; Yes; Yes; 26690
920;  Zannih; F; 28; Navajo; F; M; Wife; 919; Yes; Yes; 26691
921;  Yee-kaz-bah; F; 11; Navajo; F; S; Daughter; 920; Yes; Yes; 26692
922;  Glih-hah-nih-bah; F; 9; Navajo; F; S; Daughter; 921; Yes; Yes; 26693
923;  Adzan-chee; F; 4; Navajo; F; S; Daughter; 922; Yes; Yes; 26694

924;  Barber-bitsoih, John; M; 23; Navajo; F; M; Head; 923; Yes; Yes; 27648
925;  Hosteen-nez-bega, bitsih; F; 21; Navajo; F; M; Wife; 924; Yes; Yes; 27649

926;  Barber-bih-adzan; F; 71; Navajo; F; Wd; Head; 925; Yes; Yes; 27634
927;  Keh-yil-ee-bah; F; 15; Navajo; F; S; Grand-daughter; 926; Yes; Yes; 27635
928;  Chih-hah-bah; F; 13; Navajo; F; S; Grand-daughter; 927; Yes; Yes; 27636
929;  Bil-nah-ziz-bah; F; 17; Navajo; F; S; Grand-daughter; 928; Yes; Yes; 27637
930;  Nah-tah-yil-chel-wudt; M; 13; Navajo; F; S; Grand-Son; 929; Yes; Yes; 27638
931;  Adzan-nil-tole; F; 13; Navajo; F; S; Grand-daughter; 930; Yes; Yes; 27639
932;  Barber, Tom; M; 11; Navajo; F; S; Grand-Son; 931; Yes; Yes; 27640
933;  Barber, Willie; M; 32; Navajo; F; S; Son; 932; Yes; Yes; 27641

934;  Adzan-yazzie; F; 72; Navajo; F; Wd; Head; 933; Yes; Yes; 27622

935;  Bih-bayse-yen-bitsoih; M; Unk; Navajo; F; M; Head; 934; Yes; Yes; 20340
936;  Toh-ahk-cleenih-bitsih; F; Unk; Navajo; F; M; Wife; 935; Yes; Yes; 20341
937;  Adzan-l-bahih; F; Unk; Navajo; F; S; Daughter; 936; Yes; Yes; 20342
938;  Dinay-dih-shoh; M; Unk; Navajo; F; S; Son; 937; Yes; Yes; 20343
939;  Dinay-chee; M; Unk; Navajo; F; S; Son; 938; Yes; Yes; 20344
940;  Nah-glih-yee-dah-nih-bah; F; Unk; Navajo; F; S; Daughter; 939; Yes; Yes; 20345
941;  Yi-tah-dez-bah; F; 2; Navajo; F; S; Daughter; 940; Yes; Yes; 20436

Census of the **Northern Navajo** reservation of the **Northern Navajo** jurisdiction, as of **April 1**, 19**31,** taken by **Ernest H. Hammond, District**, Superintendent. **in Charge**

**Key:** Number; NAME: Surname, Given; Sex; Birth Year (if given), Age At Last Birthday; Tribe; Degree of Blood; Marital Status; Relationship To Head of Family; Last Census Roll Number; At Jurisdiction Where Enrolled (Yes or No); At Another Jurisdiction; ELSEWHERE: Post office, County, State; Ward (Yes or No); Allotment, Annuity, and Identification Numbers.

942;  Beleen-legaih-bitah[sic], Ben; M; 51; Navajo; F; M; Head; 941; Yes; Yes; 19216  [Name is probably Beleen-lagaih-bitah, Ben]
943;  Batoni-bize-atin-bitsih; F; 43; Navajo; F; M; Wife; 942; Yes; Yes; 19217
944;  Dah-hah-ah; F; 20; Navajo; F; S; Daughter; 943; Yes; Yes; 19218
945;  Glenda; F; 16; Navajo; F; S; Daughter; 944; Yes; Yes; 19219
946;  Hah-bah; F; 13; Navajo; F; S; Daughter; 945; Yes; Yes; 19220
947;  Yee-nah-ho-lel; M; 5; Navajo; F; S; Son; Yes; Yes; 19221
948;  Batoni-lise-atin-bih-adzanih; F; Unk; Navajo; F; Wd; Great-mother-in-law; 947; Yes; Yes; 19222
949;  Beleen-ensaz-e-yen-bitsih; F; Unk; Navajo; F; Wd; Mother-in-law; 948; Yes; Yes; 19223
950;  Hosteen-sehl-lahih; M; 23; Navajo; F; S; Grand-son; 949; Yes; Yes; 19224

951;  Bega-ith-linn; M; 45; Navajo; F; Wd; Head; 950; Yes; Yes; 19986
952;  Dinay-yazzie; M; 21; Navajo; F; S; Son; 951; Yes; Yes; 19987
953;  Bega-ith-linn, Peter; M; 17; Navajo; F; S; Son; 952; Yes; Yes; 19988
954;  Zan-bah; F; 13; Navajo; F; S; Daughter; 953; Yes; Yes; 19989
955;  Eskee-sosie; M; 8; Navajo; F; S; Son; 954; Yes; Yes; 19990

956;  Bitsee-lagaih-bega; M; 33; Navajo; F; M; Head; 955; Yes; Yes; 27565
957;  Tah-dez-bah; F; 33; Navajo; F; M; Wife; 956; Yes; Yes; 27566
958;  Nah-glih-yil-hah-bah; F; 8; Navajo; F; S; Daughter; 957; Yes; Yes; 27567
959;  Tah-nih-yah; M; 3; Navajo; F; S; Son; 958; Yes; Yes; 27568
960;  Nah-tah-yil-nih-nih-yah; M; 4; Navajo; F; S; Son; 959; Yes; Yes; 27569
961;  Bah; F; Unk; Navajo; F; Wd; Mother-in-law; 960; Yes; Yes; 27570
962;  Wudt; M; 23; Navajo; F; A; Brother-in-law; 961; Yes; Yes; 27571
963;  Haska-yil-ee-yah; M; 19; Navajo; F; S; Brother-in-law; 962; Yes; Yes; 27572

964;  Beleen-lagaih-bega, Dick; 27; Navajo; F; M; Head; 963; Yes; Yes; 18902
965;  Beleen-lagaih-bitah-bitsih; F; 21; Navajo; F; M; Wife; 964; Yes; Yes; 18903

966;  Bennet, Alfred; M; 28; Navajo; F; M; Head; 965; Yes; Yes; 27513
967;  Bin-nih-ziz-bah; F; Unk; Navajo; F; M; Wife; 966; Yes; Yes; 27514

968;  Benally, Charley; M; 31; Navajo; F; M; Head; 967; Yes; Yes; 27580
969;  Bah; F; 56; Navajo; F; Wd; Mother; 968; Yes; Yes; 27581
970;  Charles, Ethel; F; 23; Navajo; F; S; Sister; 969; Yes; Yes; 27582
971;  Chih-des-wudt; M; 21; Navajo; F; S; Brother; 970; Yes; Yes; 27583

972;  Boh-woh-atin, Howard; M; 40; Navajo; F; M; Head; 971; Yes; Yes; 28030
973;  Mamie; F; 41; Navajo; F; M; Wife; 972; Yes; Yes; 28031
974;  Willie; M; 14; Navajo; F; S; Son; 973; Yes; Yes; 28032
975;  Esther; F; 12; Navajo; F; S; Daughter; 974; Yes; Yes; 28033

31

Census of the **Northern Navajo** reservation of the **Northern Navajo**
jurisdiction, as of **April 1**, 19**31,** taken by **Ernest H. Hammond, District**,
Superintendent. **in Charge**

**Key:** Number; NAME: Surname, Given; Sex; Birth Year (if given), Age At Last Birthday; Tribe; Degree of
Blood; Marital Status; Relationship To Head of Family; Last Census Roll Number; At Jurisdiction Where
Enrolled (Yes or No); At Another Jurisdiction; ELSEWHERE: Post office, County, State; Ward (Yes or No);
Allotment, Annuity, and Identification Numbers.

976;   Mamie; F; 9; Navajo; F; S; Daughter; 975; Yes; Yes; 28034
977;   Junior; M; 7; Navajo; F; S; Son; 976; Yes; Yes; 28035
978;   Gladis; F; 5; Navajo; F; S; Daughter; 977; Yes; Yes; 28036
979;   Seginih, Mark; M; 26; Navajo; F; S; Daughter-in-law[sic]; 978; Yes; Yes;
28037                                   [Should be Brother-in-law]

980;   Bitsee-chilligi; M; 37; Navajo; F; M; Head; 979; Yes; Yes; 17377
981;   Nat-kles-yilth-desbah; F; 31; Navajo; F; M; Wife; 980; Yes; Yes; 17378
982;   Bitsees-chilligi-woody; M; 7; Navajo; F; S; Son; 981; Yes; Yes; 17379
983;   Bitsees-chilligi-bidge-ee-bah; F; 5; Navajo; F; S; Son[sic]; Yes; Yes; 17380
                                          [Should be female]

984;   Bitsee-clitsoih; M; 58; Navajo; F; Wd; Head; 983; Yes; Yes; 20098

985;   Bih-nath-lapaih-bega; M; 27; Navajo; F; M; Head; 984; Yes; Yes; 17201
986;   Bah-ahzonih-bitsih; F; 25; Navajo; F; M; Wife; 985; Yes; Yes; 17202
987;   Florence Smiley; F; 12; Navajo; F; S; Daughter; 986; Yes; Yes; 17203
988;   Bih-nath-lapaih-bega-kee; M; 10; Navajo; F; S; Son; 987; Yes; Yes; 17204
989;   Bih-nath-lapaih-bega-bah; F; 7; Navajo; F; S; Daughter; 988; Yes; Yes; 17205
990;   John Cents; M; 4; Navajo; F; S; Son; 989; Yes; Yes; 17206
991;   Baby; [M]; 1; Navajo; F; S; [Son]; 990; Yes; Yes; 17407

992;   Bayah-boh-gwoh-bega; M; 33; Navajo; F; M; Head; 991; Yes; Yes; 17349
993;   Bayah-boh-gwoh-bega's wife; F; 31; Navajo; F; M; Wife; 992; Yes; Yes;
17350
994;   Bayah-hoh-gwoh-deh-nesbah[sic]; F; 8; Navajo; F; S; Daughter; 993; Yes; Yes;
17351   [Name should be Bayah-boh-gwoh-deh-nesbah]
995;   Bayah-boh-alchi-hasbah; F; 6; Navajo; F; S; Daughter; 994; Yes; Yes; 17352
996;   Hoska-yil-dez-wudt; M; 3; Navajo; F; S; Son; 995; Yes; Yes; 17353

997;   Bah-hah-zohnih-bitah; M; 31; Navajo; F; M; Head; 996; Yes; Yes; 17026
998;   Descheeny's Daughter; F; 23; Navajo; F; M; Wife; 997; Yes; Yes; 17027

999;   Batoni-bega; M; 41; Navajo; F; M; Head; 1007; Yes; Yes; 27990
1000;   Hosteen-clitsoh-bitsih; F; 32; Navajo; F; M; Wife-1st; 1008; Yes; Yes; 27991
1001;   Eskee; M; 14; Navajo; F; S; Son; 1009; Yes; Yes; 27992
1002;   Adzan-soh; F; 9; Navajo; F; S; Daughter; 1010; Yes; Yes; 27993
1003;   Doh-yazzie; F; 7; Navajo; F; S; Daughter; 1011; Yes; Yes; 27994
1004;   Hosteen-clitsoh-bitsih; F; 30; Navajo; F; M; 2nd-Wife; 1012; Yes; Yes; 27995
1005;   Adzan-nez; F; 8; Navajo; F; S; Daughter; 1013; Yes; Yes; 27996
1006;   Dinay-l-bahih; F; 6; Navajo; F; S; Son; 1014; Yes; Yes; 27997
1007;   Chih-keh; F; 3; Navajo; F; S; Daughter; 1015; Yes; Yes; 27998
1008;   Dez-bah; F; 19; Navajo; F; S; Sister-in-law; 1016; Yes; Yes; 27999

Census of the **Northern Navajo** reservation of the **Northern Navajo** jurisdiction, as of **April 1**, 19**31,** taken by **Ernest H. Hammond, District**, Superintendent. **in Charge**

**Key:** Number; NAME: Surname, Given; Sex; Birth Year (if given), Age At Last Birthday; Tribe; Degree of Blood; Marital Status; Relationship To Head of Family; Last Census Roll Number; At Jurisdiction Where Enrolled (Yes or No); At Another Jurisdiction; ELSEWHERE: Post office, County, State; Ward (Yes or No); Allotment, Annuity, and Identification Numbers.

1009; Batoni-bitsih; F; 57; Navajo; F; Wd; Head; 1017; Yes; Yes; 27976
1010; Haska-des-wudt; M; 26; Navajo; F; S; Son; 1018; Yes; Yes; 27977
1011; Hosteen-yazzie-chic; M; 20; Navajo; F; S; Son; 1019; Yes; Yes; 27979
1012; Nah-haz-bah; F; 17; Navajo; F; S Daughter; 1020; Yes; Yes; 27980
1013; Dennis; M; 14; Navajo; F; S; Son; 1021; Yes; Yes; 27981

1014; Batoni-itso-benally; M; 31; Navajo; F; M; Head; 1022; Yes; Yes; 27962
1015; Hosteen-zannih-bitsih; F; 27; Navajo; F; M; Wife; 1023; Yes; Yes; 27963
1016; Choih; F; 8; Navajo; F; S; Daughter; 1024; Yes; Yes; 27964
1017; Curtis; M; 2; Navajo; F; S; Son; 1025; Yes; Yes; 28101

1018; Beleen-dal-suen-bitah-hosea; M; 50; Navajo; F; M; Head; 1026; Yes; Yes; 27537
1019; Bil-zihz-diz-bah; F; 49; Navajo; F; M; Wife; 1027; Yes; Yes; 27538
1020; Haska-yil-has-wudt, Tom; M; 38; Navajo; F; Wd; Step-son; 1028; Yes; Yes; 27539
1021; Hosteen-yazzie; M; 83; Navajo; F; Div.; Father-in-law; 1030; Yes; Yes; 27541

1022; Blue-eye-benally; M; Unk; Navajo; F; M; Head; 1032; Yes; Yes; 27529
1023; Jennie; F; 40; Navajo; F; M; Wife; 1033; Yes; Yes; 27530
1024; Tas-wudt; M; 22; Navajo; F; S; Son; 1034; Yes; Yes; 27531
1025; Taoz-bah; F; 18; Navajo; F; S; Daughter; 1035; Yes; Yes; 27532
1026; Yee-has-wudt; M; 14; Navajo; F; S; Daughter; 1036; Yes; Yes; 27533
1027; Tah-deyah; M; 12; Navajo; F; S; Son; 1037; Yes; Yes; 27534
1028; Nah-tah-yil-des-wudt; M; 9; Navajo; F; S; Son; 1038; Yes; Yes; 27535
1029; Al-kih-nih-bah; F; 6; Navajo; F; S; Daughter; 1039; Yes; Yes; 27536

1030; Binh-bih-tohnih-bega, Warren; M; 38; Navajo; F; M; Head; 1040; Yes; Yes; 28362
1031; Chan-tailly-benally; F; 41; Navajo; F; M; Wife; 1041; Yes; Yes; 28363
1032; Warren, John; M; 18; Navajo; F; S; Son; 1042; Yes; Yes; 28364
1033; Warren, Francis; M; 13; Navajo; F; S; Son; 1043; Yes; Yes; 28365
1034; Haska-yee-dah-nal-wudt; M; 11; Navajo; F; S; Son; 1044; Yes; Yes; 28366
1035; Amos; M; 8; Navajo; F; S; Son; 1045; Yes; Yes; 28367
1036; Mary; F; 1-4/12; Navajo; F; S; Daughter; [Blank]; Yes; Yes; 28552

1037; Bitsee-bahih-bega; M; 24; Navajo; F; M; Head; 1046; Yes; Yes; 28372
1038; Nellie; F; 21; Navajo; F; M; Wife; 1047; Yes; Yes; 28373
1039; Chester; M; 3; Navajo; F; S; Son; 1048; Yes; Yes; 28374

1040; Batoni-bitsees-chilli; M; 71; Navajo; F; M; Head; 1049; Yes; Yes; 28375
1041; Nocki-dinay-bilah; F; 79; Navajo; F; M; 1st Wife; 1050; Yes; Yes; 28376
1042; Adzan-bitsee-l-bahih; F; 62; Navajo; F; M; 2nd Wife; 1051; Yes; Yes; 28377

Census of the **Northern Navajo** reservation of the **Northern Navajo** jurisdiction, as of **April 1** , 19**31,** taken by **Ernest H. Hammond, District** , Superintendent. **in Charge**

**Key:** Number; NAME: Surname, Given; Sex; Birth Year (if given), Age At Last Birthday; Tribe; Degree of Blood; Marital Status; Relationship To Head of Family; Last Census Roll Number; At Jurisdiction Where Enrolled (Yes or No); At Another Jurisdiction; ELSEWHERE: Post office, County, State; Ward (Yes or No); Allotment, Annuity, and Identification Numbers.

1043; Denit-sosie; M; 18; Navajo; F; S; Son; 1052; Yes; Yes; 28378

1044; Boh-woh-atin-bega; M; 46; Navajo; F; M; Head; 1053; Yes; Yes; 28416
1045; Adzanih-yazzie; F; 29; Navajo; F; M; Wife; 1054; Yes; Yes; 28417
1046; Bahih; M; 13; Navajo; F; S; Step-son; 1055; Yes; Yes; 28418
1047; Yee-kih-haz-bah; F; 7; Navajo; F; S; Daughter; 1056; Yes; Yes; 28419
1048; Nah-tah-yil-yil-wudt; M; 5; Navajo; F; S; Son; 1057; Yes; Yes; 28420
1049; Harry; M; 2; Navajo; F; S; Son; 1058; Yes; Yes; 28525

1050; Bih-keh-dinnih-bega; M; 60; Navajo; F; M; Head; 1059; Yes; Yes; 28463
1051; Doh-yen-bitsih; F; 37; Navajo; F; M; Wife; 1060; Yes; Yes; 28464
1052; Doh-yen-bitsih; F; 19; Navajo; F; S; Daughter; 1061; Yes; Yes; 28465
1053; Eee-bah; F; 18; Navajo; F; S; Daughter; 1062; Yes; Yes; 28466
1054; Eddie; M; 16; Navajo; F; S; Son; 1063; Yes; Yes; 28467
1055; Bonna; F; 12; Navajo; F; S; Daughter; 1064; Yes; Yes; 28468
1056; Sosie; M; 10; Navajo; F; S; Son; 1065; Yes; Yes; 28469
1057; Haska-yah-des-wudt; M; 3; Navajo; F; S; Son; 1066; Yes; Yes; 28470
1058; Kez-bah; F; 25; Navajo; F; Div. Wd; Daughter; 1067; Yes; Yes; 28471
1059; Haska-yee-bal-wohl; M; 3; Navajo; F; S; Grand-Son; 1068; Yes; Yes; 28472
1060; Posey; M; 18; Navajo; F; S; Son; 1069; Yes; Yes; 28473

1061; Bih- keh-dinnih-benally-; M; 30; Navajo; F; M; Head; 1070; Yes; Yes; 28474
1062; An-nah-gahnih-bitsih; F; 26; Navajo; F; M; Wife; 1071; Yes; Yes; 28475
1063; Haska-yee-chih-has-wudt; M; 7; Navajo; F; S; Son; 1072; Yes; Yes; 28476
1064; Glih-hah-nih-bah; F; 5; Navajo; F; S; Daughter; 1073; Yes; Yes; 28477
1065; Glih-han-nih-bah; F; 3; Navajo; F; S; Daughter; 1074; Yes; Yes; 28478

1066; Bah-ilth-inni-bitsoih, Jumbo; M; Unk; Navajo; F; M; Head; 1075; Yes; Yes; 24948
1067; Bil-hih-ziz-bah; F; 35; Navajo; F; M; Wife; 1076; Yes; Yes; 24949
1068; Haska-yah-nil-wudt; M; 22; Navajo; F; S; Son; 1077; Yes; Yes; 24950
1069; George; M; 20; Navajo; F; S; Son; 1078; Yes; Yes; 24951
1070; Alice; F; 16; Navajo; F; S; Daughter; 1079; Yes; Yes; 24952
1071; Jimmie; M; 10; Navajo; F; S; Son; 1080; Yes; Yes; 24953
1072; Haska-inl-wudt[sic]; M; 5; Navajo; F; S; Son; 1081; Yes; Yes; 24955
      [Name is probably Haska-nil-wudt]
1073; Charley; M; 2; Navajo; F; S; Son; 1082; Yes; Yes; 25339

1074; Bih-dagah-li-cheeih; M; 93; Navajo; F; Wd; Head; 1083; Yes; Yes; 24782
1075; Nocki-dinay, Nellie; F; 22; Navajo; F; S; Grand-daughter; 1084; Yes; Yes; 24783
1076; Nocki-dinay, Eli; F[sic]; 21; Navajo; F; S; Grand-Son; 1085; Yes; Yes; 24784
1077; Nocki-dinay, Walter; M; 16; Navajo; F; S; Grand-Son; 1086; Yes; Yes; 24785

Census of the __Northern Navajo__ reservation of the __Northern Navajo__ jurisdiction, as of __April 1__, 19**31,** taken by __Ernest H. Hammond, District__, Superintendent. __in Charge__

**Key:** Number; NAME: Surname, Given; Sex; Birth Year (if given), Age At Last Birthday; Tribe; Degree of Blood; Marital Status; Relationship To Head of Family; Last Census Roll Number; At Jurisdiction Where Enrolled (Yes or No); At Another Jurisdiction; ELSEWHERE: Post office, County, State; Ward (Yes or No); Allotment, Annuity, and Identification Numbers.

1078; Carmelita; F; 5; Navajo; F; S; Great-grand-Daughter; 1087; Yes; Yes; 24786

1079; Biz-dee-bah; F; 45; Navajo; F; Wd; Head; 1088; Yes; Yes; 24747
1080; Bessie; F; 23; Navajo; F; S; Daughter; 1089; Yes; Yes; 24748
1081; Tah-yaz; M; 12; Navajo; F; S; Son; 1090; Yes; Yes; 24750
1082; Al-dah-nez-bah; F; 10; Navajo; F; S; Daughter; 1091; Yes; Yes; 24751
1083; Yee-hah-naz-bah; F; 4; Navajo; F; S; Daughter; 1092; Yes; Yes; 24752

1084; Bih-bayse-yen-bitsih; F; 58; Navajo; F; Wd; Head; 1093; Yes; Yes; 20326
1085; Bih-bayse-yen-bitsoih, Addison; M; 20; Navajo; F; S; Son; 1094; Yes; Yes; 20327
1086; Nah-glih-bah; F; 15; Navajo; F; S; Daughter; 1095; Yes; Yes; 20328

1087; Bahih; M; 71; Navajo; F; Wd; Head; 1096; Yes; Yes; 24740

1088; Bih-teece-ih-yen-bega; M; 30; Navajo; F; M; Head; 1097; Yes; Yes; 24720
1089; Keh-haz-bah; F; 27; Navajo; F; M; Wife; 1098; Yes; Yes; 24721
1090; Mary; F; 13; Navajo; F; S; Daughter; 1099; Yes; Yes; 24722
1091; Ben; M; 6; Navajo; F; S; Son; 1100; Yes; Yes; Yes; 24723
1092; Lena; F; 2; Navajo; F; S; Daughter; 1101; Yes; Yes; 25331

1093; Bitsee-yiz-bizee-bega; M; Unk; Navajo; F; M; Head; 1102; Yes; Yes; 17233
1094; Bitsee-pahih-yeetah-bah; F; 20; Navajo; F; M; Wife; 1103; Yes; Yes; 17234

1095; Bitsee-pahih-bega; M; 50; Navajo; F; M; Head; 1104; Yes; Yes; 17227
1096; Bih-hay-dih-chise-benally; F; 41; Navajo; F; M; Wife; 1105; Yes; Yes; 17228
1097; Bitsee-pahih-adzamih[sic], Tulie; F; 15; Navajo; F; S; Daughter; 1106; Yes; Yes; 17229 [Name should be Bitsee-pahih-adzanih, Tulie]
1098; Bitsee-pahih, Marie; F; 12; Navajo; F; S; Daughter; 1107; Yes; Yes; 17230
1099; Bitsee-pahih-adzanih; F; 5; Navajo; F; S; Daughter; 1108; Yes; Yes; 17231
1100; Bega, Helen S.; F; 21; Navajo; F; S; Daughter; 1109; Yes; Yes; 17232

1101; Bah-ahzonih; M; 43; Navajo; F; M; Head; 1110; Yes; Yes; 17211
1102; Natalie-ha-bah; F; 41; Navajo; F; M; Wife; 1111; Yes; Yes; 17212
1103; Bah-ahzonih- Little John; M; 20; Navajo; F; S; Son; 1112; Yes; Yes; 17213
1104; Bah-ahzonih-dinay-pahih; M; 19; Navajo; F; S; Son; 1113; Yes; Yes; 17214
1105; Smiley, Tulie; F; 17; Navajo; F; S; Daughter; 1114; Yes; Yes; 17215
1106; Smiley, Michael; M; 16; Navajo; F; S; Son; 1115; Yes; Yes; 17216
1107; Bah-ahzonih-kin-lachee-nih; M; 14; Navajo; F; S; Son; 1116; Yes; Yes; 17217
1108; Bah-ahzonih-bah-ih; F; 11; Navajo; F; S; Daughter; 1117; Yes; Yes; 17218
1109; Bah-ahzonih-adzanih-pahih; F; 8; Navajo; F; S; Daughter; 1119; Yes; Yes; 17219

Census of the **Northern Navajo** reservation of the **Northern Navajo** jurisdiction, as of **April 1**, 19**31,** taken by **Ernest H. Hammond, District**, Superintendent. **in Charge**

Key: Number; NAME: Surname, Given; Sex; Birth Year (if given), Age At Last Birthday; Tribe; Degree of Blood; Marital Status; Relationship To Head of Family; Last Census Roll Number; At Jurisdiction Where Enrolled (Yes or No); At Another Jurisdiction; ELSEWHERE: Post office, County, State; Ward (Yes or No); Allotment, Annuity, and Identification Numbers.

1110; Bah-ahzonih-ahtseeih[sic]; F; 5; Navajo; F; S; Daughter; 1120; Yes; Yes; 17220 [Name could be Bah-ahzonih-ahtseesih]

1111; Nina; F; 2; Navajo; F; S; Daughter; 1121; Yes; Yes; 17221

1112; Wezbah; F; 1; Navajo; F; S; Daughter; [Blank]; Yes; Yes; 17418

1113; Bitsee-chilli; M; 53; Navajo; F; M; Head; 1122; Yes; Yes; 20120

1114; Bitsee-chilli's wife; F; 33; Navajo; F; M; Wife; 1123; Yes; Yes; 20121

1115; Eskee-suen; M; 9; Navajo; F; S; Son; 1124; Yes; Yes; 20122

1116; Dinay-chee; M; 7; Navajo; F; S; Son; 1125; Yes; Yes; 20123

1117; Adzan; F; 5; Navajo; F; S; Daughter; 1126; Yes; Yes; 20124

1118; Harry; M; 3; Navajo; F; S; Son; 1127; Yes; Yes; 20125

1119; Bigman Frank; M; 44; Navajo; F; M; Head; 1128; Yes; Yes; 25276

1120; Adzan-sosie; F; 45; Navajo; F; M: Wife; 1129; Yes; Yes; 25277

1121; Chee, Wilson; M; 29; Navajo; F; S; Step-son; 1130; Yes; Yes; 25278

1122; Ben Frank; M; 25; Navajo; F; S; Son; 1131; Yes; Yes; 25279

1123; Frank, Ruth; F; 20; Navajo; F; S; Daughter; 1132; Yes; Yes; 25280

1124; Wilson, Lily; F; 27; Navajo; F; S; Step-daughter; 1133; Yes; Yes; 25281

1125; Nancy Frank; F; 11; Navajo; F; S; Daughter; 1134; Yes; Yes; 25282

1126; Alice; F; 7; Navajo; F; S; Daughter; 1135; Yes; Yes; 25283

1127; Bah; F; 75; Navajo; F; Wd; Cousin-in-law; 1136; Yes; Yes; 25284

1128; Benally, Bigman Lee; M; 23; Navajo; F; M; Head; 1137; Yes; Yes; 25285

1129; Glih-hah-bah; F; 18; Navajo; F; M; Wife; 1138; Yes; Yes; 25286

1130; Bigman; M; 79; Navajo; F; Wd; Head; 1139; Yes; Yes; 25295

1131; Bilah-is-chilli-bega, K. P. Jackson; M; 33; Navajo; F; Wd; Head; 1139; Yes; Yes; 18103

1132; Bay-bohgwoh; M; Unk; Navajo; F; M; Head; 1141; Yes; Yes; 17342

1133; Bay-bohgwoh's wife; F; 61; Navajo; F; M; Wife; 1142; Yes; Yes; 17343

1134; Bay-bohgwoh Adzan-stohl; F; 20; Navajo; F; S; Daughter; 1143; Yes; Yes; 17344

1135; Nah-chee-bah; F; Unk; Navajo; F; S; Daughter; 1144; Yes; Yes; 17345

1136; Bah-gee-chah-benally, Sandman; M; 49; Navajo; F; M; Head; 1145; Yes; Yes; 25259

1137; Chah-dih-tlohi-bitsih; F; 48; Navajo; F; M; Wife; 1146; Yes; Yes; 25260

1138; Guy; M; 22; Navajo; F; S; Son; 1147; Yes; Yes; 25261

1139; Allen; M; 20; Navajo; F; S; Son; 1148; Yes; Yes; 25262

1140; Grant; M; 11; Navajo; F; S; Son; 1149; Yes; Yes; 25263

1141; Key-yil-nih-bah; F; 9; Navajo; F; S; Daughter; 1150; Yes; Yes; 25264

Census of the **Northern Navajo** reservation of the **Northern Navajo** jurisdiction, as of **April 1**, 1931, taken by **Ernest H. Hammond, District**, Superintendent.                    **in Charge**

**Key:** Number; NAME: Surname, Given; Sex; Birth Year (if given), Age At Last Birthday; Tribe; Degree of Blood; Marital Status; Relationship To Head of Family; Last Census Roll Number; At Jurisdiction Where Enrolled (Yes or No); At Another Jurisdiction; ELSEWHERE: Post office, County, State; Ward (Yes or No); Allotment, Annuity, and Identification Numbers.

1142;  Belone, John; M; 41; Navajo; F; M; Head; 1151; Yes; Yes; 25114
1143;  Hasteen-bih-dagaihigi-bitsih; F; 48; Navajo; F; M; Wife; 1152; Yes; Yes; 25115
1144;  Haska-yee-nas-wudt; M; 14; Navajo; F; S; Step-grand-son; 1153; Yes; Yes; 25116

1145;  Bainbridge, Tom; M; 39; Navajo; F; M; Head; 1154; Yes; Yes; 25073
1146;  Susie; F; 43; Navajo; F; M; Wife; 1155; Yes; Yes; 25074
1147;  Herman; M; 24; Navajo; F; S; Son; 1156; Yes; Yes; 25075
1148;  Henry; F[sic]; 15; Navajo; F; S; Son; 1157; Yes; Yes; 25076
1149;  Grace; F; 6; Navajo; F; S; Daughter; 1158; Yes; Yes; 25077
1150;  Alice; F; 2; Navajo; F; S; Daughter; 1159; Yes; Yes; 25342

1151;  Bitsees-chilli-yazzie-bega; M; 26; Navajo; F; M; Head; 1164; Yes; Yes; 17338
1152;  Bitsees-chilli-yazzie-bega wife; F; 23; Navajo; F; M; Wife; 1165; Yes; Yes; 17339
1153;  Hah-hah-yis-bah; F; 6; Navajo; F; S; Daughter; 1166; Yes; Yes; 17340
1154;  Bitsees-chilli-yazzie-bega son; M; 3; Navajo; F; S; Son; 1167; Yes; Yes; 17341

1155;  Bih-clah-toh; M; 59; Navajo; F; M; Head; 1168; Yes; Yes; 17273
1156;  Bitsee-pis-gih-bitsih; F; 43; Navajo; F; M; Wife; 1169; Yes; Yes; 17274
1157;  Bih-dah-toh-etseesigih; M; 7; Navajo; F; S; Son; 1170; Yes; Yes; 17275

1158;  Bitsee-gail-lachee; F; 81; Navajo; F; Wd; Head; 1171; Yes; Yes; 17950
1159;  Tah-desbah; F; 17; Navajo; F; S; Grand-daughter; 1172; Yes; Yes; 17951

1160;  Benally-badoni, Skinny; M; 34; Navajo; F; M; Head; 1173; Yes; Yes; 18009
1161;  Benally-bitsih (Skinny); F; 27; Navajo; F; M; Wife; 1174; Yes; Yes; 18010
1162;  Pearl; F; 2; Navajo; F; S; Daughter; 1175; Yes; Yes; 18231

1163;  Bah-ilth-inni-yah-ah-yeh; M; Unk; Navajo; F; M; Head; 1176; Yes; Yes; 25043
1164;  Adzan-nez; F; 66; Navajo; F; M; Wife; 1177; Yes; Yes; 25044

1165;  Bay-ilchee; M; 51; Navajo; F; M; Head; 1178; Yes; Yes; 17867
1166;  Adzan-seeih; F; 34; Navajo; F; M; Wife; 1179; Yes; Yes; 17868
1167;  Hoska-yikih-dahih-yah; M; 17; Navajo; F; S; Son; 1180; Yes; Yes; 17869
1168;  Hoska-yih-nath; M; 12; Navajo; F; S; Son; 1181; Yes; Yes; 17870
1169;  Nah-glinn-yil-nocki-yih; F; 10; Navajo; F; S; Daughter; 1182; Yes; Yes; 17871
1170;  Hoska-yil-hah-yah; M; 7; Navajo; F; S; Son; 1183; Yes; Yes; 17872
1171;  Yil-hah-yah; M; 13; Navajo; F; S; Son; 1184; Yes; Yes; 18237

37

Census of the __Northern Navajo__ reservation of the __Northern Navajo__
jurisdiction, as of __April 1__, 1931, taken by __Ernest H. Hammond, District__,
Superintendent.                                                      __in Charge__

Key: Number; NAME: Surname, Given; Sex; Birth Year (if given), Age At Last Birthday; Tribe; Degree of
Blood; Marital Status; Relationship To Head of Family; Last Census Roll Number; At Jurisdiction Where
Enrolled (Yes or No); At Another Jurisdiction; ELSEWHERE: Post office, County, State; Ward (Yes or No);
Allotment, Annuity, and Identification Numbers.

1172;   Bah Tsihe; F; 1; Navajo; F; S; Daughter; [Blank]; Yes; Yes; 18301


1173;   Bay-gashih-lagaih; M; Unk; Navajo; F; M; Head; 1185; Yes; Yes; 25901
1174;   Watchman, Annie; F; 39; Navajo; F; M; Wife; 1186; Yes; Yes; 25902
1175;   Watchman, Glenn; M; 23; Navajo; F; S; Step-son; 1187; Yes; Yes; 25903
1176;   Watchman, Nelson; M; 12; Navajo; F; S; Step-son; 1188; Yes; Yes; 25904


1177;   Bih-yel, Clyde; M; Unk; Navajo; F; M; Head; 1189; Yes; Yes; 26418
1178;   Bil-nih-ziz-bah; F; 31; Navajo; F; M; Wife; 1190; Yes; Yes; 26419
1179;   Nah-tah-yee-neh-yah; M; 30; Navajo; F; S; Son; 1191; Yes; Yes; 26420
1180;   Yil-nah-bah, Annie; F; 6; Navajo; F; S; Daughter; 1192; Yes; Yes; 26421
1181;   Zan-bah, Eve; F; 37; Navajo; F; S; Sister; 1193; Yes; Yes; 26431


1182;   Yee-kaz-bah; F; 44; Navajo; F; M; Wife; 1195; Yes; Yes; 26405
1183;   Kayih-bah; F; 17; Navajo; F; S; Daughter; 1196; Yes; Yes; 26406
1184;   Virginia; F; 15; Navajo; F; S; Daughter; 1197; Yes; Yes; 26407
1185;   Al-kih-nih-bah; F; 8; Navajo; F; S; Daughter; 1198; Yes; Yes; 26408
1186;   Dah-al-woody; M; 7; Navajo; F; S; Son; 1199; Yes; Yes; 26409
1187;   Tah-des-wudt; M; 3; Navajo; F; S; Son; 1200; Yes; Yes; 26410


1188;   Bitsees-chilli-yazzie; M; 62; Navajo; F; M; Head; 1201; Yes; Yes; 17332
1189;   Adzanih-hartathly; F; 62; Navajo; F; M; Wife; 1202; Yes; Yes; 17333
1190;   Adzanih-hartathly-bitsih; F; 19; Navajo; F; S; Daughter; 1203; Yes; Yes;
17334
1191;   Hoska-yih-kih-deswudt; M; 16; Navajo; F; S; Son; 1204; Yes; Yes; 17335


1192;   Bitsees-chilli-yazzie-bitsih; F; 35; Navajo; F; Div Wd; Head; 1205; Yes; Yes;
17336
1193;   Bitsees-chilli-yazzie-kee-zanih-yazzie; M; 12; Navajo; F; S; Son; 1206; Yes;
Yes; 17337


1194;   Beleen-lagaih-bega, Billy; M; 22; Navajo; F; M; Head; 1207; Yes; Yes; 18863
1195;   Yah-des-bah; F; 19; Navajo; F; M; Wife; 1208; Yes; Yes; 18864


1196;   Beleen-lagaih-bega, John; M; 34; Navajo; F; M; Head; 1209; Yes; Yes; 18826
1197;   Beleen-lagaih-bega's wife; F; 31; Navajo; F; M; Wife; 1210; Yes; Yes; 18827
1198;   Adzanih-suen; F; 10; Navajo; F; S; Daughter; 1211; Yes; Yes; 18828
1199;   Kee-sosie; M; 7; Navajo; F; S; Son; 1212; Yes; Yes; 18829


1200;   Bah-gon-l-chee-bih-bizeen, Mark; M; Unk; Navajo; F; M; Head; 1213; Yes;
Yes; 26271
1201;   Bil-nih-ziz-bah; F; 27; Navajo; F; M; Wife; 1214; Yes; Yes; 26272
1202;   Mamie; F; 10; Navajo; F; S; Daughter; 1215; Yes; Yes; 26273


38

Census of the **Northern Navajo** reservation of the **Northern Navajo** jurisdiction, as of **April 1**, 19**31**, taken by **Ernest H. Hammond, District**, Superintendent. **in Charge**

**Key:** Number; NAME: Surname, Given; Sex; Birth Year (if given), Age At Last Birthday; Tribe; Degree of Blood; Marital Status; Relationship To Head of Family; Last Census Roll Number; At Jurisdiction Where Enrolled (Yes or No); At Another Jurisdiction; ELSEWHERE: Post office, County, State; Ward (Yes or No); Allotment, Annuity, and Identification Numbers.

1203; Bylilli, Steve; M; 1873, 58; Navajo; F; M; Head; 1216; Yes; Yes; 20362
1204; Bitsoih-yazzie-bitsih; F; 24; Navajo; F; M; Wife; 1217; Yes; Yes; 20363
1205; Adzan-l-bahih; F; 3; Navajo; F; S; Daughter; 1218; Yes; Yes; 20364

1206; Bee-oh-chidie; M; Unk; Navajo; F; M; Head; 1219; Yes; Yes; 17811
1207; Athochee-hasbah; F; 25; Navajo; F; M; Wife; 1220; Yes; Yes; 17812
1208; See-l-pahih; M; 7; Navajo; F; S; Son; 1221; Yes; Yes; 17813
1209; See-l-pahih-yazzie; M; 5; Navajo; F; S; Son; 1222; Yes; Yes; 17814
1210; Des-bah; F; 4; Navajo; F; S; Daughter; 1223; Yes; Yes; 17815

1211; Badoni-sani (Charley Manuelito); M; 66; Navajo; F; M; Head; 1224; Yes; Yes; 26246
1212; Chih-dez-bah; F; 54; Navajo; F; M; Wife; 1225; Yes; Yes; 26247
1213; Harry; M; 20; Navajo; F; S; Son; 1226; Yes; Yes; 26249
1214; Manuelito, Joe; M; 15; Navajo; F; S; Son; 1227; Yes; Yes; 26250
1215; Toaz-bah; F; 6; Navajo; F; S; Grand-daughter; 1228; Yes; Yes; 26251

1216; Benally, Skinny; M; 62; Navajo; F; M; Head; 1229; Yes; Yes; 17904
1217; Adzan-hosch-clish-nih; F; 37; Navajo; F; M; Wife; 1230; Yes; Yes; 17905
1218; Yih-hih-bah; F; 12; Navajo; F; S; Daughter; 1231; Yes; Yes; 17906
1219; Hoska-bah-ho-tal; M; 9; Navajo; F; S; Son; 1232; Yes; Yes; 17907
1220; Shunilla, Nita; F; 21; Navajo; F; S; Daughter; 1233; Yes; Yes; 17910
1221; Ruland; M; 2; Navajo; F; S; Son; 1234; Yes; Yes; 18221

1222; Bah-gee-chah-benally, Manuelito Armijo; M; 22; Navajo; F; M; Head; 1235; Yes; Yes; 26213
1223; Dorcas; F; 29; Navajo; F; M; Wife; 1236; Yes; Yes; 26214
1224; Marie; F; 3; Navajo; F; S; Daughter; 1237; Yes; Yes; 26215
1225; Bah-gee-chah-bah-zah-ad; F; 57; Navajo; Wd; Mother; 1238; Yes; Yes; 26216
1226; Clih-hah-nih-bah; F; 24; Navajo; F; Wd; Sister; 1239; Yes; Yes; 26217
1227; Lucille; F; 20; Navajo; F; S; Sister; 1240; Yes; Yes; 26218
1228; Dora; F; Unk; Navajo; F; Wd; Cousin; 1241; Yes; Yes; 26219
1229; Glenna; F; 12; Navajo; F; S; 2nd Cousin; 1242; Yes; Yes; 26220
1230; Mary; F; 4; Navajo; F; S; 2nd Cousin; 1243; Yes; Yes; 26221

1231; Bih-naz-linh-bitsoih; M; 39; Navajo; F; M; Head; 1244; Yes; Yes; 27040
1232; Adzan-suen; F; 31; Navajo; F; M; Wife; 1245; Yes; Yes; 27041
1233; Nahn-nih-bah; F; 17; Navajo; F; S; Daughter; 1246; Yes; Yes; 27042
1234; Gih-nih-bah; F; 14; Navajo; F; S; Daughter; 1247; Yes; Yes; 27043
1235; Nih-nil-tolih; M; 9; Navajo; F; S; Son; 1248; Yes; Yes; 27044
1236; Yil-des-bah; F; 11; Navajo; F; S; Daughter; 1249; Yes; Yes; 27045
1237; Keh-yil-naz-bah; F; 7; Navajo; F; S; Daughter; 1250; Yes; Yes; 27046

Census of the **Northern Navajo** reservation of the **Northern Navajo** jurisdiction, as of **April 1**, 1931, taken by **Ernest H. Hammond, District**, Superintendent. **in Charge**

Key: Number; NAME: Surname, Given; Sex; Birth Year (if given), Age At Last Birthday; Tribe; Degree of Blood; Marital Status; Relationship To Head of Family; Last Census Roll Number; At Jurisdiction Where Enrolled (Yes or No); At Another Jurisdiction; ELSEWHERE: Post office, County, State; Ward (Yes or No); Allotment, Annuity, and Identification Numbers.

1238; Adzan-yazzie; F; 33; Navajo; F; M; Head Wife; 1252; Yes; Yes; 26978
1239; Glih-yahn-nih-bah; F; 14; Navajo; F; S; Daughter; 1253; Yes; Yes; 26979
1240; Haska-yee-ta-nah-gah; M; 9; Navajo; F; S; Son; 1254; Yes; Yes; 26980
1241; Ha-naz-bah; F; 3; Navajo; F; S; Daughter; 1255; Yes; Yes; 27092

1242; Bilah-gohah-ye-is-kinih-benally; M; 25; Navajo; F; M; Head; 1256; Yes; Yes; 20199
1243; Gliz-bah; F; 22; Navajo; F; M; Wife; 1257; Yes; Yes; 20200

1244; Bah-dagaih, Charley; M; 65; Navajo; F; Wd; Head; 1258; Yes; Yes; 26973
1245; Nah-yil-dez-bah; F; 14; Navajo; F; S; Daughter; 1259; Yes; Yes; 26974
1246; Dah-bahih; F; 10; Navajo; F; S; Daughter; 1260; Yes; Yes; 26975
1247; Nah-yil-des-wudt; M; 13; Navajo; F; S; Grand-Son; 1261; Yes; Yes; 26976

1248; Bay-gashih-lagaih-bitsoih; M; 31; Navajo; F; M; Head; 1262; Yes; Yes; 26921
1249; Al-soh-se-bah; F; 23; Navajo; F; M; Wife; 1263; Yes; Yes; 26922
1250; Haska-yee-chih-deyah; M; 6; Navajo; F; S; Son; 1264; Yes; Yes; 26923

1251; Beleen-lizin-bitah-bega; M; 33; Navajo; F; M; Head; 1265; Yes; Yes; 18112
1252; Gliz-bah; F; 23; Navajo; F; M; Wife; 1266; Yes; Yes; 18113
1253; Adzanih-gaih; F; 10; Navajo; F; S; Daughter; 1267; Yes; Yes; 18114
1254; Adzan-bah; F; 7; Navajo; F; S; Daughter; 1268; Yes; Yes; 18115

1255; Bah-kiah-dinee-bega, Bob; M; 56; Navajo; F; M; Head; 1269; Yes; Yes; 18136
1256; Topahpahpadzan; F; 60; Navajo; F; M; Wife; 1270; Yes; Yes; 18137
1257; Bitsee-nihgih, Lloyd; M; 21; Navajo; F; S; Step-son; 1271; Yes; Yes; 18138
1258; Hoska-bahih; M; 20; Navajo; F; S; Step-son; 1272; Yes; Yes; 18139
1259; Hoska-yi-hi-dah-yis-wudt; M; 7; Navajo; F; S; Son; 1273; Yes; Yes; 18140

1260; Benally, Jim; M; Unk; Navajo; F; M; Head; 1274; Yes; Yes; 26911
1261; Yil-dez-bah; F; 22; Navajo; F; M; Wife; 1275; Yes; Yes; 26912
1262; Haska-yee-neh-yah; M; 7; Navajo; F; S; Son; 1276; Yes; Yes; 26913
1263; Haska-yee-nih-yah; M; 3; Navajo; F; S; Son; 1277; Yes; Yes; 27088

1264; Bih-bayse-yen-benally, Jack; M; 27; Navajo; F; M; Head; 1278; Yes; Yes; 20033
1265; Hosteen-ah-sosie-yen-bitah; F; 24; Navajo; F; M; Wife; 1279; Yes; Yes; 20034
1266; Yee-nah-bah; F; 6; Navajo; F; S; Daughter; 1280; Yes; Yes; 20035
1267; Nah-glih-nas-bah; F; 4; Navajo; F; S; Daughter; 1281; Yes; Yes; 20036
1268; Aht-sosie-asa; M; 13; Navajo; F; S; Brother-in-law; 1282; Yes; Yes; 20037
1269; Hosteen-thitsoe; M; 2; Navajo; F; S; Son; 1283; Yes; Yes; 20411

Census of the **Northern Navajo** reservation of the **Northern Navajo** jurisdiction, as of **April 1**, 19**31**, taken by **Ernest H. Hammond, District**, Superintendent. **in Charge**

**Key:** Number; NAME: Surname, Given; Sex; Birth Year (if given), Age At Last Birthday; Tribe; Degree of Blood; Marital Status; Relationship To Head of Family; Last Census Roll Number; At Jurisdiction Where Enrolled (Yes or No); At Another Jurisdiction; ELSEWHERE: Post office, County, State; Ward (Yes or No); Allotment, Annuity, and Identification Numbers.

1270; Bay-gashih-lagaih-bitah; M; 70; Navajo; F; M; Head; 1284; Yes; Yes; 26813
1271; Hah-nah-bah; F; 59; Navajo; F; M; Wife; 1285; Yes; Yes; 26814
1272; Jenny; F; 25; Navajo; F S; Step-daughter; 1286; Yes; Yes; 26815
1273; Bih-soh-naz-nih-bah; F; 24; Navajo; F; S; Step-daughter; 1287; Yes; Yes; 26816
1274; Haska-yee-chih-nil-wudt; M; 10; Navajo; F; S; Son; 1288; Yes; Yes; 26818

1275; Bah-dagaih-bega, Charley; M; 29; Navajo; F; M; Head; 1289; Yes; Yes; 26661
1276; Ah-hih-dee-bah; F; 26; Navajo; F; M; Wife; 1290; Yes; Yes; 26662
1277; Haska-yee-chih-deyah; M; 4; Navajo; F; S; Son; 1291; Yes; Yes; 26663
1278; Al-nah-bah; F; 3; Navajo; F; S; Daughter; 1292; Yes; Yes; 26664

1279; Beleen-li-chee-bega; M; 56; Navajo; F; M; Head; 1293; Yes; Yes; 26653
1280; Bah; F; 54; Navajo; F; M; Wife; 1294; Yes; Yes; 26654
1281; Al-nah-bah; F; 19; Navajo; F; S; Daughter; 1295; Yes; Yes; 26655
1282; Zaz-bah; F; 8; Navajo; F; S; Daughter; 1296; Yes; Yes; 26656
1283; Haska-yee-nal-wudt; M; 20; Navajo; F; S; Son; 1297; Yes; Yes; 26657
1284; Nah-tah-yil-deyh; M; 17; Navajo; F; S; Son; 1298; Yes; Yes; 26658
1285; Haska-yee-tah-yee-gahl; M; 7; Navajo; F; S; Grand-Son; 1299; Yes; Yes; 26659
1286; Marie; F; 20; Navajo; F; S; Niece; 1300; Yes; Yes; 26660

1287; Beleen-thlani-badoni; M; 60; Navajo; F; M; Head; 1301; Yes; Yes; 26618
1288; Beleen-thani-bitsih; F; 59; Navajo; F; M; Wife; 1302; Yes; Yes; 26619
1289; Haska-yee-has-wudt; M; 8; Navajo; F; S; Grand-son; 1303; Yes; Yes; 26620
1290; Dah-dee-bah; F; 42; Navajo; F; M; 2nd wife; 1304; Yes; Yes; 26621
1291; Rebecca; F; 17; Navajo; F; S; Daughter; 1305; Yes; Yes; 26622
1292; Tahn-hal-wudt; M; 8; Navajo; F; S; Son; 1306; Yes; Yes; 26623
1293; Al-soh-dez-bah; F; 5; Navajo; F; S; Daughter; 1307; Yes; Yes; 26624

1294; Bitah, Ben; M; 34; Navajo; F; M; Head; 1308; Yes; Yes; 23212
1295; Tahn-hah-bah; F; 26; Navajo; F; M; Wife; 1309; Yes; Yes; 23213
1296; Nah-tah-yil-ziz-zih; M; 3; Navajo; F; S; Son; 1310; Yes; Yes; 23214

1297; Bagashi-thlani-bega; M; 28; Navajo; F; M; Head; 1311; Yes; Yes; 23334
1298; Dinay-yazzie-bitsih; F; 23; Navajo; F; M; Wife; 1312; Yes; Yes; 23335
1299; Keh-yee-chih-hah-bah; F; 7; Navajo; F; S; Daughter; 1313; Yes; Yes; 23336
1300; Bil-nez-nih-bah; F; 5; Navajo; F; S; Daughter; 1314; Yes; Yes; 23337
1301; Keh-nih-bah; F; 3; Navajo; F; S; Daughter; 1315; Yes; Yes; 23338

1302; Batoni-nez; M; Unk; Navajo; F; M; Head; 1316; Yes; Yes; 23346
1303; Keh-yahn-nah-bah; F; 28; Navajo; F; M; Wife; 1317; Yes; Yes; 23347
1304; Yil-nih-bah; F; 7; Navajo; F; S; Daughter; 1318; Yes; Yes; 23348

Census of the **Northern Navajo** reservation of the **Northern Navajo** jurisdiction, as of **April 1** , 1931, taken by **Ernest H. Hammond, District**, Superintendent. **in Charge**

**Key:** Number; NAME: Surname, Given; Sex; Birth Year (if given), Age At Last Birthday; Tribe; Degree of Blood; Marital Status; Relationship To Head of Family; Last Census Roll Number; At Jurisdiction Where Enrolled (Yes or No); At Another Jurisdiction; ELSEWHERE: Post office, County, State; Ward (Yes or No); Allotment, Annuity, and Identification Numbers.

1305;   Nah-tah-yil-has-wudt; M; 5; Navajo; F; S; Son; 1319; Yes; Yes; 23349
1306;   John M.; M; 39; Navajo; F; S; Brother-in-law; 1320; Yes; Yes; 23351
1307;   Bega, John N.; M; 1 4/12; Navajo; F; S; Nephew; 1321; Yes; Yes; 23923

1308;   Barber, Frank; M; 39; Navajo; F; M; Head; 1322; Yes; Yes; 23365
1309;   Frank Barber's wife; F; 36; Navajo; F; M; Wife; 1323; Yes; Yes; 23366
1310;   Taylor; M; 12; Navajo; F; S; Son; 1324; Yes; Yes; 23367
1311;   Han-ziz-bah; F; 10; Navajo; F; S; Daughter; 1325; Yes; Yes; 23368
1312;   Nah-tah-yee-tah-des-wudt; M; 7; Navajo; F; S; Son; 1326; Yes; Yes; 23369
1313;   Nah-tah-yee-nah-gahl; M; 5; Navajo; F; S; Son; 1327; Yes; Yes; 23370
1314;   Bil-zoz-bah; F; 18; Navajo; F; S; Sister; 1328; Yes; Yes; 23371

1315;   Bih-oh-chidih-benally; M; 39; Navajo; F; M; Head; 1329; Yes; Yes; 23372
1316;   Yee-taz-hah; F; 21; Navajo; F; M; Wife; 1330; Yes; Yes; 23373
1317;   Tah-naz-bah; F; 6; Navajo; F; S; Daughter; 1331; Yes; Yes; 23374
1318;   Keh-yil-se-bah; F; 4; Navajo; F; S; Daughter; 1332; Yes; Yes; 23375

1319;   Nah-ah-ahih-yen-bitsih; F; 36; Navajo; F; Wd; Head; 1333; Yes; Yes; 23493
1320;   Yahn-yil-wohl; M; 20; Navajo; F; S; Son; 1334; Yes; Yes; 23494

1321;   Bitsih, Dr. John; F[sic]; 26; Navajo; F; Wd; Head; 1335; Yes; Yes; 23491
1322;   Chih-hoh-gahl; M; 5; Navajo; F; S; Son; 1336; Yes; Yes; 23492

1323;   Bitsees-chilli-bega; M; 23; Navajo; F; M; Head; 1337; Yes; Yes; 23858
1324;   Minnie; F; 23; Navajo; F; M; Wife; 1338; Yes; Yes; 23859
1325;   Han-bah; F; 5; Navajo; F; S; Daughter; 1339; Yes; Yes; 24010

1326;   Bye-otsin-bega; M; 39; Navajo; F; M; Head; 1340; Yes; Yes; 21476
1327;   Lee, Zonnie; F; 36; Navajo; F; M; Wife; 1341; Yes; Yes; 21477
1328;   Atate-soh; F; 13; Navajo; F; S; Daughter; 1342; Yes; Yes; 21478
1329;   Thelma; F; 10; Navajo; F; S; Daughter; 1343; Yes; Yes; 21479
1330;   Has-wuddy; M; 5; Navajo; F; S; Son; 1344; Yes; Yes; 21480
1331;   Has-wudt; M; 5; Navajo; F; S; Son; 1345; Yes; Yes; 21481
1332;   Don Lee; M; 23; Navajo; F; S; Brother-in-law; 1346; Yes; Yes; 21482
1333;   Hoskee, Lee; M; 25; Navajo; F; S; Brother-in-law; 1347; Yes; Yes; 21483

1334;   Bay-l-tone-bitseen-inni-bitsih; F; 46; Navajo; F; Wd; Head; 1348; Yes; Yes; 23812
1335;   Carl; M; 20; Navajo; F; S; Son; 1349; Yes; Yes; 23813
1336;   Annabel; F; 22; Navajo; F; S; Daughter; 1350; Yes; Yes; 23814
1337;   Haska-yee-chih-nah-hah-bah; M; 14; Navajo; F; S; Son; 1351; Yes; Yes; 23815
1338;   Haska-yee-keh-lahl; M; 7; Navajo; F; S; Son; 1352; Yes; Yes; 23816

Census of the __Northern Navajo__ reservation of the __Northern Navajo__ jurisdiction, as of __April 1__, 19**31,** taken by __Ernest H. Hammond, District__, Superintendent. **in Charge**

**Key:** Number; NAME: Surname, Given; Sex; Birth Year (if given), Age At Last Birthday; Tribe; Degree of Blood; Marital Status; Relationship To Head of Family; Last Census Roll Number; At Jurisdiction Where Enrolled (Yes or No); At Another Jurisdiction; ELSEWHERE: Post office, County, State; Ward (Yes or No); Allotment, Annuity, and Identification Numbers.

1339;  Yee-kah-nih-bah; F; 23; Navajo; F; Wd; Daughter; 1353; Yes; Yes; 23817
1340;  Bay-dee-bah; F; 8; Navajo; F; S; Grand-daughter; 1354; Yes; Yes; 23818
1341;  Haska-tah-yah; M; 2; Navajo; F; S; Grand-son; 1355; Yes; Yes; 23910

1342;  Bih-nee-nah; M; Unk; Navajo; F; M; Head; 1356; Yes; Yes; 23750
1343;  Bil-hah-ziz-bah; F; 21; Navajo; F; M; Wife; 1357; Yes; Yes; 23751
1344;  Mildred; F; 11; Navajo; F; S; Daughter; 1358; Yes; Yes; 23752
1345;  Robert; M; 19; Navajo; F; S; Son; 1359; Yes; Yes; 23753

1346;  Bee-yees-bitsoih, John Luke; M; 25; Navajo; F; M; Head; 1360; Yes; Yes; 23687
1347;  Yil-dah-ziz-bah; F; 23; Navajo; F; M; Wife; 1361; Yes; Yes; 23688
1348;  Bil-heh-ziz-bah; F; 7; Navajo; F; S; Daughter; 1362; Yes; Yes; 23689
1349;  Yee-hih-bah; F; 4; Navajo; F; S; Daughter; 1363; Yes; Yes; 23690

1350;  Beleen-bitsee-gah-lagaih-benally; M; 33; Navajo; F; M; Head; 1368; Yes; Yes; 23674
1351;  Yee-lah-nih-bah; F; 21; Navajo; F; M; Wife; 1369; Yes; Yes; 23675
1352;  Haska-nah-gathl; F[sic]; 1 5/12; Navajo; F; S; Son; 1370; Yes; Yes; 23940
          [Should be male.]

1353;  Beleen-bitsee-gah-lagaih-bega; M; 63; Navajo; F; M; Head; 1371; Yes; Yes; 23665
1354;  Dah-ziz-bah; F; 58; Navajo; F; M; Wife; 1372; Yes; Yes; 23666
1355;  Eva; F; 22; Navajo; F; S; Daughter; 1373; Yes; Yes; 23667
1356;  Daisy; F; 13; Navajo; F; S; Daughter; 1374; Yes; Yes; 23668

1357;  Bay-gashih-thlani-bega; M; Unk; Navajo; F; M; Head; 1375; Yes; Yes; 23646
1358;  Yee-kih-dez-bah; F; 21; Navajo; F; M; Wife; 1376; Yes; Yes; 23647
1359;  Nah-tah-yee-tah-yee-ghal; M; 4; Navajo; F; S; Son; 1377; Yes; Yes; 23648

1360;  Bay-gashih-thlani-bega; M; 26; Navajo; F; M; Head; 1378; Yes; Yes; 23619
1361;  Al-nah-bah; F; 25; Navajo; F; M; Wife; 1379; Yes; Yes; 23620
1362;  Biz-deh-bah; F; 4; Navajo; F; S; Daughter; 1380; Yes; Yes; 23621
1363;  Biz-nih-bah, Hilda; F; 15; F; S; Niece-in-law; 1381; Yes; Yes; 23622
1364;  Earl; M; 13; Navajo; F; S; Nephew-in-law; 1382; Yes; Yes; 23623

1365;  Bega John Washburn; M; 28; Navajo; F; M; Head; 1383; Yes; Yes; 23485
1366;  Ah-keh-dee-bah; F; 23; Navajo; F; M; Wife; 1384; Yes; Yes; 23486

1367;  Beleen-lizin-bitsih; M; 58; Navajo; F; M; Head; 1385; Yes; Yes; 18609
1368;  Beleen-lizin-bitsih's wife; F; 50; Navajo; F; M; Wife; 1386; Yes; Yes; 18610
1369;  Bah; F; 12; Navajo; F; S; Daughter; 1387; Yes; Yes; 18611

Census of the **Northern Navajo** reservation of the **Northern Navajo** jurisdiction, as of **April 1**, 1931, taken by **Ernest H. Hammond, District**, Superintendent. **in Charge**

**Key:** Number; NAME: Surname, Given; Sex; Birth Year (if given), Age At Last Birthday; Tribe; Degree of Blood; Marital Status; Relationship To Head of Family; Last Census Roll Number; At Jurisdiction Where Enrolled (Yes or No); At Another Jurisdiction; ELSEWHERE: Post office, County, State; Ward (Yes or No); Allotment, Annuity, and Identification Numbers.

1370; Hoska-yee-tah-dayah; M; 9; Navajo; F; S; Son; 1388; Yes; Yes; 18612

1371; Begay, Charley; M; Unk; Navajo; F; M; Head; 1389; Yes; Yes; 23545
1372; Ah-heh-nil-bah; F; 22; Navajo; F; M; Wife; 1390; Yes; Yes; 23546
1373; Hoskey Logai; M; 2/12; Navajo; F; S; Son; [Blank]; Yes; Yes; 24011

1374; Bih-bizee-bega; M; 35; Navajo; F; M; Head; 1391; Yes; Yes; 23590
1375; Dinay-yazzie-bilah; F; 33; Navajo; F; S; Daughter; 1392; Yes; Yes; 23591
1376; Dah-ye-bah; F; 20; Navajo; F; S; Daughter; 1393; Yes; Yes; 23592
1377; Dora; F; 17; Navajo; F; S; Daughter; 1394; Yes; Yes; 23593
1378; Eugene; M; 14; Navajo; F; S; Son; 1395; Yes; Yes; 23594
1379; Haska-yee-nah-bah; M; 9; Navajo; F; S; Son; 1396; Yes; Yes; 23595
1380; Haska-dah-yah; M; 1; Navajo; F; S; Son; 1397; Yes; Yes; 23596

1381; Bih-oh-chidih-benally; M; Unk; Navajo; F; M; Head; 1398; Yes; Yes; 23388

1382; Ben; M 59; Navajo; F; M; Head; 1399; Yes; Yes; 23422
1383; Clah-yazzie-bitsih; F; 51; Navajo; F; M; Wife; 1400; Yes; Yes; 23423
1384; Carl; M; 15; Navajo; F; S; Son; 1401; Yes; Yes; 23425
1385; Awa-chee; F; 13; Navajo; F; S; Daughter; 1402; Yes; Yes; 23426
1386; Haska-yil-nah-hoh-gahl; M; 11; Navajo; F; S; Son; 1403; Yes; Yes; 23427
1387; Haska-yil-nih-yah; M; 6; Navajo; F; S; Son; 1404; Yes; Yes; 23428
1388; Bega, Ben; M; 21; Navajo; F; S; Son; 1405; Yes; Yes; 23980

1389; Bih-lizee; M; 75; Navajo; F; M; Head; 1406; Yes; Yes; 23448
1390; Bih-lizee-bih-adzan; F; 51; Navajo; F; M; Son[sic]; 1407; Yes; Yes; 23449
1391; Bizee-bega; M; 21; Navajo; F; M; Son; 1408; Yes; Yes; 23450

1392; Bye-otsin-bitsih; F; 43; Navajo; F; Wd; Head; 1409; Yes; Yes; 21487
1393; William; M; 16; Navajo; F; S; Son; 1410; Yes; Yes; 21488
1394; Anita; F; 11; Navajo; F; S; Daughter; 1411; Yes; Yes; 21489
1395; Yah-yil-wudt; M; 9; Navajo; F; S; Son; 1412; Yes; Yes; 21490
1396; Dah-des-wudt; M; 6; Navajo; F; S; Son; 1413; Yes; Yes; 21491

1397; Beleen-lizin-badoni; M; 43; Navajo; F; M; Head; 1414; Yes; Yes; 21311
1398; Beleen-lizin-bitsih; F; 57; Navajo; F; M; Wife; 1415; Yes; Yes; 21312
1399; Hoska-yahl-wudt; M; 23; Navajo; F; S; Son; 1416; Yes; Yes; 21313
1400; Bernice; F; 21; Navajo; F; S; Daughter; 1417; Yes; Yes; 21314
1401; Andy; M; 19; Navajo; F; S; Son; 1418; Yes; Yes; 21315
1402; Hah-ziz-bah; F; 8; Navajo; F; S; Daughter; 1419; Yes; Yes; 21316
1403; Bil-nih-ziz-bah; F; 7; Navajo; F; S; Daughter; 1420; Yes; Yes; 21317

1404; Batoni-bitsees-chilli-bega; M; 23; Navajo; F; M; Head; 1421; Yes; Yes; 28868

44

Census of the **Northern Navajo** reservation of the **Northern Navajo** jurisdiction, as of **April 1**, 19**31**, taken by **Ernest H. Hammond, District**, Superintendent. **in Charge**

**Key:** Number; NAME: Surname, Given; Sex; Birth Year (if given), Age At Last Birthday; Tribe; Degree of Blood; Marital Status; Relationship To Head of Family; Last Census Roll Number; At Jurisdiction Where Enrolled (Yes or No); At Another Jurisdiction; ELSEWHERE: Post office, County, State; Ward (Yes or No); Allotment, Annuity, and Identification Numbers.

1405;  Adzan-nih-bah; F; 21; Navajo; F; M; Wife; 1422; Yes; Yes; 28869
1406;  Adzan-nih-bah; F; 5; Navajo; F; S; Daughter; 1423; Yes; Yes; 28870
1407;  Nah-tah-yil-deyah; M; 3; Navajo; F; S; Son; 1424; Yes; Yes; 28871

1408;  Beleen-lizin-benally; M; 27; Navajo; F; M; Head; 1425; Yes; Yes; 28859
1409;  Beleen-lagaih-bitsih; F; 25; Navajo; F; M; Wife; 1426; Yes; Yes; 28860
1410;  Yahn-yil-wohl; M; 7; Navajo; F; S; Son; 1427; Yes; Yes; 28861
1411;  Eskee-sosie; M; 5; Navajo; F; S; Son; 1428; Yes; Yes; 28862

1412;  Beleen-lizin-bitsoih; M; 29; Navajo; F; M; Head; 1429; Yes; Yes; 21321
1413;  Glih-has-bah; F; 26; Navajo; F; M; Wife; 1430; Yes; Yes; 21322
1414;  Baz-dee-bah; F; 7; Navajo; F; S; Daughter; 1431; Yes; Yes; 21323
1415;  Yan-dee-bah; F; 6; Navajo; F; S; Daughter; 1432; Yes; Yes; 21324
1416;  Nah-tah-yil-deyah; M; 4; Navajo; F; S; Son; 1433; Yes; Yes; 21325

1417;  Beleen-lizin-badoni-bega; M; 26; Navajo; F; M; Head; 1434; Yes; Yes; 21340
1418;  Adzani-l-chee; F; 38; Navajo; F; M; Wife; 1435; Yes; Yes; 21341
1419;  Ah-hae-des-hah; F; 10; Navajo; F; S; Daughter; 1436; Yes; Yes; 21342

1420;  Beleen-clitsuen; M; 64; Navajo; F; M; Head; 1437; Yes; Yes; 21389
1421;  Nocki-chee-bitsih; F; 48; Navajo; F; M; Wife; 1438; Yes; Yes; 21390
1422;  Beleen-clitsuen-bega; M; 23; Navajo; F; S; Son; 1439; Yes; Yes; 21391
1423;  Lukechukia-nih; M; 19; Navajo; F; S; Son; 1440; Yes; Yes; 21392
1424;  Kin-ban-cheeny; M; 13; Navajo; F; S; Son; 1441; Yes; Yes; 21393
1425;  Doh-des-hah; F; 21; Navajo; F; S; Daughter; 1442; Yes; Yes; 21394
1426;  Klizi-thlani; M; 10; Navajo; F; S; Son; 1443; Yes; Yes; 21395
1427;  Adzan-l-chee; F; 7; Navajo; F; S; Daughter; 1444; Yes; Yes; 21396

1428;  Haysee-boh-woh-bih-seh-kin; M; 31; Navajo; F; M; Head; 1445; Yes; Yes; 21400
1429;  Beleen-clitsuen-bitsih; F; 25; Navajo; F; M; Wife; 1446; Yes; Yes; 21401
1430;  Tuel; M; 8; Navajo; F; S; Son; 1447; Yes; Yes; 21402
1431;  Tuel-yazzie; M; 6; Navajo; F; S; Son; 1448; Yes; Yes; 21403
1432;  Awa-dah; F; 4; Navajo; F; S; Daughter; 1449; Yes; Yes; 21404

1433;  Bye-otsin-bega; M; 26; Navajo F; M; Head; 1450; Yes; Yes; 21437
1434;  Yil-has-bah; F; 27; Navajo; F; M; Wife; 1451; Yes; Yes; 21438
1435;  Al-soh-nih-bah; F; 8; Navajo; F; S; Daughter; 1452; Yes; Yes; 21439
1436;  Nah-tah-yee-kahyah; M; 6; Navajo; F; S; Son; 1453; Yes; Yes; 21440
1437;  Al-dash-nih-bah; F; 3; Navajo; F; S; Daughter; 1454; Yes; Yes; 21441

1438;  Bilah-ganih-ye-is-kinih-bega; M; 58; Navajo; F; M; Head; 1455; Yes; Yes; 20931

45

Census of the **Northern Navajo** reservation of the **Northern Navajo**
jurisdiction, as of **April 1**, 19**31,** taken by **Ernest H. Hammond, District**,
Superintendent. **in Charge**

**Key:** Number; NAME: Surname, Given; Sex; Birth Year (if given), Age At Last Birthday; Tribe; Degree of
Blood; Marital Status; Relationship To Head of Family; Last Census Roll Number; At Jurisdiction Where
Enrolled (Yes or No); At Another Jurisdiction; ELSEWHERE: Post office, County, State; Ward (Yes or No);
Allotment, Annuity, and Identification Numbers.

1439; See-l-chee-bitsih; F; 45; Navajo; F; M; Wife; 1456; Yes; Yes; 20932
1440; Irene Woods; F; 25; Navajo; F; S; Daughter; 1457; Yes; Yes; 20933
1441; Woods, Murray; M; 19; Navajo; F; S; Son; 1458; Yes; Yes; 20934
1442; Mary-Susan; F; 16; Navajo; F; S; Daughter; 1459; Yes; Yes; 20935
1443; Hoska-yee-nee-wudt; M; 13; Navajo; F; S; Son; 1460; Yes; Yes; 20936
1444; Wilma; F; 11; Navajo; F; S; Daughter; 1461; Yes; Yes; 20937
1445; Toh-nas-bah; F; 8; Navajo; F; S; Daughter; 1462; Yes; Yes; 20938
1446; Bil-nas-nih-bah; F; 7; Navajo; F; S; Daughter; 1463; Yes; Yes; 20939
1447; John; F[sic]; 4; Navajo; F; S; Daughter[sic]; 1464; Yes; Yes; 20940

1448; Bih-gail-yen-benally; M; Unk; Navajo; F; M; Head; 1465; Yes; Yes; 20969
1449; Dil-a-weeh-ih-benally-bitsih; F; 21; Navajo; F; M; Wife; 1466; Yes; Yes;
20970
1450; Bil-chie-nih-bah; F; 4; Navajo; F; S; Daughter; 1467; Yes; Yes; 20971

1451; Bah-dagaih, Francis; M; 36; Navajo; F; M; Head; 1468; Yes; Yes; 21019
1452; Nah-cheeny-benally-bitsih; F; 31; Navajo; F; M; Wife; 1469; Yes; Yes; 21020
1453; Francisco; M; 15; Navajo; F; S; Son; 1470; Yes; Yes; 21021
1454; Lewis; M; 13; Navajo; F; S; Son; 1471; Yes; Yes; 21022
1455; Gabriel; M; 11; Navajo; F; S; Son; 1472; Yes; Yes; 21023
1456; Alphonsus; M; 9; Navajo; F; S; Son; 1473; Yes; Yes; 21024
1457; Juan; M; 6; Navajo; F; S; Son; 1474; Yes; Yes; 21025

1458; Bee-nah; M; 39; Navajo; F; M: Head; 1475; Yes; Yes; 21034
1459; Bee-nah's wife; F; 25; Navajo; F; M; Wife; 1476; Yes; Yes; 21035
1460; Yee-nah-yan; M; 11; Navajo; F; S; Son; 1477; Yes; Yes; 21036
1461; Soh; F; 5; Navajo; F; S; Daughter; 1478; Yes; Yes; 21037

1462; Bah-dagaih-bega; M; 30; Navajo; F; M; Head; 1479; Yes; Yes; 21066
1463; See-dih-chasie-bitsih; F; 30; Navajo; F; M; Wife; 1480; Yes; Yes; 21067
1464; Ah-hah-gee-bah; F; 8; Navajo; F; S; Daughter; 1481; Yes; Yes; 21068
1465; Nah-tah-yee-kay-lal; M; 7; Navajo; F; S; Son; 1482; Yes; Yes; 21069
1466; Hoska-yee-chih-has-wudt; M; 5; Navajo; F; S; Son; 1483; Yes; Yes; 21070
1467; Hoska-yil-hah-nahe-wudt; M; 4; Navajo; F; S; Son; 1484; Yes; Yes; 21071
1468; Ha-nas-bah; F; 2; Navajo; F; S; Daughter; 1485; Yes; Yes; 21636

1469; Bah-dagaih, Cecil; M; 23; Navajo; F; M; Head; 1486; Yes; Yes; 21139
1470; Din-y-ye-is-kinih-bitsih; F; 23; Navajo; F; M; Wife; 1487; Yes; Yes; 21140

1471; Yoh-hah-tahly-bega; M; 28; Navajo; F; M; Head; 1488; Yes; Yes; 21141
1472; Dinay-ye-si-kinih-bitsih; F; Unk; Navajo; F; M; Wife; 1489; Yes; Yes; 21142
1473; Nah-glih-tas-bah; F; 2; Navajo; F; S; Daughter; 1490; Yes; Yes; 21659

46

Census of the **Northern Navajo** reservation of the **Northern Navajo** jurisdiction, as of **April 1** , 19**31**, taken by **Ernest H. Hammond, District** , Superintendent.                                          **in Charge**

**Key:** Number; NAME: Surname, Given; Sex; Birth Year (if given), Age At Last Birthday; Tribe; Degree of Blood; Marital Status; Relationship To Head of Family; Last Census Roll Number; At Jurisdiction Where Enrolled (Yes or No); At Another Jurisdiction; ELSEWHERE: Post office, County, State; Ward (Yes or No); Allotment, Annuity, and Identification Numbers.

1474;  Bitsee-dih-chosie-bega; M; 58; Navajo; F; M; Head; 1491; Yes; Yes; 21170
1475;  Adzan-bitsees-chilli-bih-che; F; 58; Navajo; F; M; Wife; 1492; Yes; Yes; 21171
1476;  Reed, Taylor; M; 18; Navajo; F; S; Son; 1493; Yes; Yes; 21172
1477;  Yaih-yah; M; 14; Navajo; F; S; Son; 1494; Yes; Yes; 21173
1478;  Yah-nih-bah; F; 10; Navajo; F; S; Daughter; 1495; Yes; Yes; 21174
1479;  Tah-hah-bah; F; 9; Navajo; F; S; Step-niece; 1496; Yes; Yes; 21175

1480;  Bih-gonnihigi-hosteen; M; 48; Navajo; F; M; Head; 1497; Yes; Yes; 18036
1481;  Adzan-yazzie; F; 46; Navajo; F; M; Wife; 1498; Yes; Yes; 18037
1482;  Joe, Maggie; F; 22; Navajo; F; S; Daughter; 1499; Yes; Yes; 18038
1483;  Bih-gonnihigi, Victor; M; 20; Navajo; F; S; Son; 1500; Yes; Yes; 18039
1484;  Zannie; F; 14; Navajo; F; S; Daughter; 1501; Yes; Yes; 18040
1485;  Adzanih-yazzie; F; 8; Navajo; F; S; Daughter; 1502; Yes; Yes; 18041
1486;  Dah-yih-yah; M; 5; Navajo; F; S; Son; 1503; Yes; Yes; 18042
1487;  Charles; M; 2; Navajo; F; S; Son; 1504; Yes; Yes; 18239

1488;  Brown, Joe; M; 41; Navajo; F; M; Head; 1505; Yes; Yes; 23464
1489;  Hah-tahly-yazzie-hih-dazih; F; 39; Navajo; F; M; Wife; 1506; Yes; Yes; 23465
1490;  Chih-nih-hih-yah; M; 13; Navajo; F; S; Son; 1507; Yes; Yes; 23466
1491;  Al-keh-nih-dez-bah; F; 9; Navajo; F; S; Daughter; 1508; Yes; Yes; 23467

1492;  Bega, Dr. John; M; 27; Navajo; F; M; Head; 1509; Yes; Yes; 23459
1493;  Wife, Dr. John; F; 40; Navajo; F; M; Wife; 1510; Yes; Yes; 23460
1494;  Yil-nah-gah; M; 26; Navajo; F; S; Son; 1511; Yes; Yes; 23461
1495;  Haska-yah-hoh-tahl; M; 19; Navajo; F; S; Son; 1512; Yes; Yes; 23462
1496;  Yil-hah-naz-bah; F; 11; Navajo; F; S; Daughter; 1513; Yes; Yes; 23463
1497;  Kah-nah-bah; F; 1 3/12; Navajo; F; S; Daughter; 1514; Yes; Yes; 23970

1498;  Badoni-sani-bitsih; F; 47; Navajo; F; Wd; Head; 1515; Yes; Yes; 23497
1499;  Biz-nil-bah; F; 17; Navajo; F; S; Daughter; 1516; Yes; Yes; 23498
1500;  Irene Barber; F; 13; Navajo; F; S; Daughter; 1517; Yes; Yes; 23499
1501;  Haska-yil-hah-koh-gahl; M; 10; Navajo; F; S; Son; 1518; Yes; Yes; 23500
1502;  Dah-dez-bah; F; 9; Navajo; F; S; Daughter; 1518-A; Yes; Yes; 23501
1503;  Dah-nih-bah; F; 7; Navajo; F; S; Daughter; 1519; Yes; Yes; 23502
1504;  Hask-yil-hoh-gahl[sic]; M; 3; Navajo; F; S; Son; 1520; Yes; Yes; 23503
          [Name could be Haska-yil-hoh-gahl]
1505;  Yil-has-bah; F; 28; Navajo; F; Wd; Daughter; 1521; Yes; Yes; 23504
1506;  Haska-yil-nil-wudt; M; 8; Navajo; F; S; Grand-son; 1522; Yes; Yes; 23505
1507;  Chih-dez-bah; F; 7; Navajo; F; S; Grand-daughter; 1523; Yes; Yes; 23506
1508;  Atate-yazzie; F; 3; Navajo; F; S; Grand-daughter; 1524; Yes; Yes; 23507
1509;  Kah-has-bah; F; 2; Navajo; F; S; Daughter; 1525; Yes; Yes; 23954

Census of the **Northern Navajo** reservation of the **Northern Navajo** jurisdiction, as of **April 1**, 19**31,** taken by **Ernest H. Hammond, District**, Superintendent. **in Charge**

**Key:** Number; NAME: Surname, Given; Sex; Birth Year (if given), Age At Last Birthday; Tribe; Degree of Blood; Marital Status; Relationship To Head of Family; Last Census Roll Number; At Jurisdiction Where Enrolled (Yes or No); At Another Jurisdiction; ELSEWHERE: Post office, County, State; Ward (Yes or No); Allotment, Annuity, and Identification Numbers.

1510;  Beleen-lizin-bega; M; 46; Navajo; F; M; Head; 1526; Yes; Yes; 21262
1511;  Adzanih-nez; F; 53; Navajo; F; M; Wife; 1527; Yes; Yes; 21263

1512;  Beleen-la-aihih-bitah; M; Unk; Navajo; F; M; Head; 1528; Yes; Yes; 23510
1513;  Beleen-bitsee-gah-lagaih; F; Unk; Navajo; F; M; Wife; 1529; Yes; Yes; 23511
1514;  Yee-nal-wohl; M; Unk; Navajo; F; S; Son; 1530; Yes; Yes; 23512
1515;  Bah-ah-zoz-bah; F; Unk; Navajo; F; S; Daughter; 1531; Yes; Yes; 23513

1516;  Bah-kiah-dinee; M; 59; Navajo; F; M; Head; 1532; Yes; Yes; 18080
1517;  Kin-lacheeny-bitsih; F; 35; Navajo; F; M; Wife; 1533; Yes; Yes; 18081
1518;  Bah-kiah-dinee, Atwell; M; 15; Navajo; F; S; Son; 1534; Yes; Yes; 18082
1519;  Bah-kiah-dinee, Mary; F; 11; Navajo; F; S; Daughter; 1535; Yes; Yes; 18083
1520;  Zannie; F; 9; Navajo; F; S; Daughter; 1536; Yes; Yes; 18084
1521;  Ah-key-dee-bah; F; 6; Navajo; F; S; Daughter; 1537; Yes; Yes; 18085
1522;  Hoska-yil-yl-wudt; M; 4; Navajo; F; S; Son; 1538; Yes; Yes; 18086
1523;  Pearl; F; 1; Navajo; F; S; Daughter; 1539; Yes; Yes; 18234

1524;  Bagashi-lagaih-bitsoih, Willer[sic]; M; 26; Navajo; F; M; Head; 1540; Yes; Yes; 23313  [Name should be Bagashi-lagaih-bitsoih, Miller]
1525;  Keh-yee-deh-bah; F; 20; Navajo; F; M; Wife; 1541; Yes; Yes; 23314
1526;  Haska-yil-dah-dol-nih; M; 3; Navajo; F; S; Son; 1542; Yes; Yes; 23315

1527;  Bih-oh-chilih-benally; M; Unk; Navajo; F; M; Head; 1543; Yes; Yes; 23388
1528;  Al-kih-nil-bah; F; 20; Navajo; F; M; Wife; 1544; Yes; Yes; 23389
1529;  Nah-tah-yil-nah-dahl; M; 3; Navajo; F; S; Son; 1545; Yes; Yes; 23390

1530;  Bega, Washburn; M; 26; Navajo; F; M; Head; 1546; Yes; Yes; 23400
1531;  Kih-yil-hah-bah; F; 20; Navajo; F; M; Wife; 1547; Yes; Yes; 23401

1532;  Biz-nil-bah; F; 80; Navajo; F; Wd; Head; 1548; Yes; Yes; 21500

1533;  Bitsees-chilli-hosteen-nez-bikis; M; 53; Navajo; F; M; Head; 1549; Yes; Yes; 23173
1534;  Bitsees-chilli-hosteen-nez-bikis-adzan; F; 55; Navajo; F; M; Wife; 1550; Yes; Yes; 23174
1535;  Katherine; F; Unk; Navajo; F; S; Daughter; 1551; Yes; Yes; 23175
1536;  Adzan-l-suen; F; 17; Navajo; F; S; Daughter; 1552; Yes; Yes; 23176
1537;  Hih-sanih; F; 11; Navajo; F; S; Daughter; 1553; Yes; Yes; 23177
1538;  Dah-ih; M; 8; Navajo; F; S; Son; 1554; Yes; Yes; 23178
1539;  Tah-zoz-bah; F; 10; Navajo; F; S; Daughter; 1555; Yes; Yes; 23402

1540;  Bitsees-chilli-bega; M; 29; Navajo; F; M; Head; 1556; Yes; Yes; 23179
1541;  Bil-hah-ziz-bah; F; 27; Navajo; F; M; Wife; 1557; Yes; Yes; 23180

Census of the __Northern Navajo__ reservation of the __Northern Navajo__ jurisdiction, as of __April 1__, 19**31,** taken by __Ernest H. Hammond, District__, Superintendent.                                    **in Charge**

**Key:** Number; NAME: Surname, Given; Sex; Birth Year (if given), Age At Last Birthday; Tribe; Degree of Blood; Marital Status; Relationship To Head of Family; Last Census Roll Number; At Jurisdiction Where Enrolled (Yes or No); At Another Jurisdiction; ELSEWHERE: Post office, County, State; Ward (Yes or No); Allotment, Annuity, and Identification Numbers.

1542;   Dinay-l-suen-yazzie; M; 8; Navajo; F; S; Son; 1558; Yes; Yes; 23181
1543;   Haska-yil-dah-dolnih; M; 6; Navajo; F; S; Son; 1559; Yes; Yes; 23182
1544;   Haska; M; 2; Navajo; F; S; Son; 1560; Yes; Yes; 24000

1545;   Bitah, Ben; M; 34; Navajo; F; M; Head; 1561; Yes; Yes; 23212
1546;   Tahn-hah-bah; F; 26; Navajo; F; M; Wife; 1562; Yes; Yes; 23213
1547;   Nah-tah-yil-ziz-zih; M; 3; Navajo; F; S; Son; 1563; Yes; Yes; 23214

1548;   Benally, Charley; M; 38; Navajo; F; M; Head; 1564; Yes; Yes; 23245
1549;   Doh-hal-tahih-bitsih; F; 27; Navajo; F; M; Wife; 1565; Yes; Yes; 23246
1550;   Keh-yee-nil-bah; F; 15; Navajo; F; S; Daughter; 1566; Yes; Yes; 23247
1551;   Tah-nih-yah; M; 9; Navajo; F; S; Son; 1567; Yes; Yes; 23248
1552;   Chih-yee-gahl; M; 6; Navajo; F; S; Son; 1568; Yes; Yes; 23249
1553;   Nah-glih-hah-naz-bah; F; 3; Navajo; F; S; Daughter; 1569; Yes; Yes; 23250

1554;   Benally, Charley; M; Unk; Navajo; F; M; Head; 1570; Yes; Yes; 23251
1555;   Doh-hal-tahih-bitsih; F; 38; Navajo; F; M; Wife; 1571; Yes; Yes; 23252
1556;   Haska-yee-neh-yah; M; 16; Navajo; F; S; Son; 1572; Yes; Yes; 23253
1557;   Al-chih-des-bah; F; 13; Navajo; F; S; Daughter; 1573; Yes; Yes; 23254
1558;   Tih-nih-bah; F; 10; Navajo; F; S; Daughter; 1574; Yes; Yes; 23255
1559;   Haska-yee-chih-has-wudt; M; 7; Navajo; F; S; Son; 1575; Yes; Yes; 23256
1560;   Chin-naz-bah; F; 4; Navajo; F; S; Daughter; 1576; Yes; Yes; 23257

1561;   Benally-soh; M; 38; Navajo; F; M; Head; 1577; Yes; Yes; 23258
1562;   Benally-soh-bih-adzan; F; 42; Navajo; F; M; Wife; 1578; Yes; Yes; 23259
1563;   Keh-yee-dah-nih-bah; F; 8; Navajo; F; S; Daughter; 1579; Yes; Yes; 23260
1564;   Nah-tah-yee-tah-des-wudt; M; 6; Navajo; F; S; Son; 1580; Yes; Yes; 23261
1565;   Bob Ware; M; Unk; Navajo; F; S; Grand-son; 1581; Yes; Yes; 23262
1566;   Harvey, John; M; 25; Navajo; F; S; Nephew; 1582; Yes; Yes; 23263

1567;   Bitsee-lagaih-bitsih; F; 42; Navajo; F; Wd; Head; 1583; Yes; Yes; 22469
1568;   John; M; 22; Navajo; F; S; Son; 1584; Yes; Yes; 22470
1569;   Glih-yil-nih-bah; F; 11; Navajo; F; S; Daughter; 1585; Yes; Yes; 22471

1570;   Bitsee-lagaih-bega, Tom Harry; M; 34; Navajo; F; M; Head; 1586; Yes; Yes; 22462
1571;   Ethel; F; 36; Navajo; F; M; Wife; 1587; Yes; Yes; 22463
1572;   Lucy; F; 13; Navajo; F; S; Daughter; 1588; Yes; Yes; 22464
1573;   Lily; F; 10; Navajo; F; S; Daughter; 1589; Yes; Yes; 22465
1574;   Frank; M; 8; Navajo; F; S; Son; 1590; Yes; Yes; 22466
1575;   James; M; 6; Navajo; F; S; Son; 1591; Yes; Yes; 22467
1576;   Johnson-Roy; M; 21; Navajo; F; S; Nephew-in-law; 1592; Yes; Yes; 22468
1577;   Adzan-etsosie; F; 92; Navajo; F; Wd; Mother-in-law; 1594; Yes; Yes; 22780

Census of the **Northern Navajo** reservation of the **Northern Navajo** jurisdiction, as of **April 1**, 1931, taken by **Ernest H. Hammond, District**, Superintendent. **in Charge**

**Key:** Number; NAME: Surname, Given; Sex; Birth Year (if given), Age At Last Birthday; Tribe; Degree of Blood; Marital Status; Relationship To Head of Family; Last Census Roll Number; At Jurisdiction Where Enrolled (Yes or No); At Another Jurisdiction; ELSEWHERE: Post office, County, State; Ward (Yes or No); Allotment, Annuity, and Identification Numbers.

1578; Bitsee-lah-gaih; M; 94; Navajo; F; M; Head; 1595; Yes; Yes; 22440
1579; Clah-alsosie-bitsih; F; 67; Navajo; F; M; Wife; 1596; Yes; Yes; 22441

1580; Bitsee-lah-gaih-bega; M; 40; Navajo; F; Wd; Head; 1597; Yes; Yes; 22448
1581; Keh-yil-chin-bah; F; 6; Navajo; F; S; Daughter; 1598; Yes; Yes; 22449

1582; Batoni-itso-bitah; M; 62; Navajo; F; M; Head; 1599; Yes; Yes; 17801
1583; Batoni-itso-bitah's wife; F; 53; Navajo; F; M; Wife; 1600; Yes; Yes; 17802
1584; Batoni-itso-bitah's son; M; 25; Navajo; F; S; Son; 1601; Yes; Yes; 17803
1585; Glinn-bah; F; 21; Navajo; F; S; Daughter; 1602; Yes; Yes; 17804
1586; Yazzie, Stanley; M; 20; Navajo; F; S; Son; 1603; Yes; Yes; 17805
1587; Ninn-bah; F; 17; Navajo; F; S; Daughter; 1604; Yes; Yes; 17806
1588; Batoni-itso, Emma; F; 15; Navajo; F; S; Daughter; 1605; Yes; Yes; 17807
1589; Bah-dih-holly; F; 13; Navajo; F; S; Daughter; 1606; Yes; Yes; 17808
1590; Batoni-itso, Faith; F; 11; Navajo; F; S; Daughter; 1607; Yes; Yes; 17809
1591; Natoni-yazzie; M; 9; Navajo; F; S; Son; 1608; Yes; Yes; 17810

1592; Beleen-l-chee; M; Unk; Navajo; F; M; Head; 1609; Yes; Yes; 22536
1593; Bil-nih-ziz-bah; F; 20; Navajo; F; M; Wife; 1610; Yes; Yes; 22537

1594; Bilah-gonah-ye-is-kinih; M; Unk; Navajo; F; M; Head; 1611; Yes; Yes; 22684
1595; See-chee-bitsih; F; Unk; Navajo; F; M; Wife; 1612; Yes; Yes; 22685
1596; Hubert; M; 23; Navajo; F; M; Son; 1613; Yes; Yes; 22686
1597; John; M; 21; Navajo; F; S; Son; 1614; Yes; Yes; 22687
1598; Tah-naz-bah; F; 16; Navajo; F; S; Daughter; 1615; Yes; Yes; 22688
1599; Bil-kih-ziz-bah; F; 10; Navajo; F; S; Daughter; 1616; Yes; Yes; 22689
1600; Willie; M; 5; Navajo; F; S; Son; 1617; Yes; Yes; 22690
1601; Franklin; M; 2; Navajo; F; S; Son; 1618; Yes; Yes; 22772

1602; Bay-gashih-thlani; M; Unk; Navajo; F; M; Head; 1619; Yes; Yes; 23931
1603; Dinay-yazzie-bilah; F; 41; Navajo; F; M; Wife; 1620; Yes; Yes; 23708
1604; Arthur; M; 13; Navajo; F; S; Son; 1621; Yes; Yes; 23709
1605; Haska-yahn-dee-zah; M; 11; Navajo; F; S; Son; 1622; Yes; Yes; 23710
1606; Eskee-yazzie; M; 6; Navajo; F; S; Son; 1623; Yes; Yes; 23711
1607; Bah; F; 3; Navajo; F; S; Daughter; 1624; Yes; Yes; 23712
1608; Bay-gashih-thlani; M; 2; Navajo; F; S; Son; 1625; Yes; Yes; 23930

1609; Barton, Stewart; M; 28; Navajo; F; M; Head; 1626; Yes; Yes; 31015
1610; Pauline; F; 29; Navajo; F; M; Wife; 1627; Yes; Yes; 31016
1611; Daniel; M; 6; Navajo; F; S; Son; 1628; Yes; Yes; 31017
1612; Helen; F; 4; Navajo; F; S; Daughter; 1629; Yes; Yes; 31018
1613; Margaret; F; 2; Navajo; F; S; Daughter; 1630; Yes; Yes; 31019

Census of the **Northern Navajo** reservation of the **Northern Navajo** jurisdiction, as of **April 1**, 19**31**, taken by **Ernest H. Hammond, District**, Superintendent. **in Charge**

**Key:** Number; NAME: Surname, Given; Sex; Birth Year (if given), Age At Last Birthday; Tribe; Degree of Blood; Marital Status; Relationship To Head of Family; Last Census Roll Number; At Jurisdiction Where Enrolled (Yes or No); At Another Jurisdiction; ELSEWHERE: Post office, County, State; Ward (Yes or No); Allotment, Annuity, and Identification Numbers.

1614; Bay-dih-chee-bitsouh-bega[sic], Willie; M; 30; Navajo; F; M; Head; 1631; Yes; Yes; 32420 [Name should be Bay-dih-chee-bitsoih-bega]
1615; Dinay-chilli-benally; F; 22; Navajo; F; M; Wife; 1632; Yes; Yes; 32421

1616; Bay-gasih-thlani; M; 59; Navajo; F; M; Head; 1633; Yes; Yes; 29318
1617; Al-nih-bah; F; 49; Navajo; F; M; Wife; 1634; Yes; Yes; 29319
1618; Haska-yil-nas-yiz; M; 24; Navajo; F; S; Son; 1635; Yes; Yes; 29320
1619; Bert; M; 16; Navajo; F; S; Son; 1636; Yes; Yes; 29321
1620; Nah-gil-wudt; M; 14; Navajo; F; S; Son; 1637; Yes; Yes; 29322
1621; Bil-nih-bih-bah; F; 8; Navajo; F; S; Daughter; 1638; Yes; Yes; 29323
1622; Bay-gasih-thlani-bega Joe, Tom; M; 20; Navajo; F; Div.; Son; 1639; Yes; Yes; 29371

1623; Bayse-boh-woh; M; Unk; Navajo; F; M; Head; 1640; Yes; Yes; 29079
1624; Adzanih-seesie; F; 60; Navajo; F; M; Wife; 1641; Yes; Yes; 29080
1625; Albert; M; 21; Navajo; F; S; Son; 1642; Yes; Yes; 29081
1626; Bayse-boh-woh-bega; M; 19; Navajo; F; S; Son; 1643; Yes; Yes; 29082
1627; Han-tahly-sosie-bega; M; Unk; Navajo; F; Wd; Step-son; 1644; Yes; Yes; 29083
1628; Haska-yee-tas-wudt; M; 11; Navajo; F; S; Grand-son; 1645; Yes; Yes; 29084
1629; Ninih; M; 9; Navajo; F; S; Grand-son; 1646; Yes; Yes; 29085
1630; Haska-ye-naz-wudt; M; 6; Navajo; F; S; Grand-son; 1647; Yes; Yes; 29086

1631; Bay-gashih-thlani-badoni; M; Unk; Navajo; F; M; Head; 1648; Yes; Yes; 29076
1632; Bay-gashih-thlani-bitsih; F; 19; Navajo; F; M; Wife; 1649; Yes; Yes; 29077
1633; Naz-bah; F; 9; Navajo; F; S; Daughter; 1650; Yes; Yes; 29078
1634; Bil-haz-bah; F; 3; Navajo; F; S; Daughter; 1651; Yes; Yes; 29404

1635; Begu-bega; M; 28; Navajo; F; M; Head; 1652; Yes; Yes; 32382
1636; Blue Eye's Bitsoih; F; 32; Navajo; F; M; Wife; 1653; Yes; Yes; 32383

1637; Begu-bega; M; 37; Navajo; F; M; Head; 1654; Yes; Yes; 32435
1638; Bay-gasih-lagaih-bitat-bitsih; F; 24; Navajo; F; M; Wife; 1655; Yes; Yes; 32436
1639; Eva; F; 12; Navajo; F; S; Niece; 1656; Yes; Yes; 32437

1640; Bekin-bitsoih[sic]; M; 27; Navajo; F; M; Head; 1657; Yes; Yes; 30775 [Name should be Bekis-bitsoih]
1641; Nah-glih-yil-dez-bah; F; 29; Navajo; F; M; Wife; 1658; Yes; Yes; 30776
1642; Yil-haz-bah; F; 8; Navajo; F; S; Daughter; 1659; Yes; Yes; 30777

1643; Bekis-Olive; F; 45; Navajo; F; Wd; Head; 1660; Yes; Yes; 30784

Census of the **Northern Navajo** reservation of the **Northern Navajo** jurisdiction, as of **April 1**, 19**31,** taken by **Ernest H. Hammond, District**, Superintendent. **in Charge**

Key: Number; NAME: Surname, Given; Sex; Birth Year (if given), Age At Last Birthday; Tribe; Degree of Blood; Marital Status; Relationship To Head of Family; Last Census Roll Number; At Jurisdiction Where Enrolled (Yes or No); At Another Jurisdiction; ELSEWHERE: Post office, County, State; Ward (Yes or No); Allotment, Annuity, and Identification Numbers.

1644; Grace; F; 12; Navajo; F; S; Daughter; 1661; Yes; Yes; 30785
1645; Pauline; F; 16; Navajo; F; S; Niece; 1662; Yes; Yes; 30786
1646; Glih-hah-daz-bah; F; 10; Navajo; F; S; Daughter; 1663; Yes; Yes; 30787
1647; Bihn-ziz-bah; F; 6; Navajo; F; S; Daughter; 1664; Yes; Yes; 30788
1648; Adzan-sch-dah-lah-gaih; F; 74; Navajo; F; Wd; Mother; 1665; Yes; Yes; 30789
1649; Haska-yil-nih-nih-yah; M; 3; Navajo; F; S; Son; 1666; Yes; Yes; 31271

1650; Beleen-dal-bahih-bitah; M; 42; Navajo; F; M; Head; 1667; Yes; Yes; 29864
1651; Nah-glih-hah-bah; F; 21; Navajo; F; M; Wife; 1668; Yes; Yes; 29865
1652; Kiz-bah; F; 7; Navajo; F; S; Daughter; 1669; Yes; Yes; 29866

1653; Beleen-doh-cliz-bega-navy; M; 30; Navajo; F; M; Head; 1670; Yes; Yes; 30321
1654; Bah; F; 25; Navajo; F; M; Wife; 1671; Yes; Yes; 30322
1655; Nih-daz-bah; F; 7; Navajo; F; S; Daughter; 1672; Yes; Yes; 30323
1656; Keh-yil-nah-nih-bah; F; 6; Navajo; F; S; Daughter; 1673; Yes; Yes; 30324
1657; Haska-chih-nih-yah; M; 4; Navajo; F; S; Son; 1674; Yes; Yes; 30325
1658; Nah-tah-yil-hah-yah; M; 3; Navajo; F; S; Son; 1675; Yes; Yes; 31280

1659; Beleen-dih-jadih-bega; M; 24; Navajo; F; M; Head; 1676; Yes; Yes; 29292
1660; Baz-nih-bah; F; 20; Navajo; F; M; Wife; 1677; Yes; Yes; 29293
1661; Nah-tah-yil-has-wudt; M; 5; Navajo; F; S; Son; 1678; Yes; Yes; 29294
1662; Nah-tah-yil-deyah; M; 4; Navajo; F; S; Son; 1679; Yes; Yes; 29295
1663; (Baby); F; 2; Navajo; F; S; Daughter; 1680; Yes; Yes; 29296

1664; Beleen-lizin-benally-shakey; M; 41; Navajo; F; M; Head; 1681; Yes; Yes; 30526
1665; Beleen-lagaih-bitsih; F; 35; Navajo; F; M; Wife; 1682; Yes; Yes; 30527
1666; Nih-des-sah; M; 19; Navajo; F; S; Son; 1683; Yes; Yes; 30528
1667; Trima[sic]; F; 14; Navajo; F; S; Daughter; 1684; Yes; Yes; 30529
     [Name should be Trina]
1668; Tahnaz-bah; F; 12; Navajo; F; S; Daughter; 1685; Yes; Yes; 30530
1669; Yee-chih-bih-bah; F; 6; Navajo; F; S; Daughter; 1686; Yes; Yes; 30532
1670; Haska; M; 3; Navajo; F; S; Son; 1687; Yes; Yes; 30533
1671; Yee-naz-hah; F; 9; Navajo; F; S; Daughter; 1688; Yes; Yes; 30531

1672; Beleen-la-chee-bega-, Tom; M; 31; Navajo; F; M; Head; 1689; Yes; Yes; 30821
1673; Hosteen-nez-benally; F; 30; Navajo; F; M; Wife; 1690; Yes; Yes; 30822
1674; Nah-yah; M; 11; Navajo; F; S; Son; 1691; Yes; Yes; 30823
1675; Yee-hah-naz-bah; F; 9; Navajo; F; S; Daughter; 1692; Yes; Yes; 30824
1676; Dah-has-yah; M; 5; Navajo; F; S; Son; 1693; Yes; Yes; 30825

Census of the **Northern Navajo** reservation of the **Northern Navajo** jurisdiction, as of **April 1**, 19**31,** taken by **Ernest H. Hammond, District**, Superintendent. **in Charge**

**Key:** Number; NAME: Surname, Given; Sex; Birth Year (if given), Age At Last Birthday; Tribe; Degree of Blood; Marital Status; Relationship To Head of Family; Last Census Roll Number; At Jurisdiction Where Enrolled (Yes or No); At Another Jurisdiction; ELSEWHERE: Post office, County, State; Ward (Yes or No); Allotment, Annuity, and Identification Numbers.

1677; Beleen-la-chee-bih-adzan; F; 53; Navajo; F; Div; Head; 1694; Yes; Yes; 30826

1678; Richard Hobson; M; 25; Navajo; F; S; Son; 1695; Yes; Yes; 30827

1679; Haska-hah-nadzah; M; 21; Navajo; F; S; Son; 1696; Yes; Yes; 30828

1680; Wudt; M; 19; Navajo; F; S; Son; 1697; Yes; Yes; 30829

1681; Gahl; M; 17; Navajo; F; S; Son; 1698; Yes; Yes; 30830

1682; Gah-nil-yah; M; 12; Navajo; F; S; Son; 1699; Yes; Yes; 30831

1683; Bih-gih-bah, Ruby; F; 9; Navajo; F; S; Daughter; 1700; Yes; Yes; 30832


1684; Beleen-lagaih; M; Unk; Navajo; F; M; Head; 1701; Yes; Yes; 29040

1685; Adzan-toh-sosie; F; Unk; Navajo; F; M; Wife; 1702; Yes; Yes; 29041

1686; Beleen-lagaih-bega; M; 29; Navajo; F; S; Son; 1703; Yes; Yes; 29042

1687; Harry; M; 19; Navajo; F; S; Son; 1704; Yes; Yes; 29043

1688; Goldie; F; 20; Navajo; F; S; Daughter; 1705; Yes; Yes; 29044

1689; Daniel; M; 18; Navajo; F; S; Son; 1706; Yes; Yes; 29045

1690; Fanny; F; 15; Navajo; F; S; Daughter; 1707; Yes; Yes; 29046

1691; Mike; M; 17; Navajo; F; S; Son; 1708; Yes; Yes; 29047

1692; Nah-tah-l-toly; M; 14; Navajo; F; S; Son; 1709; Yes; Yes; 29048

1693; Yee-kay-bah; F; 10; Navajo; F; S; Daughter; 1710; Yes; Yes; 29049

1694; Melba; F; 19; Navajo; F; S; Grand-daughter; 1711; Yes; Yes; 29050

1695; Beleen-lagaih-bitsih; F; 28; Navajo; F; Div; Daughter; 1712; Yes; Yes; 29051

1696; Haska-yil-hal-iz; M; 8; Navajo; F; S; Nephew; 1713; Yes; Yes; 29052

1697; Nellie; F; 3; Navajo; F; S; Grand-daughter; 1714; Yes; Yes; 29389


1698; Beleen-lizin-bega, Slim; M; 28; Navajo; F; M; Head; 1715; Yes; Yes; 32262

1699; Nocki-yazzie-bitsih; F; 24; Navajo; F; M; Wife; 1716; Yes; Yes; 32263

1700; Glih-yil-hah-bah; F; 2; Navajo; F; S; Daughter; 1717; Yes; Yes; 32264


1701; Beleen-lizin-bega; M; 48; Navajo; F; M; Head; 1718; Yes; Yes; 30348

1702; Hosteen-ashinh-bitsih; F; 26; Navajo; F; M; Wife; 1719; Yes; Yes; 30349

1703; Haska-tab-hah-bah; F; 6; Navajo; F; S; Daughter; 1720; Yes; Yes; 30350


1704; Beleen-l-chee-bega; M; 30; Navajo; F; M; Head; 1721; Yes; Yes; 32351

1705; Hosteen-nez-benally; F; 2; Navajo; F; M; Wife; 1722; Yes; Yes; 32352

1706; Bis-dee-bah; F; 6; Navajo; F; S; Daughter; 1723; Yes; Yes; 32353


1707; Benally, Cuyler; M; Unk; Navajo; F; M; Head; 1724; Yes; Yes; 30958

1708; Biniah-bitsih, Little Joe; F; 23; Navajo; F; M; Wife; 1725; Yes; Yes; 30959

1709; Nel-wudt; M; 6; Navajo; F; S; Son; 1726; Yes; Yes; 30960

1710; Keh-yil-hah-bah; F; 4; Navajo; F; S; Daughter; 1727; Yes; Yes; 30961

1711; Ah-hih-hah-bah; F; 2; Navajo; F; S; Daughter; 1728; Yes; Yes; 30962


1712; Benally-sani; M; 52; Navajo; F; M; Head; 1729; Yes; Yes; 29930

Census of the **Northern Navajo** reservation of the **Northern Navajo** jurisdiction, as of **April 1**, 19**31,** taken by **Ernest H. Hammond, District**, Superintendent.                                                                                                        **in Charge**

**Key:** Number; NAME: Surname, Given; Sex; Birth Year (if given), Age At Last Birthday; Tribe; Degree of Blood; Marital Status; Relationship To Head of Family; Last Census Roll Number; At Jurisdiction Where Enrolled (Yes or No); At Another Jurisdiction; ELSEWHERE: Post office, County, State; Ward (Yes or No); Allotment, Annuity, and Identification Numbers.

1713;   Bih-gee-bah; F; 47; Navajo; F; M; Wife; 1730; Yes; Yes; 29931
1714;   Tahn-nah-yah; M; 8; Navajo; F; S; Son; 1731; Yes; Yes; 29932
1715;   Al-chih-nil-wudt; M; 6; Navajo; F; S; Son; 1732; Yes; Yes; 29933

1716;   Benally-yazzie; M; 42; Navajo; F; M; Head; 1733; Yes; Yes; 29724
1717;   Tahn-dez-bah; F; 26; Navajo; F; M; Wife; 1734; Yes; Yes; 29725
1718;   Nah-viz-nil-bah; F; 5; Navajo; F; S; Daughter; 1735; Yes; Yes; 29726
1719;   Benally, John; M; 36; Navajo; F; S; Brother; 1736; Yes; Yes; 29727

1720;   Ben-bega; M; 32; Navajo; F; M; Head; 1737; Yes; Yes; 30729
1721;   Happy Jack's daughter; F; 30; Navajo; F; M; 1738; Wife; Yes; Yes; 30730
1722;   Yee-neh-bah; F; 11; Navajo; F; S; Daughter; 1739; Yes; Yes; 30731
1723;   Haska-yee-zih; M; 9; Navajo; F; S; Son; 1740; Yes; Yes; 30732
1724;   Des-wudt; M; 5; Navajo; F; S; Son; 1741; Yes; Yes; 30733
1725;   Nah-tah-yee-nas-wudt; M; 4; Navajo; F; S; Son; 1742; Yes; Yes; 30734

1726;   Beleen-lizin-bega; M; Unk; Navajo; F; M; Head; 1743; Yes; Yes; 30561
1727;   Clash-chee-bitsih; F; 42; Navajo; F; M; Wife; 1744; Yes; Yes; 30562
1728;   Haska-yee-chih-nil-wudt; M; 19; Navajo; F; S; Son; 1745; Yes; Yes; 30563
1729;   Peter; M; 17; Navajo; F; S; Son; 1746; Yes; Yes; 30564
1730;   Eddie; M; 14; Navajo; F; S; Son; 1747; Yes; Yes; 30565
1731;   Haska-yil-nih-yah; M; 12; Navajo; F; S; Son; 1748; Yes; Yes; 30566
1732;   Keh-hih-bah; F; 10; Navajo; F; S; Daughter; 1749; Yes; Yes; 30567
1733;   Nah-dez-bah; F; 8; Navajo; F; S; Daughter; 1750; Yes; Yes; 30568
1734;   Keh-hah-dez-bah; F; 6; Navajo; F; S; Daughter; 1751; Yes; Yes; 30570
1735;   Haska-yee-kih-nih-yah; M; 2; Navajo; F; S; Son; 1752; Yes; Yes; 30571

1736;   Badoni, Bigmouth; M; Unk; Navajo; F; M; Head; 1753; Yes; Yes; 29150
1737;   Bitsih, Bigmouth; F; Unk; Navajo; F; M; Wife; 1754; Yes; Yes; 29151
1738;   Awa-yazzie; M[sic]; 14; Navajo; F; S; Daughter; 1755; Yes; Yes; 29152
          [Should be female.]
1739;   Haska-yee-tah-deyah; M; 10; Navajo; F; S; Son; 1756; Yes; Yes; 29153
1740;   Dinay-yazzie; M; 8; Navajo; F; S; Son; 1757; Yes; Yes; 29154
1741;   Al-keh-hah-bah; F; 4; Navajo; F; S; Daughter; 1758; Yes; Yes; 29155
1742;   Haska-yah-n-nih-tih; M; 24; Navajo; F; S; Nephew; 1759; Yes; Yes; 29156
1743;   Zah-nez-bih-adzan; F; 20; Navajo; F; S; Niece; 1760; Yes; Yes; 29157
1744;   Yazzie; M; 10; Navajo; F; S; Nephew; 1761; Yes; Yes; 29158
1745;   Haska-nez-kez; M; 3; Navajo; F; S; Son; 1762; Yes; Yes; 29405

1746;   Bih-dagah-in-bih-adzan; F; 57; Navajo; F; Wd; Head; 1763; Yes; Yes; 30712
1747;   Bih-dagahih-bitsih; F; 28; Navajo; F; S; Daughter; 1764; Yes; Yes; 30713
1748;   Dan; M; 24; Navajo; F; S; Son; 1765; Yes; Yes; 30714
1749;   Eee-bah; F; 21; Navajo; F; S; Daughter; 1766; Yes; Yes; 30715

Census of the **Northern Navajo** reservation of the **Northern Navajo** jurisdiction, as of **April 1**, 19**31,** taken by **Ernest H. Hammond, District**, Superintendent.                                                                       **in Charge**

**Key:** Number; NAME: Surname, Given; Sex; Birth Year (if given), Age At Last Birthday; Tribe; Degree of Blood; Marital Status; Relationship To Head of Family; Last Census Roll Number; At Jurisdiction Where Enrolled (Yes or No); At Another Jurisdiction; ELSEWHERE: Post office, County, State; Ward (Yes or No); Allotment, Annuity, and Identification Numbers.

1750;   Harold; M; 16; Navajo; F; S; Son; 1767; Yes; Yes; 30716
1751;   Nahn-bah; F; 13; Navajo; F; S; Daughter; 1768; Yes; Yes; 30717
1752;   Tas-wudt; M; 8; Navajo; F; S; Son; 1769; Yes; Yes; 30718
1753;   Haska-yee-nah-wudt; M; 2; Navajo; F; S; Grand-son; 1770; Yes; Yes; 31240
1754;   Franklin; M; 2; Navajo; F; S; Grand-son; 1771; Yes; Yes; 31241


1755;   Bih-dagah, Lester; M; 26; Navajo; F; M; Head; 1772; Yes; Yes; 30721
1756;   Nah-hah-zahih-bitsih; F; 22; Navajo; F; M; Wife; 1773; Yes; Yes; 30722
1757;   Bihn-ziz-bah; F; 4; Navajo; F; S; Daughter; 1774; Yes; Yes; 30723


1758;   Bih-dagah-nez-bega, Tom; Unk; Navajo; F; M; Head; 1775; Yes; Yes; 30371
1759;   Hosteen-hih-des-ann-bitsih; F; 28; Navajo; F; M; Wife; 1776; Yes; Yes; 30372
1760;   Haz-bah; F; 8; Navajo; F; S; Step-daughter; 1777; Yes; Yes; 30373
1761;   Joe James; M; 5; Navajo; F; S; Step-son; 1778; Yes; Yes; 30374


1762;   Bih-gail-benally, John; M; 31; Navajo; F; M; Head; 1779; Yes; Yes; 30244
1763;   Salou-sani-bitsih; F; 24; Navajo; F; M; Wife; 1780; Yes; Yes; 30245


1764;   Bih-gail-bega; M; 59; Navajo; F; M; Head; 1781; Yes; Yes; 30238
1765;   Topah-hosteen-bitsih; F; 53; Navajo; F; M; Wife; 1782; Yes; Yes; 30239
1766;   Bih-gail-benally; M; 29; Navajo; F; S; Son; 1783; Yes; Yes; 30240
1767;   Cheeih; F; 10; Navajo; F; S; Daughter; 1784; Yes; Yes; 30241
1768;   Shee-yazzie; F; 8; Navajo; F; S; Daughter; 1785; Yes; Yes; 30242
1769;   Biz-yoh; F; 5; Navajo; F; S; Daughter; 1786; Yes; Yes; 30243


1770;   Bih-gee-ashih; M; Unk; Navajo; F; M; Head; 1787; Yes; Yes; 29181
1771;   Toh-dih-cheenybitsih[sic]; F; Unk; Navajo; F; M; Wife; 1788; Yes; Yes; 29182
          [Name should be Toh-dih-cheeny-bitsih]
1772;   Hah-nih-bah; F; 16; Navajo; F; S; Daughter; 1789; Yes; Yes; 29183
1773;   Yeilth-hah-nas-bah; F; 2; Navajo; F; S; Daughter; 1790; Yes; Yes; 29184
1774;   Natalh-dah-yah; M; 1; Navajo; F; S; Son; 1791; Yes; Yes; 29407


1775;   Bih-jah-atin; M; 53; Navajo; F; M; Head; 1792; Yes; Yes; 29347
1776;   Clah-yazzie-bitsih; F; 47; Navajo; F; M; Wife; 1793; Yes; Yes; 29348
1777;   Archie; M; 19; Navajo; F; S; Step-son; 1794; Yes; Yes; 29349
1778;   Daisy; F; 12; Navajo; F; S; Step-daughter; 1795; Yes; Yes; 29350
1779;   Bil-jih-bah; F; 9; Navajo; F; S; Step-daughter; 1796; Yes; Yes; 29351
1780;   Tah-nih-bah; F; 7; Navajo; F; S; Daughter; 1797; Yes; Yes; 29352
1781;   Bahih; M; 5; Navajo; F; S; Son; 1798; Yes; Yes; 29353


1782;   Bih-jah-atin-bega; M; 32; Navajo; F; M; Head; 1799; Yes; Yes; 31086
1783;   Clah-hah-zoh-benally; F; 27; Navajo; F; M; Wife; 1800; Yes; Yes; 31087

Census of the **Northern Navajo** reservation of the **Northern Navajo** jurisdiction, as of **April 1** , 19**31**, taken by **Ernest H. Hammond, District**, Superintendent.                                                                          **in Charge**

**Key:** Number; NAME: Surname, Given; Sex; Birth Year (if given), Age At Last Birthday; Tribe; Degree of Blood; Marital Status; Relationship To Head of Family; Last Census Roll Number; At Jurisdiction Where Enrolled (Yes or No); At Another Jurisdiction; ELSEWHERE: Post office, County, State; Ward (Yes or No); Allotment, Annuity, and Identification Numbers.

1784;  Haska-nih-nih; M; 10; Navajo; F; S; Son; 1801; Yes; Yes; 31088
1785;  Nah-tah-yil-has-wudt; M; 6; Navajo; F; S; Son; 1802; Yes; Yes; 31089
1786;  Nal-ih-woody; M; 3; Navajo; F; S; Son; 1803; Yes; Yes; 31090
1787;  Al-chah-bah; F; 2; Navajo; F; S; Daughter; 1804; Yes; Yes; 31249


1788;  Bilah-nah-yiz-colih-bega; M; 32; Navajo; F; M; Head; 1805; Yes; Yes; 32403
1789;  Dagah-dah-sah-kad-benally; F; 30; Navajo; F; M; Wife; 1806; Yes; Yes; 32404
1790;  Bil-naz-hih-bah; F; 8; Navajo; F; S; Daughter; 1807; Yes; Yes; 32405
1791;  Haska-yil-chil-wudt; M; 5; Navajo; F; S; Son; 1808; Yes; Yes; 32406


1792;  Bilah-nah-yiz-colih-bega; M; 30; Navajo; F; M; Head; 1809; Yes; Yes; 32398
1793;  Dagah-dah-sah-kad-benally Russell Simpson[sic]; F; 26; Navajo; F; M; Wife; 1810; Yes; Yes; 32399
1794;  Nah-tah-yil-chih-nih-yah; M; 6; Navajo; F; S; Son; 1811; Yes; Yes; 32400
1795;  Nah-glih-naz-bah; F; 4; Navajo; F; S; Daughter; 1812; Yes; Yes; 32401
1796;  Leslie; M; 15; Navajo; F; S; Brother-in-law; 1813; Yes; Yes; 32402


1797;  Bih-zah-nez-bega; M; 30; Navajo; F; M; Head; 1814; Yes; Yes; 30757
1798;  Bob-bikis's bitsih; F; 30; Navajo; F; M: Wife; 1815; Yes; Yes; 30758
1799;  Haska-yil-yil-wudt; M; 6; Navajo; F; S; Son; 1816; Yes; Yes; 30759
1800;  Al-soh-nih-dez-bah; F; 4; Navajo; F; S Daughter; 1817; Yes; Yes; 30760
1801;  Yil-nih-dez-bah; F; 2; Navajo; F; S; Daughter; 1818; Yes; Yes; 30761
1802;  Chis-chilli, Ben; M; 16; Navajo; F; S; Nephew-in-law; 1819; Yes; Yes; 30762


1803;  Bega, Billy; M; 59; Navajo; F; M; Head; 1820; Yes; Yes; 30881
1804;  Hosteen-bah-benally; F; 21; Navajo; F; M; Wife; 1821; Yes; Yes; 30882
1805;  Haska-yil-hah-del; M; 6; Navajo; F; S; Son; 1822; Yes; Yes; 30883
1806;  Haska-yil-nih-yah; M; 6; Navajo; F; S; Son; 1823; Yes; Yes; 30884
1807;  Haska-yil-hoh-gahl; M; 3; Navajo; F; S; Son; 1824; Yes; Yes; 30885
1808;  John Billy; M; 22; Navajo; F; S; Son; 1825; Yes; Yes; 30886
1809;  Hollis; M; 12; Navajo; F; S; Son; 1826; Yes; Yes; 30887
1810;  Casey; M; 10; Navajo; F; S; Son; 1827; Yes; Yes; 30888
1811;  Haska-yah-des-yan; M; 9; Navajo; F; S; Son; 1828; Yes; Yes; 30889


1812;  Billy-bitsoih; M; 17; Navajo; F; M; Head; 1829; Yes; Yes; 32278
1813;  Ah-nah-thlohi-bitsih; F; 18; Navajo; F; M; Wife; 1830; Yes; Yes; 32279
1814;  Nah-tih-yee-chee-dae-yah; M; 1; Navajo; F; S; Son; 1831; Yes; Yes; 27075


1815;  Bitsee-dih-chosie-bitsoih; M; 30; Navajo; F; M; Head; 1832; Yes; Yes; 29147
1816;  Hosteen-ih-ih-bitsih; F; 19; Navajo; F; M; Wife; 1833; Yes; Yes; 29148
1817;  Atate-l-bahih; F; 4; Navajo; F; S; Daughter; 1834; Yes; Yes; 29149
1818;  Adzana-at-sosie; F; 2; Navajo; F; S; Daughter; 1835; Yes; Yes; 29412

Census of the **Northern Navajo** reservation of the **Northern Navajo** jurisdiction, as of **April 1**, 19**31**, taken by **Ernest H. Hammond, District**, Superintendent. **in Charge**

**Key:** Number; NAME: Surname, Given; Sex; Birth Year (if given), Age At Last Birthday; Tribe; Degree of Blood; Marital Status; Relationship To Head of Family; Last Census Roll Number; At Jurisdiction Where Enrolled (Yes or No); At Another Jurisdiction; ELSEWHERE: Post office, County, State; Ward (Yes or No); Allotment, Annuity, and Identification Numbers.

1819; Bil-ganih-yis-kih-bega; M; 50; Navajo; F; M; Head; 1836; Yes; Yes; 29015
1820; Lily; F; 24; Navajo; F; M; Wife; 1837; Yes; Yes; 29016
1821; Lewis; M; 8; Navajo; F; S; Son; 1838; Yes; Yes; 29017
1822; Hazel; F; 5; Navajo; F; S; Daughter; 1839; Yes; Yes; 29018

1823; Bitsee-dih-chasie, Earl Curley; M; 33; Navajo; F; M; Head; 1840; Yes; Yes; 29101
1824; Ashinih-clah-bitsoih; F; 23; Navajo; F; M; Wife; 1841; Yes; Yes; 29102
1825; Toaz-bah; F; 5; Navajo; F; S; Daughter; 1842; Yes; Yes; 29103
1826; Natoni-yazzie; M; 3; Navajo; F; S; Son; 1843; Yes; Yes; 29104

1827; Bitsee-gail-ensahih-bega; M; 21; Navajo; F; M; Head; 1844; Yes; Yes; 29205
1828; Glenna; F; 23; Navajo; F; M; Wife; 1845; Yes; Yes; 29206
1829; Bah; F; 4; Navajo; F; S; Daughter; 1846; Yes; Yes; 29207
1830; Haska-yee-tah-wo-lath; M; 3; Navajo; F; S; Son; 1847; Yes; Yes; 29388

1831; Blue Eye's Son; M; 34; Navajo; F; M; Head; 1848; Yes; Yes; 32212
1832; Salou-l-sosie-bitsoih, Lucine; F; 30; Navajo; F; M; Wife; 1849; Yes; Yes; 32213
1833; Alfred; M; 10; Navajo; F; S; Son; 1850; Yes; Yes; 32214
1834; Francis; F; 8; Navajo; F; S; Daughter; 1851; Yes; Yes; 32215
1835; Frank; M; 6; Navajo; F; S; Son; 1852; Yes; Yes; 32216
1836; John; M; 4; Navajo; F; S; Son; 1853; Yes; Yes; 32217
1837; Paul; M; 3; Navajo; F; S; Daughter[sic]; 1854; Yes; Yes; 32479

1838; Bob Bikis; M; 52; Navajo; F; M; Head; 1855; Yes; Yes; 29819
1839; Aht-citty-yen-bitsih; F; 58; Navajo; F; M; Wife; 1856; Yes; Yes; 29820
1840; Tah-nih-yah; M; 12; Navajo; F; S; Son; 1857; Yes; Yes; 29821
1841; Kee-bah; F; 9; Navajo; F; S; Daughter; 1858; Yes; Yes; 29822
1842; Lowell; M; 18; Navajo; F; S; Son; 1859; Yes; Yes; 29823
1843; Dan; M; 15; Navajo; F; S; Son; 1860; Yes; Yes; 29824
1844; Dah-yil-sohl; M; 21; Navajo; F; S; Son; 1861; Yes; Yes; 29825

1845; Bob Bekis Badoni-hosteen; M; 42; Navajo; F; M; Head; 1861-A; Yes; Yes; 29826
1846; Nah-lih-il-bah; F; 28; Navajo; F; M; Wife; 1862; Yes; Yes; 29827
1847; Yee-nah-yah, Melvin; M; 12; Navajo; F; S; Step-son; 1863; Yes; Yes; 29828
1848; Haska-yee-chih-hah-yah; M; 8; Navajo; F; S; Son; 1864; Yes; Yes; 29829
1849; Haska-ziz-zih; M; 6; Navajo; F; S; Son; 1865; Yes; Yes; 29830
1850; Hah-bah-bah; F; 3; Navajo; F; S; Daughter; 1866; Yes; Yes; 29831
1851; Nellie; F; 14; Navajo; F; S; Daughter; 1867; Yes; Yes; 29832
1852; Dez-bah; F; 18; Navajo; F; S; Daughter; 1868; Yes; Yes; 29833
1853; Zah; M; 21; Navajo; F; S; Son; 1869; Yes; Yes; 29834

Census of the **Northern Navajo** reservation of the **Northern Navajo** jurisdiction, as of **April 1** , 1931, taken by **Ernest H. Hammond, District**, Superintendent. **in Charge**

**Key:** Number; NAME: Surname, Given; Sex; Birth Year (if given), Age At Last Birthday; Tribe; Degree of Blood; Marital Status; Relationship To Head of Family; Last Census Roll Number; At Jurisdiction Where Enrolled (Yes or No); At Another Jurisdiction; ELSEWHERE: Post office, County, State; Ward (Yes or No); Allotment, Annuity, and Identification Numbers.

1854; Bob Bekis; M; 31; Navajo; F; Wd; Head; 1870; Yes; Yes; 29817
1855; Tahn-biz-bah; F; 8; Navajo; F; S; Daughter; 1871; Yes; Yes; 29818

1856; Bega, Bowen; M; 28; Navajo; F; M; Head; 1872; Yes; Yes; 30995
1857; Hosch-clish-nih-bitsih; F; 25; Navajo; F; M; Wife; 1873; Yes; Yes; 30996
1858; Willie; M; 7; Navajo; F; S; Son; 1874; Yes; Yes; 20997[sic]
[ID No. should be 30997]

1859; Hosteen-nez-bitsih; F; 52; Navajo; F; Wd; Head; 1875; Yes; Yes; 30859
1860; Bah; F; 18; Navajo; F; S; Daughter; 1876; Yes; Yes; 30860
1861; Haska-yee-nah-hoh-gahl; M; 18; Navajo; F; S; Son; 1877; Yes; Yes; 30861
1862; John; M; 15; Navajo; F; S; Son; 1878; Yes; Yes; 30862
1863; Keh-yil-dez-bah; F; 10; Navajo; F; S; Daughter; 1879; Yes; Yes; 30863
1864; Yee-naz-bah; F; 6; Navajo; F; S; Daughter; 1880; Yes; Yes; 30864
1865; Nah-tah-yin-neyah; M; 4; Navajo; F; S; Son; 1881; Yes; Yes; 30865
1866; Kean, Charley; M; 30; Navajo; F; S; Nephew; 1882; Yes; Yes; 30866
1867; Joe Eee; M; 26; Navajo; F; S; Nephew; 1883; Yes; Yes; 30867
1868; Haska-yil-nil-wudt; M; 24; Navajo; F; S; Nephew; 1884; Yes; Yes; 30868

1869; Barber, Barber Tom[sic]; M; 35; Navajo; F; M; Head; 1885; Yes; Yes; 32867
[Name should be Barber, Tom]
1870; Bato-ni-bitsees-chilli-bitsih; F; 22; Navajo; F; M; Wife; 1886; Yes; Yes; 32868
1871; Yah-hah-nih-bah; F; 5; Navajo; F; S; Daughter; 1887; Yes; Yes; 32869
1872; Nah-yih-yil-nih-nih-yah; M; 3; Navajo; F; S; Son; 1888; Yes; Yes; 32870

1873; Blue Eyes, Walter; M; 31; Navajo; F; M; Head; 1889; Yes; Yes; 32899
1874; Bitsih, Francisco; F; 24; Navajo; F; M; Wife; 1890; Yes; Yes; 32900
1875; Haska-yil-chih-nihyah; M; 6; Navajo; F; S; Son; 1891; Yes; Yes; 32901
1876; Haska-yil-des-wudt; M; 2; Navajo; F; S; Son; 1892; Yes; Yes; 32902

1877; Bowen, Dan; M; 47; Navajo; F; M; Head; 1893; Yes; Yes; 21617
1878; Oss-cah-bimah-bih-dazee; F; 47; Navajo; F; M; Wife; 1894; Yes; Yes; 21618

1879; Bitsee-lagaih-bega; M; 35; Navajo; F; M; Head; 1895; Yes; Yes; 20385
1880; Aht-citty; F; 42; Navajo; F; M; Wife; 1896; Yes; Yes; 20386
1881; Aht-citty-bitsoih; M; 24; Navajo; F; S; Step-son; 1897; Yes; Yes; 20387
1882; Aht-citty, Lee; M; 19; Navajo; F; S; Step-son; 1898; Yes; Yes; 20388
1883; Dinay-chilli; M; 12; Navajo; F; S; Step-son; 1899; Yes; Yes; 20389
1884; Chih-n-bah; F; 7; Navajo; F; S; Daughter; 1900; Yes; Yes; 20390
1885; Naz-bah; F; 6; Navajo; F; S; Daughter; 1901; Yes; Yes; 20391

1886; Batoni-yen-bega (Satan); M; 46; Navajo; F; M; Head; 1902; Yes; Yes; 18058

Census of the **Northern Navajo** reservation of the **Northern Navajo** jurisdiction, as of **April 1**, 19**31**, taken by **Ernest H. Hammond, District**, Superintendent. **in Charge**

**Key:** Number; NAME: Surname, Given; Sex; Birth Year (if given), Age At Last Birthday; Tribe; Degree of Blood; Marital Status; Relationship To Head of Family; Last Census Roll Number; At Jurisdiction Where Enrolled (Yes or No); At Another Jurisdiction; ELSEWHERE: Post office, County, State; Ward (Yes or No); Allotment, Annuity, and Identification Numbers.

1887; Chah-dih-thlohi-bilah; F; 49; Navajo; F; M; Wife; 1903; Yes; Yes; 18059
1888; Batonih-yen-bega, Grant; M; 17; Navajo; F; S; Son; 1904; Yes; Yes; 18060

1889; Bih-oh-chidih-benally; M; Unk; Navajo; F; M; Head; 1905; Yes; Yes; 23388
1890; Al-kih-nil-bah; F; 20; Navajo; F; M; Wife; 1906; Yes; Yes; 23389
1891; Nah-tah-yil-nah-dahl; M; 3; Navajo; F; S; Son; 1907; Yes; Yes; 23390

1892; Bah-al-chinih-thlani-bega; M; 32; Navajo; F; M; Head; 1908; Yes; Yes; 27731
1893; Hosteen-neskahi-bitsih; F; 26; Navajo; F; M; Wife; 1909; Yes; Yes; 27732
1894; Tah-dez-bah; F; 8; Navajo; F; S; Daughter; 1910; Yes; Yes; 27733
1895; Hah-gee-bah; F; 5; Navajo; F; S; Daughter; 1911; Yes; Yes; 27734
1896; Baby; F; 2; Navajo; F; S; Daughter; 1912; Yes; Yes; 27735

1897; Batoni-bitsees-chilli-bega; M; 23; Navajo; F; S; Head; 1913; Yes; Yes; 32993

1898; Batoni-bitsee-chilli-bitah; M; Unk; Navajo; F; M; Head; 1914; Yes; Yes; 32858
1899; Gah-leesah-benally; F; 30; Navajo; F; M; Wife; 1915; Yes; Yes; 32859
1900; Dah-dez-bah; F; 13; Navajo; F; S; Daughter; 1916; Yes; Yes; 32860
1901; Yahn-dez-bah; F; 11; Navajo; F; S; Daughter; 1917; Yes; Yes; 32861
1902; Haska-yil-deyah; M; 8; Navajo; F; S; Son; 1918; Yes; Yes; 32862
1903; Yil-hah-bah; F; 6; Navajo; F; S; Daughter; 1919; Yes; Yes; 32863
1904; Nah-tah-yee-tah-deyah; M; 4; Navajo; F; S; Son; 1920; Yes; Yes; 32864

1905; Batoni-bitsees-chilli; M; 41; Navajo; F; M; Head; 1921; Yes; Yes; 32935
1906; Hah-nih-tayshih-benally; F; 19; Navajo; F; M; Wife; 1922; Yes; Yes; 32936
1907; Mac Burton; F; 22; Navajo; F; S; Daughter; 1923; Yes; Yes; 32937
1908; Dah-nih-bah; F; 18; Navajo; F; S; Daughter; 1924; Yes; Yes; 32938
1909; Glih-hah-naz-bah; F; 14; Navajo; F; S; Daughter; 1925; Yes; Yes; 32939
1910; Nah-tah-yee-nal-wohl; M; 12; Navajo; F; S; Son; 1926; Yes; Yes; 32940
1911; Nah-tah-yil-nahyah, Charley Burton; M; 10; Navajo; F; S; Son; 1927; Yes; Yes; 32941
1912; Glih-yahn-dez-bah; F; 9; Navajo; F; S; Daughter; 1928; Yes; Yes; 32942
1913; Haska-yee-tah-deyah; M; 7; Navajo; F; S; Son; 1929; Yes; Yes; 32943
1914; Nah-glih-yil-nih-nih-bah; F; 3; Navajo; F; S; Daughter; 1930; Yes; Yes; 32944

1915; Benally-bikis; M; Unk; Navajo; F; M; Head; 1931; Yes; Yes; 32807
1916; Gah-hah-daddy-bitsih; F; Unk; Navajo; F; M; Wife; 1932; Yes; Yes; 32808
1917; Johnson, Nelson; M; 17; Navajo; F; S; Son; 1933; Yes; Yes; 32809
1918; Bega, Lewis; M; 16; Navajo; F; Son; 1934; Yes; Yes; 32810

1919; Benally, Charley; M; 46; Navajo; F; M; Head; 1935; Yes; Yes; 32843
1920; Zaz-naz-lachee-bitsih; F; 46; Navajo; F; M; Wife; 1936; Yes; Yes; 32844

Census of the **Northern Navajo** reservation of the **Northern Navajo** jurisdiction, as of **April 1**, 19**31,** taken by **Ernest H. Hammond, District**, Superintendent.                                             **in Charge**

**Key:** Number; NAME: Surname, Given; Sex; Birth Year (if given), Age At Last Birthday; Tribe; Degree of Blood; Marital Status; Relationship To Head of Family; Last Census Roll Number; At Jurisdiction Where Enrolled (Yes or No); At Another Jurisdiction; ELSEWHERE: Post office, County, State; Ward (Yes or No); Allotment, Annuity, and Identification Numbers.

1921;  Tah-doz-bah; F; 16; Navajo; F; S; Daughter; 1937; Yes; Yes; 32845
1922;  Keh-yil-naz-bah, Camelia; F; 13; Navajo; F; S; Daughter; 1938; Yes; Yes; 32846
1923;  Clih-yil-nih-bah; F; 10; Navajo; F; S; Daughter; 1939; Yes; Yes; 32847

1924;  Blue Eyes; M; 66; Navajo; F; M; Head; 1940; Yes; Yes; 32218
1925;  Salon-etsosie-bitsih; F; 53; Navajo; F; M; Wife; 1941; Yes; Yes; 32219
1926;  Tah-des-wudt; M; 10; Navajo; F; S; Son; 1942; Yes; Yes; 32220
1927;  Ah-shih-kay-dal-suen-bitsih; F; 49; Navajo; F; M; 2nd wife; 1943; Yes; Yes; 32223
1928;  Haska-yil-chil-wudt; M; 10; Navajo; F; S; Son; 1944; Yes; Yes; 32224
1929;  Biz-nih-bah; F; 7; Navajo; F; S; Daughter; 1945; Yes; Yes; 32225

1930;  Beleen-lizin-bih-adzan; F; 66; Navajo; F; Wd; Head; 1946; Yes; Yes; 30622
1931;  Cheh-dez-bah; F; 11; Navajo; F; S; Grand-daughter; 1947; Yes; Yes; 30623
1932;  Eva; F; 18; Navajo; F; S; Grand-daughter; 1948; Yes; Yes; 30624
1933;  Viola; F; 18; Navajo; F; S; Daughter; 1949; Yes; Yes; 30652
1934;  Chih-naz-bah; F; 19; Navajo; F; S; Grand-daughter; 1950; Yes; Yes; 30560

1935;  Benally, Randolph; M; 41; Navajo; F; M; Head; 1951; Yes; Yes; 28096
1936;  Nocki-bitsih, Sadie; F; 25; Navajo; F; M; Wife; 1952; Yes; Yes; 28097

1937;  Clah-yazzie-bih-adzan; F; 79; Navajo; F; Wd; Head; 1953; Yes; Yes; 22721
1938;  Clah-yazzie-bega; M; Unk; Navajo; F; Wd; Son; 1954; Yes; Yes; 22722
1939;  Eskee-ashih-ih; M; Unk; Navajo; F; S; Grand-son; 1955; Yes; Yes; 22723

1940;  Clah-alsosie-bega; M; 62; Navajo; F; M; Head; 1956; Yes; Yes; 22428
1941;  Nah-glih-yee-za-nas-bah; F; 43; Navajo; F; M; Wife; 1957; Yes; Yes; 22429
1942;  Alfred; M; 18; Navajo; F; S; Son; 1958; Yes; Yes; 22430
1943;  Tah-deyah; M; 15; Navajo; F; S; Son; 1959; Yes; Yes; 22431
1944;  Nah-tah-yil-nadah; M; 12; Navajo; F; S; Son; 1960; Yes; Yes; 22432
1945;  Hoska-yee-kih-hah-yah; M; 7; Navajo; F; S; Son; 1961; Yes; Yes; 22433

1946;  Clah-nez; M; 44; Navajo; F; M; Head; 1962; Yes; Yes; 23183
1947;  Clah-nez-bih-adzan; F; 25; Navajo; F; M; Wife; 1963; Yes; Yes; 23184
1948;  Keh-yee-chih-deyah; M; 7; Navajo; F; S; Son; 1964; Yes; Yes; 23185
1949;  Bih-ziz-bah; F; 5; Navajo; F; S; Daughter; 1965; Yes; Yes; 23186
1950;  Yil-deh-bah; F; 18; Navajo; F; S; Daughter; 1966; Yes; Yes; 23187
1951;  Barbee; M; 14; Navajo; F; S; Son; 1967; Yes; Yes; 23188
1952;  Keh-nihyah; M; 10; Navajo; F; S; Son; 1968; Yes; Yes; 23189
1953;  Haska-ah-gahl; M; 2; Navajo; F; S; Son; 1969; Yes; Yes; 23982

1954;  Clah-nez-bega; M; 24; Navajo; F; M; Head; 1970; Yes; Yes; 23190

Census of the **Northern Navajo** reservation of the **Northern Navajo** jurisdiction, as of **April 1**, 19**31,** taken by **Ernest H. Hammond, District**, Superintendent. **in Charge**

**Key:** Number; NAME: Surname, Given; Sex; Birth Year (if given), Age At Last Birthday; Tribe; Degree of Blood; Marital Status; Relationship To Head of Family; Last Census Roll Number; At Jurisdiction Where Enrolled (Yes or No); At Another Jurisdiction; ELSEWHERE: Post office, County, State; Ward (Yes or No); Allotment, Annuity, and Identification Numbers.

1955; Bah; F; 22; Navajo; F; M; Wife; 1971; Yes; Yes; 23191
1956; Bah-doz-bah; F; 10; Navajo; F; S; Niece; 1972; Yes; Yes; 23193
1957; Ah-to-naz-bah; F; 2; Navajo; F; S; Daughter; 1973; Yes; Yes; 23983

1958; Clah-bega; M; 51; Navajo; F; M; Head; 1974; Yes; Yes; 23320
1959; Hosteen-l-bahih-bitsih; F; 57; Navajo; F; M; Wife; 1975; Yes; Yes; 23321
1960; Bruce; M; 26; Navajo; F; S; Son; 1976; Yes; Yes; 23322
1961; Clah-yazzie; M; 23; Navajo; F; S; Son; 1977; Yes; Yes; 23323
1962; Tap-des-bah; F; 17; Navajo; F; S; Daughter; 1978; Yes; Yes; 23324
1963; Clyde; M; 13; Navajo; F; S; Son; 1979; Yes; Yes; 23325
1964; Nah-tah-yil-dah-ziz-zih; M; 10; Navajo; F; S; Son; 1980; Yes; Yes; 23326
1965; Yahn-des-wudt; M; 7; Navajo; F; S; Son; 1981; Yes; Yes; 23327

1966; Charley; M; 63; Navajo; F; M; Head; 1982; Yes; Yes; 23296
1967; Charley's wife; F; 71; Navajo; F; M; Wife; 1983; Yes; Yes; 23297
1968; Keh-yil-des-bah; F; 9; Navajo; F; S; Grand-Daughter; 1984; Yes; Yes; 23298

1969; Clah-bega; M; Unk; Navajo; F; M; Head; 1985; Yes; Yes; 21227
1970; Clah-bega's wife; F; 60; Navajo; F; M; Wife; 1986; Yes; Yes; 21228
1971; Clah-bega, Ona; F; 23; Navajo; F; S; Daughter; 1987; Yes; Yes; 21229

1972; Capitan-benally; M; 26; Navajo; F; M; Head; 1988; Yes; Yes; 20984
1973; Tah-hah-tah-ly-bitsih; F; 21; Navajo; F; M; Wife; 1989; Yes; Yes; 20985
1974; Nah-tah-yah-nadasah; M; 3; Navajo; F; S; Son; 1990; Yes; Yes; 20986

1975; Capitan-benally; M; 29; Navajo; F; M; Head; 1991; Yes; Yes; 21449
1976; Doh-hah-nah-bah; F; 24; Navajo; F; M; Wife; 1992; Yes; Yes; 21450
1977; Hoska-yah-nihyah; M; 11; Navajo; F; S; Son; 1993; Yes; Yes; 21451
1978; Yee-has-wudt; M; 5; Navajo; F; S; Son; 1994; Yes; Yes; 21452

1979; Clah-hah-soh-goh-benally; M; 23; Navajo; F; M; Head; 1995; Yes; Yes; 28879
1980; Bah-l-saih; F; 19; Navajo; F; M; Wife; 1996; Yes; Yes; 28880
1981; Key-hahoz-ah; F; 1; Navajo; F; S; Daughter; 199[sic]; Yes; Yes; 28559

1982; Captan-bitsih[sic]; F; 70; Navajo; F; Wd; Head; 1997; Yes; Yes; 21571
      [Name should be Capitan-bitsih]
1983; Hosteen-soh-benally; M; 24; Navajo; F; S; Grand-son; 1998; Yes; Yes; 21572

1984; Chah-l-chee-bega; M; 36; Navajo; F; M: Head; 1999; Yes; Yes; 21568
1985; Polly-benally; F; 20; Navajo; F; M; Wife; 2000; Yes; Yes; 21569
1986; Hoska-yee-tah-na-wudt; M; 3; Navajo; F; S; Son; 2001; Yes; Yes; 21570
1987; Haska-yee-tah-nih-yah; M; 1; Navajo; F; S; Son; 2002; Yes; Yes; 21690

61

Census of the **Northern Navajo** reservation of the **Northern Navajo** jurisdiction, as of **April 1**, 19**31,** taken by **Ernest H. Hammond, District**, Superintendent. **in Charge**

Key: Number; NAME: Surname, Given; Sex; Birth Year (if given), Age At Last Birthday; Tribe; Degree of Blood; Marital Status; Relationship To Head of Family; Last Census Roll Number; At Jurisdiction Where Enrolled (Yes or No); At Another Jurisdiction; ELSEWHERE: Post office, County, State; Ward (Yes or No); Allotment, Annuity, and Identification Numbers.

1988; Chischilli; M; 78; Navajo; F; Wd; Head; 2003; Yes; Yes; 23793

1989; Clah-chee-yazzie; M; Unk; Navajo; F; M; Head; 2004; Yes; Yes; 23698
1990; Al-keh-nih-bah; F; 38; Navajo; F; M; Wife; 2005; Yes; Yes; 23699
1991; Al-keh-nih-bah; F; 21; Navajo; F; S; Daughter; 2006; Yes; Yes; 23700
1992; Wallace; M; 17; Navajo; F; S; Son; 2007; Yes; Yes; 23701
1993; Amy; F; 15 Navajo; F; S; Daughter; 2008; Yes; Yes; 23702
1994; Yil-kez-bah; F; 10; Navajo; F; S; Daughter; 2009; Yes; Yes; 23703
1995; Hoska-yee-chih-nal-dol; M; 8; Navajo; F; S; Son; 2010; Yes; Yes; 23704
1996; Tahn-nan-nih-bah; F; 6; Navajo; F; S; Daughter; 2011; Yes; Yes; 23705
1997; Clah-ih-bitah; M; Unk; Navajo; F; S; Nephew-in-law; 2012; Yes; Yes; 23706

1998; Clah-bekis-bega; M; 24; Navajo; F; M; Head; 2013; Yes; Yes; 23362
1999; Yee-kih-des-bah; F; 24; Navajo; F; M; Wife; 2014; Yes; Yes; 23363
2000; Nah-tah-yil-deyan; F[sic]; 5; Navajo; F; S; Son; 2015; Yes; Yes; 23364
[Should be male.]

2001; Clah-l-suen; M; 52; Navajo; F; M; Head; 2016; Yes; Yes; 23794
2002; Clah-l-suen's wife; F; 51; Navajo; F; M; Wife; 2017; Yes; Yes; 23795
2003; Bil-naz-hih-bah; F; 19; Navajo; F; S; Cousin; 2018; Yes; Yes; 23796
2004; Yahn-yee-gahl; M; 7; Navajo; F; S; Grand-son; 2019; Yes; Yes; 23797

2005; Clay-gee-hah-tahly-bih-bizee; M; 37; Navajo; F; M; Head; 2020; Yes; Yes; 26201
2006; Yee-kah-nih-bah; F; 40; Navajo; F; M; Wife; 2021; Yes; Yes; 26202
2007; Wayne; M; 15; Navajo; F; S; Son; 2022; Yes; Yes; 26203
2008; Frank; M; 10; Navajo; F; S; Son; 2023; Yes; Yes; 26204
2009; Maxine; F; 2; Navajo; F; S; Daughter; 2024; Yes; Yes; 26430

2010; Chah-dih-tlohi; M; 71; Navajo; F; M; Head; 2025; Yes; Yes; 25252
2011; Dah-dih-bah; F; 59; Navajo; F; M; Wife; 2026; Yes; Yes; 25253
2012; Lewis, Napoleon; M; 21; Navajo; F; S; Son; 2027; Yes; Yes; 25254
2013; Idabell; F; 17; Navajo; F; S; Grand-daughter; 2028; Yes; Yes; 25255

2014; Clash-cheeih-bega; M; 44; Navajo; F; M; Head; 2029; Yes; Yes; 25124
2015; Hosteen-hosch-clish-nih-bitsih; F; 28; Navajo; F; M; Wife; 2030; Yes; Yes; 25125
2016; Haska-yil-chel-wudt; M; 12; Navajo; F; S; Son; 2031; Yes; Yes; 25126
2017; Nah-tah-yee-tah-yah; M; 7; Navajo; F; S; Son; 2032; Yes; Yes; 25127
2018; Nah-tah-yee-chih-nil-wudt; M; 5; Navajo; F; S; Son; 2033; Yes; Yes; 25128

2019; Cambridge, Lewis; M; 37; Navajo; F; M; Head; 2034; Yes; Yes; 24960
2020; Ada; F; 35; Navajo; F; M; Wife; 2035; Yes; Yes; 24961

Census of the **Northern Navajo** reservation of the **Northern Navajo** jurisdiction, as of **April 1**, 19**31**, taken by **Ernest H. Hammond, District**, Superintendent.                                                                  **in Charge**

**Key:** Number; NAME: Surname, Given; Sex; Birth Year (if given), Age At Last Birthday; Tribe; Degree of Blood; Marital Status; Relationship To Head of Family; Last Census Roll Number; At Jurisdiction Where Enrolled (Yes or No); At Another Jurisdiction; ELSEWHERE: Post office, County, State; Ward (Yes or No); Allotment, Annuity, and Identification Numbers.

2021; Helen; F; 15; Navajo; F; S; Daughter; 2036; Yes; Yes; 24962
2022; Francis; M; 13; Navajo; F; S; Son; 2037; Yes; Yes; 24963
2023; Lorene; F; 10; Navajo; F; S; Daughter; 2038; Yes; Yes; 24964
2024; Amy; F; 8; Navajo; F; S; Daughter; 2039; Yes; Yes; 24965
2025; Gladis; F; 3; Navajo; F; Son[sic]; 2040; Yes; Yes; 24966
                            [Should be female.]
2026; Cambridge, James Kennedy; M; 2; Navajo; F; S; Son; 2041; Yes; Yes; 25340

2027; Clash-cheeih-sani; M; 84; Navajo; F; M; Head; 2042; Yes; Yes; 25134
2028; Clash-cheeih-sani's wife; F; 66; Navajo; F; M; Wife; 2043; Yes; Yes; 25135
2029; Ah-nah-bahih; F; 14; Navajo; F; S; Grand-daughter; 2044; Yes; Yes; 25136

2030; Chah-dih-thlohi; M; 59; Navajo; F; M; Head; 2045; Yes; Yes; 20245
2031; Chah-dih-thlohi's wife; F; 55; Navajo; F; M; Wife; 2046; Yes; Yes; 20246
2032; Nas-bah; F; 13; Navajo; F; S; Daughter; 2047; Yes; Yes; 20247

2033; Chis-chilli-bega; M; 24; Navajo; F; M; Head; 2048; Yes; Yes; 26368
2034; Chis-chilli-bega's wife; F; 20; Navajo; F; M; Wife; 2049; Yes; Yes; 26369
2035; Glih-naz-bah; F; 3; Navajo; F; S; Daughter; 2050; Yes; Yes; 26370

2036; Clah-cheeih-sosie, Frank; M; Unk; Navajo; F; M; Head; 2051; Yes; Yes; 25905
2037; Yazzie-bimah, John; F; 32; Navajo; F; M; Wife; 2052; Yes; Yes; 25906
2038; Yazzie, John; M; 18; Navajo; F; S; Step-son; 2053; Yes; Yes; 25907
2039; Glih-yil-naz-bah; F; 15; Navajo; F; S; Step-daughter; 2054; Yes; Yes; 25908
2040; Yazzie, Harry; M; 9; Navajo; F; S; Step-son; 2055; Yes; Yes; 25910
2041; Kaz-bah; F; 6; Navajo; F; S; Step-daughter; 2056; Yes; Yes; 25911

2042; Chis-chilli-benally; M; Unk; Navajo; F; M; Head; 2057; Yes; Yes; 24934
2043; Nah-glih-hah-bah; F; 19; Navajo; F; M; Wife; 2058; Yes; Yes; 24935
2044; Baz-dez-bah; F; 3; Navajo; F; S; Daughter; 2059; Yes; Yes; 24936

2045; Costillo, Tuly; M; 42; Navajo; F; M; Head; 2060; Yes; Yes; 24943
2046; Clih-hah-bah; F; 30; Navajo; F; M; Wife; 2061; Yes; Yes; 24944
2047; Sam; M; 12; Navajo; F; S; Son; 2062; Yes; Yes; 24945
2048; Dennison; M; 8; Navajo; F; S; Son; 2063; Yes; Yes; 24946
2049; Guy; M; 6; Navajo; F; S; Son; 2064; Yes; Yes; 24947

2050; Chis-chilli-bega; M; 35; Navajo; F; M; Head; 2065; Yes; Yes; 24873
2051; Ah-hih-dee-bah; F; 34; Navajo; F; M; Wife; 2066; Yes; Yes; 24874
2052; Ralph; M; 16; Navajo; F; S; Son; 2067; Yes; Yes; 24875
2053; Ona; F; 14; Navajo; F; S; Daughter; 2068; Yes; Yes; 24876
2054; Deswoody; M; 1; Navajo; F; S; Son; [Blank]; Yes; Yes; 25344

Census of the **Northern Navajo** reservation of the **Northern Navajo** jurisdiction, as of **April 1** , 19**31,** taken by **Ernest H. Hammond, District**, Superintendent.                                                              **in Charge**

Key: Number; NAME: Surname, Given; Sex; Birth Year (if given), Age At Last Birthday; Tribe; Degree of Blood; Marital Status; Relationship To Head of Family; Last Census Roll Number; At Jurisdiction Where Enrolled (Yes or No); At Another Jurisdiction; ELSEWHERE: Post office, County, State; Ward (Yes or No); Allotment, Annuity, and Identification Numbers.

2055;  Chischilli-bitah, Charley; M; 53; Navajo; F; M; Head; 2069; Yes; Yes; 24806
2056;  Dagah-li-cheeih-bitsih; F; 61; Navajo; F; M; Wife; 2070; Yes; Yes; 24807
2057;  Maurice; M; 18; Navajo; F; S; Son; 2071; Yes; Yes; 24808
2058;  Haska-yil-hol-wudt; M; 16; Navajo; F; S; Son; 2072; Yes; Yes; 24809

2059;  Chee, Joe; M; 33; Navajo; F; M; Head; 2073; Yes; Yes; 25913
2060;  Yahn-nih-bah; F; 55; Navajo; F; M; Wife; 2074; Yes; Yes; 25914
2061;  Haska-yil-nih-yah; M; 7; Navajo; F; S; Nephew; 2075; Yes; Yes; 25915

2062;  Chischilli-bega; M; 25; Navajo; F; M; Head; 2076; Yes; Yes; 20312
2063;  Kay-yah-nih-bah; F; 21; Navajo; F; M; Wife; 2077; Yes; Yes; 20312A
2064;  Yil-nas-bah; F; 3; Navajo; F; S; Daughter; 2078; Yes; Yes; 20313

2065;  Clah; M; Unk; Navajo; F; M; Head; 2079; Yes; Yes; 24758
2066;  Josephine; F; 31; Navajo; F; M; Wife; 2080; Yes; Yes; 24759
2067;  Josephine; F; 10; Navajo; F; S; Daughter; 2081; Yes; Yes; 24760
2068;  Keh-yee-tah-dez-bah; F; 8; Navajo; F; S; Daughter; 2082; Yes; Yes; 24761
2069;  Nah-tah-yil-hah-yah; M; 5; Navajo; F; S; Son; 2083; Yes; Yes; 24762

2070;  Cohoh-bega; M; Unk; Navajo; F; M; Head; 2084; Yes; Yes; 24709
2071;  Yil-dez-bah; F; 27; Navajo; F; M; Wife; 2085; Yes; Yes; 24710
2072;  Atate-yazzie; F; 3; Navajo; F; S; Daughter; 2086; Yes; Yes; 24711
2073;  Haska-yazzie; M; 2; Navajo; F; S; Son; 2087; Yes; Yes; 25330

2074;  Bikis, Custer; M; Unk; Navajo; F; M; Head; 2088; Yes; Yes; 27596
2075;  Naz-bah; F; 25; Navajo; F; M; Wife; 2089; Yes; Yes; 27597
2076;  Keh-hah-noh-bah; F; 3; Navajo; F; S; Daughter; 2090; Yes; Yes; 27598

2077;  Clash-cheeih-nez; M; 31; Navajo; F; M; Head; 2091; Yes; Yes; 27901
2078;  Toh-lizin-benally; F; 24; Navajo; F; M; Wife; 2092; Yes; Yes; 27902
2079;  Dinay-soh; M; 9; Navajo; F; M; Son; 2093; Yes; Yes; 27903
2080;  Seesie; F; 6; Navajo; F; S; Daughter; 2094; Yes; Yes; 27904
2081;  Eskie-l-bahih; M; 3; Navajo; F; S; Son; 2095; Yes; Yes; 27905
2082;  Ith-ne-pah; F; 2; Navajo; F; S; Daughter; 2096; Yes; Yes; 18273

2083;  Chah-dih-thlohi-bega; M; 31; Navajo; F; M; Head; 2097; Yes; Yes; 17242
2084;  Hohsonie-hosteen-bitsih; F; 26; Navajo; F; M; Wife; 2098; Yes; Yes; 17243
2085;  Chah-dis-lohi-kee-ahyah; M; 9; Navajo; F; S; Son; 2099; Yes; Yes; 17244
2086;  Chah-dis-lohi-eee-hay-has-bah; F; 7; Navajo; F; S; Daughter; 2100; Yes; Yes; 17245

2087;  Clah, Teddy; M; 35; Navajo; F; M; Head; 2101; Yes; Yes; 28026
2088;  Hah-nah-ziz-hih-bitsih; F; Unk; Navajo; F; M; Wife; 2102; Yes; Yes; 28027

Census of the **Northern Navajo** reservation of the **Northern Navajo** jurisdiction, as of **April 1**, 19**31**, taken by **Ernest H. Hammond, District**, Superintendent. **in Charge**

**Key:** Number; NAME: Surname, Given; Sex; Birth Year (if given), Age At Last Birthday; Tribe; Degree of Blood; Marital Status; Relationship To Head of Family; Last Census Roll Number; At Jurisdiction Where Enrolled (Yes or No); At Another Jurisdiction; ELSEWHERE: Post office, County, State; Ward (Yes or No); Allotment, Annuity, and Identification Numbers.

2089;  Dinay; M; 13; Navajo; F; S; Nephew-in-law; 2103; Yes; Yes; 28028
2090;  Hah-nah-zihih-bih-adzan; F; Unk; Navajo; F; Wd; Mother-in-law; 2104; Yes; Yes; 28029

2091;  Clah; M; 41; Navajo; F; M; Head; 2105; Yes; Yes; 18087
2092;  Nocki-bitsih; F; 40; Navajo; F; M; Wife; 2106; Yes; Yes; 18088
2093;  Clah-, Willie Tony; M; 17; Navajo; F; S; Son; 2107; Yes; Yes; 18089
2094;  Clah, John Tony; M; 15; Navajo; F; S; Son; 2108; Yes; Yes; 18090
2095;  Glih-has-bah; F; 12; Navajo; F; S; Daughter; 2109; Yes; Yes; 18091
2096;  Glih-hah-nih-bah; F; 10; Navajo; F; S; Daughter; 2110; Yes; Yes; 18092
2097;  Glih-hah-nih-Day-bah; F; 8; Navajo; F; S; Daughter; 2111; Yes; Yes; 18093
2098;  Hoska-yee-naz-wudt; M; 6; Navajo; F; S; Son; 2112; Yes; Yes; 18094
2099;  Clah, Willie; M; 4; Navajo; F; S; Son; 2113; Yes; Yes; 18095
2100;  Glene-bah; F; 3; Navajo; F; S; Daughter; 2114; Yes; Yes; 18287

2101;  Chah-dih-tlohi-badoni; M; Unk; Navajo; F; M; Head; 2115; Yes; Yes; 20235
2102;  Clah-dih-tlohi-bitsih; F; 27; Navajo; F; M; Wife; 2116; Yes; Yes; 20236
2103;  Nah-tah-l-bahih; M; 10; Navajo; F; S; Son; 2117; Yes; Yes; 20237
2104;  Yee-che-has-wudt; M; 7; Navajo; F; S; Son; 2118; Yes; Yes; 20238
2105;  Yee-tah-des-bah; F; 4; Navajo; F; S; Daughter; 2119; Yes; Yes; 20239

2106;  Clash-cheeih-soh; M; 59; Navajo; F; M; Head; 2120; Yes; Yes; 26759
2107;  Clash-cheeih-soh's wife; F; 52; Navajo; F; M; Wife; 2121; Yes; Yes; 26760
2108;  Haska-yee-chih-has-wudt; M; 22; Navajo; F; S; Son; 2122; Yes; Yes; 26761
2109;  Yahn-nah-bah; F; 21; Navajo; F; S; Daughter; 2123; Yes; Yes; 26762
2110;  Arlene; F; 19; Navajo; F; S; Daughter; 2124; Yes; Yes; 26763
2111;  Ah-hahn-nih-bah; F; 8; Navajo; F; S; Daughter; 2125; Yes; Yes; 26764
2112;  Glih-yil-naz-bah; F; 16; Navajo; F; S; Niece-in-law; 2126; Yes; Yes; 26765

2113;  Chis-chilli-boh-bizee; M; 26; Navajo; F; M; Head; 2127; Yes; Yes; 23810
2114;  Tah-dez-bah; F; 20; Navajo; F; M; Wife; 2128; Yes; Yes; 23811
2115;  Kah-yee-nah-bah; F; 2; Navajo; F; S; Daughter; 2129; Yes; Yes; 23908

2116;  Clah-hah-zoh-gah-bega; M; Unk; Navajo; F; M; Head; 2130; No; McElmo, Colo., San Juan, Utah; Yes; 19477
2117;  Bitaih, Charley; F; 46; Navajo; F; M; Wife; 2131; No; McElmo, Colo., San Juan, Utah; Yes; 19478
2118;  Wulth; M; 22; Navajo; F; S; Son; 2132;  No; McElmo, Colo., San Juan, Utah; Yes; 19479
2119;  Chah-ly; F; 12; Navajo; F; S; Daughter; 2133; No; McElmo, Colo., San Juan, Utah; Yes; 19480
2120;  Clah-hah-zoh-gah, Ellis; M; 10; Navajo; F; S; Son; 2134; No; McElmo, Colo., San Juan, Utah; Yes; 19481

Census of the **Northern Navajo** reservation of the **Northern Navajo** jurisdiction, as of **April 1**, 19**31,** taken by **Ernest H. Hammond, District**, Superintendent.                                                            **in Charge**

**Key:** Number; NAME: Surname, Given; Sex; Birth Year (if given), Age At Last Birthday; Tribe; Degree of Blood; Marital Status; Relationship To Head of Family; Last Census Roll Number; At Jurisdiction Where Enrolled (Yes or No); At Another Jurisdiction; ELSEWHERE: Post office, County, State; Ward (Yes or No); Allotment, Annuity, and Identification Numbers.

2121; Kal-ih; M; 7; Navajo; F; S; Son; 2135; No; McElmo, Colo., San Juan, Utah; Yes; 19482
2122; Nellie; F; 5; Navajo; F; S; Daughter; 2136; No; McElmo, Colo., San Juan, Utah; Yes; 19483
2123; Akee-bahe; F; 2; Navajo; F; S; Daughter; 2137; No; McElmo, Colo., San Juan, Utah; Yes; 19526

2124; Cudih-benally; M; Unk; Navajo; F; M; Head; 2138; Yes; Yes; 28368
2125; Lillian; F; 22; Navajo; F; M; Wife; 2139; Yes; Yes; 28369
2126; Yil-nah-bah; F; 7; Navajo; F; S; Daughter; 2140; Yes; Yes; 28370
2127; Keh-yil-nah-nih-bah; F; 5; Navajo; Daughter; 2141; Yes; Yes; 28371
2128; Akee; M; 3; Navajo; F; S; Son; 2142; Yes; Yes; 28553

2129; Clah-nez; M; Unk; Navajo; F; M; Head; 2143; Yes; Yes; 28527
2130; Clah-nez's wife; F; 3387; Navajo; F; M; Wife; 2144; Yes; Yes; 28528
2131; Dinay-ah-saih; M; 20; Navajo; F; S; Son; 2145; Yes; Yes; 28529
2132; James; M; 19; Navajo; F; S; Son; 2146; Yes; Yes; 28530
2133; Lyle; M; 13; Navajo; F; S; Son; 2147; Yes; Yes; 28531
2134; Haska-yil-yee-gahl; M; 8; Navajo; F; S; Son; 2148; Yes; Yes; 28532
2135; Yazih-toh; M; 6; Navajo; F; S; Son; 2149; Yes; Yes; 28533
2136; Cheh-naz-bah; F; 3; Navajo; F; S; Daughter; 2150; Yes; Yes; 28534

2137; Clah-gih-hah-tahly-bega; M; 38; Navajo; F; M; Head; 2151; Yes; Yes; 26969
2138; Bih-kih-nih-ziz-bah; F; 24; Navajo; F; M; Wife; 2152; Yes; Yes; 26970

2139; Clah-bakis-bega; M; Unk; Navajo; F; M; Head; 2157; Yes; Yes; 23362
2140; Yee-kih-des-bah; F; 25; Navajo; F; M; Wife; 2158; Yes; Yes; 23363
2141; Nah-tah-yil-deyah; M; 5; Navajo; F; S; Son; 2159; Yes; Yes; 23369

2142; Clah, Felix; M; Unk; Navajo; F; M; Head; 2160; Yes; Yes; 23115
2143; Al-naoz-bah; F; 31; Navajo; F; M; Wife; 2161; Yes; Yes; 23116
2144; Kee-soh; M; 7; Navajo; F; S; Son; 2162; Yes; Yes; 23117
2145; Sarah; F; 3; Navajo; F; S; Daughter; 2163; Yes; Yes; 23118

2146; Chise-nez-bega; M; 62; Navajo; F; M; Head; 2164; No; McElmo, Colo., San Juan, Utah; Yes; 18951
2147; Chise-nez-bega's wife; F; 48; Navajo; F; M; Wife; 2165; No; McElmo, Colo., San Juan, Utah; Yes; 18952
2148; Hoska-yee-tah-yil-ta; M; 25; Navajo; F; S; Son; 2166; No; McElmo, Colo., San Juan, Utah; Yes; 18953
2149; Hoska-yee-ha-sah; M; 23; Navajo; F; S; Son; 2167; No; McElmo, Colo., San Juan, Utah; Yes; 18954

Census of the __Northern Navajo__ reservation of the__ Northern Navajo __
jurisdiction, as of__ April 1 __, 19**31**, taken by__ Ernest H. Hammond, District __,
Superintendent.                                                      **in Charge**

**Key:** Number; NAME: Surname, Given; Sex; Birth Year (if given), Age At Last Birthday; Tribe; Degree of
Blood; Marital Status; Relationship To Head of Family; Last Census Roll Number; At Jurisdiction Where
Enrolled (Yes or No); At Another Jurisdiction; ELSEWHERE: Post office, County, State; Ward (Yes or No);
Allotment, Annuity, and Identification Numbers.

2150; Adzanih-chee; F; 17; Navajo; F; S; Daughter; 2168; No; McElmo, Colo., San
Juan, Utah; Yes; 18955
2151; Doh-bah; F; 6; Navajo; F; S; Daughter; 2169; No; McElmo, Colo., San Juan,
Utah; Yes; 18956

2152; Clah-nez-bega; M; 30; Navajo; F; M; Head; 2170; Yes; Yes; 23128
2153; Mike-bitsih; F; 22; Navajo; F; M; Wife; 2171; Yes; Yes; 23129
2154; Bil-nih-ziz-bah; F; 6; Navajo; F; S; Daughter; 2172; Yes; Yes; 23130
2155; Haska-kee-azk-wudt; M; 5; Navajo; F; S; Son; 2173; Yes; Yes; 23131
2156; Keh-yil-ee-bah; F; 3; Navajo; F; S; Daughter; 2174; Yes; Yes; 23132
2157; Baby; M; 1; Navajo; F; S; Son; 2175; Yes; Yes; 24012

2158; Cudih-yen-bega; F[sic]; 51; Navajo; F; M; Head; 2176; No; McElmo, Colo.,
San Juan, Utah; Yes; 19311
2159; Boh-woh-atin-bisih, Exie; F; 38; Navajo; F; M; Wife; 2177; No; McElmo,
Colo., San Juan, Utah; Yes; 19312
2160; Cudih, Teddy; M; 12; Navajo; F; S; Son; 2178; No; McElmo, Colo., San Juan,
Utah; Yes; 19313
2161; Cudih, Bessie; F; 9; Navajo; F; S; Daughter; 2179; No; McElmo, Colo., San
Juan, Utah; Yes; 19314
2162; Cudih, Agnes; F; 6; Navajo; F; S; Daughter; 2180; No; McElmo, Colo., San
Juan, Utah; Yes; 19315
2163; Cudih, Anna; F; 16; Navajo; F; S; Daughter; 2181; No; McElmo, Colo., San
Juan, Utah; Yes; 19492
2164; Isabelle; F; 3; Navajo; F; S; Daughter; 2182; No; McElmo, Colo., San Juan,
Utah; Yes; 19505

2165; Chah-dih-thlohi-bega; M; 32; Navajo; F; M; Head; 2183; No; McElmo, Colo.,
San Juan, Utah; Yes; 19413
2166; Hosteen-tiah-benally-bitsih; F; 23; Navajo; F; M; Wife; 2184; No; McElmo,
Colo., San Juan, Utah; Yes; 19414
2167; Dah-ih-bah; F; 7; Navajo; F; S; Daughter; 2185; No; McElmo, Colo., San
Juan, Utah; Yes; 19415
2168; Yee-yilth-naz-bah; F; 5; Navajo; F; S; Daughter; 2186; No; McElmo, Colo.,
San Juan, Utah; Yes; 19416
2169; Hoska-tah-des-wudt; M; 3; Navajo; F; S; Son; 2187; No; McElmo, Colo., San
Juan, Utah; Yes; 19417
2170; Natah-yee-tah-gah; M; 4; Navajo; F; S; Son; 2188; No; McElmo, Colo., San
Juan, Utah; Yes; 19418
2171; Haska-hah-yazzie; M; 1; Navajo; F; S; Son; 2189; No; McElmo, Colo., San
Juan, Utah; Yes; 19522

Census of the **Northern Navajo** reservation of the **Northern Navajo** jurisdiction, as of **April 1**, 19**31**, taken by **Ernest H. Hammond, District**, Superintendent. **in Charge**

2172; Clah-bega, Tony; M; 26; Navajo; F; M; Head; 2190; No; McElmo, Colo., San Juan, Utah; Yes; 19444

2173; Hosteen-gan-bitsih; F; 29; Navajo; F; M; Wife; 2191; No; McElmo, Colo., San Juan, Utah; Yes; 19445

2174; Awa-bah; F; 9; Navajo; F; S; Daughter; 2192; No; McElmo, Colo., San Juan, Utah; Yes; 19446

2175; Clah-Uintilli-bega; M; Unk; Navajo; F; M; Head; 2193; No; McElmo, Colo., San Juan, Utah; Yes; 19462

2176; Adaki-nez-bitsih; F; 22; Navajo; F; M; Wife; 2194; No; McElmo, Colo., San Juan, Utah; Yes; 19463

2177; Dah-nih-bah; F; 7; Navajo; F; S; Daughter; 2195; No; McElmo, Colo., San Juan, Utah; Yes; 19464

2178; Hoska-yah-deyah; M; 5; Navajo; F; S; Son; 2196; No; McElmo, Colo., San Juan, Utah; Yes; 19465

2179; Cudih-yen-bega; M; 45; Navajo; F; M; Head; 2197; Yes; Yes; 20001

2180; Beleen-lagaih-bitah, (Sam bitsih); F; 28; Navajo; F; M; Wife; 2198; Yes; Yes; 20002

2181; Ah-kee; M; 10; Navajo; F; S; Son; 2199; Yes; Yes; 20003

2182; Tah-des-bah; F; 6; Navajo; F; S; Daughter; 2200; Yes; Yes; 20004

2183; Clih-hah-nih-bah; F; 5; Navajo; F; S; Daughter; 2201; Yes; Yes; 20005

2184; Zanna-nih-bah-he; F; 2; Navajo; F; S; Daughter; 2202; Yes; Yes; 19516

2185; Clah-Uintilli; M; 56; Navajo; F; M; Head; 2203; No; McElmo, Colo., San Juan, Utah; Yes; 19447

2186; Bitsih, Charley; F; 47; Navajo; F; M; Wife; 2204; No; McElmo, Colo., San Juan, Utah; Yes; 19448

2187; Klizi-thlani, Ned; M; 17; Navajo; F; S; Son; 2205; No; McElmo, Colo., San Juan, Utah; Yes; 19449

2188; Hah-nah-bah; F; 17; Navajo; F; S; Daughter; 2206; No; McElmo, Colo., San Juan, Utah; Yes; 19450

2189; Atate-l-bahih; F; 15; Navajo; F; S; Daughter; 2207; No; McElmo, Colo., San Juan, Utah; Yes; 19451

2190; Adzanih-eyseeie; F; 7; Navajo; F; S; Daughter; 2208; No; McElmo, Colo., San Juan, Utah; Yes; 19453

2191; Lowell; M; 3; Navajo; F; S; Son; 2209; No; McElmo, Colo., San Juan, Utah; Yes; 19454

2192; Chah-la-bahih-yen-bega; M; 74; Navajo; F; M; Head; 2210; Yes; Yes; 20073

2193; Adzanih-bitsee-clitsohi; F; 59; Navajo; F; M; Wife; 2211; Yes; Yes; 20074

2194; Cudih-yen-bega; M; Unk; Navajo; F; M; Head; 2212; Yes; Yes; 19916

Census of the **Northern Navajo** reservation of the **Northern Navajo** jurisdiction, as of **April 1**, 1931, taken by **Ernest H. Hammond, District** Superintendent. **in Charge**

**Key:** Number; NAME: Surname, Given; Sex; Birth Year (if given), Age At Last Birthday; Tribe; Degree of Blood; Marital Status; Relationship To Head of Family; Last Census Roll Number; At Jurisdiction Where Enrolled (Yes or No); At Another Jurisdiction; ELSEWHERE: Post office, County, State; Ward (Yes or No); Allotment, Annuity, and Identification Numbers.

2195; Tah-dez-zanih-soh-bitsih; F; 38; Navajo; F; M; Wife; 2213; Yes; Yes; 19917
2196; Adzanih-soh; F; 18; Navajo; F; S; Daughter; 2214; Yes; Yes; 19918
2197; Cudih, Melissa; F; 16; Navajo; F; S; Daughter; 2215; Yes; Yes; 19919
2198; Hoska-yil-wudt; M; 14; Navajo; F; S; Son; 2216; Yes; Yes; 19920
2199; Cudih, Elmer; M; 10; Navajo; F; S; Son; 2217; Yes; Yes; 19921
2200; Tohe-nih-bah; F; 8; Navajo; F; S; Daughter; 2218; Yes; Yes; 19922
2201; Tah-des-bah; F; 6; Navajo; F; S; Daughter; 2219; Yes; Yes; 19923
2202; Nah-geih-yah-bah; F; 4; Navajo; F; S; Daughter; 2220; Yes; Yes; 19924
2203; Natoni-bihma; F; 78; Navajo; F; Wd; None; 2221; Yes; Yes; 19925
2204; Yades-wudt; M; 4; Navajo; F; S; Son; 2222; Yes; Yes; 20406
2205; Cudih, Jessie; F; 18; Navajo; F; S; Daughter; 2223; Yes; Yes; 20392
2206; Cudih-chee; M; Unk; Navajo; F; S; Son; 2224; Yes; Yes; 20393

2207; Chah-la-bahih-yen-bega; M; 63; Navajo; F; M; Head; 2225; Yes; Yes; 20103
2208; Adzan-dah-kay-ho-dih-thlohi; F; 63; Navajo; F; M; Wife; 2226; Yes; Yes; 20104
2209; Hah-tahly-soh-bega; M; 21; Navajo; F; S; Son; 2227; Yes; Yes; 20105
2210; Bahih; F; 16; Navajo; F; S; Grand-Daughter; 2228; Yes; Yes; 20313

2211; Cudih-yen-bega; M; 41; Navajo; F; M; Head; 2229; Yes; Yes; 20082
2212; See-codih-bitsih; F; 23; Navajo; F; M; Wife; 2230; Yes; Yes; 20083
2213; Nah-tah-yee-che-has-wudt; M; 4; Navajo; F; S; Son; 2231; Yes; Yes; 20084
2214; Yichin-haska-wudt; M; 2; Navajo; F; S; Son; 2232; Yes; Yes; 20424

2215; Chah-etsee-sih; M; 53; Navajo; F; M; Head; 2233; Yes; Yes; 20332
2216; Hosteen-clitsoh-bitsih; F; 21; Navajo; F; M; Wife; 2234; Yes; Yes; 20333
2217; Chah-etseeih, Hazel; F; 18; Navajo; F; S; Daughter; 2235; Yes; Yes; 20334
2218; Hosteen-soh; M; 15; Navajo; F; S; Son; 2236; Yes; Yes; 20335
2219; Al-nah-bah; F; 11; Navajo; F; S; Daughter; 2237; Yes; Yes; 20336
2220; Haska-yil-dol-nih; M; 1; Navajo; F; S; Son; 2238; Yes; Yes; 20444

2221; Crane, Leo; M; 25; Navajo; F; M; Head; 2239; Yes; Yes; 20112
2222; Crane, Callie; F; 29; Navajo; F; M; Wife; 2240; Yes; Yes; 20113
2223; Crane, Arlene; F; 3; Navajo; F; S; Daughter; 2241; Yes; Yes; 20114

2224; Chah-dih-tlohi, Leo; M; 38; Navajo; F; M; Head; 2242; Yes; Yes; 20210
2225; Bah; F; 19; Navajo; F; M; Wife; 2243; Yes; Yes; 20211

2226; Cambridge, John; M; 37; Navajo; F; M; Head; 2244; Yes; Yes; 30518
2227; Hosteen-la-bahih-bitsih; F; 26; Navajo; F; M; Wife; 2245; Yes; Yes; 30519
2228; Haska-yil-se-yah; M; 7; Navajo; F; S; Son; 2246; Yes; Yes; 30520
2229; Nah-tah-yil-mah-dahl; M; 5; Navajo; F; S; Son; 2247; Yes; Yes; 30521
2230; Nah-tah-yil-has-wudt; M; 18; Navajo; F; S; Nephew; 2248; Yes; Yes; 30522

Census of the **Northern Navajo** reservation of the **Northern Navajo** jurisdiction, as of **April 1** , 19**31,** taken by **Ernest H. Hammond, District** , Superintendent. **in Charge**

**Key:** Number; NAME: Surname, Given; Sex; Birth Year (if given), Age At Last Birthday; Tribe; Degree of Blood; Marital Status; Relationship To Head of Family; Last Census Roll Number; At Jurisdiction Where Enrolled (Yes or No); At Another Jurisdiction; ELSEWHERE: Post office, County, State; Ward (Yes or No); Allotment, Annuity, and Identification Numbers.

2231; Tah-deyah; M; 16; Navajo; F; S; Nephew; 2249; Yes; Yes; 30523


2232; Capitan-benally; M; 34; Navajo; F; M; Head; 2250; Yes; Yes; 29365
2233; Al-soh-bah; F; 28; Navajo; F; M; Wife; 2251; Yes; Yes; 29366
2234; Chih-naz-bah; F; 10; Navajo; F; S; Daughter; 2252; Yes; Yes; 29367
2235; Kees-chee; M; 8; Navajo; F; S; Son; 2253; Yes; Yes; 29368
2236; Dal-wudt; M; 6; Navajo; F; S; Son; 2254; Yes; Yes; 29369
2237; Shih-nehih; M; 4; Navajo; F; S; Son; 2255; Yes; Yes; 29370


2238; Charley badoni; M; 45; Navajo; F; M; Head; 2256; Yes; Yes; 30975
2239; Charley Bitsih; M[sic]; 34; Navajo; F; M; Wife; 2257; Yes; Yes; 30976
              [Should be female.]
2240; Charley, Edwin; M; 15; Navajo; F; S; Son; 2258; Yes; Yes; 30977
2241; Keyah; M; 11; Navajo; F; S; Son; 2259; Yes; Yes; 30978
2242; Biz-des-bah; F; 6; Navajo; F; S; Daughter; 2260; Yes; Yes; 30979
2243; Wilmer Roberts; M; 23; Navajo; F; S; Brother-in-law; 2262; Yes; Yes; 30981


2244; Charley-bikis; M; 55; Navajo; F; Wd; Head; 2263; Yes; Yes; 31055
2245; Nah-tah-yihl-yiz, Alfred; M; 13; Navajo; F; S; Son; 2264; Yes; Yes; 31056
2246; James Jenson; M; 26; Navajo; F; S; Son; 2265; Yes; Yes; 31233
2247; Haska-nah-nike-Charley Walker; M; 16; Navajo; F; S; Son; 2266; Yes; Yes; 31287


2248; Charley Bitchilli; M; 50; Navajo; F; M; Head; 2267; Yes; Yes; 30763
2249; Bekis-bitsih; F; 42; Navajo; F; M; Wife; 2268; Yes; Yes; 30764
2250; Haska-yee-nel-wudt; M; 19; Navajo; F; S; Son; 2269; Yes; Yes; 30765
2251; Yil-dez-bah, Mary; F; 16; Navajo; F; S; Daughter; 2270; Yes; Yes; 30766
2252; Tah-yazzie; M; 15; Navajo; F; S; Son; 2271; Yes; Yes; 30767
2253; Edd-bah; F; 11; Navajo; F; S; Daughter; 2272; Yes; Yes; 30768
2254; Nah-tah-yil-nah-hah-yah; M; 8; Navajo; F; S; Son; 2273; Yes; Yes; 30769
2255; Nah-glih-kih-nih-bah; F; 6; Navajo; F; S; Daughter; 2274; Yes; Yes; 30770


2256; Charley Bitsoih; M; 43; Navajo; F; M; Head; 2275; Yes; Yes; 32329
2257; Bih-jah-tlol-nih-deal-bitsoih; F; 29; Navajo; F; M; Wife; 2276; Yes; Yes; 32330
2258; Yil-nah-bah; F; 9; Navajo; F; S; Daughter; 2277; Yes; Yes; 32331
2259; Haska-yee-tah-nil-wudt; M; 8; Navajo; F; S; Son; 2278; Yes; Yes; 32332
2260; Yil-nih-bah; F; 4; Navajo; F; S; Daughter; 2279; Yes; Yes; 32333
2261; Gee-bah; F; 20; Navajo; F; S; Daughter; 2280; Yes; Yes; 32334


2262; Charley Buck Bikis; M; 26; Navajo; F; M; Head; 2281; Yes; Yes; 30897
2263; Clah-bekis-bitsih; F; 21; Navajo; F; M; Wife; 2282; Yes; Yes; 30898
2264; Nah-tah-yil-hah-yah; M; 3; Navajo; F; S; Son; 2283; Yes; Yes; 30899

Census of the **Northern Navajo** reservation of the **Northern Navajo** jurisdiction, as of **April 1**, 19**31,** taken by **Ernest H. Hammond, District**, Superintendent. **in Charge**

**Key:** Number; NAME: Surname, Given; Sex; Birth Year (if given), Age At Last Birthday; Tribe; Degree of Blood; Marital Status; Relationship To Head of Family; Last Census Roll Number; At Jurisdiction Where Enrolled (Yes or No); At Another Jurisdiction; ELSEWHERE: Post office, County, State; Ward (Yes or No); Allotment, Annuity, and Identification Numbers.

2265;  Chase, Lee; M; 31; Navajo; F; M; Head; 2284; Yes; Yes; 31041
2266;  Geraldine; F; 29; Navajo; F; M; Wife; 2285; Yes; Yes; 31042
2267;  Chase, Lee Chester; M; 2; Navajo; F; S; Son; 2286; Yes; Yes; 31218

2268;  Chih-chisih-bega; M; 32; Navajo; F; M; Head; 2287; Yes; Yes; 30402
2269;  Dinay-yazzie-bitsih; F; 30; Navajo; F; M; Wife; 2288; Yes; Yes; 30403
2270;  Haska-yil-nas-yee; M; 15; Navajo; F; S; Son; 2289; Yes; Yes; 30404
2271;  Haska-yil-nah-yah; M; 8; Navajo; F; S; Son; 2290; Yes; Yes; 30405
2272;  Glih-hagahn-nih-bah; F; 5; Navajo; F; S; Daughter; 2291; Yes; Yes; 30406
2273;  Haska-hah-kis-wudt; M; 3; Navajo; F; S; Son; 2292; Yes; Yes; 30407

2274;  Chis-chilli-benally; M; 31; Navajo; F; M; Head; 2293; Yes; Yes; 30705
2275;  Beleen-sasih-bitsoin[sic]; F; 20; Navajo; F; M; Wife; 2294; Yes; Yes; 30706
[Name should be Beleen-sasih-bitsoih]
2276;  Nah-ziz-bah; F; 4; Navajo; F; S; Daughter; 2295; Yes; Yes; 30707
2277;  John Jay; M; 18; Navajo; F; S; Brother-in-law; 2296; Yes; Yes; 30708
2278;  Bruce; M; 16; Navajo; F; S; Brother-in-law; 2297; Yes; Yes; 30709
2279;  Zannie-yazzie; F; 14; Navajo; F; S; Sister-in-law; 2298; Yes; Yes; 30710
2280;  Hah-gee-bah; F; 11; Navajo; F; S; Sister-in-law; 2299; Yes; Yes; 30711
2281;  Nah-tah-yil-nih-nih-yah; M; 12; Navajo; F; S; Son; 2300; Yes; Yes; 31242

2282;  Cho-yin-nih-benally-bega; M; Unk; Navajo; F; M; Head; 2301; Yes; Yes; 30819
2283;  Jim Buck's Daughter; F; 21; Navajo; F; M; Wife; 2302; Yes; Yes; 30820
2284;  Al-chih-hah-bah; F; 2; Navajo; F; S; Daughter; 2303; Yes; Yes; 31270

2285;  Cille, Buck; M; 43; Navajo; F; M; Head; 2304; Yes; Yes; 30419
2286;  Adzan-nanl-codih; F; 34; Navajo; F; M; Wife; 2305; Yes; Yes; 30420
2287;  Haska-yil-des-del; M; 19; Navajo; F; S; Son; 2306; Yes; Yes; 30421
2288;  Abe; M; 17; Navajo; F; S; Son; 2307; Yes; Yes; 30422
2289;  Hah-kah-hiz-bah; F; 10; Navajo; F; S; Daughter; 2308; Yes; Yes; 30423
2290;  Haska-yoh-zise; M; 8; Navajo; F; S; Son; 2309; Yes; Yes; 30424
2291;  Tom; M; 5; Navajo; F; S; Son; 2310; Yes; Yes; 30425

2292;  Clah, Billy; M; 47; Navajo; F; M; Head; 998; Yes; Yes; 28015
2293;  Ah-gee-ghaih; F; 35; Navajo; F; M; Wife; 999; Yes; Yes; 28016
2294;  Moffat, Thomas; M; 20; Navajo; F; S; Son; 1000; Yes; Yes; 28017
2295;  Haska-yil-chih-nihyah; M; 15; Navajo; F; S; Son; 1001; Yes; Yes; 28018
2296;  Kayah; M; 12; Navajo; F; S; Son; 1002; Yes; Yes; 28019
2297;  Keh-yil-naz-bah; F; 8; Navajo; F; S; Daughter; 1003; Yes; Yes; 28020
2298;  Deshna-bimah; F; 72; Navajo; F; Wd; Mother; 1004; Yes; Yes; 28021
2299;  Al-kih-nih-bah; F; 15; Navajo; F; S; Niece; 1005; Yes; Yes; 28022
2300;  Nah-glih-yil-nih-bah; F; 10; Navajo; F; S; Niece; 1006; Yes; Yes; 28023

71

Census of the **Northern Navajo** reservation of the **Northern Navajo** jurisdiction, as of **April 1**, 19**31**, taken by **Ernest H. Hammond, District**, Superintendent. **in Charge**

**Key:** Number; NAME: Surname, Given; Sex; Birth Year (if given), Age At Last Birthday; Tribe; Degree of Blood; Marital Status; Relationship To Head of Family; Last Census Roll Number; At Jurisdiction Where Enrolled (Yes or No); At Another Jurisdiction; ELSEWHERE: Post office, County, State; Ward (Yes or No); Allotment, Annuity, and Identification Numbers.

2301;  Clah-badoni; M; Unk; Navajo; F; Wd; Head; 2311; Yes; Yes; 29105
2302;  Haska-yil-nil-wudt; M; 19; Navajo; F; S; Son; 2312; Yes; Yes; 29106
2303;  Lydia; F; 13; Navajo; F; S; Daughter; 2313; Yes; Yes; 29107

2304;  Clah-bikis; M; 46; Navajo; F; Wd; Head; 2314; Yes; Yes; 30890
2305;  Raymond; M; 28; Navajo; F; S; Son; 2315; Yes; Yes; 30891
2306;  Edward; M; 22; Navajo; F; S; Son; 2316; Yes; Yes; 30892
2307;  Tohl; F; 19; Navajo; F; S; Daughter; 2317; Yes; Yes; 30893
2308;  Yee-kih-dah-yah; M; 14; Navajo; F; S; Son; 2318; Yes; Yes; 30894
2309;  Nah-bah; F; 11; Navajo; F; S; Daughter; 2319; Yes; Yes; 30895
2310;  Chih-naz-bah; F; 7; Navajo; F; S; Daughter; 2320; Yes; Yes; 30896

2311;  Clah-cheeny; M; 44; Navajo; F; M; Head; 2321; Yes; Yes; 29941
2312;  Clah-iltsuen-benally; F; 36; Navajo; F; M; Wife; 2322; Yes; Yes; 29942
2313;  Keh-hih-bah, Harriet; F; 20; Navajo; F; S; Step-daughter; 2323; Yes; Yes; 29943
2314;  Waye; M; 12; Navajo; F; S; Son; 2324; Yes; Yes; 29944
2315;  Aaron; M; 10; Navajo; F; S; Son; 2325; Yes; Yes; 29945
2316;  Yah-hah-bah; F; 8; Navajo; F; S; Daughter; 2326; Yes; Yes; 29946
2317;  Bil-naz-nih-bah; F; 6; Navajo; F; S; Daughter; 2327; Yes; Yes; 29947
2318;  Minnie; F; 3; Navajo; F; S; Daughter; 2328; Yes; Yes; 29948

2319;  Clah-chischilli-deshna; M; 39; Navajo; F; M; Head; 2329; Yes; Yes; 30218
2320;  Evelyn; F; 26; Navajo; F; M; Wife; 2330; Yes; Yes; 30219
2321;  Herbert; M; 4; Navajo; F; S; Son; 2331; Yes; Yes; 30220
2322;  Jane Elizabeth; F; 6; Navajo; F; S; Daughter; 2332; Yes; Yes; 30221
2323;  William; M; 3; Navajo; F; S; Son; 2333; Yes; Yes; 30222
2324;  Chih-ih; F; 14; Navajo; F; S; Niece; 2334; Yes; Yes; 30223

2325;  Clah-hah-zoh-bega; M; Unk; Navajo; F; M; Head; 2335; Yes; Yes; 31096
2326;  Hosteen-nah-seeih-benally; F; 52; Navajo; F; M; Wife; 2336; Yes; Yes; 31097
2327;  Dah-nih-yah; M; 20; Navajo; F; S; Son; 2337; Yes; Yes; 31098
2328;  Zonih; M; 18; Navajo; F; S; Son; 2338; Yes; Yes; 31099
2329;  Tah-bah; M; 16; Navajo; F; S; Son; 2339; Yes; Yes; 31100
2330;  Haska-yee-silth; M; 16; Navajo; F; S; Son; 2340; Yes; Yes; 31101
2331;  Bah-gee-bah; F; 11; Navajo; F; S; Daughter; 2341; Yes; Yes; 31102
2332;  Biz-nil-bah; F; 11; Navajo; F; S; Daughter; 2342; Yes; Yes; 31103
2333;  Adzan-lagaih; F; 21; Navajo; F; Div.; Daughter; 2343; Yes; Yes; 31104

2334;  Clah-hah-zoh-benally; F; 28; Navajo; F; Div.; Head; 2344; Yes; Yes; 29850
2335;  Dah-hiz-bah; F; 3; Navajo; F; S; Daughter; 2345; Yes; Yes; 29852

Census of the **Northern Navajo** reservation of the **Northern Navajo** jurisdiction, as of **April 1**, 19**31,** taken by **Ernest H. Hammond, District**, Superintendent. **in Charge**

**Key:** Number; NAME: Surname, Given; Sex; Birth Year (if given), Age At Last Birthday; Tribe; Degree of Blood; Marital Status; Relationship To Head of Family; Last Census Roll Number; At Jurisdiction Where Enrolled (Yes or No); At Another Jurisdiction; ELSEWHERE: Post office, County, State; Ward (Yes or No); Allotment, Annuity, and Identification Numbers.

2336;  Vlsh-iltsuen-bega[sic]; M; 63; Navajo; F; M; Head; 2346; Yes; Yes; 29753
[Name should be Clah-iltsuen-bega]
2337;  Clah-iltsuen-bega's wife; F; 59; Navajo; F; M; Wife; 2347; Yes; Yes; 29754
2338;  Clah-iltsuen-benally; M; 36; Navajo; F; S; Son; 2348; Yes; Yes; 29755
2339;  Ben; M; 24; Navajo; F; S; Son; 2349; Yes; Yes; 29756
2340;  Haska-yee-chih-nah-yah; M; 16; Navajo; F; S; Son; 2350; Yes; Yes; 29757
2341;  Haska-yee-tah-yil-wudt; M; 9; Navajo; F; S; Grand-son; 2351; Yes; Yes;
29758
2342;  Toh-nih-ziz-bah; F; 4; Navajo; F; S; Grand-daughter; 2352; Yes; Yes; 29759
2343;  Henry; M; 8; Navajo; F; S; Grand-son; 2353; Yes; Yes; 29760
2344;  Dah-sahih; M; 57; Navajo; F; S; Brother-in-law; 2354; Yes; Yes; 29761

2345;  Clah-iltsuen-bitsih; F; 55; Navajo; F; Div.; Head; 2355; Yes; Yes; 30685
2346;  Lily; F; 28; Navajo; F; S; Daughter; 2356; Yes; Yes; 30686

2347;  Clah-iltsuen-benally; F; 30; Navajo; F; M; Head; 2357; Yes; Yes; 29847
2348;  Nah-tah-dayah; M; 12; Navajo; F; S; Son; 2358; Yes; Yes; 29848
2349;  Nah-tah-yil-des-wudt; M; 3; Navajo; F; S; Son; 2359; Yes; Yes; 29849

2350;  Clah-zin-bega, Dave; M; 82; Navajo; F; M; Head; 2360; Yes; Yes; 29297
2351;  Al-soh-naz-bah; F; 63; Navajo; F; M; Wife; 2361; Yes; Yes; 29298
2352;  Sam; M; 32; Navajo; F; S; Son; 2362; Yes; Yes; 29299
2353;  Otto; M; 21; Navajo; F; S; Son; 2363; Yes; Yes; 29300
2354;  Eskee-l-bahih; M; 14; Navajo; F; S; Son; 2364; Yes; Yes; 29301
2355;  Mary B; F; 16; Navajo; F; S; Grand-daughter; 2365; Yes; Yes; 29302

2356;  Clash-chee-bega; M; Unk; Navajo; F; M; Head; 2366; Yes; Yes; 32422
2357;  Dinay-chilli-benally; F; 18; Navajo; F; M; Wife; 2367; Yes; Yes; 32423

2358;  Clash-chee-nez-bega; M; 30; Navajo; F; M; Head; 2368; Yes; Yes; 30680
2359;  Aht-citty-benally; F; 30; Navajo; F; M; Wife; 2369; Yes; Yes; 30682
2360;  Nih-ziz-bah; F; 10; Navajo; F; S; Daughter; 2370; Yes; Yes; 30683
2361;  Nah-glih-hahn-bah; F; 8; Navajo; F; S; Daughter; 2371; Yes; Yes; 30684
2362;  Dinay-sosie; M; 5; Navajo; F; S; Son; 2372; Yes; Yes; 30685
2363;  Glih-eebah; F; 2; Navajo; F; S; Daughter; 2373; Yes; Yes; 31259

2364;  Clash-chee-yazzie-badoni; M; 20; Navajo; F; M; Head; 2374; Yes; Yes; 32452
2365;  Al-keh-naz-bah; F; 17; Navajo; F; M; Wife; 2375; Yes; Yes; 32453

2366;  Clash-chee-yazzie-bega; M; 20; Navajo; F; M; Head; 2376; Yes; Yes; 32221
2367;  Blue Eye's daughter; F; 18; Navajo; F; M; Wife; 2377; Yes; Yes; 32222

2368;  Clash-chee-nez; M; 61; Navajo; F; M; Head; 2378; Yes; Yes; 32425

73

Census of the **Northern Navajo** reservation of the **Northern Navajo** jurisdiction, as of **April 1**, 19**31,** taken by **Ernest H. Hammond, District**, Superintendent. **in Charge**

**Key:** Number; NAME: Surname, Given; Sex; Birth Year (if given), Age At Last Birthday; Tribe; Degree of Blood; Marital Status; Relationship To Head of Family; Last Census Roll Number; At Jurisdiction Where Enrolled (Yes or No); At Another Jurisdiction; ELSEWHERE: Post office, County, State; Ward (Yes or No); Allotment, Annuity, and Identification Numbers.

2369; Begus; F; 44; Navajo; F; M; Wife; 2379; Yes; Yes; 32426
2370; Charley Lyman; M; 19; Navajo; F; S; Son; 2380; Yes; Yes; 32427
2371; Glih-ykl-nih-bah[sic]; F; 11; Navajo; F; S; Daughter; 2381; Yes; Yes; 32428
[Name should be Glih-yil-nih-bah]
2372; Nah-tah-yee-tah-des-wudt; M; 7; Navajo; F; S; Son; 2382; Yes; Yes; 32429
2373; Nah-glih-tah-nih-bah; F; 5; Navajo; F; S; Daughter; 2383; Yes; Yes; 32430
2374; Begus, Pearl; F; 7; Navajo; Sister-in-law; 2384; Yes; Yes; 32432
2375; Susan; F; 20; Navajo; F; S; Daughter; 2385; Yes; Yes; 32433
2376; John; M; 19; Navajo; F; S; Son; 2386; Yes; Yes; 32434

2377; Clash-chee-yazzie; M; 44; Navajo; F; M; Head; 2387; Yes; Yes; 32447
2378; Salou-bitsees-chilli-bitsih; F; 36; Navajo; F; M; Wife; 2388; Yes; Yes; 32448
2379; Yazzie-, Philip; M; 13; Navajo; F; S; Son; 2389; Yes; Yes; 32449
2380; Nah-tah-yil-has-wudt; M; 7; Navajo; F; S; Son; 2390; Yes; Yes; 32450
2381; Nah-tah-yil-nal-wudt; M; 5; Navajo; F; S; Son; 2391; Yes; Yes; 32451

2382; Clah-yazzie, Fritz; M; 60; Navajo; F; M; Head; 2392; Yes; Yes; 30236
2383; Aht-citty-benally; F; 19; Navajo; F; M; Wife; 2393; Yes; Yes; 30237

2384; Clash-cheeih-bega, David; M; 27; Navajo; F; M; Head; 2394; Yes; Yes; 27711
2385; Hosteen-sinnih-bitsih; F; 24; Navajo; F; M; Wife; 2395; Yes; Yes; 27712
2386; Tah-dez-bah; F; 7; Navajo; F; S; Daughter; 2396; Yes; Yes; 27713
2387; Bil-nih-ziz-bah; F; 2; Navajo; F; S; Daughter; 2397; Yes; Yes; 27714

2388; Clash-che-ih-bega; M; 37; Navajo; F; M; Head; 2398; Yes; Yes; 27715
2389; Hosteen-sihhin-bitsih; F; 27; Navajo; F; M; Wife; 2399; Yes; Yes; 27716
2390; Glih-yil-haz-bah; F; 11; Navajo; F; S; Daughter; 2400; Yes; Yes; 27717
2391; Nah-tah-yil-hah-yah; M; 7; Navajo; F; S; Son; 2401; Yes; Yes; 27718
2392; Haska-yil-nal-wohl; M; 3; Navajo; F; S; Son; 2402; Yes; Yes; 27719
2393; Hosteen-sinnih; M; 83; Navajo; F; Wd; Father-in-law; 2403; Yes; Yes; 27720

2394; Clah-benally, Horace; M; Unk; Navajo; F; M; Head; 2404; Yes; Yes; 23838
2395; Yee-kih-haz-bah; F; Unk; Navajo; F; M; Wife; 2405; Yes; Yes; 23839
2396; Etah-naz-en-pah; F; 1; Navajo; F; S; Daughter; 2406; Yes; Yes; 23914

2397; Chih-des-bah; F; Unk; Navajo; F; Wd; Head; 2407; Yes; Yes; 21420
2398; Nel-wudt; M; 8; Navajo; F; S; Son; 2408; Yes; Yes; 21421

2399; Clah-nez-bega; M; 24; Navajo; F; M; Head; 2409; Yes; Yes; 23190
2400; Bah; F; 22; Navajo; F; M; Wife; 2410; Yes; Yes; 23191
2401; Jensen; M; 9; Navajo; F; S; Nephew; 2411; Yes; Yes; 23192
2402; Bah-doz-bah; F; 10; Navajo; F; S; Niece; 2412; Yes; Yes; 23193

74

Census of the **Northern Navajo** reservation of the **Northern Navajo** jurisdiction, as of **April 1** , 19**31,** taken by **Ernest H. Hammond, District** , Superintendent. **in Charge**

**Key:** Number; NAME: Surname, Given; Sex; Birth Year (if given), Age At Last Birthday; Tribe; Degree of Blood; Marital Status; Relationship To Head of Family; Last Census Roll Number; At Jurisdiction Where Enrolled (Yes or No); At Another Jurisdiction; ELSEWHERE: Post office, County, State; Ward (Yes or No); Allotment, Annuity, and Identification Numbers.

2403; Cleh-hih-hah-tahly-bitsoih; F; 19; Navajo; F; S; Sister-in-law to Mike Bitah; 2413; Yes; Yes; 23153

2404; Cleveland, Grover; M; 31; Navajo; F; S; Head; 2414; Yes; Yes; 29372

2405; Curley, Nat; M; 28; Navajo; F; M; Head; 2415; Yes; Yes; 31023
2406; Curley, Ora; F; 22; Navajo; F; M; Wife; 2416; Yes; Yes; 31024
2407; Virginia; F; 4; Navajo; F; S; Daughter; 2417; Yes; Yes; 31025
2408; Frances; F; 3; Navajo; F; S; Daughter; 2418; Yes; Yes; 31026
2409; Lee, Henry; M; 21; Navajo; F; S; Brother-in-law; 2419; Yes; Yes; 31027

2410; Charley; M; 70; Navajo; F; M; Head; 2420; Yes; Yes; 32828
2411; Toh-sonie-bitsih; F; 64; Navajo; F; M; Wife; 2421; Yes; Yes; 32829
2412; Glih-yah-dez-bah; F; 19; Navajo; F; S; Grand-daughter; 2422; Yes; Yes; 32830
2413; Nah-tah-yil-chih-nih-yah; M; 12; Navajo; F; S; Grand-son; 2423; Yes; Yes; 32831

2414; Benally-hosteen, Charley; M; 48; Navajo; F; M; Head; 2424; Yes; Yes; 32852
2415; Yazzie-bih-jik-, Charley; F; 22; Navajo; F; S; Wife; 2425; Yes; Yes; 32853
2416; Til-dez-bah; F; 6; Navajo; F; S; Daughter; 2426; Yes; Yes; 32854
2417; Al-kih-nih-bah; F; 2; Navajo; F; S; Daughter; 2427; Yes; Yes; 32855
2418; Haska-yee-tah-yil-wohl; M; 23; Navajo; F; S; Son; 2428; Yes; Yes; 32856
2419; Nah-tah-yee-tah-des-wudt; M; 16; Navajo; F; S; Son; 2429; Yes; Yes; 32857

2420; Clah-lah-bahih-bega-bitah, Harry; M; 30; Navajo; F; M; Head; 2430; Yes; Yes; 20394
2421; Doh-hah-ih-bitsih, Netta; F; 25; Navajo; F; M; Wife; 2431; Yes; Yes; 20395
2422; Nil-wudt; M; 5; Navajo; F; S; Son; 2432; Yes; Yes; 20396
2423; Adzan-bitani; F; 3; Navajo; F; S; Daughter; 2433; Yes; Yes; 20397
2424; Doh-hah-ih-bitsih; F; 23; Navajo; F; M; 2nd Wife; 2434; Yes; Yes; 20398
2425; Glih-bah; F; 2; Navajo; F; S; Daughter; 2435; Yes; Yes; 20399

2426; Clash-chee-bega; M; Unk; Navajo; F; M; Head; 2436; Yes; Yes; 32422
2427; Dinay-chilli-benally; F; 18; Navajo; F; M; Wife; 2437; Yes; Yes; 32423

2428; Chis-chilli-bega; M; 67; Navajo; F; M; Head; 2438; Yes; Yes; 21663
2429; Ya-doz-bah; F; 21; Navajo; F; M; Wife; 2439; Yes; Yes; 21664
2430; As-auz-bah; F; 3; Navajo; F; S; Daughter; 2440; Yes; Yes; 21665
2431; Yih-niz-bah; F; 17; Navajo; F; S; Sister-in-law; 2441; Yes; Yes; 21666

2432; Dinay-sosie; M; 51; Navajo; F; M; Head; 2442; Yes; Yes; 19901
2433; Cudih-yen-bitsih; F; 49; Navajo; F; M; Wife; 2443; Yes; Yes; 19902

Census of the **Northern Navajo** reservation of the **Northern Navajo** jurisdiction, as of **April 1** , 19**31,** taken by **Ernest H. Hammond, District**, Superintendent. **in Charge**

Key: Number; NAME: Surname, Given; Sex; Birth Year (if given), Age At Last Birthday; Tribe; Degree of Blood; Marital Status; Relationship To Head of Family; Last Census Roll Number; At Jurisdiction Where Enrolled (Yes or No); At Another Jurisdiction; ELSEWHERE: Post office, County, State; Ward (Yes or No); Allotment, Annuity, and Identification Numbers.

2434; Dinay-sosie-bega; M; 23; Navajo; F; S; Son; 2444; Yes; Yes; 19903
2435; Posey; M; 21; Navajo; F; S; Son; 2445; Yes; Yes; 19904
2436; Dinay-sosie, Myrtle; F; 17; Navajo; F; S; Daughter; 2446; Yes; Yes; 19905
2437; Dinay-sosie, Grace; F; 15; Navajo; F; S; Daughter; 2447; Yes; Yes; 19906
2438; Dinay-sosie, Myra; F; 11; Navajo; F; S; Daughter; 2448; Yes; Yes; 19907
2439; Casey; M; 7; Navajo; F; S; Son; 2449; Yes; Yes; 19908

2440; Doh-hih-jadkh-bitsih; M; Unk; Navajo; F; M; Head; 2450; Yes; Yes; 20348
2441; Doh-dih-jadih-bitsih's[sic] wife; F; 21; Navajo; F; M; Wife; 2451; Yes; Yes; 20349 [Name is probably Doh-hih-jadih-bitsih's wife]
2442; Haska-yee-onl-wudt; M; 4; Navajo; F; S; Son; 2452; Yes; Yes; 20350
2443; Haska-yil-nas-wudt; M; 3; Navajo; F; S; Son; 2453; Yes; Yes; 20446

2444; David, Silas; M; 27; Navajo; F; M; Head; 2454; No; McElmo, Colo., San Juan, Utah; Yes; 19409
2445; Clah-dih-tholhi-bitsih; F; 23; Navajo; F; M; Wife; 2455; No; McElmo, Colo., San Juan, Utah; Yes; 19410
2446; Eskee-l-bah; M; 7; Navajo; F; S; Son; 2456; No; McElmo, Colo., San Juan, Utah; Yes; 19411

2447; Dinay-etsosie; M; 65; Navajo; F; M; Head; 2457; No; McElmo, Colo., San Juan, Utah; Yes; 19267
2448; Chan-tailly-bitsih; F; 50; Navajo; F; M; Wife; 2458; No; McElmo, Colo., San Juan, Utah; Yes; 19268
2449; Maz-zih; F; 17; Navajo; F; S; Daughter; 2459; No; McElmo, Colo., San Juan, Utah; Yes; 19269
2450; Dinay-etsosie, Mark; M; 14; Navajo; F; S; Son; 2460; No; McElmo, Colo., San Juan, Utah; Yes; 19270
2451; Cha-dee-bah; F; 11; Navajo; F; S; Daughter; 2461; No; McElmo, Colo., San Juan, Utah; Yes; 19271
2452; Yee-chee-has-bah; F; 7; Navajo; F; S; Grand-daughter; 2462; No; McElmo, Colo., San Juan, Utah; Yes; 19272
2453; Adzan-l-bahih; F; 19; Navajo; F; Wd; Daughter; 2463; No; McElmo, Colo., San Juan, Utah; Yes; 19273
2454; Shih-dah; F; 5; Navajo; F; S; Grand-daughter; 2464; No; McElmo, Colo., San Juan, Utah; Yes; 19274

2455; Dagah-chee; M; 42; Navajo; F; M; Head; 2465; No; McElmo, Colo., San Juan, Utah; Yes; 19301
2456; Dagah-chee's wife; F; 43; Navajo; F; M; Wife; 2466; No; McElmo, Colo., San Juan, Utah; Yes; 19302
2457; Dagah-chee bega; M; 24; Navajo; F; S; Son; 2467; No; McElmo, Colo., San Juan, Utah; Yes; 19303

Census of the **Northern Navajo** reservation of the **Northern Navajo** jurisdiction, as of **April 1**, 19**31**, taken by **Ernest H. Hammond, District**, Superintendent. **in Charge**

**Key:** Number; NAME: Surname, Given; Sex; Birth Year (if given), Age At Last Birthday; Tribe; Degree of Blood; Marital Status; Relationship To Head of Family; Last Census Roll Number; At Jurisdiction Where Enrolled (Yes or No); At Another Jurisdiction; ELSEWHERE: Post office, County, State; Ward (Yes or No); Allotment, Annuity, and Identification Numbers.

2458; Chee, Bruce; M; 20; Navajo; F; S; Son; 2468; No; McElmo, Colo., San Juan, Utah; Yes; 19304

2459; Bah; F; 19; Navajo; F; S; Daughter; 2469; No; McElmo, Colo., San Juan, Utah; Yes; 19305

2460; Atate-bis-ah-ahlani; F; 17; Navajo; F; S; Daughter; 2470; No; McElmo, Colo., San Juan, Utah; Yes; 19306

2461; Yee-dah-nih-ha-sah; M; 9; Navajo; F; S; Son; 2471; No; McElmo, Colo., San Juan, Utah; Yes; 19307

2462; Hosteen-nez-bega; M; 26; Navajo; F; S; Half-brother; 2472; No; McElmo, Colo., San Juan, Utah; Yes; 19308

2463; Dagah-lagaih-bega, Bug-eye Bill; M; 48; Navajo; F; Wd; Head; 2473; No; McElmo, Colo., San Juan, Utah; Yes; 19005

2464; Dinay-suen-benally; M; 20; Navajo; F; M; Head; 2474; No; McElmo, Colo., San Juan, Utah; Yes; 19824

2465; Aht-sosie-bega's bitsih; F; 16; Navajo; F; M; Wife; 2475; No; McElmo, Colo., San Juan, Utah; Yes; 19825

2466; Dinay-etsosie-bega, Sam Shorty; M; 26; Navajo; F; M; Head; 2476; No; McElmo, Colo., San Juan, Utah; Yes; 19352

2467; Cudih-yen-bitsih; F; 28; Navajo; F; M; Wife; 2477; No; McElmo, Colo., San Juan, Utah; Yes; 19353

2468; Dahah-lagaih-yen-bega, John; M; 49; Navajo; F; M; Head; 2478; No; McElmo, Colo., San Juan, Utah; Yes; 19237

2469; Hosteen-nes-bitsih; F; 36; Navajo; F; M; Wife; 2479; No; McElmo, Colo., San Juan, Utah; Yes; 19238

2470; Yee-nah-ho-lel; M; 19; Navajo; F; S; Son; 2480; No; McElmo, Colo., San Juan, Utah; Yes; 19239

2471; Tah-zil-de-yah, Albert Rockwell; M; 16; Navajo; F; S; Son; 2481; No; McElmo, Colo., San Juan, Utah; Yes; 19240

2472; Nez-, Oretta; F; 12; Navajo; F; S; Daughter; 2482; No; McElmo, Colo., San Juan, Utah; Yes; 19241

2473; As-wudt; M; 6; Navajo; F; S; Son; 2483; No; McElmo, Colo., San Juan, Utah; Yes; 19242

2474; Bahn-ziz-bah; F; 3; Navajo; F; S; Daughter; 2484; No; McElmo, Colo., San Juan, Utah; Yes; 19243

2475; Haska-yil-nih-wudt; M; 1; Navajo; F; S; Son; 2485; No; McElmo, Colo., San Juan, Utah; Yes; 19528

2476; Dah-yiz-jah-bitsih; F; 37; Navajo; F; Wd; Head; 2486; No; McElmo, Colo., San Juan, Utah; Yes; 18959

Census of the **Northern Navajo** reservation of the **Northern Navajo** jurisdiction, as of **April 1**, 19**31**, taken by **Ernest H. Hammond, District**, Superintendent. **in Charge**

**Key:** Number; NAME: Surname, Given; Sex; Birth Year (if given), Age At Last Birthday; Tribe; Degree of Blood; Marital Status; Relationship To Head of Family; Last Census Roll Number; At Jurisdiction Where Enrolled (Yes or No); At Another Jurisdiction; ELSEWHERE: Post office, County, State; Ward (Yes or No); Allotment, Annuity, and Identification Numbers.

2477; Yah-deyah; M; 10; Navajo; F; S; Son; 2487; No; McElmo, Colo., San Juan, Utah; Yes; 18960

2478; Kee-soh; M; 8; Navajo; F; S; Son; 2488; No; McElmo, Colo., San Juan, Utah; Yes; 18961

2479; Yee-zannie; F; 5; Navajo; F; S; Daughter; 2489; No; McElmo, Colo., San Juan, Utah; Yes; 18962

2480; Dischle-bilah; F; 70; Navajo; F; Wd; Head; 2490; No; McElmo, Colo., San Juan, Utah; Yes; 18930

2481; Dohi-yen-bitsoih; M; 43; Navajo; F; M; Head; 2491; No; McElmo, Colo., San Juan, Utah; Yes; 18916

2482; Nocki-hosteen-bitsih; F; 30; Navajo; F; M; Wife; 2492; No; McElmo, Colo., San Juan, Utah; Yes; 18917

2483; Yee-gon-bahih; F; 7; Navajo; F; S; Daughter; 2493; No; McElmo, Colo., San Juan, Utah; Yes; 18918

2484; Zan-bahih; F; 4; Navajo; F; S; Daughter; 2494; No; McElmo, Colo., San Juan, Utah; Yes; 18919

2485; Wallace; M; 3; Navajo; F; S; Son; 2495; No; McElmo, Colo., San Juan, Utah; Yes; 18920

2486; Dohi-yen-bega; M; 38; Navajo; F; M; Head; 2496; No; McElmo, Colo., San Juan, Utah; Yes; 18912

2487; Nocki-hosteen-bitsih; F; 28; Navajo; F; M; Wife; 2497; No; McElmo, Colo., San Juan, Utah; Yes; 18913

2488; Bahn-yis-bah; F; 6; Navajo; F; S; Daughter; 2498; No; McElmo, Colo., San Juan, Utah; Yes; 18914

2489; Dinay-soh; M; 3; Navajo; F; S; Son; 2499; No; McElmo, Colo., San Juan, Utah; Yes; 18915

2490; Dinay-uienth-nezzi-conn; M; 27; Navajo; F; M; Head; 2500; Yes; Yes; 20195
2491; Badih; F; 26; Navajo; F; M; Wife; 2501; Yes; Yes; 20196

2492; Dinay-al-seesih; M; 61; Navajo; F; M; Head; 2502; Yes; Yes; 22365
2493; Nah-cheeny-benelly[sic]; F; 46; Navajo; F; M; Wife; 2503; Yes; Yes; 22366
[Name should be Nah-cheeny-benally]

2494; Dinay-sosie-benally; M; 28; Navajo; F; M; Head; 2504; Yes; Yes; 22360
2495; Nah-glih-kar-nah-bah; F; 23; Navajo; F; M; Wife; 2505; Yes; Yes; 22361
2496; Nah-tah-yee-nayah; M; 7; Navajo; F; S; Son; 2506; Yes; Yes; 22362
2497; Chih-ne-nih-bah; F; 6; Navajo; F; S; Daughter; 2507; Yes; Yes; 22363
2498; Nah-tah-yah-dah-dolin; M; 4; Navajo; F; S; Son; 2508; Yes; Yes; 22791

Census of the **Northern Navajo** reservation of the **Northern Navajo** jurisdiction, as of **April 1**, 1931, taken by **Ernest H. Hammond, District**, Superintendent.                                            **in Charge**

**Key:** Number; NAME: Surname, Given; Sex; Birth Year (if given), Age At Last Birthday; Tribe; Degree of Blood; Marital Status; Relationship To Head of Family; Last Census Roll Number; At Jurisdiction Where Enrolled (Yes or No); At Another Jurisdiction; ELSEWHERE: Post office, County, State; Ward (Yes or No); Allotment, Annuity, and Identification Numbers.

2499;  Dinay-yazzie-bega; M; 44; Navajo; F; M; Head; 2509; Yes; Yes; 22321
2500;  Yil-hah-nas-bah; F; 28; Navajo; F; M; Wife; 2510; Yes; Yes; 22322
2501;  Chee; M; 5; Navajo; F; S; Son; 2511; Yes; Yes; 22323
2502;  Nah-tah-nih-bah; F; 2; Navajo; F; S; Daughter; 2512; Yes; Yes; 22792

2503;  Descheeny-benally; M; 27; Navajo; F; M; Head; 2513; Yes; Yes; 23487
2504;  Glih-hah-nih-bah; F; 28; Navajo; F; M; Wife; 2514; Yes; Yes; 23488
2505;  Edith; F; Unk; Navajo; F; S; Sister-in-law; 2515; Yes; Yes; 23489
2506;  Alvin; M; 21; Navajo; F; S; Brother-in-law; 2516; Yes; Yes; 23490

2507;  Doh-haih-in-bih-adzan; F; 59; Navajo; F; Wd; Head; 2517; Yes; Yes; 21233
2508;  Dah-nas-bah; F; 13; Navajo; F; S; Daughter; 2518; Yes; Yes; 21234

2509;  Dinay-nez; M; 83; Navajo; F; M; Head; 2519; Yes; Yes; 21176
2510;  Ah-hih-dee-bah; F; 12; Navajo; F; S; Great-Grand-Daughter; 2520; Yes; Yes; 21178
2511;  Hoska-yil-nih-yah, John; M; 23; Navajo; F; S; Grand-son; 2521; Yes; Yes; 21179

2512;  Dah-toh-badoni, John; M; Unk; Navajo; F; M; Head; 2522; Yes; Yes; 21338
2513;  Dah-toh, Sarah; F; 25; Navajo; F; M; Wife; 2523; Yes; Yes; 21339
2514;  Linee-bah, Helen; F; 3; Navajo; F; S; Daughter; 2524; Yes; Yes; 21726

2515;  Dinay-suen; M; Unk; Navajo; F; M; Head; 2525; Yes; Yes; 17183
2516;  Dinay-suen Bihadzanih; F; 43; Navajo; F; M; 2526; Wife; Yes; Yes; 17184
2517;  Cogghall, Harold; M; 26; Navajo; F; S; Son; 2527; Yes; Yes; 17185
2518;  Dinay-suen-bega; M; 22; Navajo; F; S; Son; 2528; Yes; Yes; 17186
2519;  Dinay-suen-adzanih; F; 20; Navajo; F; S; Daughter; 2529; Yes; Yes; 17187
2520;  Dinay-suen Jay-yilth-hah-pah; F; 9; Navajo; F; S; Daughter; 2530; Yes; Yes; 17188
2521;  Dinay-suen Laaz; M; 18; Navajo; F; S; Son; 2531; Yes; Yes; 17189
2522;  Larry; M; 15; Navajo; F; S; Son; 2532; Yes; Yes; 17190
2523;  Amos; M; 13; Navajo; F; S; Son; 2533; Yes; Yes; 17191
2524;  Dinay-suen-clish-bah; F; 7; Navajo; F; S; Daughter; 2534; Yes; Yes; 17192
2525;  Dinay-suen- Tah-no-bah; F; 5; Navajo; F; S; Daughter; 2535; Yes; Yes; 17193
2526;  Lukaih-hosteen-bega; M; 25; Navajo; F; S; Brother-in-law; 2536; Yes; Yes; 17200

2527;  Dil-a-wosh-ih-benally-bega; M; 27; Navajo; F; M; Head; 2537; Yes; Yes; 20965
2528;  En-clah-ihgi-bitsih; F; 25; Navajo; F; M; Wife; 2538; Yes; Yes; 20966
2529;  Hah-naz-bah; F; 7; Navajo; F; S; Daughter; 2539; Yes; Yes; 20967
2530;  Hoska-yil-has-wudt; M; 3; Navajo; F; S; Son; 2540; Yes; Yes; 20968

Census of the **Northern Navajo** reservation of the **Northern Navajo** jurisdiction, as of **April 1**, 19**31**, taken by **Ernest H. Hammond, District**, Superintendent. **in Charge**

**Key:** Number; NAME: Surname, Given; Sex; Birth Year (if given), Age At Last Birthday; Tribe; Degree of Blood; Marital Status; Relationship To Head of Family; Last Census Roll Number; At Jurisdiction Where Enrolled (Yes or No); At Another Jurisdiction; ELSEWHERE: Post office, County, State; Ward (Yes or No); Allotment, Annuity, and Identification Numbers.

2531;  Charley Yazzie; M; 2; Navajo; F; S; Son; 2541; Yes; Yes; 21687

2532;  Dee-clayt-soh; M; 62; Navajo; F; M; Head; 2542; Yes; Yes; 19938
2533;  Ah-glani-bitsih; F; 43; Navajo; F; M; Wife; 2543; Yes; Yes; 19939
2534;  Dee-clayt-soh, Carmelita; F; 25; Navajo; F; S; Daughter; 2544; Yes; Yes; 19940
2535;  Dee-clayt-soh, Margaret; F; 15; Navajo; F; S; Daughter; 2545; Yes; Yes; 19941
2536;  Dee-clayt-soh, Taft; M; 13; Navajo; F; S; Son; 2546; Yes; Yes; 19942
2537;  Dee-clayt-soh, Ella; F; 10; Navajo; F; S; Daughter; 2547; Yes; Yes; 19943
2538;  Yah-des-wudt, Thomas; F[sic]; 5; Navajo; F; S; Son; 2548; Yes; Yes; 19944
         [Should be male.]

2539;  Dinay-nez-badoni; M; 44; Navajo; F; M; Head; 2549; Yes; Yes; 21180
2540;  Dinay-nez-bitsih; F; 29; Navajo; F; M; Wife; 2550; Yes; Yes; 21181
2541;  Dah-nas-bah; F; 17; Navajo; F; S; Daughter; 2551; Yes; Yes; 21182
2542;  Hoska-yoh-tah; M; 9; Navajo; F; S; Son; 2552; Yes; Yes; 21183
2543;  Hoska-yee-nah-galh; M; 7; Navajo; F; S; Son; 2553; Yes; Yes; 21184
2544;  Dah-des-bah; F; 6; Navajo; F; S; Daughter; 2554; Yes; Yes; 21185
2545;  Yee-dah-des-bah; F; 1; Navajo; F; S; Daughter; 2555; Yes; Yes; 21711

2546;  Doh-dih-jadi-bitah; M; Unk; Navajo; F; M; Head; 2556; Yes; Yes; 17035
2547;  Dipboy-la-chee-bega's daughter; F; 21; Navajo; F; M; Wife; 2557; Yes; Yes; 17036
2548;  Donald; M; 1; Navajo; F; S; Son; 2558; Yes; Yes; 17413

2549;  Descheeny-yazzie; M; 53; Navajo; F; M; Head; 2559; Yes; Yes; 17154
2550;  Ahtsani-bega-bitsih; F; 53; Navajo; F; M; Wife; 2560; Yes; Yes; 17155
2551;  Woot-gate-woot; M; 25; Navajo; F; S; Son; 2561; Yes; Yes; 17156
2552;  Hoska-yeecheen-hoss-wudt; M; 23; Navajo; F; S; Son; 2562; Yes; Yes; 17157
2553;  Descheeny-deswoody; M; 17; Navajo; F; S; Son; 2563; Yes; Yes; 17158
2554;  Descheeny Ah-ha-ease-bah; M; 15; Navajo; F; S; Son; 2564; Yes; Yes; 17159
2555;  Descheeny, Ray; M; 13; Navajo; F; S; Son; 2565; Yes; Yes; 17160
2556;  Descheeny Dayah; M; 11; Navajo; F; S; Son; 2566; Yes; Yes; 17161
2557;  Descheeny Keeyah; M; 9; Navajo; F; S; Son; 2567; Yes; Yes; 17162

2558;  Descheeny-ahtcity-bega; M; 48; Navajo; F; M; Head; 2568; Yes; Yes; 17883
2559;  Atate-l-chee; F; 25; Navajo; F; M; Wife; 2569; Yes; Yes; 17884
2560;  Dinay-l-pahih; M; 8; Navajo; F; S; Son; 2570; Yes; Yes; 17885
2561;  Natah-yeetah-deyah; M; 5; Navajo; F; S; Son; 2571; Yes; Yes; 17886
2562;  Natah-yilth-deyah; M; 3; Navajo; F; S; Son; 2572; Yes; Yes; 17887

Census of the **Northern Navajo** reservation of the **Northern Navajo** jurisdiction, as of **April 1**, 19**31,** taken by **Ernest H. Hammond, District**, Superintendent. **in Charge**

**Key:** Number; NAME: Surname, Given; Sex; Birth Year (if given), Age At Last Birthday; Tribe; Degree of Blood; Marital Status; Relationship To Head of Family; Last Census Roll Number; At Jurisdiction Where Enrolled (Yes or No); At Another Jurisdiction; ELSEWHERE: Post office, County, State; Ward (Yes or No); Allotment, Annuity, and Identification Numbers.

2563; Dil-a-wash-ih-benally, Slim; M; 43; Navajo; F; M; Head; 2573; Yes; Yes; 20951
2564; Chas-chee-bitsih; F; 42; Navajo; F; M; Wife; 2574; Yes; Yes; 20952
2565; Nah-tah-yee-nas-wudt; M; 14; Navajo; F; S; Son; 2575; Yes; Yes; 20953
2566; Clit-sohoh; M; 13; Navajo; F; S; Son; 2576; Yes; Yes; 20954
2567; Kay-yil-nas-bah; F; 11; Navajo; F; S; Daughter; 2577; Yes; Yes; 20955
2568; Tah-bah; F; 9; Navajo; F; S; Daughter; 2578; Yes; Yes; 20956
2569; Nih-jih-bah; F; 5; Navajo; F; S; Daughter; 2579; Yes; Yes; 20957
2570; Glih-yil-nah-bah; F; 3; Navajo; F; S; Daughter; 2580; Yes; Yes; 20958

2571; Descheeny-ahtcity; M; 88; Navajo; F; M; Head; 2581; Yes; Yes; 17304
2572; Descheeny-ahtcity's wife; F; 78; Navajo; F; M; Wife; 2582; Yes; Yes; 17305
2573; Descheeny-ahtcity Tahus-eah; F; 16; Navajo; F; S; Grand-daughter; 2583; Yes; Yes; 17306

2574; Dinay-yazzie-bega; M; 26; Navajo; F; M; Head; 2584; Yes; Yes; 20948
2575; Bih-bayee-yen-bitsih; F; 23; Navajo; F; M; Wife; 2585; Yes; Yes; 20949
2576; Dinay-yazzie-benally; M; 3; Navajo; F; S; Son; 2586; Yes; Yes; 20950

2577; Glih-hah-bah; F; 58; Navajo; F; Wd; Head; 2587; Yes; Yes; 21332
2578; Batoni-yazzie; M; 30; Navajo; F; S; Son; 2588; Yes; Yes; 21333
2579; Nah-glih-yil-ee-bah; F; 22; Navajo; F; S; Step-daughter; 2589; Yes; Yes; 21334
2580; Custer; M; 16; Navajo; F; S; Grand-son; 2590; Yes; Yes; 21335
2581; Tah-hoas-bah; F; 11; Navajo; F; S; Grand-daughter; 2591; Yes; Yes; 21336
2582; Hoska-nal-wudt-ih; M; 8; Navajo; F; S; Grand-son; 2592; Yes; Yes; 21337

2583; Descheeny; M; 33; Navajo; F; M; Head; 2593; Yes; Yes; 17116
2584; Top-a-hah-yazzie-bitsih; F; 35; Navajo; F; M; Wife; 2594; Yes; Yes; 17117
2585; Descheeny, Carrie; F; 14; Navajo; F; S; Daughter; 2595; Yes; Yes; 17118
2586; Descheeny Dinay-nih-wudt; M; 11; Navajo; F; S; Daughter; 2596; Yes; Yes; 17119
2587; Descheeny-bah; F; 9; Navajo; F; S; Daughter; 2597; Yes; Yes; 17120
2588; Descheeny Nih-gee-pah; F; 7; Navajo; F; S; Daughter; 2598; Yes; Yes; 17121
2589; Descheeny Neshaih-yazzie; M; 4; Navajo; F; S; Daughter[sic]; 2599; Yes; Yes; 17122                    [Should be male.]

2590; Dipboy-lagaih-badoni, Joe; M; 24; Navajo; F; M; Head; 2600; Yes; Yes; 18015
2591; Dipboy-lagaih-bitsih; F; 30; Navajo; F; M; Wife; 2601; Yes; Yes; 18016
2592; White-sheep, Desche; F; 14; Navajo; F; S; Daughter; 2602; Yes; Yes; 18017
2593; White Sheep[sic], Lewis; M; 12; Navajo; F; S; Son; 2603; Yes; Yes; 18018
[Name could be White-sheep, Lewis]

Census of the __Northern Navajo__ reservation of the __Northern Navajo__ jurisdiction, as of __April 1__ , 1931, taken by __Ernest H. Hammond, District__, Superintendent. __in Charge__

Key: Number; NAME: Surname, Given; Sex; Birth Year (if given), Age At Last Birthday; Tribe; Degree of Blood; Marital Status; Relationship To Head of Family; Last Census Roll Number; At Jurisdiction Where Enrolled (Yes or No); At Another Jurisdiction; ELSEWHERE: Post office, County, State; Ward (Yes or No); Allotment, Annuity, and Identification Numbers.

2594; Desbah; F; 7; Navajo; F; S; Daughter; 2604; Yes; Yes; 18019
2595; White-sheep, Mark; M; 5; Navajo; F; S; Son; 2605; Yes; Yes; 18020
2596; Natoni-yazzie; M; 3; Navajo; F; S; Son; 2606; Yes; Yes; 18021
2597; White Sheep[sic], Luke; F; 2; Navajo; F; S; Daughter; 2607; Yes; Yes; 18271
[Name could be White-sheep, Luke]

2598; Dipboy Chee; M; 77; Navajo; F; M; Head; 2608; Yes; Yes; 17278
2599; Dipboy Chee Bihadzanih; F; 77; Navajo; F; M; Wife; 2609; Yes; Yes; 17279
2600; Tony-Yazzie Shonie; F; 10; Navajo; F; S; Great-Grand-daughter; 2610; Yes; Yes; 17280

2601; Dagah-soh-oh-bega; M; Unk; Navajo; F; M; Head; 2611; No; Bluff, Utah, San Juan, Utah; Yes; 28851
2602; Zahn-bah; F; 25; Navajo; F; M; Wife; 2612; No; Bluff, Utah, San Juan, Utah; Yes; 28852
2603; Baih; M; 11; Navajo; F; S; Daughter[sic]; 2613; No; Bluff, Utah, San Juan, Utah; Yes; 28853          [Should be male.]
2604; Nah-glih-nih; F; 7; Navajo; F; S; Daughter; 2614; No; Bluff, Utah, San Juan, Utah; Yes; 28854
2605; Al-nah-gee-bah; F; 5; Navajo; F; S; Daughter; 2615; No; Bluff, Utah, San Juan, Utah; Yes; 28855
2606; Baby; [F]; 1; Navajo; F; S; [Daughter]; 2616; No; Bluff, Utah, San Juan, Utah; Yes; 28558

2607; Dagah-sohoh-bega; M; 30; Navajo; F; M; Head; 2617; No; Bluff, San Juan, Utah; Yes; 28863
2608; Beleen-lagaih-bitsih; F; 27; Navajo; F; M; Wife; 2618; No; Bluff, San Juan, Utah; Yes; 28864
2609; Al-chih-naz-bah; F; 9; Navajo; F; S; Daughter; 2619; No; Bluff, San Juan, Utah; Yes; 28865
2610; Nah-glih-yil-hah-bah; F; 7; Navajo; F; S; Daughter; 2620; No; Bluff, San Juan, Utah; Yes; 28866
2611; Kah-has-bah; F; 3; Navajo; F; S; Daughter; 2621; No; Bluff, San Juan, Utah; Yes; 28867

2612; Doh-dih-jadi-bih-jaykay; F; 30; Navajo; F; Wd; Head; 2622; Yes; Yes; 17286
2613; Doh-dih-jadi, Awa etsosie; F; 8; Navajo; F; S; Daughter; 2623; Yes; Yes; 17287
2614; Doh-dih-jadi-yah-ah-no-bah; F; 6; Navajo; F; S; Daughter; 2624; Yes; Yes; 17288
2615; Doh-dih-jadi Sinn-sah-cahnih; M; 3; Navajo; F; S; Son; 2625; Yes; Yes; 17289

Census of the **Northern Navajo** reservation of the **Northern Navajo** jurisdiction, as of **April 1**, 19**31**, taken by **Ernest H. Hammond, District**, Superintendent. **in Charge**

**Key:** Number; NAME: Surname, Given; Sex; Birth Year (if given), Age At Last Birthday; Tribe; Degree of Blood; Marital Status; Relationship To Head of Family; Last Census Roll Number; At Jurisdiction Where Enrolled (Yes or No); At Another Jurisdiction; ELSEWHERE: Post office, County, State; Ward (Yes or No); Allotment, Annuity, and Identification Numbers.

2616; Dohi-benally; M; 29; Navajo; F; M; Head; 2626; Yes; Yes; 17265
2617; Chilli-hahtah; F; 39; Navajo; F; M; Wife; 2627; Yes; Yes; 17266
2618; Dohi-Ahkintlh-bah; F; 11; Navajo; F; S; Daughter; 2628; Yes; Yes; 17267
2619; Dohi-yilth-ha-ha-nilth; F; 9; Navajo; F; S; Daughter; 2629; Yes; Yes; 17268
2620; Dohi, Nah-blee-yista; F; 8; Navajo; F; S; Daughter; 2630; Yes; Yes; 17269
2621; Yih-kah-hah; F; 2; Navajo; F; S; Daughter; 2631; Yes; Yes; 20437

2622; Descheeny-bega; M; 29; Navajo; F; M; Head; 2632; Yes; Yes; 17310
2623; Destsah-benally; F; 29; Navajo; F; M; Wife; 2633; Yes; Yes; 17311
2624; Descheeny-eskee-pahih; M; 11; Navajo; F; S; Son; 2634; Yes; Yes; 17312
2625; Descheeny Hays-bah; F; 6; Navajo; F; S; Daughter; 2635; Yes; Yes; 17313
2626; Descheeny, John; M; 4; Navajo; F; S; Son; 2636; Yes; Yes; 17314
2627; Toh-dih-kozie, David; M; 20; Navajo; F; S; Cousin; 2637; Yes; Yes; 17315

2628; Dipboy-la-chee-bega; M; Unk; Navajo; F; M; Head; 2638; Yes; Yes; 17030
2629; Sinn-sah-cadnih-bitsih; F; 38; Navajo; F; M; Wife; 2639; Yes; Yes; 17031
2630; Adzanih-suie; F; 15; Navajo; F; S; Daughter; 2640; Yes; Yes; 17032
2631; Dipboy-lachee-bega's[sic] son (Eskie); M; 9; Navajo; F; S; Son; 2641; Yes; Yes; 17033
2632; Adzanih-fohly; F; 3; Navajo; F; S; Daughter; 2642; Yes; Yes; 17034

2633; Dohi-bega's Stepson; M; 30; Navajo; F; M; Head; 2643; Yes; Yes; 18022
2634; Askan-yazzie-bega-bitsih; F; 22; Navajo; F; M; Wife; 2644; Yes; Yes; 18023
2635; Eskee-chee; M; 4; Navajo; F; S; Son; 2645; Yes; Yes; 18024

2636; Dinay-yazzie, Shorty; M; 26; Navajo; F; M; Head; 2646; Yes; Yes; 18043
2637; Bith-nas-nih-bah; F; 24; Navajo; F; M; Wife; 2647; Yes; Yes; 18044
2638; Chee; M; 29; Navajo; F; S; Step-son; 2648; Yes; Yes; 18045
2639; Kee-sosie; M; 4; Navajo; F; S; Son; 2649; Yes; Yes; 18046

2640; Dipboy-lagaih, White-sheep; M; 62; Navajo; F; M; Head; 2650; Yes; Yes; 18172
2641; Bis-ah-ahlanih-bitsih; F; 58; Navajo; F; M; Wife; 2651; Yes; Yes; 18173
2642; Ahsh-ih-ih; M; 22; Navajo; F; S; Son; 2652; Yes; Yes; 18174
2643; Bis-ah-ahlanih-bitsoih; F; 28; Navajo; F; Wd; Daughter; 2653; Yes; Yes; 18175
2644; Adzanih-yazzie; F; 14; Navajo; F; S; Step-grand daughter; 2654; Yes; Yes; 18176
2645; Awa-etseesih; F; 4; Navajo; F; S; Step-grand daughter; 2655; Yes; Yes; 18177

2646; Dip-boy-lazin; M; 41; Navajo; F; M; Head; 2656; Yes; Yes; 17943
2647; Dip-boy-lazin's wife; F; 25; Navajo; F; M; Wife; 2657; Yes; Yes; 17944
2648; Hoskee-soh; M; 8; Navajo; F; S; Son; 2658; Yes; Yes; 17945

Census of the **Northern Navajo** reservation of the **Northern Navajo** jurisdiction, as of **April 1** , 19**31,** taken by **Ernest H. Hammond, District** , Superintendent. **in Charge**

**Key:** Number; NAME: Surname, Given; Sex; Birth Year (if given), Age At Last Birthday; Tribe; Degree of Blood; Marital Status; Relationship To Head of Family; Last Census Roll Number; At Jurisdiction Where Enrolled (Yes or No); At Another Jurisdiction; ELSEWHERE: Post office, County, State; Ward (Yes or No); Allotment, Annuity, and Identification Numbers.

2649;   Awa-chee; F; 6; Navajo; F; S; Daughter; 2659; Yes; Yes; 17946


2650;   Descheeny; M; Unk; Navajo; F; M; Head; 2660; Yes; Yes; 17022
2651;   Sinn-sah-dadnih-soh-bitsih; F; 41; Navajo; F; M; Wife; 2661; Yes; Yes; 17023
2652;   Descheeny, Benton; M; 12; Navajo; F; S; Son; 2662; Yes; Yes; 17024
2653;   Descheeny Adzanih-pohih; F; 4; Navajo; F; S; Daughter; 2663; Yes; Yes; 17025


2654;   Dogah-chee; M; 43; Navajo; F; M; Head; 2664; Yes; Yes; 17319
2655;   Hosteen-soh-bitsih; F; 53; Navajo; F; M; Wife; 2665; Yes; Yes; 17320
2656;   Dogah-chee-adzan-yazzie; F; 18; Navajo; F; S; Daughter; 2666; Yes; Yes; 17321
2657;   Dogah-chee-adzan, Nez; M; 16; Navajo; F; S; Son; 2667; Yes; Yes; 17322
2658;   Dogah-chee-adzan, Sosie; F; 13; Navajo; F; S; Daughter; 2668; Yes; Yes; 17323
2659;   Dogah-chee, Joe; M; 11; Navajo; F; S; Son; 2669; Yes; Yes; 17324


2660;   Dohi-Bega-toh-dis; M; 59; Navajo; F; M; Head; 2670; Yes; Yes; 17252
2661;   Descheeny-ahtcity-bitsih; F; 60; Navajo; F; M; Wife; 2671; Yes; Yes; 17253
2662;   Dohi-benally; M; 22; Navajo; F; S; Son; 2672; Yes; Yes; 17254
2663;   Dohi-benally; F; 19; Navajo; F; S; Daughter; 2673; Yes; Yes; 17255
2664;   Toh-dish-clish-had-desbah; F; 18; Navajo; F; S; Daughter; 2674; Yes; Yes; 17256
2665;   Toh-dish-clish, Ashih-Etsosie; M; 16; Navajo; F; S; Son; 2675; Yes; Yes; 17257
2666;   Toh-dish-clish, Peter; M; 13; Navajo; F; S; Son; 2676; Yes; Yes; 17258
2667;   Toh-dish-clish, Oskee-sosie; M; 11; Navajo; F; S; Son; 2677; Yes; Yes; 17259
2668;   Toh-dish-clish- Had-delth-bahih; F; 12; Navajo; F; S; Daughter; 2678; Yes; Yes; 17260


2669;   Descheeny-atcitty-bega; M; Unk; Navajo; F; M; Head; 2679; Yes; Yes; 17066
2670;   Adzanih-suie; F; Unk; Navajo; F; M; Wife; 2680; Yes; Yes; 17067
2671;   Dohopah; F; 17; Navajo; F; S; Step-daughter; 2681; Yes; Yes; 17068
2672;   Boy; M; Unk; Navajo; F; S; Step-son; 2682; Yes; Yes; 17069


2673;   Dagah-soh-oh-bega; M; 28; Navajo; F; M; Head; 2683; No; Bluff, Utah, San Juan, Utah; Yes; 28875
2674;   Toh-dil-yil-bitsih; F; 54; Navajo; F; M; Wife; 2684; No; Bluff, Utah, San Juan, Utah; Yes; 28876
2675;   Oscar; M; 14; Navajo; F; S; Son; 2685; No; Bluff, Utah, San Juan, Utah; Yes; 28877
2676;   Oskee-soh; M; 9; Navajo; F; S; Son; 2686; No; Bluff, San Juan, Utah; Yes; 28878

Census of the __Northern Navajo__ reservation of the __Northern Navajo__ jurisdiction, as of __April 1__, 19**31,** taken by __Ernest H. Hammond, District__, Superintendent. __in Charge__

Key: Number; NAME: Surname, Given; Sex; Birth Year (if given), Age At Last Birthday; Tribe; Degree of Blood; Marital Status; Relationship To Head of Family; Last Census Roll Number; At Jurisdiction Where Enrolled (Yes or No); At Another Jurisdiction; ELSEWHERE: Post office, County, State; Ward (Yes or No); Allotment, Annuity, and Identification Numbers.

2677; Dagah-sohoh; M; 79; Navajo; F; M; Head; 2687; No; Bluff, San Juan, Utah; Yes; 28872
2678; Dagah-sohoh's wife; F; 62; Navajo; F; M; Wife; 2688; No; Bluff, San Juan, Utah; Yes; 28873
2679; Unknown; M; 14; Navajo; F; S; Grand-son; 2689; No; Bluff, San Juan, Utah; Yes; 28874

2680; Dinay-suen-bitcilli; M; 40; Navajo; F; M; Head; 2690; Yes; Yes; 17194
2681; Dinay-suen-bitcilli's step-daughter; F; 27; Navajo; F; M; Wife; 2691; Yes; Yes; 17195
2682; Andson; M; 10; Navajo; F; S; Son; 2692; Yes; Yes; 17196
2683; Dinay-suen-bitcilli's son; M; 8; Navajo; F; S; Son; 2693; Yes; Yes; 17197
2684; Gathih; M; 6; Navajo; F; S; Son; 2694; Yes; Yes; 17198
2685; Sohih; M; 5; Navajo; F; S; Son; 2695; Yes; Yes; 17199
2686; Walter; M; 2; Navajo; F; S; Son; 2696; Yes; Yes; 16406

2687; Dinay-suen-benally, Tom; M; 38; Navajo; F; M; Head; 2697; Yes; Yes 26205
2688; Irene; F; 29; Navajo; F; M; Wife; 2698; Yes; Yes 26206
2689; Nah-bah, Lucy; F; 21; Navajo; F; S; Niece-in-law; 2699; Yes; Yes 26207

2690; Dinay-dih-joely; M; 60; Navajo; F; M; Head; 2700; Yes; Yes 26274
2691; Tah-nih-bah; F; 61; Navajo; F; M; Wife; 2701; Yes; Yes 26275
2692; Haska-yee-yil-wohl; M; 20; Navajo; F; S; Son; 2702; Yes; Yes 26276

2693; Dinay-dih-joely-bega; M; 25; Navajo; F; M; Head; 2703; Yes; Yes; 26294
2694; Yee-kaz-bah; F; 27; Navajo; F; M; Wife; 2704; Yes; Yes; 26295
2695; Nah-tah; M; 9; Navajo; F; S; Son; 2705; Yes; Yes; 26296
2696; Tah-nih-bah; F; 7; Navajo; F; S; Daughter; 2706; Yes; Yes; 26297
2697; Yee-zoz-bah; F; 2; Navajo; F; S; Daughter; 2707; Yes; Yes; 26443

2698; Dinay-l-suen, Sam; M; 40; Navajo; F; M; Head; 2708; Yes; Yes; 26324
2699; Dinay-l-suen's wife, Sam; F; 33; Navajo; F; M; Wife; 2709; Yes; Yes; 26325
2700; Harriet; F; 19; Navajo; F; S; Daughter; 2710; Yes; Yes; 26326
2701; Leonard; M; 18; Navajo; F; S; Son; 2711; Yes; Yes; 26327
2702; Harry; M; 14; Navajo; F; S; Son; 2712; Yes; Yes; 26328
2703; Ira; M; 7; Navajo; F; S; Son; 2713; Yes; Yes; 26329
2704; Dennis; M; 3; Navajo; F; S; Son; 2714; Yes; Yes; 26330
2705; Clah, John; M; 30; Navajo; F; S; Cousin; 2715; Yes; Yes; 26331

2706; Dinay-lah-gaih-yen-bega; M; 28; Navajo; F; M; Head; 2716; Yes; Yes; 26339
2707; Hah-dez-bah; F; 20; Navajo; F; M; Wife; 2717; Yes; Yes; 26340
2708; Arthur, Harry; M; 24; Navajo; F; S; Brother-in-law; 2718; Yes; Yes; 26341

Census of the **Northern Navajo** reservation of the **Northern Navajo** jurisdiction, as of **April 1**, 19**31,** taken by **Ernest H. Hammond, District**, Superintendent. **in Charge**

**Key:** Number; NAME: Surname, Given; Sex; Birth Year (if given), Age At Last Birthday; Tribe; Degree of Blood; Marital Status; Relationship To Head of Family; Last Census Roll Number; At Jurisdiction Where Enrolled (Yes or No); At Another Jurisdiction; ELSEWHERE: Post office, County, State; Ward (Yes or No); Allotment, Annuity, and Identification Numbers.

2709;  Ass-woody-yazzie; M; 19; Navajo; F; S; Brother-in-law; 2719; Yes; Yes; 26342

2710;  Has-woody; M; 2; Navajo; F; S; Son; 2720; Yes; Yes; 26439

2711;  Nas-wudt; M; 1; Navajo; F; S; Son; 2721; Yes; Yes; 26440

2712;  Dinay-deel-bega; M; 37; Navajo; F; M; Head; 2722; Yes; Yes; 26360

2713;  Yil-dez-bah; F; 29; Navajo; F; M; Wife; 2723; Yes; Yes; 26361

2714;  Roger; M; 9; Navajo; F; S; Son; 2724; Yes; Yes; 26362

2715;  Nah-glih-yil-naz-bah; F; 7; Navajo; F; S; Daughter; 2725; Yes; Yes; 26363

2716;  Keh-yil-naz-bah; F; 5; Navajo; F; S; Daughter; 2726; Yes; Yes; 26364

2717;  Keh-yil-naz-bah; F; 3; Navajo; F; S; Daughter; 2727; Yes; Yes; 26365

2718;  Dinay-dih-tannih, Luke; M; 73; Navajo; F; Wd; Head; 2728; Yes; Yes; 26007

2719;  Luke's son; M; 28; Navajo; F; S; Son; 2729; Yes; Yes; 26008

2720;  Etta; F; 20; Navajo; F; S; Daughter; 2730; Yes; Yes; 26009

2721;  Jennette; F; 15; Navajo; F; S; Daughter; 2731; Yes; Yes; 26010

2722;  Denet-clah, Clarence; M; 34; Navajo; F; M; Head; 2732; Yes; Yes; 25971

2723;  Bih-nih-gee-bah; F; 24; Navajo; F; M; Wife; 2733; Yes; Yes; 25972

2724;  Jones; M; 7; Navajo; F; S; Son; 2734; Yes; Yes; 25973

2725;  Gladis; F; 5; Navajo; F; S; Daughter; 2735; Yes; Yes; 25974

2726;  Paul; M; 3; Navajo; F; S; Son; 2736; Yes; Yes; 25975

2727;  Denet-clah; M; 64; Navajo; F; M; Head; 2737; Yes; Yes; 25848[sic]
             [ID No. should be 25948]

2728;  Denet-clah's wife; F; 53; Navajo; F; M; Wife; 2738; Yes; Yes; 25949

2729;  Theodore; M; 23; Navajo; F; S; Son; 2739; Yes; Yes; 25950

2730;  Tommy; M; 21; Navajo; F; S; Son; 2740; Yes; Yes; 25951

2731;  Louise; F; 18; Navajo; F; S; Daughter; 2741; Yes; Yes; 25952

2732;  Pierias; M; 15; Navajo; F; S; Son; 2742; Yes; Yes; 25953

2733;  Esther; F; 13; Navajo; F; S; Daughter; 2743; Yes; Yes; 25954

2734;  Jessie; F; 20; Navajo; F; S; Grand-daughter; 2743-A; Yes; Yes; 25955

2735;  Dinay-yazzie; M; 50; Navajo; F; S[sic]; Head; 2744; Yes; Yes; 25256

2736;  Nah-glih-nih-dee-bah; F; 19; Navajo; F; S; Wife; 2745; Yes; Yes; 25257

2737;  Keh-yil-nah-bah; F; 18; Navajo; F; S; Daughter; 2746; Yes; Yes; 25258

2738;  Dinay-dee-tannih-bega; M; Unk; Navajo; F; M; Head; 2747; Yes; Yes; 25225

2739;  Kee-kih-dez-bah; F; 32; Navajo; F; M; Wife; 2748; Yes; Yes; 25226

2740;  Bah-nih-ziz-bah; F; 7; Navajo; F; S; Daughter; 2749; Yes; Yes; 25227

2741;  Ah-hah-zeiz-bah; F; 3; Navajo; F; S; Daughter; 2750; Yes; Yes; 25228

2742;  Dinay-al-sosie; M; 29; Navajo; F; M; Head; 2751; Yes; Yes; 24892

Census of the **Northern Navajo** reservation of the **Northern Navajo** jurisdiction, as of **April 1**, 19**31**, taken by **Ernest H. Hammond, District**, Superintendent. **in Charge**

**Key:** Number; NAME: Surname, Given; Sex; Birth Year (if given), Age At Last Birthday; Tribe; Degree of Blood; Marital Status; Relationship To Head of Family; Last Census Roll Number; At Jurisdiction Where Enrolled (Yes or No); At Another Jurisdiction; ELSEWHERE: Post office, County, State; Ward (Yes or No); Allotment, Annuity, and Identification Numbers.

2743;  Ida; F; 34; Navajo; F; M; Wife; 2752; Yes; Yes; 24893
2744;  Jerome; M; 17; Navajo; F; S; Step-son; 2753; Yes; Yes; 24894
2745;  Jess; M; 12; Navajo; F; S; Step-son; 2754; Yes; Yes; 24895
2746;  Kez-bah; F; 8; Navajo; F; S; Daughter; 2755; Yes; Yes; 24896
2747;  Yil-nih-bah; F; 6; Navajo; F; S; Daughter; 2756; Yes; Yes; 24897
2748;  Baz-nih-bah; F; 3; Navajo; F; S; Daughter; 2757; Yes; Yes; 24898
2749;  Yahn-nah-nih-bah; F; 77; Navajo; F; S; Mother-in-law; 2758; Yes; Yes; 24899

2750;  Dagah-li-chesih-bitsoih; M; 39; Navajo; F; M; Head; 2759; Yes; Yes; 24800
2751;  Bih-teeceih-yen-bitsih; F; 27; Navajo; F; M; Wife; 2760; Yes; Yes; 24801
2752;  Keh-yil-hah-bah; F; 15; Navajo; F; S; Daughter; 2761; Yes; Yes; 24802
2753;  Charley; M; 11; Navajo; F; S; Son; 2762; Yes; Yes; 24803
2754;  Ah-hah-nih-bah; F; 7; Navajo; F; S; Daughter; 2763; Yes; Yes; 24804
2755;  Tah-des-wudt; M; 4; Navajo; F; S; Son; 2764; Yes; Yes; 24805
2756;  His-naz-bah; F; 2; Navajo; F; S; Daughter; 2765; Yes; Yes; 25333
2757;  John; M; 2; Navajo; F; S; Son; 2766; Yes; Yes; 25334

2758;  Dagah-li-cheeih-chee; M; 28; Navajo; F; M; Head; 2767; Yes; Yes; 24787
2759;  Daisy; F; 23; Navajo; F; M; Wife; 2768; Yes; Yes; 24788
2760;  Carl; M; 29; Navajo; F; S; Brother; 2769; Yes; Yes; 24789
2761;  Chee-nil-wudt; M; 2; Navajo; F; S; Son; 2770; Yes; Yes; 25335

2762;  Dagah-clitsoh; M; 73; Navajo; F; M; Head; 2771; Yes; Yes; 24790
2763;  Dagah-li-cheeih-bitsih; F; 49; Navajo; F; M; Wife; 2772; Yes; Yes; 24791
2764;  Dagah-clitsoh-bega; M; 26; Navajo; F; S; Son; 2773; Yes; Yes; 24792
2765;  Hoh-ho-bah; F; 15; Navajo; F; S; Daughter; 2774; Yes; Yes; 24793
2766;  Adzan-soh; F; 77; Navajo; F; M; 1st Wife; 2775; Yes; Yes; 24794
2767;  Elmer; M; 28; Navajo; F; S; Son; 2776; Yes; Yes; 24795
2768;  George; M; 24; Navajo; F; S; Son; 2777; Yes; Yes; 24796
2769;  Dagah-li-cheeih-bega; M; 61; Navajo; F; Wd; Brother-in-law; 2778; Yes; Yes; 24797

2770;  Bah-hah-hal-tahih, Vernon; M; 25; Navajo; F; M; Head; 2779; Yes; Yes; 27527
2771;  Tate-dee; F; 21; Navajo; F; M; Wife; 2780; Yes; Yes; 27527[sic]
                                                    [ID No. should be 27528]

2772;  Dixon, David; M; 44; Navajo; F; M; Head; 2781; Yes; Yes; 27573
2773;  Nah-glih-yil-chin-bah; F; 29; Navajo; F; M; Wife; 2782; Yes; Yes; 27574
2774;  Haska-yee-tah-deyah; M; 20; Navajo; F; S; Son; 2783; Yes; Yes; 27575
2775;  Dah-nih-bah; F; 16; Navajo; F; S; Daughter; 2784; Yes; Yes; 27576
2776;  Earl; M; 18; Navajo; F; S; Son; 2785; Yes; Yes; 27577
2777;  Nah-dez-bah; F; 7; Navajo; F; S; Daughter; 2786; Yes; Yes; 27578

Census of the **Northern Navajo** reservation of the **Northern Navajo** jurisdiction, as of **April 1**, 19**31,** taken by **Ernest H. Hammond, District**, Superintendent. **in Charge**

**Key:** Number; NAME: Surname, Given; Sex; Birth Year (if given), Age At Last Birthday; Tribe; Degree of Blood; Marital Status; Relationship To Head of Family; Last Census Roll Number; At Jurisdiction Where Enrolled (Yes or No); At Another Jurisdiction; ELSEWHERE: Post office, County, State; Ward (Yes or No); Allotment, Annuity, and Identification Numbers.

2778; Biz-nih-bah; F; 5; Navajo; F; S; Daughter; 2787; Yes; Yes; 27579

2779; Dah-gah-sih-kadnih-bitsoih; M; 34; Navajo; F; M; Head; 2788; Yes; Yes; 27558

2780; Hosteen-soh-bih-jah-tlel-bitsih; F; 37; Navajo; F; M; Wife; 2789; Yes; Yes; 27559

2781; Julius; M; 23; Navajo; F; S; Son; 2790; Yes; Yes; 27560

2782; Des-woody; M; 11; Navajo; F; S; Son; 2791; Yes; Yes; 27561

2783; Nah-tah-yil-nil-wudt; M; 8; Navajo; F; S; Son; 2792; Yes; Yes; 27562

2784; Glih-yil-nah-bah; F; 6; Navajo; F; S; Daughter; 2793; Yes; Yes; 27563

2785; Glih-yahn-nih-bah; F; 3; Navajo; F; S; Daughter; 2794; Yes; Yes; 27564

2786; Dagah-dah-sahad-benally; M; 34; Navajo; F; M; Head; 2795; Yes; Yes; 27602

2787; Bitsih, Jim Curley; F; 32; Navajo; F; M; Wife; 2696; Yes; Yes; 27603

2788; Haska-yee-neyah; M; 13; Navajo; F; S; Son; 2797; Yes; Yes; 27604

2789; Haska-yil-yee-ghsh[sic]; M; 8; Navajo; F; S; Son; 2798; Yes; Yes; 27605
[Name should be Haska-yil-yee-ghah]

2790; Nah-tah-yil-yil-wudt; M; 5; Navajo; F; S; Son; 2799; Yes; Yes; 27606

2791; Dagah-dah-sih-kadnih-bega; M; 40; Navajo; F; M; Head; 2800; Yes; Yes; 27623

2792; Bitsih, Barger[sic]; F; 27; Navajo; F; M; Wife; 2801; Yes; Yes; 27624
[Name should be Bitsih, Barber]

2793; Hah-yah; M; 13; Navajo; F; S; Son; 2802; Yes; Yes; 27625

2794; Tah-gah; M; 11; Navajo; F; S; Son; 2803; Yes; Yes; 27626

2795; Nah-tah-yil-dah-yee-yah; M; 10; Navajo; F; S; Son; 2804; Yes; Yes; 27627

2796; Haska-yah-nih-yah; M; 8; Navajo; F; S; Son; 2805; Yes; Yes; 27628

2797; Nah-tah-yil-chin-nih-yah; M; 4; Navajo; F; S; Son; 2806; Yes; Yes; 27629

2798; Adzan-l-suen; F; 17; Navajo; F; S; Daughter; 2807; Yes; Yes; 27630

2799; Dale, Tom; M; 36; Navajo; F; M; Head; 2808; Yes; Yes; 27660

2800; Katie; F; 31; Navajo; F; M; Wife; 2809; Yes; Yes; 27661

2801; Dah-nih-bah; F; 11; Navajo; F; S; Daughter; 2810; Yes; Yes; 27662

2802; Glinnih; F; 6; Navajo; F; S; Daughter; 2811; Yes; Yes; 27663

2803; Glih-haz-bah; F; 4; Navajo; F; S; Daughter; 2812; Yes; Yes; 27664

2804; Stephen; M; 3; Navajo; F; S; Son; 2813; Yes; Yes; 27665

2805; Dohi-hih-bih-bizee, River Jim; M; 40; Navajo; F; M; Head; 2814; Yes; Yes; 27940

2806; Nocki-nez-bitsih; F; 34; Navajo; F; M; Wife; 2815; Yes; Yes; 27941

2807; Eskie-soh; M; 18; Navajo; F; S; Son; 2816; Yes; Yes; 27942

2808; Yazzie; M; 15; Navajo; F; S; Son; 2817; Yes; Yes; 27943

Census of the **Northern Navajo** reservation of the **Northern Navajo** jurisdiction, as of **April 1**, 19**31**, taken by **Ernest H. Hammond, District**, Superintendent. **in Charge**

**Key:** Number; NAME: Surname, Given; Sex; Birth Year (if given), Age At Last Birthday; Tribe; Degree of Blood; Marital Status; Relationship To Head of Family; Last Census Roll Number; At Jurisdiction Where Enrolled (Yes or No); At Another Jurisdiction; ELSEWHERE: Post office, County, State; Ward (Yes or No); Allotment, Annuity, and Identification Numbers.

2809; Nas-jah-yen-bilah; F; 79; Navajo; F; Wd; Mother-in-law; 2818; Yes; Yes; 27944
2810; Ah-keh-dih-bah; F; 19; Navajo; F; S; Niece-in-law; 2819; Yes; Yes; 27945
2811; Wanda; F; 11; Navajo; F; S; Niece-in-law; 2820; Yes; Yes; 27946

2812; Doh-bilth-hoh-zonih; M; 47; Navajo; F; M; Head; 2821; Yes; Yes; 27969
2813; Nanl-cadih-bitsih; F; 41; Navajo; F; M; Wife; 2822; Yes; Yes; 27970
2814; Dinay-yazzie; M; 22; Navajo; F; S; Son; 2823; Yes; Yes; 27971
2815; Little John; M; 20; Navajo; F; S; Son; 2824; Yes; Yes; 27972
2816; Tah-bah; F; 15; Navajo; F; S; Daughter; 2825; Yes; Yes; 27973
2817; Ah-keh-hih-bah; F; 7; Navajo; F; S; Daughter; 2826; Yes; Yes; 27974
2818; Nah-zoh-bah; F; 6; Navajo; F; S; Daughter; 2827; Yes; Yes; 27975

2819; Dah-toh, Eddie; M; 23; Navajo; F; S; Head; 2828; Yes; Yes; 21300

2820; Doh-dih-jadih-bitah; M; 31; Navajo; F; M; Head; 2829; Yes; Yes; 28301
2821; Doh-lih-yen-bitsih; F; 28; Navajo; F; M; Wife; 2830; Yes; Yes; 28302
2822; Dinay-l-chee; M; 13; Navajo; F; S; Son; 2831; Yes; Yes; 28303
2823; Nellie; F; 11; Navajo; F; S; Daughter; 2832; Yes; Yes; 28304
2824; Tah-ly; M; 9; Navajo; F; S; Son; 2833; Yes; Yes; 28305
2825; Yil-deyah; M; 7; Navajo; F; S; Son; 2834; Yes; Yes; 28306
2826; Haska-yee-kih-nas-wudt; M; Unk; Navajo; F; S; Son; 2835; Yes; Yes; 28307
2827; Doh-iih-yen-bih-adzan; F; 66; Navajo; F; Wd; Mother-in-law; 2836; Yes; Yes; 28308
2828; Keh-yee-naz-bah; F; 2; Navajo; F; S; Daughter; 2837; Yes; Yes; 28543

2829; Dohi-ih-yen-bitsoih; F; 37; Navajo; F; Wd; Head; 2838; Yes; Yes; 28316
2830; Anna-Joe; F; 16; Navajo; F; S; Daughter; 2839; Yes; Yes; 28317
2831; Cheeih; M; 11; Navajo; F; S; Son; 2840; Yes; Yes; 28318
2832; Nih-nah-ziz-bah; F; 8; Navajo; F; S; Daughter; 2841; Yes; Yes; 28319
2833; Dohi-ih-yen-bitsih; F; 62; Navajo; F; S; Mother; 2842; Yes; Yes; 28320

2834; Doh-dih-jadih; M; 64; Navajo; F; M; Head; 2843; Yes; Yes; 28343
2835; Toh-dil-yil-bih-dazih; F; 54; Navajo; F; M; Wife; 2844; Yes; Yes; 28344
2836; Doh-hih-jadih-bitsoih; M; 21; Navajo; F; S; Grand-son; 2845; Yes; Yes; 28345
2837; Doh-hih-jadih-bitah; F; 20; Navajo; F; S; Niece; 2846; Yes; Yes; 28346
2838; Katie; F; 18; Navajo; F; S; Niece; 2847; Yes; Yes; 28347

2839; Dohi-yen-bitsoih; M; Unk; Navajo; F; M; Head; 2848; Yes; Yes; 28486
2840; Dohi-yen-bitsoih's wife; F; 41; Navajo; F; M; Wife; 2849; Yes; Yes; 28487
2841; Atate-l-bahih; F; 22; Navajo; F; S; Daughter; 2850; Yes; Yes; 28488
2842; Harry; M; 21; Navajo; F; S; Son; 2851; Yes; Yes; 28489
2843; Phillip; M; 15; Navajo; F; S; Son; 2852; Yes; Yes; 28490

89

Census of the **Northern Navajo** reservation of the **Northern Navajo** jurisdiction, as of **April 1**, 19**31,** taken by **Ernest H. Hammond, District**, Superintendent. **in Charge**

**Key:** Number; NAME: Surname, Given; Sex; Birth Year (if given), Age At Last Birthday; Tribe; Degree of Blood; Marital Status; Relationship To Head of Family; Last Census Roll Number; At Jurisdiction Where Enrolled (Yes or No); At Another Jurisdiction; ELSEWHERE: Post office, County, State; Ward (Yes or No); Allotment, Annuity, and Identification Numbers.

2844; Dah-nez-bah; F; 17; Navajo; F; S; Daughter; 2853; Yes; Yes; 28491
2845; See-l-bah; M; 14; Navajo; F; S; Son; 2854; Yes; Yes; 28492
2846; Kee-soh; M; 10; Navajo; F; S; Son; 2855; Yes; Yes; 28493
2847; Kee-chee; M; 7; Navajo; F; S; Son; 2856; Yes; Yes; 28494

2848; Dinay-l-suen; M; 29; Navajo; F; M; Head; 2857; Yes; Yes; 27062
2849; Glih-yah-nih-bah; F; 22; Navajo; F; M; Wife; 2858; Yes; Yes; 27063
2850; Keh-hah-bah; F; 8; Navajo; F; S; Daughter; 2859; Yes; Yes; 27064
2851; Nah-glih-yil-dah-yiz-bah; F; 5; Navajo; F; S; Daughter; 2860; Yes; Yes; 27065
2852; Adzan-yazzie; F; 51; Navajo; F; Wd; Mother-in-law; 2861; Yes; Yes; 27067

2853; Dinay-nez-bega; M; 62; Navajo; F; M; Head; 2862; Yes; Yes; 26914
2854; Nih-bahih; F; 56; Navajo; F; M; Wife; 2863; Yes; Yes; 26915
2855; Dah-nih-bah; F; 25; Navajo; F; S; Daughter; 2864; Yes; Yes; 26916
2856; Haska-yil-hal-wudt; M; 20; Navajo; F; S; Son; 2865; Yes; Yes; 26917
2857; George; M; 18; Navajo; F; S; Son; 2866; Yes; Yes; 26918

2858; Doh-hash-jahih-benally; M; 50; Navajo; F; M; Head; 2867; Yes; Yes; 27058
2859; Yee-kez-bah; F; 48; Navajo; F; M; Wife; 2868; Yes; Yes; 27059
2860; Wohl-benally; M; 21; Navajo; F; S; Son; 2869; Yes; Yes; 27060
2861; Yil-nih-dee-bah; F; 20; Navajo; F; S; Daughter; 2870; Yes; Yes; 27061

2862; Dinay-l-suen-bega; M; 43; Navajo; F; M; Head; 2871; Yes; Yes; 31074
2863; Adzan-soh-nih-tah-bih-cheh; F; 41; Navajo; F; M; Wife; 2872; Yes; Yes;
21075[sic]   [ID No. should be 31075]
2864; Theodore; M; 16; Navajo; F; S; Son; 2873; Yes; Yes; 31076
2865; Shih-kenh-yazzie; F; 14; Navajo; F; S; Daughter; 2874; Yes; Yes; 31077
2866; Nad-ditz-sohih; M; 10; Navajo; F; S; Son; 2875; Yes; Yes; 31078
2867; Haska-yee-chin-dael[sic]; M; 7; Navajo; F; S; Son; 2876; Yes; Yes; 31079
     [Name is probably Haska-yee-chin-deel]

2868; Dinay-l-suen-benally; M; 29; Navajo; F; M; Head; 2877; Yes; Yes; 31091
2869; Bih-jah-atin-bitsih; F; 30; Navajo; F; M; Wife; 2878; Yes; Yes; 31092
2870; Tohih; F; 21[sic]; Navajo; F; S; Daughter; 2879; Yes; Yes; 31093
2871; Gahn; F; 6; Navajo; F; S; Daughter; 2880; Yes; Yes; 31094
2872; David; M; 3; Navajo; F; S; Son; 2881; Yes; Yes; 31095
2873; Nellie; F; 2; Navajo; F; S; Daughter; 2882; Yes; Yes; 31250

2874; Dixon, Harvey; M; 36; Navajo; F; M; Head; 2883; Yes; Yes; 31043
2875; Ellen; F; 27; Navajo; F; M; Wife; 2884; Yes; Yes; 31044
2876; William David; M; 7; Navajo; F; S; Son; 2885; Yes; Yes; 31045
2877; Viola; F; 6; Navajo; F; S; Daughter; 2886; Yes; Yes; 31046
2878; Harvey, Jr.; M; 4; Navajo; F; S; Son; 2887; Yes; Yes; 31047

Census of the **Northern Navajo** reservation of the **Northern Navajo** jurisdiction, as of **April 1**, 19**31**, taken by **Ernest H. Hammond, District**, Superintendent. **in Charge**

**Key:** Number; NAME: Surname, Given; Sex; Birth Year (if given), Age At Last Birthday; Tribe; Degree of Blood; Marital Status; Relationship To Head of Family; Last Census Roll Number; At Jurisdiction Where Enrolled (Yes or No); At Another Jurisdiction; ELSEWHERE: Post office, County, State; Ward (Yes or No); Allotment, Annuity, and Identification Numbers.

2879;  Samuel Parry; M; 2; Navajo; F; S; Son; 2888; Yes; Yes; 31048

2880;  Duncan, Joe; M; Unk; Navajo; F; M; Head; 2891; Yes; Yes; 31051
2881;  Kitty bah; F; 35; Navajo; F; M; Wife; 2892; Yes; Yes; 31052
2882;  Paul Arthur; M; 29; Navajo; F; S; Son; 2893; Yes; Yes; 31053
2883;  Lenora; F; 8; Navajo; F; S; Daughter; 2894; Yes; Yes; 31054

2884;  Dinay-yazzie-bega, Frank; M; Unk; Navajo; F; M; Head; 2895; Yes; Yes; 30935
2885;  Al-soh-nih-bah, Fred Funston's daughter; F; 20; Navajo; F; M; Wife; 2896; Yes; Yes; 30936
2886;  Dinay-yazzie, Pete Billy; M; 1; Navajo; F; S; Son; 2897; Yes; Yes; 31230

2887;  Doh-hal-tahih-bega; M; 49; Navajo; F; Wd; Head; 2898; Yes; Yes; 30580
2888;  Haska-yil-chih-nih-yah; M; 14; Navajo; F; S; Son; 2899; Yes; Yes; 30581

2889;  Doh-hal-tahih; M; Unk; Navajo; F; Wd; Head; 2900; Yes; Yes; 30582
2890;  Clineth; F; 33; Navajo; F; S; Daughter; 2901; Yes; Yes; 30583
2891;  Jim; M; 27; Navajo; F; S; Son; 2902; Yes; Yes; 30584

2892;  Descheeny; M; Unk; Navajo; F; M; Head; 2903; Yes; Yes; 30551
2893;  Hosteen-ashinih-bitsih; F; 38; Navajo; F; M; Wife; 2904; Yes; Yes; 30552
2894;  Dah-nih-bah; F; 10; Navajo; F; S; Daughter; 2905; Yes; Yes; 30553
2895;  Yah-deyah; M; 8; Navajo; F; S; Son; 2906; Yes; Yes; 30554
2896;  Haska-yee-tah-dih-gah; M; 7; Navajo; F; S; Son; 2907; Yes; Yes; 30555
2897;  Nah-chih-nih-bah; F; 3; Navajo; F; S; Daughter; 2908; Yes; Yes; 30556
2898;  Hosteen-ashinh; M; 63; Navajo; F; Wd; Father-in-law; 2909; Yes; Yes; 30557
2899;  Haska-yee-nel-wudt; M; 19; Navajo; F; S; Brother-in-law; 2910; Yes; Yes; 30558

2900;  Doh-hal-tahih-bega; M; 52; Navajo; F; Wd; Head; 2911; Yes; Yes; 30586
2901;  Tah-yil-wudt; F[sic]; 8; Navajo; F; S; Son; 2912; Yes; Yes; 30587
            [Should be male.]

2902;  Dixon, John; M; 39; Navajo; F; M; Head; 2913; Yes; Yes; 30450
2903;  Frances; F; 38; Navajo; F; M; Wife; 2914; Yes; Yes; 30451
2904;  Phillip; M; 5; Navajo; F; S; Son; 2915; Yes; Yes; 30452
2905;  Vernon; M; 11; Navajo; F; S; Son; 2916; Yes; Yes; 30453
2906;  James; M; 8; Navajo; F; S; Son; 2917; Yes; Yes; 30454
2907;  Lilly; F; 6; Navajo; F; S; Daughter; 2918; Yes; Yes; 30455
2908;  Harold; M; 4; Navajo; F; S; Son; 2919; Yes; Yes; 30456

Census of the **Northern Navajo** reservation of the **Northern Navajo** jurisdiction, as of **April 1** , 19**31,** taken by **Ernest H. Hammond, District**, Superintendent. **in Charge**

**Key:** Number; NAME: Surname, Given; Sex; Birth Year (if given), Age At Last Birthday; Tribe; Degree of Blood; Marital Status; Relationship To Head of Family; Last Census Roll Number; At Jurisdiction Where Enrolled (Yes or No); At Another Jurisdiction; ELSEWHERE: Post office, County, State; Ward (Yes or No); Allotment, Annuity, and Identification Numbers.

2909; Doh-yalthih-bega, Salou; M; Unk; Navajo; F; M; Head; 2920; Yes; Yes; 30843
2910; Hosteen-nez-benally; F; 21; Navajo; F; M; Wife; 2921; Yes; Yes; 30844
2911; Hah-gee-bah; F; 5; Navajo; F; S; Daughter; 2922; Yes; Yes; 30845
2912; Yee-hah-nih-bah; F; 3; Navajo; F; S; Daughter; 2923; Yes; Yes; 30846

2913; Dih-cheez-bitah; M; 26; Navajo; F; M; Head; 2924; Yes; Yes; 30754
2914; Tah-nih-bah; F; 22; Navajo; F; M; Wife; 2925; Yes; Yes; 30755
2915; Haska-yah-nih-yah; M; 2; Navajo; F; S; Son; 2926; Yes; Yes; 30756

2916; Descheeny-aht-citty-bega; M; 48; Navajo; F; M; Head; 2927; Yes; Yes; 30457
2917; Kin-lah-cheeny-bitsih; F; 43; Navajo; F; M; Wife; 2928; Yes; Yes; 30458
2918; Yinl-bah; F; 21; Navajo; F; S; Daughter; 2929; Yes; Yes; 30459
2919; Kee-bahih; M; 11; Navajo; F; S; Son; 2930; Yes; Yes; 30460

2920; Dinay-yazzie-bega; M; 40; Navajo; F; M; Head; 2931; Yes; Yes; 30433
2921; Hosteen-hah-zah-benally; F; 31; Navajo; F; M; Wife; 2932; Yes; Yes; 30434
2922; Ah-kih-naz-bah; F; 12; Navajo; F; S; Daughter; 2933; Yes; Yes; 30435
2923; Nah-tah-hoh-lel; M; 9; Navajo; F; S; Son; 2934; Yes; Yes; 30436
2924; Yee-kin-nih-bah; F; 7; Navajo; F; S; Daughter; 2935; Yes; Yes; 30437
2925; Haska-yih-kayah; M; 3; Navajo; F; S; Son; 2936; Yes; Yes; 30438

2926; Dinay-yazzie-bih-adzan; F; 68; Navajo; F; Wd; Head; 2937; Yes; Yes; 30353
2927; Dan Lewis; M; 27; Navajo; F; S; Son; 2938; Yes; Yes; 30354

2928; Doh-hah-tahih-bitah; M; 53; Navajo; F; Wd; Head; 2940; Yes; Yes; 23547
2929; Manson; M; 31; Navajo; F; S; Son; 2941; Yes; Yes; 23548
2930; Nah-tah-yee-kih-da-ziz-zinh; M; 22; Navajo; F; S; Son; 2942; Yes; Yes; 23549
2931; Keh-yee-dee-nih-bah; F; 20; Navajo; F; S; Daughter; 2943; Yes; Yes; 23550
2932; Scott; M; 18; Navajo; F; S; Son; 2944; Yes; Yes; 23551
2933; Nas-wudt, Onus; M; 6; Navajo; F; S; Son; 2945; Yes; Yes; 23552
2934; Louise; F; 14; Navajo; F; S; Daughter; 2946; Yes; Yes; 23553
2935; Haska-yil-nah-gah; M; 10; Navajo; F; S; Son; 2947; Yes; Yes; 23554
2936; Johnson; M; 8; Navajo; F; S; Son; 2948; Yes; Yes; 23555
2937; Eskee; M; 18; Navajo; F; S; Nephew; 2949; Yes; Yes; 23557
2938; Eskee-yazzie; M; 9; Navajo; F; S; Nephew; 2950; Yes; Yes; 23668[sic]
[ID No. should be 23558]

2939; Dinay-nez-benally; M; 24; Navajo; F; M; Head; 2951; Yes; Yes; 26919
2940; Dinay-nez-benally's wife; F; Unk; Navajo; F; M; Wife; 2952; Yes; Yes; 26920

2941; Dinay-nez-bega; M; 51; Navajo; F; M; Head; 2953; Yes; Yes; 26924
2942; Dinay-nez-bega's wife; F; 50; Navajo; F; M; Wife; 2954; Yes; Yes; 26925

Census of the __Northern Navajo__ reservation of the __Northern Navajo__ jurisdiction, as of __April 1__, 1931, taken by __Ernest H. Hammond, District__, Superintendent. __in Charge__

**Key:** Number; NAME: Surname, Given; Sex; Birth Year (if given), Age At Last Birthday; Tribe; Degree of Blood; Marital Status; Relationship To Head of Family; Last Census Roll Number; At Jurisdiction Where Enrolled (Yes or No); At Another Jurisdiction; ELSEWHERE: Post office, County, State; Ward (Yes or No); Allotment, Annuity, and Identification Numbers.

2943; Yil-es-bah; F; 21; Navajo; F; S; Daughter; 2955; Yes; Yes; 26926
2944; Haska-yee-tah-yil-wudt; M; 15; Navajo; F; S; Son; 2956; Yes; Yes; 26927
2945; Al-kih-des-bah; F; 87; Navajo; F; Wd; Mother-in-law; 2957; Yes; Yes; 26928

2946; Denet, Clarence; M; 35; Navajo; F; M; Head; 2958; Yes; Yes; 26838
2947; Bah, Ethel; F; 29; Navajo; F; M; Wife; 2959; Yes; Yes; 26839
2948; Willie; M; 9; Navajo; F; S; Son; 2960; Yes; Yes; 26840
2949; Nellie; F; 8; Navajo; F; S; Daughter; 2961; Yes; Yes; 26841
2950; Hah-hoh-gahl-ih; M; 6; Navajo; F; S; Son; 2962; Yes; Yes; 26842

2951; Dinay-sosie-bitsih; F; 29; Navajo; F; Wd.; Head; 2963; Yes; Yes; 26997
2952; Nah-glih-yil-hah-naz-bah; F; 7; Navajo; F; S; Daughter; 2964; Yes; Yes; 26998
2953; Keh-yil-dez-bah; F; 26; Navajo; F; S; Sister; 2965; Yes; Yes; 26999
2954; Ah-hih-hih-bah; F; 22; Navajo; F; S; Sister; 2966; Yes; Yes; 27000
2955; Haska-yil-has-wudt; M; 16; Navajo; F; S; Brother; 2967; Yes; Yes; 27001

2956; Dinay-sosie; M; Unk; Navajo; F; M; Head; 2968; Yes; Yes; 27002
2957; Dinay-sosie's wife; F; Unk; Navajo; F; M; Wife; 2969; Yes; Yes; 27003
2958; Haska-yee-heh-lal; M; 20; Navajo; F; S; Son; 2970; Yes; Yes; 27004
2959; Chih-hoh-tahl; M; 5; Navajo; F; S; Son; 2971; Yes; Yes; 27005

2960; Doh-hah-hal-tahih, Roy; M; Unk; Navajo; F; M; Head; 2972; Yes; Yes; 23819
2961; Adzan-toh-nil-chonih; F; 66; Navajo; F; M; Wife; 2973; Yes; Yes; 23820
2962; Haska-yee-chih-nil-wudt; M; 9; Navajo; F; S; Nephew; 2974; Yes; Yes; 23821

2963; Dah-gah-dah-sah-kad-bega, William Hand; M; Unk; Navajo; F; M; Head; 2975; Yes; Yes; 23863
2964; Jeh-k-nez; F; Unk; Navajo; F; M; Wife; 2976; Yes; Yes; 23864
2965; Hand Williams; M; Unk; Navajo; F; S; Son; 2977; Yes; Yes; 23865
2966; Haska-yil-has-wudt; M; Unk; Navajo; F; S; Son; 2978; Yes; Yes; 23866
2967; Nah-gahl; M; Unk; Navajo; F; S; Son; 2979; Yes; Yes; 23867

2968; Dinay-l-suen-benally, Peter; M; 29; Navajo; F; M; Head; 2980; Yes; Yes; 26678
2969; Glih-hah-nih-bah; F; 24; Navajo; F; M; Wife; 2981; Yes; Yes; 26679
2970; Nanih-bah; F; 6; Navajo; F; S; Daughter; 2982; Yes; Yes; 26680
2971; Tah-nal-wudt; M; 4; Navajo; F; S; Son; 2983; Yes; Yes; 26681
2972; Haska-yee-tah-yil-wudt; M; 3; Navajo; F; S; Son; 2984; Yes; Yes; 26682
2973; Kah-nip-ah[sic]; F; 1; Navajo; F; S; Daughter; 2985; Yes; Yes; 27095
[Name could be Kah-ni-ah]

2974; Dinay-l-suen, Leroy; M; 27; Navajo; F; M; Head; 2986; Yes; Yes; 26675

Census of the **Northern Navajo** reservation of the **Northern Navajo** jurisdiction, as of **April 1**, 19**31,** taken by **Ernest H. Hammond, District,** Superintendent. **in Charge**

**Key:** Number; NAME: Surname, Given; Sex; Birth Year (if given), Age At Last Birthday; Tribe; Degree of Blood; Marital Status; Relationship To Head of Family; Last Census Roll Number; At Jurisdiction Where Enrolled (Yes or No); At Another Jurisdiction; ELSEWHERE: Post office, County, State; Ward (Yes or No); Allotment, Annuity, and Identification Numbers.

2975;  Happy; F; 28; Navajo; F; M; Wife; 2987; Yes; Yes; 26676
2976;  Helen; F; 4; Navajo; F; S; Step-Daughter; 2988; Yes; Yes; 26677
2977;  Alva; M; 2; Navajo; F; S; Son; 2989; Yes; Yes; 27072

2978;  Dee-nehi-glehih-bega; M; 30; Navajo; F; M; Head; 2990; Yes; Yes; 26625
2979;  Nah-glih-hah-naz-bah; F; 25; Navajo; F; M; Wife; 2991; Yes; Yes; 26626
2980;  Tah-no-tahl; M; 8; Navajo; F; S; Son; 2992; Yes; Yes; 26627
2981;  Nah-yah-yee-gahl; M; 3; Navajo; F; S; Son; 2993; Yes; Yes; 26628

2982;  Dinay-chilli-benally, Joe; M; 30; Navajo; F; M; Head; 2994; Yes; Yes; 26614
2983;  Bah-ee; F; 25; Navajo; F; M; Wife; 2995; Yes; Yes; 26615
2984;  Haska-yee-nah-hah-yah; M; 4; Navajo; F; S; Son; 2996; Yes; Yes; 26616
2985;  Tah-gee-bah; F; 2; Navajo; F; S; Daughter; 2997; Yes; Yes; 27073
2986;  Heh-hah-nih-bah; F; 3; Navajo; F; S; Daughter; 2998; Yes; Yes; 26617

2987;  Dinay-l-suen-benally-bega; M; 27; Navajo; F; M; Head; 2999; Yes; Yes; 26629
2988;  Nah-glih-yil-nih-des-bah; F; 22; Navajo; F; M; Wife; 3000; Yes; Yes; 26630
2989;  Al-soh-dah-yiz-bah; F; 3; Navajo; F; S; Daughter; 3001; Yes; Yes; 26631
2990;  Nah-glih-yahn-nih-bah; F; 2; Navajo; F; S; Daughter; 3002; Yes; Yes; 26632

2991;  Dagahih-soh-bega; M; 38; Navajo; F; M; Head; 3003; Yes; Yes; 26633
2992;  Glih-yil-nih-bah; F; 32; Navajo; F; M; Wife; 3004; Yes; Yes; 26634
2993;  Chih-des-bah; F; 17; Navajo; F; S; Daughter; 3005; Yes; Yes; 26635
2994;  Ah-kih-nih-bah; F; 14; Navajo; F; S; Daughter; 3006; Yes; Yes; 26636
2995;  Ah-hah-dee-bah; F; 65; Navajo; F; Wd; Mother-in-law; 3007; Yes; Yes; 26637

2996;  Dale, Frank; M; 31; Navajo; F; M; Head; 3008; Yes; Yes; 23573
2997;  Batoni-bitsih; F; 20; Navajo; F; M; Wife; 3009; Yes; Yes; 23574
2998;  Ah-hih-nah-nih-bah; F; 6; Navajo; F; S; Daughter; 3010; Yes; Yes; 23575

2999;  Dah-nah-al-ja-benally; M; 31; Navajo; F; M; Head;  3011; Yes; Yes; 23563
3000;  Zannie; F; 31; Navajo; F; M; Wife; 3012; Yes; Yes; 23564
3001;  Keh-yahn-nas-bah; F; 9; Navajo; F; S; Daughter; 3013; Yes; Yes; 23565
3002;  Nah-tah-yee-gahl; M; 4; Navajo; F; S; Son; 3014; Yes; Yes; 23566
3003;  Clyde; M; 22; Navajo; F; S; Nephew; 3015; Yes; Yes; 23567
3004;  Haska-yee-sas-wudt; M; 2; Navajo; F; S; Son; 3016; Yes; Yes; 23925

3005;  Dagaih-seeih-yen-bega; M; 41; Navajo; F; M; Head; 3017; Yes; Yes; 20913
3006;  Kin-lah-cheeny-bitsih; F; 41; Navajo; F; M; Wife; 3018; Yes; Yes; 20914
3007;  Chin-nih-bahih; F; 8; Navajo; F; S; Daughter; 3019; Yes; Yes; 20915
3008;  Hah-nah-bah; F; 51; Navajo; F; Wd. Div.; Wife; 3020; Yes; Yes; 20916

Census of the **Northern Navajo** reservation of the **Northern Navajo** jurisdiction, as of **April 1** , 19**31,** taken by **Ernest H. Hammond, District** , Superintendent. **in Charge**

**Key:** Number; NAME: Surname, Given; Sex; Birth Year (if given), Age At Last Birthday; Tribe; Degree of Blood; Marital Status; Relationship To Head of Family; Last Census Roll Number; At Jurisdiction Where Enrolled (Yes or No); At Another Jurisdiction; ELSEWHERE: Post office, County, State; Ward (Yes or No); Allotment, Annuity, and Identification Numbers.

3009; Dinay-yazzie-bitcilli; M; 50; Navajo; F; M; Head; 3021; Yes; Yes; 23576
3010; Nil-chi-gih-hah-tahly-bitsih; 49; Navajo; F; M; Wife; 3022; Yes; Yes; 23577
3011; Henderson, Charles; M; 24; Navajo; F; S; Son; 3023; Yes; Yes; 23578
3012; Henderson, George; M; 17; Navajo; F; S; Son; 3024; Yes; Yes; 23579
3013; Henderson, Mary; F; 15; Navajo; F; S; Daughter; 3025; Yes; Yes; 23580
3014; Bah-yazzie; F; 13; Navajo; F; S; Daughter; 3026; Yes; Yes; 23581
3015; Ah-keh-nil-bah; F; 9; Navajo; F; S; Daughter; 3027; Yes; Yes; 23582
3016; Glih-bah; F; 5; Navajo; F; S; Daughter; 3028; Yes; Yes; 23583
3017; Kee; M; 11; Navajo; F; S; Son; 3029; Yes; Yes; 23599

3018; Dale, Stephen; M; 51; Navajo; F; M; Head; 3030; Yes; Yes; 22647
3019; Stephen Dale's Wife; F; 24; Navajo; F; M; Wife; 3031; Yes; Yes; 22648
3020; Herbert; M; 7; Navajo; F; S; Son; 3032; Yes; Yes; 22649
3021; Ray; M; 6; Navajo; F; S; Son; 3033; Yes; Yes; 22650
3022; Kee; M; 4; Navajo; F; S; Son; 3034; Yes; Yes; 22651
3023; Samuel; M; Unk; Navajo; F; S; Son; 3035; Yes; Yes; 22652
3024; Kah-haz-bah; M[sic]; 1; Navajo; F; S; Daughter; 3036; Yes; Yes; 22653
        [Should be female.]

3025; Dinay-yazzie-bitcilli-bega; M; 20; Navajo; F; M; Head; 3037; Yes; Yes; 23584
3026; Nih-j-k, Mike; F; 19; Navajo; F; M; Wife; 3038; Yes; Yes; 23585

3027; Descheeny-Atcitty-bega; M; 33; Navajo; F; M; Head; 3039; Yes; Yes; 21384
3028; Hah-das-bah; F; 26; Navajo; F; M; Wife; 3040; Yes; Yes; 21385
3029; Haska-yee-silh; M; 22[sic]; Navajo; F; S; Son; 3041; Yes; Yes; 21386
        [On the 1933 Census this child is 14 years old.]
3030; Al-nah-ges-bah; F; 6; Navajo; F; S; Daughter; 3042; Yes; Yes; 21387
3031; Hah-nah-bah; F; 3; Navajo; F; S; Daughter; 3043; Yes; Yes; 21388

3032; Doh-haih-ih-badoni; M; 31; Navajo; F; M; Head; 3044; Yes; Yes; 21398
3033; Doh-haih-ih-badoni bitsih; F; Unk; Navajo; F; M; Wife; 3045; Yes; Yes;
21399

3034; Dil-a-woshih, Tas-wudt; M; 25; Navajo; F; M; Head; 3046; Yes; Yes; 21007
3035; Hoh-sohnih-hah-tahly-bitsih; F; 19; Navajo; F; M; Wife; 3047; Yes; Yes;
21008

3036; Descheeny-bega; M; 26; Navajo; F; M; Head; 3048; Yes; Yes; 21062
3037; Yee-tah-nas-bah; F; 22; Navajo; F; M; Wife; 3049; Yes; Yes; 21063
3038; Haska-yazzie; M; 8; Navajo; F; M[sic]; Son; 3050; Yes; Yes; 21064

3039; Dil-a-wash-ih-benally, Fat; M; 59; Navajo; F; M; Head; 3051; Yes; Yes;
20996

Census of the **Northern Navajo** reservation of the **Northern Navajo** jurisdiction, as of **April 1**, 19**31,** taken by **Ernest H. Hammond, District**, Superintendent. **in Charge**

**Key:** Number; NAME: Surname, Given; Sex; Birth Year (if given), Age At Last Birthday; Tribe; Degree of Blood; Marital Status; Relationship To Head of Family; Last Census Roll Number; At Jurisdiction Where Enrolled (Yes or No); At Another Jurisdiction; ELSEWHERE: Post office, County, State; Ward (Yes or No); Allotment, Annuity, and Identification Numbers.

3040; Capitan-bega, bitsih; F; 40; Navajo; F; M; Wife; 3052; Yes; Yes; 20997
3041; Dil-a-woshih, Jay; M; 11; Navajo; F; S; Son; 3053; Yes; Yes; 20998
3042; Yah-yil-wulth; M; 9; Navajo; F; S; Son; 3054; Yes; Yes; 20999
3043; El-wudt; M; 7; Navajo; F; S; Son; 3055; Yes; Yes; 21000
3044; Yil-des-wudt; M; 5; Navajo; F; S; Son; 3056; Yes; Yes; 21001
3045; Hoska-yil-yee-gah; M; 3; Navajo; F; S; Son; 3057; Yes; Yes; 21002
3046; Nel-wudt-ahtcitty; M; 20; Navajo; F; S; Step-son; 3058; Yes; Yes; 21003
3047; Capitan-bega, Walter; M; 22; Navajo; F; S; Brother-in-law; 3059; Yes; Yes; 21004
3048; Hah-bah; F; 20; Navajo; F; S; Sister-in-law; 3060; Yes; Yes; 21005
3049; Capitan, Luther; M; 16; Navajo; F; S; Brother-in-law; 3061; Yes; Yes; 21006

3050; Dagah-dah-sah[sic]; M; 62; Navajo; F; M; Head; 3062; Yes; Yes; 23234
 [1930 Census the name was Dagah-dah-sah-kad-bega]
3051; Bah-sanih; F; 57; Navajo; F; M; Wife; 3063; Yes; Yes; 23235
3052; Tah-ziz-bah; F; 19; Navajo; F; S; Daughter; 3064; Yes; Yes; 23236

3053; Dil-a-woshih-benally-bega; M; 30; Navajo; F; M; Head; 3065; Yes; Yes; 20987
3054; Bih-gail-yen-benally; F; 24; Navajo; F; M; Wife; 3066; Yes; Yes; 20988
3055; Nah-tah-yee-nah-galh; M; 9; Navajo; F; S; Son; 3067; Yes; Yes; 20989
3056; Haska-yil-chin-yah; M; 7; Navajo; F; S; Son; 3068; Yes; Yes; 20990
3057; Nah-glaih-yee-kah-nih-desbah; F; 20; Navajo; F; S; Sister-in-law; 3069; Yes; Yes; 20991
3058; Bih-gee-bah; F; 21; Navajo; F; S; Sister; 3070; Yes; Yes; 20994
3059; Bih-gail-yen-benally, Esther; F; 18; Navajo; F; S; Sister-in-law; 3071; Yes; Yes; 20992
3060; Dil-a-wosh-ih, Lola; F; 19; Navajo; F; S; Sister; 3072; Yes; Yes; 20995

3061; Dinay-ye-is-kinih, Michael; M; 31; Navajo; F; M; Head; 3073; Yes; Yes; 21115
3062; Mary; F; 35; Navajo; F; M; Wife; 3074; Yes; Yes; 21116
3063; George, Estelle; F; 22; Navajo; F; S; Sister-in-law; 3075; Yes; Yes; 21117
3064; George, Daisy; F; 20; Navajo; F; S; Sister-in-law; 3076; Yes; Yes; 21118
3065; Willer; M; 18; Navajo; F; S; Brother-in-law; 3077; Yes; Yes; 21119
3066; Kee; M; 16; Navajo; F; S; Brother-in-law; 3078; Yes; Yes; 21120
3067; Ella; F; 16; Navajo; F; S; Sister-in-law; 3079; Yes; Yes; 21121
3068; Louise; F; 6; Navajo; F; S; Niece-in-law; 3080; Yes; Yes; 21122

3069; Dinay-ye-is-kinih; M; Unk; Navajo; F; M; Head; 3081; Yes; Yes; 21109
3070; Al-chih-hah-bah; F; 35; Navajo; F; M; Wife; 3082; Yes; Yes; 21110
3071; Haska-yil-deyah; M; 17; Navajo; F; S; Son; 3083; Yes; Yes; 21111
3072; Stephen; M; 15; Navajo; F; S; Son; 3084; Yes; Yes; 21112

Census of the __Northern Navajo__ reservation of the __Northern Navajo__ jurisdiction, as of __April 1__, 19**31,** taken by __Ernest H. Hammond, District__, Superintendent.                                                         **in Charge**

**Key:** Number; NAME: Surname, Given; Sex; Birth Year (if given), Age At Last Birthday; Tribe; Degree of Blood; Marital Status; Relationship To Head of Family; Last Census Roll Number; At Jurisdiction Where Enrolled (Yes or No); At Another Jurisdiction; ELSEWHERE: Post office, County, State; Ward (Yes or No); Allotment, Annuity, and Identification Numbers.

3073;  Lester; M; 13; Navajo; F; S; Son; 3085; Yes; Yes; 21113
3074;  Adzanih-yazzie; F; 10; Navajo; F; S; Daughter; 3086; Yes; Yes; 21114

3075;  Dinay-ye-is-kinih-bega; M; Unk; Navajo; F; M; Head; 3087; Yes; Yes; 21132
3076;  Chin-nih-bah; F; 40; Navajo; F; M; Wife; 3088; Yes; Yes; 21133
3077;  Olive; F; 19; Navajo; F; S; Daughter; 3089; Yes; Yes; 21134
3078;  Haska-yil-hal-wudt; M; 17; Navajo; F; S; Son; 3090; Yes; Yes; 21135
3079;  Nel-wudt; M; 10; Navajo; F; S; Son; 3091; Yes; Yes; 21136
3080;  Tah-deyah; M; 7; Navajo; F; S; Son; 3092; Yes; Yes; 21137
3081;  Hah-jih-bah; F; 4; Navajo; F; S; Daughter; 3093; Yes; Yes; 21138
3082;  Yah-nas-bah; F; 1; Navajo; F; S; Daughter; 3094; Yes; Yes; 21638

3083;  Dinay-yazzie-bikis; M; 33; Navajo; F; M; Head; 3095; Yes; Yes; 23451
3084;  Bih-bizee-bitsih; F; 45; Navajo; F; M; Wife; 3096; Yes; Yes; 23452
3085;  Keh-yil-haz-bah; F; 21; Navajo; F; S; Daughter; 3097; Yes; Yes; 23453
3086;  Earl; M; 15; Navajo; F; S; Son; 3098; Yes; Yes; 23454
3087;  Chih-des-wudt; M; 12; Navajo; F; S; Son; 3099; Yes; Yes; 23455
3088;  Tah-dez-bah; F; 9; Navajo; F; S; Daughter; 3100; Yes; Yes; 23456
3089;  Haska-yil-des-wudt; M; 7; Navajo; F; S; Son; 3102; Yes; Yes; 23457
3090;  Yee-nil-bah; F; 4; Navajo; F; S; Daughter; 3103; Yes; Yes; 23458

3091;  Dagah-clitsuen-bega, Tall Barber; M; 63; Navajo; F; M; Head; 3104; Yes; Yes; 23514
3092;  Glih-haz-bah; F; 50; Navajo; F; M; Wife; 3105; Yes; Yes; 23515
3093;  Andrew; M; 25; Navajo; F; S; Son; 3106; Yes; Yes; 23516
3094;  Nah-tah-yil-dah-yee-yah; M; 14; Navajo; F; S; Son; 3107; Yes; Yes; 23517
3095;  Haska-yil-chih-nih-yah; M; 11; Navajo; F; S; Son; 3108; Yes; Yes; 23518
3096;  Kah-tah-bah; F; 3; Navajo; F; S; Daughter; 3109; Yes; Yes; 23995
3097;  Haska-gathl; M; 2; Navajo; F; S; Son; 3110; Yes; Yes; 23997

3098;  Dinay-nez-bega; M; 29; Navajo; F; M; Head; 3111; Yes; Yes; 21257
3099;  Yahn-hah-bah; F; 22; Navajo; F; M; Wife; 3112; Yes; Yes; 21258
3100;  Hoska-yee-chih-nil-wudt; M; 5; Navajo; F; S; Son; 3113; Yes; Yes; 21259
3101;  Al-neh-bah; F; 4; Navajo; F; S; Daughter; 3114; Yes; Yes; 21260
3102;  Hoska-yil-nil-wudt; M; 3; Navajo; F; S; Son; 3115; Yes; Yes; 21261

3103;  Dagah-dah-sah-kad-bega; M; 54; Navajo; F; M; Head; 3116; Yes; Yes; 23309
3104;  Glih-hah-bah; F; 66; Navajo; F; M; Wife; 3117; Yes; Yes; 23310

3105;  Doh-hah-hah-tahih; M; 81; Navajo; F; M; Head; 3118; Yes; Yes; 23311
3106;  Dagah-dah-sah-kad-bitsih; F; 78; Navajo; F; M; Wife; 3119; Yes; Yes; 23312

Census of the **Northern Navajo** reservation of the **Northern Navajo** jurisdiction, as of **April 1** , 19**31,** taken by **Ernest H. Hammond, District**, Superintendent. **in Charge**

**Key:** Number; NAME: Surname, Given; Sex; Birth Year (if given), Age At Last Birthday; Tribe; Degree of Blood; Marital Status; Relationship To Head of Family; Last Census Roll Number; At Jurisdiction Where Enrolled (Yes or No); At Another Jurisdiction; ELSEWHERE: Post office, County, State; Ward (Yes or No); Allotment, Annuity, and Identification Numbers.

3107; Dagah-dah-sah-kad-bitsoih; M; 33; Navajo; F; M; Head; 3120; Yes; Yes; 23316

3108; Al-soh-naz-bah; F; 43; Navajo; F; M; Wife; 3121; Yes; Yes; 23317

3109; Nah-tah-yil-yeel-wudt; M; 7; Navajo; F; S; Son; 3122; Yes; Yes; 23319

3110; Dagaih-sosie-benally; M; Unk; Navajo; F; M; Head; 3123; Yes; Yes; 23107

3111; Kih-nih-bah; F; 19; Navajo; F; M; Wife; 3124; Yes; Yes; 23108

3112; Dagah-clitsuen-benally; M; 33; Navajo; F; M; Head; 3125; Yes; Yes; 23433

3113; Bitzee-chilli-bitsih; F; 31; Navajo; F; M; Wife; 3126; Yes; Yes; 23434

3114; Yil-nih-nih-yah; M; 13; Navajo; F; S; Son; 3127; Yes; Yes; 23435

3115; Yil-nih-nih-bah; F; 11; Navajo; F; S; Daughter; 3128; Yes; Yes; 23436

3116; Yee-tah-nah-gah; M; 8; Navajo; F; S; Son; 3129; Yes; Yes; 23437

3117; Dagah-dah-say-kad-bega; M; 55; Navajo; F; M; Head; 3133; Yes; Yes; 23205

3118; Dagah-dah-say-kad-bega's wife; F; 56; Navajo; F; M; Wife; 3134; Yes; Yes; 23206

3119; Ah-louz-bah; F; 19; Navajo; F; S; Daughter; 3135; Yes; Yes; 23207

3120; Pat; M; 17; Navajo; F; S; Son; 3136; Yes; Yes; 23208

3121; Ah-keh-haz-bah; F; 14; Navajo; F; S; Daughter; 3137; Yes; Yes; 23209

3122; Dorothy; F; 13; Navajo; F; S; Daughter; 3138; Yes; Yes; 23210

3123; Ah-ha-ah-yiz-bah; F; 9; Navajo; F; S; Daughter; 3139; Yes; Yes; 23211

3124; Bitsih, Dr. John; F; 26; Navajo; F; Wd; Head; 3140; Yes; Yes; 23491

3125; Chih-hoh-gahl; M; 5; Navajo; F; S; Son; 3141; Yes; Yes; 23492

3126; Doh-bih-haltin; M; 58; Navajo; F; M; Head; 3143; Yes; Yes; 22472

3127; Doh-bih-haltin's wife; F; 32; Navajo; F; M; Wife; 3144; Yes; Yes; 22473

3128; Kee-yazzie; M; 22; Navajo; F; S; Son; 3145; Yes; Yes; 22474

3129; Dinay-sosie-bega; M; 60; Navajo; F; M; Head; 3146; Yes; Yes; 22347

3130; Aht-johih-benally; F; 32; Navajo; F; M; Wife; 3147; Yes; Yes; 22348

3131; Tah-yah; M; 13; Navajo; F; S; Son; 3148; Yes; Yes; 22349

3132; Awa-sosie; F; 10; Navajo; F; S; Daughter; 3149; Yes; Yes; 22350

3133; Al-che-chin-nih-bah; F; 5; Navajo; F; S; Daughter; 3150; Yes; Yes; 22351

3134; Dinay-sosie-benally; M; 28; Navajo; F; M; Head; 3151; Yes; Yes; 22352

3135; Toh-sonie-benally; F; 18; Navajo; F; M; Wife; 3152; Yes; Yes; 22353

3136; Dinay-al-seeih-bega; M; 23; Navajo; F; M; Head; 3153; Yes; Yes; 22372

3137; Oss-cah-bitsih; F; 18; Navajo; F; M; Wife; 3154; Yes; Yes; 22373

3138; Hoska-yil-nah-ho-gahl; M; 4; Navajo; F; S; Son; 3155; Yes; Yes; 22374

3139; Kee-des-bah; F; 3; Navajo; F; S; Daughter; 3156; Yes; Yes; 22785

Census of the **Northern Navajo** reservation of the **Northern Navajo** jurisdiction, as of **April 1**, 19**31**, taken by **Ernest H. Hammond, District**, Superintendent. **in Charge**

**Key:** Number; NAME: Surname, Given; Sex; Birth Year (if given); Age At Last Birthday; Tribe; Degree of Blood; Marital Status; Relationship To Head of Family; Last Census Roll Number; At Jurisdiction Where Enrolled (Yes or No); At Another Jurisdiction; ELSEWHERE: Post office, County, State; Ward (Yes or No); Allotment, Annuity, and Identification Numbers.

3140; Dinay-chilli-bega; M; 26; Navajo; F; M; Head; 3157; Yes; Yes; 22583
3141; Hah-des-bah; F; 21; Navajo; F; M; Wife; 3158; Yes; Yes; 22584
3142; Haska-yee-tah-yee-gah; M; 3; Navajo; F; S; Son; 3159; Yes; Yes; 22585
3143; Tah-deyah; M; 20; Navajo; F; S; Brother-in-law; 3160; Yes; Yes; 22586
3144; Awa-alsoesis; M; 10; Navajo; F; S; Nephew-in-law; 3161; Yes; Yes; 22587

3145; Dale, Stephen's Nephew; M; 21; Navajo; F; M; Head; 3162; Yes; Yes; 22656
3146; Dale, Stephen's Nephew's wife; F; 19; Navajo; F; M; Wife; 3163; Yes; Yes; 22657

3147; Tah-nih-bah; F; 5; Navajo; F; S; Daughter; 3164; Yes; Yes; 22765[sic]
                                    [ID No. should be 22658]
[3148; Haska-yil-hah-yah; M; 2; Navajo; F; S; Son; 3165; Yes; Yes; 22765]
[This child was omitted on this 1931 Census]

3149; Dinay-yee-is-kinih-bega; M; Unk; Navajo; F; M; Head; 3166; Yes; Yes; 22667
3150; Ahph-yeh-bah; F; 20; Navajo; F; M; Wife; 3167; Yes; Yes; 22668

3151; Dahah-dah-sah-kad-bitsoih; M; 30; Navajo; F; M; Head; 3169; Yes; Yes; 32250
3152; Salou-sosie-benally, Louise; F; 29; Navajo; F; M; Wife; 3170; Yes; Yes; 32251

3153; Dagah-etsosie, Pinto; M; 66; Navajo; F; M; Head; 3171; Yes; Yes; 32201
3154; Hosteen-nez-bitsih; F; 42; Navajo; F; M; Wife; 3172; Yes; Yes; 32202
3155; Tahn; M; 20; Navajo; F; S; Son; 3173; Yes; Yes; 32203
3156; Bil-chih-dez-bah; F; 16; Navajo; F; S; Daughter; 3174; Yes; Yes; 32204
3157; Haska-yil-yil-wudt, Clah; M; 14; Navajo; F; S; Son; 3175; Yes; Yes; 32205
3158; Hosteen-deel-benally; F; 30; Navajo; F; M; 2nd Wife; 3176; Yes; Yes; 32206
3159; Tah-gah; M; 17; Navajo; F; S; Son; 3177; Yes; Yes; 32207
3160; Dah-his-wudt; M; 12; Navajo; F; S; Son; 3178; Yes; Yes; 32208
3161; Haska-yah-nal-wudt; M; 5; Navajo; F; S; Son; 3179; Yes; Yes; 32209
3162; Nah-hoh-gahl; M; 8; Navajo; F; S; Grand-son; 3180; Yes; Yes; 32210
3163; Yee-dah-bah; F; 12; Navajo; F; S; Grand-daughter; 3181; Yes; Yes; 32211

3164; Dinay-chilli-benally; M; 34; Navajo; F; M; Head; 3182; Yes; Yes; 32354
3165; Salou-bitsees-chilli-bitsih; F; 30; Navajo; F; M; Wife; 3183; Yes; Yes; 32355
3166; Haska-yee-chih-hal-wudt; M; 16; Navajo; F; S; Son; 3184; Yes; Yes; 32356
3167; Curley, Timothy; M; 12; Navajo; F; S; Son; 3185; Yes; Yes; 32357
3168; Yil-chin-bah; F; 10; Navajo; F; S; Daughter; 3186; Yes; Yes; 32358
3169; Glih-yil-dez-bah; F; 8; Navajo; F; S; Daughter; 3187; Yes; Yes; 32359
3170; Adzan-l-bahih; F; 5; Navajo; F; S; Daughter; 3188; Yes; Yes; 32360
3171; Glih-yil-nih-bah; F; 3; Navajo; F; S; Daughter; 3189; Yes; Yes; 32361

Census of the **Northern Navajo** reservation of the **Northern Navajo** jurisdiction, as of **April 1**, 19**31,** taken by **Ernest H. Hammond, District**, Superintendent. **in Charge**

**Key:** Number; NAME: Surname, Given; Sex; Birth Year (if given), Age At Last Birthday; Tribe; Degree of Blood; Marital Status; Relationship To Head of Family; Last Census Roll Number; At Jurisdiction Where Enrolled (Yes or No); At Another Jurisdiction; ELSEWHERE: Post office, County, State; Ward (Yes or No); Allotment, Annuity, and Identification Numbers.

3172; Duncan, Amelia; F; Unk; Navajo; F; Wd; Head; 3190; Yes; Yes; 22677
3173; Francis; M; 21; Navajo; F; S; Son; 3191; Yes; Yes; 22678
3173; Evelyn; F; Unk; Navajo; F; S; Daughter; 3192; Yes; Yes; 22680
3175; John; M; Unk; Navajo; F; S; Son; 3193; Yes; Yes; 22679
3176; Hah-gee-bah; F; Unk; Navajo; F; S; Daughter; 3194; Yes; Yes; 22681
3177; Bahn-hah-gee-bah; F; Unk; Navajo; F; S; Daughter; 3195; Yes; Yes; 22682
3178; Kee; M; Unk; Navajo; F; S; Son; 3196; Yes; Yes; 22683

3179; Dinay-chilli-bega; M; 55; Navajo; F; M; Head; 3197; Yes; Yes; 32417
3180; Hosteen-charley-bitsih; F; 62; Navajo; F; M; Wife; 3198; Yes; Yes; 32418
3181; Gahl; M; 8; Navajo; F; S; Grandson; 3199; Yes; Yes; 32419

3182; Dinay-chilli-benally, Watson Werner; M; 24; Navajo; F; S; Head; 3200; Yes; Yes; 32424

3183; Denet-clah, Harry; M; 35; Navajo; F; M; Head; 3201; Yes; Yes; 22697
3184; Julia; F; 35; Navajo; F; M; Wife; 3202; Yes; Yes; 22698
3185; Harry, Jr.; M; 7; Navajo; F; S; Son; 3203; Yes; Yes; 22699
3186; Salou-alsosie, Esther; F; 22; Navajo; F; S; Sister-in-law; 3204; Yes; Yes; 22700
3187; Fannie; F; 28; Navajo; F; S; Sister; 3205; Yes; Yes; 22701
3188; Marian; F; 7/12; Navajo; F; S; Daughter; [Blank]; Yes; Yes; 22796

3189; Damon, Toge A.; M; 24; Navajo; F; Wd; Head; 3206; Yes; Yes; 30224
3190; Ruth; F; 3; Navajo; F; S; Daughter; 3207; Yes; Yes; 30226

3191; Dinay-chilli-benally; F; 28; Navajo; F; Wd; Head; 3208; Yes; Yes; 32438
3192; Nas-wudt; M; 8; Navajo; F; S; Son; 3209; Yes; Yes; 32439

3193; Dinay-chilli-bega, Pretty; M; 46; Navajo; F; M; Head; 3210; Yes; Yes; 32454
3194; Bah-al-chih-thalani-bitsih, Elsie; F; 47; Navajo; F; M; Wife; 3211; Yes; Yes; 32455
3195; Grey-horse, Jessie; F; 19; Navajo; F; S; Daughter; 3212; Yes; Yes; 32456
3196; Ah-kin-nih-bah; F; 13; Navajo; F; S; Daughter; 3213; Yes; Yes; 32457

3197; Dagah-ih-bega; M; Unk; Navajo; F; M; Head; 3214; Yes; Yes; 29312
3198; Adzan-hah-tahly; F; Unk; Navajo; F; M; Wife; 3215; Yes; Yes; 29313

3199; Dagah-soh-oh-bega; M; Unk; Navajo; F; M; Head; 3216; Yes; Yes; 29053
3200; Hah-naz-bah; F; 7; Navajo; F; S; Daughter; 3217; Yes; Yes; 29055
3201; Kee; M; 5; Navajo; F; S; Son; 3218; Yes; Yes; 29056
3202; Kih-gee-bah; F; 3; Navajo; F; S; Daughter; 3219; Yes; Yes; 29057
3203; John; M; 21; Navajo; F; S; Brother-in-law; 3220; Yes; Yes; 29058

Census of the **Northern Navajo** reservation of the **Northern Navajo** jurisdiction, as of **April 1**, 1931, taken by **Ernest H. Hammond, District**, Superintendent. **in Charge**

**Key:** Number; NAME: Surname, Given; Sex; Birth Year (if given), Age At Last Birthday; Tribe; Degree of Blood; Marital Status; Relationship To Head of Family; Last Census Roll Number; At Jurisdiction Where Enrolled (Yes or No); At Another Jurisdiction; ELSEWHERE: Post office, County, State; Ward (Yes or No); Allotment, Annuity, and Identification Numbers.

3199; Dagah-soh-oh-bega; M; Unk; Navajo; F; M; Head; 3216; Yes; Yes; 29053
3200; Hah-naz-bah; F; 7; Navajo; F; S; Daughter; 3217; Yes; Yes; 29055
3201; Kee; M; 5; Navajo; F; S; Son; 3218; Yes; Yes; 29056
3202; Kih-gee-bah; F; 3; Navajo; F; S; Daughter; 3219; Yes; Yes; 29057
3203; John; M; 21; Navajo; F; S; Brother-in-law; 3220; Yes; Yes; 29058
3204; Leon; M; 14; Navajo; F; S; Brother-in-law; 3221; Yes; Yes; 29059

3205; Dagah-thlani-bega; M; 37; Navajo; F; M; Head; 3222; Yes; Yes; 29035
3206; Nioh-tah-bitsih; F; 28; Navajo; F; M; Wife; 3223; Yes; Yes; 29036
3207; Haska-yee-sil; M; 8; Navajo; F; S; Son; 3224; Yes; Yes; 29037
3208; Tah-ee-bah; F; 6; Navajo; F; S; Daughter; 3225; Yes; Yes; 29038
3209; Hah-gee-bah; F; 6; Navajo; F; S; Daughter; 3226; Yes; Yes; 29039
3210; Peter; M; 3; Navajo; F; S; Son; 3227; Yes; Yes; 29401

3211; Dinay-l-seesih; M; Unk; Navajo; F; M; Head; 3228; Yes; Yes; 29853
3212; Bitsee-lagaih-bitsih; F; 45; Navajo; F; M; Wife; 3229; Yes; Yes; 29854
3213; Haska-yil-nil-wudt; M; 23; Navajo; F; S; Son; 3230; Yes; Yes; 29855
3214; Clifford; M; 22; Navajo; F; S; Son; 3231; Yes; Yes; 29856
3215; Laura; F; 18; Navajo; F; S; Daughter; 3232; Yes; Yes; 29857
3216; Naz-bah; F; 16; Navajo; F; S; Daughter; 3233; Yes; Yes; 29858
3217; Cora; F; 13; Navajo; F; S; Daughter; 3234; Yes; Yes; 29859
3218; Dee-bah; F; 9; Navajo; F; S; Daughter; 3235; Yes; Yes; 29860
3219; Yee-dil-wudt; M; 6; Navajo; F; S; Son; 3236; Yes; Yes; 29861
3220; Clah-litsuen-benally; M; 25; Navajo; F; S; Second cousin; 3237; Yes; Yes; 29862
3221; Tyler; M; 19; Navajo; F; S; Second cousin; 3238; Yes; Yes; 29863

3222; Dinay-sosie; M; 63; Navajo; F; M; Head; 3239; Yes; Yes; 29361
3223; Dinay-sosie's wife; F; 51; Navajo; F; M; Wife; 3240; Yes; Yes; 29362
3224; Dinay-a-tol; M; 27; Navajo; F; S; Son; 3241; Yes; Yes; 29363
3225; Yah-hil-wudt; M; 21; Navajo; F; S; Son; 3242; Yes; Yes; 29364

3226; Dinay-sosie-bega, Ellis; M; 34; Navajo; F; M; Head; 3243; Yes; Yes; 29241
3227; Hosteen-boh-woh-atin-bitsih; F; 34; Navajo; F; M; Wife; 3244; Yes; Yes; 29242
3228; Robert; M; 12; Navajo; F; S; Son; 3245; Yes; Yes; 29243
3229; Earl; M; 10; Navajo; F; S; Son; 3246; Yes; Yes; 29244
3230; John; M; 7; Navajo; F; S; Son; 3247; Yes; Yes; 29245
3231; Red girl; F; 3; Navajo; F; S; Daughter; 3248; Yes; Yes; 29378

3232; Dinay-yazzie-badoni; M; Unk; Navajo; F; M; Head; 3249; Yes; Yes; 29185
3233; Dinay-yazzie-bitsih; F; 26; Navajo; F; M; Wife; 3250; Yes; Yes; 29186
3234; Yee-neh-bah; F; 10; Navajo; F; S; Daughter; 3251; Yes; Yes; 29187

Census of the **Northern Navajo** reservation of the **Northern Navajo** jurisdiction, as of **April 1**, 19**31**, taken by **Ernest H. Hammond, District**, Superintendent. **in Charge**

Key: Number; NAME: Surname, Given; Sex; Birth Year (if given), Age At Last Birthday; Tribe; Degree of Blood; Marital Status; Relationship To Head of Family; Last Census Roll Number; At Jurisdiction Where Enrolled (Yes or No); At Another Jurisdiction; ELSEWHERE: Post office, County, State; Ward (Yes or No); Allotment, Annuity, and Identification Numbers.

3235; Dah-toh-lel; M; 8; Navajo; F; S; Son; 3252; Yes; Yes; 29188
3236; Yallie; M; 5; Navajo; F; S; Son; 3253; Yes; Yes; 29189
3237; Lucy; F; 2; Navajo; F; S; Daughter; 3254; Yes; Yes; 29379

3238; Dinay-yazzie-bega; M; 25; Navajo; F; M; Head; 3255; Yes; Yes; 29275
3239; Bah; F; 22; Navajo; F; M; Wife; 3256; Yes; Yes; 29276
3240; Clih-yil-nih-bah; F; 6; Navajo; F; S; Daughter; 3257; Yes; Yes; 29277
3241; Yee-tah-yah; M; 3; Navajo; F; S; Son; 3258; Yes; Yes; 29278
3242; Maybell; F; 2; Navajo; F; S; Daughter; 3259; Yes; Yes; 29279

3243; Dinay-yazzie-bega; M; 30; Navajo; F; M; Head; 3260; Yes; Yes; 29262
3244; Nah-dee-bah; F; 27; Navajo; F; M; Wife; 3261; Yes; Yes; 29263
3245; Yahn-nah-bah; F; 6; Navajo; F; S; Daughter; 3262; Yes; Yes; 29264
3246; Tah-dez-bah; F; 3; Navajo; F; S; Daughter; 3263; Yes; Yes; 29265
3247; Baby; F; 2; Navajo; F; S; Daughter; 3264; Yes; Yes; 29266

3248; Dish Nose; M; 59; Navajo; F; M; Head; 3265; Yes; Yes; 29772
3249; Oz-bah; F; 28; Navajo; F; M; Wife; 3266; Yes; Yes; 29773
3250; Bash-in; M; 26; Navajo; F; S; Son; 3267; Yes; Yes; 29774
3251; Dish Nose's daughter; F; 22; Navajo; F; S; Daughter; 3268; Yes; Yes; 29775
3252; Haska-yee-kih-des-wudt; M; 9; Navajo; F; S; Son; 3269; Yes; Yes; 29776
3253; Haska-yil-hah-hah-del; M; 7; Navajo; F; S; Son; 3270; Yes; Yes; 29777
3254; Ah-hah-yee-nih-bah; F; 5; Navajo; F; S; Daughter; 3271; Yes; Yes; 29778
3255; Nah-glih-se-bah; F; 3; Navajo; F; S; Daughter; 3272; Yes; Yes; 29779
3256; Hosteen-klizi-thlani; M; 107; Navajo; F; Wd; Father; 3273; Yes; Yes; 29780
3257; Haska-yee-tah-hah-zah; M; 16; Navajo; F; S; Son; 3274; Yes; Yes; 29949

3258; Bega, Dish Nose; M; 29; Navajo; F; M; Head; 3275; Yes; Yes; 29790
3259; Chih-gee-bah; F; 20; Navajo; F; M; Wife; 3276; Yes; Yes; 29791
3260; Kih-dez-bah; F; 9; Navajo; F; S; Daughter; 3277; Yes; Yes; 29792
3261; Yee-kah-nih-bah; F; 7; Navajo; F; S; Daughter; 3278; Yes; Yes; 29793
3262; Kah-dez-bah; F; 5; Navajo; F; S; Daughter; 3279; Yes; Yes; 29794
3263; Haska-yee-nah-hoh-lal; M; 3; Navajo; F; S; Son; 3280; Yes; Yes; 29795

3264; Doh-bil-hoh-zohn; M; 45; Navajo; F; Wd; Head; 3281; Yes; Yes; 29191
3265; Inez; F; 21; Navajo; F; S; Daughter; 3282; Yes; Yes; 29192
3266; Hosteen-tahn-bitsih; F; 67; Navajo; F; Wd; Aunt; 3283; Yes; Yes; 29193
3267; Tah-zoz-bah; F; 10; Navajo; F; S; Cousin; 3284; Yes; Yes; 29194

3268; Doh-jah-hih; M; Unk; Navajo; F; M; Head; 3285; Yes; Yes; 29090
3269; Bilah-gahih-yis-kin-bitsih; F; Unk; Navajo; F; M; Wife; 3286; Yes; Yes; 29091

Census of the **Northern Navajo** reservation of the **Northern Navajo** jurisdiction, as of **April 1**, 19**31**, taken by **Ernest H. Hammond, District**, Superintendent. **in Charge**

**Key:** Number; NAME: Surname, Given; Sex; Birth Year (if given), Age At Last Birthday; Tribe; Degree of Blood; Marital Status; Relationship To Head of Family; Last Census Roll Number; At Jurisdiction Where Enrolled (Yes or No); At Another Jurisdiction; ELSEWHERE: Post office, County, State; Ward (Yes or No); Allotment, Annuity, and Identification Numbers.

3270; Dee-nay-clay-bega; M; Unk; Navajo; F; M; Head; 3287; Yes; Yes; 32848
3271; Benally, Charley; F; 24; Navajo; F; M; Wife; 3288; Yes; Yes; 32849
3272; Nah-glih-yil-hah-nih-bah; F; 4; Navajo; F; S; Daughter; 3289; Yes; Yes; 32850
3273; Haska-yil-has-wudt; M; 2; Navajo; F; S; Son; 3290; Yes; Yes; 32851

3274; Dinay-sosie-benally; M; 38; Navajo; F; M; Head; 3291; Yes; Yes; 32885
3275; Hah-nih-tayshih-benally; F; 32; Navajo; F; M; Wife; 3292; Yes; Yes; 32886

3276; Dinay-l-suen-benally; M; 46; Navajo; F; M; Head; 3293; Yes; Yes; 32917
3277; Benally-hosteen-bitsih, Charley; F; 26; Navajo; F; M; Wife; 3294; Yes; Yes; 32918
3278; Amy; F; 22; Navajo; F; S; Daughter; 3295; Yes; Yes; 32919
3279; Glih-nih-nih-bah; F; 19; Navajo; F; S; Daughter; 3296; Yes; Yes; 32920
3280; Haska-yee-chih-deyah; M; 10; Navajo; F; S; Son; 3297; Yes; Yes; 32921
3281; Jerry-Bonito; M; 6; Navajo; F; S; Son; 3298; Yes; Yes; 32922
3282; Nah-gleeh-shen-pah; F; 3; Navajo; F; S; Daughter; 3299; Yes; Yes; 27082

3283; Dixon-Hallet; M; 26; Navajo; F; M; Head; 3300; Yes; Yes; 32909
3284; Dinay-l-suen-benally-bitsih; F; 26; Navajo; F; M; Wife; 3301; Yes; Yes; 32910
3285; Nah-tah-yee-kadt-deyah; M; 6; Navajo; F; S; Son; 3302; Yes; Yes; 32911
3286; Frank; M; 5; Navajo; F; S; Son; 3303; Yes; Yes; 32912
3287; Haska-yee-chih-has-wudt; M; 2; Navajo; F; S; Son; 3304; Yes; Yes; 32913

3288; Dogie-bega; M; 29; Navajo; F; M; Head; 3305; Yes; Yes; 32950
3289; Hah-nih-tay-shih-benally; F; 24; Navajo; F; M; Wife; 3306; Yes; Yes; 32951
3290; Nah-tah-yey-ee-gahl; M; 6; Navajo; F; S; Son; 3307; Yes; Yes; 32952
3291; Nah-glih-ee-tah-dez-bah; F; 3; Navajo; F; S; Daughter; 3308; Yes; Yes; 32953

3292; Dinay-yazzie-bega-hosteen; M; 45; Navajo; F; Div.; Head; 3309; Yes; Yes; 31163

3293; Descheeny-Sani; M; 66; Navajo; F; M; Head; 3310; Yes; Yes; 28074
3294; Hosteen-nah-seeih-benally; F; 33; Navajo; F; M; Wife; 3311; Yes; Yes; 28075
3295; Haska-yil-noh-tahl; M; 9; Navajo; F; S; Son; 3312; Yes; Yes; 28076
3296; Toh-dez-bah; F; 11; Navajo; F; S; Daughter; 3313; Yes; Yes; 28077
3297; Tahn; M; 5; Navajo; F; S; Son; 3314; Yes; Yes; 28078
3298; Yee-taz-bah; F; 3; Navajo; F; S; Daughter; 3315; Yes; Yes; 28079
3299; Nah-woody; M; 16; Navajo; F; S; Step-son; 3316; Yes; Yes; 28080

3300; Doh-bilth-haltin-bega; F; 27; Navajo; F; M; Head; 3317; Yes; Yes; 28092

Census of the **Northern Navajo** reservation of the **Northern Navajo** jurisdiction, as of **April 1**, 19**31**, taken by **Ernest H. Hammond, District**, Superintendent. **in Charge**

**Key:** Number; NAME: Surname, Given; Sex; Birth Year (if given), Age At Last Birthday; Tribe; Degree of Blood; Marital Status; Relationship To Head of Family; Last Census Roll Number; At Jurisdiction Where Enrolled (Yes or No); At Another Jurisdiction; ELSEWHERE: Post office, County, State; Ward (Yes or No); Allotment, Annuity, and Identification Numbers.

3301; Bitsee-bitsuih-bitsih, Gladys; F; 26; Navajo; F; M; Wife; 3318; Yes; Yes; 28093
3302; Rena; F; 5; Navajo; F; S; Daughter; 3319; Yes; Yes; 28094
3303; Kee; M; 2; Navajo; F; S; Son; 3320; Yes; Yes; 28095

3304; Descheeny; M; 52; Navajo; F; M; Head; 3321; Yes; Yes; 18061
3305; Descheeny's wife; F; 56; Navajo; F; M; Wife; 3322; Yes; Yes; 18062
3306; Descheeny Bega; M; 26; Navajo; F; S; Son; 3323; Yes; Yes; 18063
3307; Bah; F; 25; Navajo; F; S; Daughter; 3324; Yes; Yes; 18064
3308; Chee-ih; F; 23; Navajo; F; S; Daughter; 3325; Yes; Yes; 18065
3309; Nah-a-bah; F; 12; Navajo; F; S; Daughter; 3326; Yes; Yes; 18066
3310; Atate-l-suen; F; 5; Navajo; F; S; Daughter; 3327; Yes; Yes; 18067
3311; Descheeny, Myrtle; F; 10; Navajo; F; S; Daughter; 3328; Yes; Yes; 18068
3312; Mary; F; 2; Navajo; F; S; Daughter; 3329; Yes; Yes; 18253

3313; Dee-chees-bitsih; F; 26; Navajo; F; Wd; Head; 3330; Yes; Yes; 31235
3314; Dah-nih-bah; F; 11; Navajo; F; S; Daughter; 3331; Yes; Yes; 31236
3315; Chih-hih-bah; F; 19; Navajo; F; 3332; Yes; Yes; 31237
3316; Glih-gil-ha-bah; F; 18; Navajo; F; S; Daughter; 3333; Yes; Yes; 31238
3317; Kih-yil-haz-bah; F; 5; Navajo; F; S; Daughter; 3334; Yes; Yes; 31239

3318; Denay-yazzie-bega; M; 56; Navajo; F; M; Head; 3335; Yes; Yes; 21714
3319; Tah-cho-nih-benally; F; 54; Navajo; F; M; Wife; 3336; Yes; Yes; 21715
3320; Ad-ae-bah-ih; F; 19; Navajo; F; S; Daughter; 3337; Yes; Yes; 21716
3321; Kae-wudt; M; 11; Navajo; F; S; Son; 3338; Yes; Yes; 21717
3322; Kae-bah; F; 9; Navajo; F; S; Daughter; 3339; Yes; Yes; 21718
3323; Al-chin-des-bah; F; 17; Navajo; F; S; Grand-Daughter; 3340; Yes; Yes; 21719
3324; Chih-kal; F; 37; F; Wd; Sister-in-law; 3341; Yes; Yes; 21720
3325; Nah-gee-bah; M; 17; F; S; Nephew-in-law; 3342; Yes; Yes; 21721

3326; Denay-sosie-bega; M; Unk; Navajo; F; M; Head; 3343; Yes; Yes; 23949
3327; Clah-nea-bitsie; F; Unk; Navajo; F; M; Wife; 3344; Yes; Yes; 23950
3328; Tas-bah; F; 8; Navajo; F; S; Daughter; 3345; Yes; Yes; 23951
3329; Away-chee; M; 10; Navajo; F; S; Son; 3346; Yes; Yes; 23952

3330; En-clah-ighi; M; 55; Navajo; F; M; Head; 3347; Yes; Yes; 28348
3331; Atate-yazzie; F; 49; Navajo; F; M; Wife; 3348; Yes; Yes; 28349
3332; Portia; F; 19; Navajo; F; S; Step-daughter; 3350; Yes; Yes; 28351
3333; Marie; F; 17; Navajo; F; S; Step-daughter; 3351; Yes; Yes; 28352
3334; Doh-cheeih; M; 11; Navajo; F; S; Son; 3352; Yes; Yes; 28353
3335; Doh-bahih; M; 9; Navajo; F; S; Son; 3353; Yes; Yes; 28354
3336; Haska-yil-hah-yah; M; 7; Navajo; F; S; Son; 3354; Yes; Yes; 28355
3337; Al-kih-gee-bah; F; 5; Navajo; F; S; Daughter; 3355; Yes; Yes; 28356

Census of the **Northern Navajo** reservation of the **Northern Navajo** jurisdiction, as of **April 1**, 19**31,** taken by **Ernest H. Hammond, District**, Superintendent. **in Charge**

**Key:** Number; NAME: Surname, Given; Sex; Birth Year (if given), Age At Last Birthday; Tribe; Degree of Blood; Marital Status; Relationship To Head of Family; Last Census Roll Number; At Jurisdiction Where Enrolled (Yes or No); At Another Jurisdiction; ELSEWHERE: Post office, County, State; Ward (Yes or No); Allotment, Annuity, and Identification Numbers.

3338; Hah-nez-bah; F; 3; Navajo; F; S; Daughter; 3356; Yes; Yes; 28357
3339; Adzan-soh; F; 78; Navajo; F; S; Mother; 3357; Yes; Yes; 28358
3340; Seginih, Bill; M; 15; Navajo; F; S; Nephew; 3358; Yes; Yes; 28359
3341; Nah-glih-hah-nel; F; 16; Navajo; F; S; Niece; 3359; Yes; Yes; 28360
3342; Segnih[sic], Rosalyn; F; 13; Navajo; F; S; Niece; 3360; Yes; Yes; 28361
[Name is probably Seginih, Rosalyn]

3343; Enclah-ihgih-bega; M; 34; Navajo; F; M; Head; 3361; Yes; Yes; 20329
3344; Bah; F; 22; Navajo; F; M; Wife; 3362; Yes; Yes; 20330
3345; Ah-ih-iln-bah; F; 9; Navajo; F; S; Daughter; 3363; Yes; Yes; 20331
3346; Ashkee-yazzie; M; 2; Navajo; F; S; Son; 3364; Yes; Yes; 20447

3347; Enclahih-bitsih; F; 35; Navajo; F; Div.; Head; 3365; Yes; Yes; 30803
3348; Johnson, Willie; M; 6; Navajo; F; S; Son; 3366; Yes; Yes; 30804
3349; Al-nez-bah, Romona; F; 16; Navajo; F; S; Sister; 3367; Yes; Yes; 30805
3350; Enclahih-bega, Dan Puggy; M; 21; Navajo; F; S; Brother; 3368; Yes; Yes; 30806

3351; Enclah-ihgi-bega; M; 22; Navajo; F; M; Head; 3370; Yes; Yes; 20126
3352; Bilah-gohah-ye-is-hin-ih-bega-bitsih; F; 25; Navajo; F; M; Wife; 3371; Yes; Yes; 20127
3353; Be-tlohi, Christine; F; 16; Navajo; F; S; Sister-in-law; 3372; Yes; Yes; 20128

3354; En-clah-ihgi, Julian; M; 67; Navajo; F; M; Head; 3373; Yes; Yes; 21086
3355; Bah; F; 49; Navajo; F; M; Wife; 3374; Yes; Yes; 21087
3356; Julian, Fay; F; 12; Navajo; F; S; Daughter; 3375; Yes; Yes; 21088
3357; Yil-des-bah; F; 20; Navajo; F; S; Daughter; 3376; Yes; Yes; 21089
3358; Joih; F; 21; Navajo; F; S; Niece-in-law; 3377; Yes; Yes; 21090
3359; Nah-tah-yil-gee-gah; M; 1; Navajo; F; S; Niece-in-law; 3378; Yes; Yes; 22784

3360; Eskie, Curley; M; 42; Navajo; F; M; Head; 770; Yes; Yes; 27053
3361; Nellie; F; 42; Navajo; F; M; Wife; 771; Yes; Yes; 27054
3362; Ethel; F; 18; Navajo; F; S; Daughter; 772; Yes; Yes; 27055
3363; Emma; F; 14; Navajo; F; S; Daughter; 773; Yes; Yes; 27056
3364; Frank; M; 10; Navajo; F; S; Son; 774; Yes; Yes; 27057

3365; Eskee; M; 33; Navajo; F; M; Head; 3380; Yes; Yes; 25172
3366; Lena; F; 34; Navajo; F; M; Wife; 3381; Yes; Yes; 25173
3367; Beatrice; F; 14; Navajo; F; S; Daughter; 3382; Yes; Yes; 25174
3368; Vetna; F; 11; Navajo; F; S; Daughter; 3383; Yes; Yes; 25175
3369; Harry; M; 4; Navajo; F; S; Son; 3384; Yes; Yes; 25176

3370; Etsitty, Kee L.; M; 28; Navajo; F; M; Head; 3385; Yes; Yes; 25994

Census of the **Northern Navajo** reservation of the **Northern Navajo** jurisdiction, as of **April 1**, 19**31,** taken by **Ernest H. Hammond, District**, Superintendent. **in Charge**

Key: Number; NAME: Surname, Given; Sex; Birth Year (if given), Age At Last Birthday; Tribe; Degree of Blood; Marital Status; Relationship To Head of Family; Last Census Roll Number; At Jurisdiction Where Enrolled (Yes or No); At Another Jurisdiction; ELSEWHERE: Post office, County, State; Ward (Yes or No); Allotment, Annuity, and Identification Numbers.

3371; Tah-esbah; F; 24; Navajo; F; M; Wife; 3386; Yes; Yes; 25995
3372; Kee-kah-naz-bah; F; 3; Navajo; F; S; Daughter; 3387; Yes; Yes; 25996
3373; Stevens; M; 1; Navajo; F; S; Son; 3388; Yes; Yes; 26057

3374; Ed-Hosea; M; 39; Navajo; F; M; Head; 3389; Yes; Yes; 32964
3375; Jackson, Ruth; F; 29; Navajo; F; M; Wife; 3390; Yes; Yes; 32965
3376; Leenoh; M; 6; Navajo; F; S; Son; 3391; Yes; Yes; 32966
3377; Frederick; M; 4; Navajo; F; S; Son; 3392; Yes; Yes; 32967
3378; Louise; F; 2; Navajo; F; S; Daughter; 3393; Yes; Yes; 32968
3379; Jackson, Mary Louise; F; 20; Navajo; F; S; Sister-in-law; 3394; Yes; Yes; 32999
3380; Hosea, Johnny; M; 16; Navajo; F; S; Brother; 3395; Yes; Yes; 32998

3381; Edway, Jake; M; Unk; Navajo; F; M; Head; 3396; Yes; Yes; 32818
3382; Bih-dole-bitsih; F; 35; Navajo; F; M; Wife; 3397; Yes; Yes; 32819
3383; Mabel; F; 11; Navajo; F; S; Daughter; 3398; Yes; Yes; 32820
3384; Esther; F; 10; Navajo; F; S; Daughter; 3399; Yes; Yes; 32821
3385; Tah-hah-bah; F; 3; Navajo; F; S; Daughter; 3400; Yes; Yes; 32822
3386; John, Frank; M; 19; Navajo; F; S; Nephew; 3401; Yes; Yes; 33001

3387; Chee, Helen - Enclah-igi-bitsih's daughter; F; 18; Navajo; F; S; Head; 3402; Yes; Yes; 31198
3388; Chih-hah-bah, Lena; M; 14; Navajo; F; S; Brother; 3403; Yes; Yes; 31199
3389; Lucy; F; 12; Navajo; F; S; Sister; 3404; Yes; Yes; 31200
3390; Elsie; F; 10; Navajo; F; S; Sister; [5084]; Yes; Yes; 31201
3391; Haska-yee-nahhah, Jean; M; 8; Navajo; F; S; Sister[sic]; 3405; Yes; Yes; 31202
3392; Big Jim; M; 16; Navajo; F; S; Brother; 3406; Yes; Yes; 31203
3393; Bih-zay-yazzie; M; 29; Navajo; F; S; Cousin; 3407; Yes; Yes; 31204
3394; Nah-tah-sosie; M; 6; Navajo; F; S; Brother; 3408; Yes; Yes; 31205

3395; El-roy; M; Unk; Navajo; F; S; Head; 3409; Yes; Yes; 23934

3396; Feece-sosie-bega; M; 33; Navajo; F; M; Head; 3410; Yes; Yes; 20006
3397; Nocki-deetsah-bega, bitsih; F; 30; Navajo; F; M; Wife; 3411; Yes; Yes; 20007
3398; Nah-thl-bah-hih; M; 15; Navajo; F; S; Son; 3412; Yes; Yes; 20008
3399; Zannie-l-chee; F; 8; Navajo; F; S; Daughter; 3413; Yes; Yes; 20009
3400; Des-clah; M; 5; Navajo; F; S; Son; 3414; Yes; Yes; 20010
3401; Andrew, Carl; M; 27; Navajo; F; M; Brother-in-law; 3415; Yes; Yes; 20011
3402; Bah-dagah-ihgi-bega; M; 23; Navajo; S; Brother-in-law; 3416; Yes; Yes; 20012
3403; Eskee-l-bahih; M; 21; Navajo; F; S; Brother-in-law; 3417; Yes; Yes; 20013
3404; Dee-kaz-bah; F; 2; Navajo; F; S; Daughter; 3418; Yes; Yes; 20433

Census of the **Northern Navajo** reservation of the **Northern Navajo** jurisdiction, as of **April 1**, 19**31**, taken by **Ernest H. Hammond, District**, Superintendent. **in Charge**

**Key:** Number; NAME: Surname, Given; Sex; Birth Year (if given), Age At Last Birthday; Tribe; Degree of Blood; Marital Status; Relationship To Head of Family; Last Census Roll Number; At Jurisdiction Where Enrolled (Yes or No); At Another Jurisdiction; ELSEWHERE: Post office, County, State; Ward (Yes or No); Allotment, Annuity, and Identification Numbers.

3405; Fred Funston's Sister; F; 50; Navajo; F; Div.; Head; 3419; Yes; Yes; 30942
3406; Aht-citty, Ida; F; 18; Navajo; F; S; Daughter; 3420; Yes; Yes; 30943
3407; Haska-yee-tah-yah; M; 13; Navajo; F; S; Son; 3421; Yes; Yes; 30944
3408; Jim, John; M; 28; Navajo; F; S; Brother; 3422; Yes; Yes; 31267

3409; Funston, Fred; M; Unk; Navajo; F; M; Head; 3423; Yes; Yes; 30929
3410; Minnie; F; Unk; Navajo; F; M; Wife; 3424; Yes; Yes; 30930
3411; Nas-wudt; M; 22; Navajo; F; S; Son; 3425; Yes; Yes; 30931
3412; Haska-yil-deyah; M; 23; Navajo; F; S; Son; 3426; Yes; Yes; 30932
3413; Al-nah-bah; F; 28; Navajo; F; S; Daughter; 3427; Yes; Yes; 30933
3414; John, Billy; M; 22; Navajo; F; S; Nephew; 3428; Yes; Yes; 30886

3415; Francis, Keith; M; 36; Navajo; F; M; Head; 3429; Yes; Yes; 27982
3416; Bah; F; 31; Navajo; F; M; Wife; 3430; Yes; Yes; 27983
3417; Unknown; M; 19; Navajo; F; S; Nephew; 3431; Yes; Yes; 27984
3418; Yahn-des-bah; F; 17; Navajo; F; S; Niece; 3432; Yes; Yes; 27985
3419; Oscar; M; 36; Navajo; F; S; Nephew; 3433; Yes; Yes; 27986
3420; Navajo, Jim; M; 34; Navajo; F; S; Nephew; 3434; Yes; Yes; 27987
3421; Dot; F; 11; Navajo; F; S; Niece; F; S; Niece; 3435; Yes; Yes; 27988
3422; Zah-nez; F; 97; Navajo; F; Wd; Grand-Mother; 3436; Yes; Yes; 27989

3423; Foster, Edward; M; Unk; Navajo; F; M; Head; 3437; Yes; Yes; 20980
3424; Nocki-dinay-clitsohigi-bitsih; F; 23; Navajo; F; M; Wife; 3438; Yes; Yes; 20981
3425; Nocki-dinay-clitsohigi-bega; M; 26; Navajo; F; S; Brother-in-law; 3439; Yes; Yes; 20982
3426; Nocki-dinay-clitsohigi-bega; M; Unk; Navajo; F; Wd; Father-in-law; 3440; Yes; Yes; 20983

3427; Foster, John Jr.; M; 25; Navajo; F; M; Head; 3441; Yes; Yes; 26306
3428; Tah-nih-bah; F; 23; Navajo; F; M; Wife; 3442; Yes; Yes; 26307
3429; Alsoh-nih-bah; F; 5; Navajo; F; S; Daughter; 3443; Yes; Yes; 26308
3430; Tah-yil-wudt; M; 3; Navajo; F; S; Son; 3444; Yes; Yes; 26309

3431; Frank, George; M; 28; Navajo; F; M; Head; 3445; Yes; Yes; 21123
3432; Frank, George's wife; F; 26; Navajo; F; M; Wife; 3446; Yes; Yes; 21124
3433; Nah-tas-wudt; M; 6; Navajo; F; S; Son; 3447; Yes; Yes; 21125
3434; Hah-kayi-dah-dolni; F; 1; Navajo; F; S; Son; 3448; Yes; Yes; 21722

3435; Foster, John's wife; F; 55; Navajo; F; M; Head; 3449; Yes; Yes; 26844

3436; Funston, Fred Jr.; M; 23; Navajo; F; M; Head; 3450; Yes; Yes; 22419
3437; Fred Funston Jr's. wife; F; 23; Navajo; F; M; Wife; 3451; Yes; Yes; 22420

Census of the __Northern Navajo__ reservation of the__ Northern Navajo__
jurisdiction, as of__ April 1___, 19__31,__ taken by__ Ernest H. Hammond, District__,
Superintendent. **in Charge**

Key: Number; NAME: Surname, Given; Sex; Birth Year (if given), Age At Last Birthday; Tribe; Degree of
Blood; Marital Status; Relationship To Head of Family; Last Census Roll Number; At Jurisdiction Where
Enrolled (Yes or No); At Another Jurisdiction; ELSEWHERE: Post office, County, State; Ward (Yes or No);
Allotment, Annuity, and Identification Numbers.

3438; Frank, Pete; M; Unk; Navajo; F; M; Head; 3452; Yes; Yes; 29141
3439; Bitsee-dih-chosie-bitsih; F; 59; Navajo; F; M; Wife; 3453; Yes; Yes; 29142
3440; Ford, Davis; M; 20; Navajo; F; S; Son; 3454; Yes; Yes; 29143
3441; Awa; M; 16; Navajo; F; S; Son; 3455; Yes; Yes; 29144

3442; Francisco; M; 62; Navajo; F; M; Head; 3456; Yes; Yes; 32903
3443; Zah-nez-la-chee-bitsih; F; 62; Navajo; F; M; Wife; 3457; Yes; Yes; 32904
3444; Yil-ee-bah; F; 12; Navajo; F; S; Daughter; 3458; Yes; Yes; 32905
3445; Zah-nez-la-chee-bitsih; F; 59; Navajo; F; M; 2nd wife; 3459; Yes; Yes; 32906
3446; Glih-hah-bah; F; 15; Navajo; F; S; Daughter; 3460; Yes; Yes; 32907
3447; Nah-glih-yil-hah-nih-bah; F; 10; Navajo; F; S; Daughter; 3461; Yes; Yes;
32908

3448; Francisco bega; M; 26; Navajo; F; S; Head; 3462; Yes; Yes; 32949

3449; Francisco's son; M; 36; Navajo; F; M; Head; 3463; Yes; Yes; 32872
3450; Hah-nih-tayshih-benally; F; 36; Navajo; F; M; Wife; 3464; Yes; Yes; 32873
3451; Eskee-soh; M; 17; Navajo; F; S; Son; 3465; Yes; Yes; 32874
3452; Donald, Raymond; M; 15; F; S; Son; 3466; Yes; Yes; 32875
3453; Nah-glih-yil-naz-bah; F; 13; Navajo; F; S; Daughter; 3467; Yes; Yes; 32876
3454; Jimmy; M; 9; Navajo; F; S; Son; 3468; Yes; Yes; 32877
3455; Charley; M; 7; Navajo; F; S; Son; 3469; Yes; Yes; 32878
3456; Bih-gon-zoz-bah; F; 3; Navajo; F; S; Daughter; 3470; Yes; Yes; 32880

3457; Fulton, Robert; M; 26; Navajo; F; S; Head; 3471; Yes; Yes; 31135

3458; Frazer, Benjamin; M; 25; Navajo; F; M; Head; 3472; Yes; Yes; 22789
3459; Kol-hah-bah; F; 23; Navajo; F; M; Wife; 3473; Yes; Yes; 22787

3460; Fannie; F; 36; Navajo; F; Wd; Head; 3474; Yes; Yes; 25026

3461; Gah-leesah-bega; M; 63; Navajo; F; M; Head; 3475; Yes; Yes; 26374
3462; Glih-bah; F; 55; Navajo; F; M; Wife; 3476; Yes; Yes; 26375
3463; Naswudt; M; 19; Navajo; F; S; Son; 3477; Yes; Yes; 26376
3464; Bishop; M; 17; Navajo; F; S; Son; 3478; Yes; Yes; 26377
3465; Bah-des-wudt; M; 15; Navajo; F; S; Son; 3479; Yes; Yes; 26378
3466; Calvin; M; 13; Navajo; F; S; Son; 3480; 3480; Yes; Yes; 26379
3467; Yahn-des-wudt; M; 8; Navajo; F; S; Son; 3481; Yes; Yes; 26380
3468; Nayah; M; 6; Navajo; F; S; Son; 3482; Yes; Yes; 26381

3469; Green, Arthur; M; 35; Navajo; F; M; Head; 3483; Yes; Yes; 31119
3470; Jenny; F; 42; Navajo; F; M; Wife; 3484; Yes; Yes; Yes; 31120
3471; Rosie Bailey; F; 26; Navajo; F; S; Step-daughter; 3485; Yes; Yes; 31121

Census of the **Northern Navajo** reservation of the **Northern Navajo** jurisdiction, as of **April 1**, 1931, taken by **Ernest H. Hammond, District**, Superintendent. **in Charge**

**Key:** Number; NAME: Surname, Given; Sex; Birth Year (if given), Age At Last Birthday; Tribe; Degree of Blood; Marital Status; Relationship To Head of Family; Last Census Roll Number; At Jurisdiction Where Enrolled (Yes or No); At Another Jurisdiction; ELSEWHERE: Post office, County, State; Ward (Yes or No); Allotment, Annuity, and Identification Numbers.

3472; Bailey, Lucy; F; 22; Navajo; F; S Step-daughter; 3486; Yes; Yes; 31122
3473; Bailey, Willie; M; 18; Navajo; F; S; Step-son; 3487; Yes; Yes; 31123
3474; Bailey, Arthur; M; 15; Navajo; F; S; Step-son; 3488; Yes; Yes; 31124
3475; Bailey, Bessie; F; 12; Navajo; F; S; Step-daughter; 3489; Yes; Yes; 31125

3476; Gould, Lee; M; 29; Navajo; F; M; Head; 1160; Yes; Yes; 25050
3477; Toh-ahk-gleenih-yazzie-bitsih; F; 30, Navajo; F; M; Wife; 1161; Yes; Yes; 25051
3478; Dah-nih-bah; F; 5; Navajo; F; S; Daughter; 1162; 1162; Yes; Yes; 25052
3479; Tah-yazzie; M; 3; Navajo; F; S; Son; 1163; Yes; Yes; 25053

3480; Gould, Jay; M; Unk; Navajo; F; M; Head; 3490; Yes; Yes; 26298
3481; Gould, Jay's wife; F; Unk; Navajo; F; M; Wife; 3491; Yes; Yes; 26299
3482; Kelly; M; 12; Navajo; F; S; Son; 3492; Yes; Yes; 26301
3483; Jay Jr.; M; 10; Navajo; F; S; Son; 3493; Yes; Yes; 26302
3484; Alsoh-dez-bah; F; 18; Navajo; F; S; Daughter; 3494; Yes; Yes; 26303
3485; Naz-bah; F; 14; Navajo; F; S; Daughter; 3495; Yes; Yes; 26304
3486; Rebecca; F; 10; Navajo; F; S; Daughter; 3496; Yes; Yes; 26305

3487; Gona-nez-bitailli[sic]; M; 52; Navajo; F; M; Head; 3497; Yes; Yes; 30633
[Name could be Gona-nez-bitcilli]
3488; Natoni-bitsih; F; 52; Navajo; F; M; Wife; 3498; Yes; Yes; 30634

3489; Green, Tom; M; 49; Navajo; F; M; Head; 3499; Yes; Yes; 30368
3490; Zani-bih-cheh; F; 27; Navajo; F; M; Wife; 3500; Yes; Yes; 30369
3491; Eskee; M; 7; Navajo; F; S; Son; 3501; Yes; Yes; 30370

3492; Gish-dee-lit-dih-bega-bitsih, Anna; F; 35; Navajo; F; Wd; Head; 3502; Yes; Yes; 26207
3493; Willie; M; 19; Navajo; F; S; Son; 3503; Yes; Yes; 26208
3494; George; M; 15; Navajo; F; S; Son; 3504; Yes; Yes; 26209
3495; Lucy; F; 9; Navajo; F; S; Daughter; 3505; Yes; Yes; 26210
3496; John; M; 8; Navajo; F; S; Son; 3506; Yes; Yes; 26211

3497; Gould, James; M; 32; Navajo; F; M; Head; 3507; Yes; Yes; 26310
3498; Daisy; F; 19; Navajo; F; M; Wife; 3508; Yes; Yes; 26311
3499; Ciah-bilah; F; 57; Navajo; F; Wd; Mother-in-law; 3509; Yes; Yes; 26312
3500; Topah-ah-sosie, Lucy; F; 21; Navajo; F; S; Cousin-in-law; 3510; Yes; Yes; 26313
3501; Evelyn; F; 14; Navajo; F; S; Cousin-in-law; 3511; Yes; Yes; 26314
3502; Charlotte; F; 12; Navajo; F; S; Cousin-in-law; 3512; Yes; Yes; 26315
3503; Clah; M; 63; Navajo; F; S; Uncle-in-law; 3513; Yes; Yes; 26316

Census of the **Northern Navajo** reservation of the **Northern Navajo** jurisdiction, as of **April 1** , 19**31**, taken by **Ernest H. Hammond, District**, Superintendent. **in Charge**

Key: Number; NAME: Surname, Given; Sex; Birth Year (if given), Age At Last Birthday; Tribe; Degree of Blood; Marital Status; Relationship To Head of Family; Last Census Roll Number; At Jurisdiction Where Enrolled (Yes or No); At Another Jurisdiction; ELSEWHERE: Post office, County, State; Ward (Yes or No); Allotment, Annuity, and Identification Numbers.

3504; Adzan-nez; F; 94; Navajo; F; Wd; Grand-mother-in-law; 3514; Yes; Yes; 26317

3505; Gah-leesah-benally, Don; M; 47; Navajo; F; M; Head; 3515; Yes; Yes; 27021
3506; Nah-dez-bah; F; 44; Navajo; F; M; Wife; 3516; Yes; Yes; 27022
3507; Don Curley; M; 18; Navajo; F; S; Son; 3517; Yes; Yes; 27023
3508; Nah-tah-yil-des-wudt; M; 15; Navajo; F; S; Son; 3518; Yes; Yes; 27024
3509; Nah-tah-yee-chih-hah-yah; M; 9; Navajo; F; S; Son; 3519; Yes; Yes; 27025
3510; Glih-ee-bah; F; 7; Navajo; F; S; Daughter; 3520; Yes; Yes; 27026
3511; Dah-nez-bah; F; 2; Navajo; F; S; Daughter; 3521; Yes; Yes; 27027

3512; Gah-lessah-bega, bitsah; F; 42; Navajo; F; Wd; Head; 3528; Yes; Yes; 26389
3513; Samuel; M; 16; Navajo; F; S; Son; 3523; Yes; Yes; 26390
3514; Victoria; F; 12; Navajo; F; S; Daughter; 3524; Yes; Yes; 26391
3515; Haska-yee-nel-wudt; M; 9; Navajo; F; S; Son; 3525; Yes; Yes; 26392
3516; Haska-des-wudt; M; 3; Navajo; F; S; Son; 3526; Yes; Yes; 26393
3517; Clifford; M; 17; Navajo; F; S; Nephew; 3527; Yes; Yes; 26394
3518; Nelson; M; 24; Navajo; F; S; Brother; 3528; Yes; Yes; 26395

3519; Goath-yen-bega; M; 61; Navajo; F; M; Head; 3529; Yes; Yes; 22487
3520; Clah-alsosie-bitsih; F; 56; Navajo; F; M; Wife; 3530; Yes; Yes; 22488
3521; Dah-deyah; M; 16; Navajo; F; S; Son; 3531; Yes; Yes; 22489
3522; Hoska-yee-tah-yeyah; M; 15; Navajo; F; S; Son; 3532; Yes; Yes; 22490
3523; Katherine; F; 28; Navajo; F; S; Daughter; 3533; Yes; Yes; 22491
3524; Tyler; M; Unk; Navajo; F; S; Step-son; 3534; Yes; Yes; 22492
3525; Bah-haz-nih-bah; M; 6; Navajo; F; S; Grand-Daughter; 3535; Yes; Yes; 22493
3526; Clah-alsosie-bih-adzan; F; 99; Navajo; F; Wd; Mother-in-law; 3536; Yes; Yes; 22494

3527; Gonih-bega; M; 52; Navajo; F; M; Head; 3537; Yes; Yes; 22038
3528; Bah-dagaih-bitsih; F; 46; Navajo; F; M; Wife; 3538; Yes; Yes; 22039
3529; Gonih-benally, Grant; M; 26; Navajo; F; M; Son; 3539; Yes; Yes; 22040
3530; Nah-hah-yah; M; 21; Navajo; F; S; Son; 3540; Yes; Yes; 22041
3531; Lee; M; 17; Navajo; F; S; Son; 3541; Yes; Yes; 22042
3532; Nah-tah-yee-che-yil-wudt; M; 13; Navajo; F; S; Son; 3542; Yes; Yes; 22043
3533; Mariana; M; 64; Navajo; F; Wd; Uncle; 3543; Yes; Yes; 22044
3534; Chih-has-bah; F; 20; Navajo; F; S; Adopted Niece; 3544; Yes; Yes; 22045

3535; Gonna-nez-bitcilli; M; 51; Navajo; F; M; Head; 3534; Yes; Yes; 22515
3536; Eye-otsin-bitsih; F; 27; Navajo; F; M; Wife; 3546; Yes; Yes; 22516
3537; Kah-bahih, Nora; F; 9; Navajo; F; S; Daughter; 3547; Yes; Yes; 22517
3538; Ah-gah-gee-bah; F; 7; Navajo; F; S; Daughter; 3548; Yes; Yes; 22518
3539; Kee-l-chee-ih; M; 6; Navajo; F; S; Son; 3549; Yes; Yes; 22519

Census of the **Northern Navajo** reservation of the **Northern Navajo** jurisdiction, as of **April 1**, 19**31**, taken by **Ernest H. Hammond, District**, Superintendent. **in Charge**

**Key:** Number; NAME: Surname, Given; Sex; Birth Year (if given), Age At Last Birthday; Tribe; Degree of Blood; Marital Status; Relationship To Head of Family; Last Census Roll Number; At Jurisdiction Where Enrolled (Yes or No); At Another Jurisdiction; ELSEWHERE: Post office, County, State; Ward (Yes or No); Allotment, Annuity, and Identification Numbers.

3540; Nah-tah-yee-tah-daynah; M; 4; Navajo; F; S; Son; 3550; Yes; Yes; 22520
3541; Leroy; M; 13; Navajo; F; S; Step-son; 3551; Yes; Yes; 22521
3542; Yee-tah-bah; F; 10; Navajo; F; S; Step-daughter; 3552; Yes; Yes; 22522

3543; Gal-leesoh-benally, John Smith; M; 32; Navajo; F; M; Head; 3553; Yes; Yes; 26353
3544; Nih-glih-yee-naz-bah; F; 22; Navajo; F; M; Wife; 3554; Yes; Yes; 26354
3545; Yil-naz-bah; F; 4; Navajo; F; S; Daughter; 3555; Yes; Yes; 26355
3546; Haska-yee-kih-des-wudt; M; 3; Navajo; F; S; Son; 3556; Yes; Yes; 26356
3547; Hosteen-haska-bih-adzan; F; 78; Navajo; F; Wd; Mother-in-law; 3557; Yes; Yes; 26357
3548; Keh-hah-nih-bah; F; 18; Navajo; F; S; Sister-in-law; 3558; Yes; Yes; 26358
3549; Dinay-lah-gaih, Mary; F; 15; Navajo; F; S; Sister-in-law; 3559; Yes; Yes; 26359
3550; Alice; F; 2; Navajo; F; S; Daughter; 3560; Yes; Yes; 26441

3551; Glih-dee-bitih-yen-benally; M; 33; Navajo; F; M; Head; 3561; Yes; Yes; 24956
3552; Al-naoz-bah; F; 25; Navajo; F; M; Wife; 3562; Yes; Yes; 24957
3553; Haska-yee-chih-naz-wudt; M; 9; Navajo; F; S; Son; 3563; Yes; Yes; 24958
3554; Keh-yil-dez-bah; F; 7; Navajo; F; S; Daughter; 3564; Yes; Yes; 24959

3555; Galeesah-benally; M; 25; Navajo; F; M; Head; 3565; Yes; Yes; 26971
3556; Ah-heh-dee-bah; F; 21; Navajo; F; M; Wife; 3566; Yes; Yes; 26972

3557; Gonnah-nez-bega; M; Unk; Navajo; F; M; Head; 3567; Yes; Yes; 21605
3558; Kep-hah-ziz-bah; F; 27; Navajo; F; M; Wife; 3568; Yes; Yes; 21606
3559; Nah-tah-yee-chih-des-wudt; M; 7; Navajo; F; S; Son; 3569; Yes; Yes; 21607
3560; Yee-chih-haz-bah; F; 4; Navajo; F; S; Daughter; 3570; Yes; Yes; 21608

3561; Gonih-benally; M; 31; Navajo; F; M; Head; 3571; Yes; Yes; 21072
3562; Tah-naz-bah; F; 28; Navajo; F; M; Wife; 3572; Yes; Yes; 21073
3563; Tah-nih-bah; F; 7; Navajo; F; S; Daughter; 3573; Yes; Yes; 21075
3564; Haska-yee-tha-nil-wudt; M; 5; Navajo; F; S; Son; 3574; Yes; Yes; 21076
3565; Al-so-nas-bah; F; 4; Navajo; F; S; Daughter; 3575; Yes; Yes; 21077

3566; Gonnah-nez's wife; F; 37; Navajo; F; Wd; Head; 3576; Yes; Yes; 22507
3567; Ah-hih-nih-bah; F; 21; Navajo; F; S; Daughter; 3577; Yes; Yes; 22508
3568; Nah-tah-yazzie; M; 8; Navajo; F; S; Son; 3578; Yes; Yes; 22509
3569; Hah-gee-bah; F; 6; Navajo; F; S; Daughter; 3579; Yes; Yes; 22510
3570; Ida; F; 3; Navajo; F; S; Daughter; 3580; Yes; Yes; 22511
3571; Gonnah, Keeswudt[sic]; M; 28; Navajo; F; S; Son; 3581; Yes; Yes; 22514
   [Name could be Gonnah, Kee-wudt]

Census of the **Northern Navajo** reservation of the **Northern Navajo** jurisdiction, as of **April 1**, 1931, taken by **Ernest H. Hammond, District**, Superintendent. **in Charge**

**Key:** Number; NAME: Surname, Given; Sex; Birth Year (if given), Age At Last Birthday; Tribe; Degree of Blood; Marital Status; Relationship To Head of Family; Last Census Roll Number; At Jurisdiction Where Enrolled (Yes or No); At Another Jurisdiction; ELSEWHERE: Post office, County, State; Ward (Yes or No); Allotment, Annuity, and Identification Numbers.

3572; Gohih-nez-bega; M; 26; Navajo; F; M; Head; 3582; Yes; Yes; 22317
3573; Nah-glih-yil-has-bah; F; 24; Navajo; F; M; Wife; 3583; Yes; Yes; 22318
3574; Haska-yee-nas-wudt; M; 6; Navajo; F; S; Son; 3584; Yes; Yes; 22319
3575; Al-chih-nas-bah; F; 4; Navajo; F; S; Daughter; 3585; Yes; Yes; 22320

3576; Grey, Wallace; M; 31; Navajo; F; M; Head; 3586; Yes; Yes; 17354
3577; Grey Wallace's wife; F; Unk; Navajo; F; M; Wife; 3587; Yes; Yes; 17355
3578; Dopahpah[sic], Grey; M; 7; Navajo; F; S; Son; 3588; Yes; Yes; 17356
 [Name could be Dopah-pah, Grey]
3579; Gaih, Grey; M; 5; Navajo; F; S; Son; 3589; Yes; Yes; 17357
3580; Haska-yilth-yegath, Grey; M; 3; Navajo; F; S; Son; 3590; Yes; Yes; 17358

3581; Gonnah-nez-bitcilli-bega; M; 25; Navajo; F; Wd; Head; 3591; Yes; Yes; 22523

3582; Goodrich, Phillip; M; 28; Navajo; F; M; Head; 3592; Yes; Yes; 17947
3583; Hosch-clish-nih-benally; F; 19; Navajo; F; M; Wife; 3593; Yes; Yes; 17948
3584; Dinay-sosie; M; 3; Navajo; F; S; Son; 3594; Yes; Yes; 17949
3585; Gladys; F; 2; Navajo; F; S; Daughter; 3595; Yes; Yes; 18227

3586; Gonnah-nez-biniah; M; Unk; Navajo; F; M; Head; 3596; Yes; Yes; 22546
3587; Ahtcitty-benally; F; Unk; Navajo; F; M; Wife; 3597; Yes; Yes; 22547
3588; Seeih-kih; M; 16; Navajo; F; S; Son; 3598; Yes; Yes; 22548
3589; Tony; M; 15; Navajo; F; S; Son; 3599; .Yes; Yes; 22549
3590; Kah-naz-bah; F; 12; Navajo; F; S; Daughter; 3600; Yes; Yes; 22550
3591; Kah-nih-naz-bah; F; 10; Navajo; F; S; Daughter; 3601; Yes; Yes; 22551
3592; Kah-hah-ziz-bah; F; 8; Navajo; F; S; Daughter; 3602; Yes; Yes; 22552
3593; Nah-tah-yee-chih-deyah; M; 4; Navajo; F; S; Son; 3603; Yes; Yes; 22553
3594; Gladys; F; 19; Navajo; F; S; Niece; 3604; Yes; Yes; 22773

3595; Gonnah-nez-biniah-bega, Arthur; M; Unk; Navajo; F; M; Head; 3605; Yes; Yes; 22630
3596; Kah-ah-bah; F; Unk; Navajo; F; M; Wife; 3606; Yes; Yes; 22631
3597; Keh-yil-al-nah-bah; F; Unk; F; S; Daughter; 3607; Yes; Yes; 22632
3598; Haska-yee-chih-yee-gahl; M; Unk; Navajo; F; S; Son; 3608; Yes; Yes; 22633

3599; Gonnah-nez-bitcilli-bitsih; F; 26; Navajo; F; Wd; Head; 3609; Yes; Yes; 22621
3600; Ah-keh-dee-bah; F; 6; Navajo; F; S; Daughter; 3610; Yes; Yes; 22622
3601; Natoni-l-chee; M; 21; Navajo; F; S; Brother; 3611; Yes; Yes; 22623

3602; Gonna-bega; M; Unk; Navajo; F; M; Head; 3612; Yes; Yes; 29357
3603; Keh-yil-nah-nih-bah; F; 21; Navajo; F; M; Wife; 3613; Yes; Yes; 29358

Census of the __Northern Navajo__ reservation of the __Northern Navajo__ jurisdiction, as of __April 1__, 19**31,** taken by __Ernest H. Hammond, District__, Superintendent. **in Charge**

**Key:** Number; NAME: Surname, Given; Sex; Birth Year (if given), Age At Last Birthday; Tribe; Degree of Blood; Marital Status; Relationship To Head of Family; Last Census Roll Number; At Jurisdiction Where Enrolled (Yes or No); At Another Jurisdiction; ELSEWHERE: Post office, County, State; Ward (Yes or No); Allotment, Annuity, and Identification Numbers.

3604; Yah-deyah; M; 6; Navajo; F; S; Son; 3614; Yes; Yes; 29359
3605; Yah-dez-bah; F; 4; Navajo; F; S; Daughter; 3615; Yes; Yes; 29360
3606; Unknown; F; Unk; Navajo; F; S; Daughter; 3616; Yes; Yes; 29376
3607; Goh-naz-bah; F; 3; Navajo; F; S; Daughter; 3617; Yes; Yes; 29411

3608; Gonna-by-lylie; M; 53; Navajo; F; M; Head; 3618; Yes; Yes; 29391
3609; Nah-ja, Sadie; F; 26; Navajo; F; M; Wife; 3619; Yes; Yes; 29392
3610; Tah-nah-bah; F; 10; Navajo; F; S; Daughter; 3620; Yes; Yes; 29394
3611; Ned; M; 9; Navajo; F; S; Son; 3621; Yes; Yes; 29393
3612; Kah-yelth-ne-bah; F; 7; Navajo; F; S; Daughter; 3622; Yes; Yes; 29395
3613; Harry, Lee; M; 1; Navajo; F; S; Son; 3623; Yes; Yes; 29396

3614; George, Jack; M; 26; Navajo; F; M; Head; 3624; Yes; Yes; 22667
3615; George, Scynthia; F; Unk; Navajo; F; M; Wife; 3625; Yes; Yes; 22668
3616; Haska-yi-toh-wudt; M; 4; Navajo; F; S; Son; 3626; Yes; Yes; 22669
3617; Ada-nah-nih-bah; F; 2; Navajo; F; S; Daughter; 3627; Yes; Yes; 22670

3618; Hah-tahly; M; 59; Navajo; F; M; Head; 3628; Yes; Yes; 29235
3619; Hah-tahly's wife; F; 42; Navajo; F; M; Wife; 3629; Yes; Yes; 29236
3620; See-ih; M; 10; Navajo; F; S; Son; 3630; Yes; Yes; 29237
3621; Haska-sosie; M; 8; Navajo; F; S; Son; 3631; Yes; Yes; 29238
3622; Ah-hih-dee-bah; F; 6; Navajo; F; S; Daughter; 3632; Yes; Yes; 29239
3623; Haska-yee-kih-nayah; M; 4; Navajo; F; S; Son; 3633; Yes; Yes; 29240
3624; Singer, Lawrence; M; 21; Navajo; F; S; Son; 3634; Yes; Yes; 29402
3625; Singer, Elwood; M; 20; Navajo; F; S; Son; 3635; Yes; Yes; 29403

3626; Hosteen-al-tahih-benally; M; 23; Navajo; F; M; Head; 3636; Yes; Yes; 29354
3627; Gonna-bitsih; F; 21; Navajo; F; M; Wife; 3637; Yes; Yes; 29355
3628; Nah-glih-yil-hah-naz-bah; F; 3; Navajo; F; S; Daughter; 3638; Yes; Yes; 29356
3629; Joe; M; 2; Navajo; F; S; Son; 3639; Yes; Yes; 29390

3630; Haska-yen-bega; M; 28; Navajo; F; M; Head; 3640; Yes; Yes; 29334
3631; Ah-hih-dee-hah; F; 22; Navajo; F; M; Wife; 3641; Yes; Yes; 29335
3632; Yee-kaz-nih-bah; F; 5; Navajo; F; S; Daughter; 3642; Yes; Yes; 29336
3633; Daniel; M; 3; Navajo; F; S; Son; 3643; Yes; Yes; 29400

3634; Hosteen-haska-bega, Joe; M; 42; Navajo; F; M; Head; 3644; Yes; Yes; 29166
3635; Hosch-clish-nih-benally; F; 31; Navajo; F; M; Wife; 3645; Yes; Yes; 29167
3636; Nah-nih-bah; F; 10; Navajo; F; S; Daughter; 3646; Yes; Yes; 29168
3637; Haska-yee-nah-yah; M; 7; Navajo; F; S; Son; 3647; Yes; Yes; 29169
3638; Dal-yil-wudt; M; 5; Navajo; F; S; Son; 3638; Yes; Yes; 29170
3639; Yee-nas-wudt; M; 3; Navajo; F; S; Son; 3649; Yes; Yes; 29381

Census of the **Northern Navajo** reservation of the **Northern Navajo** jurisdiction, as of **April 1**, 19**31,** taken by **Ernest H. Hammond, District**, Superintendent. **in Charge**

**Key:** Number; NAME: Surname, Given; Sex; Birth Year (if given), Age At Last Birthday; Tribe; Degree of Blood; Marital Status; Relationship To Head of Family; Last Census Roll Number; At Jurisdiction Where Enrolled (Yes or No); At Another Jurisdiction; ELSEWHERE: Post office, County, State; Ward (Yes or No); Allotment, Annuity, and Identification Numbers.

3640; Hosteen-soh-bega; M; 26; Navajo; F; M; Head; 3650; Yes; Yes; 29331
3641; Yee-naz-bah; F; 26; Navajo; F; M; Wife; 3651; Yes; Yes; 29332
3642; Nah-tah-yee-dez-yeel; M; 3; Navajo; F; S; Son; 3652; Yes; Yes; 29333
3643; Nah-tah-yil-nah-jah; M; 2; Navajo; F; S; Son; 3653; Yes; Yes; 29387

3644; Hosteen-tohih; M; 72; Navajo; F; Wd; Head; 3654; Yes; Yes; 29211
3645; Yee-ah-bah; F; 15; Navajo; F; S; Daughter; 3655; Yes; Yes; 29213

3646; Hosteen-haska-bih-adzan; F; 75; Navajo; F; Wd; Head; 3656; Yes; Yes; 29164
3647; Nah-dah-sih; M; 14; Navajo; F; S; Grand-Son; 3657; Yes; Yes; 29165

3648; Hoh-zoh-nih-hah-tahly-badoni; M; 43; Navajo; F; M; Head; 3658; Yes; Yes; 22334
3649; Glih-hah-bah; F; 37; Navajo; F; M; Wife; 3659; Yes; Yes; Yes; 29335
3650; Alfred; M; 19; Navajo; F; S; Son; 3660; Yes; Yes; Yes; 29336
3651; Jim; M; 18; Navajo; F; S; Son; 3661; Yes; Yes; 29337
3652; Daniel; M; 16; Navajo; F; S; Son; 3662; Yes; Yes; 29338
3653; Yahn-nih-bah; F; 14; Navajo; F; S; Daughter; 3663; Yes; Yes; 29339
3654; Al-chih-has-bah; F; 12; Navajo; F; S; Daughter; 3664; Yes; Yes; 29340
3655; Kay-yil-des-bah; F; 4; Navajo; F; S; Daughter; 3665; Yes; Yes; 29341
3656; Gil-naz-bah; F; 3; Navajo; F; S; Daughter; 3666; Yes; Yes; 22788

3657; Hah-tahly-blohih-bega; M; 42; Navajo; F; M; Head; 3667; Yes; Yes; 30989
3658; Wol-ah-chee-hah-tahly-bitsih; F; 34; Navajo; F; M; Wife; 3668; Yes; Yes; 30990
3659; Jeane; F; 13; Navajo; F; S; Daughter; 3669; Yes; Yes; 30991
3660; Nah-tah-yee-chih-hahyah; M; 9; Navajo; F; S; Son; 3670; Yes; Yes; 20992[sic]
[ID No. should be 30992]
3661; Haska-yee-tah-deyah; M; 7; Navajo; F; S; Son; 3671; Yes; Yes; 30993
3662; Haska-yee-dah-nih-yah; M; 5; Navajo; F; S; Son; 3672; Yes; Yes; 30994
3663; Haska-yee-nil-wudt; M; 2; Navajo; F; S; Son; 3673; Yes; Yes; 30209

3664; Haska, Charley; M; 41; Navajo; F; M; Head; 3674; Yes; Yes; 29060
3665; Awa-seeih; F; 24; Navajo; F; M; Wife; 3675; Yes; Yes; 29061
3666; Al-soh-dez-bah; F; 4; Navajo; F; S; Daughter; 3676; Yes; Yes; 29062
3667; Hosteen-haska-yen-bega; M; 49; Navajo; F; S; Brother; 3677; Yes; Yes; 29063

3668; Hosteen-l-suen-benally; M; 21; Navajo; F; Wd; Head; 3678; Yes; Yes; 32376
3669; Nah-tah-yee-tah-yil-wohl; M; 7; Navajo; F; S; Son; 3679; Yes; Yes; 32377
3670; Yah-des-wudt; M; 3; Navajo; F; S; Son; 3680; Yes; Yes; 32378

3671; Hosteen-bah-bitah; M; 40; Navajo; F; M; Head; 3681; Yes; Yes; 30876
3672; Hah-tahly-sosie-bitsih; F; 38; Navajo; F; M; Wife; 3682; Yes; Yes; 30877

Census of the **Northern Navajo** reservation of the **Northern Navajo** jurisdiction, as of **April 1**, 19**31,** taken by **Ernest H. Hammond, District**, Superintendent. **in Charge**

**Key:** Number; NAME: Surname, Given; Sex; Birth Year (if given), Age At Last Birthday; Tribe; Degree of Blood; Marital Status; Relationship To Head of Family; Last Census Roll Number; At Jurisdiction Where Enrolled (Yes or No); At Another Jurisdiction; ELSEWHERE: Post office, County, State; Ward (Yes or No); Allotment, Annuity, and Identification Numbers.

3673; Ralph; M; 15; Navajo; F; S; Son; 3683; Yes; Yes; 30878
3674; Haska-yee-tah-yil-wohl; M; 14; Navajo; F; S; Son; 3684; Yes; Yes; 30879
3675; Yee-key-nih-bah; F; 12; Navajo; F; S; Daughter; 3685; Yes; Yes; 30880

3676; Hosteen-hah-zoh-goh-bega; M; Unk; Navajo; F; M; Head; 3686; Yes; Yes; 29029
3677; Nah-dez-bah; F; 34; Navajo; F; M; Wife; 3687; Yes; Yes; 29030
3678; Abner; M; 13; Navajo; F; S; Step-son; 3688; Yes; Yes; 29031
3679; Haska-yil-has-wudt; M; 10; F; S; Step-son; 3689; Yes; Yes; 29032
3680; Haska-yil-chel-woody; M; 7; Navajo; F; S; Son; 3690; Yes; Yes; 29033
3681; Haska-yil-yil-wudt; M; 4; Navajo; F; S; Son; 3691; Yes; Yes; 29034

3682; Hosch-clish-nih-bega; M; 42; Navajo; F; M; Head; 3692; Yes; Yes; 30267
3683; Nah-glih-yil-dez-bah; F; 38; Navajo; F; M; Wife; 3693; Yes; Yes; 30268
3684; Emmet; M; 20; Navajo; F; S; Son; 3694; Yes; Yes; 30269
3685; Bah; F; 18; Navajo; F; S; Daughter; 3695; Yes; Yes; 30270
3686; Theodore; M; 16; Navajo; F; S; Son; 3696; Yes; Yes; 30271
3687; Ziz-hih-bah; F; 12; Navajo; F; S; Daughter; 3697; Yes; Yes; 30272
3688; Yee-nih-bah; F; 10; Navajo; F; S; Daughter; 3698; Yes; Yes; 30273
3689; Cisz; F; 8; Navajo; F; S; Daughter; 3699; Yes; Yes; 30274
3690; Eskee-sosie; M; 3; Navajo; F; S; Son; 3700; Yes; Yes; 30275

3691; Hosteen-hoh-dez-ann; M; Unk; Navajo; F; Wd; Head; 3701; Yes; Yes; 30366
3692; Green, Arthur; M; 24; Navajo; F; S; Son; 3702; Yes; Yes; 30367

3693; Hosteen-al-tohih-badoni, Jim; M; 42; Navajo; F; M; Head; 3704; Yes; Yes; 30394
3694; Al-tahih-bitsih; F; 40; Navajo; F; M; Wife; 3705; Yes; Yes; 30395
3695; Nah-tah; M; 19; Navajo; F; S; Son; 3706; Yes; Yes; 30396
3696; Jane; F; 15; Navajo; F; S; Daughter; 3707; Yes; Yes; 30397
3697; Ellis; M; 11; Navajo; F; S; Son; 3708; Yes; Yes; 30398
3698; Glih; F; 8; Navajo; F; S; Daughter; 3709; Yes; Yes; 30399
3699; Haska-yil-nah-tal; M; 5; Navajo; F; S; Son; 3710; Yes; Yes; 30400

3700; Hosteen-nez-benally; M; Unk; Navajo; F; M; Head; 3711; Yes; Yes; 30869
3701; Beleen-la-chee-bitsih; F; Unk; Navajo; F; M; Wife; 3712; Yes; Yes; 30870
3702; Al-nah-zoz-bah; F; Unk; Navajo; F; S; Daughter; 3713; Yes; Yes; 30871
3703; Biz-nil-hah; F; Unk; Navajo; F; S; Daughter; 3714; Yes; Yes; 30872
3704; Bihn-gee-bah; F; Unk; Navajo; F; S; Daughter; 3715; Yes; Yes; 30873
3705; Nish-bah; F; Unk; Navajo; F; S; Daughter; 3716; Yes; Yes; 30874
3706; Yah-nan-bah; F; 1; Navajo; F; S; Daughter; 3717; Yes; Yes; 31266

Census of the **Northern Navajo** reservation of the **Northern Navajo** jurisdiction, as of **April 1**, 1931, taken by **Ernest H. Hammond, District**, Superintendent. **in Charge**

**Key:** Number; NAME: Surname, Given; Sex; Birth Year (if given), Age At Last Birthday; Tribe; Degree of Blood; Marital Status; Relationship To Head of Family; Last Census Roll Number; At Jurisdiction Where Enrolled (Yes or No); At Another Jurisdiction; ELSEWHERE: Post office, County, State; Ward (Yes or No); Allotment, Annuity, and Identification Numbers.

3707; Hosteen-soh-yah-dih-nih-sinih; M; Unk; Navajo; F; M; Head; 3718; Yes; Yes; 29919

3708; Hosteen-tahn-bitsih; F; Unk; Navajo; F; M; Wife; 3719; Yes; Yes; 29920

3709; Haska-yee-tah-gah; M; 24; Navajo; F; S; Son; 3720; Yes; Yes; 29921

3710; Nah-tah-yee-kih-has-wudt; M; 22; Navajo; F; S; Son; 3721; Yes; Yes; 29922

3711; Tah-zoz-bah; F; 18; Navajo; F; S; Daughter; 3722; Yes; Yes; 29923

3712; Nah-tah-yil-des-wudt; M; 12; Navajo; F; S; Son; 3723; Yes; Yes; 29924

3713; Biz-dee-tah; F; 5; Navajo; F; S; Grand-daughter; 3724; Yes; Yes; 29925

3714; Hosteen-clishnih-gonna-bih-adzan; F; 102; Navajo; F; Wd; Mother-in-law; 3725; Yes; Yes; 29926

3715; Hosteen-shih-yahih-bega; M; 25; Navajo; F; M; Head; 3726; Yes; Yes; 29721

3716; Hosteen-soh-bega; M; 36; Navajo; F; M; Head; 3727; Yes; Yes; 29837

3717; Shih-bah; F; 20; Navajo; F; M; Wife; 3728; Yes; Yes; 29838

3718; Hosteen-tahn; M; Unk; Navajo; F; M; Head; 3729; Yes; Yes; 30538

3719; Hosteen-gonih-benally; F; 33; Navajo; F; M; Wife; 3730; Yes; Yes; 30539

3720; Bin-gee-bah, Annie; F; 20; Navajo; F; S; Daughter; 3731; Yes; Yes; 30540

3721; Haska-yil-hal-wudt; M; 18; Navajo; F; S; Son; 3732; Yes; Yes; 30541

3722; Nah-tah-yil-wudt; M; 16; Navajo; F; S; Son; 3733; Yes; Yes; 30542

3723; Zannie-bah; F; 14; Navajo; F; S; Daughter; 3734; Yes; Yes; 30543

3724; Ah-kee; M; 9; Navajo; F; S; Son; 3735; Yes; Yes; 30544

3725; Atate-l-chee; F; 12; Navajo; F; S; Daughter; 3736; Yes; Yes; 30545

3726; Adzanih-chee; F; 12; Navajo; F; S; Daughter; 3737; Yes; Yes; 30546

3727; Hettie; F; 4; Navajo; F; S; Daughter; 3738; Yes; Yes; 30547

3728; Happy, Jack; M; 56; Navajo; F; M; Head; 3739; Yes; Yes; 30724

3729; Happy Jack's wife; F; 41; Navajo; F; M; Wife; 3740; Yes; Yes; 30725

3730; Jim; M; 21; Navajo; F; S; Son; 3741; Yes; Yes; 30726

3731; Nah-glih-yil-hah-bah; F; 19; Navajo; F; S; Daughter; 3742; Yes; Yes; 30727

3732; Al-noz-bah; F; 7; Navajo; F; S; Daughter; 3743; Yes; Yes; 30728

3733; Hosteen-Nez; M; 62; Navajo; F; M; Head; 3744; Yes; Yes; 22528

3734; Hosteen-Nez's wife; F; 39; Navajo; F; M; Wife; 3745; Yes; Yes; 22529

3735; Hosteen-l-suen; M; 21; Navajo; F; S; Son; 3746; Yes; Yes; 22530

3736; Johnson; M; 16; Navajo; F; S; Son; 3747; Yes; Yes; 22531

3737; Joe; M; 13; Navajo; F; S; Son; 3748; Yes; Yes; 22532

3738; Wudt; M; 11; Navajo; F; S; Son; 3749; Yes; Yes; 22533

3739; Al-kih-des-bah; F; 7; Navajo; F; S; Daughter; 3750; Yes; Yes; 22534

3740; Dan; M; 5; Navajo; F; S; Son; 3751; Yes; Yes; 22535

3741; Al-kee-bah; F; 2; Navajo; F; S; Daughter; 2752; Yes; Yes; 22774

Census of the **Northern Navajo** reservation of the **Northern Navajo** jurisdiction, as of **April 1**, 19**31,** taken by **Ernest H. Hammond, District**, Superintendent. **in Charge**

**Key:** Number; NAME: Surname, Given; Sex; Birth Year (if given), Age At Last Birthday; Tribe; Degree of Blood; Marital Status; Relationship To Head of Family; Last Census Roll Number; At Jurisdiction Where Enrolled (Yes or No); At Another Jurisdiction; ELSEWHERE: Post office, County, State; Ward (Yes or No); Allotment, Annuity, and Identification Numbers.

3742; Hogan-thlani; M; 43; Navajo; F; M; Head; 3753; Yes; Yes; 23776
3743; Hogan-thlani's wife; M[sic]; 39; Navajo; F; M; Wife; 3754; Yes; Yes; 23777
3744; Dorothy; F; 17; Navajo; F; S; Daughter; 3755; Yes; Yes; 23778
3745; Yil-naz-bah; F; 15; Navajo; F; S; Daughter; 3756; Yes; Yes; 23779
3746; James; M; 12; Navajo; F; S; Son; 3757; Yes; Yes; 23780
3747; Keh-hah-naz-bah; F; 8; Navajo; F; S; Daughter; 3759; Yes; Yes; 23782
3748; Kah-nah-nih-bahih; F; 6; Navajo; F; S; Daughter; 3760; Yes; Yes; 23783
3749; Bah; F; 88; Navajo; F; Wd; Grand-Mother; 3761; Yes; Yes; 23784
3750; Haska-yil-kes-wudt; M; 17; Navajo; F; S; Nephew; 3762; Yes; Yes; 23785
3751; Nih-zih-bah; F; 50; Navajo; F; S; Sister; 3763; Yes; Yes; 23786


3752; Hosteen-deel-yen-benally; M; 63; Navajo; F; M; Head; 3764; Yes; Yes; 22404
3753; Hosteen-dagih-bitsih; F; 39; Navajo; F; M; Wife; 3765; Yes; Yes; 22405
3754; Hosteen-deel-yen-benally-bega; M; 27; Navajo; F; S; Son; 3766; Yes; Yes; 22406
3755; Nah-tah-yil-yee-gahl; M; 21; Navajo; F; S; Son; 3768; Yes; Yes; 22408
3756; Coolidge; M; 15; Navajo; F; S; Son; 3769; Yes; Yes; 22409
3757; Hoska-yee-chih-sizih; M; 10; Navajo; F; S; Son; 3770; Yes; Yes; 22410
3758; Eskee; M; 7; Navajo; F; S; Son; 3771; Yes; Yes; 22411
3759; Nah-glih-yee-kih-desbah; F; 4; Navajo; F; S; Daughter; 3772; Yes; Yes; 22412
3760; Deel, Flora; F; 25; Navajo; F; S; Daughter; 3773; Yes; Yes; 22413
3761; Sherman; M; 21; Navajo; F; S; Son; 3774; Yes; Yes; 22414
3762; Nah-tah-yil-hah-yah; M; 17; Navajo; F; S; Son; 3775; Yes; Yes; 22415
3763; Adac-chee; F; 3; Navajo; F; S; Daughter; 3776; Yes; Yes; 22777
3764; Adae-elcloe; F; 3; Navajo; F; S; Daughter; 3777; Yes; Yes; 22778


3765; Hosteen-nez-bega, Frank; M; 43; Navajo; F; M; Head; 3778; Yes; Yes; 32298
3766; Bih-jah-tlol-nih-dael-bitsih[sic]; F; 48; Navajo; F; M; Wife; 3779; Yes; Yes; 32299   [Name could be Bih-jah-tlol-nih-deel-bitsih]
3767; Dale, Francis; M; 21; Navajo; F; S; Son; 3780; Yes; Yes; 32300
3768; Bih-tis-gee-bah; F; 13; Navajo; F; S; Daughter; 3781; Yes; Yes; 32301
3769; Tillie; F; 10; Navajo; F; S; Daughter; 3782; Yes; Yes; 32302
3770; Haska-yee-chin-deyah; M; 6; Navajo; F; S; Son; 3783; Yes; Yes; 32303
3771; Yah-nih-bah; F; 33; Navajo; F; S[sic]; 2nd wife; 3784; Yes; Yes; 32304
3772; Haska-dah-hih-bah; M; 13; Navajo; F; S; Son; 3785; Yes; Yes; 32305
3773; Cyrus; M; 10; Navajo; F; S; Son; 3786; Yes; Yes; 32306
3774; Bayse-dee-bah; F; 8; Navajo; F; S; Daughter; 3787; Yes; Yes; 32307
3775; Nah-tah-yil-yil-wudt; M; 5; Navajo; F; S; Son; 3788; Yes; Yes; 32308


3776; Hosteen-al-sosie-yen-bega; M; 73; Navajo; F; M; Head; 3789; Yes; Yes; 23226
3777; Hosteen-alsosie-yen-bega's[sic] wife; F; 38; Navajo; F; M; Wife; 3790; Yes; Yes; 23227     [Name could be Hosteen-al-sosie-yen-bega's wife]

Census of the **Northern Navajo** reservation of the **Northern Navajo**
jurisdiction, as of **April 1**, 19**31,** taken by **Ernest H. Hammond, District**,
Superintendent. **in Charge**

**Key:** Number; NAME: Surname, Given; Sex; Birth Year (if given), Age At Last Birthday; Tribe; Degree of
Blood; Marital Status; Relationship To Head of Family; Last Census Roll Number; At Jurisdiction Where
Enrolled (Yes or No); At Another Jurisdiction; ELSEWHERE: Post office, County, State; Ward (Yes or No);
Allotment, Annuity, and Identification Numbers.

3778; Nah-glih-yil-des-bah; F; 19; Navajo; F; S; Daughter; 3791; Yes; Yes; 23228
3779; Sylvia; F; 13; Navajo; F; S; Step-Daughter; 3792; Yes; Yes; 23229
3780; Glih-haz-bah; F; 9; Navajo; F; S; Daughter; 3793; Yes; Yes; 23230
3781; Nah-glih-yil-nih-nih-bah; F; 7; Navajo; F; S; Daughter; 3794; Yes; Yes; 23231
3782; Yil-dah-dee-bah; F; 23; Navajo; F; Wd; Daughter; 3795; Yes; Yes; 23232
3783; Haska-yil-hah-yah; M; 3; Navajo; F; S; Grand-son; 3796; Yes; Yes; 23233

3784; Bega, Happy Jack; M; 34; Navajo; F; M; Head; 3797; Yes; Yes; 30735
3785; Dan Pete's Daughter; F; 25; Navajo; F; M; Wife; 3798; Yes; Yes; 30736

3786; Hosteen-sinih-bitsoih; F; 29; Navajo; F; Wd; Head; 3799; Yes; Yes; 30515
3787; Yih-kik-nee-bah; F; 23; Navajo; F; S; Sister; 3800; Yes; Yes; 30516
3788; Walter; M; 20; Navajo; F; S; Brother; 3801; Yes; Yes; 30517

3789; Hosteen-ah-banih-bih-dazee; F; 61; Navajo; F; Wd; Head; 3802; Yes; Yes;
30524
3790; Hosteen-yazzie; M; 24; Navajo; F; S; Daughter[sic]; 3803; Yes; Yes; 30525

3791; Hosteen-al-tohih-bega, Willie; M; 37; Navajo; F; M; Head; 3804; Yes; Yes;
30380
3792; Clih-chee; F; 20; Navajo; F; M; Wife; 3805; Yes; Yes; 30381
3793; Tah-zoz-bah; F; 3; Navajo; F; S; Daughter; 3806; Yes; Yes; 31244

3794; Hosteen-hah-nih-tayshih-bega; M; 61; Navajo; F; M; Head; 3807; Yes; Yes;
32335
3795; Al-shih-kay-dal-suen-bitsih; F; 44; Navajo; F; M; 1st wife; 3808; Yes; Yes;
32336
3796; Haska-yil-hal-wudt; M; 20; Navajo; F; S; Son; 3809; Yes; Yes; 32337
3797; Al-kih-nay-bah; F; 15; Navajo; Daughter; 3810; Yes; Yes; 32338
3798; Hosteen-hah-nih-tayshih-bih-adzan; F; 84; Navajo; F; Wd; Mother; 3811; Yes;
Yes; 32339
3799; Blue eye's bitsih; F; 44; Navajo; F; M; 2nd wife; 3812; Yes; Yes; 32534
3800; Yee-nah-yah; M; 18; Navajo; F; S; Son; 3813; Yes; Yes; 32345
3801; Clih-ee-bah; F; 11; Navajo; F; S; Daughter; 3814; Yes; Yes; 32346

3802; Hosteen-ashinh-bega; M; 34; Navajo; F; M; Head; 3815; Yes; Yes; 30598
3803; Dinay-chilli-benally; F; 31; Navajo; F; M; Wife; 3816; Yes; Yes; 30599
3804; Bih-chih-hah-ziz-bah; F; 9; Navajo; F; S; Daughter; 3817; Yes; Yes; 30601
3805; Haska-yil-deyah; M; 6; Navajo; F; S; Son; 3818; Yes; Yes; 30602
3806; Waye; M; 19; Navajo; F; S; Step-son; 3819; Yes; Yes; 30603

3807; Hosea Badoni; M; 51; Navajo; F; S; Head; 3820; Yes; Yes; 30797
3808; Jim Pete; M; 23; Navajo; F; S; Son; 3821; Yes; Yes; 30798

Census of the **Northern Navajo** reservation of the **Northern Navajo** jurisdiction, as of **April 1**, 1931, taken by **Ernest H. Hammond, District**, Superintendent. **in Charge**

**Key:** Number; NAME: Surname, Given; Sex; Birth Year (if given), Age At Last Birthday; Tribe; Degree of Blood; Marital Status; Relationship To Head of Family; Last Census Roll Number; At Jurisdiction Where Enrolled (Yes or No); At Another Jurisdiction; ELSEWHERE: Post office, County, State; Ward (Yes or No); Allotment, Annuity, and Identification Numbers.

3809; Nah-glih-kee-kih-dah-hiz-bah; F; 12; Navajo; F; S; Daughter; 3822; Yes; Yes; 30799

3810; Bil-hah-gee-bah; F; 5; Navajo; F; S; Daughter; 3823; Yes; Yes; 30800

3811; Bah; F; 80; Navajo; F; Wd; Mother; 3824; Yes; Yes; 30801

3812; Navajo, Charley; M; 58; Navajo; F; Wd; Brother; 3825; Yes; Yes; 30802

3813; Hosteen-al-bahih-badoni, Willie; M; 46; Navajo; F; M; Head; 3826; Yes; Yes; 30388

3814; Ah-banih-bitsih; F; 47; Navajo; F; M; Wife; 3827; Yes; Yes; 30389

3815; Has-wudt; M; 15; Navajo; F; S; Son; 3828; Yes; Yes; 30390

3816; Keh-haz-bah; F; 14; Navajo; F; S; Daughter; 3829; Yes; Yes; 30391

3817; Chih-nil-wudt; M; 8; Navajo; F; S; Son; 3830; Yes; Yes; 30392

3818; Yil-wudt; M; 6; Navajo; F; S; Son; 3831; Yes; Yes; 30393

3819; Hah-tahly-soh; M; Unk; Navajo; F; Wd; Head; 3832; Yes; Yes; 22724

3820; Hah-naz-bahih; F; Unk; Navajo; F; Daughter; 3833; Yes; Yes; 22725

3821; Nah-tah-yazzie; M; 2; Navajo; F; S; Nephew; 3834; Yes; Yes; 21685

3822; Hah-dih-jadih-bega; M; 30; Navajo; F; M; Head; 3835; Yes; Yes; 20356

3823; Hah-dih-jadih, Oscar; M; 13; Navajo; F; S; Son; 3836; Yes; Yes; 20358

3824; Glih-bah; F; 11; Navajo; F; S; Dau; 3837; Yes; Yes; 20359

3825; Tee; M; 7; Navajo; F; S; Son; 3838; Yes; Yes; 20360

3826; Chee; M; 5; Navajo; F; S; Son; 3839; Yes; Yes; 20361

3827; Julia; F; 2; Navajo; F; S; Daughter; 3840; Yes; Yes; 20404

3828; Hosteen-yazzie-bega; M; Unk; Navajo; F; M; Head; 3841; Yes; Yes; 22717

3829; Yoh-hah-tahly-sosie-bitsih; F; 24; Navajo; F; M; Wife; 3842; Yes; Yes; 22718

3830; Ah-kah-nih-bah; F; 7; Navajo; F; S; Daughter; 3843; Yes; Yes; 22719

3831; Keh-hah-bih-bah; F; 3; Navajo; F; S; Daughter; 3844; Yes; Yes; 22720

3832; Hosteen-ah-banih-badoni; M; 42; Navajo; F; M; Head; 3845; Yes; Yes; 30376

3833; Ah-banih-bitsih; F; 44; Navajo; F; M; Wife; 3846; Yes; Yes; 30377

3834; Haska-yil-des-wudt; M; 9; Navajo; F; S; Son; [blank]; Yes; Yes; 30378

3835; Zaz-bah; F; 7; Navajo; F; S; Daughter; 3847; Yes; Yes; 30379

3836; Hosteen-en-clahih-bega; M; 21; Navajo; F; S; Brother; 3848; Yes; Yes; 30387

3837; Had-dih-chah-ly-bitsih; F; Unk; Navajo; F; Wd; Head; 3849; Yes; Yes; 17037

3838; Tahanopah; F; 18; Navajo; F; S; Niece; 3850; Yes; Yes; 17038

3839; Haska-yilth-chineyah; M; 12; Navajo; F; S; Son; 3851; Yes; Yes; 17039

3840; Kayeetah-nopah; F; 11; Navajo; F; S; Daughter; 3852; Yes; Yes; 17040

3841; Glen, James; M; 14; Navajo; F; S; Half-brother; 3853; Yes; Yes; 17042

3842; Hosteen-gon-benally; M; 40; Navajo; F; Wd; Head; 3854; Yes; Yes; 30501

Census of the **Northern Navajo** reservation of the **Northern Navajo** jurisdiction, as of **April 1** , 19**31,** taken by **Ernest H. Hammond, District** , Superintendent. **in Charge**

**Key:** Number; NAME: Surname, Given; Sex; Birth Year (if given), Age At Last Birthday; Tribe; Degree of Blood; Marital Status; Relationship To Head of Family; Last Census Roll Number; At Jurisdiction Where Enrolled (Yes or No); At Another Jurisdiction; ELSEWHERE: Post office, County, State; Ward (Yes or No); Allotment, Annuity, and Identification Numbers.

3843;   Haska-yee-tahyah; M; 16; Navajo; F; S; Son; 3855; Yes; Yes; 30503
3844;   Haska-yee-tah-nah-yah; M; 12; Navajo; F; S; Son; 3856; Yes; Yes; 30504
3845;   Yil-haz-bah; F; 10; Navajo; F; S; Daughter; 3857; Yes; Yes; 30505
3846;   Chihn-ziz-bah; F; 8; Navajo; F; S; Daughter; 3858; Yes; Yes; 30506

3847;   Hosteen-ah-banih's wife Ah-banih-bih-adzan; F; 52; Navajo; F; Wd; Head; 3860; Yes; Yes; 30383
3848;   Haska-yil-nih-nih-yah; M; 14; Navajo; F; S; Son; 3861; Yes; Yes; 30384

3849;   Hoh-zohnih-hah-tahly; M; 80; Navajo; F; M; Head; 3862; Yes; Yes; 22324
3850;   Hoh-zohnih-hah-tahly's wife; F; 53; Navajo; F; M; Wife; 3863; Yes; Yes; 22325
3851;   Nah-tah-yil-nah-dahl; M; 24; Navajo; F; S; Son; 3864; Yes; Yes; 22326
3852;   David; M; 22; Navajo; F; S; Son; 3865; Yes; Yes; 22327
3853;   Tah-des-wudt; M; 16; Navajo; F; S; Son; 3866; Yes; Yes; 22328
3854;   Hoska-yee-kih-dah-yee-yah; M; 11; Navajo; F; S; Son; 3867; Yes; Yes; 22329

3855;   Harvey, Willie; M; 23; Navajo; F; M; Head; 3868; No; McElmo, Colo., San Juan, Utah; Yes; 18973
3856;   Adzanih-klizi-lagaih; F; 36; Navajo; F; M; Wife; 3869; No; McElmo, Colo., San Juan, Utah; Yes; 18974
3857;   Tah-des-bah; F; 18; Navajo; F; S; Step-daughter; 3870; No; McElmo, Colo., San Juan, Utah; Yes; 18975
3858;   Kee-soh; M; 21; Navajo; F; S; Step-son; 3871; No; McElmo, Colo., San Juan, Utah; Yes; 18976
3859;   Nocki-yazzie, Allen; M; 15; Navajo; F; S; Step-son; 3872; No; McElmo, Colo., San Juan, Utah; Yes; 18977

3860;   Hosteen-bih-nah-atin, Jim; M; Unk; Navajo; F; M; Head; 3873; Yes; Yes; 32321
3861;   Goldie, Goldie; F; 26; Navajo; F; S; Daughter; 3874; Yes; Yes; 32322
3862;   Haska-yil-nih-nih-yah; M; 22; Navajo; F; S; Son; 3875; Yes; Yes; 32323

3863;   Had-dih-chahly-bega; M; 33; Navajo; F; M; Head; 3876; Yes; Yes; 17307
3864;   Bitsue-sani-bitsih; F; Unk; Navajo; F; M; Wife; 3877; Yes; Yes; 17308
3865;   Had--dih-chally-nah-yah[sic]; M; 7; Navajo; F; M S; Son; 3878; Yes; Yes; 17309    [Name is probably Had-dih-chally-nah-yah]

3866;   Had-dih-chahly-yazzie; M; Unk; Navajo; F; M; Head; 3879; Yes; Yes; 26869
3867;   Glihe-bah; F; 11[sic]; Navajo; F; M; Wife; 3880; Yes; Yes; 26870
3868;   Ah-hih-nih-bah; F; 5; Navajo; F; S; Daughter; 3881; Yes; Yes; 26871
3869;   Nah-tah-ye-nayah; M; 2; Navajo; F; S; Son; 3882; Yes; Yes; 27101

Census of the **Northern Navajo** reservation of the **Northern Navajo** jurisdiction, as of **April 1**, 19**31,** taken by **Ernest H. Hammond, District**, Superintendent. **in Charge**

Key: Number; NAME: Surname, Given; Sex; Birth Year (if given), Age At Last Birthday; Tribe; Degree of Blood; Marital Status; Relationship To Head of Family; Last Census Roll Number; At Jurisdiction Where Enrolled (Yes or No); At Another Jurisdiction; ELSEWHERE: Post office, County, State; Ward (Yes or No); Allotment, Annuity, and Identification Numbers.

3870; Hah-tahly-yazzie-yen-bekis; M; 77; Navajo; F; M; Head; 3883; Yes; Yes; 23119
3871; Ah-keh-dee-bah; F; 61; Navajo; F; M; Wife; 3884; Yes; Yes; 23120
3872; Nah-ah-sohoshi-yen-bilah; F; 93; Navajo; F; M; Mother-in-law; 3885; Yes; Yes; 23121

3873; Had-dil-chahly, Pete; M; Unk; Navajo; F; M; Head; 3886; Yes; Yes; 23801
3874; Nah-glih-yil-nah-bah; F; 41; Navajo; F; M; Wife; 3887; Yes; Yes; 23802
3875; Tah-dez-wudt; M; 19; Navajo; F; S; Son; 3888; Yes; Yes; 23803
3876; Esther; F; 13; Navajo; F; S; Daughter; 3889; Yes; Yes; 23804
3877; Haska-yil-haz-wudt; M; 6; Navajo; F; S; Son; 3890; Yes; Yes; 23805
3878; Tuly; M; 4; Navajo; F; S; Son; 3891; Yes; Yes; 23806

3879; Hah-tahly-yazzie-bih-bizee; M; 31; Navajo; F; M; Head; 3892; Yes; Yes; 23629
3880; Bay-gashih-thlani-bitsah; F; 33; Navajo; F; M; Wife; 3893; Yes; Yes; 23630
3881; Hask-yee-kih-dil-ez; M; 14; Navajo; F; S; Son; 3894; Yes; Yes; 23631
3882; Jessie; F; 12; Navajo; F; S; Daughter; 3895; Yes; Yes; 23632
3883; Gahl; M; 8; Navajo; F; S; Son; 3896; Yes; Yes; 23633
3884; Clah-bahih-yen-bitsih; F; 57; Navajo; F; Wd; Mother-in-law; 3897; Yes; Yes; 23634

3885; Hah-dil-chahly, Luke; M; 34; Navajo; F; Wd; Head; 3898; Yes; Yes; 23807
3886; Haska-yahn-hal-wudt; M; 7; Navajo; F; S; Son; 3899; Yes; Yes; 23808

3887; Hah-diy-jadih, Charley; M; 36; Navajo; F; M; Head; 3900; Yes; Yes; 20038
3888; Teece-sosie-bitsih; F; 36; Navajo; F; M; Wife; 3901; Yes; Yes; 20039
3889; Hah-dih-jadih, Jordan; M; 14; Navajo; F; S; Step-son; 3902; Yes; Yes; 20040
3890; Hoska-yee-nah-ho-lel; M; 11; Navajo; F; S; Son; 3903; Yes; Yes; 20041
3891; Yazzie-suen; M; 9; Navajo; F; S; Son; 3904; Yes; Yes; 20042
3892; Chee-soh; M; 7; Navajo; F; S; Son; 3905; Yes; Yes; 20043
3893; Des-bah; F; 5; Navajo; F; S; Daughter; 3906; Yes; Yes; 20044
3894; Hoska-yilt-hoh-lel; M; 3; Navajo; F; S; Son; 3907; Yes; Yes; 20045
3895; Hah-dih-jadih, Hugh; M; 20; Navajo; F; S; Brother; 3908; Yes; Yes; 20047
3896; Poyer, Martin; M; 29; Navajo; F; S; Brother; 3908-A; Yes; Yes; 20048

3897; Hah-dih-chahly-bikis-bega; M; 25; Navajo; F; M; Head; 3909; Yes; Yes; 21268
3898; Hah-nah-gah-nih-nez-bitsih; F; 25; Navajo; F; M; Wife; 3910; Yes; Yes; 21269
3899; Nah-tah-yil-deyah; M; 5; Navajo; F; S; Son; 3911; Yes; Yes; 21270
3900; Bil-naz-nih-bah; F; 3; Navajo; F; S; Daughter; 3912; Yes; Yes; 21271

Census of the **Northern Navajo** reservation of the **Northern Navajo** jurisdiction, as of **April 1**, 1931, taken by **Ernest H. Hammond, District**, Superintendent. **in Charge**

**Key:** Number; NAME: Surname, Given; Sex; Birth Year (if given), Age At Last Birthday; Tribe; Degree of Blood; Marital Status; Relationship To Head of Family; Last Census Roll Number; At Jurisdiction Where Enrolled (Yes or No); At Another Jurisdiction; ELSEWHERE: Post office, County, State; Ward (Yes or No); Allotment, Annuity, and Identification Numbers.

3901; Hah-nah-gah-nih-nez-bega; M; 26; Navajo; F; M; Head; 3913; Yes; Yes; 21545

3902; Yee-has-bah; F; 33; Navajo; F; M; Wife; 3914; Yes; Yes; 21546

3903; Amy; F; 16; Navajo; F; S; Daughter; 3915; Yes; Yes; 21547

3904; Rosalind; F; 12; Navajo; F; S; Daughter; 3916; Yes; Yes; 21548

3905; Bih-kih-gee-bah; F; 8; Navajo; F; S; Daughter; 3917; Yes; Yes; 21550

3906; Nah-tah-yee-tah-gah; M; 6; Navajo; F; S; Son; 3918; Yes; Yes; 21551

3907; Hoska-yee-no-ah; M; 4; Navajo; F; S; Son; 3919; Yes; Yes; 21552

3908; Haska-yee-cin-hah-yah; M; 3; Navajo; F; S; Son; 3920; Yes; Yes; 21687

3909; Hah-ah-sisi-bega; M; 25; Navajo; F; M; Head; 3921; Yes; Yes; 21504

3910; Beleen-doh-clizi-bitsih; F; 21; Navajo; F; M; Wife; 3922; Yes; Yes; 21505

3911; Maui-desch-kiznih-bega; M; Unk; Navajo; F; S; Cousin; 3923; Yes; Yes; 21506

3912; Haska-yee-chin-hah-wudt; M; 4; Navajo; F; S; Son; 3924; Yes; Yes; 21700

3913; Hah-tahly-sosie; M; 63; Navajo; F; M; Head; 3925; Yes; Yes; 21365

3914; Hah-tahly-sosie-bih-adzanih; F; 60; Navajo; F; M; Wife; 3926; Yes; Yes; 21366

3915; Tah-yah; M; 11; Navajo; F; S; Grand-son; 3927; Yes; Yes; 21367

3916; Ah-hahn-yiz-bah; F; 8; Navajo; F; S; Grand-daughter; 3928; Yes; Yes; 21368

3917; Hah-dih-chahly-yen-bitsoih; M; 38; Navajo; F; M; Head; 3929; Yes; Yes; 21377

3918; Hah-glih-yah-nah-bah; F; 28; Navajo; F; M; Wife; 3930; Yes; Yes; 21378

3919; Nah-glih-yil-hah-bah; F; 12; Navajo; F; S; Daughter; 3931; Yes; Yes; 21379

3920; Watt, Arthur; M; 14; Navajo; F; S; Son; 3932; Yes; Yes; 21380

3921; Dan; M; 8; Navajo; F; S; Son; 3933; Yes; Yes; 21381

3922; Nah-ziz-bah; F; 6; Navajo; F; S; Daughter; 3934; Yes; Yes; 21382

3923; Eskee-l-suen; M; 4; Navajo; F; S; Son; 3935; Yes; Yes; 21383

3924; Dah-dee-bah; F; 3; Navajo; F; S; Daughter; 3936; Yes; Yes; 21713

3925; Hah-ziz-bah; F; 60; Navajo; F; Wd; Head; 3937; Yes; Yes; 21422

3926; Yahn-des-bah; F; 22; Navajo; F; S; Daughter; 3938; Yes; Yes; 21423

3927; Be-gan-zoz-bah; F; 20; Navajo; F; S; Grand-daughter; 3939; Yes; Yes; 21424

3928; Aflock, Byron; M; 23; Navajo; F; S; Grand-son; 3940; Yes; Yes; 21425

3929; Cheh-naz-bah; F; 17; Navajo; F; S; Daughter; 3941; Yes; Yes; 21426

3930; Yah-nih-bah; F; 24; Navajo; F; Wd; Daughter; 3942; Yes; Yes; 21427

3931; Tah-nih-bah; F; 6; Navajo; F; S; Grand-daughter; 3943; Yes; Yes; 21428

3932; Hoska-yee-dah-nee-hah; M; 4; Navajo; F; S; Grand-son; 3944; Yes; Yes; 21429

3933; Hah-tahly-yazzie-bega; M; 26; Navajo; F; M; Head; 3945; Yes; Yes; 21430

Census of the **Northern Navajo** reservation of the **Northern Navajo** jurisdiction, as of **April 1**, 19**31**, taken by **Ernest H. Hammond, District**, Superintendent. **in Charge**

**Key:** Number; NAME: Surname, Given; Sex; Birth Year (if given), Age At Last Birthday; Tribe; Degree of Blood; Marital Status; Relationship To Head of Family; Last Census Roll Number; At Jurisdiction Where Enrolled (Yes or No); At Another Jurisdiction; ELSEWHERE: Post office, County, State; Ward (Yes or No); Allotment, Annuity, and Identification Numbers.

3934; Hah-glih-yazzie; F; 25; Navajo; F; M; Wife; 3946; Yes; Yes; 21431
3935; Yee-kay-bah; F; 12; Navajo; F; S; Daughter; 3947; Yes; Yes; 21432
3936; Nah-glih-nas-bah; F; 10; Navajo; F; S; Daughter; 3948; Yes; Yes; 21433
3937; Hoska-has-wudt; M; 3; Navajo; F; S; Son; 3949; Yes; Yes; 21434
3938; Yah-nih-bah; F; 1; Navajo; F; S; Daughter; 3950; Yes; Yes; 21682

3939; Hah-nah-gah-nih-ahtsosie-gih; M; Unk; Navajo; F; M; Head; 3951; Yes; Yes; 21166
3940; Beleen-clitsuen-bitsih; F; 27; Navajo; F; M; Wife; 3952; Yes; Yes; 21167
3941; Harvey; M; 13; Navajo; F; S; Son; 3953; Yes; Yes; 21168
3942; Hah-nah-gah-nih-l-chee; M; 15; Navajo; F; S; Brother; 3954; Yes; Yes; 21169

3943; Hah-tahly-yazzie-bega; M; 19; Navajo; F; M; Head; 3955; Yes; Yes; 21204
3944; Doh-haih-bitsih; F; 17; Navajo; F; M; Wife; 3956; Yes; Yes; 21205
3945; Chee; F; 59; Navajo; F; Wd; Aunt; 3957; Yes; Yes; 21206

3946; Hah-tahly-yazzie; M; 65; Navajo; F; M; Head; 3958; Yes; Yes; 21201
3947; Bih-aye-doh-cliz-bitsih; F; 66; Navajo; F; M; Wife; 3959; Yes; Yes; 21202
3948; Sossie; M; 8; Navajo; F; S; Grand-son; 3960; Yes; Yes; 21203

3949; Hah-tahly-sosie-bega; M; 30; Navajo; F; M; Head; 3961; Yes; Yes; 21186
3950; Bitsee-dih-chosie-benally; F; 24; Navajo; F; M; Wife; 3962; Yes; Yes; 21187
3951; Noh-glih-bah; F; 8; Navajo; F; S; Daughter; 3963; Yes; Yes; 21188
3952; Hoska-yil-hah-yah; M; 6; Navajo; F; S; Son; 3964; Yes; Yes; 21189
3953; Hoska-yee-chik-nil-wudt; M; 3; Navajo; F; S; Son; 3965; Yes; Yes; 21190

3954; Hah-ah-sidih-soh-bega; M; 29; Navajo; F; M; Head; 3966; Yes; Yes; 26414
3955; Nah-glih-haz-bah; F; 20; Navajo; F; M; Wife; Yes; 3967; Yes; 26415
3956; Nah-tah-yil-hah-ayh; M; 3; Navajo; F; S; Son; 3968; Yes; Yes; 26416
3957; Nah-tah-yil-gathl; M; 2; Navajo; F; S; Son; 3969; Yes; Yes; 26438

3958; Hah-nah-gah-nih, Pete; M; 58; Navajo; F; M; Head; 3970; Yes; Yes; 25246
3959; Adzan-in-lah-cheeny; F; 57; Navajo; F; M; Wife; 3971; Yes; Yes; 25247
3960; Cecil; M; 19; Navajo; F; S; Son; 3972; Yes; Yes; 25248
3961; May; F; 18; Navajo; F; S; Daughter; 3973; Yes; Yes; 25249
3962; Maxine; F; 16; Navajo; F; S; Daughter; 3974; Yes; Yes; 25250
3963; Emma; F; 22; Navajo; F; S; Grand-daughter; 3975; Yes; Yes; 25251

3964; Hah-tahly-gloh-nizenih-bitah; M; 31; Navajo; F; M; Head; 3976; Yes; Yes; 25091
3965; Nah-dez-bah; F; 18; Navajo; F; M; Wife; 3977; Yes; Yes; 25092
3966; Al-soh-dez-bah; F; 3; Navajo; F; S; Daughter; 3978; Yes; Yes; 25093
3967; Bahih, Lewis; M; 21; Navajo; F; S; Cousin-in-law; 3979; Yes; Yes; 25094

Census of the **Northern Navajo** reservation of the **Northern Navajo** jurisdiction, as of **April 1**, 1931, taken by **Ernest H. Hammond, District**, Superintendent. **in Charge**

**Key:** Number; NAME: Surname, Given; Sex; Birth Year (if given), Age At Last Birthday; Tribe; Degree of Blood; Marital Status; Relationship To Head of Family; Last Census Roll Number; At Jurisdiction Where Enrolled (Yes or No); At Another Jurisdiction; ELSEWHERE: Post office, County, State; Ward (Yes or No); Allotment, Annuity, and Identification Numbers.

3968; Yazzie, Lewis; M; 15; Navajo; F; S; Cousin-in-law; 3980; Yes; Yes; 25095
3969; Angeline; F; 13; Navajo; F; S; Cousin-in-law; 3981; Yes; Yes; 25096

3970; Hah-ah-sidih-soh-bega; M; Unk; Navajo; F; M; Head; 3982; Yes; Yes; 24848
3971; Aht-sosie-yen-bitsih; F; Unk; Navajo; F; M; Wife; 3983; Yes; Yes; 24849
3972; Keh-yil-nih-bah; F; 18; Navajo; F; S; Daughter; 3984; Yes; Yes; 24850

3973; Hah-tahly-sosie; M; 59; Navajo; F; M; Head; 3985; Yes; Yes; 28055
3974; Ah-hah-nih-bah; F; 43; Navajo; F; M; Wife; 3986; Yes; Yes; 28056
3975; Ashe-bahih; M; 18; Navajo; F; S; Son; 3987; Yes; Yes; 28057
3976; Randall; M; 13; Navajo; F; S; Son; 3988; Yes; Yes; 28058
3977; Haska-yee-kih-zol-tih; M; 8; Navajo; F; S; Son; 3989; Yes; Yes; 28059
3978; Yee-dah-nih-bah; F; 6; Navajo; F; S; Daughter; 3990; Yes; Yes; 28060
3979; Stella; F; 2; Navajo; F; S; Daughter; 3991; Yes; Yes; 28098

3980; Hah-tahly-yazzie-bega; M; 38; Navajo; F; M; Head; 3992; Yes; Yes; 23411
3981; Yah-hah-tahly-bitsih; F; 33; Navajo; F; M; Wife; 3993; Yes; Yes; 23412
3982; Yahn-naz-bah; F; 21; Navajo; F; S; Step-daughter; 3994; Yes; Yes; 23413
3983; Beh-nih-gee-bah; F; 19; Navajo; F; S; Step-daughter; 3995; Yes; Yes; 23414
3984; Cora; F; 17; Navajo; F; S; Step-daughter; 3996; Yes; Yes; 23415
3985; Glih-yil-dez-bah; F; 14; Navajo; F; S; Daughter; 3997; Yes; Yes; 23416
3986; Haska-yil-hah-gahl; M; 11; Navajo; F; S; Son; 3998; Yes; Yes; 23417
3987; Tah-gah; F[sic]; 9; Navajo; F; S; Son; 3999; Yes; Yes; 23418 [Should be male.]
3988; Taz-bah; F; 9; Navajo; F; S; Daughter; 4000; Yes; Yes; 23419
3989; Tah-gah-yazzie; M; 5; Navajo; F; S; Son; 4001; Yes; Yes; 23420
3990; Hah-tahly-yazzie-bega; M; 2; Navajo; F; S; Son; 4002; Yes; Yes; 23971

3991; Hah-nah-gahnih-yazzie; M; Unk; Navajo; F; M; Head; 4003; Yes; Yes; 22512
3992; Ah-hih-nil-bah; F; 21; Navajo; F; M; Wife; 4004; Yes; Yes; 22513
3993; Yil-des-bah; F; 3; Navajo; F; S; Daughter; 4005; Yes; Yes; 21702

3994; Hah-dih-chahly; M; Unk; Navajo; F; M; Head; 4006; Yes; Yes; 20259
3995; Nah-glih-soh; F; 46; Navajo; F; M; Wife; 4007; Yes; Yes; 20260
3996; Klizi-thalani, Lois; F; 18; F; S; Step-daughter; 4008; Yes; Yes; 20261
3997; Dah-yiz-bah; F; 7; Navajo; F; S; Daughter; 4009; Yes; Yes; 20262
3998; Gaih; M; 2; Navajo; F; S; Step-Grand-son; 4010; Yes; Yes; 20421

3999; Hah-tah-ly-yee-thlohih-yen-bega; M; 35; Navajo; F; M; Head; 4011; Yes; Yes; 20241
4000; Hah-tah-ly Yazzie-bitsih; F; 31; Navajo; F; M; Wife; 4012; Yes; Yes; 20242
4001; Tis-deyah; M; 8; Navajo; F; S; Son; 4013; Yes; Yes; 20243
4002; Eskee-l-chee; M; 3; Navajo; F; S; Son; 4014; Yes; Yes; 20244

Census of the **Northern Navajo** reservation of the **Northern Navajo** jurisdiction, as of **April 1**, 19**31**, taken by **Ernest H. Hammond, District**, Superintendent. **in Charge**

**Key:** Number; NAME: Surname, Given; Sex; Birth Year (if given), Age At Last Birthday; Tribe; Degree of Blood; Marital Status; Relationship To Head of Family; Last Census Roll Number; At Jurisdiction Where Enrolled (Yes or No); At Another Jurisdiction; ELSEWHERE: Post office, County, State; Ward (Yes or No); Allotment, Annuity, and Identification Numbers.

4003; Hah-nah-gah-nih-soh; M; 43; Navajo; F; M; Head; 4015; Yes; Yes; 24724
4004; Natoni-bitsih; F; 55; Navajo; F; M; Wife; 4016; Yes; Yes; 24725
4005; Joe; M; 21; Navajo; F; S; Son; 4017; Yes; Yes; 24726
4006; Abner; M; 15; Navajo; F; S; Son; 4018; Yes; Yes; 24727
4007; Nih-bah; F; 10; Navajo; F; S; Daughter; 4019; Yes; Yes; 24728
4008; Dinay-soh; M; 8; Navajo; F; S; Son; 4020; Yes; Yes; 24729
4009; Yaz; M; 6; Navajo; F; S; Son; 4021; Yes; Yes; 24730
4010; Bessie; F; 3; Navajo; F; S; Daughter; 4022; Yes; Yes; 24731

4011; Hah-tahly-sosie-bega; M; 25; Navajo; F; M; Head; 4023; Yes; Yes; 27947
4012; Adzan-seeih; F; 19; Navajo; F; M; Wife; 4024; Yes; Yes; 27948

4013; Hah-sidih-soh-bega; M; 49; Navajo; F; M; Head; 4025; Yes; Yes; 26769
4014; Nahn-nih-bah; F; 22; Navajo; F; M; Wife; 4026; Yes; Yes; 26770
4015; Adzan-seesie; F; 22; Navajo; F; S; Daughter; 4027; Yes; Yes; 26771
4016; Vincent; M; 21; Navajo; F; S; Son; 4028; Yes; Yes; 26772
4017; Hah-wudt; M; 18; Navajo; F; S; Son; 4029; Yes; Yes; 26773
4018; Ghih-nil-yah; F; 17; Navajo; F; S; Daughter; 4030; Yes; Yes; 26774
4019; Tah-yah; M; 14; Navajo; F; S; Son; 4031; Yes; Yes; 26775
4020; Chih-hah-yah; M; 10; Navajo; F; S; Son; 4032; Yes; Yes; 26776

4021; Hah-tahly-gloh-nih-zen-nih; M; 64; Navajo; F; M; Head; 4033; Yes; Yes; 25976
4022; Adzan-batoni; F; 77; Navajo; F; M; Wife; 4034; Yes; Yes; 25977
4023; Martin; M; 22; Navajo; F; S; Son; 4035; Yes; Yes; 25978
4024; Hah-nih-bahih; F; 18; Navajo; F; S; Daughter; 4036; Yes; Yes; 25979
4025; Kih-hih-bah; F; 12; Navajo; F; S; Grand-daughter; 4037; Yes; Yes; 25980
4026; Yazzie, Emerson; M; 17; Navajo; F; S; Grand-son; 4038; Yes; Yes; 25981

4027; Hah-dil-chahly-bega; M; 25; Navajo; F; M; Head; 4039; Yes; Yes; 23830
4028; Aloh-nih-bah; F; 23; Navajo; F; M; Wife; 4040; Yes; Yes; 23831
4029; Glih-yil-hah-bah; F; 6; Navajo; F; S; Daughter; 4041; Yes; Yes; 23832
4030; Kah-yil-naz-bah; F; 4; Navajo; F; S; Daughter; 4042; Yes; Yes; 23833
4031; Al-chih-hah-ziz-bah; F; 3; Navajo; F; S; Dai; 4043; Yes; Yes; 23834

4032; Hah-tah-ly-soh-bega; M; 43; Navajo; F; Wd; Head; 4044; Yes; Yes; 20119

4033; Hah-dih-chahly-bega; M; 32; Navajo; F; M; Head; 4045; Yes; Yes; 21301
4034; Bitsoih-yazzie-bih-bize; F; 25; Navajo; F; M; Wife; 4046; Yes; Yes; 21302
4035; Top-ah-hoh-soh; M; 7; Navajo; F; S; Son; 4047; Yes; Yes; 21303
4036; Hah-yah-sosie; M; 5; Navajo; F; S; Son; 4048; Yes; Yes; 21304

Census of the **Northern Navajo** reservation of the **Northern Navajo** jurisdiction, as of **April 1**, 19**31,** taken by **Ernest H. Hammond, District**, Superintendent. **in Charge**

Key: Number; NAME: Surname, Given; Sex; Birth Year (if given), Age At Last Birthday; Tribe; Degree of Blood; Marital Status; Relationship To Head of Family; Last Census Roll Number; At Jurisdiction Where Enrolled (Yes or No); At Another Jurisdiction; ELSEWHERE: Post office, County, State; Ward (Yes or No); Allotment, Annuity, and Identification Numbers.

4037;  Hah-dih-jadih-bitah, Edward Lee Simpson; M; 37; Navajo; F; M; Head; 4049; Yes; Yes; 18201
4038;  Adzanih-nez; F; 38; Navajo; F; M; Wife; 4050; Yes; Yes; 18202
4039;  Naz-bah; F; 12; Navajo; F; S; Daughter; 4051; Yes; Yes; 18203
4040;  Hah-dih-jadih-benally, Henry; M; 9; Navajo; F; S; Son; 4052; Yes; Yes; 18204
4041;  Hah-dih-jadih-benally; M; 8; Navajo; F; S; Son; 4053; Yes; Yes; 18205

4042;  Hah-tahly-yazzie; M; 58; Navajo; F; Wd; Head; 4054; Yes; Yes; 23473
4043;  Haska-yee-chih-dah-yee-gah; M; 17; Navajo; F; S; Son; 4055; Yes; Yes; 23476
4044;  Clyde; M; 15; Navajo; F; S; Son; 4056; Yes; Yes; 23477
4045;  Haska-yil-dah-yis-wudt; M; 11; Navajo; F; S; Son; 4057; Yes; Yes; 23478
4046;  Haska-yil-ziz-zih; M; 9; Navajo; F; S; Son; 4058; Yes; Yes; 23479
4047;  Bih-kah-ziz-bah; F; 49; Navajo; F; M; 1st wife; 4059; Yes; Yes; 23480
4048;  Ah-hahn-yee-bah; F; 19; Navajo; F; S; Daughter; 4060; Yes; Yes; 23481
4049;  Frank; M; 15; Navajo; F; S; Son; 4061; Yes; Yes; 23482
4050;  Bradley; M; 12; Navajo; F; S; Son; 4062; Yes; Yes; 23483
4051;  Haska-yil-kes-wudt; M; 7; Navajo; F; S; Son; 4063; Yes; Yes; 23484
4052;  Kee-kih-bah; F; 20; Navajo; F; S; Sister-in-law; 4064; Yes; Yes; 23686

4053;  Hah-nah-gah-nih; M; Unk; Navajo; F; M; Head; 4065; Yes; Yes; 23868
4054;  Yahn-dez-bah; F; Unk; Navajo; F; M; Wife; 4066; Yes; Yes; 23869
4055;  Unknown; F; Unk; Navajo; F; S; Daughter; 4067; Yes; Yes; 23870
4056;  Nah-tah-yah-zil-wohl; M; Unk; Navajo; F; S; Son; 4068; Yes; Yes; 23871
4057;  Chih-nih-nih-yah; M; Unk; Navajo; F; S; Brother-in-law; 4069; Yes; Yes; 23872
4058;  James, Mark; M; Unk; Navajo; F; S; Brother-in-law; 4070; Yes; Yes; 23873

4059;  Hah-dih-jadih, George; M; 27; Navajo; F; M; Head; 4071; Yes; Yes; 20201
4060;  Teece-sosie-bitsih; F; 24; Navajo; F; M; Wife; 4072; Yes; Yes; 20202
4061;  Denny; M; 7; Navajo; F; S; Son; 4073; Yes; Yes; 20203
4062;  Annie; F; 5; Navajo; F; S; Daughter; 4074; Yes; Yes; 20204
4063;  May; F; 2; Navajo; F; S; Daughter; 4075; Yes; Yes; 20401

4064;  Hah-tahly, Marshall; M; 38; Navajo; F; M; Head; 4076; Yes; Yes; 22380
4065;  Dah-gee-bah; F; 24; Navajo; F; M; Wife; 4077; Yes; Yes; 22381
4066;  Hoska-yil-hal-wudt; M; 5; Navajo; F; S; Son; 4078; Yes; Yes; 22382
4067;  Nah-tah-sosie; M; 3; Navajo; F; S; Son; 4079; Yes; Yes; 22383
4068;  Nah-gee-bah; M[sic]; 2; Navajo; F; S; Daughter; 4080; Yes; Yes; 22782
        [Should be female.]

4069;  Hartathly-sosie-bega; M; 31; Navajo; F; M; Head; 4081; Yes; Yes; 20065
4070;  Dagah-sohoh-benally; F; 21; Navajo; F; M; Wife; 4082; Yes; Yes; 20066

Census of the **Northern Navajo** reservation of the **Northern Navajo** jurisdiction, as of **April 1**, 19**31,** taken by **Ernest H. Hammond, District**, Superintendent. **in Charge**

Key: Number; NAME: Surname, Given; Sex; Birth Year (if given), Age At Last Birthday; Tribe; Degree of Blood; Marital Status; Relationship To Head of Family; Last Census Roll Number; At Jurisdiction Where Enrolled (Yes or No); At Another Jurisdiction; ELSEWHERE: Post office, County, State; Ward (Yes or No); Allotment, Annuity, and Identification Numbers.

4071; Bil-jee-bah; F; 3; Navajo; F; S; Daughter; 4083; Yes; Yes; 20067
4072; Yilth-deyah; M[sic]; 2; Navajo; F; S; Daughter; 4084; Yes; Yes; 20448
      [Should be female.]

4073; Harvey, John; M; 27; Navajo; F; M; Head; 4085; Yes; Yes; 23224
4074; Mamie; F; 22; Navajo; F; M; Wife; 4086; Yes; Yes; 23225

4075; Harley, Mark; M; Unk; Navajo; F; M; Head; 4087; Yes; Yes; 23284
4076; Dagah-l-chee-benally; F; Unk; Navajo; F; M; Wife; 4088; Yes; Yes; 23285
4077; Yil-hah-naz-bah; F; Unk; Navajo; F; S; Daughter; 4089; Yes; Yes; 23286
4078; Nah-tah-yah-nih-hih-yah; M; Unk; Navajo; F; S; Son; 4090; Yes; Yes; 23287
4079; Dixon, Henry; M; Unk; Navajo; F; S; Brother-in-law; 4091; Yes; Yes; 23288
4080; Dixon, Jessie; F; Unk; Navajo; F; S; Sister-in-law; 4092; Yes; Yes; 23289
4081; Dixon, Taylor; M; 17; Navajo; F; S; Brother-in-law; 4093; Yes; Yes; 23290

4082; Haska-bega, Julian; M; 40; Navajo; F; M; Head; 4094; Yes; Yes; 23237
4083; Dahah-dah-sah-kad-bitsih; F; 46; Navajo; F; M; Wife; 4095; Yes; Yes; 23238
4084; Hugh; M; 18; Navajo; F; S; Son; 4096; Yes; Yes; 23239
4085; Naz-nih-bakih; F; 14; Navajo; F; S; Daughter; 4097; Yes; Yes; 23240
4086; Keh-yil-hah-bah; F; 11; Navajo; F; S; Daughter; 4098; Yes; Yes; 23241
4087; Tah-nil-wudt; M; 8; Navajo; F; S; Son; 4099; Yes; Yes; 23242
4088; Tahn-hah-nih-bah; F; 7; Navajo; F; S; Daughter; 4100; Yes; Yes; 23243
4089; Harry; M; Unk; Navajo; F; S; Brother; 4101; Yes; Yes; 23244
4090; Nah-clah-tas-bah; F; 2; Navajo; F; S; Daughter; 4102; Yes; Yes; 24003

4091; Hartathle-bega; M; 26; Navajo; F; M; Head; 4103; No; McElmo, Colo., San Juan, Utah; Yes; 18860
4092; Holkidney-bitsih; F; 20; Navajo; F; M; Wife; 4104; No; McElmo, Colo., San Juan, Utah; Yes; 18861
4093; Hoska-yis-taa; M; 4; Navajo; F; S; Son; 4105; No; McElmo, Colo., San Juan, Utah; Yes; 18862

4094; Hartathle-bega; M; 32; Navajo; F; M; Head; 4106; No; McElmo, Colo., San Juan, Utah; Yes; 18865
4095; Adzanih-yazzie; F; 22; Navajo; F; M; Wife; 4107; No; McElmo, Colo., San Juan, Utah; Yes; 18866
4096; Zan-oh-pah; F; 10; Navajo; F; S; Daughter; 4108; No; McElmo, Colo., San Juan, Utah; Yes; 18867
4097; Eskee; M; 8; Navajo; F; S; Son; 4109; No; McElmo, Colo., San Juan, Utah; Yes; 18868
4098; Oh-zih; M; 5; Navajo; F; S; Son; 4110; No; McElmo, Colo., San Juan, Utah; Yes; 18869

Census of the **Northern Navajo** reservation of the **Northern Navajo** jurisdiction, as of **April 1**, 19**31,** taken by **Ernest H. Hammond, District**, Superintendent. **in Charge**

Key: Number; NAME: Surname, Given; Sex; Birth Year (if given), Age At Last Birthday; Tribe; Degree of Blood; Marital Status; Relationship To Head of Family; Last Census Roll Number; At Jurisdiction Where Enrolled (Yes or No); At Another Jurisdiction; ELSEWHERE: Post office, County, State; Ward (Yes or No); Allotment, Annuity, and Identification Numbers.

4099; Atate-l-bahih; F; 4; Navajo; F; S; Daughter; 4111; No; McElmo, Colo., San Juan, Utah; Yes; 18870

4100; Hartathle, Jim; M; 61; Navajo; F; M; Head; 4112; No; McElmo, Colo., San Juan, Utah; Yes; 18845
4101; Hartathle's wife; F; 58; Navajo; F; M: Wife; 4113; No; McElmo, Colo., San Juan, Utah; Yes; 18846
4102; Whay, Juan; M; 25; Navajo; F; S; Son; 4114; No; McElmo, Colo., San Juan, Utah; Yes; 18847
4103; Hah-ish-, James; M; 23; Navajo; F; S; Son; 4115; No; McElmo, Colo., San Juan, Utah; Yes; 18848
4104; Kee-yazzie; M; 21; Navajo; F; S; Son; 4116; No; McElmo, Colo., San Juan, Utah; Yes; 18849
4105; Hartathle, Ruel; M; 16; Navajo; F; S; Son; 4117; No; McElmo, Colo., San Juan, Utah; Yes; 18850
4106; Yah-des-bah; F; 11; Navajo; F; S; Daughter; 4118; No; McElmo, Colo., San Juan, Utah; Yes; 18851

4107; Hartathe-bega, Jim; M; 39; Navajo; F; M; Head; 4119; No; McElmo, Colo., San Juan, Utah; Yes; 18852
4108; Nocki-dinay-bitsih; F; 42; Navajo; F; M; Wife; 4120; No; McElmo, Colo., San Juan, Utah; Yes; 18853
4109; Kee-soh; M; 11; Navajo; F; S; Son; 4121; No; McElmo, Colo., San Juan, Utah; Yes; 18854
4110; Samuel; M; 3; Navajo; F; S; Son; 4122; No; McElmo, Colo., San Juan, Utah; Yes; 18855

4111; Hartathly-etsosie-bekis; M; Unk; Navajo; F; Wd; Head; 4123; Yes; Yes; 17931[sic] [ID No. should be 17831]
4112; Hartathly-etsosie, Paula; F; 18; Navajo; F; S; Daughter; 4124; Yes; Yes; 17832
4113; Adzan-etsosie; F; 15; Navajo; F; S; Daughter; 4125; Yes; Yes; 17833
4114; Hartathly-etsosie, Ed; M; 11; Navajo; F; S; Son; 4126; Yes; Yes; 17834
4115; Ah-kay-des-bah; F; 9; Navajo; F; S; Daughter; 4127; Yes; Yes; 17835

4116; Haska-nad-zah; M; Unk; Navajo; F; M; Head; 4128; Yes; Yes; 24763
4117; Keh-yil-nih-bah; F; 51; Navajo; F; M; Wife; 4129; Yes; Yes; 24764
4118; Belons, Carrie; F; 20; Navajo; F; S; Step-daughter; 4130; Yes; Yes; 24765
4119; Tahn-nih-dez-bah; F; 19; Navajo; F; S; Step-daughter; 4131; Yes; Yes; 24766
4120; Haska-yahn-yil-wohl; M; 24; Navajo; F; S; Step-son; 4132; Yes; Yes; 24767
4121; Haska-yil-has-wudt; M; 10; Navajo; F; S; Step-son; 4133; Yes; Yes; 24768
4122; Glih-yil-nih-bah; F; 7; Navajo; F; S; Step-grand daughter; 4134; Yes; Yes; 24769

Census of the **Northern Navajo** reservation of the **Northern Navajo** jurisdiction, as of **April 1**, 19**31**, taken by **Ernest H. Hammond, District**, Superintendent. **in Charge**

**Key:** Number; NAME: Surname, Given; Sex; Birth Year (if given), Age At Last Birthday; Tribe; Degree of Blood; Marital Status; Relationship To Head of Family; Last Census Roll Number; At Jurisdiction Where Enrolled (Yes or No); At Another Jurisdiction; ELSEWHERE: Post office, County, State; Ward (Yes or No); Allotment, Annuity, and Identification Numbers.

4123; Haska-yee-nih-tih; M; 51; Navajo; F; M; Head; 4135; Yes; Yes; 25989
4124; Bih-naz-nih-bah; F; 63; Navajo; F; M; Wife; 4136; Yes; Yes; 25990
4125; Ah-kih-gee-bah; F; 22; Navajo; F; S; Daughter; 4137; Yes; Yes; 25991
4126; Haska-yil-nas-wudt; M; 18; Navajo; F; S; Son; 4138; Yes; Yes; 25992
4127; Ah-hih-dee-bah; F; 6; Navajo; F; S; Daughter; 4139; Yes; Yes; 25993

4128; Hosch-cliznih-bega; M; 40; Navajo; F; M; Head; 4140; Yes; Yes; 23439
4129; Bih-bizee-bitsih; F; 36; Navajo; F; M; Wife; 4141; Yes; Yes; 23440
4130; Awa-soh; M; 16; Navajo; F; S; Son; 4142; Yes; Yes; 23441
4131; Evan; M; 13; Navajo; F; S; Son; 4143; Yes; Yes; 23442
4132; Kay-yah; M; 11; Navajo; F; S; Son; 4144; Yes; Yes; 23443
4133; Kay-yil-chin-bah; F; 9; Navajo; F; S; Daughter; 4145; Yes; Yes; 23444
4134; Keh-yil-chen-nih-bah; F; 5; Navajo; F; S; Daughter; 4146; Yes; Yes; 23445
4135; Adzan-ah-nah-thlohi; F; 44[sic]; Navajo; F; Wd; Mother-in-law; 4147; Yes; Yes; 23446
4136; Yee-yah-hal-wudt; M; 21; Navajo; F; S; Nephew-in-law; 4148; Yes; Yes; 23447
4137; Haska-yee-tah-des-wudt; M; 1; Navajo; F; S; Son; 4149; Yes; Yes; 23943

4138; Hosteen-nez-bega, Tom; M; 60; Navajo; F; M; Head; 4150; Yes; Yes; 32347
4139; Niota-hosteen-benally; F; 50; Navajo; F; M; Wife; 4151; Yes; Yes; 32348
4140; Donald; M; 23; Navajo; F; S; Son; 4152; Yes; Yes; 32349
4141; Haska-yil-yee-gahl; M; 8; Navajo; F; S; Grand-son; 4153; Yes; Yes; 32350

4142; Hosteen-yazzie-bega, Lee, Joe; M; 26; Navajo; F; M; Head; [Blank]; Yes; Yes; 20175
4143; Toh-ah-k-glin-nih-bitsih; F; 23; Navajo; F; M; Wife; [Blank]; Yes; Yes; 20176
4144; Yazzie, Sarah; F; 5; Navajo; F; S; Daughter; [Blank]; Yes; Yes; 20177

4145; Hosteen-etsosie-bitsih; F; 39; Navajo; F; Wd; Head; 4154; Yes; Yes; 17134
4146; Hosteen-etsosie-bitsih's daughter; F; 22; Navajo; F; S; Daughter; 4155; Yes; Yes; 17135
4147; Etsosie, Laura; F; 11; Navajo; F; S; Daughter; 4156; Yes; Yes; 17136
4148; Hosteen-etsosie-bitsih-hoskee-seeih; M; 8; Navajo; F; S; Son; 4157; Yes; Yes; 17137
4149; Hosteen-etsosie-bitsih-nasbah; F; 5; Navajo; F; S; Daughter; 4158; Yes; Yes; 17138

4150; Hosteen-yazzie-bih-adzan; F; 67; Navajo; F; Wd; Head; 4159; Yes; Yes; 22705
4151; Nah-naz-nah; F; 98; Navajo; F; Wd; Mother; 4160; Yes; Yes; 22706
4152; Hosteen-yazzie-bega; F[sic]; 29; Navajo; F; S; Son; 4161; Yes; Yes; 22707

Census of the **Northern Navajo** reservation of the **Northern Navajo** jurisdiction, as of **April 1**, 19**31,** taken by **Ernest H. Hammond, District**, Superintendent. **in Charge**

Key: Number; NAME: Surname, Given; Sex; Birth Year (if given), Age At Last Birthday; Tribe; Degree of Blood; Marital Status; Relationship To Head of Family; Last Census Roll Number; At Jurisdiction Where Enrolled (Yes or No); At Another Jurisdiction; ELSEWHERE: Post office, County, State; Ward (Yes or No); Allotment, Annuity, and Identification Numbers.

4153; Hosteen-bitsee-lagaih; M; 62; Navajo; F; M; Head; 4162; Yes; Yes; 22599
4154; Neekiha-bitsih; F; 62; Navajo; F; M; Wife; 4163; Yes; Yes; 22600

4155; Hosteen-bih-dagaih-bitah; M; Unk; Navajo; F; M; Head; 4164; Yes; Yes; 22442
4156; Keh-hah-nih-bah; F; 29; Navajo; F; M; Wife; 4165; Yes; Yes; 22443
4157; Yee-nah-oh-gahl; M; 13; Navajo; F; S; Son; 4166; Yes; Yes; 22444
4158; Hoska-yil-nah-dahl; M; 10; Navajo; F; S; Son; 4167; Yes; Yes; 22445
4159; Nah-tah-ah-yah; M; 7; Navajo; F; S; Son; 4168; Yes; Yes; 22446
4160; Cheh-bah; F; 4; Navajo; F; S; Daughter; 4169; Yes; Yes; 22447

4161; Hosteen, Joe; M; 62; Navajo; F; M; Head; 4170; Yes; Yes; 22421
4162; Kay-yil-nas-bah; F; 62; Navajo; F; M; Wife; 4171; Yes; Yes; 22422
4163; Yah-dee-yah; M; 8; Navajo; F; S; Grand-son; 4172; Yes; Yes; 22424
4164; Shause-bega, Joe; M; 22; Navajo; F; S; Son; 4173; Yes; Yes; 22738

4165; Hosteen-ahshin-bega-et-seesihgi; M; 41; Navajo; F; M; Head; 4174; Yes; Yes; 17246
4166; Hosteen-ashan-bitsih; F; 41; Navajo; F; M; Wife; 4175; Yes; Yes; 17247
4167; Ahshin, Walter; M; 18; Navajo; F; S; Son; 4176; Yes; Yes; 17248
4168; Ahshin-athanah-abah; F; 8; Navajo; F; S; Daughter; 4177; Yes; Yes; 17249
4169; Hosteen-ahahin-bega-Etseesihigi-bitsih; F; 20; Navajo; F; S; Daughter; 4178; Yes; Yes; 17250
4170; Athnah-hahnasbah; F; 4; Navajo; F; S; Daughter; 4179; Yes; Yes; 17251

4171; Hosteen-soh-ah-tah; M; Unk; Navajo; F; M; Head; 4180; Yes; Yes; 22375
4172; Nah-cheeny-benally; F; 43; Navajo; F; M; Wife; 4181; Yes; Yes; 22376
4173; Laura; F; 16; Navajo; F; S; Daughter; 4182; Yes; Yes; 22377
4174; Awa-yazzie; F; 13; Navajo; F; S; Daughter; 4183; Yes; Yes; 22378
4175; Bil-hah-des-bah; F; 6; Navajo; F; S; Grand-daughter; 4184; Yes; Yes; 22379

4176; Hosteen-nez, Long-John; M; 36; Navajo; F; M; Head; 4185; Yes; Yes; 22475
4177; Hah-nah-bah; F; 24; Navajo; F; M; Wife; 4186; Yes; Yes; 22476
4178; Glih-hah-bah; F; 9; Navajo; F; S; Daughter; 4187; Yes; Yes; 22477
4179; Dinay-soh; M; 7; Navajo; F; S; Son; 4188; Yes; Yes; 22478
4180; Bah-hah-zohnih; M; 4; Navajo; F; S; Son; 4189; Yes; Yes; 22479
4181; Yil-hah-wudt; M; 1; Navajo; F; S; Son; 4190; Yes; Yes; 22793

4182; Hosteen-sah-hah-ah-atin-bega; M; 26; Navajo; F; M; Head; 4191; Yes; Yes; 23264
4183; Kih-des-bah; F; 21; Navajo; F; M; Wife; 4192; Yes; Yes; 23265
4184; Nah-tah-yah-yil-wohl; M; 4; Navajo; F; S; Son; 4193; Yes; Yes; 23266

Census of the **Northern Navajo** reservation of the **Northern Navajo** jurisdiction, as of **April 1**, 19**31,** taken by **Ernest H. Hammond, District**, Superintendent. **in Charge**

**Key:** Number; NAME: Surname, Given; Sex; Birth Year (if given), Age At Last Birthday; Tribe; Degree of Blood; Marital Status; Relationship To Head of Family; Last Census Roll Number; At Jurisdiction Where Enrolled (Yes or No); At Another Jurisdiction; ELSEWHERE: Post office, County, State; Ward (Yes or No); Allotment, Annuity, and Identification Numbers.

4185; Hosteen-hosch-cliznih-bitsih; F; 43; Navajo; F; Wd; Head; 4194; Yes; Yes; 23203
4186; Nocki-yazzie; M; 13; Navajo; F; S; Son; 4195; Yes; Yes; 23204

4187; Hosteen-l-suen-bega, Juan; M; 50; Navajo; F; M; Head; 4196; Yes; Yes; 23215
4188; Hosteen-l-suen-bega's wife; F; 47; Navajo; F; M; Wife; 4197; Yes; Yes; 23216
4189; Russell; M; 18; Navajo; F; S; Son; 4198; Yes; Yes; 23217
4190; Yee-nil-bah; F; 12; Navajo; F; S; Daughter; 4199; Yes; Yes; 23218
4191; Lewis; M; 16; Navajo; F; S; Son; 4200; Yes; Yes; 23219
4192; Nah-yah; M; 10; Navajo; F; S; Son; 4201; Yes; Yes; 23220
4193; David; M; 5; Navajo; F; S; Son; 4202; Yes; Yes; 23221
4194; Glih-deh-bah; F; 18; Navajo; F; S; Niece; 4203; Yes; Yes; 23222
4195; Edmund; M; 16; Navajo; F; S; Nephew; 4204; Yes; Yes; 23223
4196; Haska-nez-wudt; M; 2; Navajo; F; S; Son; 4205; Yes; Yes; 23927

4197; Hosteen-l-suen; M; Unk; Navajo; F; M; Head; 4206; Yes; Yes; 23199
4198; Hosteen-hosch-cliznih-bitsih; F; 32; Navajo; F; M; Wife; 4207; Yes; Yes; 23200
4199; Clyde; M; 21; Navajo; F; S; Son; 4208; Yes; Yes; 23201

4200; Hosteen-bih-dagaih-bilah; F; 76; Navajo; F; Wd; Head; 4209; Yes; Yes; 22393
4201; Hoska-yee-dal-wudt; M; 10; Navajo; F; S; Great-grand-son; 4210; Yes; Yes; 22394

4202; Hortathly-soh; M; 60; Navajo; F; M; Head; 4211; Yes; Yes; 17104
4203; Ahath-map-bah; F; 78; Navajo; F; M; Wife; 4212; Yes; Yes; 17105

4204; Hortathly-soh-bega; M; 33; Navajo; F; M; Head; 4213; Yes; Yes; 17102
4205; Hosteen-ezanih-bitsih; F; 33; Navajo; F; M; Wife; 4214; Yes; Yes; 17103

4206; Hosteen-ezanih; M; 88; Navajo; F; Wd; Head; 4215; Yes; Yes; 17099
4207; Hosteen-ezanih; M; 10; Navajo; F; S; Son; 4216; Yes; Yes; 17100
4208; Hosteen-ezanih-klizi-soh; M; 8; Navajo; F; S; Son; 4217; Yes; Yes; 17101

4209; Hosteen-yen-bega; M; 85; Navajo; F; Wd; Head; 4218; Yes; Yes; 23495
4210; Benally-yazzie; M; 25; Navajo; F; S; Son; 4219; Yes; Yes; 23496

4211; Hosteen-clitsoh-bega; M; 30; Navajo; F; M; Head; 4220; Yes; Yes; 17207
4212; Bah-ahzonih-bitsih; F; 24; Navajo; F; M; Wife; 4221; Yes; Yes; 17208
4213; Hosteen-clitsoh-bega-Oskiehaih; M; 6; Navajo; F; S; Son; 4222; Yes; Yes; 17209
4214; Askee Tuly; M; 3/12; Navajo; F; S; Son; 4223; Yes; Yes; 17420

**Key:** Number; NAME: Surname, Given; Sex; Birth Year (if given), Age At Last Birthday; Tribe; Degree of Blood; Marital Status; Relationship To Head of Family; Last Census Roll Number; At Jurisdiction Where Enrolled (Yes or No); At Another Jurisdiction; ELSEWHERE: Post office, County, State; Ward (Yes or No); Allotment, Annuity, and Identification Numbers.

4215; Hosteen-deel-benally-bega; M; 39; Navajo; F; M; Head; 4224; Yes; Yes; 21191
4216; Gil-hah-yazzie; F; 21; Navajo; F; M; Wife; 4225; Yes; Yes; 21192
4217; Nah-glih-hah-bah; F; 21; Navajo; F; S; Niece; 4226; Yes; Yes; 21200

4218; Hah-nah-gahnih; M; 75; Navajo; F; Wd; Head; 4227; Yes; Yes; 21157
4219; Hah-nah-gah-nih-bitsih; F; 31; Navajo; F; Wd.; Daughter; 4228; Yes; Yes; 21158
4220; Yee-nil-bah; F; 16; Navajo; F; S; Grand-daughter; 4229; Yes; Yes; 21159
4221; Grace; F; 14; Navajo; F; S; Grand-daughter; 4230; Yes; Yes; 21160
4222; Yah-hoh-tahl; M; 8; Navajo; F; S; Grand-son; 4231; Yes; Yes; 21161
4223; Hoska-yil-deyah; M; 5; Navajo; F; S; Grand-son; 4232; Yes; Yes; 21162
4224; Hah-yis-bah; F; 2; Navajo; F; S; Grand-daughter; 4233; Yes; Yes; 21706

4225; Hosteen-deel-benally-bitsih; F; 39; Navajo; F; Wd; Head; 4234; Yes; Yes; 21143
4226; Yil-has-wudt; M; 19; Navajo; F; S; Son; 4235; Yes; Yes; 21144
4227; Dah-yis-bah; F; 15; Navajo; F; S; Daughter; 4236; Yes; Yes; 21145
4228; Charles Kelly; M; 18; Navajo; F; S; Nephew; 4237; Yes; Yes; 21146
4229; Kelly, James; M; 15; Navajo; F; S; Nephew; 4238; Yes; Yes; 21147
4230; Kelly, Henry; M; 12; Navajo; F; S; Nephew; 4239; Yes; Yes; 21148
4231; Nas-wudt; M; 7; Navajo; F; S; Nephew; 4240; Yes; Yes; 21149

4232; Hosteen-nez-bega; M; 26; Navajo; F; M; Head; 4241; Yes; Yes; 21091
4233; See-dih-chosie-yen-bitsih; F; 21; Navajo; F; M; Wife; 4242; Yes; Yes; 21092
4234; Kah-des-bah; F; 5; Navajo; F; S; Daughter; 4243; Yes; Yes; 21093
4235; Dah-yis-bah; F; 3; Navajo; F; S; Daughter; 4244; Yes; Yes; 21094

4236; Hosteen-nez; M; 43; Navajo; F; M; Head; 4245; Yes; Yes; 21095
4237; Clah-ilt-suen-benally; F; 33; Navajo; F; M; 4246; Wife; Yes; Yes; 21096
4238; Nez, Ben; M; 19; Navajo; F; S; Son; 4247; Yes; Yes; 21097
4239; Nah-tah-yil-nah-gah; M; 18; Navajo; F; S; Son; 4248; Yes; Yes; 21098
4240; Kee-yazzie; M; 8; Navajo; F; S; Son; 4249; Yes; Yes; 21099
4241; Zab-nih-bah; F; 6; Navajo; F; S; Daughter; 4250; Yes; Yes; 21100
4242; Awae-yazzie; F; 2; Navajo; F; S; Daughter; 4251; Yes; Yes; 21637

4243; Hosteen-yazzie-bega; M; 35; Navajo; F; M; Head; 4252; Yes; Yes; 21101
4244; Yah-hah-tahly-bitsih; F; 40; Navajo; F; M; Wife; 4253; Yes; Yes; 21102
4245; Nah-tah-yil-yee-yah; M; 19; Navajo; F; S; Son; 4254; Yes; Yes; 21103
4246; Mollie; F; 17; Navajo; F; S; Daughter; 4255; Yes; Yes; 21104
4247; Nah-tah-yee-che-hah-gahl; M; 13; Navajo; F; S; Son; 4256; Yes; Yes; 21105
4248; Dinay-l-chee; M; 7; Navajo; F; S; Son; 4257; Yes; Yes; 21106
4249; Nah-glih-yee-nas-bah; F; 4; Navajo; F; S; Daughter; 4258; Yes; Yes; 21107

Census of the **Northern Navajo** reservation of the **Northern Navajo** jurisdiction, as of **April 1**, 1931, taken by **Ernest H. Hammond, District**, Superintendent. **in Charge**

Key: Number; NAME: Surname, Given; Sex; Birth Year (if given), Age At Last Birthday; Tribe; Degree of Blood; Marital Status; Relationship To Head of Family; Last Census Roll Number; At Jurisdiction Where Enrolled (Yes or No); At Another Jurisdiction; ELSEWHERE: Post office, County, State; Ward (Yes or No); Allotment, Annuity, and Identification Numbers.

4250;  Adzanih-yazzie; F; 80; Navajo; F; Wd; Great-grandmother; 4259; Yes; Yes; 21108

4251;  Hosteen-l-chee's aunt, Capitan-bih-adzan; F; 93; Navajo; F; Wd; Head; 4260; Yes; Yes; 20973

4252;  Hoska-yil-ee-yah, Lee Dan; M; 33; Navajo; F; M; Head; 4261; Yes; Yes; 20925
4253;  Ah-kays-bah; F; 27; Navajo; F; M; Wife; 4262; Yes; Yes; 20926
4254;  Wash; M; 10; Navajo; F; S; Son; 4263; Yes; Yes; 20927
4255;  Hoska-yil-nah-yah; M; 9; Navajo; F; S; Son; 4264; Yes; Yes; 20928
4256;  Hoska-yil-hah-yah; M; 7; Navajo; F; S; Son; 4265; Yes; Yes; 20929
4257;  Nah-tah-yah-nal-wudt; M; 5; Navajo; F; S; Son; 4266; Yes; Yes; 20930

4258;  Hosteen-tahn; M; 66; Navajo; F; Wd; Head; 4267; Yes; Yes; 21474
4259;  Yil-nas-bah; F; 13; Navajo; F; S; Daughter; 4268; Yes; Yes; 21475

4260;  Hosteen-deel-benally-bega; M; 29; Navajo; F; M; Head; 4269; Yes; Yes; 21609
4261;  Julian's daughter; F; Unk; Navajo; F; M; Wife; 4270; Yes; Yes; 21610
4262;  Clih-bah; F; 4; Navajo; F; S; Daughter; 4271; Yes; Yes; 21611

4263;  Hosteen-badoni; M; 98; Navajo; F; M; Head; 4272; Yes; Yes; 21435
4264;  Hosteen-badoni's wife; F; 86; Navajo; F; M; Wife; 4273; Yes; Yes; 21436

4265;  Hosteen-l-chee-bih-adzan; F; 72; Navajo; F; Wd; Head; 4274; ~~Yes~~ No; Bluff, San Juan, Utah; Yes; 28856
4266;  Al-soh-naz-bah; F; 15; Navajo; F; S; Niece; 4275; No; Bluff, San Juan, Utah; Yes; 28857
4267;  Zahn-nih-bah; F; 9; Navajo; F; S; Grand-daughter; 4276; No; Bluff, San Juan, Utah; Yes; 28858

4268;  Hoh-zoh-nih-bah-tahly-bega; M; Unk; Navajo; F; M; Head; 4277; Yes; Yes; 21594
4269;  Jessie; F; Unk; Navajo; F; M; Wife; 4278; Yes; Yes; 21595
4270;  Glih-yazzie; F; 6; Navajo; F; S; Daughter; 4279; Yes; Yes; 21596
4271;  Al-dah-nih-bah; F; 4; Navajo; F; S; Daughter; 4280; Yes; Yes; 21597

4272;  Hosteen Yazzie; M; 51; Navajo; F; M; Head; 4281; Yes; Yes; 21553
4273;  Bitzoih, Polly; F; 48; Navajo; F; M; Wife; 4282; Yes; Yes; 21554
4274;  Ashinh-l-chee; M; 7; Navajo; F; S; Son; 4283; Yes; Yes; 21555

Census of the __Northern Navajo__ reservation of the __Northern Navajo__ jurisdiction, as of __April 1__ , 1931, taken by __Ernest H. Hammond, District__, Superintendent. **in Charge**

Key: Number; NAME: Surname, Given; Sex; Birth Year (if given), Age At Last Birthday; Tribe; Degree of Blood; Marital Status; Relationship To Head of Family; Last Census Roll Number; At Jurisdiction Where Enrolled (Yes or No); At Another Jurisdiction; ELSEWHERE: Post office, County, State; Ward (Yes or No); Allotment, Annuity, and Identification Numbers.

4275; Hosteen-tahn-bega, Henry; M; 23; Navajo; F; M; Head; 4284; Yes; Yes; 21501
4276; Nah-des-bah; F; 16; Navajo; F; M; Wife; 4285; Yes; Yes; 21502
4277; Hosch-cliznih-ahtcitty-yen-bih-adzan; F; 73; Navajo; F; Wd; Grand-mother; 4286; Yes; Yes; 21503
4278; Awae-yazzie; F; 1; Navajo; F; S; Daughter; 4287; Yes; Yes; 21676

4279; Hosteen-wo-daih-bega, Dick; M; Unk; Navajo; F; M; Head; 4288; Yes; Yes; 23299
4280; Hosteen-wo-daih-bega's wife; F; 41; Navajo; F; M; Wife; 4289; Yes; Yes; 23300
4281; Tah-gah; M; 20; Navajo; F; S; Son; 4290; Yes; Yes; 23301
4282; Haska-yee-no-sh[sic]; M; 19; Navajo; F; S; Son; 4291; Yes; Yes; 23302
    [Name is probably Haska-yee-no-ah]
4283; Johl; M; 18; Navajo; F; S; Son; 4292; Yes; Yes; 23303
4284; Kih-kenih-bah; F; 17; Navajo; F; S; Daughter; 4293; Yes; Yes; 23304
4285; Haska-yil-kee-gahl; M; 11; Navajo; F; S; Son; 4294; Yes; Yes; 23305
4286; Haska-yee-chih-dah-dee-yah; M; 7; Navajo; F; S; Son; 4295; Yes; Yes; 23306
4287; Hosteen-wo-daih-bih-adzan; F; 73; Navajo; F; Wd; Mother; 4297; Yes; Yes; 23308

4288; Hosteen-suen, Grant; M; 45; Navajo; F; M; Head; 4298; Yes; Yes; 23291
4289; Sheepman-bitsih; F; 36; Navajo; F; M; Wife; 4299; Yes; Yes; 23292
4290; Harry; M; 13; Navajo; F; S; Son; 4300; Yes; Yes; 23293
4291; Ruby; F; 10; Navajo; F; S; Daughter; 4301; Yes; Yes; 23294
4292; Frances; F; 7; Navajo; F; S; Son[sic]; 4302; Yes; Yes; 23295
    [Should be female]
4293; Han-nes-bah; F; 1; Navajo; F; S; Daughter; 4303; Yes; Yes; 23296

4294; Hosteen-sani-bega; M; 46; Navajo; F; M; Head; 4304; Yes; Yes; 17106
4295; Hortathly-bitsih; F; 36; Navajo; F; M; Wife; 4305; Yes; Yes; 17107
4296; Hosteen-sani-bega's daughter; F; 25; Navajo; F; S; Daughter; 4306; Yes; Yes; 17108
4297; Hosteen-sani-bega, Mable; F; Unk; Navajo; F; S; Daughter; 4307; Yes; Yes; 17109
4298; Yah-dih-bah-sani-bega; F; 25; Navajo; F; S; Daughter; 4308; Yes; Yes; 17110
4299; Sani-bega, Talth-chee; M; 18; Navajo; F; S; Son; 4309; Yes; Yes; 17111
4300; Sani-bega, Della; F; 14; Navajo; F; S; Daughter; 4310; Yes; Yes; 17112
4301; Sani-bega, Jerry; M; 12; Navajo; F; S; Son; 4311; Yes; Yes; 17113
4302; Sani-bega Alchinn-haspah; F; 8; Navajo; F; S; Daughter; 4312; Yes; Yes; 17114
4303; Sani-bega Hoska-la-chee; M; 5; Navajo; F; S; Son; 4313; Yes; Yes; 17115

Census of the **Northern Navajo** reservation of the **Northern Navajo** jurisdiction, as of **April 1**, 19**31**, taken by **Ernest H. Hammond, District**, Superintendent. **in Charge**

**Key:** Number; NAME: Surname, Given; Sex; Birth Year (if given), Age At Last Birthday; Tribe; Degree of Blood; Marital Status; Relationship To Head of Family; Last Census Roll Number; At Jurisdiction Where Enrolled (Yes or No); At Another Jurisdiction; ELSEWHERE: Post office, County, State; Ward (Yes or No); Allotment, Annuity, and Identification Numbers.

4304; Hosteen-shah-hah-ah-atin-bega; M; 25; Navajo; F; M; Head; 4314; Yes; Yes; 23264
4305; Kih-des-bah; F; 21; Navajo; F; M; Wife; 4315; Yes; Yes; 23265
4306; Nah-tah-yah-yil-wohl; M; 4; Navajo; F; S; Son; 4316; Yes; Yes; 23266
4307; Wdut[sic]; M; 1; Navajo; F; S; Son; 4317; Yes; Yes; 24006
[Name should be Wudt]

4308; Hosteen-l-suen; M; 78; Navajo; F; M; Head; 4318; Yes; Yes; 23267
4309; Hosteen-l-suen's wife; F; 60; Navajo; F; M; Wife; 4319; Yes; Yes; 23268
4310; Nah-tah-yee-tah-yee-gahl; M; 12; Navajo; F; S; Grand-son; 4320; Yes; Yes; 23269

4311; Hosteen-l-suen bega; M; 47; Navajo; F; M; Head; 4321; Yes; Yes; 23274
4312; Sheepman-bitsih; F; 38; Navajo; F; M; Wife; 4322; Yes; Yes; 23275
4313; Al-hoh-yis-bah; F; 24; Navajo; F; S; Daughter; 4323; Yes; Yes; 23276
4314; Guy; M; 20; Navajo; F; S; Son; 4324; Yes; Yes; 23277
4315; Bah-yis-bah; F; 12; Navajo; F; S; Daughter; 4325; Yes; Yes; 23278
4316; Al-kih-dah-yis-bah; F; 9; Navajo; F; S; Daughter; 4326; Yes; Yes; 23279
4317; Haska-yil-nih-nih-yah; M; 4; Navajo; F; S; Son; 4327; Yes; Yes; 23280
4318; Adzan-zin-nih; F; 79; Navajo; F; Wd; Grand-mother; 4328; Yes; Yes; 23281
4319; Eskee-l-gaih; M; 13; Navajo; F; S; Grand-son; 4329; Yes; Yes; 23282

4320; Hosteen-l-bahih-benally; M; 25; Navajo; F; M; Head; 4330; Yes; Yes; 23860
4321; Bitsees-chillibitsih[sic]; F; 25; Navajo; F; M; Wife; 4331; Yes; Yes; 23861
[Name should be Bitsees-chilli-bitsih]
4322; Keh-yee-tah-nih-bah; F; 4; Navajo; F; S; Daughter; 4332; Yes; Yes; 23862

4323; Hosteen-yen-benally; M; Unk; Navajo; F; M; Head; 4333; Yes; Yes; 23635
4324; Stephen's mother; F; 65; Navajo; F; M; Wife; 4334; Yes; Yes; 23636
4325; Nah-tah-yee-nah-gah; M; 17; Navajo; F; S; Son; 4335; Yes; Yes; 23637
4326; Benally-bitsih; F; 27; Navajo; F; Wd; Daughter; 4336; Yes; Yes; 23638
4327; Bih-nih-ziz-bah; F; 8; Navajo; F; S; Grand-daughter; 4337; Yes; Yes; 23639
4328; Yil-naz-bah; F; 7; Navajo; F; S; Grand-daughter; 4338; Yes; Yes; 23640
4329; Yil-nih-bah; F; 4; Navajo; F; S; Grand-daughter; 4339; Yes; Yes; 23641

4330; Hosteen-ashinhi-bega; M; 44; Navajo; F; M; Head; 4340; Yes; Yes; 17281
4331; Doh-dihadi-belah; F; 62; Navajo; F; M; Wife; 4341; Yes; Yes; 17282
4332; Dohdihjadi-bih-jay-kay; F; 39; Navajo; F; S; Daughter; 4342; Yes; Yes; 17283
4333; Bah-seeih; F; 24; Navajo; F; S; Step-daughter; 4343; Yes; Yes; 17284
4334; Sohie; F; 9; Navajo; F; S; Step-granddaughter; 4344; Yes; Yes; 17285

4335; Hosteen-li-che; M; 66; Navajo; F; M; Head; 4345; Yes; Yes; 23642
4336; Clah-yen-bitsih; F; 36; Navajo; F; M; Wife; 4346; Yes; Yes; 23643

Census of the **Northern Navajo** reservation of the **Northern Navajo** jurisdiction, as of **April 1**, 19**31**, taken by **Ernest H. Hammond, District**, Superintendent. **in Charge**

**Key:** Number; NAME: Surname, Given; Sex; Birth Year (if given), Age At Last Birthday; Tribe; Degree of Blood; Marital Status; Relationship To Head of Family; Last Census Roll Number; At Jurisdiction Where Enrolled (Yes or No); At Another Jurisdiction; ELSEWHERE: Post office, County, State; Ward (Yes or No); Allotment, Annuity, and Identification Numbers.

4337; Cora; F; 19; Navajo; F; S; Daughter; 4347; Yes; Yes; 23644
4338; Bih-nih-ziz-bah; F; 17; Navajo; F; S; Daughter; 4348; Yes; Yes; 23645

4339; Hosteen-haska-bega; M; Unk; Navajo; F; M; Head; 4349; Yes; Yes; 23740
4340; Dah-naz-bah; F; 23; Navajo; F; M; Wife; 4350; Yes; Yes; 23741
4341; Keh-yee-taz-bah; F; 4; Navajo; F; S; Daughter; 4351; Yes; Yes; 23742

4342; Hosteen-li-chee-bitsih; F; 36; Navajo; F; Wd; Head; 4352; Yes; Yes; 23735
4343; Keh-haz-bah; F; 18; Navajo; F; S; Daughter; 4353; Yes; Yes; 23736
4344; Tah-nih-bah, Matilda; F; 15; Navajo; F; S; Daughter; 4354; Yes; Yes; 23737
4345; Al-nah-ee-bah; F; 11; Navajo; F; S; Daughter; 4355; Yes; Yes; 23738
4346; Chih-nah-dahl; M; 18; Navajo; F; S; Nephew; 4356; Yes; Yes; 23739

4347; Hosteen-l-bahih-benally; M; 35; Navajo; F; M; Head; 4357; Yes; Yes; 23154
4348; Bitsih, Washburn; F; 35; Navajo; F; M; Wife; 4358; Yes; Yes; 23155
4349; Keh-l-yah; M; 10; Navajo; F; S; Son; 4359; Yes; Yes; 23156
4350; Keh-yil-nan-nih-bah; F; 6; Navajo; F; S; Daughter; 4360; Yes; Yes; 23157
4351; Keh-yil-chin-bah; F; 4; Navajo; F; S; Daughter; 4361; Yes; Yes; 23158
4352; Keh-ah-des-bah; F; 16; Navajo; F; S; Sister-in-law; 4362; Yes; Yes; 23159

4353; Haska-ye-chee-has-wudt; M; Unk; Navajo; F; M; Head; 4363; Yes; Yes; 23937
4354; Ye-nas-bah; F; Unk; Navajo; F; M; Wife; 4364; Yes; Yes; 23938
4355; Enal-wudt; M; 8; Navajo; F; S; Son; 4365; Yes; Yes; 23939

4356; Hosteen-dih-jeely-benally; M; 25; Navajo; F; M; Head; 4366; Yes; Yes; 26222
4357; Kee-Joe, Lelia; F; 25; Navajo; F; M; Wife; 4367; Yes; Yes; 26223
4358; Wilson; M; Unk; Navajo; F; S; Son; 4368; Yes; Yes; 26433

4359; Hosteen-aht-sosie-men-bega; M; 36; Navajo; F; M; Head; 4369; Yes; Yes; 23822
4360; Yil-nih-bah; F; 39; Navajo; F; M; Wife; 4370; Yes; Yes; 23823
4361; Nah-tah-yil-dey-yah; M; 19; Navajo; F; S; Son; 4371; Yes; Yes; 23824
4362; Dah-dee-bah; F; 14; Navajo; F; S; Daughter; 4372; Yes; Yes; 23825
4363; Christine; F; 9; Navajo; F; S; Daughter; 4373; Yes; Yes; 23826
4364; Al-chih-haz-bah; F; 7; Navajo; F; S; Daughter; 4374; Yes; Yes; 23827
4365; Keh-yil-nah-nih-bah; F; 5; Navajo; F; S; Daughter; 4375; Yes; Yes; 23828
4366; Keh-hah-dez-bah; F; 2; Navajo; F; S; Daughter; 4376; Yes; Yes; 23829

4367; Hosteen-bih-dagaihih-bitah; F; 62; Navajo; F; Wd; Head; 4377; Yes; Yes; 23835
4368; Arlene; F; 13; Navajo; F; S; Grand-Daughter; 4378; Yes; Yes; 23836
4369; Glih-yazzie; F; 10; Navajo; F; S; Daughter; 4379; Yes; Yes; 23837

Census of the __Northern Navajo__ reservation of the __Northern Navajo__ jurisdiction, as of __April 1___, 19**31**, taken by __Ernest H. Hammond, District__, Superintendent. **in Charge**

**Key:** Number; NAME: Surname, Given; Sex; Birth Year (if given), Age At Last Birthday; Tribe; Degree of Blood; Marital Status; Relationship To Head of Family; Last Census Roll Number; At Jurisdiction Where Enrolled (Yes or No); At Another Jurisdiction; ELSEWHERE: Post office, County, State; Ward (Yes or No); Allotment, Annuity, and Identification Numbers.

4370; Hosteen-seeih-gih-bega; M; Unk; Navajo; F; M; Head; 4380; Yes; Yes; 32236
4371; Blue Eye's daughter; F; 22; Navajo; F; M; Wife; 4381; Yes; Yes; 32237

4372; Hosteen-l-suen-bega; M; 33; Navajo; F; M; Head; 4382; Yes; Yes; 32238
4373; Blue Eye's daughter; F; 27; Navajo; F; M; Wife; 4383; Yes; Yes; 32239
4374; Nah-tah-yil-has-wudt; M; 11; Navajo; F S; Son; 4384; Yes; Yes; 32240
4375; Yil-nil-wudt; M; 7; Navajo; F; S; Son; 4385; Yes; Yes; 32241
4376; Yee-nah-gah; M; 5; Navajo; F; S; Son; 4386; Yes; Yes; 32242
4377; Yil-nih-bah; F; 3; Navajo; F; S; Daughter; 4387; Yes; Yes; 32243

4378; Hosteen-clitsoih; M; 66; Navajo; F; M; Head; 4388; Yes; Yes; 30698
4379; Hosteen-suen-bitah; F; 54; Navajo; F; M; Wife; 4389; Yes; Yes; 30699
4380; John Joe; M; 25; Navajo; F; S; Step-son; 4390; Yes; Yes; 30700
4381; Tas-wudt; M; 21; Navajo; F; S; Step-son; 4391; Yes; Yes; 30701
4382; Nas-wudt; M; 17; Navajo; F; S; Step-son; 4392; Yes; Yes; 30702
4383; Haska-yil-gahl; M; 15; Navajo; F; S; Step-son; 4393; Yes; Yes; 30703
4384; Yee-hah-nih-bah; F; 13; Navajo; F; S; Step-daughter; 4394; Yes; Yes; 30704

4385; Hogan-thalni-badoni; M; 43; Navajo; F; M; Head; 4395; Yes; Yes; 23847
4386; Bah-nih-ziz-bah; F; 23; Navajo; F; M; Wife; 4396; Yes; Yes; 23848
4387; Haska-yee-chih-nil-wudt; M; 16; Navajo; F; S; Son; 4397; Yes; Yes; 23849
4388; Yil-dez-bah; F; 10; Navajo; F; S; Daughter; 4398; Yes; Yes; 23850
4389; Nah-tah-yee-sih-yil-wohl; M; 6; Navajo; F; S; Son; 4399; Yes; Yes; 23851
4390; Hah-ziz-bahih; M[sic]; 3; Navajo; F; S; Daughter; 4400; Yes; Yes; 23852
          [Should be female.]

4391; Hosteen-l-bahih-bega; M; 48; Navajo; F; M; Head; 4401; Yes; Yes; 23853
4392; Chis-chilli-bih-j-k; F; 41; Navajo; F; M; Wife; 4402; Yes; Yes; 23854
4393; Edith; F; 21; Navajo; F; S; Daughter; 4403; Yes; Yes; 23855
4394; Sarah; F; 19; Navajo; F; S; Daughter; 4404; Yes; Yes; 23856
4395; Keh-hah-dez-bah; F; 12; Navajo; F; S; Daughter; 4405; Yes; Yes; 23857

4396; Hosteen-yazzie; M; 53; Navajo; F; M; Head; 4406; Yes; Yes; 31060
4397; Salou-nez-bitsih; F; 41; Navajo; F; M; Wife; 4407; Yes; Yes; 31061
4398; Peter; M; 23; Navajo; F; S; Son; 4408; Yes; Yes; 31062
4399; Elizabeth; F; 21; Navajo; F; S; Daughter; 4409; Yes; Yes; 31063
4400; Zah; M; 19; Navajo; F; S; Son; 4410; Yes; Yes; 31064
4401; Naus; M; 16; Navajo; F; S; Son; 4411; Yes; Yes; 31065
4402; Bah-yazzie; F; 12; Navajo; F; S; Daughter; 4412; Yes; Yes; 31066
4403; Jah; F; 9; Navajo; F; S; Daughter; 4413; Yes; Yes; 31067
4404; Nahn-bah; F; 6; Navajo; F; S; Daughter; 4414; Yes; Yes; 31068

4405; Hosteen-hah-nih-nih-bega; M; 37; Navajo; F; M; Head; 4415; Yes; Yes; 31080

Census of the **Northern Navajo** reservation of the **Northern Navajo**
jurisdiction, as of **April 1**, 19**31**, taken by **Ernest H. Hammond, District**,
Superintendent. **in Charge**

**Key:** Number; NAME: Surname, Given; Sex; Birth Year (if given), Age At Last Birthday; Tribe; Degree of
Blood; Marital Status; Relationship To Head of Family; Last Census Roll Number; At Jurisdiction Where
Enrolled (Yes or No); At Another Jurisdiction; ELSEWHERE: Post office, County, State; Ward (Yes or No);
Allotment, Annuity, and Identification Numbers.

4406;  Dinay-suen-benally; F; 30; Navajo; F; M; Wife; 4416; Yes; Yes; 31081
4407;  Haska-en; M; 12; Navajo; F; S; Son; 4417; Yes; Yes; 31082
4408;  Bih-gee-bah; F; 9; Navajo; F; S; Daughter; 4418; Yes; Yes; 31083

4409;  Hosteen-deel-yen-benally; M; 33; Navajo; F; M; Head; 4419; Yes; Yes; 20280
4410;  Adzanih-beleen-bidzee-lih-bih-chah; F; 21; Navajo; F; M; Wife; 4420; Yes;
Yes; 20281
4411;  Nah-tah-yil-neyah; M; 5; Navajo; F; S; Son; 4421; Yes; Yes; 20282
4412;  Eskee-yazzie; M; 3; Navajo; F; S; Son; 4422; Yes; Yes; 20283
4413;  Alna-jibah; F; 1; Navajo; F; S; Daughter; 4423; Yes; Yes; 20413
4414;  Adzanih-beleen-bidaeelih[sic]; F; Unk; Navajo; F; Wd; Mother-in-law; 4424;
Yes; Yes; 20284    [Name could be Adzanih-beleen-bidzeelih]
4415;  Adzanih-beleen-bidzeelihe-bih-yaz; M; 19; Navajo; F; S; Brother-in-law;
4425; Yes; Yes; 20285
4416;  Beleen-bidzeel, Deshna; M; 12; Navajo; F; S; Brother-in-law; 4426; Yes; Yes;
20286
4417;  Nah-nih-bahih; F; 7; Navajo; F; S; Sister-in-law; 4427; Yes; Yes; 20287

4418;  Hosteen-seeih-bega; M; 68; Navajo; F; M; Head; 4428; Yes; Yes; 27523
4419;  Adzan-yazzie; F; 65; Navajo; F; M; Wife; 4429; Yes; Yes; 27524
4420;  Etta; F; 23; Navajo; F; S; Daughter; 4430; Yes; Yes; 27525
4421;  Eskee; M; 22; Navajo; F; S; Son; 4431; Yes; Yes; 27526

4422;  Hosteen-nez-bitsih; M; 39; Navajo; F; M; Head; 4432; Yes; Yes; 27543
4423;  Glih-yil-nah-nih-bah; F; 26; Navajo; F; M; Wife; 4433; Yes; Yes; 27544
4424;  Nah-yah; M; 12; Navajo; F; S; Son; 4434; Yes; Yes; 27545
4425;  Chah-nih-bah; F; 7; Navajo; F; S; Daughter; 4435; Yes; Yes; 27546
4426;  Hah-dez-bah; F; 5; Navajo; F; S; Daughter; 4436; Yes; Yes; 27547
4427;  Chel-wudt; M; 4; Navajo; F; S; Son; 4437; Yes; Yes; 27548

4428;  Hosteen-sinnih-bega, Leo; M; 38; Navajo; F; M; Head; 4438; Yes; Yes; 27584
4429;  Glih-yah-nih-bah; F; 24; Navajo; F; M; Wife; 4439; Yes; Yes; 27585
4430;  Nah-glih-yil-chin-bah; F; 8; Navajo; F; S; Daughter; 4440; Yes; Yes; 27586
4431;  Haska-yil-wudt; M; 5; Navajo; F; S; Son; 4441; Yes; Yes; 27587
4432;  Nih-dez-bah; F; 4; Navajo; F; S; Daughter; 4442; Yes; Yes; 27588
4433;  Yil-naz-bah; F; 2; Navajo; F; S; Daughter; 4443; Yes; Yes; 27589

4434;  Hosteen-l-bega, Horace; M; 44; Navajo; F; M; Head; 4444; Yes; Yes; 27599
4435;  Chah-naz-bah; F; 25; Navajo; F; M; Wife; 4445; Yes; Yes; 27600
4436;  Hah-tah-yee-tah-hoh-lel; M; 3; Navajo; F; S; Son; 4446; Yes; Yes; 27601

4437;  Hosteen-bitsee-lagaih; M; Unk; Navajo; F; M; Head; 4447; Yes; Yes; 27592
4438;  Bay-dih-chee-bitsih; F; 60; Navajo; F; M; Wife; 4448; Yes; Yes; 27593

Census of the **Northern Navajo** reservation of the **Northern Navajo** jurisdiction, as of **April 1**, 19**31**, taken by **Ernest H. Hammond, District**, Superintendent. **in Charge**

Key: Number; NAME: Surname, Given; Sex; Birth Year (if given), Age At Last Birthday; Tribe; Degree of Blood; Marital Status; Relationship To Head of Family; Last Census Roll Number; At Jurisdiction Where Enrolled (Yes or No); At Another Jurisdiction; ELSEWHERE: Post office, County, State; Ward (Yes or No); Allotment, Annuity, and Identification Numbers.

4439; Haska-yee-chih-has-wudt; M; 16; Navajo; F; S; Son; 4449; Yes; Yes; 27594
4440; Nah-glah-yil-ee-bah; F; 7; Navajo; F; S; Grand-daughter; 4450; Yes; Yes; 27595

4441; Hosteen-ashinhih; M; 59; Navajo; F; M; Head; 4451; Yes; Yes; 27614
4442; Dinay-chilli-bitsih; F; 37; Navajo; F; M; Wife; 4452; Yes; Yes; 27615
4443; Haska-yil-nih-sonh; M; 21; Navajo; F; S; Son; 4453; Yes; Yes; 27616
4444; Cecil; M; 19; Navajo; F; S; Son; 4454; Yes; Yes; 27617
4445; Nah-tah-yee-nah-wudt; M; 13; Navajo; F; S; Son; 4455; Yes; Yes; 27618
4446; Haska-yil-woh-yah; M; 5; Navajo; F; S; Son; 4456; Yes; Yes; 27619

4447; Hosteen-chash-cheeih; M; Unk; Navajo; F; M; Head; 4457; Yes; Yes; 27653
4448; Bis-ah-ahlani-bih-che; F; 61; Navajo; F; M; Wife; 4458; Yes; Yes; 27654
4449; Glih-ee-bah; F; 4; Navajo; F; S; Step-grand-daughter; 4459; Yes; Yes; 27655
4450; Lah-bah; M; 21; Navajo; F; S; Son; 4460; Yes; Yes; 27656
4451; Cheeih; M; 17; Navajo; F; S; Son; 4461; Yes; Yes; 27657
4452; Way-choih; M; 16; Navajo; F; S; Son; 4462; Yes; Yes; 27658
4453; Chih-des-wudt; M; 14; Navajo; F; S; Grand-son; 4463; Yes; Yes; 27659

4454; Hosteen-nez-benally Roy, Joe; M; 32; Navajo; F; M; Head; 4464; Yes; Yes; 27678
4455; Salou-enclah-ihgi-bitsih; F; 22; Navajo; F; M; Wife; 4465; Yes; Yes; 27679

4456; Hosteen-nez-bega; M; 53; Navajo; F; M; Head; 4466; Yes; Yes; 27672
4457; Beleen-dal-suen-bitsih; F; 53; Navajo; F; M; Wife; 4467; Yes; Yes; 27673
4458; Yee-gonh-yih-bah; F; 21; Navajo; F; S; Daughter; 4468; Yes; Yes; 27674
4459; Haska-yil-nah-zah; M; 18; Navajo; F; S; Son; 4469; Yes; Yes; 27675
4460; Haska-yee-kih-des-wudt; M; 14; Navajo; F; S; Son; 4470; Yes; Yes; 27676
4461; Haska-yil-nah-hah-yah; M; 12; Navajo; F; S; Son; 4471; Yes; Yes; 27677

4462; Hosteen-tahn-badoni; M; Unk; Navajo; F; M; Head; 4472; Yes; Yes; 27695
4463; Hosteen-tahn-bitsih; F; Unk; Navajo; F; M; Wife; 4473; Yes; Yes; 27696
4464; Yee-kih-nih-bah; F; 24; Navajo; F; S; Daughter; 4474; Yes; Yes; 27697
4465; Nah-tah-yil-chel-wudt; M; 22; Navajo; F; S; Son; 4475; Yes; Yes; 27698
4466; Tah-bah; F; 20; Navajo; F; S; Daughter; 4476; Yes; Yes; 27699
4467; Washburn; M; 18; Navajo; F; S; Son; 4477; Yes; Yes; 27700
4468; Haska-yee-chih-nil-wudt; M; 12; Navajo; F; S; Son; 4478; Yes; Yes; 27701
4469; Keh-yil-nil-naz-bah; F; 8; Navajo; F; S; Daughter; 4479; Yes; Yes; 27702
4470; Pettigrew, Manson; M; 21; Navajo; F; S; Grand-son; 4480; Yes; Yes; 27703

4471; Hosteen-l-chee-bega, John; M; 23; Navajo; F; M; Head; 4481; Yes; Yes; 27692
4472; Kee-ah-annih-nez-bitsih; F; 20; Navajo; F; M; Wife; 4482; Yes; Yes; 27693

Census of the **Northern Navajo** reservation of the **Northern Navajo**
jurisdiction, as of **April 1** , 19**31**, taken by **Ernest H. Hammond, District**,
Superintendent. **in Charge**

Key: Number; NAME: Surname, Given; Sex; Birth Year (if given), Age At Last Birthday; Tribe; Degree of
Blood; Marital Status; Relationship To Head of Family; Last Census Roll Number; At Jurisdiction Where
Enrolled (Yes or No); At Another Jurisdiction; ELSEWHERE: Post office, County, State; Ward (Yes or No);
Allotment, Annuity, and Identification Numbers.

4473; Nah-tah-yil-ee-gahl; M; 3; Navajo; F; S; Son; 4483; 4483; Yes; Yes; 27694

4474; Hosteen-sinnih-bega; M; Unk; Navajo; F; M; Head; 4484; Yes; Yes; 27686
4475; Hosteen-clash-cheeih-bitsih; F; 24; Navajo; F; M; Wife; 4485; Yes; Yes; 27687
4476; Keh-hah-nih-bah; F; 6; Navajo; F; S; Daughter; 4486; Yes; Yes; 27688
4477; Yee-naz-bah; F; 3; Navajo; F; S; Daughter; 4487; Yes; Yes; 27689
4478; Nah-tah-yee-nah-yah; M; 13; Navajo; F; S; Nephew; 4488; Yes; Yes; 27690
4479; Gaih; M; 8; Navajo; F; S; Nephew; 4489; Yes; Yes; 27691

4480; Hosteen-hosch-clish-nih; M; Unk; Navajo; F; Wd; Head; 4490; Yes; Yes; 27684
4481; Beleen-dal-suen-bikis-bih-adzan; F; 76; Navajo; F; Wd; Sister; 4491; Yes; Yes; 27685

4482; Hosteen-l-bahih-yen-bega; M; 44; Navajo; F; M; Head; 4492; Yes; Yes; 23610
4483; Yen-bitsih, Charley; F; 25; Navajo; F; M; Wife; 4493; Yes; Yes; 23611
4484; Howard; M; 17; Navajo; F; S; Son; 4494; Yes; Yes; 23612
4485; Herman; M; 15; Navajo; F; S; Son; 4495; Yes; Yes; 23613
4486; Nellie; F; 25; Navajo; F; S; Sister-in-law; 4496; Yes; Yes; 23614
4487; Haska-yee-nel-wudt; M; 13; Navajo; F; S; Brother-in-law; 4497; Yes; Yes; 23615

4488; Hosteen-topah-ah-bih-dazih; F; 58; Navajo; F; Wd; Head; 4498; Yes; Yes; 26224
4489; Josephine; F; 21; Navajo; F; S; Daughter; 4499; Yes; Yes; 26225
4490; Jerry; M; 18; Navajo; F; S; Son; 4500; Yes; Yes; 26226
4491; Nah-glih-yee-nih-bah; F; 11; Navajo; F; S; Grand-daughter; 4501; Yes; Yes; 26227

4492; Hosteen-clitsoh; M; Unk; Navajo; F; M; Head; 4502; Yes; Yes; 27914
4493; Toh-lizin-bitsih; F; Unk; Navajo; F; M; Wife; 4503; Yes; Yes; 27915
4494; Shoih; M; Unk; Navajo; F; S; Son; 4504; Yes; Yes; 27916
4495; Woody; M; 24; Navajo; F; S; Son; 4505; Yes; Yes; 27917
4496; Ah-bah; F; 18; Navajo; F; S; Daughter; 4506; Yes; Yes; 27918
4497; Dinay-yazzie; M; 14; Navajo; F; S; Son; 4507; Yes; Yes; 27919
4498; Tah-hah; M; 9; Navajo; F; S; Grand-son; 4508; Yes; Yes; 27920
4499; Haska-ith-no-teath; M; 1; Navajo; F; S; Son; 4509; Yes; Yes; 18272

4500; Hosteen-zin-bega; M; 60; Navajo; F; M; Head; 4510; Yes; Yes; 27923
4501; Toh-ahk-gleenih-adzan; F; 39; Navajo; F; M; Wife; 4511; Yes; Yes; 27924
4502; Deh; M; 15; Navajo; F; S; Son; 4512; Yes; Yes; 27925
4503; Al-kih-gee-bah; F; 13; Navajo; F; S; Daughter; 4513; Yes; Yes; 27926

Census of the **Northern Navajo** reservation of the **Northern Navajo** jurisdiction, as of **April 1**, 1931, taken by **Ernest H. Hammond, District**, Superintendent. **in Charge**

**Key:** Number; NAME: Surname, Given; Sex; Birth Year (if given), Age At Last Birthday; Tribe; Degree of Blood; Marital Status; Relationship To Head of Family; Last Census Roll Number; At Jurisdiction Where Enrolled (Yes or No); At Another Jurisdiction; ELSEWHERE: Post office, County, State; Ward (Yes or No); Allotment, Annuity, and Identification Numbers.

4504; Jack; M; 29; Navajo; F; S; Brother-in-law; 4514; Yes; Yes; 27927
4505; Ned; M; 23; Navajo; F; S; Brother-in-law; 4515; Yes; Yes; 27928
4506; Dah-yiz-bah; F; 18; Navajo; F; S; Daughter; 4516; Yes; Yes; 27929
4507; Maxie; M; 12; Navajo; F; S; Son; 4517; Yes; Yes; 27930

4508; Hosteen-belone-bega, Allen; M; 57; Navajo; F; M; Head; 4518; Yes; Yes; 26252
4509; Ah-hahn-yiz-bah; F; 35; Navajo; F; M; Wife; 4519; Yes; Yes; 26253
4510; Nah-glih-yee-taz-bah; F; 11; Navajo; F; S; Daughter; 4520; Yes; Yes; 26254
4511; Tah-deyah; M; 6; Navajo; F; S; Son; 4521; Yes; Yes; 26256
4512; Tah-yee-gahl; M; 3; Navajo; F; S; Son; 4522; Yes; Yes; 26257
4513; Belone, Charley; M; 22; Navajo; F; S; Son; 4523; Yes; Yes; 26258

4514; Hosteen-zin-benally; M; 25; Navajo; F; M; Head; 4524; Yes; Yes; 27931
4515; Zannie-bah; F; 19; Navajo; F; M; Wife; 4525; Yes; Yes; 27932
4516; Ah-hih-bah; F; 3; Navajo; F; S; Daughter; 4526; Yes; Yes; 27933
4517; Atwell; M; 23; Navajo; F; S; Brother; 4527; Yes; Yes; 27934

4518; Hosteen-soh; M; 47; Navajo; F; M; Head; 4528; Yes; Yes; 27949
4519; Batoni-bitsih; F; 42; Navajo; F; M; Wife; 4529; Yes; Yes; 27950
4520; Wallace; M; 22; Navajo; F; S; Son; 4530; Yes; Yes; 27951
4521; Al-sah-bah; F; 20; Navajo; F; S; Daughter; 4531; Yes; Yes; 27952
4522; Nah-glih; F; 18; Navajo; F; S; Daughter; 4532; Yes; Yes; 27953
4523; Haska; M; 11; Navajo; F; S; Son; 4533; Yes; Yes; 27954
4524; Nil-bah; F; 9; Navajo; F; S; Daughter; 4534; Yes; Yes; 27955
4525; Kee-yaz; M; 7; Navajo; F; S; Son; 4535; Yes; Yes; 27956

4526; Hosteen-soh-bitsih; F; 24; Navajo; F; Wd.; Head; 4536; Yes; Yes; 27958
4527; Yil-des-wudt; M; 5; Navajo; F; S; Son; 4537; Yes; Yes; 27959
4528; Adzan-kin-lacheeny; F; 84; Navajo; F; Wd; Grand-mother; 4538; Yes; Yes; 27961

4529; Hosteen-yazzie; M; Unk; Navajo; F; M; Head; 4539; Yes; Yes; 28005
4530; Al-nah-bah; F; 17; Navajo; F; M; Wife; 4540; Yes; Yes; 28006
4531; Yah-nih-bah; F; 10; Navajo; F; S; Cousin-in-law; 4541; Yes; Yes; 28007

4532; Hosteen-hah-zohgoh; M; 55; Navajo; F; M; Head; 4542; Yes; Yes; 28024
4533; Hah-nah-gahnih-bitsih; F; 25; Navajo; F; M; Wife; 4543; Yes; Yes; 28025

4534; Hosteen-choh-hoh-nih-tael-, Frank; M; Unk; Navajo; F; M; Head; 4544; Yes; Yes; 26944
4535; Kih-hih-bah; F; 61; Navajo; F; M; 1st Wife; 4545; Yes; Yes; 26945

Census of the **Northern Navajo** reservation of the **Northern Navajo** jurisdiction, as of **April 1**, 1931, taken by **Ernest H. Hammond, District**, Superintendent. **in Charge**

**Key:** Number; NAME: Surname, Given; Sex; Birth Year (if given), Age At Last Birthday; Tribe; Degree of Blood; Marital Status; Relationship To Head of Family; Last Census Roll Number; At Jurisdiction Where Enrolled (Yes or No); At Another Jurisdiction; ELSEWHERE: Post office, County, State; Ward (Yes or No); Allotment, Annuity, and Identification Numbers.

4536; Nah-glih-yee-tah-dez-bah; F; 31; Navajo; F; M; 2nd Wife; 4546; Yes; Yes; 26946

4537; Ah-hih-nel-bah; F; 3; Navajo; F; S; Daughter; 4547; Yes; Yes; 26947

4538; Nas-wudt; M; 21; Navajo; F; S; Son; 4548; Yes; Yes; 26948

4539; Ned; M; 17; Navajo; F; S; Son; 4549; Yes; Yes; 26949

4540; Dah-naz-bah; F; 14; Navajo; F; S; Daughter; 4550; Yes; Yes; 26950

4541; Nah-glih-yee-tah-bah; F; 9; Navajo; F; S; Daughter; 4551; Yes; Yes; 26951

4542; Chih-has-wudt; M; 8; Navajo; F; S; Son; 4552; Yes; Yes; 26952

4543; Hosteen-al-sosie-bega; M; 30; Navajo; F; M; Head; 4553; Yes; Yes; 26893

4544; Adobe-bega-bitsih; F; 25; Navajo; F; M; Wife; 4554; Yes; Yes; 26894

4545; Nah-tah-yil-hah-yah; M; 7; Navajo; F; S; Son; 4555; Yes; Yes; 26895

4546; Nah-tah-nal-wohl; M; 4; Navajo; F; S; Son; 4556; Yes; Yes; 26896

4547; Glih-hod-dez-bah; F; 3; Navajo; F; S; Daughter; 4557; Yes; Yes; 27094

4548; Hosteen-sahah-tah-badoni; M; Unk; Navajo; F; M; Head; 4558; Yes; Yes; 26897

4549; Nah-glih-yil-dez-bah; F; 28; Navajo; F; M; Wife; 4559; Yes; Yes; 26898

4550; Keh-yil-nih-nih-bah; F; 9; Navajo; F; S; Daughter; 4560; Yes; Yes; 26899

4551; Haska-yil-has-wudt; M; 8; Navajo; F; S; Son; 4561; Yes; Yes; 26900

4552; Haska-yee-chih-has-wudt; M; 7; Navajo; F; S; Son; 4562; Yes; Yes; 26901

4553; Haska-yee-chih-des-wudt; M; 3; Navajo; F; S; Son; 4563; Yes; Yes; 26902

4554; Hosteen-sehah-tah; M; Unk; Navajo; F; M; Head; 4564; Yes; Yes; 26903

4555; Bih-nah-la-bahih-benally; F; Unk; Navajo; F; M; Wife; 4565; Yes; Yes; 26904

4556; Haska-yah-yil-wohl; M; 19; Navajo; F; S; Son; 4566; Yes; Yes; 26905

4557; Yil-haz-bah; F; 17; Navajo; F; S; Daughter; 4567; Yes; Yes; 26906

4558; Esther; F; 14; Navajo; F; S; Daughter; 4568; Yes; Yes; 26907

4559; Keh-nih-bah; F; 10; Navajo; F; S; Daughter; 4569; Yes; Yes; 26908

4560; Tah-wudt; M; 8; Navajo; F; S; Son; 4570; Yes; Yes; 26909

4561; Yee-nah-bah; F; 4; Navajo; F; S; Daughter; 4571; Yes; Yes; 26910

4562; Yee-chee-noz-bah; F; 2; Navajo; F; S; Daughter; 4572; Yes; Yes; 27087

4563; Hosteen-soh-lagaih-dez-eye; M; Unk; Navajo; F; M; Head; 4573; Yes; Yes; 26866

4564; Hosteen-soh-lagaih-dez-eye's wife; F; Unk; Navajo; F; M; Wife; 4574; Yes; Yes; 26867

4565; Haska-ye-nel-wudt; M; 16; Navajo; F; S; Grand-son; 4575; Yes; Yes; 26868

4566; Hosteen-lizinih-bega; M; Unk; Navajo; F; Wd; Head; 4576; Yes; Yes; 26873

4567; Martin; M; 18; Navajo; F; S; Son; 4577; Yes; Yes; 26874

4568; Al-chih-nih-nih-bah; F; 16; Navajo; F; S; Daughter; 4578; Yes; Yes; 26875

4569; Yil-nih-nih-yah; M; 7; Navajo; F; S; Son; 4580; Yes; Yes; 26877

Census of the **Northern Navajo** reservation of the **Northern Navajo** jurisdiction, as of **April 1**, 19**31,** taken by **Ernest H. Hammond, District**, Superintendent. **in Charge**

**Key:** Number; NAME: Surname, Given; Sex; Birth Year (if given), Age At Last Birthday; Tribe; Degree of Blood; Marital Status; Relationship To Head of Family; Last Census Roll Number; At Jurisdiction Where Enrolled (Yes or No); At Another Jurisdiction; ELSEWHERE: Post office, County, State; Ward (Yes or No); Allotment, Annuity, and Identification Numbers.

4570;  Glih-yahn-nih-bah; F; 5; Navajo; F; S; Daughter; 4581; Yes; Yes; 26878

4571;  Hosteen-goh; M; 72; Navajo; F; M; Head; 4582; Yes; Yes; 26825
4572;  Sisih-bah; F; 34; Navajo; F; M; Wife; 4583; Yes; Yes; 26826
4573;  Haska-yee-chih-has-wudt; M; 17; Navajo; F; S; Son; 4584; Yes; Yes; 26827
4574;  Nah-tah-yee-nal-wudt; M; 9; Navajo; F; S; Son; 4585; Yes; Yes; 26828
4575;  Yil-nih-bah; F; 5; Navajo; F; S; Daughter; 4586; Yes; Yes; 26829
4576;  Haska-yee-kes-wudt; M; 2; Navajo; F; S; Son; 4587; Yes; Yes; 26830

4577;  Hosteen-sosie-bega; M; 39; Navajo; F; M; Head; 4588; Yes; Yes; 26953
4578;  Al-kih-nih-bah; F; 40; Navajo; F; M; Wife; 4589; Yes; Yes; 26954
4579;  John Arthur; M; 17; Navajo; F; S; Son; 4590; Yes; Yes; 26955
4580;  Haska-yee-chih-des-wudt; M; 8; Navajo; F; S; Son; 4591; Yes; Yes; 26956
4581;  Nah-glih-yil-naz-bah; F; 6; Navajo; F; S; Daughter; 4592; Yes; Yes; 26957
4582;  Haska-yil-chel-wudt; M; 4; Navajo; F; S; Son; 4593; Yes; Yes; 26958

4583;  Hosteen-skonihih-bega Hosteen-nihgi; M; Unk; Navajo; F; M; Head; 4594; Yes; Yes; 26807
4584;  Yahn-nah-bah; F; Unk; Navajo; F; M; Wife; 4595; Yes; Yes; 26808
4585;  Gah; F; 16; Navajo; F; S; Daughter; 4596; Yes; Yes; 26809
4586;  Haska-yee-kih-dah-has-wudt; M; 10; Navajo; F; S; Son; 4597; Yes; Yes; 26810
4587;  Hah-yazzie; M; 8; Navajo; F; S; Son; 4598; Yes; Yes; 26811
4588;  Ah-kih-des-bah; F; 4; Navajo; F; S; Daughter; 4599; Yes; Yes; 26812

4589;  Hogan-thani-bega; M; 33; Navajo; F; M; Head; 4600; Yes; Yes; 26766
4590;  Yee-naz-bah; F; 28; Navajo; F; M; Wife; 4601; Yes; Yes; 26767
4591;  Haska-yee-keh-lal; M; 8; Navajo; F; S; Son; 4602; Yes; Yes; 26768

4592;  Hosea-bih-bizee; M; Unk; Navajo; F; M; Head; 4603; Yes; Yes; 27028
4593;  Nah-dez-bah; F; 24; Navajo; F; M; Wife; 4604; Yes; Yes; 27029
4594;  Nah-glih-yee-tah-yih-bah; F; 4; Navajo; F; S; Daughter; 4605; Yes; Yes; 27030
4595;  Al-kih-haz-bah; F; 50; Navajo; F; Wd; Mother-in-law; 4606; Yes; Yes; 27031
4596;  Al-keh-ee-bah; F; 16; Navajo; F; S; Cousin-in-law; 4607; Yes; Yes; 27032
4597;  Alchee-dez-bah[sic]; F; 3; Navajo; F; S; Daughter; 4608; Yes; Yes; 27102
        [Name should be Al-chee-dez-bah]

4598;  Hosteen-lizinih-bitsoih, Willie; M; 25; Navajo; F; M; Head; 4609; Yes; Yes; 27019
4599;  Hah-glih-naz-bah; F; 29; Navajo; F; M; Wife; 4610; Yes; Yes; 27020

4600;  Hosteen-yazzie; M; 41; Navajo; F; M; Head; 4611; Yes; Yes; 26277

Census of the **Northern Navajo** reservation of the **Northern Navajo** jurisdiction, as of **April 1**, 19**31,** taken by **Ernest H. Hammond, District**, Superintendent. **in Charge**

4601;  Yil-naz-behih; F; 57; Navajo; F; M; Wife; 4612; Yes; Yes; 26278
4602;  Yazzie, Harry; M; 24; Navajo; F; S; Son; 4613; Yes; Yes; 26279
4603;  Chester; M; 22; Navajo; F; S; Son; 4614; Yes; Yes; 26280
4604;  Haska-yee-tah-yil-wudt; M; 14; Navajo; F; S; Cousin; 4615; Yes; Yes; 26281

4605;  Hosteen-deel-benally; M; 39; Navajo; F; M; Head; 4616; Yes; Yes; 20248
4606;  Hosteen-deel-benally's wife; F; 43; Navajo; F; M; Wife; 4617; Yes; Yes; 20249
4607;  Nah-tah-zoh-nih; M; 13; Navajo; F; S; Son; 4618; Yes; Yes; 20250
4608;  Wudt; M; 11; Navajo; F; S; Son; 4619; Yes; Yes; 20251
4609;  Tis-wudt; M; 6; Navajo; F; S; Son; 4620; Yes; Yes; 20252
4610;  Ashkee; M; 1; Navajo; F; S; Son; 4621; Yes; Yes; 20423

4611;  Hosteen-bib-keh-dinnihih-benally; M; 39; Navajo; F; M; Head; 4622; Yes; Yes; 26700
4612;  Hosteen-en-clahih-bitsih; F; 38; Navajo; F; M; Wife; 4623; Yes; Yes; 26701
4613;  Haska-yil-hoh-lel; M; 18; Navajo; F; S; Son; 4624; Yes; Yes; 26702
4614;  Marion; F; 14; Navajo; F; S; Daughter; 4625; Yes; Yes; 26703
4615;  Mamie; F; 11; Navajo; F; S; Daughter; 4626; Yes; Yes; 26704
4616;  Kih-zoz-bah; F; 8; Navajo; F; S; Daughter; 4627; Yes; Yes; 26705
4617;  John; M; 6; Navajo; F; S; Son; 4628; Yes; Yes; 26706
4618;  Haska-yee-tah-des-wudt; M; 3; Navajo; F; S; Son; 4629; Yes; Yes; 26707
4619;  Dinay-l-suen-bitsih; F; 71; Navajo; F; Wd; Grand-mother-in-law; 4630; Yes; Yes; 26708

4620;  Hosteen-shonih-bitsoih; M; Unk; Navajo; F; M; Head; 4631; Yes; Yes; 26709
4621;  Tah-nih-bah; F; 41; Navajo; F; M; Wife; 4632; Yes; Yes; 26710
4622;  Theodore, Faye; F; 20; Navajo; F; S; Step-daughter; 4633; Yes; Yes; 26711
4623;  Haska-yee-nehyah; M; 16; Navajo; F; S; Son; 4634; Yes; Yes; 26712
4624;  Haska-yee-chih-has-wudt; M; 13; Navajo; F; S; Son; 4635; Yes; Yes; 26713
4625;  Sosie; M; 11; Navajo; F; S; Son; 4636; Yes; Yes; 26714
4626;  Haska-yee-nah-gahl; M; 9; Navajo; F; S; Son; 4637; Yes; Yes; 26715
4627;  Haska-yee-ba-doh-yah; M; 7; Navajo; F; S; Son; 4638; Yes; Yes; 26716
4628;  Keh-hah-nih-bah; F; 3; Navajo; F; S; Daughter; 4639; Yes; Yes; 26717
4629;  Bay-gashih-lagaih-bih-adzan; F; 59; Navajo; F; Wd; Mother-in-law; 4640; Yes; Yes; 26718

4630;  Hosteen-bih-kih-dinnee-bitsih; F; 58; Navajo; F; Wd.; Head; 4641; Yes; Yes; 26683
4631;  Cheebo; M; 22; Navajo; F; S; Son; 4642; Yes; Yes; 26624

4632;  Hosteen-goh-bega; M; 22; Navajo; F; M; Head; 4643; Yes; Yes; 26665
4633;  Yahn-nih-bah; F; 22; Navajo; F; M; Wife; 4644; Yes; Yes; 26666

Census of the **Northern Navajo** reservation of the **Northern Navajo** jurisdiction, as of **April 1** , 19**31,** taken by **Ernest H. Hammond, District** , Superintendent. **in Charge**

4634; Sarah; F; 2; Navajo; F; S; Daughter; 4645; Yes; Yes; 27074

4635; Hosteen-soh-bikis; M; Unk; Navajo; F; M; Head; 4646; Yes; Yes; 26601
4636; Adzan-Uintilli; F; 60; Navajo; F; M; Wife; 4647; Yes; Yes; 26602
4637; Al-chih-nih-nih-bah; F; 28; Navajo; F; Wd; Daughter; 4648; Yes; Yes; 26603
4638; Dih-nih-ziz-bah; F; 6; Navajo; F; S; Grand-daughter; 4649; Yes; Yes; 26604
4639; Adzan-l-chee; F; 3; Navajo; F; S; Grand-daughter; 4650; Yes; Yes; 26605
4640; Yahn-nih-bah; F; 4; Navajo; F; S; Grand-daughter; 4651; Yes; Yes; 26606
4641; Nas-woody; M; 10; Navajo; F; S; Grand-son; 4652; Yes; Yes; 26607
4642; Yee-hah-bah; F; 38; Navajo; F; M; Wife; 4653; Yes; Yes; 26608
4643; Haska-yee-chih-hah-yah; M; 22; Navajo; F; S; Son; 4654; Yes; Yes; 26609
4644; Tah-cheey; F; 17; Navajo; F; S; Daughter; 4655; Yes; Yes; 26610
4645; Alfred; M; 14; Navajo; F; S; Son; 4656; Yes; Yes; 26611
4646; Nah-nih-bahih; F; 26; Navajo; F; S; Daughter; 4657; Yes; Yes; 26612
4647; Yahn-hah-nih-bah; F; 7; Navajo; F; S; Grand-daughter; 4658; Yes; Yes; 26613
4648; Asath-li-kih; F; 3; Navajo; F; S; Grand-daughter; 4659; Yes; Yes; 27091

4649; Hosch-clish-nih-hosteen-nez; M; 53; Navajo; F; M; Head; 4660; Yes; Yes; 25008
4650; Adzanih-clash-chee; F; 53; Navajo; F; M; Wife; 4661; Yes; Yes; 25009
4651; Shelton; M; 28; Navajo; F; S; Son; 4662; Yes; Yes; 25010
4652; Adzan-nez; F; 27; Navajo; F; S; Daughter; 4663; Yes; Yes; 25011
4653; Bates, Kenneth; M; 25; Navajo; F; S; Son; 4664; Yes; Yes; 25012
4654; Adzanih-yazzie; F; 20; Navajo; F; S; Son[sic]; 4665; Yes; Yes; 25013
[Should be female]
4655; Martha; F; 17; Navajo; F; S; Daughter; 4666; Yes; Yes; 25014
4656; Kee-seeih; M; 10; Navajo; F; S; Son; 4667; Yes; Yes; 25015

4657; Hosteen-ashinhih; M; 56; Navajo; F; M; Head; 4668; Yes; Yes; 25027
4658; Adzan-yazzie; F; 42; Navajo; F; M; Wife; 4669; Yes; Yes; 25028
4659; Howard; M; 21; Navajo; F; S; Son; 4670; Yes; Yes; 25029
4660; Richard; M; 17; Navajo; F; S; Son; 4671; Yes; Yes; 25030
4661; Haska-yazzie; M; 12; Navajo; F; S; Son; 4672; Yes; Yes; 25031
4662; Sarah; F; 10; Navajo; F; S; Daughter; 4673; Yes; Yes; 25032
4663; Dorothy; F; 8; Navajo; F; S; Daughter; 4674; Yes; Yes; 25033
4664; Arlene; F; 7; Navajo; F; S; Daughter; 4675; Yes; Yes; 25034
4665; Al-nah-bah; F; 3; Navajo; F; S; Daughter; 4676; Yes; Yes; 25035

4666; Hosch-clish-nih-bega, Harry; M; 34; Navajo; F; M; Head; 4677; Yes; Yes; 25040
4667; Hosteen-yazzie-bitsih, Lois; F; 21; Navajo; F; M; Wife; 4678; Yes; Yes; 25041
4668; Kee-; M; 4; Navajo; F; S; Son; 4679; Yes; Yes; 25042

Census of the **Northern Navajo** reservation of the **Northern Navajo** jurisdiction, as of **April 1**, 19**31**, taken by **Ernest H. Hammond, District**, Superintendent. **in Charge**

**Key:** Number; NAME: Surname, Given; Sex; Birth Year (if given), Age At Last Birthday; Tribe; Degree of Blood; Marital Status; Relationship To Head of Family; Last Census Roll Number; At Jurisdiction Where Enrolled (Yes or No); At Another Jurisdiction; ELSEWHERE: Post office, County, State; Ward (Yes or No); Allotment, Annuity, and Identification Numbers.

4669; Hosch-clish-nih-Hosteen-nez-bega; M; 54; Navajo; F; M; Head; 4680; Yes; Yes; 25036
4670; Badoni-sani-bitsih; F; 27; Navajo; F; M; Wife; 4681; Yes; Yes; 25037
4671; Sylvia; F; 10; Navajo; F; S; Daughter; 4682; Yes; Yes; 25038
4672; Tah-noaz-bah; F; 7; Navajo; F; S; Daughter; 4683; Yes; Yes; 25039

4673; Hosteen-sosie-bega; M; 26; Navajo; F; M; Head; 4684; Yes; Yes; 26753
4674; Yah-dez-bah; F; 25; Navajo; F; M; Wife; 4685; Yes; Yes; 26754
4675; Haska-yil-hah-yah; M; 6; Navajo; F; S; Son; 4686; Yes; Yes; 26755
4676; Haska-yee-neh-yah; M; 3; Navajo; F; S; Son; 4687; Yes; Yes; 26756
4677; Adobe-bitsih; F; 49; Navajo; F; Wd; Mother-in-law; 4688; Yes; Yes; 26757
4678; Nah-tah-yee-chih-des-wudt; M; 13; Navajo; F; S; Brother-in-law; 4689; Yes; Yes; 26758

4679; Hosteen-soh-hoh-bega; M; Unk; Navajo; F; M; Head; 4690; Yes; Yes; 26967
4680; Yah-nee-pah; F; 3; Navajo; F; S; Daughter; 4691; Yes; Yes; 27080

4681; Hosteen-bihnah-atinih-bitsih-Bihyaz, Olden, William; M; 29; Navajo; F; Wd; Head; 4692; Yes; Yes; 17015
4682; Hosteen-bihnah-atinih-bitsih Rehyaz, nanah-bakih; F; 5; Navajo; F; S; Daughter; 4693; Yes; Yes; 17016

4683; Hosteen-nez-bega; M; 30; Navajo; F; M; Head; 4694; Yes; Yes; 24819
4684; Dagah-li-cheeih-bitsoih; F; 28; Navajo; F; M; Wife; 4695; Yes; Yes; 24820
4685; David; M; 12; Navajo; F; S; Son; 4696; Yes; Yes; 24821
4686; Nah-tah-yil-nih-yah; M; 10; Navajo; F; S; Son; 4697; Yes; Yes; 24822
4687; Nah-tah-yil-hah-yah; M; 7; Navajo; F; S; Son; 4698; Yes; Yes; 24823
4688; Yil-nah-nih-bah; F; 5; Navajo; F; S; Daughter; 4699; Yes; Yes; 24824
4689; Haska-yee-tah-dez-wudt; M; 17; Navajo; F; S; Brother-in-law; 4700; Yes; Yes; 24825
4690; Dah-pah-ah-bah; F; 2; Navajo; F; S; Daughter; 4701; Yes; Yes; 25336

4691; Hosteen-nez; M; 53; Navajo; F; M; Head; 4702; Yes; Yes; 24826
4692; Hosteen-nez's wife; F; 35; Navajo; F; M; Wife; 4703; Yes; Yes; 24827
4693; John; M; 13; Navajo; F; S; Step-son; 4704; Yes; Yes; 24828
4694; Elizabeth; F; 11; Navajo; F; S; Step-daughter; 4705; Yes; Yes; 24829
4695; Nah-nih-bah; F; 8; Navajo; F; S; Daughter; 4706; Yes; Yes; 24830
4696; Yil-nih-bah; F; 4; Navajo; F; S; Daughter; 4707; Yes; Yes; 24831
4697; Lewis; F[sic]; 27; Navajo; F; S; Daughter[sic]; 4708; Yes; Yes; 24832
4698; Winona; F; 27; Navajo; F; S; Daughter; 4709; Yes; Yes; 24833
4699; Murray; M; 20; Navajo; F; S; Son; 4710; Yes; Yes; 24834

4700; Hosteen-haska; M; Unk; Navajo; F; M; Head; 4711; Yes; Yes; 24835

Census of the **Northern Navajo** reservation of the **Northern Navajo** jurisdiction, as of **April 1** , 1931, taken by **Ernest H. Hammond, District**, Superintendent. **in Charge**

**Key:** Number; NAME: Surname, Given; Sex; Birth Year (if given), Age At Last Birthday; Tribe; Degree of Blood; Marital Status; Relationship To Head of Family; Last Census Roll Number; At Jurisdiction Where Enrolled (Yes or No); At Another Jurisdiction; ELSEWHERE: Post office, County, State; Ward (Yes or No); Allotment, Annuity, and Identification Numbers.

4701; Hosteen-haska's wife; F; 53; Navajo; F; M; Wife; 4712; Yes; Yes; 24836
4702; Donald; M; 24; Navajo; F; S; Son; 4713; Yes; Yes; 24837
4703; Mark; M; 22; Navajo; F; S; Son; 4714; Yes; Yes; 24838

4704; Hosteen-toh-dih-koz; M; unk; Navajo; F; Wd; Head; 4715; Yes; Yes; 24839
4705; Keh-yil-nih-bah; F; 17; Navajo; F; S; Daughter; 4716; Yes; Yes; 24841

4706; Hosteen-haska-bega; M; 38; Navajo; F; M; Head; 4717; Yes; Yes; 24842
4707; Hah-ah-sidih-soh-benally; F; 28; Navajo; F; M; Wife; 4718; Yes; Yes; 24843
4708; Linnette; F; 12; Navajo; F; S; Daughter; 4719; Yes; Yes; 24844
4709; Chih-des-woody; M; 8; Navajo; F; S; Son; 4720; Yes; Yes; 24845
4710; Ed; M; 6; Navajo; F; S; Son; [Blank]; Yes; Yes; 24846
4711; Dah-dez-bah; F; 5; Navajo; F; S; Daughter; 4721; Yes; Yes; 24847

4712; Hosteen-haska-bega, John; M; Unk; Navajo; F; M; Head; 4722; Yes; Yes; 24857
4713; Hah-ah-sidih-soh-benally; F; Unk; Navajo; F; M; Wife; 4723; Yes; Yes; 24858
4714; Nah-hah-yah; M; 7; Navajo; F; S; Son; 4724; Yes; Yes; 24859
4715; Toh-nil-wudt; M; 2; Navajo; F; S; Son; 4725; Yes; Yes; 25337

4716; Hosteen-deel; M; 62; Navajo; F; M; Head; 4726; Yes; Yes; 24900
4717; Hosteen-deel-bih-adzan; F; 48; Navajo; F; M; 4727; Wife; Yes; Yes; 24901
4718; Roy; M; 24; Navajo; F; M; Son; 4728; Yes; Yes; 24902
4719; Oscar; F[sic]; 19; Navajo; F; S; Son; 4729; Yes; Yes; 24903
4720; Ah-hah-hah-bah; F; 17; Navajo; F; S; Daughter; 4730; Yes; Yes; 24904
4721; Julia; F; 11; Navajo; F; S; Daughter; 4731; Yes; Yes; 24905
4722; Nah-tah-yil-des-wudt; M; 7; Navajo; F; S; Son; 4732; Yes; Yes; 24906
4723; Fred; M; 5; Navajo; F; S; Son; 4733; Yes; Yes; 24907
4724; Deel, Joe; M; 5/12; Navajo; F; S; Son (of Roy); [Blank]; Yes; Yes; 25345

4725; Hosteen-bih-chi-bega, Curley; M; Unk; Navajo; F; M; Head; 4734; Yes; Yes; 24972
4726; Nellie; F; 42; Navajo; F; M; Wife; 4735; Yes; Yes; 24973
4727; Curley, Pete; M; 21; Navajo; F; S; Son; 4736; Yes; Yes; 24974
4728; George; M; 21; Navajo; F; S; Son; 4737; Yes; Yes; 24975
4729; Leo; M; 18; Navajo; F; S; Son; 4738; Yes; Yes; 24976
4730; Nah-tah-yil-yee-gahl; M; 15; Navajo; F; S; Son; 4739; Yes; Yes; 24977
4731; Joe; M; 14; Navajo; F; S; Son; 4740; Yes; Yes; 24978
4732; John; M; 12; Navajo; F; S; Son; 4741; Yes; Yes; 24979
4733; Nellie; F; 10; Navajo; F; S; Daughter; 4742; Yes; Yes; 24980
4734; Yee-chih-haz-bah; F; 8; Navajo; F; S; Daughter; 4743; Yes; Yes; 24981

Census of the **Northern Navajo** reservation of the **Northern Navajo** jurisdiction, as of **April 1**, 19**31,** taken by **Ernest H. Hammond, District,** Superintendent. **in Charge**

Key: Number; NAME: Surname, Given; Sex; Birth Year (if given), Age At Last Birthday; Tribe; Degree of Blood; Marital Status; Relationship To Head of Family; Last Census Roll Number; At Jurisdiction Where Enrolled (Yes or No); At Another Jurisdiction; ELSEWHERE: Post office, County, State; Ward (Yes or No); Allotment, Annuity, and Identification Numbers.

4735; Hosteen-hosch-clizhih-bilah; F; 61; Navajo; F; Div; Head; 4744; Yes; Yes; 24982

4736; Anna; F; 30; Navajo; F; Div; Daughter; 4745; Yes; Yes; 24983

4737; Bayse-lagaih, John; M; 8; Navajo; F; S; Grand-son; 4746; Yes; Yes; 24984

4738; Tah-des-wudt; M; 6; Navajo; F; S; Grand-son; 4747; Yes; Yes; 24985


4739; Hosteen-thlani-bega. (Ft. Defiance Dist.); Head; 4748;

4740; Toh-cheeny-benally, Clara; F; 23; Navajo; F; M; Wife; 4749; Yes; Yes; 25069

4741; Mary; F; 3; Navajo; F; S; Daughter; 4750; Yes; Yes; 25070


4742; Hosteen-nez-yen-bega; M; Unk; Navajo; F; M; Head; 4751; Yes; Yes; 25088

4743; Nellie; F; 43; Navajo; F; M; Wife; 4752; Yes; Yes; 25089

4744; Dez-bah; F; 78; Navajo; F; Wd; Mother; 4753; Yes; Yes; 25090


4745; Hosteen-Utintilli, Joe Brown; M; 52; Navajo; F; M; Head; 4754; Yes; Yes; 25097

4746; Bah; F; 36; Navajo; F; M; Wife; 4755; Yes; Yes; 25098

4747; Philip; M; 19; Navajo; F; S; Son; 4756; Yes; Yes; 25099

4748; Al-chih-haz-bah; F; 16; Navajo; F; S; Daughter; 4757; Yes; Yes; 25100

4749; Elizabeth; F; 11; Navajo; F; S; Daughter; 4758; Yes; Yes; 25101

4750; Hahn-nih-bah; F; 9; Navajo; F; S; Daughter; 4759; Yes; Yes; 25102

4751; Adzan-l-chee; F; 6; Navajo; F; S; Daughter; 4760; Yes; Yes; 25103

4752; Adzan-l-suen; F; 6; Navajo; F; S; Daughter; 4761; Yes; Yes; 25104

4753; Yil-dez-bah; F; 3; Navajo; F; S; Daughter; 4762; Yes; Yes; 25105


4754; Hosteen-yazzie; M; 39; Navajo; F; M; Head; 4763; Yes; Yes; 25117

4755; Chah-dih-tlohi-bitsih; F; 38; Navajo; F; M; Wife; 4764; Yes; Yes; 25118

4756; Donald; M; 16; Navajo; F; S; Son; 4765; Yes; Yes; 25119

4757; Chih-dez-bah; F; 9; Navajo; F; S; Daughter; 4766; Yes; Yes; 25120

4758; Haska-yee-nas-wudt; M; 7; Navajo; F; S; Son; 4767; Yes; Yes; 25121

4759; Haska-yee-kih-dee-wudt; M; 6; Navajo; F; S; Son; 4768; Yes; Yes; 25122

4760; Glih-yil-naz-bah; F; 3; Navajo; F; S; Daughter; 4769; Yes; Yes; 25123


4761; Hosteen-dih-chalih-bega; M; 58; Navajo; F; M; Head; 4770; Yes; Yes; 25165

4762; Salou-yazzie-bitsih; F; 53; Navajo; F; M; Wife; 4771; Yes; Yes; 25166

4763; Kenapah, Martinez; M; 24; Navajo; F; S; Son; 4772; Yes; Yes; 25167

4764; Adzanih-yazzie; F; 18; Navajo; F; S; Daughter; 4773; Yes; Yes; 25168

4765; Kenapah, Glena; F; 16; Navajo; F; S; Daughter; 4774; Yes; Yes; 25169

4766; Kenapah, Gladys; F; 14; Navajo; F; S; Daughter; 4775; Yes; Yes; 25170

4767; Hubert; M; 11; Navajo; F; S; Son; 4776; Yes; Yes; 25171


4768; Hosteen-hosch-clish-nih; M; Unk; Navajo; F; M; Head; 4777; Yes; Yes; 25202

Census of the **Northern Navajo** reservation of the **Northern Navajo** jurisdiction, as of **April 1** , 1931, taken by **Ernest H. Hammond, District** , Superintendent. **in Charge**

**Key:** Number; NAME: Surname, Given; Sex; Birth Year (if given), Age At Last Birthday; Tribe; Degree of Blood; Marital Status; Relationship To Head of Family; Last Census Roll Number; At Jurisdiction Where Enrolled (Yes or No); At Another Jurisdiction; ELSEWHERE: Post office, County, State; Ward (Yes or No); Allotment, Annuity, and Identification Numbers.

4769; Hosteen-hosch-clish-nih's wife; F; 48; Navajo; F; M; Wife; 4778; Yes; Yes; 25203

4770; Bil-nah-ziz-bah; F; 15; Navajo; F; S; Daughter; 4779; Yes; Yes; 25204

4771; Yil-nih-naz-bah; F; 13; Navajo; F; S; Daughter; 4780; Yes; Yes; 25205

4772; Haska-yee-tah-des-wudt; M; 11; Navajo; F; S; Son; 4781; Yes; Yes; 25206

4773; Nah-tah-yee-kih-has-wudt; M; 9; Navajo; F; S; Son; 4782; Yes; Yes; 25207

4774; Haska-yil-nih-nih-yah; M; 7; Navajo; F; S; Son; 4783; Yes; Yes; 25208

4775; Haska-yee-la-dos-wudt; M; 5; Navajo; F; S; Son; 4784; Yes; Yes; 25209

4776; Hosteen-nez-bega; M; 38; Navajo; F; M; Head; 4785; Yes; Yes; 25229

4777; Yee-naz-bah; F; 32; Navajo; F; M; Wife; 4786; Yes; Yes; 25230

4778; Haska-yil-nah-yah; M; 11; Navajo; F; S; Son; 4787; Yes; Yes; 25231

4779; Larry; M; 9; Navajo; F; S; Son; 4788; Yes; Yes; 25232

4780; Haska-yee-neh-yah; M; 8; Navajo; F; S; Son; 4789; Yes; Yes; 25233

4781; Haska-yil-nah-yah; M; 5; Navajo; F; S; Son; 4790; Yes; Yes; 25234

4782; Haska-yil-nil-wudt; M; 4; Navajo; F; S; Son; 4791; Yes; Yes; 25235

4783; Hosch-clish-nih-bega; M; 38; Navajo; F; M; Head; 4792; Yes; Yes; 25240

4784; Fannie; F; 36; Navajo; F; M; Wife; 4793; Yes; Yes; 25241

4785; Elinora; F; 18; Navajo; F; S; Daughter; 4794; Yes; Yes; 25242

4786; Hosteen-yazzie; M; 48; Navajo; F; M; Head; 4795; Yes; Yes; 25966

4787; Yee-nil-bah; F; 26; Navajo; F; M; Wife; 4796; Yes; Yes; 25967

4788; Glih-yee-tah-nil-bah; F; 5; Navajo; F; S; Daughter; 4797; Yes; Yes; 25968

4789; Nah-tah-yee-tah-nih-yah; M; 3; Navajo; F; S; Son; 4798; Yes; Yes; 25969

4790; Uienth-nez-ai-bega, Nez, Joe; M; 11; Navajo; F; S; Sheep-herder; 4799; Yes; Yes; 25970

4791; Hosteen-bitsee-lagaih; M; 69; Navajo; F; M; Head; 4800; Yes; Yes; 26422

4792; Hosteen-bitsee-lagaih-bih-adzan; F; 59; Navajo; F; M; Wife; 4801; Yes; Yes; 26423

4793; Hosteen-bitah, Sleepy; M; 30; Navajo; F; M; Head; 4802; Yes; Yes; 26411

4794; Glih-yee-tah-nih-bah; F; 19; Navajo; F; M; Wife; 4803; Yes; Yes; 26412

4795; Yil-naz-bah; F; 5; Navajo; F; S; Daughter; 4804; Yes; Yes; 26413

4796; Hosteen-haska-benally; M; 33; Navajo; F; M; Head; 4805; Yes; Yes; 26382

4797; Keh-yil-dez-bah; F; 31; Navajo; F; M; Wife; 4806; Yes; Yes; 26383

4798; Haska-yee-chih-dez-wudt; M; 6; Navajo; F; S; Son; 4807; Yes; Yes; 26384

4799; Hah-noh-tahl; M; 4; Navajo; F; S; Son; 4808; Yes; Yes; 26385

4800; Hosteen-haska-bega Ahtcitty's wife; F; 46; Navajo; F; Wd; Head; 4809; Yes; Yes; 26371

Census of the **Northern Navajo** reservation of the **Northern Navajo** jurisdiction, as of **April 1**, 19**31**, taken by **Ernest H. Hammond, District**, Superintendent. **in Charge**

**Key:** Number; NAME: Surname, Given; Sex; Birth Year (if given), Age At Last Birthday; Tribe; Degree of Blood; Marital Status; Relationship To Head of Family; Last Census Roll Number; At Jurisdiction Where Enrolled (Yes or No); At Another Jurisdiction; ELSEWHERE: Post office, County, State; Ward (Yes or No); Allotment, Annuity, and Identification Numbers.

4801;  Russell; M; 15; Navajo; F; S; Son; 4810; Yes; Yes; 26372
4802;  Raymond; M; 12; Navajo; F; S; Son; 4811; Yes; Yes; 26373


4803;  Hosteen-Ashinih; M; 68; Navajo; F; M; Head; 4812; Yes; Yes; 17385
4804;  Hosteen-Ashinih's wife; F; 25; Navajo; F; M; Wife; 4813; Yes; Yes; 17386
4805;  Atate-chee; F; 5; Navajo; F; S; Daughter; 4814; Yes; Yes; 17387
4806;  Adzanih-tah-cheeny; F; 64; Navajo; F; Wd; Mother-in-law; 4815; Yes; Yes; 17388
4807;  Casy[sic]; M; 2; Navajo; F; S; Son; 4816; Yes; Yes; 17412
      [Name is probably Casey]


4808;  Hosteen-bihnah-atinih-bitsih; F; 58; Navajo; F; Wd; Head; 4817; Yes; Yes; 17012
4809;  Hosteen-bihnah-atinih-bitsih's daughter; F; 24; Navajo; F; Wd; Daughter; 4818; Yes; Yes; 17013
4810;  Hosteen-bihnah-atinih-bitsih's daughter; F; 21; Navajo; F; S; Daughter; 4819; Yes; Yes; 17014


4811;  Hosteen-ashinih-bega; M; Unk; Navajo; F; M; Head; 4820; Yes; Yes; 17346
4812;  See-pahih; F; 25; Navajo; F; M; Wife; 4821; Yes; Yes; 17347
4813;  Nat-glin-yilt-hay-ah; F; 3; Navajo; F; S; Daughter; 4822; Yes; Yes; 17348


4814;  Hosteen-Tahn; M; 77; Navajo; F; Wd; Head; 4823; Yes; Yes; 17331


4815;  Hosteen-bih-gennihgi-bega; M; 28; Navajo; F; M; Head; 4824; Yes; Yes; 18030
4816;  Eskee-l-suih; M; 10; Navajo; F; S; Son; 4825; Yes; Yes; 18032
4817;  Bih-ayaih; M; 8; Navajo; F; S; Son; 4826; Yes; Yes; 18033
4818;  Dah-yis-wudt; M; 6; Navajo; F; S; Son; 4827; Yes; Yes; 18034
4819;  Hoska-yilth-nah-del; M; 4; Navajo; F; S; Son; 4828; Yes; Yes; 18035


4820;  Hoska-yilth-des-del-askan-Yazzie-benally; M; 25; Navajo; F; M; Head; 4829; Yes; Yes; 18056
4921;  Batonih-in-bega-bitsih; F; 21; Navajo; F; M; Wife; 4830; Yes; Yes; 18057
4822;  Edith; F; 2; Navajo; F; S; Daughter; 4831; Yes; Yes; 18232
4823;  Jane; F; 1; Navajo; F; S; Daughter; 4832; Yes; Yes; 18298


4824;  Holkidnay-bilah; F; 60; Navajo; F; Wd; Head; 4833; Yes; Yes; 18096
4825;  Dewey, Grey; M; 29; Navajo; F; S; Son; 4834; Yes; Yes; 18097
4826;  Zannie; F; 15; Navajo; F; S; Daughter; 4835; Yes; Yes; 18098


4827;  Hosteen-lagaih-yen-bitsoih Jones, Scotty; M; 34; Navajo; F M; Head; 4836; Yes; Yes; 18126

Census of the **Northern Navajo** reservation of the **Northern Navajo** jurisdiction, as of **April 1**, 19**31**, taken by **Ernest H. Hammond, District**, Superintendent. **in Charge**

**Key:** Number; NAME: Surname, Given; Sex; Birth Year (if given), Age At Last Birthday; Tribe; Degree of Blood; Marital Status; Relationship To Head of Family; Last Census Roll Number; At Jurisdiction Where Enrolled (Yes or No); At Another Jurisdiction; ELSEWHERE: Post office, County, State; Ward (Yes or No); Allotment, Annuity, and Identification Numbers.

4828; Hosteen-bitseenihgi-bitsih; F; 24; Navajo; F; M; Wife; 4837; Yes; Yes; 18127
4829; Zannie; F; 4; Navajo; F; S; Son[sic]; 4838; Yes; Yes; 18128
[Should be female]
4830; Peter; M; 2; Navajo; F; S; Son; 4839; Yes; Yes; 18224

4831; Hosteen-bitsee-nihgih; M; 53; Navajo; F; M; Head; 4840; Yes; Yes; 18131
4832; Hosteen-bitsee-nihgih's wife; F; 37; Navajo; F; M; Wife; 4841; Yes; Yes; 18132
4833; Lo-nih; F; 13; Navajo; F; S; Daughter; 4842; Yes; Yes; 18133
4834; Yis-clayih; M; 6; Navajo; F; S; Son; 4843; Yes; Yes; 18134
4835; Betty; F; 2; Navajo; F; S; Daughter; 4844; Yes; Yes; 18225

4836; Hosteen-hoska-ih; M; 61; Navajo; F; M; Head; 4845; Yes; Yes; 17874
4837; Toh-nih-bilah; F; 47; Navajo; F; M; Wife; 4846; Yes; Yes; 17875
4838; Hoska-hah-no-tahl; M; 22; Navajo; F; S; Son; 4847; Yes; Yes; 17876
4839; Hosteen, Harold; M; 19; Navajo; F; S; Son; 4848; Yes; Yes; 17877
4840; Teller, Margaret; F; 18; Navajo; F; S; Daughter; 4849; Yes; Yes; 17878
4841; Teller, Ida; F; 16; Navajo; F; S; Daughter; 4850; Yes; Yes; 17879
4842; Yah-desbah; F; 20; Navajo; F; S; Daughter; 4851; Yes; Yes; 17880
4843; Yee-tah-nibah; F; 12; Navajo; F; S; Daughter; 4852; Yes; Yes; 17881
4844; Yee-tah-desbah; F; 9; Navajo; F; S; Daughter; 4853; Yes; Yes; 17882

4845; Hosteen-bih-kay-atsosie; F; 63; Navajo; F; Wd; Head; 4854; Yes; Yes; 18135

4846; Hosteen-Uintilli-bega; M; 30; Navajo; F; M; Head; 4855; Yes; Yes; 18141
4847; Hosteen-dohi-hih-bitsih; F; 30; Navajo; F; M; Wife; 4856; Yes; Yes; 18142
4848; Hosteen-Uintilli-bega; M; 18; Navajo; F; S; Brother; 4857; Yes; Yes; 18143
4849; Eskee-l-cheeih; M; 9; Navajo; F; S; Son; 4858; Yes; Yes; 18144
4850; Adzan-sinih; F; 6; Navajo; F; S; Daughter; 4859; Yes; Yes; 18145
4851; Atate-sosie; F; 4; Navajo; F; S; Daughter; 4860; Yes; Yes; 18146

4852; Hosteen-bitseeshi; M; Unk; Navajo; F; M; Head; 4861; Yes; Yes; 18147
4853; Adzan-bihteesih; F; 73; Navajo; F; M; Wife; 4862; Yes; Yes; 18148
4854; Hosteen-bih-teesih-bega Bitseez-chilligi; M; 25; Navajo; F; S; Son; 4863; Yes; Yes; 18149
4855; Haska-yee-ch-has-wudt; M; 13; Navajo; F; S; Son; 4864; Yes; Yes; 18150

4856; Hosteen-Uintilli-bega, Dan; M; 33; Navajo; F; M; Head; 4865; Yes; Yes; 18151
4857; Hosteen-bihtessih-bitsih; F; 35; Navajo; F; M; Wife; 4866; Yes; Yes; 18152
4858; Bah; F; 11; Navajo; F; S; Daughter; 4867; Yes; Yes; 18153

4859; Hosteen-sani; M; 32; Navajo; F; M; Head; 4868; Yes; Yes; 18160

Census of the **Northern Navajo** reservation of the **Northern Navajo**
jurisdiction, as of **April 1** , 1931, taken by **Ernest H. Hammond, District**,
Superintendent. **in Charge**

Key: Number; NAME: Surname, Given; Sex; Birth Year (if given), Age At Last Birthday; Tribe; Degree of
Blood; Marital Status; Relationship To Head of Family; Last Census Roll Number; At Jurisdiction Where
Enrolled (Yes or No); At Another Jurisdiction; ELSEWHERE: Post office, County, State; Ward (Yes or No);
Allotment, Annuity, and Identification Numbers.

4860; Tah-nes-zanih-adzan; F; 24; Navajo; F; M; Wife; 4869; Yes; Yes; 18161
4861; Shi-bah; F; 10; Navajo; F; S; Daughter; 4870; Yes; Yes; 18162
4862; Hosteen-l-suen; M; 6; Navajo; F; S; Son; 4871; Yes; Yes; 18163
4863; Bitsee-lachee; M; 3; Navajo; F; S; Son; 4872; Yes; Yes; 18164

4864; Hosteen-bih-chah-lizin; M; 63; Navajo; F; Wd; Head; 4873; Yes; Yes; 18194

4865; Hosteen-yazzie-bega; M; Unk; Navajo; F; M; Head; 4874; Yes; Yes; 18198
4866; Hosteen-yazzie-bega's wife; F; 22; Navajo; F; M; Wife; 4875; Yes; Yes;
18199
4867; Awa-yazzie-eskin; M; 3; Navajo; F; S; Son; 4876; Yes; Yes; 18274

4868; Hol-kidnay[sic]; M; 52; Navajo; F; M; Head; 4877; Yes; Yes; 17850
[Name could be Hol-kidney]
4869; Toh-sonie-bitsih; F; 37; Navajo; F; M; Wife; 4878; Yes; Yes; 17851
4870; Hol-kidney; Jack; M; 23; Navajo; F; S; Son; 4879; Yes; Yes; 17852
4871; Sazie- Holkidney; F; 15; Navajo; F; S; Daughter; 4880; Yes; Yes; 17853
4872; Hol-kidnay, Leila; F; 9; Navajo; F; S; Daughter; 4881; Yes; Yes; 17854
4873; Aholtah-yazzie; F; 6; Navajo; F; S; Daughter; 4882; Yes; Yes; 17855
4874; Toh-sonih-bitsih; F; 35; Navajo; F; M; 2nd wife; 4883; Yes; Yes; 17857
4875; Hol-kidney, Homer; M; 14; Navajo; F; S; Son; 4884; Yes; Yes; 17858
4876; Hol-kidney, Una; F; 13; Navajo; F; S; Daughter; 4885; Yes; Yes; 17859
4877; Hol-kidney, Alma; F; 10; Navajo; F; S; Daughter; 4886; Yes; Yes; 17860
4878; Haska-tah-alegade; M; 2; Navajo; F; S; Son; 4887; Yes; Yes; 18289

4879; Hoschih; M; 45; Navajo; F; M; Head; 4888; Yes; Yes; 17927
4880; Adzan-Topahah; F; 40; Navajo; F; M; Wife; 4889; Yes; Yes; 17928
4881; Hoschinh-bega; M; 26; Navajo; F; S; Son; 4890; Yes; Yes; 17929
4882; Hoschnih, Dick; M; 12; Navajo; F; S; Son; 4891; Yes; Yes; 17930
4883; Zohne-yazzie; M; 10; Navajo; F; S; Son; 4892; Yes; Yes; 17931
4884; Enchico-Yazzie; M; 3; Navajo; F; S; Son; 4893; Yes; Yes; 17932

4885; Hosteen-lagaih-yen-bega; M; 56; Navajo; F; M; Head; 4894; Yes; Yes; 17963
4886; Adzanih-Telly; F; 67; Navajo; F; M; Wife; 4910; Yes; Yes; 17964
4887; Ath-chah-bah; F; 17; Navajo; F; S; Step-daughter; 4911; Yes; Yes; 17965

4888; Hosteen-askan-bitsih; F; 48; Navajo; F; Wd; Head; 4912; Yes; Yes; 17966
4889; Mays, Oliver; M; 23; Navajo; F; S; Son; 4913; Yes; Yes; 17967
4890; Conna, Edna; F; 18; Navajo; F; S; Daughter; 4914; Yes; Yes; 17968
4891; Hosteen Nocki, Peairs; M; 13; Navajo; F; S; Son; 4915; Yes; Yes; 17969
4892; Nocki-Hosteen, Tully; M; 10; Navajo; F; S; Son; 4916; Yes; Yes; 17970
4893; Dah-yis-wudt; M; 6; Navajo; F; S; Son; 4917; Yes; Yes; 17971
4894; Eh-no-pah; F; 4; Navajo; F; S; Daughter; 4918; Yes; Yes; 18293

Census of the **Northern Navajo** reservation of the **Northern Navajo** jurisdiction, as of **April 1** , 1931, taken by **Ernest H. Hammond, District** , Superintendent. **in Charge**

**Key:** Number; NAME: Surname, Given; Sex; Birth Year (if given), Age At Last Birthday; Tribe; Degree of Blood; Marital Status; Relationship To Head of Family; Last Census Roll Number; At Jurisdiction Where Enrolled (Yes or No); At Another Jurisdiction; ELSEWHERE: Post office, County, State; Ward (Yes or No); Allotment, Annuity, and Identification Numbers.

4895; Hol-kidney-bilah; F; 59; Navajo; F; Wd; Head; 4919; Yes; Yes; 17995
4896; Grey, Zane; M; 30; Navajo; F; S; Son; 4920; Yes; Yes; 17996
4897; Nocki-, Lewis; M; 19; Navajo; F; S; Son; 4921; Yes; Yes; 17997
4898; Yah-nih-hah; F; 17; Navajo; F; S; Daughter; 4922; Yes; Yes; 17998
4899; Ason-kly; F; 3; Navajo; F; S; Daughter; 4923; Yes; Yes; 18294

4900; Hosteen-bih-teeceih-bega; M; 41; Navajo; F; M; Head; 4895; Yes; Yes; 18007
4901; Toh-oh-sosie-bitsih; F; 1; Navajo; F; M; Wife; 4896; Yes; Yes; 18008
4902; Bertha; F; 2; Navajo; F; S; Daughter; 4897; Yes; Yes; 18230

4903; Hoska-nih-nih-bega-badoni; M; 40; Navajo; F; M; Head; 4898; Yes; Yes; 18011
4904; Hoska-nih-nih-bega-bitsih; F; 23; Navajo; F; M; Wife; 4899; Yes; Yes; 18012
4905; Ahseesih; M; 8; Navajo; F; S; Son; 4900; Yes; Yes; 18013
4906; Dah-yiy-bah; F; 4; Navajo; F; S; Daughter; 4901; Yes; Yes; 18014

4907; Hosch-clishnih-bega; M; Unk; Navajo; F; M; Head; 4902; Yes; Yes; 17816
4908; Toh-lizin-bitsih; F; 35; Navajo; F; M; Wife; 4903; Yes; Yes; 17817
4909; Johnson, Mabel; F; 20; Navajo; F; S; Daughter; 4904; Yes; Yes; 17818
4910; Hosch-clishnih, Bennie; F; 15; Navajo; F; S; Daughter; 4905; Yes; Yes; 17819
4911; Hosch-clishnin[sic], Perry; M; 10; Navajo; F; S; Son; 4906; Yes; Yes; 17820
[Name is probably Hosch-clishnih, Perry]
4912; Hosch-clishnih, Mike; M; 8; Navajo; F; S; Son; 4907; Yes; Yes; 17821
4913; Hosch-clish-nih-bah; F; 5; Navajo; F; S; Daughter; 4908; Yes; Yes; 17822
4914; Hosha-tah-yil-wudt; M; 3; Navajo; F; S; Son; 4909; Yes; Yes; 17823

4915; Hosch-clish-nih-hosteen's wife; F; 61; Navajo; F; Wd; Head; 4924; Yes; Yes; 17825
4916; Hah-tah-yil-dayah; M; 24; Navajo; F; S; Son; 4925; Yes; Yes; 17826
4917; Yazzie, Lowell; M; 23; Navajo; F; S; Grand-son; 4926; Yes; Yes; 17827
4918; Kee Yazzie; M; 17; Navajo; F; S; Grand-son; 4927; Yes; Yes; 17828
4919; Oskee-zunih; M; 9; Navajo; F; S; Grand-son; 4928; Yes; Yes; 17829
4920; Hosch-clish-nih, Flander; M; 16; Navajo; F; S; Grand-son; 4929; Yes; Yes; 17830

4921; Hosteen-bihnes-dihthlohi; M; 61; Navajo; F; M; Head; 4930; Yes; Yes; 17896
4922; Toh-dih-cheeny-bitsih; F; 35; Navajo; F; M; Wife; 4931; Yes; Yes; 17897
4923; Kin-lacheeny-soh; F; 71; Navajo; F; Wd; Grand-mother-in-law; 4932; Yes; Yes; 17898

4924; Hosteen-gah-bitsoih; M; 48; Navajo; F; M; Head; 4933; Yes; Yes; 20094
4925; Dagah-sohoh-benally; F; 24; Navajo; F; M; Wife; 4934; Yes; Yes; 20095
4926; Al-kay-dez-bah; F; 9; Navajo; F; S; Daughter; 4935; Yes; Yes; 20096

Census of the **Northern Navajo** reservation of the **Northern Navajo** jurisdiction, as of **April 1**, 1931, taken by **Ernest H. Hammond, District**, Superintendent. **in Charge**

4927; Yee-nas-wudt; M; 7; Navajo; F; S; Son; 4936; Yes; Yes; 20098

4928; Holkidney; M; Unk; Navajo; F; M; Head; 4937; No; McElmo, Colo., San Juan, Utah; Yes; 18871
4929; Holkidney's wife; F; 33; Navajo; F; M; Wife; 4938; No; McElmo, Colo., San Juan, Utah; Yes; 18872
4930; Holkidney-bega; M; 26; Navajo; F; S; Son; 4939; No; McElmo, Colo., San Juan, Utah; Yes; 18873
4931; Dagah-lachee, Tuly; M; 19; Navajo; F; S; Son; 4940; No; McElmo, Colo., San Juan, Utah; Yes; 18874
4932; Zannie-l-chee; F; 6; Navajo; F; S; Daughter; 4941; No; McElmo, Colo., San Juan, Utah; Yes; 18875
4933; Kee; M; 11; Navajo; F; S; Nephew-in-law; 4942; No; McElmo, Colo., San Juan, Utah; Yes; 18876

4934; Hosteen-dischle-yen-bega; M; 30; Navajo; F; M; Head; 4943; No; McElmo, Colo., San Juan, Utah; Yes; 19346
4935; Askan-shiz-yah-ih-bitsih; F; 21; Navajo; F; M; Wife; 4944; No; McElmo, Colo., San Juan, Utah; Yes; 19347
4936; Suen; F; 6; Navajo; F; S; Daughter; 4945; No; McElmo, Colo., San Juan, Utah; Yes; 19348
4937; Bah-Yazzie; F; 3; Navajo; F; S; Daughter; 4946; No; McElmo, Colo., San Juan, Utah; Yes; 19349
4938; Bahih; M; 19; Navajo; F; S; Nephew; 4947; No; McElmo, Colo., San Juan, Utah; Yes; 19350
4939; Gadt-ee-eyeih-bega; M; 43; Navajo; F; Wd; Uncle; 4948; No; McElmo, Colo., San Juan, Utah; Yes; 19351

4940; Hosteen-bih-teeceih-bega; M; 27; Navajo; F; M; Head; 4949; Yes; Yes; 18004
4941; Nocki-bitsih; F; 21; Navajo; F; M; Wife; 4950; Yes; Yes; 18005
4942; Shih-gee; M; 4; Navajo; F; S; Son; 4951; Yes; Yes; 18006
4943; Zellz[sic]; F; 2; Navajo; F; S; Daughter; 4952; Yes; Yes; 18229
[Name should be Zella]

4944; Hosteen-soh; M; 37; Navajo; F; M; Head; 4953; No; McElmo, Colo., San Juan, Utah; Yes; 18992
4945; Bitsih Thomas Jones; F; 30; Navajo; F; M; Wife; 4954; No; McElmo, Colo., San Juan, Utah; Yes; 18993
4946; Chu-lah; F; 9; Navajo; F; S; Daughter; 4955; No; McElmo, Colo., San Juan, Utah; Yes; 18994
4947; Asch-dee; M; 5; Navajo; F; S; Son; 4956; No; McElmo, Colo., San Juan, Utah; Yes; 18995

Census of the **Northern Navajo** reservation of the **Northern Navajo** jurisdiction, as of **April 1**, 1931, taken by **Ernest H. Hammond, District**, Superintendent. **in Charge**

**Key:** Number; NAME: Surname, Given; Sex; Birth Year (if given), Age At Last Birthday; Tribe; Degree of Blood; Marital Status; Relationship To Head of Family; Last Census Roll Number; At Jurisdiction Where Enrolled (Yes or No); At Another Jurisdiction; ELSEWHERE: Post office, County, State; Ward (Yes or No); Allotment, Annuity, and Identification Numbers.

4948; Nah-tah-soh; M; 3; Navajo; F; S; Son; 4957; No; McElmo, Colo., San Juan, Utah; Yes; 18996

4949; Hosteen-tiah-benally; M; 51; Navajo; F; Wd; Head; 4958; No; McElmo, Colo., San Juan, Utah; Yes; 19405
4950; Vincent; M; 19; Navajo; F; S; Son; 4959; No; McElmo, Colo., San Juan, Utah; Yes; 19407
4951; Adzan-soh; F; 9; Navajo; F; S; Daughter; 4960; No; McElmo, Colo., San Juan, Utah; Yes; 19408

4952; Hosteen-nez-bega-li; M; 42; Navajo; F; M; Head; 4961; No; McElmo, Colo., San Juan, Utah; Yes; 19436
4953; Topah-ah-bitsih; F; 27; Navajo; F; M; Wife; 4962; No; McElmo, Colo., San Juan, Utah; Yes; 19437
4954; Lee, Joe; M; 11; Navajo; F; S; Son; 4963; No; McElmo, Colo., San Juan, Utah; Yes; 19438
4955; Al-cha-des-bah; F; 7; Navajo; F; S; Daughter; 4964; No; McElmo, Colo., San Juan, Utah; Yes; 19439
4956; Nah-glih-l-bah; F; 5; Navajo; F; S; Daughter; 4965; No; McElmo, Colo., San Juan, Utah; Yes; 19440
4957; Des-wudt-yazzie; M; 3; Navajo; F; S; Son; 4966; No; McElmo, Colo., San Juan, Utah; Yes; 19441
4958; Hosteen-nez-bega, Ellis Lansing; M; 21; Navajo; F; S; Brother; 4967; No; McElmo, Colo., San Juan, Utah; Yes; 19442
4959; Hosteen-nez-bega, Roy Lansing; M; 18; Navajo; F; S; Brother; 4968; No; McElmo, Colo., San Juan, Utah; Yes; 19443
4960; Nah-glin-ye-tah-bah; F; 1; Navajo; F; S; Daughter; 4969; No; McElmo, Colo., San Juan, Utah; Yes; 19523

4961; Hosteen-hoska-yen-benally, Phillip; M; 43; Navajo; F; M; Head; 4970; No; McElmo, Colo., San Juan, Utah; Yes; 19805
4962; Toh-dih-cheeny-bitsih; F; 37; Navajo; F; M; Wife; 4971; No; McElmo, Colo., San Juan, Utah; Yes; 19806
4963; Hoska-yil-dayah; M; 18; Navajo; F; S; Son; 4972; No; McElmo, Colo., San Juan, Utah; Yes; 19807
4964; Philip, Felix; M; 16; Navajo; F; S; Son; 4973; No; McElmo, Colo., San Juan, Utah; Yes; 19808
4965; Toh-dih-cheeny, Victoria; F; 14; Navajo; F; S; Daughter; 4974; No; McElmo, Colo., San Juan, Utah; Yes; 19809
4966; Awa-l-bahih; F; 13; Navajo; F; S; Daughter; 4975; No; McElmo, Colo., San Juan, Utah; Yes; 19810
4967; Philip, Ned; M; 12; Navajo; F; S; Son; 4976; No; McElmo, Colo., San Juan, Utah; Yes; 19811

Census of the **Northern Navajo** reservation of the **Northern Navajo** jurisdiction, as of **April 1**, 19**31**, taken by **Ernest H. Hammond, District**. Superintendent. **in Charge**

**Key:** Number; NAME: Surname, Given; Sex; Birth Year (if given), Age At Last Birthday; Tribe; Degree of Blood; Marital Status; Relationship To Head of Family; Last Census Roll Number; At Jurisdiction Where Enrolled (Yes or No); At Another Jurisdiction; ELSEWHERE: Post office, County, State; Ward (Yes or No); Allotment, Annuity, and Identification Numbers.

4968; Hoska-ye-nas-wudt; M; 9; Navajo; F; S; Son; 4977; No; McElmo, Colo., San Juan, Utah; Yes; 19812

4969; Yee-nih-bah; F; 8; Navajo; F; S; Daughter; 4978; No; McElmo, Colo., San Juan, Utah; Yes; 19813

4970; Doh-nih-bah; F; 5; Navajo; F; S; Daughter; 4979; No; McElmo, Colo., San Juan, Utah; Yes; 19814

4971; Doh-des-bah; F; 3; Navajo; F; S; Daughter; 4980; No; McElmo, Colo., San Juan, Utah; Yes; 19815

4972; Hosteen-tohih-bega, John; M; 40; Navajo; F; M; Head; 4981; No; McElmo, Colo., San Juan, Utah; Yes; 19339

4973; Beleen-lagaih-bih-j-k; F; 41; Navajo; F; M; Wife; 4982; No; McElmo, Colo., San Juan, Utah; Yes; 19340

4974; Hoska-yee-chah-alwudt; M; 17; Navajo; F; S; Son; 4983; No; McElmo, Colo., San Juan, Utah; Yes; 19341

4975; Ah-kih-se-bah; F; 13; Navajo; F; S; Daughter; 4984; No; McElmo, Colo., San Juan, Utah; Yes; 19342

4976; Ep-nah-sh-dih; M; 9; Navajo; F; S; Son; 4985; No; McElmo, Colo., San Juan, Utah; Yes; 19343

4977; Dah-shih-bah; F; 7; Navajo; F; S; Daughter; 4986; No; McElmo, Colo., San Juan, Utah; Yes; 19344

4978; Seesih; F; 4; Navajo; F; S; Daughter; 4987; No; McElmo, Colo., San Juan, Utah; Yes; 19345

4979; Yun-nih-bah-i; F; 1; Navajo; F; S; Daughter; 4988; No; McElmo, Colo., San Juan, Utah; Yes; 19510

4980; Hosteen-bih-gizih; M; 54; Navajo; F; M; Head; 4989; Yes; Yes; 20291

4981; Atate-l-chee; F; 30; Navajo; F; M; Wife; 4990; Yes; Yes; 20292

4982; Bih-gizih, Barton; M; 22; Navajo; F; S; Son; 4991; Yes; Yes; 20293

4983; Nah-tahl-suen; M; 12; Navajo; F; S; Son; 4992; Yes; Yes; 20294

4984; Woody; M; 10; Navajo; F; S; Son; 4993; Yes; Yes; 20295

4985; Hah-ziz-bah; F; 8; Navajo; F; S; Daughter; 4994; Yes; Yes; 20296

4986; Dinay-chee; M; 7; Navajo; F; S; Son; 4995; Yes; Yes; 20297

4987; Hosh-cliznih; M; 5; Navajo; F; S; Son; 4996; Yes; Yes; 20298

4988; Adzan-deel; F; 59; Navajo; F; M; 1st wife; 4997; Yes; Yes; 20299

4989; Naglee-nas-bah; F; 2; Navajo; F; S; Daughter; 4998; Yes; Yes; 20420

4990; Hosteen, Sleepy; M; 88; Navajo; F; M; Head; 4999; No; McElmo, Colo., San Juan, Utah; Yes; 18966

4991; Natoni-bitsih; F; 45; Navajo; F; M; Wife; 5000; No; McElmo, Colo., San Juan, Utah; Yes; 18967

4992; Tah-nas-bah; F; 9; Navajo; F; S; Daughter; 5001; No; McElmo, Colo., San Juan, Utah; Yes; 18968

Census of the **Northern Navajo** reservation of the **Northern Navajo** jurisdiction, as of **April 1**, 1931, taken by **Ernest H. Hammond, District**, Superintendent. **in Charge**

**Key:** Number; NAME: Surname, Given; Sex; Birth Year (if given), Age At Last Birthday; Tribe; Degree of Blood; Marital Status; Relationship To Head of Family; Last Census Roll Number; At Jurisdiction Where Enrolled (Yes or No); At Another Jurisdiction; ELSEWHERE: Post office, County, State; Ward (Yes or No); Allotment, Annuity, and Identification Numbers.

4993; Yee-chih-has-bah; F; 7; Navajo; F; S; Daughter; 5002; No; McElmo, Colo., San Juan, Utah; Yes; 18969

4994; Eskee; M; 5; Navajo; F; S; Son; 5003; No; McElmo, Colo., San Juan, Utah; Yes; 18970

4995; Natah-yil-des-wudt, Charley; M; 15; Navajo; F; S; Step-son; 5004; No; McElmo, Colo., San Juan, Utah; Yes; 18971

4996; Biz-dee-bah; F; 25; Navajo; F; S; Step-daughter; 5005; No; McElmo, Colo., San Juan, Utah; Yes; 18972

4997; Hosteen-tah-yen-bega; M; 59; Navajo; F; M; Head; 5006; Yes; Yes; 19971

4998; Cudih-yen-bitsih; F; 38; Navajo; F; M; Wife; 5007; Yes; Yes; 19972

4999; Atate-sosie; F; 26; Navajo F; S; Daughter; 5008; Yes; Yes; 19973

5000; Hosteen, Pat; M; 12; Navajo; F; S; Son; 5009; Yes; Yes; 19974

5001; Tah, Wilma; F; 13; Navajo; F; S; Daughter; 5010; Yes; Yes; 19975

5002; Chee-cudih; M; 17; Navajo; F; S; Brother-in-law; 5011; Yes; Yes; 19977

5003; Hosteen-teece-sosie; M; 74; Navajo; F; M; Head; 5012; Yes; Yes; 20090

5004; Hoh-zinegih-bih-dazih; F; 45; Navajo; F; M; Wife; 5013; Yes; Yes; 20091

5005; Teece-sosie, Ralph; M; 18; Navajo; F; S; Son; 5014; Yes; Yes; 20092

5006; Kay-yil-hih-bah; F; 2; Navajo; F; S; Daughter; 5015; Yes; Yes; 20093

5007; Hosteen-bitsee-lakaihin-bega; M; 26; Navajo; F; M; Head; 5016; Yes; Yes; 17028

5008; Decheeny's Daughter; F; 19; Navajo; F; M; Wife; 5017; Yes; Yes; 17029

5009; Lucy; F; 3; Navajo; F; S; Daughter; 5018; Yes; Yes; 17405

5010; Hosteen-hoska-yen-bitsoih, Ned; M; 40; Navajo; F; S; Head; 5019; Yes; Yes; 20022

5011; Hosteen-hoska-yen-bitsih; F; 62; Navajo; F; Wd; Mother; 5020; Yes; Yes; 20023

5012; Clah-lizin; M; 36; Navajo; F; S; Brother; 5021; Yes; Yes; 20025

5013; Yee-nah-ho-dal; M; 42; Navajo; F; S; Brother; 5022; Yes; Yes; 20026

5014; Little, Wilmer; M; 18; Navajo; F; S; Nephew; 5023; Yes; Yes; 20027

5015; Little, Madge; F; 16; Navajo; F; S; Niece; 5024; Yes; Yes; 20028

5016; Little, Bob; M; 13; Navajo; F; S; Nephew; 5025; Yes; Yes; 20029

5017; Hosteen-hoska-yen-benally; M; 41; Navajo; F; M; Head; 5026; Yes; Yes; 19926

5018; Cudih-bega-bitsih; F; 40; Navajo; F; M; Wife; 5027; Yes; Yes; 19927

5019; Maurice; M; 12; Navajo; F; S; Son; 5028; Yes; Yes; 19928

5020; Hoska-yil-hahlel; M; 11; Navajo; F; S; Son; 5029; Yes; Yes; 19929

5021; Nah-tah-sosie; M; 6; Navajo; F; S; Son; 5030; Yes; Yes; 19930

5022; Nah-tah-yahi; M; 2; Navajo; F; S; Son; 5031; Yes; Yes; 20405

Census of the **Northern Navajo** reservation of the **Northern Navajo** jurisdiction, as of **April 1**, 1931, taken by **Ernest H. Hammond, District**, Superintendent. **in Charge**

Key: Number; NAME: Surname, Given; Sex; Birth Year (if given), Age At Last Birthday; Tribe; Degree of Blood; Marital Status; Relationship To Head of Family; Last Census Roll Number; At Jurisdiction Where Enrolled (Yes or No); At Another Jurisdiction; ELSEWHERE: Post office, County, State; Ward (Yes or No); Allotment, Annuity, and Identification Numbers.

5023; Hosteen-bihnah-atnih-bitsoih[sic]; F; 38; Navajo; F; Wd; Head; 5038; Yes; Yes; 17017 [Name could be Hosteen-bihnah-atinih-bitsoih]
5024; Hosteen-bihnah-atinih-bitsoih's Daughter; F; 19; Navajo; F; S; Daughter; 5039; Yes; Yes; 17018
5025; Hosteen-bihnah-atinih-bitsoih's daughter Ruby; F; 17; Navajo; F; S; Daughter; 5040; Yes; Yes; 17019
5026; Bihnah-atin, Artie; F; 15; Navajo; F; S; Daughter; 5041; Yes; Yes; 17020
5027; Hosteen-bihnah-atinih-bitsoih-bihyaz (Dinay Yazzie); M; 23; Navajo; F; S; Son; 5042; Yes; Yes; 17021
5028; Tsi-Tse; [Blank]; 4/12; Navajo; F; S; child of #17021 [Blank]; Yes; Yes; 17421

5029; Hosteen-nez-bega; M; 51; Navajo; F; M; Head; 5043; Yes; Yes; 21318
5030; Chin-nih-bah; F; 37; Navajo; F; M; Wife; 5044; Yes; Yes; 21319
5031; Beleen-lizin, Matthew; M; 12; Navajo; F; S; Son; 5045; Yes; Yes; 21320

5032; Hosteen-l-chee-yen-bega; M; 30; Navajo; F; M; Head; 5046; Yes; Yes; 20945
5033; Yee-kee-has-bah; F; 19; Navajo; F; M; Wife; 5047; Yes; Yes; 20946
5034; Glih-yil-nan-bah; F; 3; Navajo; F; S; Daughter; 5048; Yes; Yes; 20947

5035; Hosteen-ahtsosie-bega; M; Unk; Navajo; F; M; Head; 5049; Yes; Yes; 19945
5036; Has-bah; F; 26; Navajo; F; M; Wife; 5050; Yes; Yes; 19946

5037; Hah-dih-chahly; M; 68; Navajo; F; M; Head; 5051; Yes; Yes; 21264
5038; Hah-dih-chahly's wife; F; 63; Navajo; F; M; Wife; 5052; Yes; Yes; 21265
5039; Nah-glih-has-bah; F; 21; Navajo; F; S; Daughter; 5053; Yes; Yes; 21266
5040; Gal-les-soh; M; 17; Navajo; F; S; Son; 5054; Yes; Yes; 21267

5041; Hoh-zone-gih; M; 61; Navajo; F; Wd; Head; 5055; Yes; Yes; 20106

5042; Hosteen-yazzie; M; 59; Navajo; F; M; Head; 5056; Yes; Yes; 20166
5043; Hosteen-yazzie's wife; F; 48; Navajo; F; M; Wife; 5057; Yes; Yes; 20167
5044; Yazzie, Lee; M; 28; Navajo; F; S; Son; 5058; Yes; Yes; 20168
5045; Hosteen-yazzie-bitsih; F; 21; Navajo; F; S; Daughter; 5059; Yes; Yes; 20169
5046; Hosteen-ih; M; 18; Navajo; F; S; Son; 5060; Yes; Yes; 20170
5047; Yazzie, Mary; F; 15; Navajo; F; S; Daughter; 5061; Yes; Yes; 20171
5048; Hosteen-nez; M; 13; Navajo; F; S; Son; 5062; Yes; Yes; 20172
5049; Yazzie, Emma; F; 10; Navajo; F; S; Daughter; 5063; Yes; Yes; 20173
5050; Yah-shih; M; 8; Navajo; F; S; Son; 5064; Yes; Yes; 20174

5051; Hosteen-boh-woh-stinih-bih-adzani[sic]; F; 60; Navajo; F; Wd; Head; 5065; Yes; Yes; 19931 [Name should be Hosteen-boh-woh-atinih-bih-adzani]
5052; Hah-hi-dih-bah; F; 21; Navajo; F; S; Niece; 5066; Yes; Yes; 19932

Census of the **Northern Navajo** reservation of the **Northern Navajo** jurisdiction, as of **April 1**, 19**31,** taken by **Ernest H. Hammond, District**, Superintendent. **in Charge**

**Key:** Number; NAME: Surname, Given; Sex; Birth Year (if given), Age At Last Birthday; Tribe; Degree of Blood; Marital Status; Relationship To Head of Family; Last Census Roll Number; At Jurisdiction Where Enrolled (Yes or No); At Another Jurisdiction; ELSEWHERE: Post office, County, State; Ward (Yes or No); Allotment, Annuity, and Identification Numbers.

5053; Scott, William; M; 26; Navajo; F; S; Nephew; 5067; Yes; Yes; 19933
5054; Scott, Flora; F; 17; Navajo; F; S; Niece; 5068; Yes; Yes; 19934
5055; Aht-sosie, Ben; M; 15; Navajo; F; S; Nephew; 5069; Yes; Yes; 19935
5056; Nah-gee-bah; F; 7; Navajo; F; S; Niece; 5070; Yes; Yes; 19936
5057; Dah-hah-bah; F; 3; Navajo; F; S; Grand-daughter; 5071; Yes; Yes; 19937

5058; Hoh-zone-gih-bitcilli, Charley; M; 52; Navajo; F; M; Head; 5072; Yes; Yes; 20108
5059; Nah-tah-ly-sh-bitsih; F; 40; Navajo; F; M; Wife; 5073; Yes; Yes; 20109
5060; Yazzie, Charley; M; 12; Navajo; F; S; Son; 5074; Yes; Yes; 20110
5061; Charles, Mae; F; 16; Navajo; F; S; Daughter; 5075; Yes; Yes; 20111

5062; Hosteen-yazzie; M; Unk; Navajo; F; M; Head; 5076; Yes; Yes; 19949
5063; Nah-nih-bah; F; 44; Navajo; F; M; Wife; 5077; Yes; Yes; 19950
5064; Hoska-yee-chi-hah-yah; M; 12; Navajo; F; S; Son; 5078; Yes; Yes; 19951
5065; Yee-hih-bah; F; 16; Navajo; F; S; Daughter; 5079; Yes; Yes; 19952
5066; By-lilli, Warren; M; 12; Navajo; F; S; Son; 5080; Yes; Yes; 19953

5067; Hosteen-etsosie; M; 65; Navajo; F; M; Head; 5081; Yes; Yes; 17131
5068; Hosteen-etsosie-ba-adzanih; F; 62; Navajo; F; M; Wife; 5082; Yes; Yes; 17132
5069; Hosteen-etsosie bega; M; 35; Navajo; F; S; Son; 5083; Yes; Yes; 17133

5070; Hosteen-l-bahih-benally, Pretty Boy; M; 35; Navajo; F; M; Head; 5085; Yes; Yes; 23154
5071; Bitsih, Washburn; F; 35; Navajo; F; M; Wife; 5086; Yes; Yes; 23155
5072; Keh-l-yah; M; 10; Navajo; F; S; Son; 5087; Yes; Yes; 23156
5073; Keh-yil-nan-nih-bah; F; 6; Navajo; F; S; Daughter; 5088; Yes; Yes; 23157
5074; Keh-yil-chin-bah; F; 4; Navajo; F; S; Daughter; 5089; Yes; Yes; 23158
5075; Keh-hah-des-bah; F; 16; Navajo; F; S; Sister-in-law; 5090; Yes; Yes; 23159

5076; Hosteen-wo-daih-bega, Dick; M; Unk; Navajo; F; M; Head; 5091; Yes; Yes; 23299
5077; Hosteen-wo-daih-bega, Dick's wife; F; 41; Navajo; F; M; Wife; 5092; Yes; Yes; 23300
5078; Toh-gah; M; 20; Navajo; F; S; Son; 5093; Yes; Yes; 23301
5079; Hoska-yee-no-ah; M; 19; Navajo; F; S; Son; 5094; Yes; Yes; 23302
5080; Johl; M; 18; Navajo; F; S; Son; 5095; Yes; Yes; 23303
5081; Nih-henih-bah; F; 17; Navajo; F; S; Daughter; 5096; Yes; Yes; 23304
5082; Haska-yil-yee-gahl; M; 11; Navajo; F; S; Son; 5097; Yes; Yes; 23305
5083; Haska-yee-chih-dah-des-yah; M; 7; Navajo; F; S; Son; 5098; Yes; Yes; 23306
5084; Yahn-nah-bah; F; 5; Navajo; F; S; Daughter; 5099; Yes; Yes; 23307

Census of the **Northern Navajo** reservation of the **Northern Navajo** jurisdiction, as of **April 1**, 19**31,** taken by **Ernest H. Hammond, District**, Superintendent. **in Charge**

Key: Number; NAME: Surname, Given; Sex; Birth Year (if given), Age At Last Birthday; Tribe; Degree of Blood; Marital Status; Relationship To Head of Family; Last Census Roll Number; At Jurisdiction Where Enrolled (Yes or No); At Another Jurisdiction; ELSEWHERE: Post office, County, State; Ward (Yes or No); Allotment, Annuity, and Identification Numbers.

5085; Hosteen-wo-daih-bih-adzane; F; 74; Navajo; F; Wd; Mother; 5100; Yes; Yes; 23308

5086; Hosteen-hah-tah-yen-bega; M; 41; Navajo; F; M; Head; 5101; Yes; Yes; 23662
5087; Hah-glih-yil-nih-nih-bah; F; 35; Navajo; F; M; Wife; 5102; Yes; Yes; 23663
5088; Des-bah; F; 11; Navajo; F; S; Daughter; 5103; Yes; Yes; 23664

5089; Hosteen-yazzie; M; 45; Navajo; F; M; Head; 5104; Yes; Yes; 23538
5090; Nellie; F; 40; Navajo; F; M; Wife; 5105; Yes; Yes; 23539
5091; Naz-bah, Helen; F; 20; Navajo; F; S; Daughter; 5106; Yes; Yes; 23540
5092; Julius; M; 16; Navajo; F; S; Son; 5107; Yes; Yes; 23541
5093; Nah-tah-yil-nih-nih-yah; M; 11; Navajo; F; S; Son; 5108; Yes; Yes; 23542

5094; Hosteen-nez-bega; M; 61; Navajo; F; M; Head; 5109; Yes; Yes; 30833
5095; Bih-jah-tlol-nih-tael-bisih; F; 68; Navajo; F; M; Wife; 5110; Yes; Yes; 30834
5096; Ak-kee, Alfred; M; 39; Navajo; F; S; Son; 5111; Yes; Yes; 30835
5097; Teddy; M; 25; Navajo; F; S; Son; 5112; Yes; Yes; 30836
5098; Ah-kin-l-bah; F; 18; Navajo; F; S; Daughter; 5113; Yes; Yes; 30837
5099; Es-has-wudt; M; 8; Navajo; F; S; Son; 5114; Yes; Yes; 23933

5100; Hosteen-soh's wife Bah-ahk-thlani-bitsih; F; 63; Navajo; F; Wd; Head; 5115; Yes; Yes; 21376

5101; Hosteen-hal-nih-tay-sih-benally; M; 37; Navajo; F; M; Head; 5116; Yes; Yes; 32269
5102; Kay-ah-kayih-bitsih; F; 36; Navajo; F; M; Wife; 5117; Yes; Yes; 32270
5103; Nah-tay-yil-nal-s-wol; M; 15; Navajo; F; S; Son; 5118; Yes; Yes; 32271
5104; Biz-dee-bah; F; 13; Navajo; F; S; Daughter; 5119; Yes; Yes; 32272
5105; Yil-has-wudt; M; 9; Navajo; F; S; Son; 5120; Yes; Yes; 32273
5106; Ah-kih-hih-bah; F; 8; Navajo; F; S; Daughter; 5121; Yes; Yes; 32274
5107; Al-chih-nih-bah; F; 5; Navajo; F; S; Daughter; 5122; Yes; Yes; 32275
5108; Nah-tah-yee-chih; M; 3; Navajo; F; S; Son; 5123; Yes; Yes; 32276
5109; Salou-sani-bitsih; F; 47; Navajo; F; Div; Mother; 5124; Yes; Yes; 32277
5110; Ath-nez-bah; F; 1; Navajo; F; S; Daughter; 5125; Yes; Yes; 27083

5111; Hosteen-deel; M; Unk; Navajo; F; M; Head; 5126; Yes; Yes; 32292
5112; Bih-nah-atin, Bitsih Jim; F; 26; Navajo; F; M; Wife; 5127; Yes; Yes; 32293
5113; Naz-bah; F; 10; Navajo; F; S; Daughter; 5128; Yes; Yes; 32294
5114; Al-soh-nih-bah; F; 8; Navajo; F; S; Daughter; 5129; Yes; Yes; 32295
5115; Nah-tah-yil-nih-yah; M; 5; Navajo; F; S; Son; 5130; Yes; Yes; 32296
5116; Glih-yah-dez-bah; F; 3; Navajo; F; S; Daughter; 5131; Yes; Yes; 32297

Census of the **Northern Navajo** reservation of the **Northern Navajo** jurisdiction, as of **April 1**, 19**31**, taken by **Ernest H. Hammond, District**, Superintendent. **in Charge**

**Key:** Number; NAME: Surname, Given; Sex; Birth Year (if given), Age At Last Birthday; Tribe; Degree of Blood; Marital Status; Relationship To Head of Family; Last Census Roll Number; At Jurisdiction Where Enrolled (Yes or No); At Another Jurisdiction; ELSEWHERE: Post office, County, State; Ward (Yes or No); Allotment, Annuity, and Identification Numbers.

5117; Nah-dih-chahly-bikis, Jimmy; M; Unk; Navajo; F; M; Head; 5132; Yes; Yes; 21272

5118; Yoh-inih-bitsih; F; Unk; Navajo; F; M; Wife; 5133; Yes; Yes; 21273

5119; Awa-seesie; F; 17; Navajo; F; S; Daughter; 5134; Yes; Yes; 21274
[Name on 1930 Census was Awa-sosie]

5120; Hosteen-clah-bega; M; 32; Navajo; F; M; Head; 5135; Yes; Yes; 26797

5121; Bessie; F; 30; Navajo; F; M; Wife; 5136; Yes; Yes; 26798

5122; Keh-yee-nih-bah; F; 7; Navajo; F; S; Daughter; 5137; Yes; Yes; 26799

5123; Rhodes, Charles; M; 2; Navajo; F; S; Son; 5138; Yes; Yes; 29075

5124; Hah-nih-tayshih-bega; M; 58; Navajo; F; M; Head; 5139; Yes; Yes; 32945

5125; Hosteen-bitsih, Julian; F; 62; Navajo; F; M; Wife; 5140; Yes; Yes; 32946

5126; Joe-Lee; M; 29; Navajo; F; S; Son; 5141; Yes; Yes; 32947

5127; Jerry Harwood; M; 26; Navajo; F; S; Son; 5142; Yes; Yes; 32948

5128; Hah-nih-tayshih-benally; M; 31; Navajo; F; M; Head; 5143; Yes; Yes; 32823

5129; Benally-bitsih, Charley; F; 26; Navajo; F; M: 5144; Wife; Yes; Yes; 32824

5130; Nah-tah-yil-yee-gahl; M; 9; Navajo; F; S; Son; 5145; Yes; Yes; 32825

5131; Al-nah-haz-bah; F; 6; Navajo; F; S; Daughter; 5146; Yes; Yes; 32826

5132; Haska-yil-nih-yah; M; 2; Navajo; F; S; Son; 5147; Yes; Yes; 23827[sic]
[ID No. should be 32827]

5133; Hah-tahly-nah-tlohi-bitsih, Joann; F; 47; Navajo; F; Wd; Head; 5148; Yes; Yes; 32994

5134; Yil-nih-bah, Ruth; F; 7; Navajo; F; S; Daughter; 5149; Yes; Yes; 32995

5135; Hosteen, Jake; M; Unk; Navajo; F; Wd; Head; 5150; Yes; Yes; 32982

5136; Yazzie, Charley; M; 12; Navajo; F; S; Grand-son; 5151; Yes; Yes; 32983

5137; Hosteen-bega, Jimmy; M; 53; Navajo; F; M; Head; 5152; Yes; Yes; 32865

5138; Batoni-bitsees-chilli-bilah; F; Unk; Navajo; F; M; Wife; 5153; Yes; Yes; 32866

5139; Hosteen-bih-adzan, Jimmy; F; 76; Navajo; F; Wd; Head; 5154; Yes; Yes; 32871

5140; Hosteen-uintilli-bega, John Dick; M; 26; Navajo; F; M; Head; 5155; Yes; Yes; 31194

5141; Enc-ah-ighi-bitsoih; F; 20; Navajo; F; M; Wife; 5156; Yes; Yes; 31195

5142; Mina; F; 2; Navajo; F; S; Daughter; 5157; Yes; Yes; 31196

Census of the **Northern Navajo** reservation of the **Northern Navajo** jurisdiction, as of **April 1**, 19**31**, taken by **Ernest H. Hammond, District**, Superintendent. **in Charge**

Key: Number; NAME: Surname, Given; Sex; Birth Year (if given), Age At Last Birthday; Tribe; Degree of Blood; Marital Status; Relationship To Head of Family; Last Census Roll Number; At Jurisdiction Where Enrolled (Yes or No); At Another Jurisdiction; ELSEWHERE: Post office, County, State; Ward (Yes or No); Allotment, Annuity, and Identification Numbers.

5143; Hosteen-la-chee-badoni, Lansing, Frank; M; Unk; Navajo; F; M; Head; 5158; Yes; Yes; 31178
5144; Aramada; F; 24; Navajo; F; M; Wife; 5159; Yes; Yes; 31179
5145; Nah-tah-yil-wudt; M; 4; Navajo; F; S; Son; 5160; Yes; Yes; 31180
5146; Aspaas, Jerry; M; 20; Navajo; F; S; Brother; 5161; Yes; Yes; 31181

5147; Hosteen-neskahi; M; 62; Navajo; F; M; Head; 5162; Yes; Yes; 27721
5148; Hosteen-bah-bih-j-k; F; 42; Navajo; F; M; Wife; 5163; Yes; Yes; 27722
5149; John; M; 24; Navajo; F; S; Son; 5164; Yes; Yes; 27723
5150; Bah; F; 12; Navajo; F; S; Daughter; 5165; Yes; Yes; 27724
5151; Chih-nil-wudt; M; 10; Navajo; F; S; Son; 5166; Yes; Yes; 27725
5152; Glih-bah; F; 3; Navajo; F; S; Daughter; 5167; Yes; Yes; 27726

5153; Hosteen-toh-dih-cheeny; M; 71; Navajo; F; M; Head; 5168; Yes; Yes; 27704
5154; Adzanih-yazzie; F; 84; Navajo; F; M; Wife; 5169; Yes; Yes; 27705

5155; Hah-tahly-sosie-bega; M; 32; Navajo; F; M; Head; 5170; Yes; Yes; 27727
5156; Hosteen-neskahi-bitsih; F; 21; Navajo; F; M; Wife; 5171; Yes; Yes; 27728
5157; Haska-yil-has-wudt; M; 7; Navajo; F; S; Son; 5172; Yes; Yes; 27729
5158; Haska-yee-tah-yah; M; 5; Navajo; F; S; Son; 5173; Yes; Yes; 27730
5159; Gih-diz-bah; F; 4; Navajo; F; S; Daughter; 5174; Yes; Yes; 27746

5160; Hosteen-Uintilli; M; 55; Navajo; F; M; Head; 5175; Yes; Yes; 31182
5161; Yellow Hair's Daughter; F; 24; Navajo; F; M; Wife; 5176; Yes; Yes; 31183
5162; Calvin Coolidge; M; 21; Navajo; F; S; Son; 5177; Yes; Yes; 31184
5163; Hasch-clish-nih-bega, Samuel; M; 18; Navajo; F; S; Son; 5178; Yes; Yes; 31185
5164; Ah-hih-bah, Janette; F; 15; Navajo; F; S; Daughter; 5179; Yes; Yes; 31186
5165; Richard; M; 14; Navajo; F; S; Son; 5180; Yes; Yes; 31187
5166; Keh-yil-se-bah; F; 9; Navajo; F; S; Daughter; 5181; Yes; Yes; 31188
5167; Bah; M; 7; Navajo; F; S; Son; 5182; Yes; Yes; 31189
5168; Bob; M; 3; Navajo; F; S; Son; 5183; Yes; Yes; 31190
5169; Yellow Hair, Pearl; F; 16; Navajo; F; S; Sister-in-law; 5184; Yes; Yes; 31191

5170; Hosteen-yazzie, Domingo; M; 40; Navajo; F; M; Head; 5185; Yes; Yes; 27736
5171; Hosteen-neskahi-bitsih; F; 25; Navajo; F; M; Wife; 5186; Yes; Yes; 27737
5172; Dah-nih-bah; F; 14; Navajo; F; S; Daughter; 5187; Yes; Yes; 27738
5173; Al-chih-nih-bah; F; 10; Navajo; F; S; Daughter; 5188; Yes; Yes; 27739
5174; Nah-bah-bah; F; 8; Navajo; F; S; Daughter; 5189; Yes; Yes; 27740
5175; Kiz-bah; F; 6; Navajo; F; S; Daughter; 5190; Yes; Yes; 27741
5176; Hosteen-Neskihi-bega-wayih; M; 8; Navajo; F; S; Brother-in-law; 5191; Yes; Yes; 27742
5177; Nata-chin-yah; M; 2; Navajo; F; S; Son; 5192; Yes; Yes; 27744

Census of the **Northern Navajo** reservation of the **Northern Navajo** jurisdiction, as of **April 1**, 19**31,** taken by **Ernest H. Hammond, District**, Superintendent. **in Charge**

**Key:** Number; NAME: Surname, Given; Sex; Birth Year (if given), Age At Last Birthday; Tribe; Degree of Blood; Marital Status; Relationship To Head of Family; Last Census Roll Number; At Jurisdiction Where Enrolled (Yes or No); At Another Jurisdiction; ELSEWHERE: Post office, County, State; Ward (Yes or No); Allotment, Annuity, and Identification Numbers.

5178; Bennett, Ray; M; 2; Navajo; F; S; Son; 5193; Yes; Yes; 27747

5179; Hah-dih-jadih-bitsih; F; 32; Navajo; F; Wd; Head; 5194; Yes; Yes; 20380
5180; Nocki-Dinay, Jenny; F; 18; Navajo; F; S; Daughter; 5195; Yes; Yes; 20381
5181; Nocki-Dinay, Samuel; M; 13; Navajo; F; S; Son; 5197; Yes; Yes; 20382
5182; Nocki-Dinay, Julius; M; 11; Navajo; F; S; Son; 5198; Yes; Yes; 20383

5183; Hah-dih-jadih; M; Unk; Navajo; F; M; Head; 5199; Yes; Yes; 20370
5184; Teece-sosie-bitsih; F; Unk; Navajo; F; M; Wife; 5200; Yes; Yes; 20371
5185; Everett; M; 17; Navajo; F; S; Son; 5201; Yes; Yes; 20372
5186; Teece-sosie-, Elliott; M; 15; Navajo; F; S; Son; 5202; Yes; Yes; 20373
5187; Roger; M; 14; Navajo; F; S; Son; 5203; Yes; Yes; 20374
5188; Bih-seesie; M; 11; Navajo; F; S; Son; 5204; Yes; Yes; 20375
5189; Ah-keh-ee-bah; F; 7; Navajo; F; S; Daughter; 5205; Yes; Yes; 20376
5190; Yee-tah-dol-nih; M; 4; Navajo; F; S; Son; 5206; Yes; Yes; 20377
5191; Dinay-bahih; M; 22; Navajo; F; S; Step-son; 5207; Yes; Yes; 20378
5192; Katy; F; 20; Navajo; F; S; Step-daughter; 5208; Yes; Yes; 20379
5193; Teece-sosie-bitsih; M; 25; Navajo; F; S; Son; 5209; Yes; Yes; 20452

5194; Hosteen-toh-lizin-bega; M; 30; Navajo; F; M; Head; 5210; Yes; Yes; 18069
5195; Descheeny-bitih; F; 26; Navajo; F; M; Wife; 5211; Yes; Yes; 18070
5196; Dinay-lachee; M; 7; Navajo; F; S; Son; 5212; Yes; Yes; 18071
5197; Haska-yah-nas-wudt; M; 6; Navajo; F; S; Son; 5213; Yes; Yes; 18072

5198; Hah-tahly-bega; M; 27; Navajo; F; M; Head; 5214; Yes; Yes; 28081
5199; Descheeny-sahi-bitsih; F; 24; Navajo; F; M; Wife; 5215; Yes; Yes; 28082
5200; Yah-dey-yah; F[sic]; 5; Navajo; F; S; Son; 5216; Yes; Yes; 28083
  [Should be male]
5201; Adzan-l-bahin; F; 4; Navajo; F; S; Daughter; 5217; Yes; Yes; 28084
5202; Baby Joan; F; 2; Navajo; F; S; Daughter; 5218; Yes; Yes; 28085
5203; Dean; M; 14; Navajo; F; S; Brother-in-law; 5219; Yes; Yes; 28086

5204; Hosteen-soh-bega, Joe; M; 31; Navajo; F; M; Head; 5220; Yes; Yes; 27068
5205; Adobe-bitsoih; F; 29; Navajo; F; M; Wife; 5221; Yes; Yes; 27069
5206; Nih-yah; M; 8; Navajo; F; S; Son; 5222; Yes; Yes; 27070
5207; Nah-tah-yee-chih-nel-wudt; M; 4; Navajo; F; S; Son; 5223; Yes; Yes; 27071

5208; Mother and father enrolled at Western Navajo Agency 5224; Hosteen-Nationia Head; 70147
5209; Luke; M; 24; Navajo; F; Wd; Son; 5225; Yes; Yes; 18299
5210; Askeez-yazzie; M; 5; Navajo; F; S; Grand-son; 5226; Yes; Yes; 18300

Census of the **Northern Navajo** reservation of the **Northern Navajo** jurisdiction, as of **April 1** , 19**31**, taken by **Ernest H. Hammond, District**, Superintendent. **in Charge**

**Key:** Number; NAME: Surname, Given; Sex; Birth Year (if given), Age At Last Birthday; Tribe; Degree of Blood; Marital Status; Relationship To Head of Family; Last Census Roll Number; At Jurisdiction Where Enrolled (Yes or No); At Another Jurisdiction; ELSEWHERE: Post office, County, State; Ward (Yes or No); Allotment, Annuity, and Identification Numbers.

5211; Inky-tohsonih-bega's wife Bay-ilchee-bitsih; F; 21; Navajo; F; M; Wife; 5228; Yes; Yes; 17863

5212; Inky, John; M; 4; Navajo; F; S; Son; 5229; Yes; Yes; 17864

5213; Iltan-zesihgi; M; 45; Navajo; F; M; Head; 5230; No; McElmo, Colo., San Juan, Utah; Yes; 19251

5214; Nocki-Dinay-bitsih; F; 29; Navajo; F; M; Wife; 5231; No; McElmo, Colo., San Juan, Utah; Yes; 19252

5215; Iltan-zeeihgi, Jess; M; 22; Navajo; F; S; Son; 5232; No; McElmo, Colo., San Juan, Utah; Yes; 19253

5216; Iltan-zeeihgi, Louise; F; 18; Navajo; F; S; Daughter; 5233; No; McElmo, Colo., San Juan, Utah; Yes; 19254

5217; Seesce; F; 11; Navajo; F; S; Daughter; 5234; No; McElmo, Colo., San Juan, Utah; Yes; 19255

5218; Bah; F; 8; Navajo; F; S; Daughter; 5235; No; McElmo, Colo., San Juan, Utah; Yes; 19256

5219; Tah-des-bah; F; 5; Navajo; F; S; Daughter; 5236; No; McElmo, Colo., San Juan, Utah; Yes; 19257

5220; Jay Gould, Bitcilli; M; 48; Navajo; F; M; Head; 5237; Yes; Yes; 24887

5221; Yil-nih-naz-bah; F; 33; Navajo; F; M; Wife; 5238; Yes; Yes; 24888

5222; Kay-yah; M; 12; Navajo; F; S; Son; 5239; Yes; Yes; 24889

5223; Eee-dee-bah; F; 9; Navajo; F; S; Daughter; 5240; Yes; Yes; 24890

5224; Mary; F; 22; Navajo; F; S; Daughter; 5241; Yes; Yes; 24938

5225; Mae; F; 20; Navajo; F; S; Daughter; 5242; Yes; Yes; 24939

5226; Tah-yazzie, Alex; M; 18; Navajo; F; S; Son; 5243; Yes; Yes; 24940

5227; Bih-nih-ziz-bah, Cora; F; 15; Navajo; F; S; Daughter; 5244; Yes; Yes; 24941

5228; Beth; F; 11; Navajo; F; S; Daughter; 5245; Yes; Yes; 24942

5229; Jay-Gould, bega; M; 28; Navajo; F; M; Head; 5246; Yes; Yes; 23798

5230; Yil-haz-bah; F; 27; Navajo; F; M; Wife; 5247; Yes; Yes; 23799

5231; Gilh-yil-hah-ziz-bah; F; 4; Navajo; F; S; Daughter; 5248; Yes; Yes; 23800

5232; Jelly, Cyrus; M; Unk; Navajo; F; M; Head; 5249; No; McElmo, Colo., San Juan, Utah; Yes; 18985

5233; Mazih, Cyrus Jelly's wife; F; 23; Navajo; F; M; Wife; 5250; No; McElmo, Colo., San Juan, Utah; Yes; 18986

5234; Joely; M; 28; Navajo; F; M; Head; 5251; No; McElmo, Colo., San Juan, Utah; Yes; 18963

5235; Joely, Mary; F; 22; Navajo; F; M; Wife; 5252; No; McElmo, Colo., San Juan, Utah; Yes; 18964

Census of the **Northern Navajo** reservation of the **Northern Navajo** jurisdiction, as of **April 1**, 19**31**, taken by **Ernest H. Hammond, District**, Superintendent. **in Charge**

**Key:** Number; NAME: Surname, Given; Sex; Birth Year (if given), Age At Last Birthday; Tribe; Degree of Blood; Marital Status; Relationship To Head of Family; Last Census Roll Number; At Jurisdiction Where Enrolled (Yes or No); At Another Jurisdiction; ELSEWHERE: Post office, County, State; Ward (Yes or No); Allotment, Annuity, and Identification Numbers.

5236; Hoska-yee-chih-hah-yah; F; 3; Navajo; F; S; Daughter; 5253; No; McElmo, Colo., San Juan, Utah; Yes; 18965

5237; Jim Buck; M; 45; Navajo; F; M; Head; 5254; Yes; Yes; 30807
5238; Hosteen-nez-benally; F; 41; Navajo; F; M; Wife; 5255; Yes; Yes; 30808
5239; Nah-tah-yee-nal-wohl; M; 24; Navajo; F; S; Son; 5256; Yes; Yes; 30809
5240; Nez, Marion; F; 18; Navajo; F; S; Daughter; 5257; Yes; Yes; 30810
5241; Ah-hih-naz-bah; F; 14; Navajo; F; S; Daughter; 5258; Yes; Yes; 30811
5242; Haska-yil-chil-wudt; M; 12; Navajo; F; S; Son; 5259; Yes; Yes; 30812
5243; Chih-yil-wohl; M; 10; Navajo; F; S; Son; 5260; Yes; Yes; 30813
5244; Nah-tah-yil-nih-nih-yah; M; 8; Navajo; F; S; Son; 5261; Yes; Yes; 30814
5245; Chih-deyah; M; 5; Navajo; F; S; Son; 5262; Yes; Yes; 30815
5246; Haska-yil-des-wudt; M; 3; Navajo; F; S; Son; 5263; Yes; Yes; 30816
5247; Haska-yee-nah-gahl; M; 23; Navajo; F; S; Brother; 5264; Yes; Yes; 30818

5248; Joe, Charley; M; 44; Navajo; F; M; Head; 5265; Yes; Yes; 30782
5249; Bah-glih-yil-ee-bah; F; 48; Navajo; F; M; Wife; 5266; Yes; Yes; 30783

5250; John, Charley; M; 25; Navajo; F; M; Head; 5267; Yes; Yes; 30771
5251; Taz-bah; F; 19; Navajo; F; M; Wife; 5268; Yes; Yes; 30772
5252; Nah-tah-yil-has-wudt; M; 4; Navajo; F; S; Son; 5269; Yes; Yes; 30773
5253; Charley-yazzie; M; 2; Navajo; F; S; Son; 5270; Yes; Yes; 30774

5254; Joe Bikis; M; 43; Navajo; F; M; Head; 5271; Yes; Yes; 27554
5255; Yee-zaz-bah; F; 56; Navajo; F; M; Wife; 5272; Yes; Yes; 27555
5256; Glih-yee-deh-bah; F; 17; Navajo; F; S; Step-daughter; 5273; Yes; Yes; 27556
5257; Bil-nih-ziz-bah; F; 9; Navajo; F; S; Daughter; 5274; Yes; Yes; 27557
5258; Glih-nih-ziz-bah; F; 3; Navajo; F; S; Step-daughter; 5275; Yes; Yes; 26880

5259; Young, Frank; Full; White; Head
5260; Joely, Joe Young, Frank M.; F; 30; Navajo; F; M; Wife; 5277; Yes; Yes; 18613
5261; Young, Leroy Frederick; M; 3; Navajo; 1/4+; S; Son; 5278; Yes; Yes; 18615
5262; Young, Frank Evan; M; 17; Navajo; 1/4+; S; Son; 5279; Yes; Yes; 18614
5263; Young, Mary Mae; F; 2; Navajo; 1/4+; S; Daughter; 5280; Yes; Yes; 31257
5264; Young, William Henry; M; 6/12; Navajo; 1/4+; S; Son; [Blank]; Yes; Yes; 18616

5265; Johnson, Harry; M; 28; Navajo; F; M; Head; 5281; Yes; Yes; 30301
5266; Mary; F; 19; Navajo; F; M; Wife; 5282; Yes; Yes; 30302

5267; John, Harry; M; 31; Navajo; F; M; Head; 5283; Yes; Yes; 30719
5268; Grace; F; 23; Navajo; F; M; Wife; 5284; Yes; Yes; 30720

Census of the **Northern Navajo** reservation of the **Northern Navajo** jurisdiction, as of **April 1** , 19**31,** taken by **Ernest H. Hammond, District**, Superintendent. **in Charge**

**Key:** Number; NAME: Surname, Given; Sex; Birth Year (if given), Age At Last Birthday; Tribe; Degree of Blood; Marital Status; Relationship To Head of Family; Last Census Roll Number; At Jurisdiction Where Enrolled (Yes or No); At Another Jurisdiction; ELSEWHERE: Post office, County, State; Ward (Yes or No); Allotment, Annuity, and Identification Numbers.

5269;   Johnson, Edwin; M; 35; Navajo; F; M; Head; 5285; Yes; Yes; 24867
5270;   Mary; F; 33; Navajo; F; M; Wife; 5286; Yes; Yes; 24868
5271;   Frank; M; 16; Navajo; F; S; Son; 5287; Yes; Yes; 24869
5272;   Frances; F; 14; Navajo; F; S; Daughter; 5288; Yes; Yes; 24870
5273;   Peter; M; 9; Navajo; F; S; Son; 5289; Yes; Yes; 24871
5274;   Lucy; F; 3; Navajo; F; S; Daughter; 5290; Yes; Yes; 24872
5275;   Martha Rosie; F; 6/12; Navajo; F; S; Daughter; 5291[sic]; Yes; Yes; 25346
[This number should not be here because this child was not on the last census.]

5276;   John, Frank; M; 30; Navajo; F; M; Head; 5291; Yes; Yes; 23559
5277;   Keh-yee-hih-bah; F; 26; Navajo; F; M; Wife; 5292; Yes; Yes; 23560
5278;   Haska-yee-chih-calth; M; 2; Navajo; F; S; Son; 5293; Yes; Yes; 23924

5279;   John, Billy; M; 44; Navajo; F; M; Head; 5294; Yes; Yes; 21295
5280;   Bah; F; 35; Navajo; F; M; Wife; 5295; Yes; Yes; 21296
5281;   Dinay-l-chee; M; 19; Navajo; F; S; Son; 5296; Yes; Yes; 21297
5282;   Dorothy; F; 17; Navajo; F; S; Daughter; 5297; Yes; Yes; 21298
5283;   Kay-yil-nih-bah; F; 6; Navajo; F; S; Step-daughter; 5298; Yes; Yes; 21299

5284;   Johnson, Enos; M; Unk; Navajo; F; Wd; Head; 5299; Yes; Yes; 23624
5285;   Bimah, Woody; F; 59; Navajo; F; Wd.; Mother; 5300; Yes; Yes; 23625
5286;   Haska-yil-nah-hah-gah, Roy; M; 21; Navajo; F; S; Brother; 5301; Yes; Yes; 23626
5287;   Woody, Clara; F; 18; Navajo; F; S; Sister; 5302; Yes; Yes; 23627
5288;   Yee-nih-bah; F; 14; Navajo; F; S; Sister; 5303; Yes; Yes; 23628

5289;   Johnson, Jordan; M; 31; Navajo; F; M; Head; 5304; Yes; Yes; 31028
5290;   Cleo; F; 26; Navajo; F; M; Wife; 5305; Yes; Yes; 31029

5291;   Johnson, Herbert; M; 30; Navajo; F; M; Head; 5307; Yes; Yes; 26643
5292;   Joely; F; 26; Navajo; F; M; Wife; 5308; Yes; Yes; 26644
5293;   Mabel; F; 3; Navajo; F; S; Daughter; 5309; Yes; Yes; 26645

5294;   Johnson, Carl; M; 25; Navajo; F; M; Head; 5310; Yes; Yes; 26651
5295;   Dinay-deel-bitsih; F; 20; Navajo; F; M; Wife; 5311; Yes; Yes; 26652

5296;   Jones, Paul; M; 34; Navajo; F; M; Head; 5312; No; McElmo, Colo., San Juan, Utah; Yes; 19261
5297;   Jones, Edith; F; 29; Navajo; F; M; Wife; 5313; No; McElmo, Colo., San Juan, Utah; Yes; 19262
5298;   Natah-yee-chi-nil-wudt; M; 6; Navajo; F; S; Son; 5314; No; McElmo, Colo., San Juan, Utah; Yes; 19263

Census of the **Northern Navajo** reservation of the **Northern Navajo** jurisdiction, as of **April 1**, 19**31,** taken by **Ernest H. Hammond, District**, Superintendent. **in Charge**

**Key:** Number; NAME: Surname, Given; Sex; Birth Year (if given), Age At Last Birthday; Tribe; Degree of Blood; Marital Status; Relationship To Head of Family; Last Census Roll Number; At Jurisdiction Where Enrolled (Yes or No); At Another Jurisdiction; ELSEWHERE: Post office, County, State; Ward (Yes or No); Allotment, Annuity, and Identification Numbers.

5299; Eoe-des-pah[sic]; M; 2; Navajo; F; S; Son; 5315; No; McElmo, Colo., San Juan, Utah; Yes; 19511 [Name could be Eee-des-pah]

5300; Jones, Thomas; M; Unk; Navajo; F; M; Head; 5316; No; McElmo, Colo., San Juan, Utah; Yes; 18987
5301; Jones, Jane; F; Unk; Navajo; F; M; Wife; 5317; No; McElmo, Colo., San Juan, Utah; Yes; 18988
5302; Jones, Clinton; M; Unk; Navajo; F; S; Son; 5318; No; McElmo, Colo., San Juan, Utah; Yes; 18989
5303; Jones, Keh; F; Unk; Navajo; F; S; Step-daughter; 5319; No; McElmo, Colo., San Juan, Utah; Yes; 18990
5304; Whitehorse, Beulah; F; Unk; Navajo; F; S; Step-daughter; 5320; No; McElmo, Colo., San Juan, Utah; Yes; 18991

5305; Jones, Tom Jr.; M; 36; Navajo; F; M; Head; 5321; No; McElmo, Colo., San Juan, Utah; Yes; 18830
5306; Nocki-dinay-Uienth-nez-bitsih; F; 23; Navajo; F; M; Wife; 5322; No; McElmo, Colo., San Juan, Utah; Yes; 18831
5307; Jones, Nellie; F; 8; Navajo; F; S; Daughter; 5323; No; McElmo, Colo., San Juan, Utah; Yes; 18832
5308; Jones, Harry; M; 4; Navajo; V; S; Son; 5324; No; McElmo, Colo., San Juan, Utah; Yes; 18833
5309; Adzanih-yo-oh; F; 62; Navajo; F; Wd; Mother; 5325; No; McElmo, Colo., San Juan, Utah; Yes; 18834
5310; Glih-yaz; F; 20; Navajo; F; Wd; Sister; 5326; No; McElmo, Colo., San Juan, Utah; Yes; 18835
5311; Toh-des-wudt; M; 10; Navajo; F; S; Nephew; 5328; No; McElmo, Colo., San Juan, Utah; Yes; 18836
5312; Jones, Clinton; M; 19; Navajo; F; S; Nephew; 5327; No; McElmo, Colo., San Juan, Utah; Yes; 18837

5313; Jones, Albert; M; 58; Navajo; F; M; Head; 5329; No; McElmo, Colo., San Juan, Utah; Yes; 18978
5314; Albert Jone's[sic] wife; F; 28; Navajo; F; M; Wife; 5330; No; McElmo, Colo., San Juan, Utah; Yes; 18979 [Name is probably Albert Jones' wife]
5315; Jones, Jack; M; 12; Navajo; F; S; Son; 5331; No; McElmo, Colo., San Juan, Utah; Yes; 18980
5316; Jones, Harry; M; 6; Navajo; F; S; Son; 5332; No; McElmo, Colo., San Juan, Utah; Yes; 18981
5317; Jones, (Nuk); M; 3; Navajo; F; S; Son; 5333; No; McElmo, Colo., San Juan, Utah; Yes; 18982

Census of the **Northern Navajo** reservation of the **Northern Navajo** jurisdiction, as of **April 1**, 19**31,** taken by **Ernest H. Hammond, District**, Superintendent. **in Charge**

5318; Hosteen-bihnahatinih-bitsih, Clinton Jones' wife; F; 25; Navajo; F; Wd; Head; 5334; Yes; Yes; 17395

5319; Beleen-dihjadih; M; 21; Navajo; F; S; Brother-in-law; 5335; Yes; Yes; 17396

5320; Gathle; M; 17; Navajo; F; S; Brother-in-law; 5336; Yes; Yes; 17397

5321; Eih-noth-inthle; M; 15; Navajo; F; S; Brother-in-law; 5337; Yes; Yes; 17398

5322; Jones, Tom; M; 32; Navajo; F; M; Head; 5338; Yes; Yes; 30969

5323; Benally-bitsih; F; 29; Navajo; F; M; Wife; 5339; Yes; Yes; 30970

5324; Nah-tah-yah-nih-yah; M; 6; Navajo; F; S; Son; 5340; Yes; Yes; 30971

5325; Hah-dez-bah; F; 4; Navajo; F; S; Daughter; 5341; Yes; Yes; 30972

5326; Benally-bega, Funny; M; 24; Navajo; F; S; Brother-in-law; 5342; Yes; Yes; 30973

5327; Benally-bega, Dinay-soh; M; 19; Navajo; F; S; Brother-in-law; 5343; Yes; Yes; 30974

5328; Nah-tah-yil-hah-dih-yah; M; 3; Navajo; F; S; Son; 5344; Yes; Yes; 31268

5329; Jumbo Bitcilli; M; 34; Navajo; F; M; Head; 5345; Yes; Yes; 25061

5330; Hosteen-clah-bitsih; F; 51; Navajo; F; M; Wife; 5346; Yes; Yes; 25062

5331; Lewis, John; M; 27; Navajo; F; S; Step-son; 5347; Yes; Yes; 25063

5332; Juanita; F; 25; Navajo; F; M; 2nd wife; 5348; Yes; Yes; 25064

5333; Eskee-yazzie; M; 19; Navajo; F; S; Step-son; 5349; Yes; Yes; 25065

5334; Jacob; M; 16; Navajo; F; S; Step-son; 5350; Yes; Yes; 25066

5335; Annie; F; 9; Navajo; F; S; Daughter; 5351; Yes; Yes; 25067

5336; Lewis; M; 4; Navajo; F; S; Son; 5352; Yes; Yes; 25068

5337; Julian, Bitsoih; M; 4; Navajo; F; M; Head; 5353; Yes; Yes; 23133

5338; Mike, Bitsih; F; 21; Navajo; F; M; Wife; 5354; Yes; Yes; 23134

5339; Haska-yahn-yil-wohl; M; 4; Navajo; F; S; Son; 5355; Yes; Yes; 23135

5340; Nah-bah; F; 67; Navajo; F; Wd; Aunt-in-law; 5356; Yes; Yes; 23136

5341; Keh-yil-hah-nih-bah; F; 20; Navajo; F; S; Niece-in-law; 5357; Yes; Yes; 23137

5342; Jim, George; M; 37; Navajo; F; M; Head; 5359; Yes; Yes; 32960

5343; Seese-pishih-bitsih, Katherine; F; 31; Navajo; F; M; Wife; 5360; Yes; Yes; 32961

5344; Elizabeth Grace; F; 5; Navajo; F; S; Daughter; 5361; Yes; Yes; 32962

5345; Ray Junior; M; 3; Navajo; F; S; Son; 5362; Yes; Yes; 32963

5346; Jaquez, Sarah; F; 16; Navajo; F; S; Head; 5363; Yes; Yes; 33000

5347; John Joe; M; 25; Navajo; F; M; Head; 5364; Yes; Yes; 30700

5348; Hosteen-nez-benally-ah-in; F; 23; Navajo; F; M; Wife; 5365; Yes; Yes; 32309

Census of the **Northern Navajo** reservation of the **Northern Navajo** jurisdiction, as of **April 1**, 19**31,** taken by **Ernest H. Hammond, District**, Superintendent. **in Charge**

**Key:** Number; NAME: Surname, Given; Sex; Birth Year (if given), Age At Last Birthday; Tribe; Degree of Blood; Marital Status; Relationship To Head of Family; Last Census Roll Number; At Jurisdiction Where Enrolled (Yes or No); At Another Jurisdiction; ELSEWHERE: Post office, County, State; Ward (Yes or No); Allotment, Annuity, and Identification Numbers.

5349;   Joe, John; M; 28; Navajo; F; M; Head; 5366; Yes; Yes; 31225
5350;   Bitsoue; F; 21; Navajo; F; M; Wife; 5367; Yes; Yes; 31226
5351;   Haska-kah-yah-nih-yah; M; 3; Navajo; F; S; Son; 5368; Yes; Yes; 31227

5352;   Bitsee, Jake; M; Unk; Navajo; F; M; Head; 5369; Yes; Yes; 23946
5353;   Ka-tah-nas-bah; F; Unk; Navajo; F; M; Wife; 5370; Yes; Yes; 23947
5354;   Akee-be-yazzie; M; 2; Navajo; F; S; Son; 5371; Yes; Yes; 23948

5355;   Jake Samuel; M; Unk; Navajo; F; S; Head; 5372; Yes; Yes; 23909

5356;   Kadt-dahshih-jah; M; 58; Navajo; F; M; Head; 5373; Yes; Yes; 30612
5357;   Dinay-yazzie-bitsih; F; Unk; Navajo; F; M; Wife; 5374; Yes; Yes; 30613
5358;   Nah-tah-yil-nah-bah; M; 18; Navajo; F; S; Son; 5375; Yes; Yes; 30614
5359;   Ella wene; F; 21; Navajo; F; S; Daughter; 5376; Yes; Yes; 30615
5360;   Sueih; M; 13; Navajo; F; S; Son; 5377; Yes; Yes; 30616
5361;   Dah-nez-gah; M; 12; Navajo; F; S; Son; 5378; Yes; Yes; 30617
5362;   Yah-nih-han-haz-bah; F; 8; Navajo; F; S; Daughter; 5379; Yes; Yes; 30618

5363;   Kadt-dah-shih-jah-bega; M; Unk; Navajo; F; M; Head; 5380; Yes; Yes; 30918
5364;   Benally-bitsih; F; 21; Navajo; F; M; Wife; 5381; Yes; Yes; 30919
5365;   Haska-dah-yah; M; 2; Navajo; F; S; Son; 5382; Yes; Yes; 31269

5366;   Kadt-ee-ahih-bih-bizee, Scott[sic]; F; 27; Navajo; F; S; Head; 5383; Yes; Yes; 30254

5367;   Kadt-ee-ahih-bega; M; 32; Navajo; F; M; Head; 5384; Yes; Yes; 30252
5368;   Zah-nez-bitsih; F; 20; Navajo; F; M; Wife; 5385; Yes; Yes; 30253

5369;   Kadt-ee-badoni-ahih; M; 39; Navajo; F; M; Head; 5386; Yes; Yes; 30246
5370;   Kadt-ee-ahih-bitsih; F; 41; Navajo; F; M; Wife; 5387; Yes; Yes; 30247
5371;   Foster; M; 12; Navajo; F; S; Son; 5388; Yes; Yes; 30248
5372;   Wohl-bah; M; 8; Navajo; F; S; Son; 5389; Yes; Yes; 30249
5373;   Haska-yee-chih-nil-wudt; M; 3; Navajo; F; S; Son; 5390; Yes; Yes; 30250
5374;   Kadt-ee-ahih-bih-adzan; F; 74; Navajo; F; Wd; Mother-in-law; 5391; Yes; Yes; 30251

5375;   Kadt-ee-ahih-bikis; M; 61; Navajo; F; M; Head; 5392; Yes; Yes; 30227
5376;   Bilah-gonah-yee-ishin-bit-sih[sic]; F; 41; Navajo; F; M; Wife; 5393; Yes; Yes; 30228   [Name is probably Bilah-gonah-yee-ishin-bitsih]
5377;   Sadie; F; 21; Navajo; F; S; Daughter; 5394; Yes; Yes; 30229
5378;   Pauline; F; 10; Navajo; F; S; Daughter; 5395; Yes; Yes; 30231
5379;   Rosalind[sic]; F; 9; Navajo; F; S; Daughter; 5396; Yes; Yes; 30232
         [Name is probably Rosaline]

Census of the **Northern Navajo** reservation of the **Northern Navajo** jurisdiction, as of **April 1**, 19**31**, taken by **Ernest H. Hammond, District**, Superintendent. **in Charge**

**Key:** Number; NAME: Surname, Given; Sex; Birth Year (if given), Age At Last Birthday; Tribe; Degree of Blood; Marital Status; Relationship To Head of Family; Last Census Roll Number; At Jurisdiction Where Enrolled (Yes or No); At Another Jurisdiction; ELSEWHERE: Post office, County, State; Ward (Yes or No); Allotment, Annuity, and Identification Numbers.

5380; Yee-kih-nih-bah; F; 6; Navajo; F; S; Daughter; 5397; Yes; Yes; 30233
5381; Mary; F; 2; Navajo; F; S; Daughter; 5398; Yes; Yes; 30234
5382; Nah-glih-yee-haz-bah; F; 8; Navajo; F; S; Daughter; 5399; Yes; Yes; 30235

5383; Kadt-ee-eye-bitah; M; 42; Navajo; F; M; Head; 5400; Yes; Yes; 22538
5384; Seh-ah-tah-badoni-bihdazih; F; 37; Navajo; F; M; Wife; 5401; Yes; Yes; 22539
5385; Nah-haz-bah; F; 18; Navajo; F; S; Daughter; 5402; Yes; Yes; 22540
5386; Lucille; F; 14; Navajo; F; S; Daughter; [Blank]; Yes; Yes; 22541
5387; Hoska-yee-dah-nihyah; M; 11; Navajo; F; S; Son; 5403; Yes; Yes; 22542
5388; Yil-nih-bah; F; 7; Navajo; F; S; Daughter; 5404; Yes; Yes; 22543
5389; Haska-yil-dah-yah; M; 4; Navajo; F; S; Son; 5405; Yes; Yes; 21671

5390; Kadt-ee-ahih-bega; M; 48; Navajo; F; M; Head; 5406; Yes; Yes; 29225
5391; Adaki-sosie-bitsih; F; 39; Navajo; F; M; Wife; 5407; Yes; Yes; 29226
5392; Henry; M; 22; Navajo; F; S; Son; 5408; Yes; Yes; 29227
5393; Zannie-sosie; F; 11; Navajo; F; S; Daughter; 5409; Yes; Yes; 29228
5394; Kase-woody; M; 10; Navajo; F; S; Son; 5410; Yes; Yes; 29229
5395; Bay-a-zannie; F; 8; Navajo; F; S; Daughter; 5411; Yes; Yes; 29230
5396; Yil-dez-bah; F; 2; Navajo; F; S; Daughter; 5412; Yes; Yes; 29232

5397; Kadt-ee-ahih-bega; M; 39; Navajo; F; M; Head; 5413; Yes; Yes; 29339
5398; Dinay-nez-bitsih; F; 31; Navajo; F; M; Wife; 5414; Yes; Yes; 29340
5399; Nah-haz-bah; F; 16; Navajo; F; S; Daughter; 5415; Yes; Yes; 29341
5400; May; F; 14; Navajo; F; S; Daughter; 5416; Yes; Yes; 29342
5401; Al-neh-hah-bah; F; 11; Navajo; F; S; Daughter; 5417; Yes; Yes; 29343
5402; Tah-zonih; M; 8; Navajo; F; S; Son; 5418; Yes; Yes; 29344
5403; Yee-gah-dez-bah; F; 4; Navajo; F; S; Daughter; 5419; Yes; Yes; 29345
5404; Haska-hal-wudt; M; 25; Navajo; F; S; Brother-in-law; 5420; Yes; Yes; 29346
5405; Yil-hon-nas-bah; F; 3; Navajo; F; S; Daughter; 5421; Yes; Yes; 29386

5406; Keedah, Marie; F; 32; Navajo; F; Wd; Head; 5422; Yes; Yes; 31020
5407; Ann Isobel; F; 9; Navajo; F; S; Daughter; 5423; Yes; Yes; 31021
5408; Evelyn Elizabeth; F; 7; Navajo; F; S; Daughter; 5424; Yes; Yes; 31022

5409; Keese-annih-bitsih; F; 61; Navajo; F; Wd; Head; 5425; Yes; Yes; 21598
5410; Hoska-yee-nah-gah; M; 20; Navajo; F; S; Son; 5426; Yes; Yes; 21599
5411; Toh-sonie, Bruce; M; 16; Navajo; F; S; Son; 5427; Yes; Yes; 21600
5412; Nah-tah-yee-tahs-wudt; M; 10; Navajo; F; S; Son; 5428; Yes; Yes; 21601

5413; Kee-ah-annih-soh-bikis; M; 32; Navajo; F; M; Head; 5429; Yes; Yes; 26989
5414; Nah-gee-bah; F; 26; Navajo; F; M; Wife; 5430; Yes; Yes; 26990
5415; Keh-hah-bah; F; 7; Navajo; F; S; Daughter; 5431; Yes; Yes; 26991

Census of the **Northern Navajo** reservation of the **Northern Navajo**
jurisdiction, as of **April 1**, 19**31**, taken by **Ernest H. Hammond, District**,
Superintendent. **in Charge**

**Key:** Number; NAME: Surname, Given; Sex; Birth Year (if given), Age At Last Birthday; Tribe; Degree of
Blood; Marital Status; Relationship To Head of Family; Last Census Roll Number; At Jurisdiction Where
Enrolled (Yes or No); At Another Jurisdiction; ELSEWHERE: Post office, County, State; Ward (Yes or No);
Allotment, Annuity, and Identification Numbers.

5416; Tah-naz-bah; F; 5; Navajo; F; S; Daughter; 5432; Yes; Yes; 26992
5417; Nah-glih-yil-nah-bah; F; 3; Navajo; F; S; Daughter; 5433; Yes; Yes; 26993
5418; Yah-niph-bah; F; 2; Navajo; F; S; Daughter; 5434; Yes; Yes; 27078
5419; Yah-in-daz-bah; F; 2; Navajo; F; S; Daughter; 5435; Yes; Yes; 27077

5420; Kee-ah-annih-sosie; M; 24; Navajo; F; M; Head; 5436; Yes; Yes; 26940
5421; Glih-yil-ee-bah; F; 31; Navajo; F; M; Wife; 5437; Yes; Yes; 26941
5422; Keh-yil-ta-e; M; 7; Navajo; F; S; Son; 5438; Yes; Yes; 26942
5423; Yahn-nah-nih-bah; F; 3; Navajo; F; S; Daughter; 5439; Yes; Yes; 26943

5424; Keh-ilth-inni-bega; M; 31; Navajo; F; M; Head; 5440; Yes; Yes; 25196
5425; Al-soh-dez-bah; F; 25; Navajo; F; M; Wife; 5441; Yes; Yes; 25197
5426; Bigman, John; M; 9; Navajo; F; S; Step-son; 5442; Yes; Yes; 25198

5427; Keeahannih-nez-bitah, Captain Bogus; M; 31; Navajo; F; M; Head; 5443; Yes;
Yes; 17933
5428; Glin-yil-hah-bah; F; 18; Navajo; F; M; Wife; 5444; Yes; Yes; 17934
5429; Geronimo; M; 2; Navajo; F; S; Son; 5445; Yes; Yes; 18236

5430; Keh-ilth-inni; M; 55; Navajo; F; M; Head; 5446; Yes; Yes; 25182
5431; Hosteen-clash-cheeih-bitscih[sic]; F; 46; Navajo; F; M; Wife; Yes; Yes; 25183
[Name is probably Hosteen-clash-cheeih-bitsoih]
5432; Jennette; F; 24; Navajo; F; S; Daughter; Yes; Yes; 25184
5433; Nih-chee; M; 15; Navajo; F; S; Son; Yes; Yes; 25185
5434; Hosteen-clash-cheeih-bitsoih; F; 44; Navajo; F; M; 2nd wife; 5450; Yes; Yes;
25186
5435; Yil-nah-bah; F; 17; Navajo; F; S; Daughter; 5451; Yes; Yes; 25187
5436; Opal; F; 14; Navajo; F; S; Daughter; 5452; Yes; Yes; 25188
5437; Nah-naz-bah; F; 9; Navajo; F; S; Daughter; 5453; Yes; Yes; 25190
5438; Dah-naz-bah; F; 6; Navajo; F; S; Daughter; 5454; Yes; Yes; 25191

5439; Kee-ahannih-nez; M; 51; Navajo; F; M; Head; 5455; Yes; Yes; 17952
5440; Kee-ah-annih-nez's wife; F; 29; Navajo; F; M; Wife; 5456; Yes; Yes; 17953
5441; Hoska-yilt-ee-dale; M; 26; Navajo; F; S; Brother-in-law; 5457; Yes; Yes;
17954
5442; Aholtaih-soh; M; 30; Navajo; F; S; Brother-in-law; 5458; Yes; Yes; 17955
5443; Kee-ah-annih-nez-, Miles; M; 21; Navajo; F; S; Brother-in-law; 5459; Yes;
Yes; 17956
5444; Keeah-annih-nez, Allen Kneale; M; 17; Navajo; F; S; Brother-in-law; 5460;
Yes; Yes; 17957
5445; Yee-aah-bah; F; 7; Navajo; F; S; Daughter; 5461; Yes; Yes; 17959
5446; Zannie; F; 20; Navajo; F; Wd; Sister-in-law; 5462; Yes; Yes; 17960
5447; Nan-bahih; F; 3; Navajo; F; S; Niece-in-law; 5463; Yes; Yes; 17961

Census of the **Northern Navajo** reservation of the **Northern Navajo** jurisdiction, as of **April 1**, 1931, taken by **Ernest H. Hammond, District**, Superintendent. **in Charge**

**Key:** Number; NAME: Surname, Given; Sex; Birth Year (if given), Age At Last Birthday; Tribe; Degree of Blood; Marital Status; Relationship To Head of Family; Last Census Roll Number; At Jurisdiction Where Enrolled (Yes or No); At Another Jurisdiction; ELSEWHERE: Post office, County, State; Ward (Yes or No); Allotment, Annuity, and Identification Numbers.

5448; Kee-seely; M; 64; Navajo; F; M; Head; 5464; Yes; Yes; 28505
5449; Bahih; F; 39; Navajo; F; M; Wife; 5465; Yes; Yes; 28506
5450; Zannie-suen; F; 18; Navajo; F; S; Daughter; 5466; Yes; Yes; 28507
5451; Lucy; F; 15; Navajo; F; S; Daughter; 5467; Yes; Yes; 28508
5452; Daniel; M; 14; Navajo; F; S; Son; 5468; Yes; Yes; 28509
5453; Grace; F; 10; Navajo; F; S; Daughter; 5469; Yes; Yes; 28510
5454; Glih-haz-bah; F; 7; Navajo; F; S; Daughter; 5470; Yes; Yes; 28511

5455; Kin-seely-badoni; M; 26; Navajo; F; M; Head; 5471; Yes; Yes; 28512
5456; Zahn; F; 25; Navajo; F; M; Wife; 5472; Yes; Yes; 28513
5457; Unknown; M; 7; Navajo; F; S; Son; 5473; Yes; Yes; 28514
5458; Haska-yoh-schol; M; 4; Navajo; F; S; Son; 5474; Yes; Yes; 28515
5459; Awae-chee; F; 1; Navajo; F; S; Daughter; 5475; Yes; Yes; 28547

5460; Kee-ith-linni-bega; M; Unk; Navajo; F; M; Head; 5476; Yes; Yes; 17082
5461; Adzanih-bah-yazzie; F; 21; Navajo; F; M; Wife; 5477; Yes; Yes; 17083
5462; Alchinn-hasbah; F; 4; Navajo; F; S; Daughter; 5478; Yes; Yes; 17084

5463; Kelly, Frank; M; 34; Navajo; F; M; Head; 5479; Yes; Yes; 21222
5464; Kelly, Rita; F; 21; Navajo; F; M; Wife; 5480; Yes; Yes; 21223
5465; Kelly, George; M; 11; Navajo; F; S; Son; 5481; Yes; Yes; 21224
5466; Kelly, Abe; M; 19; Navajo; F; S; Nephew; 5482; Yes; Yes; 21225
5467; Kelly, James; M; 6; Navajo; F; S; Step-son; 5483; Yes; Yes; 21226

5468; Kee-tuly; M; 38; Navajo; F; M; Head; 5484; Yes; Yes; 24810
5469; Nora; F; 38; Navajo; F; M; Wife; 5485; Yes; Yes; 24811
5470; Catherine; F; 11; Navajo; F; S; Daughter; 5486; Yes; Yes; 24812
5471; Benjamin; M; 8; Navajo; F; S; Son; 5487; Yes; Yes; 24813
5472; Mary-anna; F; 7; Navajo; F; S; Daughter; 5488; Yes; Yes; 24814
5473; Taz-bah; F; 3; Navajo; F; S; Daughter; 5489; Yes; Yes; 24815

5474; Kelwood, Harry; M; 38; Navajo; F; M; Head; 5490; Yes; Yes; 31031
5475; Nellie; F; 28; Navajo; F; M; Wife; 5491; Yes; Yes; 31032
5476; Harrison, Sam; M; 7; Navajo; F; S; Son; 5492; Yes; Yes; 31033
5477; Mary Janine; F; 5; Navajo; F; S; Daughter; 5493; Yes; Yes; 31034
5478; Helen May; F; 3; Navajo; F; S; Daughter; 5494; Yes; Yes; 31035
5479; Elsie; F; 1; Navajo; F; S; Daughter; 5495; Yes; Yes; 31261

5480; Kee-ah-ahnih-nez; M; 45; Navajo; F; M; Head; 5496; Yes; Yes; 30443
5481; Yee-naz-bah; F; 32; Navajo; F; M; Wife; 5497; Yes; Yes; 30444
5482; Chee-nez; M; 13; Navajo; F; S; Son; 5498; Yes; Yes; 30445
5483; Yazzie; M; 11; Navajo; F; S; Son; 5499; Yes; Yes; 30446
5484; Yil-dez-bah; F; 10; Navajo; F; S; Daughter; 5500; Yes; Yes; 30447

Census of the **Northern Navajo** reservation of the **Northern Navajo** jurisdiction, as of **April 1**, 19**31,** taken by **Ernest H. Hammond, District**, Superintendent. **in Charge**

**Key:** Number; NAME: Surname, Given; Sex; Birth Year (if given), Age At Last Birthday; Tribe; Degree of Blood; Marital Status; Relationship To Head of Family; Last Census Roll Number; At Jurisdiction Where Enrolled (Yes or No); At Another Jurisdiction; ELSEWHERE: Post office, County, State; Ward (Yes or No); Allotment, Annuity, and Identification Numbers.

5485; Yil-nee-bah; F; 5; Navajo; F; S; Daughter; 5501; Yes; Yes; 30448
5486; Haska-yih-nih-yah; M; 3; Navajo; F; S; Son; 5502; Yes; Yes; 30449

5487; Kesh-colih-benally; M; 64; Navajo; F; M; Head; 5503; Yes; Yes; 30439
5488; Kesh-colih-benally's wife; F; 58; Navajo; F; M; Wife; 5504; Yes; Yes; 30440
5489; Biz-dee-bah; F; 23; Navajo; F; S; Daughter; 5505; Yes; Yes; 30441
5490; See-cahih; M; 17; Navajo; F; S; Grand-son; 5506; Yes; Yes; 30442
5491; Yil-nah-das-bah; F; 3; Navajo; F; S; Daughter; 5507; Yes; Yes; 31252

5492; Kah-yee-tah-des-bah; F; 66; Navajo; F; Wd; Head; 5508; Yes; Yes; 21397

5493; Kelwood, David; M; 31; Navajo; F; M; Head; 5509; Yes; Yes; 22702
5494; Hosteen-yazzie-bitsih; F; 25; Navajo; F; M; Wife; 5510; Yes; Yes; 22703
5495; Eskee-l-suen; M; 5; Navajo; F; S; Son; 5511; Yes; Yes; 22704
5496; Kih-des-bah; F; 4; Navajo; F; S; Daughter; 5512; Yes; Yes; 21689

5497; Kin-lah-cheeny; M; 57; Navajo; F; M; Head; 5513; Yes; Yes; 29263
5498; Al-soh-naz-bah; F; 40; Navajo; F; M; Wife; 5514; Yes; Yes; 29264
5499; Alden; M; 12; Navajo; F; S; Son; 5515; Yes; Yes; 29265
5500; Helen; F; 10; Navajo; F; S; Daughter; 5516; Yes; Yes; 29266
5501; Dah-yil-woh; M; 6; Navajo; F; S; Son; 5517; Yes; Yes; 29267
5502; Haska-yah-nih-hah-zah; M; 3; Navajo; F; S; Son; 5518; Yes; Yes; 29268
5503; Al-chih-hah-bah; F; 56; Navajo; F; M; 1st wife; 5519; Yes; Yes; 29269
5504; Leo; M; 20; Navajo; F; S; Son; 5520; Yes; Yes; 29270
5505; Dah-yiz-bah; F; 18; Navajo; F; S; Daughter; 5521; Yes; Yes; 29271
5506; Leon; M; 16; Navajo; F; S; Son; 5522; Yes; Yes; 29272
5507; Rodney; M; 12; Navajo; F; S; Son; 5523; Yes; Yes; 29273
5508; Hoh-dee-bah; F; 9; Navajo; F; S; Daughter; 5524; Yes; Yes; 29274
5509; Esther; F; 2; Navajo; F; S; Daughter; 5525; Yes; Yes; 29408

5510; Kin-lah-cheeny-bega; M; 24; Navajo; F; M; Head; 5526; Yes; Yes; 29233
5511; Toh-dihcheeny-soh-bitsih; F; 18; Navajo; F; M; Wife; 5527; Yes; Yes; 29234
5512; Haska-yee-dah-wudt; M; 2; Navajo; F; S; Son; 5528; Yes; Yes; 29380

5513; Kin-lah-cheeny-nez-bega; M; 30; Navajo; F; M; Head; 5529; Yes; Yes; 23754
5514; Hosteen-deel-bitsih; F; 25; Navajo; F; M; Wife; 5530; Yes; Yes; 23755
5515; Haska-yee-chih-nih-nih-yah; M; 10; Navajo; F; S; Son; 5531; Yes; Yes; 23756
5516; Yil-hah-bah; F; 9; Navajo; F; S; Daughter; 5532; Yes; Yes; 23757
5517; Yil-chin-bah; F; 7; Navajo; F; S; Daughter; 5533; Yes; Yes; 23758
5518; Keh-yil-ee-bah; F; 6; Navajo; F; S; Daughter; 5534; Yes; Yes; 23759
5519; Glih-yil-nan-bah; F; 3; Navajo; F; S; Daughter; 5535; Yes; Yes; 23760

5520; Kin-le-cheeny; M; 39; Navajo; F; M; Head; 5536; Yes; Yes; 20129

Census of the **Northern Navajo** reservation of the **Northern Navajo** jurisdiction, as of **April 1**, 1931, taken by **Ernest H. Hammond, District**, Superintendent. **in Charge**

Key: Number; NAME: Surname, Given; Sex; Birth Year (if given), Age At Last Birthday; Tribe; Degree of Blood; Marital Status; Relationship To Head of Family; Last Census Roll Number; At Jurisdiction Where Enrolled (Yes or No); At Another Jurisdiction; ELSEWHERE: Post office, County, State; Ward (Yes or No); Allotment, Annuity, and Identification Numbers.

5521; Charley Bitsih; F; 23; Navajo; F; M; Wife; 5537; Yes; Yes; 20130

5522; King, Paul; M; 28; Navajo; F; M; Head; 5538; Yes; Yes; 31036
5523; Hah-tahly-bitsih; F; 31; Navajo; F; M; Wife; 5539; Yes; Yes; 31037
5524; Dinay-sosie, John; M; 12; Navajo; F; S; Step-son; 5540; Yes; Yes; 31038
5525; Al-nahn-bah; F; 4; Navajo; F; S; Daughter; 5541; Yes; Yes; 31039

5526; Kin-lacheeny-sosie; M; 39; Navajo; F; M; Head; 5542; Yes; Yes; 17899
5527; Nocki-bitsih; F; 33; Navajo; F; M; Wife; 5543; Yes; Yes; 17900
5528; White-sheep, Lee; M; 20; Navajo; F; S; Son; 5544; Yes; Yes; 17901
5529; Kin-lacheeny-sosie, Nelson; M; 17; Navajo; F; S; Son; 5545; Yes; Yes; 17902
5530; Shi-bahih; M; 10; Navajo; F; S; Son; 5546; Yes; Yes; 17903
5531; Woh-chee; M; 4; Navajo; F; S; Son; 5547; Yes; Yes; 18290

5532; Kin-lah-cheeny; M; 35; Navajo; F; M; Head; 5548; Yes; Yes; 30619
5533; Aht-citty-benally; F; 28; Navajo; F; M; Wife; 5549; Yes; Yes; 30620
5534; Bil-nih-ziz-bah; F; 6; Navajo; F; S; Daughter; 5550; Yes; Yes; 30621
5536[sic];Yee-kah-dez-bah; F; 3; Navajo; F; S; Daughter; 5551; Yes; Yes; 31248

5537; Kin-ilth-innih, Stony; M; 57; Navajo; F; M; Head; 5552; Yes; Yes; 27965
5538; Doh-bilth-hohzonih-bitsih; F; 23; Navajo; F; M; Wife; 5553; Yes; Yes; 27966
5539; Al-kih-doz-bah; F; 2; Navajo; F; S; Daughter; 5554; Yes; Yes; 27967
5540; Yee-kee-bah; F; 17; Navajo; F; S; Niece; 5555; Yes; Yes; 27968

5541; Kinsel, George; M; 26; Navajo; F; M; Head; 5556; Yes; Yes; 22484
5542; Nah-yil-ee-bah; F; 38; Navajo; F; M; Wife; 5557; Yes; Yes; 22485
5543; Yes-kas-bah; F; 5; Navajo; F; S; Daughter; Yes; Yes; 22586[sic]
                    [ID No. should be 22486]

5544; Kin-lachee-hih-bega; M; 33; Navajo; F; M; Head; 5559; Yes; Yes; 17276
5545; Bih-doh-toh-dihdazih; F; 43; Navajo; F; M; Wife; 5560; Yes; Yes; 17277

5546; Kin-seely-bega; M; Unk; Navajo; F; M; Head; 5561; No; McElmo, Colo., San Juan, Utah-; Yes; 19258
5547; Iltan-zeeihgi-bitsih; F; 20; Navajo; F; M; Wife; 5562; No; McElmo, Colo., San Juan, Utah; Yes; 19259
5548; Zaay; M; 4; Navajo; F; S; Son; 5563; No; McElmo, Colo., San Juan, Utah; Yes; 19260

5549; Kin-lacheeny-bitsees-lagaih Natoni; M; 53; Navajo; F; M; Head; 5564; Yes; Yes; 18104
5550; Descheeny-sani-bitsih; F; 40; Navajo; F; M; Wife; 5565; Yes; Yes; 18105
5551; Kin-lacheeny, Lula; F; 22; Navajo; F; S; Daughter; 5566; Yes; Yes; 18106

Census of the **Northern Navajo** reservation of the **Northern Navajo** jurisdiction, as of **April 1** , 1931, taken by **Ernest H. Hammond, District**, Superintendent. **in Charge**

**Key:** Number; NAME: Surname, Given; Sex; Birth Year (if given), Age At Last Birthday; Tribe; Degree of Blood; Marital Status; Relationship To Head of Family; Last Census Roll Number; At Jurisdiction Where Enrolled (Yes or No); At Another Jurisdiction; ELSEWHERE: Post office, County, State; Ward (Yes or No); Allotment, Annuity, and Identification Numbers.

5552; Ah-kay-nah-bah; F; 17; Navajo; F; S; Daughter; 5567; Yes; Yes; 18107
5553; Kin-lacheeny, Smith, Clover; F; 13; Navajo; F; S; Daughter; 5568; Yes; Yes; 18108
5554; Wudt; M; 11; Navajo; F; S; Son; 5569; Yes; Yes; 18109
5555; Eskee-l-gaih; M; 9; Navajo; F; S; Son; 5570; Yes; Yes; 18110
5556; Yee-haa-bah; F; 5; Navajo; F; S; Daughter; 5571; Yes; Yes; 18111

5557; Kih-yah-ahinih; M; 55; Navajo; F; M; Head; 5572; Yes; Yes; 26782
5558; Hosteen-shonhih-bitsoih; F; 44; Navajo; F; M; Wife; 5573; Yes; Yes; 26783
5559; Haska-dah-cih-lah; M; 22; Navajo; F; S; Son; 5574; Yes; Yes; 26784
5560; Priscilla; F; 15; Navajo; F; S; Daughter; 5575; Yes; Yes; 26785
5561; Daniel; M; 13; Navajo; F; S; Son; 5576; Yes; Yes; 26786
5562; Haska-yil-nas-wudt; M; 11; Navajo; F; S; Son; 5577; Yes; Yes; 26787
5563; Atate-keh-haz-bah; F; 7; Navajo; F; S; Daughter; 5578; Yes; Yes; 26788
5564; Haska-yil-hah-d-chit; M; 4; Navajo; F; S; Son; 5579; Yes; Yes; 26789
5565; Atate-keh-biz-dih-bah; F; 2; Navajo; F; S; Daughter; 5580; Yes; Yes; 26790

5566; Kin-lacheeny-bega-bih-nee-dih-thlohigi; M; 28; Navajo; F; M; Head; 5581; Yes; Yes; 18121
5567; Yee-thloni-bitah; F; 26; Navajo; F; M; Wife; 5582; Yes; Yes; 18122
5568; Wudt; M; 9; Navajo; F; S; Son; 5583; Yes; Yes; 18123
5569; Dah-nah-nih-bah; F; 7; Navajo; F; S; Daughter; 5584; Yes; Yes; 18124
5570; Tah-shee-bah; F; 3; Navajo; F; S; Daughter; 5585; Yes; Yes; 18125

5571; Klizi-thlani-benally; M; 22; Navajo; F; M; Head; 5586; Yes; Yes; 31071
5572; See-cody-bitsih F; 22; Navajo; F; M; Wife; 5587; Yes; Yes; 31072
5573; Hah-ziz-bah; F; 3; Navajo; F; S; Daughter; 5588; Yes; Yes; 31073
5574; Emma; F; 19; Navajo; F; S; Sister-in-law; 5589; Yes; Yes; 31252

5575; Klizi-dal-cheeih-yen-bega; M; 54; Navajo; F; Wd; Head; 5590; Yes; Yes; 25151
5576; Elinor Glen; F; 23; Navajo; F; S; Daughter; 5591; Yes; Yes; 25152
5577; Albert; M; 21; Navajo; F; S; Son; 5592; Yes; Yes; 25153

5578; Kin-yah-ahnih-soh; M; Unk; Navajo; F; M; Head; 5593; Yes; Yes; 26646
5579; Taoz-bah; F; 42; Navajo; F; M; Wife; 5594; Yes; Yes; 26647
5580; Doh-dez-hah; F; 23; Navajo; F; M; 2nd wife; 5595; Yes; Yes; 26648
5581; Glih-hah-bah; F; 4; Navajo; F; S; Daughter; 5596; Yes; Yes; 26649
5582; Haska-yil-nal-wudt; M; 3; Navajo; F; S; Son; 5597; Yes; Yes; 26650

5583; Kin-lah-cheeny-bitsih; F; 23; Navajo; F; Wd; Head; 5598; Yes; Yes; 20917
5584; Atate-l-chee; F; 10; Navajo; F; S; Daughter; 5599; Yes; Yes; 20918
5585; Kay-des-bah; F; 7; Navajo; F; S; Daughter; 5600; Yes; Yes; 20919

Census of the **Northern Navajo** reservation of the **Northern Navajo**
jurisdiction, as of **April 1** , 19**31,** taken by **Ernest H. Hammond, District** ,
Superintendent. **in Charge**

**Key:** Number; NAME: Surname, Given; Sex; Birth Year (if given), Age At Last Birthday; Tribe; Degree of Blood; Marital Status; Relationship To Head of Family; Last Census Roll Number; At Jurisdiction Where Enrolled (Yes or No); At Another Jurisdiction; ELSEWHERE: Post office, County, State; Ward (Yes or No); Allotment, Annuity, and Identification Numbers.

5586;  Klizi-lagaih; M; 50; Navajo; F; M; Head; 5601; Yes; Yes; 21492
5587;  Klizi-lagaih's wife; F; 62; Navajo; F; M; Wife; 5602; Yes; Yes; 21493
5588;  Nocki-dinay-bega, Jim; M; 24; Navajo; F; S; Grand-son; 5603; Yes; Yes;
21494
5589;  Hosteen-yah-benally; M; 21; Navajo; F; S; Grand-son; 5604; Yes; Yes; 21495
5590;  Yahn-des-bah; F; 17; Navajo; F; S; Grand-daughter; 5605; Yes; Yes; 21496

5591;  Klizi-yen-benally; M; 34; Navajo; F; M; Head; 5606; Yes; Yes; 25078
5592;  Hosteen-sosie-bitsih; F; 42; Navajo; F; M; Wife; 5607; Yes; Yes; 25079
5593;  Gahl; M; 26; Navajo; F; S; Son; 5608; Yes; Yes; 25080
5594;  Yahn-dez-bah; F; 17; Navajo; F; S; Daughter; 5609; Yes; Yes; 25081
5595;  Chee; M; 22; Navajo; F; S; Son; 5610; Yes; Yes; 25082
5596;  Bahih; M; 20; Navajo; F; S; Son; 5611; Yes; Yes; 25083
5597;  Haska-yee-nas-wudt; M; 11; Navajo; F; S; Son; 5612; Yes; Yes; 25084
5598;  Haska-yee-chih-nil-wudt; M; 7; Navajo; F; S; Son; 5613; Yes; Yes; 25085
5599;  Biz-dee-bah; F; 4; Navajo; F; S; Daughter; 5614; Yes; Yes; 25086
5600;  Nah-tah-yee-chih-nih-yah; M; 3; Navajo; F; S; Son; 5615; Yes; Yes; 25087

5601;  Klizi-dal-cheeih-benally, Jim; M; 31; Navajo; F; M; Head; 5616; Yes; Yes;
25157
5602;  Hosteen-yazzie-bitsih; F; 21; Navajo; F; M; Wife; 5617; Yes; Yes; 25158
5603;  Yee-nih-bah; F; 5; Navajo; F; S; Daughter; 5618; Yes; Yes; 25159

5604;  Klizi-dal-cheeih-bitsoih; M; 41; Navajo; F; M; Head; 5619; Yes; Yes; 25160
5605;  Hosteen-dih-chalih-bitsih; F; 38; Navajo; F; M; Wife; 5620; Yes; Yes; 25161
5606;  Richard; M; 19; Navajo; F; S; Son; 5621; Yes; Yes; 25162
5607;  Haska-yil-dah-yil-wohl; M; 8; Navajo; F; S; Son; 5622; Yes; Yes; 25163
5608;  Adzan-deel; F; 4; Navajo; F; S; Daughter; 5623; Yes; Yes; 25164

5609;  Klay-jinnih, Aleck; M; 31; Navajo; F; M; Head; 5624; Yes; Yes; 28433
5610;  Klay-jinnih-bih-adzan; F; 52; Navajo; F; M; Wife; 5625; Yes; Yes; 28434
5611;  Hosteen-nez-bega, Moapa; M; 41; Navajo; F; S; Cousin; 5626; Yes; Yes;
28435

5612;  Klizi-thlani-bega; M; 44; Navajo; F; M; Head; 5627; Yes; Yes; 24770
5613;  Hah-nah-bah; F; 34; Navajo; F; M; Wife; 5628; Yes; Yes; 24771
5614;  Yee-kah-naz-bah; F; 20; Navajo; F; S; Daughter; 5629; Yes; Yes; 24772
5615;  Haska-yee-kih-dah-yis-wudt; M; 17; Navajo; F; S; Son; 5630; Yes; Yes;
24773
5616;  Paul; M; 15; Navajo; F; S; Son; 5631; Yes; Yes; 24774
5617;  Nah-tah-yil-yee-gahl; M; 11; Navajo; F; S; Son; 5632; Yes; Yes; 24775
5618;  Raymond; M; 9; Navajo; F; S; Son; 5633; Yes; Yes; 24776
5619;  Yah-nah-nih-bah; F; 5; Navajo; F; S; Daughter; 5634; Yes; Yes; 24777

Census of the __Northern Navajo__ reservation of the __Northern Navajo__ jurisdiction, as of __April 1__, 19**31,** taken by __Ernest H. Hammond, District__, Superintendent. **in Charge**

**Key:** Number; NAME: Surname, Given; Sex; Birth Year (if given), Age At Last Birthday; Tribe; Degree of Blood; Marital Status; Relationship To Head of Family; Last Census Roll Number; At Jurisdiction Where Enrolled (Yes or No); At Another Jurisdiction; ELSEWHERE: Post office, County, State; Ward (Yes or No); Allotment, Annuity, and Identification Numbers.

5620; Bah; F; 48; Navajo; F; M; 1st Wife; 5635; Yes; Yes; 24779
5621; Hastaih; M; 16; Navajo; F; S; Son; 5636; Yes; Yes; 24780
5622; Adzan-yazzie; F; 86; Navajo; F; Wd; Mother-in-law; 5637; Yes; Yes; 24781

5623; Klizi-thlani; M; 67; Navajo; F; Wd; Head; 5638; No; McElmo, Colo., San Juan, Utah; Yes; 19264

5624; Klizi-thlani, Tom; M; 28; Navajo; F; M; Head; 5639; No; McElmo, Colo., San Juan, Utah; Yes; 19309
5625; Beleen-dih-jadih-bitsih; F; 24; Navajo; F; M; Wife; 5640; No; McElmo, Colo., San Juan, Utah; Yes; 19310

5626; Klizi-lazin-bitah; M; 31; Navajo; F; M; Head; 5641; Yes; Yes; 20305
5627; Bih-gizih-bitsih; F; 27; Navajo; F; M; Wife; 5642; Yes; Yes; 20306
5628; Black-goat, Julia; F; 12; Navajo; F; S; Daughter; 5643; Yes; Yes; 20307
5629; Nah-tah-l-bahih; M; 10; Navajo; F; S; Son; 5644; Yes; Yes; 20308
5630; Bil-zozbah; F; 8; Navajo; F; S; Daughter; 5645; Yes; Yes; 20309
5631; Nah-tah-yil-deyah; M; 6; Navajo; F; S; Son; 5646; Yes; Yes; 20310
5632; Bil-nih-ziz-bah; F; 3; Navajo; F; S; Daughter; 5647; Yes; Yes; 20311
5633; Haska-yel-deya; M; 1; Navajo; F; S; Son; 5648; Yes; Yes; 20408

5634; Klizi-thlani, Johnson, Billy; M; 58; Navajo; F; M; Head; 5649; No; McElmo, Colo., San Juan, Utah; Yes; 19384
5635; Batoni-bitsees-chillinge-bitsih[sic]; F; 43; Navajo; F; M; Wife; 5650; No; McElmo, Colo., San Juan, Utah; Yes; 19385 [Name should be Batoni-bitsees-chillige-bitsih]
5636; Joely, Robert; M; 20; Navajo; F; S; Son; 5651; No; McElmo, Colo., San Juan, Utah; Yes; 19386
5637; Bitsee-clitsoh; M; 18; Navajo; F; S; Son; 5652; No; McElmo, Colo., San Juan, Utah; Yes; 19387
5638; Ah-keh; F; 12; Navajo; F; S; Daughter; 5653; No; McElmo, Colo., San Juan, Utah; Yes; 19389
5639; Wazzih; F; 10; Navajo; F; S; Daughter; 5654; No; McElmo, Colo., San Juan, Utah; Yes; 19390
5640; Hosteen-l-bahih; M; 5; Navajo; F; S; Son; 5655; No; McElmo, Colo., San Juan, Utah; Yes; 19392

5641; Klizi-thlani-bega; M; 47; Navajo; F; M; Head; 5657; Yes; Yes; 31112
5642; Hosteen-al-taih-bitsih; F; 45; Navajo; F; M; Wife; 5658; Yes; Yes; 31113
5643; Haska-yee-nah-yah; M; 18; Navajo; F; S; Son; 5659; Yes; Yes; 31114
5644; Keh-yil-hah-naz-bah; F; 14; Navajo; F; S; Daughter; 5660; Yes; Yes; 31115
5645; Haska-yil-hah-yah; M; 11; Navajo; F; S; Son; 5661; Yes; Yes; 31116
5646; Nah-tah-yil-hoh-lel; M; 8; Navajo; F; S; Son; 5662; Yes; Yes; 31117

Census of the__Northern Navajo__reservation of the__Northern Navajo__
jurisdiction, as of__April 1___, 19**31**, taken by__Ernest H. Hammond, District__,
Superintendent. **in Charge**

**Key:** Number; NAME: Surname, Given; Sex; Birth Year (if given), Age At Last Birthday; Tribe; Degree of
Blood; Marital Status; Relationship To Head of Family; Last Census Roll Number; At Jurisdiction Where
Enrolled (Yes or No); At Another Jurisdiction; ELSEWHERE: Post office, County, State; Ward (Yes or No);
Allotment, Annuity, and Identification Numbers.

5647;  Keh-yil-haz-bah; F; 2; Navajo; F; S; Daughter; 5663; Yes; Yes; 31118

5648;  Klizi-dal-cheeih; M; Unk; Navajo; F; M; Head; 5664; Yes; Yes; 23194
5649;  Klizi-dal-cheeih's wife; F; 59; Navajo; F; M; Wife; 5665; Yes; Yes; 23195
5650;  Nora; F; 21; Navajo; F; S; Grand-daughter; 5666; Yes; Yes; 23196
5651;  Nah-tah-yil-ah-nahzah, Sam; M; 28; Navajo; F; S; Son; 5667; Yes; Yes; 23197
5652;  Chee-ih-sosie; M; 10; Navajo; F; S; Cousin; 5668; Yes; Yes; 23198

5653;  Klizi-lizin; M; 59; Navajo; F; M; Head; 5669; Yes; Yes; 20049
5654;  Nocki-hosteen-bitsih; F; 47; Navajo; F; M; Wife; 5670; Yes; Yes; 20050

5655;  Klizi-lizin-bega; M; 37; Navajo; F; M; Head; 5671; Yes; Yes; 19994
5656;  Batoni-tahih-bitsih; F; 22; Navajo; F; M; Wife; 5672; Yes; Yes; 19995
5657;  Kay-yil-nih-bah; F; 5; Navajo; F; S; Daughter; 5673; Yes; Yes; 19996
5658;  Adzanih-batoni; F; Unk; Navajo; F; Wd; Step-Grand-Mother; 5674; Yes; Yes;
19997

5659;  Klee-nanl-cadih-bega, Roy; M; Unk; Navajo; F; M; Head; 5676; Yes; Yes;
29706
5660;  Nettie; F; 31; Navajo; F; M; Wife; 5677; Yes; Yes; 29707
5661;  Robert; M; 4; Navajo; F; S; Son; 5678; Yes; Yes; 29708
5662;  Maud; F; 19; Navajo; F; S; Sister-in-law; 5679; Yes; Yes; 29709
5663;  Red Sheep, Dora; F; 19; Navajo; F; S; Niece-in-law; 5680; Yes; Yes; 29710
5664;  Dinay-Seesih; M; 23; Navajo; F; S; Cousin-in-law; 5681; Yes; Yes; 29711

5665;  Klizi-thlani-bega; M; 25; Navajo; F; M; Head; 5682; Yes; Yes; 19947
5666;  Kee-nas-bah; F; 17; Navajo; F; M; Wife; 5683; Yes; Yes; 19948

5667;  Klizi-thlani-bega; M; Unk; Navajo; F; M; Head; 5684; Yes; Yes; 29087
5668;  Dinay-sosie-bitsih; F; 38; Navajo; F; M; Wife; 5685; Yes; Yes; 29088
5669;  Dayton; M; 9; Navajo; F; S; Step-cousin; 5686; Yes; Yes; 29089

5670;  Klizi-thlani; M; Unk; Navajo; F; M; Head; 5687; Yes; Yes; 29279
5671;  Klizi-thlani's wife; F; 57; Navajo; F; M; Wife; 5688; Yes; Yes; 29280
5672;  Pearl; F; 18; Navajo; F; S; Daughter; 5689; Yes; Yes; 29281
5673;  Haz-bah; F; 15; Navajo; F; S; Daughter; 5690; Yes; Yes; 29282
5674;  Edith; F; 12; Navajo; F; S; Daughter; 5691; Yes; Yes; 29283
5675;  Nah-tahih; M; 11; Navajo; F; S; Grand-son; 5692; Yes; Yes; 29284
5676;  Kee-kih-dez-bah; F; 9; Navajo; F; S; Grand-daughter; 5693; Yes; Yes; 29285
5677;  Nal-ja-, Walter; M; 24; Navajo; F; S; Grand-son; 5694; Yes; Yes; 29377

5678;  Kolie; M; 31; Navajo; F; M; Head; 5695; Yes; Yes; 29064
5679;  Hosteen-soh-bitsih; F; 24; Navajo; F; M; Wife; 5696; Yes; Yes; 29065

Census of the **Northern Navajo** reservation of the **Northern Navajo** jurisdiction, as of **April 1**, 19**31,** taken by **Ernest H. Hammond, District**, Superintendent. **in Charge**

**Key:** Number; NAME: Surname, Given; Sex; Birth Year (if given), Age At Last Birthday; Tribe; Degree of Blood; Marital Status; Relationship To Head of Family; Last Census Roll Number; At Jurisdiction Where Enrolled (Yes or No); At Another Jurisdiction; ELSEWHERE: Post office, County, State; Ward (Yes or No); Allotment, Annuity, and Identification Numbers.

5680; Toh-naz-bah; F; 7; Navajo; F; S; Daughter; 5697; Yes; Yes; 29066
5681; Ah-gee; M; 5; Navajo; F; S; Son; 5698; Yes; Yes; 29067
5682; Bah-yazzie; F; 4; Navajo; F; S; Daughter; 5699; Yes; Yes; 29068
5683; Nih-den-nah-bah (Baby); F; 2; Navajo; F; S; Daughter; 5700; Yes; Yes; 29069
5684; Gonnah-Bylilli, Jim; M; 26; Navajo; F; S; Cousin-in-law; 5701; Yes; Yes; 29070
5685; Hosteen-soh-bih-adzan; F; 53; Navajo; F; S; Mother-in-law; 5702; Yes; Yes; 29071
5686; Chester; M; 22; Navajo; F; S; Brother-in-law; 5703; Yes; Yes; 29072
5687; Gonnah-bylilli, Lewis; M; 25; Navajo; F; S; Cousin-in-law; 5704; Yes; Yes; 29073

5688; Koz-bah-belone-benally; M; 24; Navajo; F; Wd; Head; 5705; Yes; Yes; 24816
5689; Haska-yil-hal-wudt; M; 10; Navajo; F; S; Son; 5706; Yes; Yes; 24817
5690; Nih-gee-wudt; M; 8; Navajo; F; S; Son; 5707; Yes; Yes; 24818

5691; Kesh-colih-benally-bitsoih; M; 26; Navajo; F; S; Head; 5708; Yes; Yes; 31208

5692; Kin-la-cheeny-bitsih-Beena; M; 42; Navajo; F; M; Head; 5709; Yes; Yes; 21612
5693; Dagaih-bega-bitsih, Alma; F; 26; Navajo; F; M; Wife; 5710; Yes; Yes; 21613
5694; Yil-chin-nih-bah; F; 5; Navajo; F; S; Daughter; 5711; Yes; Yes; 21614
5695; Yah-dee-bah; F; 3; Navajo; F; S; Daughter; 5712; Yes; Yes; 21615
5696; Haska-yee-hah-yah; M; 11; Navajo; F; S; Brother-in-law; 5713; Yes; Yes; 21616

5697; Kin-la-cheeny-nez-bega, Wade; M; 34; Navajo; F; M; Head; 5714; Yes; Yes; 21620
5698; Dinay-ye-iekin-bitsih; F; 31; Navajo; F; M; Wife; 5715; Yes; Yes; 21621
5699; Nah-tah-yazzie; M; 9; Navajo; F; S; Son; 5716; Yes; Yes; 21622
5700; Tah-des-wudt; M; 8; Navajo; F; S; Son; 5717; Yes; Yes; 21623
5701; Bil-yih-gee-bah; F; 4; Navajo; F; S; Daughter; 5718; Yes; Yes; 21624

5702; Kin-la-cheeny-yazzie; M; Unk; Navajo; F; M; Head; 5719; Yes; Yes; 22750
5703; Hosteen-hah-seeih-benally; F; Unk; Navajo; F; M; Wife; 5720; Yes; Yes; 22751
5704; El-woody; M; 11; Navajo; F; S; Son; 5721; Yes; Yes; 22752
5705; Chis-chilli; M; 10; Navajo; F; S; Son; 5722; Yes; Yes; 22753
5706; Nah-yazzie; F; 8; Navajo; F; S; Daughter; 5723; Yes; Yes; 22754
5707; Nis-zan; F; 5; Navajo; F; S; Daughter; 5724; Yes; Yes; 22755

5708; Kin-lacheeny; M; 36; Navajo; F; M; Head; 5725; Yes; Yes; 28087
5709; Bitsee-litsuih-bitsih; F; 27; Navajo; F; M; Wife; 5726; Yes; Yes; 28088

179

Census of the **Northern Navajo** reservation of the **Northern Navajo** jurisdiction, as of **April 1**, 19**31**, taken by **Ernest H. Hammond, District**, Superintendent. **in Charge**

**Key:** Number; NAME: Surname, Given; Sex; Birth Year (if given), Age At Last Birthday; Tribe; Degree of Blood; Marital Status; Relationship To Head of Family; Last Census Roll Number; At Jurisdiction Where Enrolled (Yes or No); At Another Jurisdiction; ELSEWHERE: Post office, County, State; Ward (Yes or No); Allotment, Annuity, and Identification Numbers.

5710; Cheeih; M; 12; Navajo; F; S; Son; 5727; Yes; Yes; 28089
5711; Azinih; M; 9; Navajo; F; S; Son; 5728; Yes; Yes; 28090
5712; Seeih; M; 6; Navajo; F; S; Son; 5729; Yes; Yes; 28091

5713; Keith, James; M; 24; Navajo; F; M; Head; 5730; Yes; Yes; 21630
5714; Cornelia; F; 23; Navajo; F; M; Wife; 5731; Yes; Yes; 21632

5715; Kerwood, Timothy; M; 23; Navajo; F; M; Head; 5732; Yes; Yes; 31263
5716; Kerwood, Ethel; F; 25; Navajo; F; M; Wife; 5733; Yes; Yes; 31264
5717; Kerwood, Charles; M; 2; Navajo; F; S; Son; 5734; Yes; Yes; 31265

5718; Lansing, Joe; M; 28; Navajo; F; S; Head; 5735; Yes; Yes; 28526

5719; La-paihih, Hugh; M; Unk; Navajo; F; M; Head; 5736; Yes; Yes; 27666
5720; Dinay-yazzie-bitsih; F; 32; Navajo; F; M; Wife; 5737; Yes; Yes; 27667
5721; Nah-tah-yee-chih-yee-gahl; M; 11; Navajo; F; S; Son; 5738; Yes; Yes; 27669
5722; Yah-dez-bah; F; 9; Navajo; F; S; Daughter; 5739; Yes; Yes; 27670
5723; Atate-yazzie; F; 2; Navajo; F; S; Daughter; 5740; Yes; Yes; 27671

5724; La-bahih, Willie; M; 30; Navajo; F; M; Head; 5741; Yes; Yes; 23761
5725; Cora; F; 31; Navajo; F; M; Wife; 5742; Yes; Yes; 23762
5726; Harrison; M; 9; Navajo; F; S; Son; 5743; Yes; Yes; 23763
5727; Jensein; M; 3; Navajo; F; S; Son; 5744; Yes; Yes; 23764
5728; Natoni-alsosie-bih-adzan; F; 75; Navajo; F; Wd; Mother-in-law; 5745; Yes; Yes; 23765
5729; Chih-haz-bah; F; 16; Navajo; F; S; Niece-in-law; 5746; Yes; Yes; 23766

5730; Lee, Harry; M; 27; Navajo; F; M; Head; 5747; Yes; Yes; 30955
5731; Yee-deh-bah; F; 21; Navajo; F; M; Wife; 5748; Yes; Yes; 30956
5732; Kee-ah-ahnih-nez-bimah; F; 64; Navajo; F; Wd; Mother; 5749; Yes; Yes; 30957

5733; Lee, Tom; M; 33; Navajo; F; M; Head; 5750; Yes; Yes; 30778
5734; Lee, Ethel; F; 41; Navajo; F; M; Wife; 5751; Yes; Yes; 30779
5735; Lee, Mary; F; 6; Navajo; F; S; Daughter; 5752; Yes; Yes; 30780
5736; Bih-zah-nez-bitsih; F; 20; Navajo; F; Wd; Sister; 5753; Yes; Yes; 30781
5737; Haska-yah-hih-gahl; M; 3; Navajo; F; S; Son; 5754; Yes; Yes; 31234

5738; Lee, Dan; M; 36; Navajo; F; S; Head; 5755; Yes; Yes; 30375

5739; Lee, Ben; M; Unk; Navajo; F; M; Head; 5756; Yes; Yes; 22734
5740; Lee, Beulah; F; Unk; Navajo; F; M; Wife; 5757; Yes; Yes; 22735
5741; Lee, William Henry; M; Unk; Navajo; F; S; Son; 5758; Yes; Yes; 22736

Census of the **Northern Navajo** reservation of the **Northern Navajo** jurisdiction, as of **April 1**, 19**31,** taken by **Ernest H. Hammond, District**, Superintendent. **in Charge**

**Key:** Number; NAME: Surname, Given; Sex; Birth Year (if given), Age At Last Birthday; Tribe; Degree of Blood; Marital Status; Relationship To Head of Family; Last Census Roll Number; At Jurisdiction Where Enrolled (Yes or No); At Another Jurisdiction; ELSEWHERE: Post office, County, State; Ward (Yes or No); Allotment, Annuity, and Identification Numbers.

5742; Elizabeth May; F; 3; Navajo; F; S; Daughter; 5759; Yes; Yes; 22737
5743; Awae-chee; F; 58; Navajo; F; Wd; Mother of John Lee; 5760; Yes; Yes; 22786

5744; Lee, Fritz; M; 52; Navajo; F; M; Head; 5761; Yes; Yes; 22659
5745; Ruth; F; 40; Navajo; F; M; Wife; 5762; Yes; Yes; 22660
5746; Robert; M; 21; Navajo; F; S; Son; 5763; Yes; Yes; 22661
5747; Jim; M; 19; Navajo; F; S; Son; 5764; Yes; Yes; 22662
5748; Stella Mae; F; 9; Navajo; F; S; Daughter; 5765; Yes; Yes; 22663

5749; Lee, Wilson; M; 52; Navajo; F; M; Head; 5766; Yes; Yes; 22669
5750; Yee-kaz-bah; F; 41; Navajo; F; M; Wife; 5767; Yes; Yes; 22670
5751; Lucy; F; 20; Navajo; F; S; Daughter; 5768; Yes; Yes; 22671
5752; Paul; M; 16; Navajo; F; S; Son; 5769; Yes; Yes; 22672
5753; Haska-yee-kih-hoh-gah; M; 13; Navajo; F; S; Son; 5770; Yes; Yes; 22673
5754; No Name; M; 11; Navajo; F; S; Son; 5771; Yes; Yes; 22674
5755; Adzanih-yazzie; F; 3; Navajo; F; S; Daughter; 5772; Yes; Yes; 22675

5756; Lee, Harry; M; 45; Navajo; F; M; Head; 5773; No; McElmo, Colo., San Juan, Utah; Yes; 19230
5757; Hosteen-nez-bitsoih; F; 31; Navajo; F; M; Wife; 5774; No; McElmo, Colo., San Juan, Utah; Yes; 19231
5758; Dinay-Yazzie; M; 20; Navajo; F; S; Son; 5775; No; McElmo, Colo., San Juan, Utah; Yes; 19232
5759; Lee, Annie; F; 14; Navajo; F; S; Daughter; 5776; No; McElmo, Colo., San Juan, Utah; Yes; 19233
5760; Yah-de-yah; M; 11; Navajo; F; S; Son; 5777; No; McElmo, Colo., San Juan, Utah; Yes; 19234
5761; Yah-des-bah; F; 9; Navajo; F; S; Daughter; 5778; No; McElmo, Colo., San Juan, Utah; Yes; 19235
5762; Yah-nih-bah; F; 6; Navajo; F; S; Daughter; 5779; No; McElmo, Colo., San Juan, Utah; Yes; 19236
5763; Haska, Lee; M; 3; Navajo; F; S; Son; 5780; No; McElmo, Colo., San Juan, Utah; Yes; 19527

5764; Lee, Jack; M; 34; Navajo; F; M; Head; 5781; Yes; Yes; 22330
5765; Pauline; F; 26; Navajo; F; M; Wife; 5782; Yes; Yes; 22331
5766; Lee, Abraham; M; 12; Navajo; F; S; Son; 5783; Yes; Yes; 22332
5767; Glih-has-bah; F; 10; Navajo; F; S; Daughter; 5784; Yes; Yes; 22333

5768; Lee, Robert; M; 34; Navajo; F; M; Head; 5785; Yes; Yes; 23429
5769; Bitsih, Ben; F; 27; Navajo; F; M; Wife; 5786; Yes; Yes; 23430
5770; Haska-yee-chih-nil-wudt; M; 8; Navajo; F; S; Son; 5787; Yes; Yes; 23431

Census of the **Northern Navajo** reservation of the **Northern Navajo** jurisdiction, as of **April 1**, 19**31,** taken by **Ernest H. Hammond, District**, Superintendent. **in Charge**

**Key:** Number; NAME: Surname, Given; Sex; Birth Year (if given), Age At Last Birthday; Tribe; Degree of Blood; Marital Status; Relationship To Head of Family; Last Census Roll Number; At Jurisdiction Where Enrolled (Yes or No); At Another Jurisdiction; ELSEWHERE: Post office, County, State; Ward (Yes or No); Allotment, Annuity, and Identification Numbers.

5771; Haska-yil-hal-wudt; M; 4; Navajo; F; S; Son; 5788; Yes; Yes; 23432
5772; Haska-e-tah-egath; M; 1; Navajo; F; S; Son; 5789; Yes; Yes; 23979

5773; Lee, Charley; M; 28; Navajo; F; M; Head; 5790; No; McElmo, Colo., San Juan, Utah; Yes; 19265
5774; Dagah-chee-bitsih; F; 21; Navajo; F; M; Wife; 5791; No; McElmo, Colo., San Juan, Utah; Yes; 19266

5775; Leonard Thomas; M; 32; Navajo; F; M; Head; 5792; Yes; Yes; 17893
5776; Toh-dih-cheeny-bitsih; F; 23; Navajo; F; M; Wife; 5793; Yes; Yes; 17894
5777; Dah-debah; F; 6; Navajo; F; S; Daughter; 5794; Yes; Yes; 17895

5778; Lewis, Henry; M; 40; Navajo; F; M; Head; 5795; Yes; Yes; 30357
5779; See-chisih-bitsih; F; 40; Navajo; F; M; Wife; 5800; Yes; Yes; 30358
5780; Reed; M; 24; Navajo; F; S; Step-son; 5801; Yes; Yes; 30360
5781; Lee; M; 22; Navajo; F; S; Step-son; 5802; Yes; Yes; 30361
5782; Benjamin; M; 18; Navajo; F; S; Step-son; 5803; Yes; Yes; 30362
5783; Nah-dez-bah; F; 13; Navajo; F; S; Step-daughter; 5804; Yes; Yes; 30363
5784; Nih-nih-bah; F; 5; Navajo; F; S; Daughter; 5805; Yes; Yes; 30364

5785; Lagaith-beleen; M; 32; Navajo; F; M; Head; 5796; Yes; Yes; 23957
5786; Bah; F; 37; Navajo; F; M; Wife; 5797; Yes; Yes; 23958
5787; Enah-gathl; M; 11; Navajo; F; S; Son; 5798; Yes; Yes; 23960
5788; Tah-nas-bah; F; 1; Navajo; F; S; Daughter; 5799; Yes; Yes; 23959

5789; Light Ray; M; 23; Navajo; F; M; Head; 5806; Yes; Yes; 30653
5790; Toh-dih-kozee-bitsih; F; 18; Navajo; F; M; Wife; 5807; Yes; Yes; 30654
5791; Paul Ray; M; 2; Navajo; F; S; Son; 5808; Yes; Yes; 30655

5792; Little, Joe; M; 36; Navajo; F; M; Head; 5809; Yes; Yes; 30951
5793; Dinay-nez-bitsih; F; 41; Navajo; F; M; Wife; 5810; Yes; Yes; 30952
5794; Has-wudt-dinay-nez; M; 21; Navajo; F; S; Step-son; 5811; Yes; Yes; 30953
5795; Johnson; M; 19; Navajo; F; S; Son; 5812; Yes; Yes; 30954

5796; Long John; M; 54; Navajo; F; M; Head; 5813; No; Bluff, San Juan, Utah; Yes; 28828
5797; Long John's wife; F; 52; Navajo; F; M; Wife; 5814; No; Bluff, San Juan, Utah; Yes; 28829
5798; Nesbit; M; 28; Navajo; F; S; Son; 5815; No; Bluff, San Juan, Utah; Yes; 28830
5799; Jean; M; 27; Navajo; F; S; Son; 5816; No; Bluff, San Juan, Utah; Yes; 28831
5800; Sam; M; 9; Navajo; F; S; Son; 5817; No; Bluff, San Juan, Utah; Yes; 28832

Census of the __Northern Navajo__ reservation of the __Northern Navajo__ jurisdiction, as of __April 1__, 19**31,** taken by __Ernest H. Hammond, District__, Superintendent. **in Charge**

Key: Number; NAME: Surname, Given; Sex; Birth Year (if given), Age At Last Birthday; Tribe; Degree of Blood; Marital Status; Relationship To Head of Family; Last Census Roll Number; At Jurisdiction Where Enrolled (Yes or No); At Another Jurisdiction; ELSEWHERE: Post office, County, State; Ward (Yes or No); Allotment, Annuity, and Identification Numbers.

5801;  Long, John Bega; M; 30; Navajo; F; M; Head; 5818; No; Bluff, San Juan, Utah; Yes; 28814   [1930 Census was listed as Bega, Long John]
5802;  Yee-kih-dah-yiz-bah; F; 29; Navajo; F; M; Wife; 5819; No; Bluff, San Juan, Utah; Yes; 28815
5803;  Haska-yee-tah-yil-wohl; M; 15; Navajo; F; S; Son; 5820; No; Bluff, San Juan, Utah; Yes; 28816
5804;  Dah-nih-bah; F; 11; Navajo; F; S; Daughter; 5821; No; Bluff, San Juan, Utah; Yes; 28817

5805;  London, Jack; M; Unk; Navajo; F; M; Head; 5822; Yes; Yes; 22459
5806;  Happy; F; 23; Navajo; F; M; Wife; 5823; Yes; Yes; 22460
5807;  Hoska-yil-nil-wudt; M; 6; Navajo; F; S; Son; 5824; Yes; Yes; 22461

5808;  Lukai-ch-gaih-nih, Harvey Harry; M; 36; Navajo; F; M; Head; 5825; No; McElmo, Colo., San Juan, Utah; Yes; 19362
5809;  Lukai-ch-gaih-nih's wife; F; 36; Navajo; F; M; Wife; 5826; No; McElmo, Colo., San Juan, Utah; Yes; 19363
5810;  Nih-nah-has-bah; F; 9; Navajo; F; S; Daughter; 5827; No; McElmo, Colo., San Juan, Utah; Yes; 19364

5811;  Lancing[sic], Lee; M; 25; Navajo; F; M; Head; 5828; Yes; Yes; 31176
        [Name is probably Lansing, Lee]
5812;  Hosteen-la-chee-bitsih, Netty; F; 20; Navajo; F; M; Wife; 5829; Yes; Yes; 31177

5813;  Lansing, Robert; M; 33; Navajo; F; M; Head; 5830; Yes; Yes; 31164
5814;  Hosteen-la-chee-bitsih, Ella; F; 35; Navajo; F; M; Wife; 5831; Yes; Yes; 31165
5815;  Charley Morris; M; 14; Navajo; F; S; Step-son; 5832; Yes; Yes; 31166
5816;  John Morris; M; 10; Navajo; F; S; Step-son; 5833; Yes; Yes; 31167
5817;  Betty; F; 5; Navajo; F; S; Daughter; 5834; Yes; Yes; 31168
5818;  Ben; M; 4; Navajo; F; S; Son; 5835; Yes; Yes; 31169
5819;  Hosteen-la-chee; F[sic]; 76; Navajo; F; Wd; Father-in-law; 5836; Yes; Yes; 31170

5820;  Lowe, John; M; 27; Navajo; F; S; Head; 5837; Yes; Yes; 22764

5821;  Manuelito, Frank; M; 31; Navajo; F; M; Head; 5838; Yes; Yes; 26233
5822;  Frances; F; 21; Navajo; F; M; Wife; 5839; Yes; Yes; 26234
5823;  Nellie; F; 6; Navajo; F; S; Daughter; 5840; Yes; Yes; 26235
5824;  Lucy; F; 3; Navajo; F; S; Daughter; 5841; Yes; Yes; 26236
5825;  Maggie; F; 23; Navajo; F; Wd; Sister-in-law; 5842; Yes; Yes; 26237
5826;  James; M; 7; Navajo; F; S; Nephew-in-law; 5843; Yes; Yes; 26238

Census of the **Northern Navajo** reservation of the **Northern Navajo** jurisdiction, as of **April 1**, 19**31,** taken by **Ernest H. Hammond, District**, Superintendent. **in Charge**

**Key:** Number; NAME: Surname, Given; Sex; Birth Year (if given), Age At Last Birthday; Tribe; Degree of Blood; Marital Status; Relationship To Head of Family; Last Census Roll Number; At Jurisdiction Where Enrolled (Yes or No); At Another Jurisdiction; ELSEWHERE: Post office, County, State; Ward (Yes or No); Allotment, Annuity, and Identification Numbers.

5827;  Sherman, Luke; M; 14; Navajo; F; S; Brother-in-law; 5844; Yes; Yes; 26239
5828;  Sherman, Paul; M; 29; Navajo; F; S; Brother-in-law; 5845; Yes; Yes; 26240

5829;  Manuelito, Stephen; M; 31; Navajo; F; M; Head; 5846; Yes; Yes; 26259
5830;  Manuelito, Glenna; F; 30; Navajo; F; M; Wife; 5847; Yes; Yes; 26260
5831;  Nettie; F; 6; Navajo; F; S; Daughter; 5848; Yes; Yes; 26261

5832;  Martin, Robert; M; 52; Navajo; F; M; Head; 5849; Yes; Yes; 28479
5833;  Martin, Mrs. Robert; F; 39; Navajo; F; M; Wife; 5850; Yes; Yes; 28480
5834;  Martin, Robert Jr.; M; 18; Navajo; F; S; Son; 5851; Yes; Yes; 28481
5835;  Martin, Fred; M; 16; Navajo; F; S; Son; 5852; Yes; Yes; 28482
5836;  Martin, Geronimo; M; 13; Navajo; F; S; Son; 5853; Yes; Yes; 28483
5837;  Martin, Susen[sic]; F; 11; Navajo; F; S; Daughter; 5854; Yes; Yes; 28484
       [Name is probably Martin, Susan]
5838;  Martin, Ruthie; F; 9; Navajo; F; S; Daughter; 5855; Yes; Yes; 28485
5839;  Martin, Marie; F; 7/12; Navajo; F; S; Daughter; [Blank]; Yes; Yes; 28546

5840;  Manih-desch-kiznih-bega; M; 27; Navajo; F; M; Head; 5856; Yes; Yes; 29314
5841;  Dagah-thlani-bitsih; F; 26; Navajo; F; M; Wife; 5857; Yes; Yes; 29315
5842;  Haska-yil-nas-wudt; M; 3; Navajo; F; S; Son; 5859; Yes; Yes; 29317

5843;  Manih-desch-gienih[sic]; M; 57; Navajo; F; M; Head; 5860; Yes; Yes; 29001
       [1930 Census name was Manih-desch-gienis, and this is probably correct.]
5844;  Rose; F; 26; Navajo; F; M; Wife; 5861; Yes; Yes; 29002
5845;  Vera; F; 23; Navajo; F; S; Daughter; 5862; Yes; Yes; 29003
5846;  Ah-bahih; M; 18; Navajo; F; S; Son; 5863; Yes; Yes; 29004
5847;  Hazel; F; 22; Navajo; F; S; Daughter; 5864; Yes; Yes; 29005
5848;  Carl; M; 14; Navajo; F; S; Son; 5865; Yes; Yes; 29006
5849;  Maybell; F; 8; Navajo; F; S; Daughter; 5866; Yes; Yes; 29008
5850;  Edward; M; 7; Navajo; F; S; Son; 5867; Yes; Yes; 29009
5851;  King; M; 4; Navajo; F; S; Son; 5868; Yes; Yes; 29010

5852;  McDonald, Harry; M; Unk; Navajo; F; M; Head; 5869; Yes; Yes; 26282
5853;  Nah-glih-yee-naz-bah; F; 39; Navajo; F; M; Wife; 5870; Yes; Yes; 26283
5854;  Tah-dez-bah; F; 5; Navajo; F; S; Daughter; 5871; Yes; Yes; 26284
5855;  Sarah; F; 22; Navajo; F; S; Daughter; 5872; Yes; Yes; 26285
5856;  Frank; M; 22; Navajo; F; S; Son; 5873; Yes; Yes; 26286
5857;  Bessie; F; 18; Navajo; F; S; Daughter; 5874; Yes; Yes; 26287
5858;  Mary; F; 16; Navajo; F; S; Daughter; 5875; Yes; Yes; 26288
5859;  Bah-hoh-zohnih; M; 30; Navajo; F; S; Nephew; 5876; Yes; Yes; 26289
5860;  Baker, Grace; F; 12; Navajo; F; S; Sister; 5877; Yes; Yes; 26442

5861;  McKenzie, John; M; 35; Navajo; F; M; Head; 5878; Yes; Yes; 31000

Census of the **Northern Navajo** reservation of the **Northern Navajo** jurisdiction, as of **April 1**, 19**31**, taken by **Ernest H. Hammond, District**, Superintendent. **in Charge**

**Key:** Number; NAME: Surname, Given; Sex; Birth Year (if given), Age At Last Birthday; Tribe; Degree of Blood; Marital Status; Relationship To Head of Family; Last Census Roll Number; At Jurisdiction Where Enrolled (Yes or No); At Another Jurisdiction; ELSEWHERE: Post office, County, State; Ward (Yes or No); Allotment, Annuity, and Identification Numbers.

5862;  Amelia; F; 38; Navajo; F; M; Wife; 5879; Yes; Yes; 31001
5863;  Calvin; M; 6; Navajo; F; S; Son; 5880; Yes; Yes; 31002
5864;  Mary Lou; F; 11; Navajo; F; S; Sister; 5881; Yes; Yes; 31003

5865;  Bitah, Mike; M; 31; Navajo; F; M; Head; 5882; Yes; Yes; 23144
5866;  Cleh-gih-hah-tahly-bitsih; F; 29; Navajo; F; M; Wife; 5883; Yes; Yes; 23145
5867;  Russell; M; 24; Navajo; F; S; Brother-in-law; 5884; Yes; Yes; 23146
5868;  Toh-ahk-gleenih-bega; M; 22; Navajo; F; S; Brother-in-law; 5885; Yes; Yes; 23147
5869;  Cleh-gih-hah-tahly-bitsih; F; 19; Navajo; F; S; Sister-in-law; 5886; Yes; Yes; 23153
5870;  Kah-nez-bah; F; 8; Navajo; F; S; Daughter; 5887; Yes; Yes; 23985
5871;  Nas-bah; F; 4; Navajo; F; S; Daughter; 5888; Yes; Yes; 23986
5872;  Haska-chen-yah; M; 2; Navajo; F; S; Son; 5889; Yes; Yes; 23987
5873;  Haska-yee-tah-ha-laith; M; 2; Navajo; F; S; Son; 5890; Yes; Yes; 23988

5874;  Bitah, Mike; M; 43; Navajo; F; M; Head; 5891; Yes; Yes; 23160
5875;  Ah-hah-nih-bah; F; 24; Navajo; F; M; Wife; 5892; Yes; Yes; 23161
5876;  Keh-yil-naz-bah; F; 8; Navajo; F; S; Daughter; 5893; Yes; Yes; 23162
5877;  Keh-yil-naz-bah; F; 5; Navajo; F; S; Daughter; 5894; Yes; Yes; 23163
5878;  Keh-yee-chih-hah-bah; F; 11; Navajo; F; S; Sister-in-law; 5895; Yes; Yes; 23164

5879;  Bitah, Mike; M; 22; Navajo; F; Wd; Head; 5896; Yes; Yes; 23138

5880;  Mike; M; 57; Navajo; F; M; Head; 5897; Yes; Yes; 23122
5881;  Martha, Mike's Wife; F; 30; Navajo; F; M; Wife; 5898; Yes; Yes; 23123
5882;  Haska-yee-nal-wohl; M; 11; Navajo; F; S; Son; 5899; Yes; Yes; 23124
5883;  Chih-des-hah; F; 9; Navajo; F; S; Daughter; 5900; Yes; Yes; 23125
5884;  Yah-nih-yah; M; 4; Navajo; F; S; Son; 5901; Yes; Yes; 23126
5885;  Herbert; M; 20; Navajo; F; S; Son; 5902; Yes; Yes; 23127

5886;  Mike-bega, John; M; 27; Navajo; F; M; Head; 5903; Yes; Yes; 30635
5887;  Hosteen-clitsoih-bitsih; F; 26; Navajo; F; M; Wife; 5904; Yes; Yes; 30636
5888;  Keh-yil-haz-bah; F; 4; Navajo; F; S; Daughter; 5905; Yes; Yes; 30637
5889;  Woody, John; M; 30; Navajo; F; S; Brother-in-law; 5906; Yes; Yes; 30638
5890;  Nih-bah; F; 17; Navajo; F; S; Sister-in-law; 5907; Yes; Yes; 30639
5891;  Hah-nih-bah; F; 12; Navajo; F; S; Sister-in-law; 5908; Yes; Yes; 30640

5892;  Morgan, Francis; M; 39; Navajo; F; M; Head; 5909; Yes; Yes; 25177
5893;  Klizi-dal-cheeih-benally; F; 27; Navajo; F; M; Wife; 5910; Yes; Yes; 25178
5894;  Adzan-sosie; F; 53; Navajo; F; Wd; Aunt-in-law; 5911; Yes; Yes; 25179

Census of the **Northern Navajo** reservation of the **Northern Navajo** jurisdiction, as of **April 1**, 1931, taken by **Ernest H. Hammond, District**, Superintendent. **in Charge**

**Key:** Number; NAME: Surname, Given; Sex; Birth Year (if given), Age At Last Birthday; Tribe; Degree of Blood; Marital Status; Relationship To Head of Family; Last Census Roll Number; At Jurisdiction Where Enrolled (Yes or No); At Another Jurisdiction; ELSEWHERE: Post office, County, State; Ward (Yes or No); Allotment, Annuity, and Identification Numbers.

5895; Mitchen, John; M; 33; Navajo; F; M; Head; 5912; Yes; Yes; 17935
5896; John Mitchen's wife; F; 34; Navajo; F; M; Wife; 5913; Yes; Yes; 17936
5897; Bih-jah-entsazo-bega, Fritz; M; 19; Navajo; F; S; Step-son; 5914; Yes; Yes; 17937
5898; Atate-yazzie; F; 13; Navajo; F; S; Daughter; 5915; Yes; Yes; 17938
5899; Atate-bahih; F; 9; Navajo; F; S; Daughter; 5916; Yes; Yes; 17939
5900; Hoska-yilt-yil-wudt; M; 6; Navajo; F; S; Son; 5917; Yes; Yes; 17940
5901; Nah-glih-yilth-hah-bah; F; 4; Navajo; F; S; Daughter; 5918; Yes; Yes; 17941
5902; Kay-hah-bah; F; 4; Navajo; F; S; Daughter; 5919; Yes; Yes; 17942

5903; Morgan, J. C.; M; 51; Navajo; F; M; Head; 5920; Yes; Yes; 32890
5904; Morgan, Azhrina T.; F; 40; Navajo; F; M; Wife; 5921; Yes; Yes; 32891
5905; Morgan, Irwin Roderick; M; 19; Navajo; F; S; Son; 5922; Yes; Yes; 32892
5906; Morgan, Wilbur Edmond; M; 18; Navajo; F; S; Son; 5923; Yes; Yes; 32893
5907; Morgan, Jacob C. Jr.; M; 14; Navajo; F; S; Son; 5924; Yes; Yes; 32894

5908; Myressa, Clyde; M; 29; Navajo; F; M; Head; 5925; No; McElmo, Colo., San Juan, Utah; Yes; 19499
5909; Dorothy; F; 20; Navajo; F; M; Wife; 5926; No; McElmo, Colo., San Juan, Utah; Yes; 19500
5910; Lewis; M; 2; Navajo; F; S; Son; 5927; No; McElmo, Colo., San Juan, Utah; Yes; 19501

5911; Myressa, Leo; M; 23; Navajo; F; M; Head; 5928; Yes; Yes; 31174
5912; Osscah-bihdazee; F; 20; Navajo; F; M; Wife; 5929; Yes; Yes; 31175

5913; Martinez; M; 66; Navajo; F; M; Head; 5930; Yes; Yes; 31171
5914; Aht-citty-sosie-bitsih; F; 60; Navajo; F; M; Wife; 5931; Yes; Yes; 31172
5915; Clyde; M; 3; Navajo; F; S; Step-son; 5932; Yes; Yes; 31173

5916; Martin Johnson; M; 25; Navajo; F; M; Head; 5933; Yes; Yes; 31274
5917; Jenett[sic]; F; 26; Navajo; F; M; Wife; 5934; Yes; Yes; 31275
         [1930 Census name was spelled Jennett]
5918; Joe; M; 5; Navajo; F; S; Son; 5935; Yes; Yes; 31276
5919; Martin, Jr.; M; 3; Navajo; F; S; Son; 5936; Yes; Yes; 31277
5920; Irene; F; 2; Navajo; F; S; Daughter; 5937; Yes; Yes; 31278

5921; Nanl-cadih-bega; M; 33; Navajo; F; M; Head; 5938; Yes; Yes; 18099
5922; Hosteen-chahih-bitsih; F; Unk; Navajo; F; M; Wife; 5939; Yes; Yes; 18100
5923; Bah; F; 6; Navajo; F; S; Daughter; 5940; Yes; Yes; 18101
5924; Hoska-yil-des-wudt; M; 3; Navajo; F; S; Son; 5941; Yes; Yes; 18102

5925; Natoni-al-sosie-bega; M; 43; Navajo; F; Wd; Head; 5942; Yes; Yes; 23767

Census of the __Northern Navajo__ reservation of the __Northern Navajo__ jurisdiction, as of __April 1__ , 19__31,__ taken by __Ernest H. Hammond, District__, Superintendent. __in Charge__

**Key:** Number; NAME: Surname, Given; Sex; Birth Year (if given), Age At Last Birthday; Tribe; Degree of Blood; Marital Status; Relationship To Head of Family; Last Census Roll Number; At Jurisdiction Where Enrolled (Yes or No); At Another Jurisdiction; ELSEWHERE: Post office, County, State; Ward (Yes or No); Allotment, Annuity, and Identification Numbers.

5926;   Clyde; M; 21; Navajo; F; S; Son; 5943; Yes; Yes; 23768
5927;   Keh-yee-nah-yah; M; 10; Navajo; F; S; Son; 5944; Yes; Yes; 23769

5928;   Nah-al-ah-hih-bega; M; 43; Navajo; F; M; Head; 5945; Yes; Yes; 23669
5929;   Baz-nih-bah; F; 31; Navajo; F; M; Wife; 5946; Yes; Yes; 23670
5930;   Chel-wudt; M; 13; Navajo; F; S; Son; 5947; Yes; Yes; 23671
5931;   Nah-hoh-gahl; M; 8; Navajo; F; S; Son; 5948; Yes; Yes; 23672
5932;   Nah-tah-yil-nah-hoh-gahl; M; 4; Navajo; F; S; Son; 5949; Yes; Yes; 23673

5933;   Natoni-el-sosie-bega; M; 29; Navajo; F; M; Head; 5950; Yes; Yes; 23770
5934;   Kin-lah-cheeny-nez-bitsih; F; 25[sic]; Navajo; F; M; Wife; 5951; Yes; Yes; 23771    [Age on 1930 Census was 34, 25 is probably the correct age.]
5935;   Nah-glih-yah-nih-bah; F; 17; Navajo; F; S; Daughter; 5952; Yes; Yes; 23772
5936;   Yil-nih-nih-bah; F; 10; Navajo; F; S; Daughter; 5953; Yes; Yes; 23773
5937;   Haska-yee-tah-yee-gahl; M; 7; Navajo; F; S; Son; 5954; Yes; Yes; 23774
5938;   Glih-yil-dez-bah; F; 5; Navajo; F; S; Daughter; 5955; Yes; Yes; 23775

5939;   Natoni, Bega; M; Unk; Navajo; F; M; Head; 5956; Yes; Yes; 23148
5940;   Natini-bega-bih-adzan[sic]; F; 24; Navajo; F; M; Wife; 5957; Yes; Yes; 23149    [Name is probably Natoni-bega-bih-adzan]
5941;   Mike-bih-dazih; F; Unk; Navajo; F; Wd; Mother-in-law; 5958; Yes; Yes; 23150

5942;   Natoni-bitsih; F; 29; Navajo; F; Wd; Head; 5033; Yes; Yes; 19911
5943;   Chung; M: 10; Navajo; F; S; Son; 5034; Yes; Yes; 19912
5944;   Nas-wudt-de; M; 8; Navajo; F; S; Son; 5035; Yes; Yes; 19913
5945;   Yee-che-des-bah; F; 5; Navajo; F; S; Daughter; 5036; Yes; Yes; 19914
5946;   Nah-glih-yil-nah-bah; F; 3; Navajo; F; S; Daughter; 5037; Yes; Yes; 19915

5947;   Nah-ah-toh-ih-hah-tahly-benally; M; Unk; Navajo; F; M; Head; 5959; Yes; Yes; 23140
5948;   Toh-ahk-bleenih-bitsih; F; 25; Navajo; F; M; Wife; 5960; Yes; Yes; 23141
5949;   Haska-yee-nah-yah; M; 7; Navajo; F; S; Son; 5961; Yes; Yes; 23142
5950;   Nah-tah-yil-chin-yah; M; 5; Navajo; F; S; Son; 5962; Yes; Yes; 23143
5951;   Haska-ah-gathl; M; 2; Navajo; F; S; Son; 5963; Yes; Yes; 23981

5952;   Nah-ah-ahih-yen-bitsih; F; 36; Navajo; F; Wd; Head; 5964; Yes; Yes; 23493
5953;   Yahn-yil-wohl; M; 20; Navajo; F; S; Son; 5965; Yes; Yes; 23494

5954;   Nal-zayih-bitsoih; M; 47; Navajo; F; M; Head; 5966; Yes; Yes; 21249
5955;   Beleen-lizin-bitsih; F; 43; Navajo; F; M; Wife; 5967; Yes; Yes; 21250
5956;   Randal[sic]; M; 17; Navajo; F; S; Son; 5968; Yes; Yes; 21251
        [1930 Census name was spelled Randall however this one may be correct.]

Census of the **Northern Navajo** reservation of the **Northern Navajo** jurisdiction, as of **April 1**, 19**31**, taken by **Ernest H. Hammond, District**, Superintendent. **in Charge**

**Key:** Number; NAME: Surname, Given; Sex; Birth Year (if given), Age At Last Birthday; Tribe; Degree of Blood; Marital Status; Relationship To Head of Family; Last Census Roll Number; At Jurisdiction Where Enrolled (Yes or No); At Another Jurisdiction; ELSEWHERE: Post office, County, State; Ward (Yes or No); Allotment, Annuity, and Identification Numbers.

5957; Yil-has-bah; F; 15; Navajo; F; S; Daughter; 5969; Yes; Yes; 21252
5958; Hoska-yil-chel-wudt; M; 10; Navajo; F; S; Son; 5971; Yes; Yes; 21254
5959; Bil-hah-ziz-bah; F; 7; Navajo; F; S; Daughter; 5972; Yes; Yes; 21255
5960; Haska-yee-nel-wudt; M; 3; Navajo; F; S; Son; 5973; Yes; Yes; 21256
5961; Bah-ni-bah; F; 2; Navajo; F; S; Daughter; 5974; Yes; Yes; 21673

5962; Nanlcadi-bitsih; F; 58; Navajo; F; Wd; Head; 5975; Yes; Yes; 17123

5963; Nal-zayih-bitah; F; 88; Navajo; F; Wd; Head; 5976; Yes; Yes; 21280
5964; Yee-kaz-bah; F; 44; Navajo; F; Wd; Daughter; 5977; Yes; Yes; 21281
5965; Askan-sosie-bega; M; 20; Navajo; F; S; Grandson; 5978; Yes; Yes; 21282
5966; Askan-sosie-bitsih; F; 41; Navajo; F; Wd; Daughter; 5979; Yes; Yes; 21283
5967; Nah-tah-seeih; M; 8; Navajo; F; S; Grand-son; 5980; Yes; Yes; 21284
5968; Toh, Willie; M; 3; Navajo; F; S; Grand-son; 5981; Yes; Yes; 21725

5969; Nah-cheeny-bega; M; 62; Navajo; F; M; Head; 5982; Yes; Yes; 22301
5970; Clah-yen-bitsih; F; 48; Navajo; F; M; Wife; 5983; Yes; Yes; 22302
5971; Kay-yah-des-bah; F; 25; Navajo; F; S; Daughter; 5984; Yes; Yes; 22303
5972; Koska-tah-nas-wudt[sic]; M; 23; Navajo; F; S; Son; 5985; Yes; Yes; 22304
[Name is probably Hoska-tah-nas-wudt]
5973; Koska-yee-kih-has-wudt[sic]; M; 21; Navajo; F; S; Son; 5986; Yes; Yes; 22305
[Name is probably Hoska-yee-kih-has-wudt]
5974; Nora; F; 19; Navajo; F; S; Daughter; 5987; Yes; Yes; 22306
5975; Mattie; F; 16; Navajo; F; S; Daughter; 5988; Yes; Yes; 22307
5976; Hoska-yee-kih-nil-wudt; M; 13; Navajo; F; S; Son; 5989; Yes; Yes; 22308
5977; Yil-hah-ziz-bah; F; 10; Navajo; F; S; Daughter; 5990; Yes; Yes; 22309
5978; Hoska-yee-tah-yah; M; 8; Navajo; F; S; Son; 5991; Yes; Yes; 22310
5979; Martha; F; 39; Navajo; F; M; 2nd wife; 5992; Yes; Yes; 22311
5980; Jane; F; 18; Navajo; F; S; Daughter; 5993; Yes; Yes; 22312
5981; Nize-nih-bah; F; 16; Navajo; F; S; Daughter; 5994; Yes; Yes; 22313
5982; Jimmy; M; 12; Navajo; F; S; Son; 5995; Yes; Yes; 22314
5983; Yin-nih-bah; F; 9; Navajo; F; S; Daughter; 5996; Yes; Yes; 22315
5984; Zannie-soh; F; 5; Navajo; F; S; Daughter; 5997; Yes; Yes; 22316

5985; Narge, Ed; M; 66; Navajo; F; M; Head; 5998; Yes; Yes; 20223
5986; By-lilli-yen-bilah; F; 77; Navajo; F; Div. Wife; 5999; Yes; Yes; 20224
5987; Adzan-l-bah; F; 43; Navajo; F; M; Wife; 6000; Yes; Yes; 20225
5988; Dinay-yazzie; M; 17; Navajo; F; S; Son; 6001; Yes; Yes; 20226
5989; Narge, Leonard; M; 13; Navajo; F; S; Son; 6002; Yes; Yes; 20227
5990; Glih-bah; F; 6; Navajo; F; S; Daughter; 6003; Yes; Yes; 20228
5991; Nih-nih-bah; F; 3; Navajo; F; S; Daughter; 6004; Yes; Yes; 20229

Census of the **Northern Navajo** reservation of the **Northern Navajo** jurisdiction, as of **April 1**, 19**31**, taken by **Ernest H. Hammond, District**, Superintendent. **in Charge**

**Key:** Number; NAME: Surname, Given; Sex; Birth Year (if given), Age At Last Birthday; Tribe; Degree of Blood; Marital Status; Relationship To Head of Family; Last Census Roll Number; At Jurisdiction Where Enrolled (Yes or No); At Another Jurisdiction; ELSEWHERE: Post office, County, State; Ward (Yes or No); Allotment, Annuity, and Identification Numbers.

5992; Natcle-bihyaz[sic]; M; 40; Navajo; F; M; Head; 6005; No; McElmo, Colo., San Juan, Utah; Yes; 19330 [Name is probably Natale-bihyaz]

5993; Dinay-etsosie-bitsih; F; 32; Navajo; F; M; Wif[sic]; 6006; No; McElmo, Colo., San Juan, Utah; Yes; 19331

5994; Sosih; M; 17; Navajo; F; S; Son; 6007; No; McElmo, Colo., San Juan, Utah; Yes; 19332

5995; Ah-khe-nih-bah; F; 13; Navajo; F; S; Daughter; 6008; No; McElmo, Colo., San Juan, Utah; Yes; 19333

5996; Natcle-bih-yaz[sic], Wilma; F; 10; Navajo; F; S; Daughter; 6009; No; McElmo, Colo., San Juan, Utah; Yes; 19334 [Name could be Natale-bih-yaz, Wilma]

5997; Kee-soh; M; 8; Navajo; F; S; Son; 6010; No; McElmo, Colo., San Juan, Utah; Yes; 19335

5998; Kee-bahih; M; 6; Navajo; F; S; Son; 6011; No; McElmo, Colo., San Juan, Utah; Yes; 19336

5999; Hah-jih-bah; F; 4; Navajo; F; S; Daughter; 6012; No; McElmo, Colo., San Juan, Utah; Yes; 19337

6000; Tah-ziz-bah; F; 1; Navajo; F; S; Daughter; 6013; No; McElmo, Colo., San Juan, Utah; Yes; 19529

6001; Naranjo, Helen; F; 36; Navajo; F; M; Wife of Pueblo Indian; 6014; Yes; Yes; 22731

6002; Naranjo, William; M; 18; Navajo; F; S; Son; 6015; Yes; Yes; 22732

6003; Naranjo, Harriet; F; 15; Navajo; F; S; Daughter; 6016; Yes; Yes; 22733

6004; Nanl-cadih-bega; M; 26; Navajo; F; M; Head; 6017; Yes; Yes; 19969

6005; Hosteen-tah-benally, Atate Yazzie; F; 24; Navajo; F; M; Wife; 6018; Yes; Yes; 19970

6006; Natoni; M; 35; Navajo; F; M; Head; 6019; No; McElmo, Colo., San Juan, Utah; Yes; 19002

6007; Chise-nez-bitsih; F; 29; Navajo; F; M; Wife; 6020; No; McElmo, Colo., San Juan, Utah; Yes; 19003

6008; Nal-got, John; F[sic]; 29; Navajo; F; S; Nephew; 6021; No; McElmo, Colo., San Juan, Utah; Yes; 19004

6009; Nah-cheeny-benally-bega; M; 28; Navajo; F; M; Head; 6022; Yes; Yes; 26634

6010; Hah-tahly-yen-bitsih; F; 23; Navajo; F; M; Wife; 6023; Yes; Yes; 26635

6011; Yil-nah-bah; F; 8; Navajo; F; S; Daughter; 6024; Yes; Yes; 26636

6012; Nah-tah-yahih; M; 7; Navajo; F; S; Son; 6025; Yes; Yes; 26637

6013; Titus; M; 3; Navajo; F; S; Son; 6026; Yes; Yes; 26638

6014; Nah-goshih-bega; M; 27; Navajo; F; M; Head; 6027; No; McElmo, Colo., San Juan, Utah; Yes; 18939

Census of the __Northern Navajo__ reservation of the __Northern Navajo__
jurisdiction, as of __April 1__, 19**31,** taken by __Ernest H. Hammond, District__,
Superintendent. **in Charge**

Key: Number; NAME: Surname, Given; Sex; Birth Year (if given), Age At Last Birthday; Tribe; Degree of
Blood; Marital Status; Relationship To Head of Family; Last Census Roll Number; At Jurisdiction Where
Enrolled (Yes or No); At Another Jurisdiction; ELSEWHERE: Post office, County, State; Ward (Yes or No);
Allotment, Annuity, and Identification Numbers.

6015; Nah-goshih-bega's wife; F; 43; Navajo; F; M; Wife; 6028; No; McElmo,
Colo., San Juan, Utah; Yes; 18940

6016; Yah-nez; M; 28; Navajo; F; S; Step-son; 6029; No; McElmo, Colo., San Juan,
Utah; Yes; 18941

6017; Kee; M; 25; Navajo; F; S; Step-son; 6030; No; McElmo, Colo., San Juan,
Utah; Yes; 18942

6018; Jones, Zonnie; F; 19; Navajo; F; S; Step-daughter; 6031; No; McElmo, Colo.,
San Juan, Utah; Yes; 18943

6019; Nah-goshih, Madelene; F; 18; Navajo; F; S; Step-daughter; 6032; No;
McElmo, Colo., San Juan, Utah; Yes; 18944

6020; Jones, Walter; M; 16; Navajo; F; S; Step-son; 6033; No; McElmo, Colo., San
Juan, Utah; Yes; 18945

6021; Jones, Allen West; M; 15; Navajo; F; S; Step-son; 6034; No; McElmo, Colo.,
San Juan, Utah; Yes; 18946

6022; Tis-des-bah; F; 11; Navajo; F; S; Daughter; 6035; No; McElmo, Colo., San
Juan, Utah; Yes; 18947

6023; Biz-nil-bah; F; 9; Navajo; F; S; Daughter; 6036; No; McElmo, Colo., San
Juan, Utah; Yes; 18948

6024; Atate-yazzie; F; 7; Navajo; F; S; Daughter; 6037; No; McElmo, Colo., San
Juan, Utah; Yes; 18949

6025; Atate; F; 4; Navajo; F; S; Daughter; 6038; No; McElmo, Colo., San Juan,
Utah; Yes; 18950

6026; Navajo, John Bega; M; 22; Navajo; F; M; Head; 6039; Yes; Yes; 22608
6027; Yahn-hah-bah; F; 22; Navajo; F; M; Wife; 6040; Yes; Yes; 22609
6028; Keh-yil-hah-bah; F; 5; Navajo; F; S; Daughter; 6041; Yes; Yes; 22610
6029; Eskee-e-soh; M; 3; Navajo; F; S; Son; 6042; Yes; Yes; 22611
6030; May; F; 2; Navajo; F; S; Daughter; 6043; Yes; Yes; 22775

6031; Naltass-bega, Dick; M; 71; Navajo; F; Wd; Head; 6044; Yes; Yes; 17139
6032; Naltass, Lucy; F; 21; Navajo; F; S; Daughter; 6045; Yes; Yes; 17140

6033; Nah-gohih[sic]; M; 60; Navajo; F; M; Head; 6046; No; McElmo, Colo., San
Juan, Utah; Yes; 18983  [Name should be Nah-goshih]
6034; Nah-goshih's wife; F; 77; Navajo; F; M; Wife; 6047; No; McElmo, Colo., San
Juan, Utah; Yes; 18984

6035; Nanl-cadih-bega; M; 22; Navajo; F; M; Head; 6048; Yes; Yes; 20137
6036; Ah-has-nih-bah; F; 22; Navajo; F; M; Wife; 6049; Yes; Yes; 20138
6037; Awa-l-bahih; F; 7; Navajo; F; S; Daughter; 6050; Yes; Yes; 20139
6038; Whey-kee; M; 4; Navajo; F; S; Son; 6051; Yes; Yes; 20140
6039; Asdzan-l-bahih; F; 2; Navajo; F; S; Daughter; 6052; Yes; Yes; 20427

Census of the **Northern Navajo** reservation of the **Northern Navajo** jurisdiction, as of **April 1**, 19**31,** taken by **Ernest H. Hammond, District**, Superintendent. **in Charge**

**Key:** Number; NAME: Surname, Given; Sex; Birth Year (if given), Age At Last Birthday; Tribe; Degree of Blood; Marital Status; Relationship To Head of Family; Last Census Roll Number; At Jurisdiction Where Enrolled (Yes or No); At Another Jurisdiction; ELSEWHERE: Post office, County, State; Ward (Yes or No); Allotment, Annuity, and Identification Numbers.

6040; Nah-cheeny-bega; M; Unk; Navajo; F; M; Head; 6053; No; McElmo, Colo., San Juan, Utah; Yes; 19467

6041; Bih-nah-atin-bitsih; F; 62; Navajo; F; M; Wife; 6054; No; McElmo, Colo., San Juan, Utah; Yes; 19468

6042; Bih-kiz-nih-bah; F; 78; Navajo; F; Wd; Mother-in-law; 6055; No; McElmo, Colo., San Juan, Utah; Yes; 19469

6043; Nanl-cadih; M; 58; Navajo; F; M; Head; 6056; Yes; Yes; 20115

6044; Klizi-thlani-bih-dagah-ihgi-bitsih, Anna; F; 25; Navajo; F; M; Wife; 6057; Yes; Yes; 20116

6045; Nanl-cadih, Willie; M; 20; Navajo; F; S; Son; 6058; Yes; Yes; 20117

6046; Nanl-cadih, Ambrose; M; 10; Navajo; F; S; Son; 6059; Yes; Yes; 20118

6047; Navajo John badoni; M; 28; Navajo; F; M; Head; 6060; Yes; Yes; 30206

6048; Navajo John bitsih; F; 28; Navajo; F; M; Wife; 6061; Yes; Yes; 30207

6049; Yil-haz-bah; F; 8; Navajo; F; S; Daughter; 6062; Yes; Yes; 30208

6050; Nah-glih-yil-haz-bah; F; 6; Navajo; F; S; Daughter; 6063; Yes; Yes; 30209

6051; Yil-chee; F; 4; Navajo; F; S; Daughter; 6064; Yes; Yes; 30210

6052; Navajo John bega, Albert; M; 26; Navajo; F; S; Brother-in-law; 6065; Yes; Yes; 30211

6053; Raymond, John; M; 22; Navajo; F; S; Brother-in-law; 6066; Yes; Yes; 30212

6054; Yee-hah-naz-bah; F; 20; Navajo; F; S; Sister-in-law; 6067; Yes; Yes; 30213

6055; Kee-shone; M; 14; Navajo; F; S; Brother-in-law; 6068; Yes; Yes; 30214

6056; Dinay-shih; M; 12; Navajo; F; S; Brother-in-law; 6069; Yes; Yes; 30215

6057; Gee; M; 10; Navajo; F; S; Brother-in-law; 6070; Yes; Yes; 30216

6058; Adzan-yazzie; F; 68; Navajo; F; Wd; Grand-mother-in-law; 6071; Yes; Yes; 30217

6059; Natoni; M; 35; Navajo; F; M; Head; 6072; Yes; Yes; 30311

6060; Adzanih-yazzie; F; 26; Navajo; F; M; Wife; 6073; Yes; Yes; 30312

6061; Sam; M; 6; Navajo; F; S; Son; 6074; Yes; Yes; 30313

6062; Zannie; F; 5; Navajo; F; S; Daughter; 6075; Yes; Yes; 30314

6063; (Baby); M; 2; Navajo; F; S; Son; 6076; Yes; Yes; 30315

6064; Nal-got-yazzie; M; 36; Navajo; F; M; Head; 6077; Yes; Yes; 30647

6065; Yee-ah-nih-bah; F; 34; Navajo; F; M; Wife; 6078; Yes; Yes; 30648

6066; Harry; M; 14; Navajo; F; S; Son; 6079; Yes; Yes; 30650

6067; Robert; M; 9; Navajo; F; S; Son; 6080; Yes; Yes; 30651

6068; Leonard; M; 2; Navajo; F; S; Son; 6081; Yes; Yes; 31216

6069; Nahtle-soh-bitsih; F; 62; Navajo; F; Wd; Head; 6082; Yes; Yes; 30492

6070; Yee-hah-nih-bih; F; 26; Navajo; F; Wd; Daughter; 6083; Yes; Yes; 30493

Census of the **Northern Navajo** reservation of the **Northern Navajo** jurisdiction, as of **April 1** , 19**31,** taken by **Ernest H. Hammond, District**, Superintendent. **in Charge**

Key: Number; NAME: Surname, Given; Sex; Birth Year (if given), Age At Last Birthday; Tribe; Degree of Blood; Marital Status; Relationship To Head of Family; Last Census Roll Number; At Jurisdiction Where Enrolled (Yes or No); At Another Jurisdiction; ELSEWHERE: Post office, County, State; Ward (Yes or No); Allotment, Annuity, and Identification Numbers.

6071; Navajo, John; M; 52; Navajo; F; M; Head; 6084; Yes; Yes; 30982
6072; Charley-badoni-bitsih; F; 20; Navajo; F; M; Wife; 6085; Yes; Yes; 30983
6073; Kate; F; 26; Navajo; F; S; Daughter; 6086; Yes; Yes; 31224

6074; Nah-cheeny-bitah, Frank; M; 42; Navajo; F; M; Head; 6087; Yes; Yes; 29900
6075; Nellie; F; 40; Navajo; F; M; Wife; 6088; Yes; Yes; 29901
6076; Gladys; F; 16; Navajo; F; S; Daughter; 6089; Yes; Yes; 29902
6077; Clara; F; 14; Navajo; F; S; Daughter; 6090; Yes; Yes; 29903
6078; Willie; M; 10; Navajo; F; S; Son; 6091; Yes; Yes; 29904
6079; Francis; M; 7; Navajo; F; S; Son; 6092; Yes; Yes; 29905
6080; Clarence; M; 5; Navajo; F; S; Son; 6093; Yes; Yes; 29906
6081; Hah-gis-wudt; M; 3; Navajo; F; S; Son; 6094; Yes; Yes; 29907

6082; Nah-cheeny-bitah; F; 62; Navajo; F; Wd; Head; 6095; Yes; Yes; 29912
6083; Ah-keh-yee-nihbah[sic]; F; 22; Navajo; F; S; Daughter; 6096; Yes; Yes; 29913
      [Name should be Ah-keh-yee-nih-bah]
6084; Willard; F[sic]; 20; Navajo; F; S; Grand-son; 6097; Yes; Yes; 29914

6085; Navajo, John Birah[sic]; M; Unk; Navajo; F; M; Head; 6098; Yes; Yes; 29934
      [Name should be Navajo, John Bitah]
6086; Minnie; F; 32; Navajo; F; M; Wife; 6099; Yes; Yes; 29935
6087; Yee-chih-nih-nih-bah; F; 7; Navajo; F; S; Step-daughter; 6100; Yes; Yes;
29936
6088; Ah-hih-nih-bah; F; 11; Navajo; F; S; Step-daughter; 6101; Yes; Yes; 29937
6089; Haska-yil-nah-yah; M; 7; Navajo; F; S; Son; 6102; Yes; Yes; 29938
6090; Haska-yil-ee-yah; M; 6; Navajo; F; S; Son; 6103; Yes; Yes; 29939
6091; Nah-tah-yil-nah-yah; M; 3; Navajo; F; S; Son; 6104; Yes; Yes; 29940

6092; Nah-seeih-bega; M; 75; Navajo; F; Wd; Head; 6105; Yes; Yes; 29261
6093; Nah-tahs-nez; M; 19; Navajo; F; S; Son; 6106; Yes; Yes; 29262

6094; Nah-cheeny-benally; M; Unk; Navajo; F; M; Head; 6107; Yes; Yes; 21054
6095; Bih-dagaih-bitsih; F; 41; Navajo; F; M; Wife; 6108; Yes; Yes; 21055
6096; Nah-cheeny, Maurice; M; 19; Navajo; F; S; Son; 6109; Yes; Yes; 21056
6097; Haska-yil-hal-wudt; M; 17; Navajo; F; S; Son; 6110; Yes; Yes; 21057
6098; Billy; M; 15; Navajo; F; S; Son; 6111; Yes; Yes; 21058
6099; Gahl; M; 13; Navajo; F; S; Son; 6112; Yes; Yes; 21059
6100; Hoska-yee-dah-hah-zah; M; 7; Navajo; F; S; Son; 6113; Yes; Yes; 21060
6101; Hoska-yah-deyah; M; 4; Navajo; F; S; Son; 6114; Yes; Yes; 21061

6102; Natoni-yen-bega, Tom; M; 65; Navajo; F; M; Head; 6115; Yes; Yes; 21026
6103; Ah-hih-dee-bah; F; 58; F; M; Wife; 6116; Yes; Yes; 21027
6104; Hoska-yee-tah-des-wudt; M; 20; Navajo; F; S; Son; 6117; Yes; Yes; 21028

Census of the **Northern Navajo** reservation of the **Northern Navajo** jurisdiction, as of **April 1** , 1931, taken by **Ernest H. Hammond, District** , Superintendent. **in Charge**

**Key:** Number; NAME: Surname, Given; Sex; Birth Year (if given), Age At Last Birthday; Tribe; Degree of Blood; Marital Status; Relationship To Head of Family; Last Census Roll Number; At Jurisdiction Where Enrolled (Yes or No); At Another Jurisdiction; ELSEWHERE: Post office, County, State; Ward (Yes or No); Allotment, Annuity, and Identification Numbers.

6105;   Glih-naz-bah; F; 25; Navajo; F; Wd; Daughter; 6118; Yes; Yes; 21029
6106;   Yee-nas-bah; F; 6; Navajo; F; S; Grand-daughter; 6119; Yes; Yes; 21030
6107;   Tah-zoz-bah; F; 3; Navajo; F; S; Grand-Daughter; 6120; Yes; Yes; 21031
6108;   Glih; F; 14; Navajo; F; S; Grand-Daughter; 6121; Yes; Yes; 21032
6109;   Natoni-bega, Barbara; F; 15; Navajo; F; S; Adopted Niece; 6122; Yes; Yes; 21033

6110;   Nanl-cadih; M; 75; Navajo; F; Wd; Head; 6123; Yes; Yes; 18129

6111;   Nahtle; M; 47; Navajo; F; M; Head; 6124; Yes; Yes; 28839
6112;   Aht-citty-sosie-bega; M; 21; Navajo; F; S; Nephew; 6125; Yes; Yes; 28840
6113;   Keedah; M; 20; Navajo; F; S; Nephew; 6126; Yes; Yes; 28841
6114;   Charley; M; 15; Navajo; F; S; Nephew; 6127; Yes; Yes; 28842
6115;   Robert; M; 14; Navajo; F; S; Nephew; 6128; Yes; Yes; 28843
6116;   Jackson; M; 13; Navajo; F; S; Nephew; 6129; Yes; Yes; 28844
6117;   Dinay-soh; M; 9; Navajo; F; S; Nephew; 6130; Yes; Yes; 28845

6118;   Nal-geed, Lame Joe; M; 58; Navajo; F; M; Head; 6131; Yes; Yes; 18165
6119;   Nanl-cadih-bitsih; F; 31; Navajo; F; M; Wife; 6132; Yes; Yes; 18166
6120;   Atate-l-bahih; F; 16; Navajo; F; S; Daughter; 6133; Yes; Yes; 18167
6121;   Nal-geed, Mark; M; 12; Navajo; F; S; Son; 6134; Yes; Yes; 18168
6122;   Ah-kay-hes-bah; F; 10; Navajo; F; S; Daughter; 6135; Yes; Yes; 18169
6123;   Haska-yee-ch-nil-wudt; M; 8; Navajo; F; S; Son; 6136; Yes; Yes; 18170
6124;   Nah-gliy-ah-nah-bah; F; 6; Navajo; F; S; Daughter; 6137; Yes; Yes; 18171

6125;   Naltsos-nah-yehih; M; 52; Navajo; F; M; Head; 6138; Yes; Yes; 26291
6126;   Yahn-nih-bah; F; 60; Navajo; F; M; Wife; 6139; Yes; Yes; 26292
6127;   Allen; M; 15; Navajo; F; S; Son; 6140; Yes; Yes; 26293

6128;   Nah-cheeny-benally; M; 38; Navajo; F; M; Head; 6141; No; McElmo, Colo., San Juan, Utah; Yes; 19470
6129;   Hosteen-etseesie-bitsih; F; 35; Navajo; F; M; Wife; 6142; No; McElmo, Colo., San Juan, Utah; Yes; 19471
6130;   Nah-cheeny-benally, Florence; F; 13; Navajo; F; S; Daughter; 6143; No; McElmo, Colo., San Juan, Utah; Yes; 19472
6131;   Das-tah; F; 10; Navajo; F; S; Daughter; 6144; No; McElmo, Colo., San Juan, Utah; Yes; 19473
6132;   Bah; F; 8; Navajo; F; S; Daughter; 6145; No; McElmo, Colo., San Juan, Utah; Yes; 19474
6133;   Etseesie; F; 6; Navajo; F; S; Daughter; 6146; No; McElmo, Colo., San Juan, Utah; Yes; 19475
6134;   Eskee; M; 5; Navajo; F; S; Son; 6147; No; McElmo, Colo., San Juan, Utah; Yes; 19476

Census of the **Northern Navajo** reservation of the **Northern Navajo** jurisdiction, as of **April 1** , 19**31**, taken by **Ernest H. Hammond, District** , Superintendent. **in Charge**

6135; Nal-al-ihih-nez-benally; M; Unk; Navajo; F; M; Head; 6148; Yes; Yes; 26011
6136; Tee-bah; F; 22; Navajo; F; M; Wife; 6149; Yes; Yes; 26012
6137; Yee-kih-dah-yiz-bah; F; 3; Navajo; F; S; Daughter; 6150; Yes; Yes; 26013

6138; Natoni-nih-dah-gih-bega; M; 31; Navajo; F; M; Head; 6151; Yes; Yes; 25960
6139; Al-keh-dez-bah; F; 32; Navajo; F; M; Wife; 6152; Yes; Yes; 25961
6140; Nah-tah-hah-dey-nah; M; 7; Navajo; F; S; Son; 6153; Yes; Yes; 25962
6141; Yil-hah-naz-bah; F; 5; Navajo; F; S; Daughter; 6154; Yes; Yes; 25963
6142; Nah-dez-bah; F; 5; Navajo; F; S; Daughter; 6155; Yes; Yes; 25964
6143; Yee-hah-zoz-bah; F; 61; Navajo; F; Wd; Mother; 6156; Yes; Yes; 25965

6144; Natoni, Morris; M; 31; Navajo; F; M; Head; 6157; Yes; Yes; 25019
6145; Grace; F; 29; Navajo; F; M; Wife; 6158; Yes; Yes; 25020
6146; Morris, Clifford; M; 3; Navajo; F; S; Son; 6159; Yes; Yes; 25021

6147; Naltsos-nih-yehih-bega, John; M; 28; Navajo; F; M; Head; 6160; Yes; Yes; 24995
6148; Bessie; F; 25; Navajo; F; M; Wife; 6161; Yes; Yes; 24996
6149; Helen; F; 1; Navajo; F; S; Daughter; 6162; Yes; Yes; 25341

6150; Natoni-bega; M; 36; Navajo; F; M; Head; 6163; Yes; Yes; 24967
6151; Gish-des-bitih-bega-bitsoih; F; 28; Navajo; F; M; Wife; 6164; Yes; Yes; 24968
6152; May; F; 16; Navajo; F; S; Daughter; 6165; Yes; Yes; 24969
6153; Kee; M; 8; Navajo; F; S; Son; 6166; Yes; Yes; 24970
6154; Haske-yee-kih-des-glish; M; 3; Navajo; F; S; Son; 6167; Yes; Yes; 24971

6155; Natoni-bitsih, Nellie; F; 36; Navajo; F; Wd; Head; 6168; Yes; Yes; 24911
6156; Warren; M; 20; Navajo; F; S; Son; 6169; Yes; Yes; 24912
6157; Peter; M; 18; Navajo; F; S; Son; 6170; Yes; Yes; 24913
6158; John; M; 12; Navajo; F; S; Son; 6171; Yes; Yes; 24914
6159; Hosteen-zeen; M; 11; Navajo; F; S; Son; 6172; Yes; Yes; 24915
6160; Haska-yil-yeel-wohl; M; 9; Navajo; F; S; Son; 6173; Yes; Yes; 24916
6161; Keh-yil-nih-bah; F; 7; Navajo; F; S; Daughter; 6174; Yes; Yes; 24917
6162; Al-chah-bah; F; 5; Navajo; F; S; Daughter; 6175; Yes; Yes; 24918

6163; Nas-clah-benally; M; 60; Navajo; F; M; Head; 6176; Yes; Yes; 24741
6164; Hosteen-belone-bitsih; F; 62; Navajo; F; M; Wife; 6177; Yes; Yes; 24742
6165; Keh-yil-dez-bah; F; 17; Navajo; F; S; Niece; 6178; Yes; Yes; 24743
6166; Abner; M; 15; Navajo; F; S; Nephew; 6179; Yes; Yes; 24744
6167; Belone-yen-bih-adzan; F; 65; Navajo; F; Wd; Mother-in-law; 6180; Yes; Yes; 24745

Census of the **Northern Navajo** reservation of the **Northern Navajo** jurisdiction, as of **April 1**, 1931, taken by **Ernest H. Hammond, District**, Superintendent. **in Charge**

Key: Number; NAME: Surname, Given; Sex; Birth Year (if given), Age At Last Birthday; Tribe; Degree of Blood; Marital Status; Relationship To Head of Family; Last Census Roll Number; At Jurisdiction Where Enrolled (Yes or No); At Another Jurisdiction; ELSEWHERE: Post office, County, State; Ward (Yes or No); Allotment, Annuity, and Identification Numbers.

6168; Nah-thlani-bega, John Billy; M; 34; Navajo; F; M; Head; 6181; Yes; Yes; 26332
6169; Nah-thlani-bega, John Billy's wife; F; 30; Navajo; F; M; Wife; 6182; Yes; Yes; 26333
6170; Dah-yiz-bah; F; 4; Navajo; F; S; Daughter; 6183; Yes; Yes; 26334

6171; Natoni; M; 53; Navajo; F; M; Head; 6184; Yes; Yes; 24712
6172; Natoni's wife; F; 60; Navajo; F; M; Wife; 6185; Yes; Yes; 24713
6173; Enos; M; 22; Navajo; F; S; Son; 6186; Yes; Yes; 24714
6174; Hosteen-nez; M; 19; Navajo; F; S; Son; 6187; Yes; Yes; 24715
6175; Kee-yazzie, Thomas; M; 10; Navajo; F; S; Grand-son; 6188; Yes; Yes; 24716
6176; Zannie; F; 25; Navajo; F; Wd; Daughter; 6189; Yes; Yes; 24717
6177; Atate-sosie; F; 3; Navajo; F; S; Grand-daughter; 6190; Yes; Yes; 24718
6178; Lee; M; 7; Navajo; F; S; Grand-son; 6191; Yes; Yes; 24719

6179; Natoh-hahtahly-bega[sic]; M; Unk; Navajo; F; M; Head; 6192; Yes; Yes; 27642
[Name is probably Natoh-hah-tahly-bega]
6180; Bitsih, Barbara; F; 45; Navajo; F; M; Wife; 6193; Yes; Yes; 27643
6181; Raymond; M; 19; Navajo; F; S; Son; 6194; Yes; Yes; 27644
6182; Al-soh-nah-nih-bah; F; 13; Navajo; F; S; Daughter; 6195; Yes; Yes; 27645
6183; Yah-nah-bah; F; 7; Navajo; F; S; Daughter; 6196; Yes; Yes; 27646
6184; Kih-haz-bah; F; 10; Navajo; F; S; Daughter; 6197; Yes; Yes; 27647

6185; Nah-cheeny-benally; M; 37; Navajo; F; Wd; Head; 6198; Yes; Yes; 28535
6186; Chih-nil-wudt; M; 4; Navajo; F; S; Son; 6199; Yes; Yes; 28537

6187; Navajo Tom; M; Unk; Navajo; F; M; Head; 6200; Yes; Yes; 26934
6188; Bah; F; 37; Navajo; F; M; Wife; 6201; Yes; Yes; 26935
6189; Billy; M; 26; Navajo; F; S; Son; 6202; Yes; Yes; 26936
6190; Dick; M; 24; Navajo; F; S; Son; 6203; Yes; Yes; 26937
6191; Keh-hah-nih-bah; F; 17; Navajo; F; S; Daughter; 6204; Yes; Yes; 26938
6192; Jule; M; 16; Navajo; F; S; Son; 6205; Yes; Yes; 26939

6193; Nah-thlani; M; 54; Navajo; F; M; Head; 6206; Yes; Yes; 26831
6194; Hosteen-bih-chie-bitsih; F; 53; Navajo; F; M; Wife; 6207; Yes; Yes; 26832
6195; Florence; F; 21; Navajo; F; S; Daughter; 6208; Yes; Yes; 26833
6196; Frank; M; 20; Navajo; F; S; Son; 6209; Yes; Yes; 26834
6197; Ellen; F; 19; Navajo; F; S; Daughter; 6210; Yes; Yes; 26835
6198; Nah-tah-sosie; M; 7; Navajo; F; S; Son; 6211; Yes; Yes; 26836
6199; John; M; 23; Navajo; F; S; Adopted Son; 6212; Yes; Yes; 26837

6200; Nohtah-sosie; M; 45; Navajo; F; M; Head; 6213; Yes; Yes; 26672
6201; Dez-bah; F; 23; Navajo; F; M; Wife; 6214; Yes; Yes; 26673

Census of the **Northern Navajo** reservation of the **Northern Navajo** jurisdiction, as of **April 1** , 19**31**, taken by **Ernest H. Hammond, District** , Superintendent. **in Charge**

**Key:** Number; NAME: Surname, Given; Sex; Birth Year (if given), Age At Last Birthday; Tribe; Degree of Blood; Marital Status; Relationship To Head of Family; Last Census Roll Number; At Jurisdiction Where Enrolled (Yes or No); At Another Jurisdiction; ELSEWHERE: Post office, County, State; Ward (Yes or No); Allotment, Annuity, and Identification Numbers.

6202; Haska-yee-kas-wudt; M; 3; Navajo; F; S; Son; 6215; Yes; Yes; 26674
6203; Nah-tah-yee-hah-yah; M; 1; Navajo; F; S; Son; 6216; Yes; Yes; 27086

6204; Nocki, John; M; 47; Navajo; F; M; Head; 6217; Yes; Yes; 25000
6205; Nocki, John's wife; F; 41; Navajo; F; M; Wife; 6218; Yes; Yes; 25001
6206; Ah-yih-nil-bah; F; 23; Navajo; F; S; Daughter; 6219; Yes; Yes; 25002
6207; George; M; 13; Navajo; F; S; Son; 6220; Yes; Yes; 25003
6208; Haska-yil-nal-tah; M; 8; Navajo; F; S; Son; 6221; Yes; Yes; 25004
6209; Tah-dez-bah; F; 5; Navajo; F; S; Daughter; 6222; Yes; Yes; 25005
6210; Fred; M; 3; Navajo; F; S; Son; 6223; Yes; Yes; 25006
6211; Bilah, Shorty; F; 71; Navajo; F; Wd; Mother-in-law; 6224; Yes; Yes; 25007

6212; Nocki-bega, John; M; 25; Navajo; F; M; Head; 6225; Yes; Yes; 25243
6213; Nah-glih-yee-lah-naz-bah; F; 20; Navajo; F; M; Wife; 6226; Yes; Yes; 25244
6214; Cheh-nih-bah; F; 3; Navajo; F; S; Daughter; 6227; Yes; Yes; 25245

6215; Nez, John; M; 27; Navajo; F; Wd; Head; 6228; No; McElmo, Colo., San Juan, Utah; Yes; 19338
6216; Nez, Tom; M; 2; Navajo; F; S; Son; 6229; No; McElmo, Colo., San Juan, Utah; Yes; 19513

6217; Neskahia-bega, Fred; M; 48; Navajo; F; M; Head; 6230; Yes; Yes; 27680
6218; Beleen-dal-suen-bikis-bitsih; F; 41; Navajo; F; M; Wife; 6231; Yes; Yes; 27681
6219; Haska-yil-hih-gahl; M; 8; Navajo; F; S; Son; 6232; Yes; Yes; 27682
6220; Bih-kah-ziz-bah; F; 3; Navajo; F; S; Daughter; 6233; Yes; Yes; 27683

6221; Neskahi-bikis; M; 61; Navajo; F; M; Head; 6234; Yes; Yes; 27501
6222; Beleen-dal-suen-bitsih; F; 47; Navajo; F; M; Wife; 6235; Yes; Yes; 27502
6223; Nah-tah-yil-nil-wudt; M; 32; Navajo; F; S; Son; 6236; Yes; Yes; 27503
6224; Big Joe; M; 29; Navajo; F; S; Son; 6237; Yes; Yes; 27504
6225; Baldwin; M; 27; Navajo; F; S; Son; 6238; Yes; Yes; 27505
6226; La-bahih; M; 20; Navajo; F; S; Son; 6239; Yes; Yes; 27506
6227; Simpson; M; 13; Navajo; F; S; Son; 6240; Yes; Yes; 27507
6228; Hosteen; M; 11; Navajo; F; S; Son; 6241; Yes; Yes; 27508
6229; Ann; F; 10; Navajo; F; S; Daughter; 6242; Yes; Yes; 27509
6230; Tahn-dez-bah; F; 8; Navajo; F; S; Daughter; 6243; Yes; Yes; 27510
6231; Al-keh-haz-bah; F; 25; Navajo; F; Wd; Daughter; 6244; Yes; Yes; 27511
6232; Nah-tah-yil-had-dol-nih; M; 4; Navajo; F; S; Grand-son; 6245; Yes; Yes; 27512

6233; Nil-chiz-hartathy-bilah; F; 47; Navajo; F; Wd; Head; 6246; Yes; Yes; 17962

Census of the **Northern Navajo** reservation of the **Northern Navajo** jurisdiction, as of **April 1**, 1931, taken by **Ernest H. Hammond, District**, Superintendent. **in Charge**

**Key:** Number; NAME: Surname, Given; Sex; Birth Year (if given); Age At Last Birthday; Tribe; Degree of Blood; Marital Status; Relationship To Head of Family; Last Census Roll Number; At Jurisdiction Where Enrolled (Yes or No); At Another Jurisdiction; ELSEWHERE: Post office, County, State; Ward (Yes or No); Allotment, Annuity, and Identification Numbers.

6234; Noskiha-benally; M; 35; Navajo; F; M; Head; 6247; Yes; Yes; 22561
6235; Capitan-benally; F; 29; Navajo; F; M; Wife; 6248; Yes; Yes; 22562
6236; Woodrow; M; 12; Navajo F; S; Son; 6249; Yes; Yes; 22563
6237; Bih-hah-ziz-bah; F; 10; Navajo; F; S; Daughter; 6250; Yes; Yes; 22564
6238; Haska-yil-deyah; M; 8; Navajo; F; S; Son; 6251; Yes; Yes; 22565
6239; Haska-yil-nal-wudt; M; 4; Navajo; F; S; Son; 6252; Yes; Yes; 22566
6240; Capitan-benally; M; 25; Navajo; F; S; Brother-in-law; 6253; Yes; Yes; 22567
6241; Capitan, John; M; 16; Navajo; F; S; Brother-in-law; 6254; Yes; Yes; 22568

6242; Neskahi-bega; M; 60; Navajo; F; M; Head; 6255; Yes; Yes; 30298
6243; Neskahi-bega-bih-adzan; F; 62; Navajo; F; M; Wife; 6256; Yes; Yes; 30299
6244; Frank Allen; M; 21; Navajo; F; S; Son; 6257; Yes; Yes; 30300

6245; Nelson, John; M; 35; Navajo; F; M; Head; 6258; Yes; Yes; 25287
6246; Bigman-bitsih; F; 39; Navajo; F; M; Wife; 6259; Yes; Yes; 25288
6247; Brown, Archie; M; 24; Navajo; F; S; Step-son; 6260; Yes; Yes; 25289
6248; Brown, Glenn; M; 22; Navajo; F; S; Step-son; 6261; Yes; Yes; 25290
6249; Brown, Johnson; M; 19; Navajo; F; S; Step-son; 6262; Yes; Yes; 25291
6250; Yazzie Billy, Norma; F; 15; Navajo; F; S; Step-daughter; 6263; Yes; Yes; 25292
6251; Brown, Billy, M; 11; Navajo; F; S; Step-son; 6264; Yes; Yes; 25293
6252; Al-keh-dez-bah; F; 8; Navajo; F; S; Step-daughter; 6265; Yes; Yes; 25294

6253; Nes-kin-dih, David; M; 37; Navajo; F; M: Head; 6266; Yes; Yes; 30316
6254; Neh-bah; F; 29; Navajo; F; M; Wife; 6267; Yes; Yes; 30317
6255; Haska-tay-yah; M; 10; Navajo; F; S; Son; 6268; Yes; Yes; 30318
6256; Yil-day-bah; F; 7; Navajo; F; S; Daughter; 6269; Yes; Yes; 30319
6257; Haska-yil-nal-wudt; M; 3; Navajo; F; S; Son; 6270; Yes; Yes; 30320

6258; Neskiha, Allen; M; 42; Navajo; F; M; Head; 6271; Yes; Yes; 30663
6259; Emma; F; 40; Navajo; F; M; Wife; 6272; Yes; Yes; 30664
6260; Mary Louise; F; 16; Navajo; F; S; Daughter; 6273; Yes; Yes; 30665
6261; Hannah; F; 13; Navajo; F; S; Daughter; 6274; Yes; Yes; 30666
6262; Bessie; F; 11; Navajo; F; S; Daughter; 6275; Yes; Yes; 30667
6263; Allen, Jr.; M; 3; Navajo; F; S; Son; 6276; Yes; Yes; 30668

6264; Neskahi-yazzie; M; 44; Navajo; F; Wd; Head; 6277; Yes; Yes; 29839
6265; Haska-yah-hal-wudt; M; 24; Navajo; F; S; Son; 6278; Yes; Yes; 29841
6266; Haska-yee-chih-has-wudt; M; 22; Navajo; F; S; Son; 6279; Yes; Yes; 29842
6267; Phillip; M; 16; Navajo; F; S; Son; 6280; Yes; Yes; 29843
6268; Haska-yee-tah-des-wudt; M; 10; Navajo; F; S; Son; 6281; Yes; Yes; 29844

Census of the **Northern Navajo** reservation of the **Northern Navajo** jurisdiction, as of **April 1**, 19**31,** taken by **Ernest H. Hammond, District**, Superintendent. **in Charge**

**Key:** Number; NAME: Surname, Given; Sex; Birth Year (if given), Age At Last Birthday; Tribe; Degree of Blood; Marital Status; Relationship To Head of Family; Last Census Roll Number; At Jurisdiction Where Enrolled (Yes or No); At Another Jurisdiction; ELSEWHERE: Post office, County, State; Ward (Yes or No); Allotment, Annuity, and Identification Numbers.

6269; Nih-gih-gih-hah-tahly-bega; M; 48; Navajo; F; M; Head; 6282; Yes; Yes; 23729

6270; Hosteen-li-chee-bitsih; F; 40; Navajo; F; M; Wife; 6283; Yes; Yes; 23730

6271; Warren; M; 21; Navajo; F; S; Son; 6284; Yes; Yes; 23731

6272; Ah-hih-nih-bah; F; 19; Navajo; F; S; Daughter; 6285; Yes; Yes; 23732

6273; Haska-yee-chih-dah-yee-gah; M; 11; Navajo; F; S; Son; 6286; Yes; Yes; 23733

6274; Haska-yee-chih-yee-gahl; M; 8; Navajo; F; S; Son; 6287; Yes; Yes; 23734

6275; Nil-chih-gih-hah-tahly-bega; M; Unk; Navajo; F; M; Head; 6288; Yes; Yes; 23691

6276; Hosteen-l-suen-sana-bitsih; F; Unk; Navajo; F; M; Wife; 6289; Yes; Yes; 23692

6277; Yee-nal-gahl; M; 13; Navajo; F; S; Son; 6290; Yes; Yes; 23693

6278; Keh-yil-haz-bah; F; 8; Navajo; F; S; Daughter; 6291; Yes; Yes; 23694

6279; Haska-yah-nal-wudt; M; 5; Navajo; F; S; Son; 6292; Yes; Yes; 23695

6280; Katherine; F; 25; Navajo; F; S; daughter[sic]; 6293; Yes; Yes; 23696
[Should be Step-daughter]

6281; Robert; M; 21; Navajo; F; S; Step-son; 6294; Yes; Yes; 23697

6282; Neskahi-bitah; M; 40; Navajo; F; M; Head; 6295; Yes; Yes; 23339

6283; Neskahi-bitah's wife; F; 42; Navajo; F; M; Wife; 6296; Yes; Yes; 23340

6284; Sidney; M; 16; Navajo; F; S; Son; 6297; Yes; Yes; 23341

6285; Al-kih-nih-bah; F; 10; Navajo; F; S; daughter[sic]; 6298; Yes; Yes; 23342

6286; Yahn-nih-bah; F; 8; Navajo; F; S; Daughter; 6299; Yes; Yes; 23343

6287; Nah-tah-yee-chih-dah-yee-gah; M; 5; Navajo; F; S; Son; 6300; Yes; Yes; 23344

6288; Nah-tah-yil-chel-wudt; M; 3; Navajo; F; S; Son; 6301; Yes; Yes; 23345

6289; Nih-chih-gih-hah-tahly-bega; M; 33; Navajo; F; M; Head; 6302; Yes; Yes; 23328

6290; Keh-yil-naz-bah; F; 33; Navajo; F; M; Wife; 6303; Yes; Yes; 23329

6291; Keh-haz-bah; F; 10; Navajo; F; S; daughter[sic]; 6304; Yes; Yes; 23330

6292; Haska-yee-tah-nihyah; M; 8; Navajo; F; S; Son; 6305; Yes; Yes; 23331

6293; Nah-tah-yee-kih-nih-yah; M; 3; Navajo; F; S; Son; 6306; Yes; Yes; 23332

6294; Dagah-clit-suen-bitsih; F; 78; Navajo; F; Wd; Grand-mother; 6307; Yes; Yes; 23333

6295; Nil-chih-gih-hah-tahly-bega; M; 44; Navajo; F; M; Head; 6308; Yes; Yes; 26351

6296; Bah; F; 42; Navajo; F; M; Wife; 6309; Yes; Yes; 26352

6297; Niohtah; M; Unk; Navajo; F; M; Head; 6310; Yes; Yes; 29019

Census of the **Northern Navajo** reservation of the **Northern Navajo** jurisdiction, as of **April 1**, 19**31,** taken by **Ernest H. Hammond, District**, Superintendent. **in Charge**

**Key:** Number; NAME: Surname, Given; Sex; Birth Year (if given), Age At Last Birthday; Tribe; Degree of Blood; Marital Status; Relationship To Head of Family; Last Census Roll Number; At Jurisdiction Where Enrolled (Yes or No); At Another Jurisdiction; ELSEWHERE: Post office, County, State; Ward (Yes or No); Allotment, Annuity, and Identification Numbers.

6298; Clah-chis-chilli-bitsih; F; 54; Navajo; F; M; Wife; 6311; Yes; Yes; 29020
6299; Haska-yah-dil-wudt; M; 22; Navajo; F; S; Son; 6312; Yes; Yes; 29021
6300; Cleveland; M; 20; Navajo; F; S; Son; 6313; Yes; Yes; 29022
6301; Jackson; M; 19; Navajo; F; S; Son; 6314; Yes; Yes; 29023
6302; Yah-dez-bah; F; 7; Navajo; F; S; daughter[sic]; 6315; Yes; Yes; 29024

6303; Nil-chih-gih-hah-tahly-bega; M; Unk; Navajo; F; M; Head; 6316; Yes; Yes; 25192
6304; Al-kih-nih-bah; F; 26; Navajo; F; M; Wife; 6317; Yes; Yes; 25193
6305; Yee-kah-nez-bah; F; 9; Navajo; F; S; daughter; 6318; Yes; Yes; 25194
6306; Haska-yee-nas-wudt; M; 4; Navajo; F; S; Son; 6319; Yes; Yes; 25195

6307; Noon, Jimmy; M; Unk; Navajo; F; M; Head; 6320; Yes; Yes; 29246
6308; Yah-nih-bah; F; 62; Navajo; F; M; Wife; 6321; Yes; Yes; 29247
6309; Zah-see; M; 35; Navajo; F; S; Step-son; 6322; Yes; Yes; 29248
6310; Dinay-seeih; M; 26; Navajo; F; S; Step-son; 6323; Yes; Yes; 29249
6311; Bahih; M; 23; Navajo; F; S; Step-son; 6324; Yes; Yes; 29250
6312; Secih; M; 20; Navajo; F; S; Step-son; 6325; Yes; Yes; 29251
6313; Al-zil-seeih; F; 11; Navajo; F; S; Step-grand-daughter; 6326; Yes; Yes; 29252

6314; Nocki Yazzie's Mother; F; 61; Navajo; F; Wd; Head; 6327; Yes; Yes; 32268

6315; Nocki-Yazzie-bitah; M; 23; Navajo; F; M; Head; 6328; Yes; Yes; 18210
6316; Yee-nil-bah; F; 23; Navajo; F; M; Wife; 6329; Yes; Yes; 18211
6317; Charles; M; 4; Navajo; F; S; Son; 6330; Yes; Yes; 18280

6318; Nocki-yazzie's wife, Aht-citty-bitsih; F; 47; Navajo; F; Wd; Head; 6332; Yes; Yes; 30327
6319; Minnie; F; 22; Navajo; F; S; Daughter; 6333; Yes; Yes; 30328
6320; Bertha; F; 17; Navajo; F; S; Daughter; 6334; Yes; Yes; 30330
6321; Woody; M; 14; Navajo; F; S; Son; 6335; Yes; Yes; 30331
6322; Daniel; M; 7; Navajo; F; S; Son; 6336; Yes; Yes; 30332
6323; Esther; F; 14; Navajo; F; S; Grand-daughter; 6337; Yes; Yes; 30334
6324; Ray Harvey (son of Minnie); M; 6/12; Navajo; F; S; Grand-son; [Blank]; Yes; Yes; 31295

6325; Nocki-dinay, Charley Stanley; M; 32; Navajo; F; M: Head; 6338; Yes; Yes; 30255
6326; Kadt-se-ahih-bitsih; F; 32; Navajo; F; M; Wife; 6339; Yes; Yes; 30256
6327; Yee-kih-nih-yah; M; 10; Navajo; F; S; Son; 6340; Yes; Yes; 30257
6328; Charley Harris; M; 8; Navajo; F; S; Son; 6341; Yes; Yes; 30258

6329; Nocki-dinay-bega, Ben; M; 9; Navajo; F; M; Head; 6342; Yes; Yes; 19957

Census of the **Northern Navajo** reservation of the **Northern Navajo** jurisdiction, as of **April 1**, 19**31,** taken by **Ernest H. Hammond, District**, Superintendent. **in Charge**

**Key:** Number; NAME: Surname, Given; Sex; Birth Year (if given), Age At Last Birthday; Tribe; Degree of Blood; Marital Status; Relationship To Head of Family; Last Census Roll Number; At Jurisdiction Where Enrolled (Yes or No); At Another Jurisdiction; ELSEWHERE: Post office, County, State; Ward (Yes or No); Allotment, Annuity, and Identification Numbers.

6330;  Bega-ith-linn-bitsih; F; 29; Navajo; F; M; Wife; 6343; Yes; Yes; 19958

6331;  Bega-ith-lin-bitsih-Emily; F; 15; Navajo; F; S; Step-daughter; 6344; Yes; Yes; 19959

6332;  Kee-soh; M; 7; Navajo; F; S; Son; 6345; Yes; Yes; 19960

6333;  Ah-hah-yis-bah; F; 5; Navajo; F; S; Daughter; 6346; Yes; Yes; 19961

6334;  Zannie-seeih; F; 9; Navajo; F; S; Sister-in-law; 6347; Yes; Yes; 19962


6335;  Nocki-yazzie; M; Unk; Navajo; F; Wd; Head; 6348; Yes; Yes; 32265

6336;  Julian-bih-adzan; F; 82; Navajo; F; Wd; Grand-mother; 6349; Yes; Yes; 32266

6337;  Haska-yil-ee-yah; M; 18; Navajo; F; S; Nephew; 6350; Yes; Yes; 32267


6338;  Nocki-dinay-Uienth-nez-bega; M; 37; Navajo; F; M; Head; 6351; No; McElmo, Colo., San Juan, Utah; Yes; 18812

6339;  Bitsih, Little Jane; F; 43; Navajo; F; M; Wife; 6352; No; McElmo, Colo., San Juan, Utah; Yes; 18813

6340;  Hoska-yee-nal-wul; M; 19; Navajo; F; S; daughter[sic]; 6353; No; McElmo, Colo., San Juan, Utah; Yes; 18814          [This should be Son]

6341;  McKean, Ida; F; 17; Navajo; F; S; daughter[sic]; 6354; No; McElmo, Colo., San Juan, Utah; Yes; 18815

6342;  Yilth-ah-yah; M; 10; Navajo; F; S; Son; 6355; No; McElmo, Colo., San Juan, Utah; Yes; 18816

6343;  Yee-tah-dez-bah; F; 9; Navajo; F; S; Daughter; 6356; No; McElmo, Colo., San Juan, Utah; Yes; 18817

6344;  Yinl-l-bah; F; 3; Navajo; F; S; daughter; 6357; No; McElmo, Colo., San Juan, Utah; Yes; 18818


6345;  Nocki-dinay-Uienth-nez; M; Unk; Navajo; F; Wd; Head; 6358; No; McElmo, Colo., San Juan, Utah; Yes; 18819

6346;  Jones, Elizabeth; F; 19; Navajo; F; S; Daughter; 6359; No; McElmo, Colo., San Juan, Utah; Yes; 18820

6347;  Hoska-ye-dah-hah-zah; M; 14; Navajo; F; S; Son; 6360; No; McElmo, Colo., San Juan, Utah; Yes; 18821

6348;  Yazzie-l-bahih; M; 10; Navajo; F; S; Son; 6361; No; McElmo, Colo., San Juan, Utah; Yes; 18822


6349;  Nocki-yazzie-yan-bih-zanih; F; 73; Navajo; F; Wd; Head; 6362; No; McElmo, Colo., San Juan, Utah; Yes; 18825


6350;  Nocki-l-chee-bega; M; Unk; Navajo; F; M; Head; 6363; Yes; Yes; 22708

6351;  Adzan-l-bahih; F; 33; Navajo; F; M; Wife; 6364; Yes; Yes; 22709

Census of the **Northern Navajo** reservation of the **Northern Navajo** jurisdiction, as of **April 1**, 1931, taken by **Ernest H. Hammond, District**, Superintendent. **in Charge**

**Key:** Number; NAME: Surname, Given; Sex; Birth Year (if given), Age At Last Birthday; Tribe; Degree of Blood; Marital Status; Relationship To Head of Family; Last Census Roll Number; At Jurisdiction Where Enrolled (Yes or No); At Another Jurisdiction; ELSEWHERE: Post office, County, State; Ward (Yes or No); Allotment, Annuity, and Identification Numbers.

6361; Nocki-deetsah-bega, Willard; M; 13; Navajo; F; S; Son; 6374; Yes; Yes; 20018

6362; Zannie-l-chee; F; 9; Navajo; F; S; Daughter; 6375; Yes; Yes; 20019

6363; Chee-yazzie; F; 6; Navajo; F; S; Daughter; 6376; Yes; Yes; 20020

6364; Nocki-Destsah-Bega[sic], Tom; M; 4; Navajo; F; S; Son; 6377; Yes; Yes; 20021    [Name is probably Nocki-Deetsah-Bega, Tom]

6365; Nocki-deetsah-benally; F; 26; Navajo; F; S; Head; 6378; No; McElmo, Colo., San Juan, Utah; Yes; 19466

6366; Nocki-dinay-bega; M; 29; Navajo; F; M; Head; 6379; Yes; Yes; 19963

6367; Bega-ith-linn-bitsih; F; 27; Navajo; F; M; Wife; 6380; Yes; Yes; 19964

6368; Zannie-l-chee; F; 8; Navajo; F; S; Son[sic]; 6381; Yes; Yes; 19965
[Should be female.]

6369; Eskee-l-bahih; M; 5; Navajo; F; S; Son; 6382; Yes; Yes; 19966

6370; Bega-ith-linn, David; M; 25; Navajo; F; S; Brother-in-law; 6383; Yes; Yes; 19968

6371; Nocki-Dinay-bega-bilatsoh; M; 36; Navajo; F; M; Head; 6384; No; McElmo, Colo., San Juan, Utah; Yes; 18933

6372; West, Jessie; F; 37; Navajo; F; M; Wife; 6385; No; McElmo, Colo., San Juan, Utah; Yes; 18934

6373; Emma; F; 9; Navajo; F; S; Daughter; 6386; No; McElmo, Colo., San Juan, Utah; Yes; 18935

6374; Hoska-yestah-noh-tih; M; 8; Navajo; F; S; Son; 6387; No; McElmo, Colo., San Juan, Utah; Yes; 18936

6375; George; M; 6; Navajo; F; S; Son; 6388; No; McElmo, Colo., San Juan, Utah; Yes; 18937

6376; Arthur; M; 3; Navajo; F; S; Son; 6389; No; McElmo, Colo., San Juan, Utah; Yes; 18938

6377; Nocki-chee-bega, Lee-Joe; F[sic]; 40; Navajo; F; M; Head; 6390; No; McElmo, Colo., San Juan, Utah; Yes; 19249

6378; Adzan-l-suen; F; 42; Navajo; F; M; Wife; 6391; No; McElmo, Colo., San Juan, Utah; Yes; 19250

6379; Nocki-chee, Mr. Lee; M; 7; Navajo; F; M; Head; 6392; No; McElmo, Colo., San Juan, Utah; Yes; 19245

6380; Nocki-chee, Susie; F; 49; Navajo; F; M; Wife; 6393; No; McElmo, Colo., San Juan, Utah; Yes; 19246

6381; Yee-nih-bah; F; 10; Navajo; F; S; Daughter; 6394; No; McElmo, Colo., San Juan, Utah; Yes; 19247

Census of the **Northern Navajo** reservation of the **Northern Navajo** jurisdiction, as of **April 1** , 1931, taken by **Ernest H. Hammond, District**, Superintendent. **in Charge**

**Key:** Number; NAME: Surname, Given; Sex; Birth Year (if given), Age At Last Birthday; Tribe; Degree of Blood; Marital Status; Relationship To Head of Family; Last Census Roll Number; At Jurisdiction Where Enrolled (Yes or No); At Another Jurisdiction; ELSEWHERE: Post office, County, State; Ward (Yes or No); Allotment, Annuity, and Identification Numbers.

6382;  Hoska-yih-nil-wudt; M; 4; Navajo; F; S; Son; 6395; No; McElmo, Colo., San Juan, Utah; Yes; 19248

6383;  Nocki-dinay's Second Wife; F; 62; Navajo; F; Wd; Head; 6396; No; McElmo, Colo., San Juan, Utah; Yes; 18931
6384;  Nocki-dinay-bega; M; 22; Navajo; F; S; Son; 6397; No; McElmo, Colo., San Juan, Utah; Yes; 18932

6385;  Nocki-Destsah-bitsoih[sic]; M; 32; Navajo; F; M; Head; 6398; No; McElmo, Colo., San Juan, Utah; Yes; 19226   [Name is probably Nocki-Deetsah-bitsoih]
6386;  Tahn-des-bah; F; 22; Navajo; F; M; Wife; 6399; No; McElmo, Colo., San Juan, Utah; Yes; 19227
6387;  Tah-deyah; M; 6; Navajo; F; S; Son; 6400; No; McElmo, Colo., San Juan, Utah; Yes; 19228
6388;  Tah-nih-bah; F; 4; Navajo; F; S; Daughter; 6401; No; McElmo, Colo., San Juan, Utah; Yes; 19229

6389;  Nocki-Dinay; M; Unk; Navajo; F; Wd; Head; 6402; Yes; Yes; 17329
6390;  Nocki-dinay-bahih; M; 6; Navajo; F; S; Son; 6403; Yes; Yes; 17330

6391;  Nocki-Dinay-bega, badone, Clifford; M; 24; Navajo; F; M; Head; 6404; Yes; Yes; 21017
6392;  Tah-dez-bah; F; 20; Navajo; F; M; Wife; 6405; Yes; Yes; 21018
6393;  Peter Clifford; M; 2; Navajo; F; S; Son; 6406; Yes; Yes; 21698

6394;  Nocki-l-chee-bega; M; 23; Navajo; F; M; Head; 6407; Yes; Yes; 21163
6395;  Hah-nah-gah-nih-bitsih; F; 25; Navajo; F; M; Wife; 6408; Yes; Yes; 21164
6396;  Tah-zoz-bah; F; 7; Navajo; F; S; Daughter; 6409; Yes; Yes; 21165

6397;  Nocki-dinay-bega; M; 46; Navajo; F; M: Head; 6410; Yes; Yes; 21009
6398;  Dinay-yazzie-bitsih; F; 40; Navajo; F; M; Wife; 6411; Yes; Yes; 21010
6399;  Bil-nas-nih-bah; F; 13; Navajo; F; S; Daughter; 6412; Yes; Yes; 21011
6400;  Nocki-Dinay, Elnora; F; 12; Navajo; F; S; Daughter; 6413; Yes; Yes; 21012
6401;  Nah-tah-yil-ninih-yah; M; 10; Navajo; F; S; Son; 6414; Yes; Yes; 21013
6402;  Hoska-yee-tah-nas-wudt; M; 9; Navajo; F; S; Son; 6415; Yes; Yes; 21014
6403;  Bah-nih-ziz-bah; F; 6; Navajo; F; S; Daughter; 6416; Yes; Yes; 21015
6404;  Haska-yee-tah-deyah; M; 4; Navajo; F; S; Son; 6417; Yes; Yes; 21016
6405;  Nah-dah-yil-hah-wudt; M; 2; Navajo; F; S; Son; 6418; Yes; Yes; 21699

6406;  Nocki-Dinay-Clitsohigi-bega's wife, Hosteen-Gonih-benally; F; 23; Navajo; F; Wd; Head; 6419; Yes; Yes; 20975
6407;  Hoska-yee-tah-yee-galh; M; 11; Navajo; F; S; Son; 6420; Yes; Yes; 20976
6408;  Al-kin-nih-bah; F; 9; Navajo; F; S; Daughter; 6421; Yes; Yes; 20977

Census of the **Northern Navajo** reservation of the **Northern Navajo** jurisdiction, as of **April 1**, 19**31,** taken by **Ernest H. Hammond, District**, Superintendent. **in Charge**

**Key:** Number; NAME: Surname, Given; Sex; Birth Year (if given), Age At Last Birthday; Tribe; Degree of Blood; Marital Status; Relationship To Head of Family; Last Census Roll Number; At Jurisdiction Where Enrolled (Yes or No); At Another Jurisdiction; ELSEWHERE: Post office, County, State; Ward (Yes or No); Allotment, Annuity, and Identification Numbers.

6409; Doh-yah-o-lih; M; 7; Navajo; F; S; Son; 64222[sic]; Yes; Yes; 20978
[Last Roll No. 6422]
6410; Alh-nee-nas-wudt; M; 5; Navajo; F; S; Son; 6423; Yes; Yes; 20979

6411; Nocki-Dinay-nez-bega; M; 33; Navajo; F; M; Head; 6424; Yes; Yes; 20920
6412; Kin-lah-cheeny-bitsoih; F; 23; Navajo; F; M; Wife; 6425; Yes; Yes; 20921
6413; Nas-bah; F; 10; Navajo; F; S; Daughter; 6426; Yes; Yes; 20922
6414; Nah-glih-hah-nas-bah; F; 8; Navajo; F; S; Daughter; 6427; Yes; Yes; 20923
6415; Nah-tah-naz-wudt; M; 5; Navajo; F; S; Son; 6428; Yes; Yes; 20924

6416; Nocki-Hosteen; M; 63; Navajo; F; M; Head; 6429; Yes; Yes; 17987
6417; Nocki-Hosteen's wife; F; 37; Navajo; F; M; Wife; 6430; Yes; Yes; 17988
6418; Grey, Raymond; M; 21; Navajo; F; S; Son; 6431; Yes; Yes; 17989
6419; Hoske-l-wudt-Nocki; M; 16; Navajo; F; S; Son; 6432; Yes; Yes; 17990
6420; Nocki, Fay; F; 12; Navajo; F; S; Daughter; 6433; Yes; Yes; 17991
6421; Nocki-Blih; F; 9; Navajo; F; S; Daughter; 6434; Yes; Yes; 17992
6422; Adzan-l-suen; F; 7; Navajo; F; S; Daughter; 6435; Yes; Yes; 17993

6423; Nocki-bega; M; 30; Navajo; F; M; Head; 6437; Yes; Yes; 17999
6424; Tony-Yazzie-bitsih; F; 25; Navajo; F; M; Wife; 6438; Yes; Yes; 18000
6425; Nocki-bega-nez; M; 9; Navajo; F; S; Son; 6439; Yes; Yes; 18001
6426; Adzan-ih-etseesol; F; 7; Navajo; F; S; Daughter; 6440; Yes; Yes; 18002
6427; Adzan-ih-yazzie; F; 3; Navajo; F; S; Daughter; 6441; Yes; Yes; 18003
6428; Haska-chan-has-gade; M; 2; Navajo; F; S; Daughter[sic]; 6442; Yes; Yes; 18295
[Should be male]

6429; Nocki-Hosteen; M; 38; Navajo; F; M; Head; 6443; Yes; Yes; 18025
6430; Ditsees-ish-bize-bitsih; F; 31; Navajo; F; M; Wife; 6444; Yes; Yes; 18026
6431; Seeih; F; 15; Navajo; F; S; Daughter; 6445; Yes; Yes; 18027
6432; Shenih; M; 8; Navajo; F; S; Son; 6446; Yes; Yes; 18028

6433; Nocki-dinay, First Wife; F; 55; Navajo; F; Wd; Head; 6447; Yes; Yes; 13886
6434; Nocki-Dinay, Paul; M; 25; Navajo; F; M; Head; 6448; Yes; Yes; 20909
6435; Kin-lah-cheeny-bitsoih; F; 20; Navajo; F; M; Wife; 6449; Yes; Yes; 20910
6436; Yee-nas-bah, Mary; F; 5; Navajo; F; S; Daughter; 6450; Yes; Yes; 20911
6437; Beleen-la-bahih, Paul Jr; M; 3; Navajo; F; S; Son; 6451; Yes; Yes; 20912
6438; Aht-nas-gee-bah; F; 1; Navajo; F; S; Daughter; 6452; Yes; Yes; 21729

6439; Nocki-Dinay-Nez; M; 69; Navajo; F; M; Head; 6453; Yes; Yes; 20901
6440; Kin-lah-cheeny-bitsih; F; 63; Navajo; F; M; Wife; 6454; Yes; Yes; 20902
6441; Nocki-Dinay-Nez-, Sidney; M; 20; Navajo; F; S; Son; 6455; Yes; Yes; 20903
6442; Dinay-l-chee; M; 20; Navajo; F; S; Step-son; 6456; Yes; Yes; 20904

Census of the **Northern Navajo** reservation of the **Northern Navajo** jurisdiction, as of **April 1**, 19**31,** taken by **Ernest H. Hammond, District**, Superintendent. **in Charge**

**Key:** Number; NAME: Surname, Given; Sex; Birth Year (if given), Age At Last Birthday; Tribe; Degree of Blood; Marital Status; Relationship To Head of Family; Last Census Roll Number; At Jurisdiction Where Enrolled (Yes or No); At Another Jurisdiction; ELSEWHERE: Post office, County, State; Ward (Yes or No); Allotment, Annuity, and Identification Numbers.

6443; Nocki-Dinay-Nez-, Lucille; F; 17; Navajo; F; S; Step-daughter; 6457; Yes; Yes; 20905

6444; Nocki-Dinay-Nez, Ida; F; 17; Navajo; F; S; Grand-daughter; 6458; Yes; Yes; 20906

6445; Houh-has-bah; F; 16; Navajo; F; S; Grand-daughter; 6459; Yes; Yes; 20907

6446; Toh-dih-kozie, Gilbert; M; 19; Navajo; F; S; Grand-son; 6460; Yes; Yes; 20908

6447; Nocki-l-chee-bih-adzan; F; 45; Navajo; F; M; Head; 6461; Yes; Yes; 21534

6448; Steve; M; 16; Navajo; F; S; Son; 6462; Yes; Yes; 21535

6449; Hoska-yee-dah-wudt; M; 12; Navajo; F; S; Son; 6463; Yes; Yes; 21536

6450; Dah-hah-bah; F; 7; Navajo; F; S; Daughter; 6464; Yes; Yes; 21537

6451; Nocki-Yazzie-bega, John; M; 42; Navajo; F; Wd; Head; 6465; No; McElmo, Colo., San Juan, Utah; Yes; 18844

6452; Nocki-l-chee; M; 50; Navajo; F; M; Head; 6466; Yes; Yes; 21521

6453; Toh-sonie-bitsih; F; 49; Navajo; F; M; Wife; 6467; Yes; Yes; 21522

6454; Hoska-yee-tah-hah-zah; M; 19; Navajo; F; S; Son; 6468; Yes; Yes; 21523

6455; Nip-bahih; F; 16; Navajo; F; S; Daughter; 6469; Yes; Yes; 21524

6456; Yee-kih-nih-bah; F; 8; Navajo; F; S; Daughter; 6470; Yes; Yes; 21525

6457; Nos-bah; F; 2; Navajo; F; S; Daughter; 6471; Yes; Yes; 21629

6458; Nocki-dinay-bega's wife, Dinay-yazzie-bitsih; F; 47; Navajo; F; Wd; Head; 6472; Yes; Yes; 21579

6459; Toh-des-wudt-ih; M; 23; Navajo; F; S; Son; 6473; Yes; Yes; 21580

6460; Nah-glih-hah-nah-bah; F; 18; Navajo; F; S; Daughter; 6474; Yes; Yes; 21581

6461; Katherine; F; 16; Navajo; F; S; Daughter; 6475; Yes; Yes; 21582

6462; Nora; F; 14; Navajo; F; S; Daughter; 6476; Yes; Yes; 21583

6463; Yahn-bah; F; 11; Navajo; F; S; Daughter; 6477; Yes; Yes; 21584

6464; Chih-nil-wudt; M; 9; Navajo; F; S; Son; 6478; Yes; Yes; 21585

6465; Nocki-l-chee-badoni; M; 33; Navajo; F; M; Head; 6479; Yes; Yes; 21150

6466; Nocki-l-chee-bitsih; F; 25; Navajo; F; M; Wife; 6480; Yes; Yes; 21151

6467; Nih-gee-bah; F; 10; Navajo; F; S; Daughter; 6481; Yes; Yes; 21152

6468; Tah-hih; M; 7; Navajo; F; S; Son; 6482; Yes; Yes; 21153

6469; Toh-sonie-benally; M; 22; Navajo; F; S; Nephew; 6483; Yes; Yes; 21155

6470; Dah-yazzie; M; 10; Navajo; F; S; Nephew; 6484; Yes; Yes; 21156

6471; Nocki-dinay, Eddie; M; 31; Navajo; F; M; Head; 6485; No; McElmo, Colo., San Juan, Utah; Yes; 18856

6472; Hartathle, Jim's daughter; F; 28; Navajo; F; M; Wife; 6486; No; McElmo, Colo., San Juan, Utah; Yes; 18857

Census of the __Northern Navajo__ reservation of the __Northern Navajo__ jurisdiction, as of __April 1__, 1931, taken by __Ernest H. Hammond, District__, Superintendent. **in Charge**

**Key:** Number; NAME: Surname, Given; Sex; Birth Year (if given), Age At Last Birthday; Tribe; Degree of Blood; Marital Status; Relationship To Head of Family; Last Census Roll Number; At Jurisdiction Where Enrolled (Yes or No); At Another Jurisdiction; ELSEWHERE: Post office, County, State; Ward (Yes or No); Allotment, Annuity, and Identification Numbers.

6473; Nah-gliz-bah[sic]; F; 11; Navajo; F; S; Daughter; 6487; No; McElmo, Colo., San Juan, Utah; Yes; 18858    [Name should be Nah-cliz-bah]
6474; Hoska-yee-nah-ch-dahl; M; 6; Navajo; F; S; Son; 6488; No; McElmo, Colo., San Juan, Utah; Yes; 18859

6475; Nocki-Yazzie-bega; M; 42; Navajo; F; M; Head; 6489; No; McElmo, Colo., San Juan, Utah; Yes; 18877
6476; Nocki-Yazzie-bega's wife; F; 38; Navajo; F; M; Wife; 6490; No; McElmo, Colo., San Juan, Utah; Yes; 18878
6577; Nocki-Yazzie, Dora; F; 19; Navajo; F; S; Daughter; 6491; No; McElmo, Colo., San Juan, Utah; Yes; 18879
6478; Fah-hah-bah; F; 13; Navajo; F; S; Daughter; 6492; No; McElmo, Colo., San Juan, Utah; Yes; 18880
6479; Hoska-yee-tah-dyah; M; 8; Navajo; F; S; Son; 6493; No; McElmo, Colo., San Juan, Utah; Yes; 18881
6480; Hoska-yil-des-wudt; M; 4; Navajo; F; S; Son; 6494; No; McElmo, Colo., San Juan, Utah; Yes; 18882

6481; Nocki, James; M; 33; Navajo; F; M; Head; 6495; Yes; Yes; 21573
6482; Allie; F; 33; Navajo; F; M; Wife; 6496; Yes; Yes; 21574
6483; Jimmie; M; 7; Navajo; F; S; Son; 6497; Yes; Yes; 21575
6484; Christine; F; 5; Navajo; F; S; Daughter; 6498; Yes; Yes; 21576
6485; Raymond; M; 1; Navajo; F; S; Son; 6499; Yes; Yes; 21722

6486; Nocki-suen; M; 23; Navajo; F; M; Head; 6500; Yes; Yes; 24738
6487; Josephine; F; 38; Navajo; F; M; Wife; 6501; Yes; Yes; 24739

6488; Nocki-sosie; M; 41; Navajo; F; M; Head; 6502; Yes; Yes; 24732
6489; Tah-nih-bah; F; 25; Navajo; F; M; Wife; 6503; Yes; Yes; 24733
6490; Tahn-hah-naz-bah, Mary; F; 12; Navajo; F; S; Daughter; 6504; Yes; Yes; 24734
6491; Jessie; F; 10; Navajo; F; S; Daughter; 6505; Yes; Yes; 24735
6492; Nah-sah-yil-wudt; M; 8; Navajo; F; S; Son; 6506; Yes; Yes; 24736
6493; Bil-nih-ziz-bah; F; 4; Navajo; F; S; Daughter; 6507; Yes; Yes; 24737

6494; Nocki-Yazzie, Harry; M; 42; Navajo; F; M; Head; 6508; Yes; Yes; 28038
6495; Harry's wife; F; 33; Navajo; F; M; Wife; 6509; Yes; Yes; 28039
6496; Mary; F; 6; Navajo; F; S; Daughter; 6510; Yes; Yes; 28040
6497; Robert; M; 4; Navajo; F; S; Son; 6511; Yes; Yes; 28041
6498; Woh-yah; M; 10; Navajo; F; S; Nephew; 6512; Yes; Yes; 28042
6499; Eddie; M; 8; Navajo; F; S; Nephew; 6513; Yes; Yes; 28043

6500; Nocki-dinay, James; M; 38; Navajo; F; M; Head; 6514; Yes; Yes; 28321

205

Census of the **Northern Navajo** reservation of the **Northern Navajo** jurisdiction, as of **April 1**, 19**31**, taken by **Ernest H. Hammond, District**, Superintendent. **in Charge**

**Key:** Number; NAME: Surname, Given; Sex; Birth Year (if given), Age At Last Birthday; Tribe; Degree of Blood; Marital Status; Relationship To Head of Family; Last Census Roll Number; At Jurisdiction Where Enrolled (Yes or No); At Another Jurisdiction; ELSEWHERE: Post office, County, State; Ward (Yes or No); Allotment, Annuity, and Identification Numbers.

6501; Dohi-ih-yen-bitsoih; F; 32; Navajo; F; M: 6515; Wife; Yes; Yes; 28322
6502; Nah-glih; F; 11; Navajo; F; S; Daughter; 6516; Yes; Yes; 28323
6503; Yazzie; F; 10; Navajo; F; S; Daughter; 6517; Yes; Yes; 28324
6504; Nih-bah; F; 6; Navajo; F; S; Daughter; 6518; Yes; Yes; 28325
6505; Nah-tah-yee-tah-gah; M; 3; Navajo; F; S; Son; 6519; Yes; Yes; 28326
6506; Kee; M; 14; Navajo; F; S; Nephew; 6520; Yes; Yes; 28333

6507; Nocki-Dinay-Ensasighi; M; 35; Navajo; F; Wd; Head; 6521; Yes; Yes; 28392
6508; Zannie-bah; F; 9; Navajo; F; S; Daughter; 6522; Yes; Yes; 28393

6509; Nocki-destsah-ah-bih-bize; M; 24; Navajo; F; M; Head; 6523; Yes; Yes; 28410
6510; Noh-toh-bitsih; F; 24; Navajo; F; M; Wife; 6524; Yes; Yes; 28521
6511; Nah-se-dil-kidih-bega, David; M; 6; Navajo; F; S; Brother; 6525; Yes; Yes; 28422
6512; Awie; M; 1; Navajo; F; S; Son; 6526; Yes; Yes; 28548

6513; Nocki-dinay-bega; M; 29; Navajo; F; M; Head; 6527; Yes; Yes; 28394
6514; Cudih-yen-bitsih; F; 28; Navajo; F; M; Wife; 6528; Yes; Yes; 28395
6515; Gee-yazzie; F; 6; Navajo; F; S; Daughter; 6529; Yes; Yes; 28396

6516; Nat-cle-bikis-bega; M; 27; Navajo; F; M; Head; 6530; Yes; Yes; 32991
6517; Al-dah-nahn-bah, Little John's daughter; F; 19; Navajo; F; M; Wife; 6531; Yes; Yes; 32992

6518; Natoni-bega; M; 25; Navajo; F; M; Head; 6532; Yes; Yes; 32815
6519; Charley-benally-bitsih; F; 24; Navajo; F; M; Wife; 6533; Yes; Yes; 32816
6520; Nah-tah-yee-tah-deyah; M; 5; Navajo; F; S; Son; 6534; Yes; Yes; 32817

6521; Natoni-bih-adzan; F; 62; Navajo; F; Wd; Head; 6535; Yes; Yes; 32811
6522; Natoni-bitsih; M; 29; Navajo; F; Wd; Grand-son; 6536; Yes; Yes; 32812
6523; Haska-yil-deyah; M; 20; Navajo; F; S; Grand-son; 6537; Yes; Yes; 32813
6524; Dinay-l-suen-benally-bega; M; 9; Navajo; F; S; Grand-son; 6538; Yes; Yes; 32814

6525; Niotah-hosteen-bitsih; M; 86; Navajo; F; M; Head; 6539; Yes; Yes; 32832
6526; Hosteen-nil-chih-lih-bitsih; F; 76; Navajo; F; M; Wife; 6540; Yes; Yes; 32833
6527; Glih-hah-bah; F; 14; Navajo; F; S; Grand-daughter; 6541; Yes; Yes; 32834
6528; Haska-yee-nas-wudt; M; 13; Navajo; F; S; Grand-son; 6542; Yes; Yes; 32835
6529; Haska-yil-hal-wudt, Willie; M; 12; Navajo; F; S; Grand-son; 6543; Yes; Yes; 32836

6530; Nocki-Clah, Tom Lee; M; 34; Navajo; F; M; Head; 6544; Yes; Yes; 32954

Census of the **Northern Navajo** reservation of the **Northern Navajo** jurisdiction, as of **April 1** , 19**31,** taken by **Ernest H. Hammond, District**, Superintendent. **in Charge**

**Key:** Number; NAME: Surname, Given; Sex; Birth Year (if given), Age At Last Birthday; Tribe; Degree of Blood; Marital Status; Relationship To Head of Family; Last Census Roll Number; At Jurisdiction Where Enrolled (Yes or No); At Another Jurisdiction; ELSEWHERE: Post office, County, State; Ward (Yes or No); Allotment, Annuity, and Identification Numbers.

6531;   Sih-nah-gahnih-bitsih; F; 25; Navajo; F; M; Wife; 6545; Yes; Yes; 32955
6532;   Yazzie, Charley; M; 13; Navajo; F; S; Son; 6546; Yes; Yes; 32956
6533;   Tah-dez-bah; F; 9; Navajo; F; S; Son[sic]; 6547; Yes; Yes; 32957
                         [Should be female]
6534;   Haska-yee-kih-des-wudt; M; 5; Navajo; F; S; Son; 6548; Yes; Yes; 32958
6535;   Nah-tah-yee-kih-des-wudt; M; 7; Navajo; F; S; Son; 6549; Yes; Yes; 32959

6536;   Nanl-cadih, John; M; Unk; Navajo; F; Div; Head; 6550; Yes; Yes; 31206
6537;   Herman; M; 13; Navajo; F; S; Son; 6551; Yes; Yes; 31207

6538;   Nocki-Destsah-bikis; M; Unk; Navajo; F; M; Head; 6552; No; McElmo, Colo., San Juan, Utah; Yes; 19493
6539;   Hosteen-nez-bitsih; F; 45; Navajo; F; M; Wife; 6553; No; McElmo, Colo., San Juan, Utah; Yes; 19494
6540;   Frank; M; 28; Navajo; F; S; Son; 6554; No; McElmo, Colo., San Juan, Utah; Yes; 19495
6541;   Albert Wilson; M; 12; Navajo; F; S; Son; 6555; No; McElmo, Colo., San Juan, Utah; Yes; 19496
6542;   Jessie Lansing; F; 9; Navajo; F; S; Daughter; 6556; No; McElmo, Colo., San Juan, Utah; Yes; 19497
6543;   Yee-tas-bah; M; 6; Navajo; F; S; Son; 6557; No; McElmo, Colo., San Juan, Utah; Yes; 19498

6544;   Nah-seeih-benally; M; Unk; Navajo; F; M; Head; 6558; Yes; Yes; 22760
6545;   Nah-cheeny-bitah-bega-bitsih; F; 23; Navajo; F; M; Wife; 6559; Yes; Yes; 22761
6546;   Naz-bah; F; 5; Navajo; F; S; Daughter; 6560; Yes; Yes; 22762
6547;   Yah-dee-bah; F; 4; Navajo; F; S; Daughter; 6561; Yes; Yes; 22763
6548;   Yee-zas-dah-bah; F; 3; Navajo; F; S; Daughter; 6562; Yes; Yes; 22781

6549;   Nocki-Hosteen; M; 82; Navajo; F; Wd; Head; 6563; Yes; Yes; 28102
6550;   Keith; M; 22; Navajo; F; S; Son; 6564; Yes; Yes; 28103

6551;   Nocki-Dinay; M; 84; Navajo; F; M; Head; 6565; Yes; Yes; 21625
6552;   Bah-ah-heh-ith-thlani-bitsih; F; 48; Navajo; F; M; Wife; 6566; Yes; Yes; 21626
6553;   Keh-yah-nih-bah, Vera; F; 16; Navajo; F; S; Daughter; 6567; Yes; Yes; 21627
6554;   Keh-yil-nahn-bah; F; 12; Navajo; F; S; Daughter; 6568; Yes; Yes; 21628

6555;   Nah-gi-athla-beshi; M; Unk; Navajo; F; M; Head; 6569; Yes; Yes; 23942
6556;   Bith-pih-dah-bah; F; Unk; Navajo; F; M; Wife; 6570; Yes; Yes; 23941

Census of the **Northern Navajo** reservation of the **Northern Navajo** jurisdiction, as of **April 1**, 19**31**, taken by **Ernest H. Hammond, District**, Superintendent. **in Charge**

**Key:** Number; NAME: Surname, Given; Sex; Birth Year (if given), Age At Last Birthday; Tribe; Degree of Blood; Marital Status; Relationship To Head of Family; Last Census Roll Number; At Jurisdiction Where Enrolled (Yes or No); At Another Jurisdiction; ELSEWHERE: Post office, County, State; Ward (Yes or No); Allotment, Annuity, and Identification Numbers.

6557; Oh-hoh-dee-tel; M; 59; Navajo; F; M; Head; 6571; No; McElmo, Colo., San Juan, Utah; Yes; 19295

6558; Adzan-Oh-hoh-des-tel; F; 60; Navajo; F; M; Wife; 6572; No; McElmo, Colo., San Juan, Utah; Yes; 19296

6559; Adzan-Chilli; F; 32; Navajo; F; Wd; Daughter; 6573; No; McElmo, Colo., San Juan, Utah; Yes; 19297

6560; Chee; M; 29; Navajo; F; S; Son; 6574; No; McElmo, Colo., San Juan, Utah; Yes; 19298

6561; Ervin; M; 20; Navajo; F; S; Sons; 6575; No; McElmo, Colo., San Juan, Utah; Yes; 19299

6562; Bah; F; 17; Navajo; F; S; Daughter; 6576; No; McElmo, Colo., San Juan, Utah; Yes; 19300

6563; Oltaih, Yazzie; M; Unk; Navajo; F; M; Head; 6577; Yes; Yes; 22367
6564; Bah-yazzie; F; 25; Navajo; M; Wife; 6578; Yes; Yes; 22368
6565; Tah-yah; M; 6; Navajo; F; S; Son; 6579; Yes; Yes; 22369
6566; Bil-hah-ziz-bah; F; 4; Navajo; F; S; Daughter; 6580; Yes; Yes; 22370
6567; Nah-glih-hah-des-bah; F; Unk; Navajo; F; Wd; Grand-mother; 6581; Yes; Yes; 22371

6568; Oliver, Howard; M; 42; Navajo; F; M; Head; 6582; Yes; Yes; 31005
6569; Olive; F; 40; Navajo; F; M; Wife; 6583; Yes; Yes; 31006
6570; Willard; M; 10; Navajo; F; S; Son; 6584; Yes; Yes; 31007
6571; Lloyd; M; 9; Navajo; F; S; Son; 6585; Yes; Yes; 31008
6572; Mabel; F; 6; Navajo; F; S; Daughter; 6586; Yes; Yes; 31009
6573; Helen; F; 3; Navajo; F; S; Daughter; 6587; Yes; Yes; 31010

6574; Oliver, John; M; 41; Navajo; F; M; Head; 6588; Yes; Yes; 20365
6575; Aht-citty-bega, bitsih; F; 36; Navajo; F; M; Wife; 6589; Yes; Yes; 20366
6576; Tah-des-bah; F; 11; Navajo; F; S; Daughter; 6590; Yes; Yes; 20367
6577; Eskee-ach; M; 9; Navajo; F; S; Son; 6591; Yes; Yes; 20368

6578; Ola, bega, Mitchell, Jimmy; M; 34; Navajo; F; Wd; Head; 6592; Yes; Yes; 21484
6579; Juanita; F; 4; Navajo; F; S; Daughter; 6593; Yes; Yes; 21486

6580; Oltahih-nez; M; Unk; Navajo; F; M; Head; 6594; Yes; Yes; 26002
6581; Dah-nih-bah; F; 33; Navajo; F; M; Wife; 6595; Yes; Yes; 26003
6582; Haska-yee-nas-wudt; M; 9; Navajo; F; S; Son; 6596; Yes; Yes; 26004
6583; Haska-yee-nal-wohl; M; 7; Navajo; F; S; Son; 6597; Yes; Yes; 26005
6584; Biz-nee-bah; F; 3; Navajo; F; S; Daughter; 6598; Yes; Yes; 26006

6585; Oltahih-soh-bikis, John; M; 47; Navajo; F; M; Head; 6599; Yes; Yes; 26855

Census of the **Northern Navajo** reservation of the **Northern Navajo** jurisdiction, as of **April 1**, 1931, taken by **Ernest H. Hammond, District**, Superintendent. **in Charge**

**Key:** Number; NAME: Surname, Given; Sex; Birth Year (if given), Age At Last Birthday; Tribe; Degree of Blood; Marital Status; Relationship To Head of Family; Last Census Roll Number; At Jurisdiction Where Enrolled (Yes or No); At Another Jurisdiction; ELSEWHERE: Post office, County, State; Ward (Yes or No); Allotment, Annuity, and Identification Numbers.

6586; Al-kih-dah-yiz-bah; F; 38; Navajo; F; M; Wife; 6600; Yes; Yes; 26856
6587; Hogus[sic], Charles; M; 20; Navajo; F; S; Son; 6601; Yes; Yes; 26857
[Name should be Hogue, Charles]
6588; Mildred; F; 18; Navajo; F; S; Step-daughter; 6602; Yes; Yes; 26858
6589; Salou-bega, Nathan; M; 16; Navajo; F; S; Step-son; 6603; Yes; Yes; 26859
6590; Nocki, John Norman; M; 18; Navajo; F; S; Nephew-in-law; 6604; Yes; Yes; 26860
6591; Haska-yil-nes-des-sah; M; 5; Navajo; F; S; Step-son; 6605; Yes; Yes; 26861
6592; Haska-yee-nah-yah; M; 4; Navajo; F; S; Son; 6606; Yes; Yes; 26862
6593; Keh-yil-haz-bah; F; 6; Navajo; F; S; Daughter; 6607; Yes; Yes; 26863
6594; Keh-yee-tah-dez-bah; F; 5; Navajo; F; S; Daughter; 6608; Yes; Yes; 26864
6595; Haska-yil-has-wudt; M; 4; Navajo; F; S; Son; 6609; Yes; Yes; 26865
6596; Nah-tah-yee-has-wudt; M; 3; Navajo; F; S; Son; 6610; Yes; Yes; 27081
6597; Hogue, Carl; M; 13; Navajo; F; S; Son; 6611; Yes; Yes; 27090

6598; Oltahih-soh, Alva; M; 46; Navajo; F; M; Head; 6612; Yes; Yes; 26719
6599; Al-kih-dez-bah; F; 48; Navajo; F; M; Wife; 6613; Yes; Yes; 26720
6600; Ford, Henry; M; 18; Navajo; F; S; Son; 6614; Yes; Yes; 26721
6601; Yee-tah-dez-bah; F; 12; Navajo; F; S; Daughter; 6615; Yes; Yes; 26722
6602; Haska-yil-des-wudt; M; 10; Navajo; F; S; Son; 6616; Yes; Yes; 26723
6603; Haska-yee-nal-wohl; M; 7; Navajo; F; S; Son; 6617; Yes; 26724
6604; Tah-nih-bah; F; 5; Navajo; F; S; Daughter; 6618; Yes; Yes; 26725
6605; Nah-glih-yil-des-bah; F; 3; Navajo; F; S; Daughter; 6619; Yes; Yes; 26726
6606; Haska-yil-ee-yah; M; 3; Navajo; F; S; Son; 6620; Yes; Yes; 26727
6607; Sannie[sic]; F; 66; Navajo; F; Wd; Mother; 6621; Yes; Yes; 26728
[Name should be Zannie]

6608; Oltahih-soh-badoni, Harry; M; 27; Navajo; F; M; Head; 6622; Yes; Yes; 26729
6609; Al-hih-nih-bah; F; 21; Navajo; F; M; Wife; 6623; Yes; Yes; 26730
6610; Yee-kih-nas-wudt; M; 7; Navajo; F; S; Son; 6624; Yes; Yes; 26731
6611; Haska-yee-kih-des-wudt; M; 6; Navajo; F; S; Son; 6625; Yes; Yes; 26732
6612; Al-soh-dez-bah; F; 4; Navajo; F; S; Daughter; 6626; Yes; Yes; 26733
6613; Eddie; M; 1; Navajo; F; S; Son; 6627; Yes; Yes; 27096

6614; Oltahih-soh-bega-chee; M; 27; Navajo; F; M; Head; 6628; Yes; Yes; 26734
6615; Dinay-deel-bitsoih; F; 25; Navajo; F; M; Wife; 6629; Yes; Yes; 26735
6616; Ah-hih-nil-bah; F; 7; Navajo; F; S; Daughter; 6630; Yes; Yes; 26736
6617; Nah-ti-yee-chee-dayaha; M; 2; Navajo; F; S; Son; 6631; Yes; Yes; 27097

6618; Oltahih-soh-bikis, Jim; M; Unk; Navajo; F; M; Head; 6632; Yes; Yes; 26737
6619; Bahih; F; 28; Navajo; F; M; Wife; 6633; Yes; Yes; 26738
6620; Yil-hah-bah; F; 12; Navajo; F; S; Daughter; 6634; Yes; Yes; 26739

Census of the **Northern Navajo** reservation of the **Northern Navajo** jurisdiction, as of **April 1**, 19**31,** taken by **Ernest H. Hammond, District**, Superintendent. **in Charge**

Key: Number; NAME: Surname, Given; Sex; Birth Year (if given), Age At Last Birthday; Tribe; Degree of Blood; Marital Status; Relationship To Head of Family; Last Census Roll Number; At Jurisdiction Where Enrolled (Yes or No); At Another Jurisdiction; ELSEWHERE: Post office, County, State; Ward (Yes or No); Allotment, Annuity, and Identification Numbers.

6621; Al-keh-nih-bah; F; 10; Navajo; F; S; Daughter; 6635; Yes; Yes; 26740
6622; Haska-yee-tah-yil-wohl; M; 7; Navajo; F; S; Son; 6636; Yes; Yes; 26741
6623; Chih-hah-yah; M; 4; Navajo; F; S; Son; 6637; Yes; Yes; 26742
6624; Nah-tah-yee-neyah; M; 3; Navajo; F; S; Son; 6638; Yes; Yes; 27098

6625; Oltahih-soh-bega, Sim's wife, Teece-yazzie-benally; F; 24; Navajo; F; Wd; Head; 6639; Yes; Yes; 26751
6626; Keh-yil-haz-bah; F; 4; Navajo; F; S; Daughter; 6640; Yes; Yes; 26752
6627; Glih-nee-pah; F; 3; Navajo; F; S; Daughter; 6641; Yes; Yes; 27093

6628; Oltaih-soh-bikis-bega, Karl Hogue; M; Unk; Navajo; F; M; Head; 6642; Yes; Yes; 26366
6629; Mildred; F; 21; Navajo; F; M; Wife; 6643; Yes; Yes; 26367

6630; Oliver, James; M; 32; Navajo; F; M; Head; 6644; No; McElmo, Colo., San Juan, Utah; Yes; 19328
6631; Della; F; 30; Navajo; F; M; Wife; 6645; No; McElmo, Colo., San Juan, Utah; Yes; 19329

6632; Oss-cah; M; 50; Navajo; F; M; Head; 6646; Yes; Yes; 22395
6633; Hosteen-schien-bitsih; F; 39; Navajo; F; M; Wife; 6647; Yes; Yes; 22396
6634; John; M; 20; Navajo; F; S; Son; 6648; Yes; Yes; 22397
6635; Hoska-litsun; M; 16; Navajo; F; S; Son; 6649; Yes; Yes; 22398
6636; Emma; F; 14; Navajo; F; S; Daughter; 6650; Yes; Yes; 22399
6637; Hoska-yil-hah-yah; M; 12; Navajo; F; S; Son; 6651; Yes; Yes; 22400
6638; Kes-bah; F; 10; Navajo; F; S; Daughter; 6652; Yes; Yes; 22401
6639; Gee-bah; F; 7; Navajo; F; S; Daughter; 6653; Yes; Yes; 22402
6640; Colon, George; M; 47; Navajo; F; S; Brother-in-law; 6654; Yes; Yes; 22403

6641; Palmer, Roy; M; Unk; Navajo; F; M; Head; 6655; Yes; Yes; 28457
6642; Yabney-bitsih; F; 29; Navajo; F; M; Wife; 6656; Yes; Yes; 28458
6643; Wudt; M; 12; Navajo; F; S; Son; 6657; Yes; Yes; 28459
6644; Aht-citty; M; 9; Navajo; F; S; Son; 6658; Yes; Yes; 28460
6645; Al-kih-nih-bah; F; 8; Navajo; F; S; Daughter; 6659; Yes; Yes; 28461
6646; Deswudt; M; 6; Navajo; F; S; Son; 6660; Yes; Yes; 28462
6647; Pat, Lee; M; 32; Navajo; F; M; Head; 6661; Yes; Yes; 22425
6648; Ah-hah-nih-bah; F; 29; Navajo; F; M; Wife; 6662; Yes; Yes; 22426
6649; Tah-nas-bah; F; 3; Navajo; F; S; Daughter; 6663; Yes; Yes; 22427

6650; Patrick, Joe; M; 26; Navajo; F; S; Head; 6664; Yes; Yes; 25022
6651; Amos; M; 24; Navajo; F; S; Brother; 6665; Yes; Yes; 25023
6652; Clyde; M; 21; Navajo; F; S; Brother; 6666; Yes; Yes; 25024

Census of the **Northern Navajo** reservation of the **Northern Navajo** jurisdiction, as of **April 1** , 19**31,** taken by **Ernest H. Hammond, District**, Superintendent. **in Charge**

**Key:** Number; NAME: Surname, Given; Sex; Birth Year (if given), Age At Last Birthday; Tribe; Degree of Blood; Marital Status; Relationship To Head of Family; Last Census Roll Number; At Jurisdiction Where Enrolled (Yes or No); At Another Jurisdiction; ELSEWHERE: Post office, County, State; Ward (Yes or No); Allotment, Annuity, and Identification Numbers.

6653; Patrick, Paul; M; Unk; Navajo; F; M; Head; 2889; Yes; Yes; 31049
6654; Ida; F; 43; Navajo; F; M; Wife; 2890; Yes; Yes; 31050
6655; Kenneth; M; 4/12; Navajo; F; S; Son; [Blank] Yes; Yes; 31298

6656; Posh-lagaih, Boyd; M; 41; Navajo; F; M; Head; 6667; Yes; Yes; 30985
6657; Evelyn; F; 26; Navajo; F; M; Wife; 6668; Yes; Yes; 30986
6658; Harriet; F; 1; Navajo; F; S; Daughter; 6669; Yes; Yes; 31231

6659; Billy Pete's Wife; F; 40; Navajo; F; Wd; Head; 6670; Yes; Yes; 30790
6660; Haska-yil-nal-wudt, Billy; M; 23; Navajo; F; S; Son; 6671; Yes; Yes; 30791
6661; John; M; 21; Navajo; F; S; Son; 6672; Yes; Yes; 30792
6662; Billy; M; 20; Navajo; F; S; Son; 6673; Yes; Yes; 30793
6663; Nah-glih-yee-naz-bah; F; 16; Navajo; F; S; Daughter; 6674; Yes; Yes; 30794
6664; Haska-yee-chih-has-wudt; M; 11; Navajo; F; S; Son; 6675; Yes; Yes; 30795
6665; Hosteen-l-suen; M; 7; Navajo; F; S; Son; 6676; Yes; Yes; 30796

6666; Pettigrew, Dick; M; 45; Navajo; F; M; Head; 6677; Yes; Yes; 30588
6667; Hosteen-nah-hah-gosih-benally; F; 51; Navajo; F; M; Wife; 6678; Yes; Yes; 30590
6668; Edward; M; 19; Navajo; F; S; Son; 6679; Yes; Yes; 30592
6669; Manson; M; 23; Navajo; F; S; Step-son; 6680; Yes; Yes; 30593
6670; Beatrice; F; 15; Navajo; F; S; Daughter; 6681; Yes; Yes; 30594
6671; Ah-kih-naz-bah; F; 11; Navajo; F; S; Daughter; 6682; Yes; Yes; 30595
6672; Ida; F; 9; Navajo; F; S; Daughter; 6683; Yes; Yes; 30596
6673; Lewis; M; 6; Navajo; F; S; Son; 6684; Yes; Yes; 30597

6674; Pettigrew, Low; M; Unk; Navajo; F; M; Head; 6685; Yes; Yes; 30572
6675; Beleen-lizin-benally; F; 23; Navajo; F; M; Wife; 6686; Yes; Yes; 30573
6676; Gliz-bah; F; 5; Navajo; F; S; Daughter; 6687; Yes; Yes; 30574
6677; Haska-yee-chih-nih-nih-yah; M; 3; Navajo; F; S; Son; 6688; Yes; Yes; 30575

6678; Pettigrew, Sam; M; 34; Navajo; F; S; Head; 6689; Yes; Yes; 30500

6679; Peterson, Clah George; M; 51; Navajo; F; Wd; Head; 6690; Yes; Yes; 29092
6680; George, Joe; M; 16; Navajo; F; S; Son; 6691; Yes; Yes; 29094
6681; Wilson; M; 15; Navajo; F; S; Son; 6692; Yes; Yes; 29095
6682; Amelia; F; 13; Navajo; F; S; Daughter; 6693; Yes; Yes; 29096
6683; James; M; 11; Navajo; F; S; Son; 6694; Yes; Yes; 29097
6684; Lee; M; 9; Navajo; F; S; Son; 6695; Yes; Yes; 29098
6685; Annie; F; 7; Navajo; F; S; Daughter; 6696; Yes; Yes; 29099
6686; Vera; F; 4; Navajo; F; S; Daughter; 6697; Yes; Yes; 29100

6687; Pete, Dan; M; Unk; Navajo; F; M; Head; 6698; Yes; Yes; 30737

Census of the **Northern Navajo** reservation of the **Northern Navajo** jurisdiction, as of **April 1** , 19**31**, taken by **Ernest H. Hammond, District**, Superintendent. **in Charge**

**Key:** Number; NAME: Surname, Given; Sex; Birth Year (if given), Age At Last Birthday; Tribe; Degree of Blood; Marital Status; Relationship To Head of Family; Last Census Roll Number; At Jurisdiction Where Enrolled (Yes or No); At Another Jurisdiction; ELSEWHERE: Post office, County, State; Ward (Yes or No); Allotment, Annuity, and Identification Numbers.

6688; Chis-chilli-benally; F; 41; Navajo; F; M; Wife; 6699; Yes; Yes; 30738
6689; Nah-tah-yil-dee-wudt-Harry; M; 26; Navajo; F; S; Son; 6700; Yes; Yes; 30739
6690; Nah-glih-yee-ah-naz-bah; F; 17; Navajo; F; S; Daughter; 6701; Yes; Yes; 30740
6691; Mildred; F; 15; Navajo; F; S; Daughter; 6702; Yes; Yes; 30741
6692; Nah-tah-yil-hah-yah; M; 11; Navajo; F; S; Son; 6703; Yes; Yes; 30742
6693; Haska-yee-chih-nil-wudt; M; 9; Navajo; F; S; Son; 6704; Yes; Yes; 30743
6694; Hah-ziz-bah; F; 3; Navajo; F; S; Daughter; 6705; Yes; Yes; 30744
6695; Walter; M; 22; Navajo; F; S; Son; 6706; Yes; Yes; 30745

6696; Phillips, Sydney; M; Unk; Navajo; F; M; Head; 6707; Yes; Yes; 30465
6697; Mary; F; 34; Navajo; F; M; Wife; 6708; Yes; Yes; 30466
6698; Josephine; F; 19; Navajo; F; S; Daughter; 6709; Yes; Yes; 30467
6699; Ida; F; 17; Navajo; F; S; Daughter; 6710; Yes; Yes; 30468
6700; Lucy; F; 15; Navajo; F; S; Daughter; 6711; Yes; Yes; 30469
6701; Wilson; M; 10; Navajo; F; S; Son; 6712; Yes; Yes; 30470
6702; Abe; M; 7; Navajo; F; S; Son; 6713; Yes; Yes; 30471
6703; James; M; 2; Navajo; F; S; Son; 6714; Yes; Yes; 30472

6704; Pinto-bega; M; 30; Navajo; F; M; Head; 6715; Yes; Yes; 27549
6705; Beleen-yis-clin-nih-bega-bitsih; F; 28; Navajo; F; M; Wife; 6716; Yes; Yes; 27550
6706; Nah-bah; F; 8; Navajo; F; S; Daughter; 6717; Yes; Yes; 27551
6707; Tah-yil-wohl; M; 6; Navajo; F; S; Son; 6718; Yes; Yes; 27552
6708; Yahn-yil-wudt; M; 2; Navajo; F; S; Son; 6719; Yes; Yes; 27553

6709; Pinto, Willie; M; 50; Navajo; F; M; Head; 6720; Yes; Yes; 27607
6710; Glih-yee-naz-bah; F; 42; Navajo; F; M; Wife; 6721; Yes; Yes; 27608
6711; Yahn-nih-bah; F; 12; Navajo; F; S; Daughter; 6722; Yes; Yes; 27609
6712; Yahn-hah-bah; F; 10; Navajo; F; S; Daughter; 6723; Yes; Yes; 27610
6713; Nah-tah-yil-dah-ziz-zinh; M; 7; Navajo; F; S; Son; 6724; Yes; Yes; 27611
6714; Yahn-hal-wudt; M; 5; Navajo; F; S; Son; 6725; Yes; Yes; 27612
6715; Keh-hah-nih-bah; F; 3; Navajo; F; S; Daughter; 6726; Yes; Yes; 27613

6716; Pinto-bega, Jay; M; 32; Navajo; F; M; Head; 6727; Yes; Yes; 32310
6717; Bih-jah-tlol-nih-dael-bit-soih, Hester; F; 31; Navajo; F; M; Wife; 6728; Yes; Yes; 32311
6718; Ah-hah-naz-bah; F; 12; Navajo; F; S; Daughter; 6729; Yes; Yes; 32312
6719; Haska-yil-chih-naihyah; M; 10; Navajo; F; S; Son; 6730; Yes; Yes; 32313
6720; Gahl; M; 8; Navajo; F; S; Son; 6731; Yes; Yes; 32314

6721; Polly; M; 59; Navajo; F; M; Head; 6732; Yes; Yes; 29915
6722; Uienth-nezzi-bitsih; F; 25; Navajo; F; M; Wife; 6733; Yes; Yes; 29916

Census of the **Northern Navajo** reservation of the **Northern Navajo** jurisdiction, as of **April 1**, 1931, taken by **Ernest H. Hammond, District**, Superintendent. **in Charge**

**Key:** Number; NAME: Surname, Given; Sex; Birth Year (if given), Age At Last Birthday; Tribe; Degree of Blood; Marital Status; Relationship To Head of Family; Last Census Roll Number; At Jurisdiction Where Enrolled (Yes or No); At Another Jurisdiction; ELSEWHERE: Post office, County, State; Ward (Yes or No); Allotment, Annuity, and Identification Numbers.

6723; Glih-zoz-bah; F; 6; Navajo; F; S; Daughter; 6734; Yes; Yes; 29917
6724; Haska-yee-l-tihih; M; 4; Navajo; F; S; Son; 6735; Yes; Yes; 29918

6725; Polly-bega; M; 31; Navajo; F; M; Head; 6736; Yes; Yes; 29908
6726; Topah-hah-soh-bitsih; F; 27; Navajo; F; M; Wife; 6737; Yes; Yes; 29909
6727; Haska-yah-nal-wudt; M; 10; Navajo; F; S; Son; 6738; Yes; Yes; 29910
6728; Keh-tah-dez-bah; F; 7; Navajo; F; S; Daughter; 6739; Yes; Yes; 29911

6729; Polly-bega, Willie; M; 29; Navajo; F; M; Head; 6740; Yes; Yes; 21560
6730; Yahn-dee-bah; F; 29; Navajo; F; M; Wife; 6741; Yes; Yes; 21561
6731; Hoska-nah-ho-des-nil-kad; M; 12; Navajo; F; S; Nephew; 6742; Yes; Yes; 21562

6732; Puggy, Jim; M; 33; Navajo; F; M; Head; 6743; Yes; Yes; 30838
6733; Hosteen-nez-benally; F; 27; Navajo; F; M; Wife; 6744; Yes; Yes; 30839
6734; Tah-yee-gahl; M; 7; Navajo; F; S; Son; 6745; Yes; Yes; 30840
6735; Haska-yil-nil-wudt; M; 4; Navajo; F; S; Son; 6746; Yes; Yes; 30841

6736; Peter, Lee; M; 30; Navajo; F; M; Head; 6747; Yes; Yes; 31150
6737; Salle-bikis-bitsih; F; 22; Navajo; F; M; Wife; 6748; Yes; Yes; 31151
6738; Cheh-naz-bah; F; 4; Navajo; F; S; Daughter; 6749; Yes; Yes; 31152
6739; Billy; M; 2; Navajo; F; S; Son; 6750; Yes; Yes; 31153

6740; Ramone; M; 36; Navajo; F; M; Head; 6756; Yes; Yes; 26819
6741; Ramone's wife; F; 32; Navajo; F; M; Wife; 6757; Yes; Yes; 26820
6742; Evangeline; F; 11; Navajo; F; S; Daughter; 6758; Yes; Yes; 26821
6743; Tah-zoaz-bah; F; 9; Navajo; F; S; Daughter; 6759; Yes; Yes; 26822
6744; Nah-tah-yee-chih-hal-wudt; M; 7; Navajo; F; S; Son; 6760; Yes; Yes; 26823
6745; Yahn-yil-wudt; M; 5; Navajo; F; S; Son; 6761; Yes; Yes; 26824
6746; Nah-tah-yee-ish-has-wudt; M; 3; Navajo; F; S; Son; 6762; Yes; Yes; 27084

6747; Rafael, Joe (Papage[sic] Indian) Head of House
6748; Rafael, Jessie; F; 31; Navajo; F; M; Wife; 6764; Yes; Yes; 22729
6749; Rafael, Josephine; F; 12; Navajo; M; S; Daughter; 6765; Yes; Yes; 22730

6750; Red Goat; M; 54; Navajo; F; M; Head; 6766; Yes; Yes; 29737
6751; Aht-citty-bitsih; F; 45; Navajo; F; M; Wife; 6767; Yes; Yes; 29738
6752; Nah-glih-yil-nah-nih-bah; F; 19; Navajo; F; S; Daughter; 6768; Yes; Yes; 29739
6753; Verne; M; 17; Navajo; F; S; Son; 6769; Yes; Yes; 29740
6754; Sally; F; 14; Navajo; F; S; Daughter; 6770; Yes; Yes; 29741
6755; Chih-dez-bah; F; 9; Navajo; F; S; Daughter; 6771; Yes; Yes; 29742
6756; Chih-nih-ziz-bah; F; 7; Navajo; F; S; Daughter; 6772; Yes; Yes; 29743

Census of the **Northern Navajo** reservation of the **Northern Navajo** jurisdiction, as of **April 1**, 19**31,** taken by **Ernest H. Hammond, District,** Superintendent. **in Charge**

**Key:** Number; NAME: Surname, Given; Sex; Birth Year (if given), Age At Last Birthday; Tribe; Degree of Blood; Marital Status; Relationship To Head of Family; Last Census Roll Number; At Jurisdiction Where Enrolled (Yes or No); At Another Jurisdiction; ELSEWHERE: Post office, County, State; Ward (Yes or No); Allotment, Annuity, and Identification Numbers.

6757; Haska-yee-chih-nal-wohl; M; 5; Navajo; F; S; Son; 6773; Yes; Yes; 29744
6758; Haska-yah-nal-wudt; M; 3; Navajo; F; S; Son; 6774; Yes; Yes; 29745
6759; Aht-citty-bih-adzan; F; 85; Navajo; F; Wd; Mother-in-law; 6775; Yes; Yes; 29746
6760; Virginia; F; 17; Navajo; F; S; Cousin; 6776; Yes; Yes; 29747

6761; Red Shirt; M; Unk; Navajo; F; Wd.; Head; 6777; Yes; Yes; 22726
6762; Hoska; M; Unk; Navajo; F; S; Son; 6778; Yes; Yes; 22727
6763; Mary; F; Unk; Navajo; F; S; Daughter; 6779; Yes; Yes; 22728

6764; Red-shirt, John; M; 31; Navajo; F; M; Head; 6780; Yes; Yes; 30641
6765; Irene; F; 36; Navajo; F; M; Wife; 6781; Yes; Yes; 30642
6766; Jim John; M; 11; Navajo; F; S; Son; 6782; Yes; Yes; 30643
6767; Jessie; F; 9; Navajo; F; S; Daughter; 6783; Yes; Yes; 30644
6768; Richard; M; 7; Navajo; F; S; Son; 6784; Yes; Yes; 30645
6769; Yee-tah-deyah; M; 4; Navajo; F; S; Son; 6785; Yes; Yes; 30646
6770; Sarah; F; 2; Navajo; F; S; Daughter; 6786; Yes; Yes; 31256

6771; Reed, Wendell; M; 27; Navajo; F; M: Head; 6787; Yes; Yes; 21193
6772; Reed, Amy; F; 24; Navajo; F; M; Wife; 6788; Yes; Yes; 21194
6773; Reed, Fern; F; 4; Navajo; F; S; Daughter; 6789; Yes; Yes; 21195

6774; Rentz, Hugh (White) Head of house; 6790
6775; Rentz, Hugh's wife; F; 58; Navajo; F; M; Wife; 6791; No.; McElmo, Colo., San Juan, Utah; Yes; Yes; 18957
6776; Woody; M; 42; Navajo; F; S; Step-son; 6792; No; McElmo, Colo., San Juan, Utah; Yes; Yes; 18958

6777; Russell, Harry; M; Unk; Navajo; F; M; Head; 6793; Yes; Yes; 23523
6778; Rachel[sic]; F; 33; Navajo; F; M; Wife; 6794; Yes; Yes; 23524
[Name could be Russell, Rachel]
6779; Russell, Irene Josephine; F; 2; Navajo; F; S; Daughter; 6795; Yes; Yes; 23880

6780; Sandoval-benally's wife Hosteen-sinih-bitsih; F; 25; Navajo; F; Wd; Head; 6797; Yes; Yes; 30490
6781; Haska-yil-yee-gahl; M; 3; Navajo; F; S; Son; 6798; Yes; Yes; 30491
6782; Mary; F; 2; Navajo; F; S; Daughter; 6799; Yes; Yes; 31272

6783; Sandoval's wife Bil-nih-ziz-bah; F; 70; Navajo; F; Wd; Head; 6800; Yes; Yes; 30474
6784; Harry; M; 27; Navajo; F; S; Son; 6801; Yes; Yes; 30475
6785; Joe; M; 24; Navajo; F; S; Son; 6802; Yes; Yes; 30476

Census of the **Northern Navajo** reservation of the **Northern Navajo** jurisdiction, as of **April 1**, 19**31**, taken by **Ernest H. Hammond, District**, Superintendent. **in Charge**

**Key:** Number; NAME: Surname, Given; Sex; Birth Year (if given), Age At Last Birthday; Tribe; Degree of Blood; Marital Status; Relationship To Head of Family; Last Census Roll Number; At Jurisdiction Where Enrolled (Yes or No); At Another Jurisdiction; ELSEWHERE: Post office, County, State; Ward (Yes or No); Allotment, Annuity, and Identification Numbers.

6786; Sandoval-bega-Hosteen; M; 48; Navajo; F; M; Head; 6803; Yes; Yes; 30482
6787; Hosteen-en-olshih-bitsih; F; 50; Navajo; F; M; Wife; 6804; Yes; Yes; 30483
6788; Nita; F; 22; Navajo; F; S; Daughter; 6805; Yes; Yes; 30485
6789; Belle; F; 19; Navajo; F; S; Daughter; 6806; Yes; Yes; 30486
6790; Nah-tah-yee-cah-gah; M; 16; Navajo; F; S; Son; 6807; Yes; Yes; 30487
6791; Yee-chih-dez-bah; F; 13; Navajo; F; S; Daughter; 6808; Yes; Yes; 30488

6792; Sani, Willie; M; 40; Navajo; F; M; Head; 6809; Yes; Yes; 30945
6793; Aht-citty-nez-bitsih; F; 29; Navajo; F; M; Wife; 6810; Yes; Yes; 30946
6794; Nah-tah-yil-ee-yah; M; 10; Navajo; F; S; 6811; Yes; Yes; 30947
6795; Nah-tah-yee-chih-nil-wudt; M; 4; Navajo; F; S; Son; 6812; Yes; Yes; 30948
6796; Nah-glih-yil-nih-bah; F; 2; Navajo; F; S; Daughter; 6813; Yes; Yes; 30949
6797; Bowen; M; 32; Navajo; F; S; Nephew; 6814; Yes; Yes; 30950

6798; Salou-ahtsosie-benally; M; 25; Navajo; F; M; Head; 6815; Yes; Yes; 22544
6799; Nah-glih-yee-kaz-bah; F; 18; Navajo; F; M; Wife; 6816; Yes; Yes; 22545
6800; Dinay-be-toh; M; 80; Navajo; F Wd; Grand-mother-in-law[sic]; 6817; Yes; Yes;
21672                                                                  [Should be male.]

6801; Sandoval Bega, Sanderson; M; Unk; Navajo; F; M; Head; 6818; Yes; Yes;
30461
6802; Aht-citty-benally; F; 23; Navajo; F; M; Wife; 6819; Yes; Yes; 30462
6803; Peterson; M; 4; Navajo; F; S; Son; 6820; Yes; Yes; 30463
6804; Luke; F[sic]; 3; Navajo; F; S; Son; Yes; Yes; 30464
       [Should be male.]

6805; Sandoval-bega, John; M; 38; Navajo; F; M; Head; 6822; Yes; Yes; 30477
6806; Chih-nih-bah; F; 31; Navajo; F; M; Wife; 6823; Yes; Yes; 30478
6807; Tom; M; 10; Navajo; F; S; Son; 6824; Yes; Yes; 30479
6808; Edison; M; 7; Navajo; F; S; Son; 6825; Yes; Yes; 30480
6809; Paul; M; 3; Navajo; F; S; Son; 6826; Yes; Yes; 30481

6810; Salou-Sani-benally's wife  Aht-citty-benally; F; 29; Navajo; F; Wd; Head;
6827; Yes; Yes; 30513
6811; Marie; F; 3; Navajo; F; S; Daughter; 6828; Yes; Yes; 31273

6812; Salou-bitsees-chilli-bega; M; 44; Navajo; F; M; Head; 6829; Yes; Yes; 32440
6813; Hosteen-hah-nih-tayshih-benally; F; 37; Navajo; F; M; Wife; 6830; Yes; Yes;
32441
6814; Nel-wudt, Joe; M; 14; Navajo; F; S; Son; 6831; Yes; Yes; 32442
6815; Tah-yil-yil-wohl; M; 11; Navajo; F; S; Son; 6832; Yes; Yes; 32443
6816; Tah-yil-yee-gahl; M; 7; Navajo; F; S; Son; 6833; Yes; Yes; 32444
6817; Nah-tah-yil-chil-wudt; M; 5; Navajo; F; S; Son; 6834; Yes; Yes; 32445

Census of the **Northern Navajo** reservation of the **Northern Navajo** jurisdiction, as of **April 1**, 19**31,** taken by **Ernest H. Hammond, District**, Superintendent. **in Charge**

**Key:** Number; NAME: Surname, Given; Sex; Birth Year (if given), Age At Last Birthday; Tribe; Degree of Blood; Marital Status; Relationship To Head of Family; Last Census Roll Number; At Jurisdiction Where Enrolled (Yes or No); At Another Jurisdiction; ELSEWHERE: Post office, County, State; Ward (Yes or No); Allotment, Annuity, and Identification Numbers.

6818; Bil-hah-gee-bah; F; 3; Navajo; F; S; Daughter; 6835; Yes; Yes; 32446

6819; Salou-bitsees-chilli-bega; M; 32; Navajo; F; M; Head; 6836; Yes; Yes; 32392
6820; Katie; F; 26; Navajo; F; M; Wife; 6837; Yes; Yes; 32393
6821; Stephen; M; 11; Navajo; F; S; Son; 6838; Yes; Yes; 32394
6822; Ah-kih-dez-bah; F; 9; Navajo; F; S; Daughter; 6839; Yes; Yes; 32395
6823; Dillih; M; 7; Navajo; F; S; Son; 6840; Yes; Yes; 32396
6824; Glih-hah-bah; F; 4; Navajo; F; S; Daughter; 6841; Yes; Yes; 32397

6825; Salou-En-clahih-gi-bega, Bruce; M; 30; Navajo; F; M; Head; 6842; Yes; Yes; 32389
6826; Woodih-bitsih; F; 20; Navajo; F; M; Wife; 6843; Yes; Yes; 32390
6827; Yale-wudt; M; 3; Navajo; F; S; Son; 6844; Yes; Yes; 32391

6828; Salou-sosie-bega; M; 36; Navajo; F; M; Head; 6845; Yes; Yes; 29748
6829; Tah-nah-bah; F; 25; Navajo; F; M; Wife; 6846; Yes; Yes; 29749
6830; Haska-yee-chih-hoh-gahl; M; 8; Navajo; F; S; Son; 6847; Yes; Yes; 29750
6831; Nah-glih-yil-nih-bah; F; 6; Navajo; F; S; Daughter; 6848; Yes; Yes; 29751
6832; Nah-glih-yil-nah-bah; F; 4; Navajo; F; S; Daughter; 6849; Yes; Yes; 29752

6833; Salou-bitsees-chilli-bega; M; 28; Navajo; F; M; Head; 6850; Yes; Yes; 32379
6834; Batoni-bitsees-chilli-bitsih; F; 25; Navajo; F; M; Wife; Yes; 6851; Yes; 32380
6835; Yah-nih-nih-yah; M; 8; Navajo; F; S; Son; 6852; Yes; Yes; 32381

6836; Salou-bitsee-chilli-bitah; M; 25; Navajo; F; Wd; Head; 6853; Yes; Yes; 32372
6837; Kih-des-wudt; M; 12; Navajo; F; S; Son; 6854; Yes; Yes; 32373
6838; Yil-hah-yah; M; 5; Navajo; F; S; Son; 6855; Yes; Yes; 32374
6839; Kih-zoz-bah; F; 3; Navajo; F; S; Daughter; 6856; Yes; Yes; 32375

6840; Salou-bitsees-chilli-bih-dazee; F; 54; Navajo; F; Div; Head; 6857; Yes; Yes; 32364
6841; Nah-tah-yee-chee-has-wudt; M; 22; Navajo; F; S; Son; 6858; Yes; Yes; 32365
6842; Tah-des-wudt; M; 18; Navajo; F; S; Son; 6859; Yes; Yes; 32366
6843; Haska-yah-hal-wudt; M; 13; Navajo; F; S; Son; 6860; Yes; Yes; 32367
6844; Yil-has-bah; F; 11; Navajo; F; S; Daughter; 6861; Yes; Yes; 32368
6845; Yil-hah-naz-bah; F; 25; Navajo; F; Div; Daughter; 6862; Yes; Yes; 32369
6846; Yee-hah-bah; F; 7; Navajo; F; S; Grand-Daughter; 6863; Yes; Yes; 32370
6847; Yee-hahal-wudt; M; 4; Navajo; F; S; Grand-son; 6864; Yes; Yes; 32371

6848; Salou-bitsee-chilli, Jim Curley; M; Unk; Navajo; F; M; Head; 6865; Yes; Yes; 32362
6849; Nopahih-bitsih; F; Unk; Navajo; F; M; Wife; 6866; Yes; Yes; 32363

Census of the **Northern Navajo** reservation of the **Northern Navajo** jurisdiction, as of **April 1**, 1931, taken by **Ernest H. Hammond, District**, Superintendent. **in Charge**

**Key:** Number; NAME: Surname, Given; Sex; Birth Year (if given), Age At Last Birthday; Tribe; Degree of Blood; Marital Status; Relationship To Head of Family; Last Census Roll Number; At Jurisdiction Where Enrolled (Yes or No); At Another Jurisdiction; ELSEWHERE: Post office, County, State; Ward (Yes or No); Allotment, Annuity, and Identification Numbers.

6850; Saltwater, Earl; M; 28; Navajo; F; M; Head; 6867; Yes; Yes; 29116
6851; Saltwater, Exie; F; 25; Navajo; F; M; Wife; 6868; Yes; Yes; 29117
6852; Ernest; M; 6; Navajo; F; S; Son; 6869; Yes; Yes; 29118
6853; Yee-kik-nih-bah; F; 4; Navajo; F; S; Daughter; 6870; Yes; Yes; 29119

6854; Sah-bah-golih-bega; M; 47; Navajo; F; M; Head; 6871; Yes; Yes; 26981
6855; Yil-hah-bah; F; 40; Navajo; F; M; Wife; 6872; Yes; Yes; 26982
6856; Haska-yil-nih-nih-yah; M; 23; Navajo; F; S; Son; 6873; Yes; Yes; 26983
6857; Keh-yee-hih-bah; F; 15; Navajo; F; S; Daughter; 6874; Yes; Yes; 26984
6858; Rosella; F; 14; Navajo; F; S; Daughter; 6875; Yes; Yes; 26985
6859; Lester; M; 11; Navajo; F; S; Son; 6876; Yes; Yes; 26986
6860; Keh-yil-hah-bah; F; 8; Navajo; F; S; Daughter; 6877; Yes; Yes; 26987
6861; Haska-yee-tah-nil-wudt; M; 6; Navajo; F; S; Son; 6878; Yes; Yes; 26988

6862; Salou-l-sosie-bega, Charley; M; 34; Navajo; F; M; Head; 6879; Yes; Yes; 32230
6863; Blue Eye's daughter; F; 29; Navajo; F; M; Wife; 6880; Yes; Yes; 32231
6864; Nah-tah-yee-tah-yil-wohl; M; 11; Navajo; F; S; Son; 6881; Yes; Yes; 32232
6865; Glih-yee-dah-bah; F; 8; Navajo; F; S; Daughter; 6882; Yes; Yes; 32233
6866; Nah-tah-yil-nih-nih-yah; M; 5; Navajo; F; S; Son; 6883; Yes; Yes; 32234
6867; Keh-yih-kih-dez-bah; F; 2; Navajo; F; S; Daughter; 6884; Yes; Yes; 32235

6868; Salou-L-sosie; M; 73; Navajo; F; M; Head; 6885; Yes; Yes; 32252
6869; Salou-L-sosie's wife; F; 72; Navajo; F; M; Wife; 6886; Yes; Yes; 32253
6870; Al-kih-nih-bah; F; 15; Navajo; F; S; Grand-daughter; 6887; Yes; Yes; 32254
6871; Bih-kih-gee-bah; F; 7; Navajo; F; S; Grand-daughter; 6888; Yes; Yes; 32255

6872; Salou-l-sosie-bega; M; 28; Navajo; F; M; Head; 6889; Yes; Yes; 32226
6873; Blue Eye's daughter; F; 26; Navajo; F; M; Wife; 6890; Yes; Yes; 32227
6874; Say-bah; F; 9; Navajo; F; S; Daughter; 6891; Yes; Yes; 32228
6875; Haska-yil-has-wudt; M; 3; Navajo; F; S; Son; 6892; Yes; Yes; 32229

6876; Salou-l-sosie-bega; M; 47; Navajo; F; M; Head; 6893; Yes; Yes; 32244
6877; Seh-bih-jah-tlol-bitsih[sic]; F; 42; Navajo; F; M; 6894; Wife; Yes; Yes; 32245
       [Name could be Sah-bih-jah-tlol-bitsih]
6878; Homer; M; 16; Navajo; F; S; Son; 6895; Yes; Yes; 32246
6879; Nah-tah-yil-nih-deesah; M; 14; Navajo; F; S; Son; 6896; Yes; Yes; 32247
6880; Dah-hah-zah; M; 10; Navajo; F; S; Son; 6897; Yes; Yes; 32248
6881; Glih-zoz-bah; F; 4; Navajo; F; S; Daughter; 6898; Yes; Yes; 32249

6882; Salou-go-zani-bih-adzan; F; 66; Navajo; F; Wd; Head; 6899; Yes; Yes; 25997
6883; Ada; F; 24; Navajo; F; S; Daughter; 6900; Yes; Yes; 25998
6884; Rudolph; M; 23; Navajo; F; S; Son; 6901; Yes; Yes; 25999

Census of the **Northern Navajo** reservation of the **Northern Navajo** jurisdiction, as of **April 1** , 19**31**, taken by **Ernest H. Hammond, District** , Superintendent. **in Charge**

**Key:** Number; NAME: Surname, Given; Sex; Birth Year (if given), Age At Last Birthday; Tribe; Degree of Blood; Marital Status; Relationship To Head of Family; Last Census Roll Number; At Jurisdiction Where Enrolled (Yes or No); At Another Jurisdiction; ELSEWHERE: Post office, County, State; Ward (Yes or No); Allotment, Annuity, and Identification Numbers.

6885;  Fanny; F; 19; Navajo; F; S; Grand-daughter; 6902; Yes; Yes; 26000
6886;  Yil-hah-bah; F; 11; Navajo; F; S; Grand-daughter; 6903; Yes; Yes; 26001

6887;  Salou-yazzie; M; Unk; Navajo; F; M; Head; 6904; Yes; Yes; 28430
6888;  Hosteen-soh-bitsih; F; 21; Navajo; F; M; Wife; 6905; Yes; Yes; 28431
6889;  See-l-bahih; M; 3; Navajo; F; S; Son; 6906; Yes; Yes; 28432

6890;  Salou-etseesie-bega, John Sam; M; 34; Navajo; F; M; Head; 6907; Yes; Yes; 27047
6891;  Hosteen-dagaihih-bitsih; F; 31; Navajo; F; M; Wife; 6908; Yes; Yes; 27048
6892;  Etta; F; 11; Navajo; F; S; Daughter; 6909; Yes; Yes; 27049
6893;  Joann; F; 9; Navajo; F; S; Daughter; Yes; 6910; Yes; 27050
6894;  Haska-yee-tah-nih-yah; M; 7; Navajo; F; S; Son; 6911; Yes; Yes; 27051
6895;  Yazzie, John; M; 3; Navajo; F; S; Son; 6912; Yes; Yes; 27052

6896;  Salou-altseessie-bilah; F; 59; Navajo; F; Wd; Head; 6913; Yes; Yes; 25129
6897;  Haska-yee-tah-yah; M; 31; Navajo; F; S; Son; 6914; Yes; Yes; 25130
6898;  Adzan-l-suen; F; 6; Navajo; F; S; Grand-daughter; 6915; Yes; Yes; 25131

6899;  Salou-alsosie-bitsih; F; 32; Navajo; F; Wd; Head; 6916; Yes; Yes; 22616
6900;  Hah-nih-bah; F; 14; Navajo; F; S; Daughter; 6917; Yes; Yes; 22617
6901;  Nah-nih-bah; F; 8; Navajo; F; S; Daughter; 6918; Yes; Yes; 22618
6902;  Chih-dez-bah; F; 4; Navajo; F; S; Daughter; 6919; Yes; Yes; 22619
6903;  Haska-yee-chih-nalwudt; M; 3; Navajo; F; S; Son; 6920; Yes; Yes; 22620

6904;  Salou-Alsosie; M; Unk; Navajo; F; M; Head; 6921; Yes; Yes; 22612
6905;  Salou-Alsosie's wife; F; 23; Navajo; F; M; Wife; 6922; Yes; Yes; 22613
6906;  Haska-yil-yee-gahl; M; 5; Navajo; F; S; Son; 6923; Yes; Yes; 22614
6907;  Salou-Alsosie-bega; M; 20; Navajo; F; S; Son; 6924; Yes; Yes; 22615

6908;  Salou-Nez-bitsih; M; Unk; Navajo; F; M; Head; 6925; Yes; Yes; 22601
6909;  Minnie; F; 32; Navajo; F; M; Wife; 6926; Yes; Yes; 22602
6910;  Chih-nih-nih-bah; F; 16; Navajo; F; S; Step-daughter; 6927; Yes; Yes; 22603
6911;  Mina; F; 11; Navajo; F; S; Step-daughter; 6928; Yes; Yes; 22604
6912;  Haska-yil-nah-yah; M; 6; Navajo; F; S; Son; 6929; Yes; Yes; 22605
6913;  Haska-yil-ee-yah; M; 5; Navajo; F; S; Son; 6930; Yes; Yes; 22606
6914;  Rex; M; 4; Navajo; F; S; Son; 6931; Yes; Yes; 22607

6915;  Salou-sani-badoni; M; Unk; Navajo; F; M; Head; 6932; Yes; Yes; 21417
6916;  Salou-sani-bitsih; F; Unk; Navajo; F; M; Wife; 6933; Yes; Yes; 21418
6917;  No-talh; M; 5; Navajo; F; S; Son; 6934; Yes; Yes; 21419

6918;  Salou-Sani; M; Unk; Navajo; F; M; Head; 6935; Yes; Yes; 21348

Census of the **Northern Navajo** reservation of the **Northern Navajo** jurisdiction, as of **April 1**, 1931, taken by **Ernest H. Hammond, District**, Superintendent. **in Charge**

**Key:** Number; NAME: Surname, Given; Sex; Birth Year (if given), Age At Last Birthday; Tribe; Degree of Blood; Marital Status; Relationship To Head of Family; Last Census Roll Number; At Jurisdiction Where Enrolled (Yes or No); At Another Jurisdiction; ELSEWHERE: Post office, County, State; Ward (Yes or No); Allotment, Annuity, and Identification Numbers.

6919;  Askan-sosie-bitsih; F; 34; Navajo; F; M; Wife; 6936; Yes; 21349
6920;  Yee-gahn-hee-bah; F; 14; Navajo; F; S; Daughter; 6937; Yes; Yes; 21350

6921;  Salou-nes[sic]; M; 58; Navajo; F; Wd; Head; 6938; Yes; Yes; 31057
       [Name should be Salou-nez]
6922;  Dah-dez-bah; F; 25; Navajo; F; S; Daughter; 6939; Yes; Yes; 31058
6923;  Sarah; F; 20; Navajo; F; S; Daughter; 6940; Yes; Yes; 31059

6924;  Sam-bega, Bruce; M; 22; Navajo; F; M; Head; 6941; No; McElmo, Colo., San Juan, Utah; Yes; 19275
6925;  Zannie; F; 21; Navajo; F; M; Wife; 6942; No; McElmo, Colo., San Juan, Utah; Yes; 19276
6926;  Elsie; F; 2; Navajo; F; S; Daughter; 6943; No; McElmo, Colo., San Juan, Utah; Yes; 19504

6927;  Scott, Roy; M; 31; Navajo; F; M; Head; 6944; Yes; Yes; 19991
6928;  Scott, Mable; F; 24; Navajo; F; M; Wife; 6945; Yes; Yes; 19992
6929;  Glih-hah-bah; M; 3; Navajo; F; S; Son; 6946; Yes; Yes; 19993
6930;  Pearl; F; 2; Navajo; F; S; Daughter; 6947; Yes; Yes; 19994

6931;  Scott, Richard; M; 26; Navajo; F; M; Head; 6948; Yes; Yes; 25956
6932;  Scott, Jennie; F; 33; Navajo; F; M; Wife; 6949; Yes; Yes; 25957
6933;  Scott, Ruth; F; 4; Navajo; F; S; Daughter; [Blank]; Yes; Yes; 25958
6934;  Nah-tah-yil-nah-deyah, Bennie; M; 3; Navajo; F; S; Son; 6950; Yes; Yes; 25959
6935;  No-pah; F; 2; Navajo; F; S; Daughter; 6951; Yes; Yes; 26034

6936;  Scott, Andrew; M; 28; Navajo; F; M; Head; 6952; Yes; Yes; 21362
6937;  Yee-kih-has-bah; M[sic]; 18; Navajo; F; M; Wife; 6953; Yes; Yes; 21363
       [Should be female.]
6938;  Kay-nas-bah; F; 4; Navajo; F; S; Daughter; 6954; Yes; Yes; 21364
6939;  Haska-yee-tas-hah-zah; M; 3; Navajo; F; S; Son; 6955; Yes; Yes; 21708

6940;  Scott, Harold; M; 24; Navajo; F; M; Head; 6956; Yes; Yes; 21235
6941;  Scott, Lily; F; 34; Navajo; F; M; Wife; 6957; Yes; Yes; 21236
6942;  Yee-nih-bah; F; 5; Navajo; F; S; Daughter; 6958; Yes; Yes; 21237
6943;  Dinay-yazzie; M; 4; Navajo; F; S; Son; 6959; Yes; Yes; 21238

6944;  Sells, Cato; M; 26; Navajo; F; M; Head; 6960; Yes; Yes; 30998
6945;  Sells, Mary; F; 24; Navajo; F; M; Wife; 6961; Yes; Yes; 30999
6946;  Wilber; M; 1; Navajo; F; S; Son; 6962; Yes; Yes; 31219
6947;  Vera Mae; F; 5/12; Navajo; F; S; Daughter; 6963; Yes; Yes; 31296

Census of the **Northern Navajo** reservation of the **Northern Navajo** jurisdiction, as of **April 1**, 1931, taken by **Ernest H. Hammond, District**, Superintendent. **in Charge**

Key: Number; NAME: Surname, Given; Sex; Birth Year (if given), Age At Last Birthday; Tribe; Degree of Blood; Marital Status; Relationship To Head of Family; Last Census Roll Number; At Jurisdiction Where Enrolled (Yes or No); At Another Jurisdiction; ELSEWHERE: Post office, County, State; Ward (Yes or No); Allotment, Annuity, and Identification Numbers.

6948; Seh-al-ch-nah-gaih-nih-bega, Charley; M; 53; Navajo; F; M; Head; 6963; No; McElmo, Colo., San Juan, Utah; Yes; 19354

6949; Bitoni-Yazzie-bitsih; F; 47; Navajo; F; M; Wife; 6964; No; McElmo, Colo., San Juan, Utah; Yes; 19355

6950; Tah-zose-bah, Lula; F; 12; Navajo; F; S; Daughter; 6965; No; McElmo, Colo., San Juan, Utah; Yes; 19356

6951; Hamlin, Lena; F; 24; Navajo; F; S; Sister-in-law; 6966; No; McElmo, Colo., San Juan, Utah; Yes; 19357

6952; Florence Charley; F; 15; Navajo; F; S; Step-niece; 6967; No; McElmo, Colo., San Juan, Utah; Yes; 19358

6953; Woody, Herbert; M; 15; Navajo; F; S; Step-nephew; 6968; No; McElmo, Colo., San Juan, Utah; Yes; 19359

6954; Senopas-Zoni-bega; M; 31; Navajo; F; M; Head; 6969; Yes; Yes; 17221
6955; Bih-dahton-bihjaykay; F; 24; Navajo; F; M; Wife; 6970; Yes; Yes; 17222
6956; Hoska-yil-wollyah; M; 8; Navajo; F; S; Son; 6971; Yes; Yes; 17223
6957; Hoska-yilt-hahyah; M; 6; Navajo; F; S; Son; 6972; Yes; Yes; 17224
6958; Thi-pahih; M; 5; Navajo; F; S; Son; 6973; Yes; Yes; 17225
6959; Chin-bah; F; 2; Navajo; F; S; Daughter; 6974; Yes; Yes; 20414

6960; Soh-ah-tah-bega; M; 24; Navajo; F; M; Head; 6975; Yes; Yes; 22710
6961; Al-sah-bah; F; 21; Navajo; F; M; Wife; 6976; Yes; Yes; 22711

6962; Soh-ah-tah-badoni; M; 40; Navajo; F; M; Head; 6977; Yes; Yes; 22495
6963; Soh-ah-tah-bitsih; F; 39; Navajo; F; M; Wife; 6978; Yes; Yes; 22496
6964; Yee-kih-des-bah; F; 17; Navajo; F; S; Daughter; 6979; Yes; Yes; 22498
6965; Kenneth; M; 14; Navajo; F; S; Son; 6980; Yes; Yes; 22499
6966; Yee-nas-bah; F; 12; Navajo; F; S; Daughter; 6981; Yes; Yes; 22500
6967; Alfred; M; 11; Navajo; F; S; Son; 6982; Yes; Yes; 22501
6968; Marshall; M; 9; Navajo; F; S; Son; 6983; Yes; Yes; 22502
6969; Hoska-yee-Nah-gahl; M; 7; Navajo; F; S; Son; 6984; Yes; Yes; 22503
6970; Hoska-yee-chih-nil-wudt; M; 5; Navajo; F; S; Son; 6985; Yes; Yes; 22504
6971; Harry; M; 3; Navajo; F; S; Son; 6986; Yes; Yes; 22505

6972; See-codih, Randall; M; 23; Navajo; F; M; Head; 6987; Yes; Yes; 22354
6973; Kih-des-bah; F; 23; Navajo; F; M; Wife; 6988; Yes; Yes; 22355
6974; Daniel; M; 5; Navajo; F; S; Step-Son; 6989; Yes; Yes; 22356
6975; Randall, Jr.; M; 3; Navajo; F; S; Son; 6990; Yes; Yes; 22357

6976; See-codih-yen-benally; M; 31; Navajo; F; M; Head; 6991; Yes; Yes; 22595
6977; Dil-awosh-ih-bitsih; F; 29; Navajo; F; M; Wife; 6992; Yes; Yes; 22596
6978; Kah-nas-bah; F; 5; Navajo; F; S; Daughter; 6993; Yes; Yes; 22597
6979; Haska-hah-noh-tahl; M; 4; Navajo; F; S; Son; 6994; Yes; Yes; 22598

Census of the **Northern Navajo** reservation of the **Northern Navajo** jurisdiction, as of **April 1**, 19**31**, taken by **Ernest H. Hammond, District**, Superintendent. **in Charge**

**Key:** Number; NAME: Surname, Given; Sex; Birth Year (if given), Age At Last Birthday; Tribe; Degree of Blood; Marital Status; Relationship To Head of Family; Last Census Roll Number; At Jurisdiction Where Enrolled (Yes or No); At Another Jurisdiction; ELSEWHERE: Post office, County, State; Ward (Yes or No); Allotment, Annuity, and Identification Numbers.

6980;  See-chisih-bega, John; M; 30; Navajo; F; S; Head; 6995; Yes; Yes; 30356

6981;  See-chisih-bitsih, Lucy; F; 38; Navajo; F; Wd; Head; 6996; Yes; Yes; 30345
6982;  Janet; F; 18; Navajo; F; S; Daughter; 6997; Yes; Yes; 30346
6983;  John; M; 11; Navajo; F; S; Son; 6998; Yes; Yes; 30347
6984;  Joe; M; 5; Navajo; F; S; Son; 6999; Yes; Yes; 30348
6985;  Bin-gee-bah, Helen; F; 2; Navajo; F; S; Daughter; 7000; Yes; Yes; 31243

6986;  See-chisih-bega; M; Unk; Navajo; F; M; Head; 7001; Yes; Yes; 30412
6987;  Dinay-yazzie-bitsih; F; 32; Navajo; F; M; Wife; 7002; Yes; Yes; 30413
6988;  Mary Lou; F; 19; Navajo; F; S; Daughter; 7003; Yes; Yes; 30414
6989;  Haska-kih-deyah; M; 13; Navajo; F; S; Son; 7004; Yes; Yes; 30415
6990;  Nah-binl-bah; F; 11; Navajo; F; S; Daughter; 7005; Yes; Yes; 30416
6991;  John; M; 7; Navajo; F; S; Son; 7006; Yes; Yes; 30417
6992;  Nah-keh-hah-bah; F; 5; Navajo; F; S; Daughter; 7007; Yes; Yes; 30418
6993;  Haska-yee-kih-nah-tahl; M; 2; Navajo; F; S; Son; 7008; Yes; Yes; 31254

6994;  See-chisih-benally; M; 36; Navajo; F; M; Head; 7009; Yes; Yes; 29712
6995;  Clah-yazzie-bitsih; F; 40; Navajo; F; M; Wife; 7010; Yes; Yes; 29713
6996;  Tahih, Hildan; F; 23; Navajo; F; S; Step-daughter; 7011; Yes; Yes; 29714
6997;  Florence; F; 16; Navajo; F; S; Daughter; 7012; Yes; Yes; 29715
6998;  Hester; F; 14; Navajo; F; S; Daughter; 7013; Yes; Yes; 29716
6999;  Ox-bah; F; 9; Navajo; F; S; Daughter; 7014; Yes; Yes; 29717
7000;  Nah-tah-yil-yee-gahl; M; 8; Navajo; F; S; Son; 7015; Yes; Yes; 29718
7001;  Nah-tah-yil-hah-yah; M; 5; Navajo; F; S; Son; 7016; Yes; Yes; 29719
7002;  Yah-nah-nih-bah; F; 3; Navajo; F; S; Daughter; 7017; Yes; Yes; 29720

7003;  See-chosie; M; 47; Navajo; F; M; Head; 7018; Yes; Yes; 29806
7004;  See-chosie-bih-adzan; M[sic]; 70; Navajo; F; M; Wife; 7019; Yes; Yes; 29807
7005;  Haska-yee-nah-hah-tal; M; 19; Navajo; F; S; Son; 7020; Yes; Yes; 29808

7006;  See-codih-benally; M; Unk; Navajo; F; M; Head; 7021; Yes; Yes; 29767
7007;  Ah-yazzie; F; 28; Navajo; F; M; Wife; 7022; Yes; Yes; 29768
7008;  Dinay-ho-lel; M; 5; Navajo; F; S; Son; 7023; Yes; Yes; 29771

7009;  See-codih; M; 51; Navajo; F; M; Head; 7024; Yes; Yes; 29159
7010;  Hosteen-soh-bitsih; F; 23; Navajo; F; M; Wife; 7025; Yes; Yes; 29160
7011;  Dah-ziz-bah; F; 2; Navajo; F; S; Daughter; 7026; Yes; Yes; 29161
7012;  Ella; M[sic]; 18; Navajo; F; S; Daughter; 7027; Yes; Yes; 29162
7013;  Soh, Horace; M; 20; Navajo; F; S; Brother-in-law; 7028; Yes; Yes; 29163
7014;  Ruth; F; 3; Navajo; F; S; Daughter; 7029; Yes; Yes; 29406

7015;  See-codih-nez; M; 51; Navajo; F; M; Head; 7030; Yes; Yes; 29011

Census of the **Northern Navajo** reservation of the **Northern Navajo** jurisdiction, as of **April 1**, 19**31,** taken by **Ernest H. Hammond, District,** Superintendent. **in Charge**

**Key:** Number; NAME: Surname, Given; Sex; Birth Year (if given), Age At Last Birthday; Tribe; Degree of Blood; Marital Status; Relationship To Head of Family; Last Census Roll Number; At Jurisdiction Where Enrolled (Yes or No); At Another Jurisdiction; ELSEWHERE: Post office, County, State; Ward (Yes or No); Allotment, Annuity, and Identification Numbers.

7016; Laura; F; 57; Navajo; F; M; Wife; 7031; Yes; Yes; 29012
7017; Thomas, Herbert; M; 37; Navajo; F; S; Step-son; 7032; Yes; Yes; 29013
7018; Philip; M; 32; Navajo; F; S; Step-son; 7033; Yes; Yes; 29014

7019; See-l-chee, Jack; M; Unk; Navajo; F; M; Head; 7034; Yes; Yes; 29216
7020; Hah-tahly-bitsih; M[sic]; 41; Navajo; F; M; Wife; 7035; Yes; Yes; 29217
        [Should be female]
7021; Joseph; M; 22; Navajo; F; S; Step-son; 7036; Yes; Yes; 29218
7022; Eskie-Yazzie; M; 19; Navajo; F; S; Step-son; 7037; Yes; Yes; 29219
7023; Edna; F; 17; Navajo; F; S; Step-daughter; 7038; Yes; Yes; 29220
7024; Jeane; F; 15; Navajo; F; S; Daughter; 7039; Yes; Yes; 29221
7025; Woody; M; 9; Navajo; F; S; Son; 7040; Yes; Yes; 29222
7026; Hah-gee-bah; F; 7; Navajo; F; S; Daughter; 7041; Yes; Yes; 29223
7027; Kih-dee-wudt; M; 2; Navajo; F; S; Son; 7042; Yes; Yes; 29224

7028; See-codih-yen-bega; M; 49; Navajo; F; M; Head; 7043; Yes; Yes; 21511
7029; Kin-lah-cheeny-bitsih; F; 39; Navajo; F; M; Wife; 7044; Yes; Yes; 21512
7030; Kin-lah-cheeny-bitsih; F; 37; Navajo; F; S; Sister-in-law; 7045; Yes; Yes; 21513
7031; Nah-tah-yah-nal-wudt; M; 15; Navajo; F; S; Grand-son; 7046; Yes; Yes; 21514

7032; See-gail-thlani-benally; M; 41; Navajo; F; M; Head; 7047; Yes; Yes; 21563
7033; Chah-la-bahih-benally; F; 32; Navajo; F; M; Wife; 7048; Yes; Yes; 21564
7034; Josephine; F; 13; Navajo; F; S; Daughter; 7049; Yes; Yes; 21565
7035; Richmond; M; 11; Navajo; F; S; Son; 7050; Yes; Yes; 21566
7036; Soh-yazzie; F; 7; Navajo; F; S; Daughter; 7051; Yes; Yes; 21567
7037; Bahee; F; 16; Navajo; F; S; Daughter; 7052; Yes; Yes; 21728

7038; Seese-chilli's wife, Adzan-bitsee-chilli-bih-che; F; 59; Navajo; F; M; Head; 7053; Yes; Yes; 21197
7039; Nee-ee-as-chee; M; 32; Navajo; F; S; Son; 7054; Yes; Yes; 21198
7040; Away-l-chee; M; 14; Navajo; F; S; Son; 7055; Yes; Yes; 21199

7041; See-chill-yazzie-bega; M; 24; Navajo; F; M; Head; 7056; Yes; Yes; 21497
7042; Klizi-lazaih-bitsih; F; 21; Navajo; F; M; Wife; 7057; Yes; Yes; 21498
7043; Eskee-bih-klizi; M; 4; Navajo; F; S; Son; 7058; Yes; Yes; 21499

7044; Seese-chilli-yazzie; M; 29; Navajo; F; M; Head; 7059; Yes; Yes; 21538
7045; Dah-yis-bah; M[sic]; 20; Navajo; F; M; Wife; 7060; Yes; Yes; 21539
        [Should be female]

Census of the **Northern Navajo** reservation of the **Northern Navajo** jurisdiction, as of **April 1**, 19**31**, taken by **Ernest H. Hammond, District**, Superintendent. **in Charge**

**Key:** Number; NAME: Surname, Given; Sex; Birth Year (if given), Age At Last Birthday; Tribe; Degree of Blood; Marital Status; Relationship To Head of Family; Last Census Roll Number; At Jurisdiction Where Enrolled (Yes or No); At Another Jurisdiction; ELSEWHERE: Post office, County, State; Ward (Yes or No); Allotment, Annuity, and Identification Numbers.

7046;  Seh-nah-hahbil-nih-bega[sic], Long John; M; 26; Navajo; F; S; Head; 7061; Yes; Yes; 27033    [Name could be Seh-nah-nah-bil-nih-bega, Long John]
7047;  Dash-nih-bah; F; 23; Navajo; F; S; Sister; 7062; Yes; Yes; 27034
7048;  Glenn, Jim; M; 25; Navajo; F; S; Brother; 7063; Yes; Yes; 27035
7049;  Hah-nih-bah; F; 17; Navajo; F; S; Sister; 7064; Yes; Yes; 27036
7050;  Kih-dih-bah; F; 15; Navajo; F; S; Sister; 7065; Yes; Yes; 27037
7051;  Wudt; M; 12; Navajo; F; S; Brother; 7066; Yes; Yes; 27038
7052;  Zahz; M; 10; Navajo; F; S; Brother; 7067; Yes; Yes; 27039

7053;  See-clitsuen; M; Unk; Navajo; F; M; Head; 7068; Yes; Yes; 27921
7054;  Adzan-l-tohly; F; Unk; Navajo; F; M; Wife; 7069; Yes; Yes; 27822[sic]
                                                [ID No. should be 27922]

7055;  Soh-bih-ajh-tlol-bega; M; 36; Navajo; F; M; Head; 7070; Yes; Yes; 27590
7056;  Yahn-naz-bah; F; 36; Navajo; F; M; Wife; 7071; Yes; Yes; 27591

7057;  Seh-nah-hah-bil-nih; M; Unk; Navajo; F; M; Head; 7072; Yes; Yes; 24908
7058;  Al-kah-ee-bah; M[sic]; 26; Navajo; F; M; Wife; 7073; Yes; Yes; 24909
7059;  Nah-tah-yah-nih-yah; M; 7; Navajo; F; S; Son; 7074; Yes; Yes; 24910

7060;  Senopas-yazzie; M; 42; Navajo; F; M; Head; 7075; Yes; Yes; 20271
7061;  Senopas-Yazzie's wife; F; 42; Navajo; F; M; Wife; 7076; Yes; Yes; 20272
7062;  Senopas-Sanih-benally; M; 20; Navajo; F; S; Son; 7077; Yes; Yes; 20273
7063;  Fred; M; 16; Navajo; F; S; Son; 7078; Yes; Yes; 20274
7064;  Ah-ghei; M; 6; Navajo; F; S; Son; 7079; Yes; Yes; 20275

7065;  Seese-chilli-yen-benally; M; 22; Navajo; F; M; Head; 7080; Yes; Yes; 22384
7066;  Seeih; F; 21; Navajo; F; M; Wife; 7081; Yes; Yes; 22385
7067;  Nah-glih-yazzie; F; 2; Navajo; F; S; Daughter; 7082; Yes; Yes; 22783

7068;  See-l-chee-bih-adzan; F; 61; Navajo; F; Wd; Head; 7083; Yes; Yes; 22664
7069;  Emma; F; 24; Navajo; F; S; Daughter; 7084; Yes; Yes; 22665
7070;  Bessie; F; 22; Navajo; F; S; Daughter; 7085; Yes; Yes; 22666

7071;  Seh-ah-tah-bega; M; 43; Navajo; F; M; Head; 7086; Yes; Yes; 21465
7072;  Biz-nih-bah; F; 39; Navajo; F; M; Wife; 7087; Yes; Yes; 21466
7073;  Kee-yah; M; 16; Navajo; F; S; Son; 7088; Yes; Yes; 21467
7074;  Leah; F; 10; Navajo; F; S; Daughter; 7089; Yes; Yes; 21468
7075;  Glih-yazzie; F; 9; Navajo; F; S; Daughter; 7090; Yes; Yes; 21469
7076;  Kee-doh-yazzie; M; 6; Navajo; F; S; Son; 7091; Yes; Yes; 21470
7077;  Nah-tah-yee-noh-innl; M; 4; Navajo; F; S; Son; 7092; Yes; Yes; 21471
7078;  Karl; M; 17; Navajo; F; S; Step-son; 7093; Yes; Yes; 21472
7079;  Vera; F; 13; Navajo; F; S; Step-daughter; 7094; Yes; Yes; 21473

Census of the **Northern Navajo** reservation of the **Northern Navajo** jurisdiction, as of **April 1**, 1931, taken by **Ernest H. Hammond, District**, Superintendent. **in Charge**

**Key:** Number; NAME: Surname, Given; Sex; Birth Year (if given), Age At Last Birthday; Tribe; Degree of Blood; Marital Status; Relationship To Head of Family; Last Census Roll Number; At Jurisdiction Where Enrolled (Yes or No); At Another Jurisdiction; ELSEWHERE: Post office, County, State; Ward (Yes or No); Allotment, Annuity, and Identification Numbers.

7080; See-codih-yen-bega; M; Unk; Navajo; F; M; Head; 7095; Yes; Yes; 22588
7081; See-codih-yen-bega-bih-adzan; F; 53; Navajo; F; M; Wife; 7096; Yes; Yes; 22589
7082; Haska-kih-deyah; M; 16; Navajo; F; S; Son; 7097; Yes; Yes; 22590
7083; Haska-yee-ziz-zinh; M; 10; Navajo; F; S; Son; 7098; Yes; Yes; 22591
7084; Rita; F; 13; Navajo; F; S; Daughter; 7099; Yes; Yes; 22592

7085; Soh-lagaih-se-nilih; M; 63; Navajo; F; M; Head; 7100; Yes; Yes; 20132
7086; Kin-le-cheeny-nez-bitsih; F; 36; Navajo; F; M; Wife; 7101; Yes; Yes; 20133
7087; Yanh-des-bah[sic]; F; 16; Navajo; F; S; Daughter; 7102; Yes; Yes; 20134
[Name should be Yahn-des-bah]
7088; Kee-bah-ih; M; 12; Navajo; F; S; Son; 7103; Yes; Yes; 20135
7089; Chah-la-bahih-yen-bitsih; F; 76; Navajo; F; Wd; Divorced wife; 7104; Yes; Yes; 20136

7090; Soh-n-del-koh; M; 47; Navajo; F; M; Head; 7105; Yes; Yes; 20141
7091; Dah-dee-bah; F; 20; Navajo; F; M; Wife; 7106; Yes; Yes; 20142
7092 Toas-bah; F; 9; Navajo; F; S; Daughter; 7107; Yes; Yes; 20165
7093; Lena; F; 2; Navajo; F; S; Daughter; 7108; Yes; 20403

7094; Soh-lagaih-se-nilih-bitcilli; M; 50; Navajo; F; M; Head; 7109; Yes; Yes; 20143
7095; Aht-sosie-yen-bitsih; M[sic]; 53; Navajo; F; M; Wife; 7110; Yes; Yes; 20144
7096; Kee-soeih; M; 16; Navajo; F; S; Son; 7111; Yes; Yes; 20145
7097; White-Rock, Annabel; F; 14; Navajo; F; S; Daughter; 7112; Yes; Yes; 20146
7098; Kee-ah-sheih; M; 12; Navajo; F; S; Son; 7113; Yes; Yes; 20147
7099; Chih-kenh-bahih; F; 8; Navajo; F; S; Daughter; 7114; Yes; Yes; 20148
7100; Hoska-l-chee; M; 6; Navajo; F; S; Son; 7115; Yes; 20149
7101; Glih-bah; F; 35; Navajo; F; M; 2nd Wife; 7116; Yes; Yes; 20150
7102; Awa-Yazzie; F; 13; Navajo; F; S; Daughter; 7117; Yes; Yes; 20151
7103; Batoni-l-chee; M; 10; Navajo; F; S; Son; 7118; Yes; Yes; 20152
7104; Nah-tah-chee; M; 7; Navajo; F; S; Son; 7119; Yes; Yes; 20153
7105; Ah-kee; M; 5; Navajo; F; S; Son; 7120; Yes; Yes; 20154

7106; See-codih-yen-bega; M; 46; Navajo; F; M; Head; 7121; Yes; Yes; 21369
7107; Tah-nih-bah; F; 33; Navajo; F; M; Wife; 7122; Yes; Yes; 21370
7108; See-codih, Rex; M; 10; Navajo; F; S; Son; 7123; Yes; Yes; 21371
7109; Nah-tah-yil-nahzah; M; 9; Navajo; F; S; Son; 7124; Yes; Yes; 21372
7110; Dah-yis-bah; F; 6; Navajo; F; S; Daughter; 7125; Yes; Yes; 21373
7111; Yil-nah-bah; F; 4; Navajo; F; S; Daughter; 7126; Yes; Yes; 21374

7112; Sen-opas-sanih-bega; M; 45; Navajo; F; M; Head; 7127; Yes; Yes; 20068
7113; Askan-deel-bih-cha-K; F; 29; Navajo; F; M; Wife; 7128; Yes; Yes; 20069

Census of the **Northern Navajo** reservation of the **Northern Navajo** jurisdiction, as of **April 1**, 19**31,** taken by **Ernest H. Hammond, District**, Superintendent. **in Charge**

**Key:** Number; NAME: Surname, Given; Sex; Birth Year (if given), Age At Last Birthday; Tribe; Degree of Blood; Marital Status; Relationship To Head of Family; Last Census Roll Number; At Jurisdiction Where Enrolled (Yes or No); At Another Jurisdiction; ELSEWHERE: Post office, County, State; Ward (Yes or No); Allotment, Annuity, and Identification Numbers.

7114; Dah-hah-bah; F; 9; Navajo; F; S; Daughter; 7129; Yes; Yes; 20070
7115; Glih-ne; F; 7; Navajo; F; S; Daughter; 7130; Yes; Yes; 20071
7116; Nah-tah-yil-has-le; M; 5; Navajo; F; S; Son; 7131; Yes; Yes; 20072
7117; Dinay-Yazzie; M; 2; Navajo; F; S; Son; 7132; Yes; Yes; 20417

7118; Senopas-Yazzie; M; 48; Navajo; F; M; Head; 7133; No; McElmo, Colo., San Juan, Utah; Yes; 18921
7119; Senopas-Yazzie's wife; F; 49; Navajo; F; M; Wife; 7134; No; McElmo, Colo., San Juan, Utah; Yes; 18922
7120; Kee-yah-bah; F; 20; Navajo; F; S; Daughter; 7135; No; McElmo, Colo., San Juan, Utah; Yes; 18923
7121; Senopas Yazzie[sic], Eldon; M; 20; Navajo; F; S; Son; 7136; No; McElmo, Colo., San Juan, Utah; Yes; 18924   [Name could be Senopas-Yazzie, Eldon]

7122; See-l-chee-bega; M; Unk; Navajo; F; M; Head; 7137; Yes; Yes; 21275
7123; Adzan-sceih; F; Unk; Navajo; F; M; Wife; 7138; Yes; Yes; 21276
7124; Hah-ee-bah; F; 9; Navajo; F; S; Daughter; 7139; Yes; Yes; 21277
7125; Kes-bah; F; 7; Navajo; F; S; Daughter; 7140; Yes; Yes; 21278
7126; Bil-ah-gee-bah; F; 3; Navajo; F; S; Daughter; 7141; Yes; Yes; 21279

7127; See-codih; M; 57; Navajo; F; M; Head; 7142; Yes; Yes; 20075
7128; Klizi-lagaih-bih-daysih; F; 59; Navajo; F; M; Wife; 7143; Yes; Yes; 20076
7129; See-codih, Mack; F[sic]; 27; Navajo; F; S; Son; 7144; Yes; Yes; 20077
7130; See-codih, Marshall; M; 21; Navajo; F; S; Son; 7145; Yes; Yes; 20078
7131; See-codih, Eda; F; 18; Navajo; F; S; Daughter; 7146; Yes; Yes; 20079
7132; Eskee-nanl-cadih; M; 16; Navajo; F; S; Son; 7147; Yes; Yes; 20080
7133; Yil-des-bah; F; 11; Navajo; F; S; Daughter; 7148; Yes; Yes; 20081

7134; Senopas-Sanih-badoni; M; 43; Navajo; F; M; Head; 7149; Yes; Yes; 20085
7135; Senopas-Sanih-bitsih; F; 33; Navajo; F; M; Wife; 7150; Yes; Yes; 20086
7136; Biz-dee-bah; F; 8; Navajo; F; S; Daughter; 7151; Yes; Yes; 20087
7137; Senopas-Sanih; M; Unk; Navajo; F; Wd; Father-in-law; 7152; Yes; Yes; 20089

7138; Soh-chil-yah-toh-bega; M; 25; Navajo; F; M; Head; 7153; Yes; Yes; 21354
7139; Top-ah-hah-bitsih; F; 21; Navajo; F; M; Wife; 7154; Yes; Yes; 21355
7140; Hoska-yil-hah-yah; M; 4; Navajo; F; S; Son; 7155; Yes; Yes; 21356
7141; Chin-nas-bah; M; 1; Navajo; F; S; Son; 7156; Yes; Yes; 21712
7142; Top-ah-hah; M; Unk; Navajo; F; Wd; Father-in-law; 7157; Yes; Yes; 21357
7143; Top-ah-hah-bega; M; 25; Navajo; FE; S; Brother-in-law; 7158; Yes; Yes; 21358
7144; Top-ah-hah, Thomas; M Unk; Navajo; F; S; Brother-in-law; 7159; Yes; Yes; 21359

Census of the **Northern Navajo** reservation of the **Northern Navajo** jurisdiction, as of **April 1**, 19**31**, taken by **Ernest H. Hammond, District**, Superintendent. **in Charge**

Key: Number; NAME: Surname, Given; Sex; Birth Year (if given), Age At Last Birthday; Tribe; Degree of Blood; Marital Status; Relationship To Head of Family; Last Census Roll Number; At Jurisdiction Where Enrolled (Yes or No); At Another Jurisdiction; ELSEWHERE: Post office, County, State; Ward (Yes or No); Allotment, Annuity, and Identification Numbers.

7145; Top-ah-hah, Nila; F; Unk; Navajo; F; S; Sister-in-law; 7160; Yes; Yes; 21360
7146; Hoska-yee-kee-dah-yis-wudt; M; 12; Navajo; F; S; Brother-in-law; 7161; Yes; Yes; 21361

7147; See-codih-yen-benally; M; Unk; Navajo; F; M; Head; 7162; Yes; Yes; 21351
7148; Yee-nas-bah; F; 18; Navajo; F; M; Wife; 7163; Yes; Yes; 21352
7149; Hoska-yee-tah-deyah; M; 3; Navajo; F; S; Son; 7164; Yes; Yes; 21353
7150; Hah-nah-bah; F; 1; Navajo; F; S; Daughter; 7165; Yes; Yes; 21688

7151; See-l-chee-bitsih; F; 49; Navajo; F; Wd; Head; 7166; Yes; Yes; 20959
7152; Foster, Heuben; M; 23; Navajo; F; S; Son; 7167; Yes; Yes; 20960
7153; Hoska-yee-tah-gah; M; 10; Navajo; F; S; Son; 7168; Yes; Yes; 20961
7154; Nah-tah-yee-tah-gah; M; 7; Navajo; F; S; Son; 7169; Yes; Yes; 20962

7155; See-dih-chosie-benally, Jim; M; 30; Navajo; F; M; Head; 7170; Yes; Yes; 21243
7156; Hah-tahly-sosie-bitsih; F; 29; Navajo; F; M; Wife; 7171; Yes; Yes; 21244
7157; Nah-tah-yil-nah-zah; M; 9; Navajo; F; S; Son; 7172; Yes; Yes; 21245
7158; Baz-nih-bah; F; 7; Navajo; F; S; Daughter; 7173; Yes; Yes; 21247
7159; Kih-yee-nih-bah; F; 2/12; Navajo; F; S; Daughter; 7174; Yes; Yes; 21724

7160; See-codih; M; 56; Navajo; F; M; Head; 7175; Yes; Yes; 20301
7161; Bylilli-yen-bitsih; F; 41; Navajo; F; M; Wife; 7176; Yes; Yes; 20302
7162; Yil-des-bah; F; 9; Navajo; F; S; Daughter; 7177; Yes; Yes; 20303
7163; Yee-nih-bah; F; 3; Navajo; F; S; Daughter; 7178; Yes; Yes; 20304

7164; Senopas-Sanih-bega, Slim; M; 32; Navajo; F; M; Head; 7179; Yes; Yes; 20205
7165; Nargo-bitsih; F; 21; Navajo; F; M; Wife; 7180; Yes; Yes; 20206
7166; Bih-gee-bah; F; 11; Navajo; F; S; Daughter; 7181; Yes; Yes; 20207
7167; Kay-ah-bah; F; 7; Navajo; F; S; Daughter; 7182; Yes; Yes; 20208
7168; Glih-des-bah; F; 5; Navajo; F; S; Daughter; 7183; Yes; Yes; 20209

7169; Seh-al-ch-nah-gaih-nih-bega, Boatman Jim; M; 61; Navajo; F; Wd; Head; 7184; No; McElmo, Colo., San Juan, Utah; Yes; 19431
7170; Es-kee-stoley; M; 24; Navajo; F; S; Son; 7185; No; McElmo, Colo., San Juan, Utah; Yes; 19432
7171; Watson, Tom; M; 21; Navajo; F; S; Son; 7186; No; McElmo, Colo., San Juan, Utah; Yes; 19433
7172; Kee-soh, Boatman; M; 15; Navajo; F; S; Son; 7187; No; McElmo, Colo., San Juan, Utah; Yes; 19434
7173; Awa-is-bah; F; 12; Navajo; F; S; Daughter; 7188; No; McElmo, Colo., San Juan, Utah; Yes; 19435

226

Census of the __Northern Navajo__ reservation of the __Northern Navajo__ jurisdiction, as of __April 1__, 19**31,** taken by __Ernest H. Hammond, District__, Superintendent. **in Charge**

**Key:** Number; NAME: Surname, Given; Sex; Birth Year (if given), Age At Last Birthday; Tribe; Degree of Blood; Marital Status; Relationship To Head of Family; Last Census Roll Number; At Jurisdiction Where Enrolled (Yes or No); At Another Jurisdiction; ELSEWHERE: Post office, County, State; Ward (Yes or No); Allotment, Annuity, and Identification Numbers.

7174;  Seh-akizee; M; 48; Navajo; F; M; Head; 7189; No; McElmo, Colo., San Juan, Utah; Yes; 19282

7175;  Top-ah-ah-bit-sih; F; 45; Navajo; F; M; Wife; 7190; No; McElmo, Colo., San Juan, Utah; Yes; 19283

7176;  Seh-ekizee-bega; M; 19; Navajo; F; S; Son; 7191; No; McElmo, Colo., San Juan, Utah; Yes; 19284

7177;  Zanie-Tuley; F; 16; Navajo; F; S; Daughter; 7192; No; McElmo, Colo., San Juan, Utah; Yes; 19285

7178;  Seh-akizee, Nora; F; 14; Navajo; F; S; Daughter; 7193; No; McElmo, Colo., San Juan, Utah; Yes; 19286

7179;  Seh-akizee, Leola; F; 12; Navajo; F; S; Daughter; 7194; McElmo, Colo., San Juan, Utah; Yes; 19287

7180;  Kee-soh; M; 9; Navajo; F; S; Son; 7195; No; McElmo, Colo., San Juan, Utah; Yes; 19288

7181;  Schiz-zah; M; 5; Navajo; F; S; Son; 7196; No; McElmo, Colo., San Juan, Utah; Yes; 19289

7182;  Seginih-soh; M; 41; Navajo; F; M; Head; 7197; No; McElmo, Colo., San Juan, Utah; Yes; 19367

7183;  Batoni-Yazzie-bitsih; M[sic]; 38; Navajo; F; M; Wife; 7198; No; McElmo, Colo., San Juan, Utah; Yes; 19368

7184;  Seginih-soh, Margaret; F; 20; Navajo; F; S; Daughter; 7199; No; McElmo, Colo., San Juan, Utah; Yes; 19369

7185;  Kee-l-bahih; M; 12; Navajo; F; S; Son; 7200; No; McElmo, Colo., San Juan, Utah; Yes; 19370

7186;  Zannie-bahih; F; 10; Navajo; F; S; Daughter; 7201; No; McElmo, Colo., San Juan, Utah; Yes; 19371

7187;  Seginih-Soh, Lewis; M; 6; Navajo; F; S; Son; 7202; No; McElmo, Colo., San Juan, Utah; Yes; 19372

7188;  Bil-zose-bahih; F; 4; Navajo; F; S; Daughter; 7203; No; McElmo, Colo., San Juan, Utah; Yes; 19373

7189;  James; M; 1; Navajo; F; S; Son; 7204; No; McElmo, Colo., San Juan, Utah; Yes; 19315[sic] [ID No. for 1930 was 19515]

7190;  Shorty-bega's wife, Glih-dez-bah; F; 27; Navajo; F; Wd; Head; 7205; Yes; Yes; 26229

7191;  John Stephen; M; 8; Navajo; F; S; Son; 7206; Yes; Yes; 26230

7192;  Marie; F; 6; Navajo; F; S; Daughter; 7207; Yes; Yes; 26231

7193;  Ruth; F; 4; Navajo; F; S; Daughter; 7208; Yes; Yes; 26232

7194;  Margaret; F; 2; Navajo; F; S; Daughter; 7209; Yes; Yes; 26437

7195;  Shorty; M; 81; Navajo; F; M; Head; 7210; Yes; Yes; 24998

7196;  Shorty's Wife; F; 79; Navajo; F; M; Wife; 7211; Yes; Yes; 24999

Census of the **Northern Navajo** reservation of the **Northern Navajo** jurisdiction, as of **April 1**, 19**31,** taken by **Ernest H. Hammond, District**, Superintendent. **in Charge**

**Key:** Number; NAME: Surname, Given; Sex; Birth Year (if given), Age At Last Birthday; Tribe; Degree of Blood; Marital Status; Relationship To Head of Family; Last Census Roll Number; At Jurisdiction Where Enrolled (Yes or No); At Another Jurisdiction; ELSEWHERE: Post office, County, State; Ward (Yes or No); Allotment, Annuity, and Identification Numbers.

7197; Shorty-Nez, Little George; M; Unk; Navajo; F; M; Head; 7212; Yes; Yes; 22639

7198; Nah-glih-Yazzie; F; 37; Navajo; F; M; Wife; 7213; Yes; Yes; 22640

7199; Haska-yee-nah-yah; M; 16; Navajo; F; S; Son; 7214; Yes; Yes; 22641

7200; George, Bobbie; M; 13; Navajo; F; S; Son; 7215; Yes; Yes; 22642

7201; Haska-yee-tah-hah-zah; M; 10; Navajo; F; S; Son; 7216; Yes; Yes; 22643

7202; Yee-hah-nih-bah; F; 7; Navajo; F; S; Daughter; 7217; Yes; Yes; 22644

7203; George, John; M; 5; Navajo; F; S; Son; 7218; Yes; Yes; 22645

7204; Shorty-John; M; 31; Navajo; F; M; Head; 7219; Yes; Yes; 26241

7205; Glih-haz-bah; F; 28; Navajo; F; M; Wife; 7220; Yes; Yes; 26242

7206; Dorcas; F; 12; Navajo; F; S; Daughter; 7221; Yes; Yes; 26243

7207; Jimmy; M; 3; Navajo; F; S; Son; 7222; Yes; Yes; 26244

7208; Manuelito, James; M; 22; Navajo; F; S; Brother-in-law; 7223; Yes; Yes; 26245

7209; Shorty Guy; M; 48; Navajo; F; M; Head; 7224; Yes; Yes; 26262

7210; Al-chih-nih-nih-bah; F; 50; Navajo; F; M; Wife; 7225; Yes; Yes; 26263

7211; Manley; M; 24; Navajo; F; S; Son; 7226; Yes; Yes; 26264

7212; Chin-nih-bahih; F; 18; Navajo; F; S; Daughter; 7227; Yes; Yes; 26265

7213; Dah-hah-zah; M; 16; Navajo; F; S; Son; 7228; Yes; Yes; 26266

7214; Barton, Belle; F; 12; Navajo; F; S; Daughter; 7229; Yes; Yes; 26267

7215; Barton, Paul; M; 10; Navajo; F; S; Son; 7230; Yes; Yes; 26268

7216; Nah-naz-bah; F; 6; Navajo; F; S; Daughter; 7231; Yes; Yes; 26269

7217; Glih-yil-nah-nih-bah; F; 3; Navajo; F; S; Daughter; 7232; Yes; Yes; 26270

7218; Shorty Tom; M; 47; Navajo; F; M; Head; 7233; Yes; Yes; 26318

7219; Nettie; F; 32; Navajo; F; M; Wife; 7234; Yes; Yes; 26319

7220; Carrie; F; 20; Navajo; F; S; Daughter; 7235; Yes; Yes; 26320

7221; Violet; F; 16; Navajo; F; S; Daughter; 7236; Yes; Yes; 26321

7222; Nellie; F; 9; Navajo; F; S; Daughter; 7237; Yes; Yes; 26322

7223; Robert; M; 6; Navajo; F; S; Son; 7238; Yes; Yes; 26323

7224; Sho-yih-nih-benally; M; 52; Navajo; F; M; Head; 7239; Yes; Yes; 30921

7225; Shause-bih-dazee; F; 47; Navajo; F; M; Wife; 7240; Yes; Yes; 30922

7226; Baz-ee-bah; F; 15; Navajo; F; S; Daughter; 7241; Yes; Yes; 30923

7227; Doh-nih-bah; F; 10; Navajo; F; S; Daughter; 7242; Yes; Yes; 30924

7228; Bil-naz-dee-bah; F; 8; Navajo; F; S; Daughter; 7243; Yes; Yes; 30925

7229; Yil-ee-bah; F; 6; Navajo; F; S; Daughter; 7244; Yes; Yes; 30926

7230; Dee; M; 16; Navajo; F; S; Son; 7245; Yes; Yes; 30927

7231; John; M; 13; Navajo; F; S; Son; 7246; Yes; Yes; 30928

7232; Shouse-bitah; M; 36; Navajo; F; M; Head; 7247; Yes; Yes; 30913

Census of the **Northern Navajo** reservation of the **Northern Navajo** jurisdiction, as of **April 1**, 19**31,** taken by **Ernest H. Hammond, District**, Superintendent. **in Charge**

**Key:** Number; NAME: Surname, Given; Sex; Birth Year (if given), Age At Last Birthday; Tribe; Degree of Blood; Marital Status; Relationship To Head of Family; Last Census Roll Number; At Jurisdiction Where Enrolled (Yes or No); At Another Jurisdiction; ELSEWHERE: Post office, County, State; Ward (Yes or No); Allotment, Annuity, and Identification Numbers.

7233; Beeleen-lizin-bitsih[sic]; F; 34; Navajo; F; M; Wife; 7248; Yes; Yes; 30914
[Name is probably Beleen-lizin-bitsih]
7234; Jane; F; 14; Navajo; F; S; Daughter; 7249; Yes; Yes; 30915
7235; Nah-tah-yil-sizih; M; 9; Navajo; F; S; Son; 7250; Yes; Yes; 30916

7236; Shouse-yah-hah-yehih; M; 32; Navajo; F; M; Head; 7251; Yes; Yes; 30904
7237; Shouse-bih-dazee; F; 30; Navajo; F; M; Wife; 7252; Yes; Yes; 30905
7238; Haska-yil-hah-yah; M; 10; Navajo; F; S; Son; 7253; Yes; Yes; 30906
7239; Bil-naz-nih-bah; F; 8; Navajo; F; S; Daughter; 7254; Yes; Yes; 30907
7240; Haska-yil-nih-nih-yah; M; 4; Navajo; F; S; Son; 7255; Yes; Yes; 30908
7241; Biz-dez-bah; F; 3; Navajo; F; S; Daughter; 7256; Yes; Yes; 31229

7242; Shouse-bekis; M; 30; Navajo; F; M; Head; 7257; Yes; Yes; 30900
7243; Hosteen-l-bahih-bitsih; F; 21; Navajo; F; M; 7258; Wife; Yes; Yes; 30901
7244; Yee-kaz-bah; F; 5; Navajo; F; S; Daughter; 7259; Yes; Yes; 30902
7245; Nah-tah-yil-dah-dee-yah; M; 2; Navajo; F; S; Son; 7260; Yes; Yes; 30903

7246; Shorty; M; 46; Navajo; F; M; Head; 7261; Yes; Yes; 30349
7247; Dinay-yazzie-bitsih; F; 30; Navajo; F; M; Wife; 7262; Yes; Yes; 30350
7248; Nih-dez-bah; F; 11; Navajo; F; S; Daughter; 7263; Yes; Yes; 30351
7249; Haska-yee-nal-wudt; M; 7; Navajo; F; S; Son; 7264; Yes; Yes; 30352
7250; Nah-kih-hah-nahz-bah; F; 3; Navajo; F; S; Daughter; 7265; Yes; Yes; 31245

7251; Sheepman; M; 87; Navajo; F; S; Head; 7266; Yes; Yes; 23284

7252; Shorty-Nez; M; 41; Navajo; F; M; Head; 7267; Yes; Yes; 30847
7253; Doh-hal-tahih-bitsih; F; 38; Navajo; F; M; 7268; Wife; Yes; Yes; 30848
7254; Haska-hah-bah; M; 20; Navajo; F; S; Son; 7269; Yes; Yes; 30849
7255; Tuly; M; 18; Navajo; F; S; Son; 7270; Yes; Yes; 30850
7256; Yil-nih-bah; F; 13; Navajo; F; S; Daughter; 7271; Yes; Yes; 30851
7257; Nah-tah-yil-yil-wudt; M; 10; Navajo; F; S; Son; 7272; Yes; Yes; 30852
7258; Glih-ee-bah; F; 8; Navajo; F; S; Daughter; 7273; Yes; Yes; 30853
7259; Chih-dah-hiz-bah; F; 7; Navajo; F; S; Daughter; 7274; Yes; Yes; 30854
7260; Nel-wudt, Matthew; M; 14; Navajo; F; S; Brother-in-law; 7275; Yes; Yes; 30857

7261; Shorty-clah-bih-adzan; F; 36; Navajo; F; Wd; Head; 7276; Yes; Yes; 26685
7262; Martin, Harry; M; 20; Navajo; F; S; Son; 7277; Yes; Yes; 26686
7263; Manda; F; 18; Navajo; F; S; Daughter; 7278; Yes; Yes; 26687
7264; George; M; 14; Navajo; F; S; Son; 7279; Yes; Yes; 26688
7265; Bih-nih-ziz-bah; F; 9; Navajo; F; S; Daughter; 7280; Yes; Yes; 26689

7266; Sims, Custer; M; 45; Navajo; F; M; Head; 7281; Yes; Yes; 32407

Census of the **Northern Navajo** reservation of the **Northern Navajo** jurisdiction, as of **April 1**, 1931, taken by **Ernest H. Hammond, District**, Superintendent. **in Charge**

**Key:** Number; NAME: Surname, Given; Sex; Birth Year (if given), Age At Last Birthday; Tribe; Degree of Blood; Marital Status; Relationship To Head of Family; Last Census Roll Number; At Jurisdiction Where Enrolled (Yes or No); At Another Jurisdiction; ELSEWHERE: Post office, County, State; Ward (Yes or No); Allotment, Annuity, and Identification Numbers.

7267; Dinay-Chilli-benally; F; 36; Navajo; F; M; Wife; 7282; Yes; Yes; 32408
7268; Has-wudt; M; 19; Navajo; F; S; Son; 7283; Yes; Yes; 32409
7269; Keh-yee-naz-bah; F; 18; Navajo; F; S; Daughter; 7284; Yes; Yes; 32410
7270; Charley; M; 16; Navajo; F; S; Son; 7285; Yes; Yes; 32411
7271; Red; M; 12; Navajo; F; S; Son; 7286; Yes; Yes; 32412
7272; Yah-ee-gahl; M; 10; Navajo; F; S; Son; 7287; Yes; Yes; 32413
7273; Yee-nay-yah; M; 8; Navajo; F; S; Son; 7288; Yes; Yes; 32414
7274; Yil-dez-bah; F; 6; Navajo; F; S; Daughter; 7289; Yes; Yes; 32415
7275; Hah-yah; M; 4; Navajo; F; S; Son; 7290; Yes; Yes; 32416

7276; Sih-nah-gahih-bega; M; 39; Navajo; F; M; Head; 7291; Yes; Yes; 25142
7277; Adzan-sinn-clah; F; 43; Navajo; F; M; Wife; 7292; Yes; Yes; 25143
7278; Beulah; F; 18; Navajo; F; S; Daughter; 7293; Yes; Yes; 25144
7279; Rena; F; 16; Navajo; F; S; Daughter; 7294; Yes; Yes; 25145
7280; Rita; F; 14; Navajo; F; S; Daughter; 7295; Yes; Yes; 25146
7281; Tah-deyah; M; 12; Navajo; F; S; Son; 7296; Yes; Yes; 25147
7282; Ross; M; 10; Navajo; F; S; Son; 7297; Yes; Yes; 25148
7283; Hah-yah; M; 9; Navajo; F; S; Son; 7298; Yes; Yes; 25149
7284; Hah-yah; M; 4; Navajo; F; S; Son; 7299; Yes; Yes; 25150

7285; Sinn-l-clahnih; M; 63; Navajo; F; M; Head; 7300; Yes; Yes; 25265
7286; Adzan-clash-chee; F; 44; Navajo; F; M; Wife; 7301; Yes; Yes; 25266
7287; Peter; M; 8; Navajo; F; S; Son; 7302; Yes; Yes; 25267
7288; Nocki-l-suen, Pearl; F; 15; Navajo; F; S; Niece-in-law; 7303; Yes; Yes; 25268
7289; Nocki-l-suen, Elsie; F; 13; Navajo; F; S; Niece-in-law; 7304; Yes; Yes; 25269
7290; Adzan-clash-chee; F; 78; Navajo; F; Div.; 1st wife; 7305; Yes; Yes; 25270

7291; Sinn-l-clah-nih-bega; M; 33; Navajo; F; M; Head; 7306; Yes; Yes; 25271
7292; Tah-cheeih-yazzie-bitsih; F; 25; Navajo; F; M; Wife; 7307; Yes; Yes; 25272
7293; Kee-soh; M; 11; Navajo; F; S; Son; 7308; Yes; Yes; 25273
7294; Kee-yazzie; M; 8; Navajo; F; S; Son; 7309; Yes; Yes; 25274
7295; Tahn-hah-gee-bah; F; 4; Navajo; F; S; Daughter; 7310; Yes; Yes; 25275

7296; Sih-nah-gahih; M; 74; Navajo; F; Wd; Head; 7311; Yes; Yes; 25296

7297; Sinn-clah-nih-yazzie-bega, Antees; M; 37; Navajo; F; M; Head; 7313; No; McElmo, Colo., San Juan, Utah; Yes; 18801
7298; Sinn-clah-nih-yazzie-bega's wife; F; 32; Navajo; F; M; Wife; 7314; No; McElmo, Colo., San Juan, Utah; Yes; 18802
7299; Sinn-clah-nih-yazzie-bega, John; M; 14; Navajo; F; S; Step-son; 7315; No; McElmo, Colo., San Juan, Utah; Yes; 18803
7300; Hoska-yee-dah-nil; M; 10; Navajo; F; S; Son; 7316; No; McElmo, Colo., San Juan, Utah; Yes; 18804

Census of the **Northern Navajo** reservation of the **Northern Navajo** jurisdiction, as of **April 1**, 1931, taken by **Ernest H. Hammond, District**, Superintendent. **in Charge**

Key: Number; NAME: Surname, Given; Sex; Birth Year (if given), Age At Last Birthday; Tribe; Degree of Blood; Marital Status; Relationship To Head of Family; Last Census Roll Number; At Jurisdiction Where Enrolled (Yes or No); At Another Jurisdiction; ELSEWHERE: Post office, County, State; Ward (Yes or No); Allotment, Annuity, and Identification Numbers.

7301; Hoska-yilth-dobnih; M; 8; Navajo; F; S; Son; 7317; No; McElmo, Colo., San Juan, Utah; Yes; 18805
7302; Nun-nih-bah; F; 6; Navajo; F; S; Daughter; 7318; No; McElmo, Colo., San Juan, Utah; Yes; 18806

7303; Sinn-sah-cadnih-bih-daznih; F; Unk; Navajo; F; Wd; Head; 7319; Yes; Yes; 17399
7304; Sin-sah-cadnih-bih-adzanih's daughter; F; Unk; Navajo; F; S; Daughter; 7320; Yes; Yes; 17400

7305; Sinn-sah-cadnih-soh-bega, Natoni; M; 46; Navajo; F; M; Head; 7321; Yes; Yes; 17001
7306; Bitsee-pahih-Botsih[sic]; F; 40; Navajo; F; M; Wife; 7322; Yes; Yes; 17002
[Name should be Bitsee-pahih-Bitsih]
7307; Sinn-sah-cadnih-soh-bega, Awa-l-chee; F; 21; Navajo; F; S; Daughter; 7323; Yes; Yes; 17003
7308; Soh, Franklin; M; 18; Navajo; F; S; Son; 7324; Yes; Yes; 17004
7309; Sin-sah-cadnih-soh-bega, Kee-sosie; M; 14; Navajo; F; S; Son; 7325; Yes; Yes; 17005
7310; Sin-sah-cadnih-soh-bega, Tom; M; 13; Navajo; F; S; Son; 7326; Yes; Yes; 17006
7311; Soh, Bessie; F; 11; Navajo; F; S; Daughter; 7327; Yes; Yes; 17007
7312; Sin-sah-cadnih-soh-bega, Ye-tah-yil-wolth; M; 8; Navajo; F; S; Son; 7328; Yes; Yes; 17008
7313; Sin-sah-cadnih-woh-bega-Til-wudt; M; 5; Navajo; F; S; Son; 7329; Yes; Yes; 17009
7314; Sinn-sah-cadnih-woh-bega, Ason-Bie; F; 1; Navajo; F; S; Daughter; 7330; Yes; Yes; 18268

7315; Silas, Richard; M; 29; Navajo; F; M; Head; 7331; No; McElmo, Colo., San Juan, Utah; Yes; 19488
7316; Sen-it-taih-neskahai, Bitsih; F; 24; Navajo; F; M; Wife; 7332; No; McElmo, Colo., San Juan, Utah; Yes; 19489
7317; Tah-yil-wudt; M; 7; Navajo; F; S; Son; 7333; No; McElmo, Colo., San Juan, Utah; Yes; 19490
7318; Ah-tahnih; F; 4; Navajo; F; S; Daughter; 7334; No; McElmo, Colo., San Juan, Utah; Yes; 19491
7319; Tah-nah-bah; F; 1; Navajo; F; S; Daughter; 7335; No; McElmo, Colo., San Juan, Utah; Yes; 19524

7320; Sinay-chilli; M; Unk; Navajo; F; Wd; Head; 7336; Yes; Yes; 22576
7321; Haska-yil-dah-yee-wudt; M; Unk; Navajo; F; S; Son; 7337; Yes; Yes; 22578
7322; Jacob; M; Unk; Navajo; F; S; Son; 7338; Yes; Yes; 22579

Census of the **Northern Navajo** reservation of the **Northern Navajo** jurisdiction, as of **April 1**, 19**31**, taken by **Ernest H. Hammond, District**, Superintendent. **in Charge**

Key: Number; NAME: Surname, Given; Sex; Birth Year (if given), Age At Last Birthday; Tribe; Degree of Blood; Marital Status; Relationship To Head of Family; Last Census Roll Number; At Jurisdiction Where Enrolled (Yes or No); At Another Jurisdiction; ELSEWHERE: Post office, County, State; Ward (Yes or No); Allotment, Annuity, and Identification Numbers.

7323; Nah-tah-yil-has-wudt; M; Unk; Navajo; F; S; Son; 7339; Yes; Yes; 22580
7324; Nah-toh-yil-nahyah; M; 8; Navajo; F; S; Son; 7340; Yes; Yes; 22581

7325; Sina-clah-nih-nez; M; 42; Navajo; F; M; Head; 7341; Yes; Yes; 22569
7326; Hosteen-seeih-bitsih; F; 37; Navajo; F; M; Wife; 7342; Yes; Yes; 22570
7327; Eva; F; 14; Navajo; F; S; Step-daughter; 7343; Yes; Yes; 22571
7328; Bella; F; 11; Navajo; F; S; Step-daughter; 7344; Yes; Yes; 22572
7329; Ben; M; 9; Navajo; F; S; Son; 7345; Yes; Yes; 22573
7330; Yee-deh-bah; F; 7; Navajo; F; S; Daughter; 7346; Yes; Yes; 22574
7331; Oscar; M; 4; Navajo; F; S; Son; 7347; Yes; Yes; 22575

7332; Smith, Lucy; F; 24; Navajo; F; Wd; Head; 7348; Yes; Yes; 18118
7333; Smith, Frank; M; 5; Navajo; F; S; Son; 7349; Yes; Yes; 18119
7334; Smith, Hattie; F; 3; Navajo; F; S; Daughter; 7350; Yes; Yes; 18120

7335; Smith, Frank W.; M; 25; Navajo; F; M; Head; 7351; Yes; Yes; 23684
7336; Clash-chee-yazzie-bitsih; F; 21; Navajo; F; M; Wife; 7352; Yes; Yes; 23685

7337; Smith, John; M; 38; Navajo; F; M; Head; 7353; Yes; Yes; 26014
7338; Hah-ziz-bahih; F; 33; Navajo; F; M; Wife; 7354; Yes; Yes; 26015
7339; Alexander; M; 14; Navajo; F; S; Son; 7355; Yes; Yes; 26016
7340; Dah-ee-bah; F; 12; Navajo; F; S; Daughter; 7356; Yes; Yes; 26017
7341; Keh-yee-nah-yah; M; 7; Navajo; F; S; Son; 7357; Yes; Yes; 26018
7342; Haska-yee-kih-dah-yes-wudt; M; 4; Navajo; F; S; Son; 7358; Yes; Yes; 26019

7343; Soh; M; 29; Navajo; F; Wd; Head; 7359; No; McElmo, Colo., San Juan, Utah; Yes; 19484
7344; Cah-ih; F; 5; Navajo; F; S; Daughter; 7360; No; McElmo, Colo., San Juan, Utah; Yes; 19485
7345; Yazzie, Tony; M; 3; Navajo; F; S; Son; 7361; No; McElmo, Colo., San Juan, Utah; Yes; 19486

7346; Sosie, Richard; M; Unk; Navajo; F; M; Head; 7362; Yes; Yes; 30201
7347; Genevieve; F; 30; Navajo; F; M; Wife; 7363; Yes; Yes; 30202
7348; David; M; 8; Navajo; F; S; Son; 7364; Yes; Yes; 30203
7349; Bye-ye; M; 6; Navajo; F; S; Son; 7365; Yes; Yes; 30204
7350; Fannie; F; 4; Navajo; F; S; Daughter; 7366; Yes; Yes; 30205

7351; Salou-bitsees-chilli-bikis- Jim Long; M; Unk; Navajo; F; M; Head; 7367; Yes; Yes; 32974
7352; Ah-doloh-bitsih[sic]; F; 48; Navajo; F; M; Wife; 7368; Yes; Yes; 32975
      [Name could be Ah-coloh-bitsih]
7353; Paul; M; 15; Navajo; F; S; Son; 7369; Yes; Yes; 32976

Census of the __Northern Navajo__ reservation of the __Northern Navajo__ jurisdiction, as of __April 1__, 1931, taken by __Ernest H. Hammond, District__, Superintendent. **in Charge**

**Key:** Number; NAME: Surname, Given; Sex; Birth Year (if given), Age At Last Birthday; Tribe; Degree of Blood; Marital Status; Relationship To Head of Family; Last Census Roll Number; At Jurisdiction Where Enrolled (Yes or No); At Another Jurisdiction; ELSEWHERE: Post office, County, State; Ward (Yes or No); Allotment, Annuity, and Identification Numbers.

7354; Kah-dah-hiz-bah; F; 13; Navajo; F; S; Daughter; 7370; Yes; Yes; 32977
7355; Edna May; F; 10; Navajo; F; S; Daughter; 7371; Yes; Yes; 32978
7356; Bahih; M; 8; Navajo; F; S; Son; 7372; Yes; Yes; 32979
7357; Haska-yil-yil-gahl; M; 5; Navajo; F; S; Son; 7373; Yes; Yes; 32980
7358; Nah-dez-bah; F; 2; Navajo; F; S; Daughter; 7374; Yes; Yes; 32981

7359; Salou-bitsee-chilli-bega, Little John; M; 51; Navajo; F; M; Head; 7375; Yes; Yes; 32984
7360; Salou-Sank-bitsih[sic]; F; 39; Navajo; F; M; Wife; 7476; Yes; Yes; 32985
    [Name should be Salou-Sani-bitsih
7361; Nah-tah-yee-tah-hoh-lel; M; 21; Navajo; F; S; Son; 7377; Yes; Yes; 32986
7362; Keh-ee-bah, Elizabeth; F; 14; Navajo; F; S; Daughter; 7378; Yes; Yes; 32987
7363; Yil-naz-bah; F; 12; Navajo; F; S; Daughter; 7379; Yes; Yes; 32988
7364; Haska-yil-yil-wohl; M; 9; Navajo; F; S; Son; 7380; Yes; Yes; 32989
7365; Haska-yee-chih-hayah; M; 7; Navajo; F; S; Son; 7381; Yes; Yes; 32990

7366; Sandoval, bitcilli-bega; M; 36; Navajo; F; M; Head; 7382; Yes; Yes; 32801
7367; Hosteen-toh-lakan-bitsih; F; 23; Navajo; F; M; Wife; 7383; Yes; Yes; 32802
7368; Nah-tah-yil-nih-yah; M; 7; Navajo; F; S; Son; 7384; Yes; Yes; 32803
7369; Haska-yil-yee-gahl; M; 6; Navajo; F; S; Son; 7385; Yes; Yes; 32804
7370; Haska-dah-dal-nih; M; 4; Navajo; F; S; Son; 7386; Yes; Yes; 32805
7371; Mr. Mason; M; 22; Navajo; F; S; Son; 7387; Yes; Yes; 32806

7372; Sih-nah-gahih-bega; M; 23; Navajo; F; M; Head; 7388; Yes; Yes; 32887
7373; Hah-nih-tay-shih-benally; F; 21; Navajo; F; M; Wife; 7389; Yes; Yes; 32888
7374; Yil-dez-bah; F; 4; Navajo; F; S; Daughter; 7390; Yes; Yes; 32889

7375; R. T. F. Simpson (White man) Head of house 7391
7376; Blanche; F; 19; Navajo; 1/4+; S; Daughter; 7392; Yes; Yes; 32931
7377; George R.; M; 16; Navajo; 1/4+; S; Son; 7393; Yes; Yes; 32932
7378; Mary Dora; F; 15; Navajo; 1/4+; S; Daughter; 7394; Yes; Yes; 32933
7379; Annie Mae; F; 13; Navajo; 1/4+; S; Daughter; 7395; Yes; Yes; 32934

7380; Shorty-bega; M; Unk; Navajo; F; M; Head; 7396; Yes; Yes; 30335
7381; Hosteen-Ashih-bitsih; F; 31; Navajo; F; M; Wife; 7397; Yes; Yes; 30336
7382; Tahn-dez-bah; F; 16; Navajo; F; S; Daughter; 7398; Yes; Yes; 30337
7383; Yee-kah-haz-bah; M; 13; Navajo; F; S; Son; 7399; Yes; Yes; 30338
7384; Haska-yil-hah-yah; M; 9; Navajo; F; S; Son; 7400; Yes; Yes; 30341
7385; Haska-yee-tah-deyah; M; 19; Navajo; F; S; Brother; 7401; Yes; Yes; 30342
7386; Naz-bah; F; 17; Navajo; F; S; Sister; 7402; Yes; Yes; 30343
7387; Haska-yil-nah-yah; M; 14; Navajo; F; S; Brother; 7403; Yes; Yes; 30344
7388; Haska-hah-la; M; 3; Navajo; F; S; Son; 7404; Yes; Yes; 31246

Census of the **Northern Navajo** reservation of the **Northern Navajo**
jurisdiction, as of **April 1** , 19**31,** taken by **Ernest H. Hammond, District** ,
Superintendent. **in Charge**

**Key:** Number; NAME: Surname, Given; Sex; Birth Year (if given), Age At Last Birthday; Tribe; Degree of Blood; Marital Status; Relationship To Head of Family; Last Census Roll Number; At Jurisdiction Where Enrolled (Yes or No); At Another Jurisdiction; ELSEWHERE: Post office, County, State; Ward (Yes or No); Allotment, Annuity, and Identification Numbers.

7389; Soh-ah-tah-badoni Wilson, Pete; M; 40; Navajo; F; M; Head; 7405; Yes; Yes; 22739

7390; Soh-ah-tah-bitsih; F; 32; Navajo; F; M; Wife; 7406; Yes; Yes; 22740

7391; Yee-lah-naz-bah; F; 15; Navajo; F; S; Daughter; 7407; Yes; Yes; 22741

7392; Logan; F; 13; Navajo; F; S; Son; 7408; Yes; Yes; 22742

7393; Tah-nas-wudt; F[sic]; 11; Navajo; F; S; Son; 7409; Yes; Yes; 22743

7394; Haska-yee-tah-nihyah; F; 9; Navajo; F; S; Son; 7410; Yes; Yes; 22744

7395; Bil-naz-nih-bah; F; 7; Navajo; F; S; Daughter; 7411; Yes; Yes; 22745

7396; Yee-chih-nih-bah; F; 4; Navajo; F; S; Daughter; 7412; Yes; Yes; 22746

7397; Yee-haz-bah; F; 2; Navajo; F; S; Daughter; 7413; Yes; Yes; 22747

7398; Wilson's Mother; F; 76; Navajo; F; Wd; Grand-mother-in-law; 7414; Yes; Yes; 22748

7399; Seh-ah-tah-bilah; F; Unk; Navajo; F; Wd; Head; 7415; Yes; Yes; 22756

7400; Yee-deh-bah; F; 21; Navajo; F; S; Daughter; 7416; Yes; Yes; 22757

7401; Nah-yah; M; 16; Navajo; F; S; Son; 7417; Yes; Yes; 22758

7402; Chin-bah; F; 11; Navajo; F; S; Daughter; 7418; Yes; Yes; 22759

7403; Seh-chil-yah-toh; M; 69; Navajo; F; M; Head; 7419; Yes; Yes; 22766

7404; Batoni-nez-bitsih; F; 36; Navajo; F; M; Wife; 7420; Yes; Yes; 22767

7405; Nah-bah; F; 10; Navajo; F; S; Daughter; 7421; Yes; Yes; 22768

7406; Haska-yah-nah-sah; M; 8; Navajo; F; S; Son; 7422; Yes; Yes; 22769

7407; Kih-dez-bah; F; 6; Navajo; F; S; Daughter; 7423; Yes; Yes; 22770

7408; Haska-yil-dah-hih-yah; M; 3; Navajo; F; S; Son; 7424; Yes; Yes; 22771

7409; See-coh; M; 66; Navajo; F; M; Head; 7425; Yes; Yes; 19846

7410; Adzan-Hahtahly; F; 66; Navajo; F; M; Wife; 7426; Yes; Yes; 19847

7411; Salle's Son  Teddy Brown; M; 27; Navajo; F; S; Head; 7427; Yes; Yes; 31155

7412; Harvey; M; 25; Navajo; F; S; Brother; 7428; Yes; Yes; 31156

7413; Don Grey; M; 23; Navajo; F; S; Brother; 7429; Yes; Yes; 31157

7414; Navajo Thomas; M; 18; Navajo; F; S; Brother; 7430; Yes; Yes; 31158

7415; Salle-bega; M; 32; Navajo; F; M; Head; 7431; Yes; Yes; 31162

7416; Sale-bega[sic], Tom Fred; M; 29; Navajo; F; M; Head; 7432; Yes; Yes; 31159
[Name is probably Salle-bega, Tom Fred]

7417; Jah-kehih-bitsih, May Ellis; F; 24; Navajo; F; M; Wife; 7433; Yes; Yes; 31160

7418; Salle Bikis; M; 47; Navajo; F; M; Head; 7434; Yes; Yes; 31141

7419; Custer Sim's Sister; F; 45; Navajo; F; M; Wife; 7435; Yes; Yes; 31142

7420; Dodge, Chee; M; 22; Navajo; F; S; Son; 7436; Yes; Yes; 31143

7421; Dodge, John; M; 14; Navajo; F; S; Son; 7437; Yes; Yes; 31144

Census of the **Northern Navajo** reservation of the **Northern Navajo** jurisdiction, as of **April 1**, 1931, taken by **Ernest H. Hammond, District**, Superintendent. **in Charge**

**Key:** Number; NAME: Surname, Given; Sex; Birth Year (if given), Age At Last Birthday; Tribe; Degree of Blood; Marital Status; Relationship To Head of Family; Last Census Roll Number; At Jurisdiction Where Enrolled (Yes or No); At Another Jurisdiction; ELSEWHERE: Post office, County, State; Ward (Yes or No); Allotment, Annuity, and Identification Numbers.

7422; Has-wudt-Asa; M; 8; Navajo; F; S; Son; 7438; Yes; Yes; 31145

7423; Salou-Sani-bih-adzan; F; 79; Navajo; F; Div.; Head; 7439; Yes; Yes; 21629

7424; Sherman, Thomas; M; 25; Navajo; F; M; Head; 7440; Yes; Yes; 26424
7425; Laura; F; 22; Navajo; F; M; Wife; 7441; Yes; Yes; 26425
7426; Lauretta; F; 4; Navajo; F; S; Daughter; 7442; Yes; Yes; 26426
7427; Wade; M; 2; Navajo; F; S; Son; 7443; Yes; Yes; 26427
7428; Duke; M; 2; Navajo; F; S; Son; 7444; Yes; Yes; 26428
7429; Tah-ba-hah-nez-bega, Stephen; M; 18; Navajo; F; S; Brother-in-law; 7445; Yes; Yes; 26429

7430; Tah-nes-zah-nih; M; 25; Navajo; F; M; Head; 7446; No; McElmo, Colo., San Juan, Utah; Yes; 19290
7431; Seh-akizee-bitsih; F; 25; Navajo; F; M; Wife; 7447; No; McElmo, Colo., San Juan, Utah; Yes; 19291
7432; Tah-des-bah; F; 7; Navajo; F; S; Daughter; 7448; No; McElmo, Colo., San Juan, Utah; Yes; 19292
7433; Natah-l-gaih; M; 3; Navajo; F; S; Son; 7449; No; McElmo, Colo., San Juan, Utah; Yes; 19293
7434; Tah-ah-ah-yen-bih-adzanih; F; 83; Navajo; F; Wd; Grand-mother; 7450; No; McElmo, Colo., San Juan, Utah; Yes; 19294

7435; Tah-nes-zan-nih, Archie; M; 29; Navajo; F; M; Head; 7451; Yes; Yes; 25045
7436; Yah-nih-nih-bah; F; 25; Navajo; F; M; Wife; 7452; Yes; Yes; 25046
7437; Nih-nih-bah; F; 7; Navajo; F; S; Daughter; 7453; Yes; Yes; 25047
7438; Haska-yee-nih-yah; M; 5; Navajo; F; S; Son; 7454; Yes; Yes; 25048
7439; Atate-Yazzie; F; 3; Navajo; F; S; Daughter; 7455; Yes; Yes; 25049

7440    Tah-nez-zanth   Dist 11   Head   7456
7441; Tahn-hah-bah; F; 59; Navajo; F; M; 2nd Wife; 7457; Yes; Yes; 26800
7442; Richard; M; 24; Navajo; F; S; Step-son; 7458; Yes; Yes; 26801
7443; Clinton; M; 22; Navajo; F; S; Step-son; 7459; Yes; Yes; 26802
7444; Peter; M; 21; Navajo; F; S; Step-son; 7460; Yes; Yes; 26803

7445; Tah-nes-zanih, John; M; Unk; Navajo; F; Wd; Head; 7461; Yes; Yes; 28061
7446; Woody; M; 16; Navajo; F; S; Step-son; 7462; Yes; Yes; 28062
7447; Katherine; F; 14; Navajo; F; S; Step-daughter; 7463; Yes; Yes; 28063
7448; Caroline; F; 11; Navajo; F; S; Daughter; 7464; Yes; Yes; 28064
7449; Shih-kee; M; 8; Navajo; F; S; Son; 7465; Yes; Yes; 28065

7450; Tah-zoz-bah, McCarty; F; 33; Navajo; F; Wd; Head; 7466; Yes; Yes; 24919
7451; Julia; F; 17; Navajo; F; S; Daughter; 7467; Yes; Yes; 24920

Census of the **Northern Navajo** reservation of the **Northern Navajo** jurisdiction, as of **April 1**, 19**31**, taken by **Ernest H. Hammond, District**, Superintendent. **in Charge**

Key: Number; NAME: Surname, Given; Sex; Birth Year (if given), Age At Last Birthday; Tribe; Degree of Blood; Marital Status; Relationship To Head of Family; Last Census Roll Number; At Jurisdiction Where Enrolled (Yes or No); At Another Jurisdiction; ELSEWHERE: Post office, County, State; Ward (Yes or No); Allotment, Annuity, and Identification Numbers.

7452; Ascher; M; 10; Navajo; F; S; Son; 7468; Yes; Yes; 24921
7453; Nah-tah-cha-yah; F[sic]; 1; Navajo; F; S; Son; 7469; Yes; Yes; 25338

7454; Tah-nez-zahnih; M; 54; Navajo; F; M; Head; 7470; Yes; Yes; 25106
7455; Adzan-kin-li-cheeny; F; 54; Navajo; F; M; Wife; 7471; Yes; Yes; 25107
7456; Haska-yil-hoh-hal-dil Theodore; M; 26; Navajo; F; S; 7472; Son; Yes; Yes; 25108
7457; Yee-nih-bah; F; 19; Navajo; F; S; Daughter; 7473; Yes; Yes; 25109
7458; Dorothy; F; 16; Navajo; F; S; Daughter; 7474; Yes; Yes; 25110
7459; Hunt, Ralph; M; 31; Navajo; F; S; Son; 7475; Yes; Yes; 25111
7460; Dodge, Mary; F; 7; Navajo; F; S; Grand-daughter; 7476; Yes; Yes; 25112
7461; Dodge, Emma; F; 5; Navajo; F; S; Grand-daughter; 7477; Yes; Yes; 25113

7462; Tah-cheen-nez; M; 42; Navajo; F; M; Head; 7478; Yes; Yes; 17290
7463; Tah-cheen-nez's wife; F; 41; Navajo; F; M; Wife; 7479; Yes; Yes; 17291
7464; Tah-cheen-nez-soh; M; 18; Navajo; F; S; Son; 7480; Yes; Yes; 17292
7465; Betche, Mack; M; 15; Navajo; F; S; Son; 7481; Yes; Yes; 17293

7466; Taliman, Ada; F; 41; Navajo; F; S; Head; 7482; Yes; Yes; 31004

7467; Tawk badoni, James Thomas; M; 26; Navajo; F; M; Head; 7483; Yes; Yes; 30308
7468; Bertha; F; 35; Navajo; F; M; Wife; 7484; Yes; Yes; 30310

7469; Tawk, Alfred; M; 33; Navajo; F; M; Head; 7485; Yes; Yes; 30534
7470; Beleen-lagaih-bitsih; F; 28; Navajo; F; M; Wife; 7486; Yes; Yes; 30535
7471; Keh-yil-nih-bah; F; 7; Navajo; F; S; Daughter; 7487; Yes; Yes; 30536
7472; Haska-yee-nah-oh-gahl; M; 5; Navajo; F; S; Son; 7488; Yes; Yes; 30537

7473; Tah-nah-zanih-etsosie; M; 28; Navajo; F; M; Head; 7489; Yes; Yes; 17325
7474; Bih-hay-yilth-nasbah; F; 21; Navajo; F; M; Wife; 7490; Yes; Yes; 17326
7475; Glin-yilt-basbah; F; 6; Navajo; F; S; Daughter; 7491; Yes; Yes; 17327
7476; Tah-nah-zanih-etsosie, Sani; M; 3; Navajo; F; S; Son; 7492; Yes; Yes; 17328

7477; Tawk; M; 61; Navajo; F; M; Head; 7493; Yes; Yes; 30303
7478; Hosteen-clitschih-bitsih; F; 42; Navajo; F; M; Wife; 7494; Yes; Yes; 30304
7479; Dorothy; F; 23; Navajo; F; S; Daughter; 7495; Yes; Yes; 30305
7480; Nil-wudt, Joe; M; 21; Navajo; F; S; Son; 7496; Yes; Yes; 30306
7481; Dahl; M; 5; Navajo; F; S; Son; 7497; Yes; Yes; 30307

7482; Taz-nih-benally, Slim; M; 40; Navajo; F; M; Head; 7498; Yes; Yes; 25916
7483; Al-noaz-bah; F; 30; Navajo; F; M; Wife; 7499; Yes; Yes; 25917
7484; Price; M; 18; Navajo; F; S; Son; 7500; Yes; Yes; 25918

Census of the **Northern Navajo** reservation of the **Northern Navajo** jurisdiction, as of **April 1**, 19**31**, taken by **Ernest H. Hammond, District**, Superintendent. **in Charge**

**Key:** Number; NAME: Surname, Given; Sex; Birth Year (if given), Age At Last Birthday; Tribe; Degree of Blood; Marital Status; Relationship To Head of Family; Last Census Roll Number; At Jurisdiction Where Enrolled (Yes or No); At Another Jurisdiction; ELSEWHERE: Post office, County, State; Ward (Yes or No); Allotment, Annuity, and Identification Numbers.

7485; Yazzie; M; 15; Navajo; F; S; Son; 7501; Yes; Yes; 25919
7486; Annie; F; 11; Navajo; F; S; Daughter; 7502; Yes; Yes; 25920
7487; Margaret; F; 9; Navajo; F; S; Daughter; 7503; Yes; Yes; 25921
7488; Haska-yee-chih-nih-nih-yah; F; 4; Navajo; F; S; Daughter; 7504; Yes; Yes; 25922
7489; Hosteen-dih-joely-bitsih; F; 56; Navajo; F; Wd.; Mother-in-law; 7505; Yes; Yes; 25923
7490; Violet; F; 12; Navajo; F; S; Niece-in-law; 7506; Yes; Yes; 25924
7491; Kee-soh; M; 20; Navajo; F; S; Brother; 7507; Yes; Yes; 25925
7492; Lee; M; 18; Navajo; F; S; Nephew; 7508; Yes; Yes; 25926
7493; Andrew; M; 13; Navajo; F; S; Nephew; 7509; Yes; Yes; 25927

7494; Teece-shih-zodih-bih-adzan; F; 48; Navajo; F; Wd; Head; 7510; Yes; Yes; 26638
7495; Nas-clah, Albert; M; 20; Navajo; F; S; Nephew; 7511; Yes; Yes; 26639
7496; Nas-clah, Lola; F; 18; Navajo; F; S; Niece; 7512; Yes; Yes; 26640
7497; Grace; F; 24; Navajo; F; S; Niece; 7513; Yes; Yes; 26641
7498; Bertha; F; 22; Navajo; F; S; Niece; 7514; Yes; Yes; 26642

7499; Teece-yazzie-bega; M; 51; Navajo; F; M; Head; 7515; Yes; Yes; 26743
7500; Bay-gashih-lagaih-benally; F; 37; Navajo; F; M; Wife; 7516; Yes; Yes; 26744
7501; Teece-yazzie-benally, Everett; M; 23; Navajo; F; S; Son; 7517; Yes; Yes; 26745
7502; Bil-ah-gee-bah; F; 19; Navajo; F; S; Daughter; 7518; Yes; Yes; 26746
7503; Jerome; M; 20; Navajo; F; S; Son; 7519; Yes; Yes; 26747
7504; Al-soh-dez-bah; F; 18; Navajo; F; S; Daughter; 7520; Yes; Yes; 26748
7505; Yil-nih-nih-bah; F; 8; Navajo; F; S; Daughter; 7521; Yes; Yes; 26749

7506; Teece-yazzie-bih-adzan's grand-daughter, Glih-naz-bah; F; 8; Navajo; F; S; Orphan; 7522; Yes; Yes; 26880

7507; Teece-yazzie-bega, Lew; M; Unk; Navajo; F; M; Head; 7523; Yes; Yes; 26881
7508; Bih-keh-kah-kehih-bitsih; F; Unk; Navajo; F; M; Wife; 7524; Yes; Yes; 26882
7509; Nah-tah-hah-yah; M; 9; Navajo; F; S; Son; 7525; Yes; Yes; 26883
7510; Hah-dez-bah; F; 7; Navajo; F; S; Daughter; 7526; Yes; Yes; 26884
7511; Nah-tah-yil-has-wudt; M; 4; Navajo; F; S; Son; 7527; Yes; Yes; 26885
7512; Parker, Jackson; M; Unk; F; S; Nephew; 7528; Yes; Yes; 26886

7513; Teece-shih-zodih-bitsoih; M; 29; Navajo; F; M; Head; 7529; Yes; Yes; 25199
7514; Ah-kih-deh-bah; F; 26; Navajo; F; M; Wife; 7530; Yes; Yes; 25200
7515; Haska-yee-nas-wudt; M; 5; Navajo; F; S; Son; 7531; Yes; Yes; 25201

Census of the **Northern Navajo** reservation of the **Northern Navajo** jurisdiction, as of **April 1**, 19**31**, taken by **Ernest H. Hammond, District**, Superintendent. **in Charge**

**Key:** Number; NAME: Surname, Given; Sex; Birth Year (if given), Age At Last Birthday; Tribe; Degree of Blood; Marital Status; Relationship To Head of Family; Last Census Roll Number; At Jurisdiction Where Enrolled (Yes or No); At Another Jurisdiction; ELSEWHERE: Post office, County, State; Ward (Yes or No); Allotment, Annuity, and Identification Numbers.

7516; Teece-shih-zodih-benally, Frank; M; 28; Navajo; F; M; Head; 7533; Yes; Yes; 23789
7517; Mary; F; 43; Navajo; F; M; Wife; 7534; Yes; Yes; 23790
7518; Chee; M; 19; Navajo; F; S; Step-son; 7535; Yes; Yes; 23791
7519; Catherine; F; 17; Navajo; F; S; Step-son[sic]; 7536; Yes; Yes; 23792
7520; Kee-yazzie; M; 8; Navajo; F; S; Step-son; 7537; Yes; Yes; 24009

7521; Teece-shih-zodih-bega; M; 39; Navajo; F; M; Head; 7538; Yes; Yes; 23840
7522; Hogah-thlani-bitsih; F; 33; Navajo; F; M; Wife; 7539; Yes; Yes; 23841
7523; Haska-yil-dah-dolnih; M; 16; Navajo; F; S; Son; 7540; Yes; Yes; 23842
7524; Haska-yee-sih-yil-wohl; M; 8; Navajo; F; S; Son; 7541; Yes; Yes; 23843
7525; Bil-zoz-bah; F; 7; Navajo; F; S; Daughter; 7542; Yes; Yes; 23844
7526; Haska-yil-hoh-gahl; M; 5; Navajo; F; S; Son; 7543; Yes; Yes; 23845
7527; Tuly; M; 20; Navajo; F; S; Brother-in-law; 7544; Yes; Yes; 23846
7528; Beh-gun-dez-bah; F; 4; Navajo; F; S; Daughter; 7545; Yes; Yes; 23915

7529; Teece-yazzie-bega, Puggy; M; 45; Navajo; F; M; Head; 7546; Yes; Yes; 30625
7530; Dinay-l-chee-bitsih; F; 39; Navajo; F; M; Wife; 7547; Yes; Yes; 30626
7531; Bega, Puggy; M; 23; Navajo; F; S; Daughter[sic]; 7548; Yes; Yes; 30627
7532; Tahn-zih-bah; F; 19; Navajo; F; S; Daughter; 7549; Yes; Yes; 30628
7533; Sam; M; 16; Navajo; F; S; Son; 7550; Yes; Yes; 30629
7534; Nah-glih-yil-dez-bah; F; 12; Navajo; F; S; Daughter; 7551; Yes; Yes; 30630
7535; Naz-bah; F; 10; Navajo; F; S; Daughter; 7552; Yes; Yes; 30631
7536; Nah-tah-yil-nih-deet-sah; M; 3; Navajo; F; S; Son; 7553; Yes; Yes; 30632

(Titus P. Lamson, Hopi Indian, head of family)
7537; Des-bah, Lamson; F; 26; Navajo; F; M; Wife; 7554; Yes; Yes; 22526
7538; Anna May; F; 4; Navajo; F; S; Daughter; 7555; Yes; Yes; 22527

7539; Thomas, Pete; M; 27; Navajo; F; M; Head; 7556; Yes; Yes; 31217
7540; Laura Buck; F; 24; Navajo; F; M; Wife; 7557; Yes; Yes; 30817

7541; Tide, James; M; Unk; Navajo; F; M; Head; 7558; Yes; Yes; 23743
7542; Hah-tahly-yazzie-bitsih; F; 38; Navajo; F; M; Wife; 7559; Yes; Yes; 23744
7543; Anderson, Clara; F; 19; Navajo; F; S; Step-daughter; 7560; Yes; Yes; 23745
7544; Keh-hah-naz-bah; F; 16; Navajo; F; S; Daughter; 7561; Yes; Yes; 23747
7545; Bernard; M; 14; Navajo; F; S; Son; 7562; Yes; Yes; 23748
7546; Des-wudt; M; 6; Navajo; F; S; Son; 7563; Yes; Yes; 23749
7547; Mildred; F; 19; Navajo; F; S; Daughter; 7564; Yes; Yes; 23965
7548; Nota-ih-nee-ah; F; 3; Navajo; F; S; Daughter; 7565; Yes; Yes; 23962
7549; Nah-glin-tha-bah; F; 1; Navajo; F; S; Daughter; 7566; Yes; Yes; 23963

Census of the **Northern Navajo** reservation of the **Northern Navajo** jurisdiction, as of **April 1** , 1931, taken by **Ernest H. Hammond, District** , Superintendent. **in Charge**

**Key:** Number; NAME: Surname, Given; Sex; Birth Year (if given), Age At Last Birthday; Tribe; Degree of Blood; Marital Status; Relationship To Head of Family; Last Census Roll Number; At Jurisdiction Where Enrolled (Yes or No); At Another Jurisdiction; ELSEWHERE: Post office, County, State; Ward (Yes or No); Allotment, Annuity, and Identification Numbers.

7550; Todue-chee; M; 34; Navajo; F; M; Head; 2153; Yes; Yes 25016
7551; Glenn; F; 35; Navajo; F; M; Wife; 2154; Yes; Yes 25017
7552; Chester; M; 3; Navajo; F; S; Son; 2155; Yes; Yes; 25018
7553; Arthur; M; 2; Navajo; F; S; Son; 2156; Yes; Yes 25301

7554; Toh-lizin-bega, Puggy; M; Unk; Navajo; F; M; Head; 7567; Yes; Yes; 27906
7555; Hosteen-clitsoh-bilah; F; 42; Navajo; F; M; Wife; 7568; Yes; Yes; 27907
7556; Haska-yee-tah-yil-ta-a; M; 20; Navajo; F; S; Son; 7569; Yes; Yes; 27908
7557; Harvey; M; 11; Navajo; F; S; Son; 7570; Yes; Yes; 27909
7558; Gone; M; 19; Navajo; F; S; Son; 7571; Yes; Yes; 27910
7559; Zannie; F; 8; Navajo; F; S; Daughter; 7572; Yes; Yes; 27911
7560; Dah-dee-bah; F; 5; Navajo; F; S; Daughter; 7573; Yes; Yes; 27912
7561; Zannie-yazzie; F; 3; Navajo; F; S; Daughter; 7574; Yes; Yes; 27913

7562; Toh-nil-cho-nih-bega; M; 63; Navajo; F; M; Head; 7575; Yes; Yes; 24753
7563; Nah-glih-yee-nah-bah; F; 63; Navajo; F; M; Wife; 7576; Yes; Yes; 24754
7564; Della; F; 21; Navajo; F; S; Daughter; 7577; Yes; Yes; 24755
7565; Samuel; M; 19; Navajo; F; S; Son; 7578; Yes; Yes; 24756
7566; Katie; F; 14; Navajo; F; S; Daughter; 7579; Yes; Yes; 24757

7567; Toh-ahk-gleenih-bega; M; 33; Navajo; F; M; Head; 7580; Yes; Yes; 27935
7568; Ah-heh-nih-bah; F; 27; Navajo; F; M; Wife; 7581; Yes; Yes; 27936
7569; Eskee-soh; M; 9; Navajo; F; S; Son; 7582; Yes; Yes; 27937
7570; Glih-yil-dez-bah; F; 7; Navajo; F; S; Daughter; 7583; Yes; Yes; 27938
7571; Keh-haz-bah; F; 3; Navajo; F; S; Daughter; 7584; Yes; Yes; 27939

7572; Toh-bih-kisih; M; 80; Navajo; F; M; Head; 7585; Yes; Yes; 28051
7573; Bah; F; 21; Navajo; F; M; Wife; 7586; Yes; Yes; 28052

7574; Toh-dil-yil-bega; M; 35; Navajo; F; M; Head; 7587; Yes; Yes; 28044
7575; Toh-bih-nah-misih-bitsih; F; 29; Navajo; F; M; Wife; 7588; Yes; Yes; 28045
7576; Nah-dez-bah; F; 13; Navajo; F; S; Daughter; 7589; Yes; Yes; 28046
7577; Yil-dez-bah; F; 11; Navajo; F; S; Daughter; 7590; Yes; Yes; 28047
7578; Tas-bah; F; 8; Navajo; F; S; Daughter; 7591; Yes; Yes; 28048
7579; Yee-Nel-wudt; M; 6; Navajo; F; S; Son; 7592; Yes; Yes; 28049
7580; Yee-tah-del-nih; M; 3; Navajo; F; S; Son; 7593; Yes; Yes; 28050

7581; Toh-lizin-benally; M; 26; Navajo; F; M; Head; 7594; Yes; Yes; 28066
7582; Aht-citty-yen-bitsih; F; Unk; Navajo; F; M; Wife; 7595; Yes; Yes; 28067
7583; Hah-tahly-sosie-bilah; F; 56; Navajo; F; Wd; Aunt; 7596; Yes; Yes; 28068
7584; Chah-dah-hah-sosie; M; 23; Navajo; F; S; Brother; 7597; Yes; Yes; 28069

7585; Toh-lizin-bega, Charley; M; 27; Navajo; F; M; Head; 7598; Yes; Yes; 28327

Census of the **Northern Navajo** reservation of the **Northern Navajo** jurisdiction, as of **April 1**, 19**31**, taken by **Ernest H. Hammond, District**, Superintendent. **in Charge**

**Key:** Number; NAME: Surname, Given; Sex; Birth Year (if given), Age At Last Birthday; Tribe; Degree of Blood; Marital Status; Relationship To Head of Family; Last Census Roll Number; At Jurisdiction Where Enrolled (Yes or No); At Another Jurisdiction; ELSEWHERE: Post office, County, State; Ward (Yes or No); Allotment, Annuity, and Identification Numbers.

7586; Bih-bayse-yen-bitsih; F; 27; Navajo; F; M; Wife; 7599; Yes; Yes; 28328
7587; Kee-seeih; M; 6; Navajo; F; S; Son; 7600; Yes; Yes; 28329
7588; Gee-woody; M; 5; Navajo; F; S; Son; 7601; Yes; Yes; 28330
7589; Woody-Yazzie; M; 4; Navajo; F; S; Son; 7602; Yes; Yes; 28331
7590; Kah-naz-bah; F; 2; Navajo; F; S; Daughter; 7603; Yes; Yes; 28332

7591; Toh-dil-yil-bimah; F; 80; Navajo; F; Wd.; Head; 7604; Yes; Yes; 28334
7592; Adzan-hoh-zoh-gee; F; 57; Navajo; F; Wd.; Daughter; 7605; Yes; Yes; 28335
7593; Doh-dih-jadih-bitsih; F; 40; Navajo; F; Wd.; Grand-daughter; 7606; Yes; Yes; 28336
7594; Doh-dih-jadih-bitsoih; M; 23; Navajo; F; S; Great-grand-son; 7607; Yes; Yes; 28337
7595; Sam; M; 19; Navajo; F; S; Great-grand-son; 7608; Yes; Yes; 28338
7596; Eskee-nanl-cadih; M; 16; Navajo; F; S; Great-grand-son; 7610; Yes; Yes; 28339
7597; Eskee-l-bahih; M; 12; Navajo; F; S; Great-grand-son; 7609; Yes; Yes; 28340
7598; Bah; F; 16; Navajo; F; S; Great-grand-daughter; 7611; Yes; Yes; 28341
7599; See-l-bah; F[sic]; 8; Navajo; F; S; Great-grand-son; 7612; Yes; Yes; 28342

7600; Toh-dih-cheeny-soh-bega; M; 24; Navajo; F; M; Head; 7613; Yes; Yes; 28455
7601; Bah; F; 20; Navajo; F; M; Wife; 7614; Yes; Yes; 28456

7602; Toh-dih-cheeny-boh-woh-atin; M; 65; Navajo; F; M; Head; 7615; Yes; Yes; 28398
7603; Toh-dih-cheeny-boh-woh-atin's wife; F; 32; Navajo; F; M; Wife; 7616; Yes; Yes; 28399
7604; Adzan-l-gaih; F; 21; Navajo; F; S; Step-daughter; 7617; Yes; Yes; 28400
7605; Rosalyn; F; 19; Navajo; F; S; Daughter; 7618; Yes; Yes; 28401
7606; Hazel; F; 17; Navajo; F; S; Daughter; 7619; Yes; Yes; 28402
7607; Kay-yah-; M; 16; Navajo; F; S; Son; 7620; Yes; Yes; 28403
7608; Cora; F; 5; Navajo; F; S; Daughter; 7621; Yes; Yes; 28404
7609; Yee-kaz-bah; F; 11; Navajo; F; S; Daughter; 7622; Yes; Yes; 28405
7610; Adzan-ih-soh; F; 9; Navajo; F; S; Daughter; 7623; Yes; Yes; 28406
7611; Haska-yee-nel-wudt; M; 7; Navajo; F; S; Son; 7624; Yes; Yes; 28407
7612; Tah-dez-bah; F; 5; Navajo; F; S; Daughter; 7625; Yes; Yes; 28408
7613; Dinay-chilli-bih-adzan; F; 57; Navajo; F; Wd; Mother-in-law; 7626; Yes; Yes; 28409
7614; Nocki-deetsah-bih-bizee; M; 24; Navajo; F; S; Brother-in-law; 7627; Yes; Yes; 28410
7615; Laura; F; 21; Navajo; F; S; Sister-in-law; 7628; Yes; Yes; 28411
7616; Nah-tah-tah-des-wudt; M; 4; Navajo; F S; Son; 7629; Yes; Yes; 28545

7617; Toh-dih-cheeny-soh; M; Unk; Navajo; F; M; Head; 7630; Yes; Yes; 28516

Census of the **Northern Navajo** reservation of the **Northern Navajo** jurisdiction, as of **April 1**, 19**31,** taken by **Ernest H. Hammond, District**, Superintendent. **in Charge**

**Key:** Number; NAME: Surname, Given; Sex; Birth Year (if given), Age At Last Birthday; Tribe; Degree of Blood; Marital Status; Relationship To Head of Family; Last Census Roll Number; At Jurisdiction Where Enrolled (Yes or No); At Another Jurisdiction; ELSEWHERE: Post office, County, State; Ward (Yes or No); Allotment, Annuity, and Identification Numbers.

7618; Adaki-sosie-bitsih; F; 37; Navajo; F; M; Wife; 7631; Yes; Yes; 28517
7619; Dez-bah; F; 19; Navajo; F; S; Daughter; 7632; Yes; Yes; 28518
7620; Haska-yil-nih-dec-zah[sic]; M; 11; Navajo; F; S; Son; 7633; Yes; Yes; 28519
[Name should be Haska-yil-nih-dee-zah]
7621; Nah-tah-yil-nah-dahl; M; 5; Navajo; F; S; Son; 7634; Yes; Yes; 28520
7622; Nah-gee-bah; F; 3; Navajo; F; S; Daughter; 7635; Yes; Yes; 28521
7623; Hosteen-talhih-bitsih; F; 62; Navajo; F; Wd.; Mother-in-law; 7636; Yes; Yes; 28522
7624; Tiah, Daniel; M; 25; Navajo; F; S; Brother-in-law; 7637; Yes; Yes; 28523
7625; Bih-dagah-nash-jinnih-gih; M; 28; Navajo; F; S; Brother-in-law; 7638; Yes; Yes; 28524

7626; Toh-nah-sani-soh; M; Unk; Navajo; F; M; Head; 7639; Yes; Yes; 17163
7627; Aht-sani-benally; F; 32; Navajo; F; M; Wife; 7640; Yes; Yes; 17164
7628; Hoh-des-bah; F; Unk; Navajo; F; S; Daughter; 7641; Yes; Yes; 17165
7629; Kee-hasbah; F; 10; Navajo; F; S; Daughter; 7642; Yes; Yes; 17166
7630; Nihnih-bah; F; Unk; Navajo; F; S; Daughter; 7643; Yes; Yes; 17167
7631; Hoska-tah-lil-wudt; M; 4; Navajo; F; S; Son; 7644; Yes; Yes; 17169
7632; Benny; M; Unk; Navajo; F; Unk; Brother; 7645; Yes; Yes; 17402
7633; Ah-shoh; M; Unk; Navajo; F; Unk; Brother; 7646; Yes; Yes; 17403
7634; Helen; F; 2; Navajo; F; S; Daughter; 7647; Yes; Yes; 17410

7635; Toh-dih-kozie, Tom; M; 37; Navajo; F; M; Head; 7648; Yes; Yes; 17056
7636; Askan-shscoh-bitsih; F; 31; Navajo; F; M; Wife; 7649; Yes; Yes; 17057
7637; Toh-dih-kozie, Hoska-ye-tah-deyah; M; 16; Navajo; F; S; Step-son; 7650; Yes; Yes; 17058
7638; Toh-dih-kozie-Eay-yahanopah; F; 13; Navajo; F; S; Daughter; 7651; Yes; Yes; 17059
7639; Toh-dih-kozie-Nasbah; F; 10; Navajo; F; S; Daughter; 7652; Yes; Yes; 17060
7640; Tom, Jr.; M; 2; Navajo; F; S; Son; 7653; Yes; Yes; 17408
7641; Utso; M; 1; Navajo; F; S; Son; [Blank]; Yes; Yes; 17422
7642; Ket-sosie; M; 2/12; Navajo; F; S; Son; [Blank]; Yes; Yes; 17423

7643; Top-ah-ah-nez-benally; M; 28; Navajo; F; M; Head; 7654; Yes; Yes; 22593
7644; Keh-yil-nan-bah; F; 19; Navajo; F; M; Wife; 7655; Yes; Yes; 22594

7645; Top-ah-hah-nez; M; 35; Navajo; F; M; Head; 7656; Yes; Yes; 21556
7646; Kin-lah-cheeny-bitsih; F; 29; Navajo; F; M; Wife; 7657; Yes; Yes; 21557
7647; Kay-has-bah; F; 6; Navajo; F; S; Daughter; 7658; Yes; Yes; 21558
7648; Hoska-yil-nil-wudt; M; 10; Navajo; F; S; Nephew; 7659; Yes; Yes; 21559
7649; Nah-dah-hah-nal-tah; M; 4; Navajo; F; S; Son; 7660; Yes; Yes; 21677

7650; Toh-begish-teze, Leo; M; 24; Navajo; F; M; Head; 7661; Yes; Yes; 17848

Census of the **Northern Navajo** reservation of the **Northern Navajo** jurisdiction, as of **April 1**, 19**31,** taken by **Ernest H. Hammond, District**, Superintendent. **in Charge**

Key: Number; NAME: Surname, Given; Sex; Birth Year (if given), Age At Last Birthday; Tribe; Degree of Blood; Marital Status; Relationship To Head of Family; Last Census Roll Number; At Jurisdiction Where Enrolled (Yes or No); At Another Jurisdiction; ELSEWHERE: Post office, County, State; Ward (Yes or No); Allotment, Annuity, and Identification Numbers.

7651; Hol-kidney-bitsih; F; 18; Navajo; F; M; Wife; 7662; Yes; Yes; 17849

7652; Topah-ah-nez-benally; M; 30; Navajo; F; M; Head; 7663; Yes; Yes; 22557
7653; Seebah; F; 21; Navajo; F; M; Wife; 7664; Yes; Yes; 22558
7654; Haska-yee-kes-wudt; M; 6; Navajo; F; S; Son; 7665; Yes; Yes; 22559
7655; Dah-yiz-bah; F; 3; Navajo; F; S; Daughter; 7666; Yes; Yes; 22560

7656; Toh-dih-cheeny; M; 56; Navajo; F; M; Head; 7667; Yes; Yes; 25932
7657; Glih-haz-bah; F; 32; Navajo; F; M; 2nd wife; 7669; Yes; Yes; 25934
7658; Has-bah; F; 11; Navajo; F; S; Daughter; 7670; Yes; Yes; 25935
7659; Elinora; F; 10; Navajo; F; S; Daughter; 7671; Yes; Yes; 25936
7660; Kes-woody; M; 6; Navajo; F; S; Son; 7672; Yes; Yes; 25937
7661; Nah-tah-yil-nas-wudt; M; 4; Navajo; F; S; Son; 7673; Yes; Yes; 25938

7662; Toh-dih-cheeny-badoni; M; 46; Navajo; F; M; Head; 7674; Yes; Yes; 25928
7663; Toh-dih-cheeny-bitsih; F; 38; Navajo; F; M; Wife; 7675; Yes; Yes; 25929
7664; Ah-hiz-nil-bah; F; 17; Navajo; F; S; Daughter; 7676; Yes; Yes; 25930
7665; Glih-hah-nih-bahih; F; 8; Navajo; F; S; Daughter; 7677; Yes; Yes; 25931

7666; Tih-dih-cheeny, Frank; M; 50; Navajo; F; M; Head; 7678; Yes; Yes; 31106
7667; Maggie; F; 33; Navajo; F; M; Wife; 7679; Yes; Yes; 31107
7668; Jimmy; M; 20; Navajo; F; S; Son; 7680; Yes; Yes; 31108
7669; Yah-dee-bah; F; 18; Navajo; F; S; Daughter; 7681; Yes; Yes; 31109
7670; Jim; M; 32; Navajo; F; S; Nephew; 7682; Yes; Yes; 31110
7671; Lee; M; 14; Navajo; F; S; Nephew-in-law; 7683; Yes; Yes; 31111
7672; Mary Francis; F; 6/12; Navajo; F; S; Daughter; [Blank]; Yes; Yes; 31297

7673; Top-ah-hah; M; 46; Navajo; F; M; Head; 7684; Yes; Yes; 25132
7674; Hosch-clish-nih-bitsih; F; 23; Navajo; F; M; Wife; 7685; Yes; Yes; 25133

7675; Toh-ahk-gleenih-yazzie; M; Unk; Navajo; F; M; Head; 7686; Yes; Yes; 25054
7676; Tahn-hah-naz-bah; F; 53; Navajo; F; M; Wife; 7687; Yes; Yes; 25055
7677; Henry; M; 21; Navajo; F; S; Son; 7688; Yes; Yes; 25056
7678; Haska-yee-kih-naz-wudt; M; 17; Navajo; F; S; Son; 7689; Yes; Yes; 25057
7679; Glih-yil-nih-bah; F; 10; Navajo; F; S; Niece; 7690; Yes; Yes; 25058

7680; Toh-ahk-gleenih-yazzie-bega; M; Unk; Navajo; F; M; Head; 7691; Yes; Yes; 25059
7681; Adzan-suen; F; Unk; Navajo; F; M; Wife; 7692; Yes; Yes; 25060

7682; Toh-dih-cheeny-benally, Wilson, Jim; M; 23; Navajo; F; M; Head; 7693; Yes; Yes; 25072
7683; Susie; F; 21; Navajo; F; M; Wife; 7694; Yes; Yes; 25072

Census of the **Northern Navajo** reservation of the **Northern Navajo** jurisdiction, as of **April 1**, 19**31**, taken by **Ernest H. Hammond, District**, Superintendent. **in Charge**

**Key:** Number; NAME: Surname, Given; Sex; Birth Year (if given), Age At Last Birthday; Tribe; Degree of Blood; Marital Status; Relationship To Head of Family; Last Census Roll Number; At Jurisdiction Where Enrolled (Yes or No); At Another Jurisdiction; ELSEWHERE: Post office, County, State; Ward (Yes or No); Allotment, Annuity, and Identification Numbers.

7684;  Topahah; M; 56; Navajo; F; Wd; Head; 7695; Yes; Yes; 26994
7685;  Dodge, Charley; F[sic]; 32; Navajo; F; S; Son; 7696; Yes; Yes; 26995
7686;  Al-keh-so-bah; F; 14; Navajo; F; S; Daughter; 7697; Yes; Yes; 26996

7687;  Toh-cheeny-nez-yen-bega; M; 40; Navajo; F; M; Head; 7698; Yes; Yes; 24922
7688;  Shih-bah; F; 28; Navajo; F; M; Wife; 7699; Yes; Yes; 24923
7689;  Chil-nil-wudt-elah; M; 20; Navajo; F; S; Brother-in-law; 7700; Yes; Yes; 24925
7690;  Clarence; M; 15; Navajo; F; S; Brother-in-law; 7701; Yes; Yes; 24927
7691;  Adzan-l-suen; F; 12; Navajo; F; S; Sister-in-law; 7702; Yes; Yes; 24928
7692;  Yee-kaz-bah; F; 19; Navajo; F; S; Sister-in-law; 7703; Yes; Yes; 24929
7693;  Kih-des-woody; M; 7; Navajo; F; S; Brother-in-law; 7704; Yes; Yes; 24930

7694;  Toh-dih-cheeny-badoni-bih-dazih; F; 42; Navajo; F; Wd; Head; 7705; Yes; Yes; 25943
7695;  Sosie, Stafford; M; 18; Navajo; F; S; Son; 7706; Yes; Yes; 25944
7696;  Sosie, Nora; F; 16; Navajo; F; S; Daughter; 7707; Yes; Yes; 25945
7697;  Gordon; M; 10; Navajo; F; S; Son; 7708; Yes; Yes; 25946
7698;  Yil-haz-bah; F; 3; Navajo; F; S; Daughter; 7709; Yes; Yes; 25947

7699;  Toh-dih-cheeny-nez-bega; M; 29; Navajo; F; M; Head; 7710; Yes; Yes; 32256
7700;  Hosteen-l-sosie-bitsih; F; 27; Navajo; F; M; Wife; 7711; Yes; Yes; 32257
7701;  Guy; M; 28; Navajo; F; S; Brother-in-law; 7712; Yes; Yes; 32259
7702;  Nah-tah-yil-nas-wudt, Victor; M; 18; Navajo; F; S; Brother-in-law; 7713; Yes; Yes; 32260
7703;  Gahl, Wilfred; M; 15; Navajo; F; S; Brother-in-law; 7714; Yes; Yes; 32261

7704;  Toh-cheeny-yazzie; M; 66; Navajo; F; Wd; Head; 7715; Yes; Yes; 25180
7705;  Tuly-yazzie; M; 30; Navajo; F; S; Son; 7716; Yes; Yes; 25181

7706;  Topah-ah, Hugh; M; Unk; Navajo; F; M; Head; 7717; Yes; Yes; 22624
7707;  Dagah-zin-bitsih; F; Unk; Navajo; F; M; Wife; 7718; Yes; Yes; 22625
7708;  Nah-tah-yee-chih-nih-wudt; M; 10; Navajo; F; S; Son; 7719; Yes; Yes; 22626
7709;  Al-zah-hah-ziz-bah; F; 6; Navajo; F; S; Daughter; 7720; Yes; Yes; 22627
7710;  Al-zah-nih-ziz-bah; F; 5; Navajo; F; S; Daughter; 7721; Yes; Yes; 22628
7711;  Lily; F; 17; Navajo; F; S; Daughter; 7722; Yes; Yes; 22629

7712;  Top-dih-cheeny-bega; M; 50; Navajo; F; M; Head; 7723; Yes; Yes; 21046
7713;  Dinay-etsosie-benally; F; 50; Navajo; F; M; Wife; 7724; Yes; Yes; 21047
7714;  Toh-des-wudt; M; 19; Navajo; F; S; Son; 7725; Yes; Yes; 21048
7715;  Kay-yil-se-bah; F; 17; Navajo; F; S; Daughter; 7726; Yes; Yes; 21049
7716;  Nas-wudt; M; 13; Navajo; F; S; Son; 7727; Yes; Yes; 21050
7717;  Yee-kis-bah; F; 9; Navajo; F; S; Daughter; 7728; Yes; Yes; 21051

Census of the **Northern Navajo** reservation of the **Northern Navajo** jurisdiction, as of **April 1**, 1931, taken by **Ernest H. Hammond, District**, Superintendent. **in Charge**

**Key:** Number; NAME: Surname, Given; Sex; Birth Year (if given), Age At Last Birthday; Tribe; Degree of Blood; Marital Status; Relationship To Head of Family; Last Census Roll Number; At Jurisdiction Where Enrolled (Yes or No); At Another Jurisdiction; ELSEWHERE: Post office, County, State; Ward (Yes or No); Allotment, Annuity, and Identification Numbers.

7718; Hoska-yee-nahs-wudt, Charley; M; 6; Navajo; F; S; Son; 7729; Yes; Yes; 21052
7719; Glih-yil-nas-bah; F; 3; Navajo; F; S; Daughter; 7730; Yes; Yes; 21053

7720; Toh-dih-kozie-sosie-bega, Jim; M; 29; Navajo; F; M; Head; 7731; Yes; Yes; 19998
7721; Nah-dih-jadih-bitsih; F; 18; Navajo; F; M; Wife; 7732; Yes; Yes; 19999
7722; Bah-dos-wudt; M; 3; Navajo; F; S; Son; 7733; Yes; Yes; 20000

7723; Toh-begish-tize; M; 57; Navajo; F; M; Head; 7734; Yes; Yes; 17837
7724; Kin-lachee-nih-bitsih; F; 35; Navajo; F; M; Wife; 7735; Yes; Yes; 17838
7725; Toh-begish-tize, Buddy; M; 23; Navajo; F; S; Son; 7736; Yes; Yes; 17839
7726; Ah-noh-bah; F; 21; Navajo; F; S; Daughter; 7737; Yes; Yes; 17840
7727; Toh-begish-teze, Charles; M; 17; Navajo; F; S; Son; 7738; Yes; Yes; 17841
7728; Toh-begish-teze, Sarah; F; 13; Navajo; F; S; Daughter; 7739; Yes; Yes; 17842
7729; Hoover; M; 2; Navajo; F; S; Son; 7740; Yes; Yes; 18235
7730; Eskee-pahih; M; 11; Navajo; F; S; Son; 7741; Yes; Yes; 17843
7731; Awa-l-pahih; F; 15; Navajo; F; S; Daughter; 7742; Yes; Yes; 17844
7732; Toh-begish-teze, Tom; M; 10; Navajo; F; S; Son; 7743; Yes; Yes; 17845
7733; Atate-la-kaih; F; 8; Navajo; F; S; Daughter; 7744; Yes; Yes; 17846
7734; Dinay-pa-ih; M; 5; Navajo; F; S; Son; 7745; Yes; Yes; 17847

7735; Toh-sonie-badoni; M; 64; Navajo; F; M; Head; 7746; Yes; Yes; 21540
7736; Toh-sonie-bitsih; F; 53; Navajo; F; M; Wife; 7747; Yes; Yes; 21541
7737; Haska-yahn-yil-wohl; M; 23; Navajo; F; S; Son; 7748; Yes; Yes; 21542
7738; Nah-tah-yee-hah-gah; M; 19; Navajo; F; S; Son; 7749; Yes; Yes; 21543
7739; Nah-tah-yee-has-wudt; M; 6; Navajo; F; S; Grandson; 7750; Yes; Yes; 21544

7740; Toh-dih-cheeny-bega; M; 28; Navajo; F; M; Head; 7751; Yes; Yes; 17363
7741; Toh-dih-cheeny, Esther; F; 24; Navajo; F; M; Wife; 7752; Yes; Yes; 17364
7742; Toh-dih-cheeny-kee-seeih; M; 9; Navajo; F; S; Son; 7753; Yes; Yes; 17365
7743; Toh-dih-cheeny, Nah-glin-yil-hisbah; F; 5; Navajo; F; S; Daughter; 7754; Yes; Yes; 17366

7744; Toh-sonie-bega; M; 35; Navajo; F; M; Head; 7755; Yes; Yes; 21526
7745; Ah-kay-nih-bah; F; 33; Navajo; F; M; Wife; 7756; Yes; Yes; 21527
7746; Ah-kay-dee-bah; F; 17; Navajo; F; S; Daughter; 7757; Yes; Yes; 21528
7747; Homer; M; 13; Navajo; F; S; Son; 7758; Yes; Yes; 21529
7748; Yil-nih-bah; F; 11; Navajo; F; S; Daughter; 7759; Yes; Yes; 21530
7749; Nah-tah-yil-hah-yah; M; 9; Navajo; F; S; Son; 7760; Yes; Yes; 21531
7750; Dah-deyah; M; 7; Navajo; F; S; Son; 7761; Yes; Yes; 21532
7751; Al-chih-hah-bah; F; 3; Navajo; F; S; Daughter; 7762; Yes; Yes; 21533
7752; Yee-kee-bah; F; 1; Navajo; F; S; Daughter; 7763; Yes; Yes; 21686

244

Census of the __Northern Navajo__ reservation of the __Northern Navajo__ jurisdiction, as of __April 1__, 19**31**, taken by __Ernest H. Hammond, District__, Superintendent. **in Charge**

Key: Number; NAME: Surname, Given; Sex; Birth Year (if given), Age At Last Birthday; Tribe; Degree of Blood; Marital Status; Relationship To Head of Family; Last Census Roll Number; At Jurisdiction Where Enrolled (Yes or No); At Another Jurisdiction; ELSEWHERE: Post office, County, State; Ward (Yes or No); Allotment, Annuity, and Identification Numbers.

7753; Topahah-soh; F; 68; Navajo; F; Wd; Head; 7764; Yes; Yes; 17926

7754; Toh-dih-cheeny-boh-woh-atin-bega; M; 29; Navajo; F; M; Head; 7765; Yes; Yes; 18116
7755; Dah-dee-bah; F; 18; Navajo; F; M; Wife; 7766; Yes; Yes; 18117
7756; Dah-dee-bah-yae-elegade[sic]; M; 3; Navajo; F; S; Son; 7767; Yes; Yes; 18269
[Name should be Dah-dee-bah-yae-alegade]

7757; Tohsoni-Hosteen; M; 72; Navajo; F; Wd; Head; 7768; Yes; Yes; 17237
7758; Tohsonie-bega; M; 22; Navajo; F; S; Son; 7769; Yes; Yes; 17238
7759; Tohsonie, Edward; M; 13; Navajo; F; S; Son; 7770; Yes; Yes; 17239
7760; Tohsonie, Anita; F; 16; Navajo; F; S; Daughter; 7771; Yes; Yes; 17240
7761; Tohsonie, Iris; F; 11; Navajo; F; S; Daughter; 7772; Yes; Yes; 17241

7762; Topahah-Yazzie's wife-Askan-sohoh-bitsih; F; 54; Navajo; F; Wd; Head; 7773; Yes; Yes; 17086
7763; Klih-has-bah; F; 36; Navajo; F; S; Daughter; 7774; Yes; Yes; 17087
7764; Topahah-Yazzie, Jefferson; M; 20; Navajo; F; S; Son; 7775; Yes; Yes; 17088
7765; Topahah-Yazzie, Fannie; F; 17; Navajo; F; S; Daughter; 7776; Yes; Yes; 17089
7766; Topahah-Yazzie Bah; F; 21; Navajo; F; S; Grand-daughter; 7777; Yes; Yes; 17090
7767; Topahah-Yazzie Natah-ilth-nala-wudt; M; 6; Navajo; F; S; Grand-son; 7778; Yes; Yes; 17091
7768; Topahah-Yazzie-Kay-yilth-nih-bah; F; 21; Navajo; F; S; Daughter; 7779; Yes; Yes; 17414

7769; Toh-dih-kozie-soh-bidazih; F; Unk; Navajo; F; Wd; Head; 7780; Yes; Yes; 17049
7770; Toh-dih-kozie, Rex; M; 16; Navajo; F; S; Son; 7781; Yes; Yes; 17050
7771; Glih-pah; F; 9; Navajo; F; S; Daughter; 7782; Yes; Yes; 17051
7772; Adzanih-bahih; F; 7; Navajo; F; S; Daughter; 7783; Yes; Yes; 17052
7773; Dinay-Yazzie; M; 5; Navajo; F; S; Son; 7784; Yes; Yes; 17053

7774; Toh-dih-cheeny-benally; M; 21; Navajo; F; M; Head; 7785; Yes; Yes; 20963
7775; Adzan-l-bahih; F; 23; Navajo; F; M; Wife; 7786; Yes; Yes; 20964

7776; Toh-nih-yazzie; M; 58; Navajo; F; M; Head; 7787; Yes; Yes; 17972
7777; Toh-nih-yazzie's wife; F; 40; Navajo; F; M; Wife; 7788; Yes; Yes; 17973
7778; Toh-nih-yazzie-bega; M; 21; Navajo; F; S; Son; 7789; Yes; Yes; 17974
7779; Toh-nih-yazzie, Fern; F; 19; Navajo; F; S; Daughter; 7790; Yes; Yes; 17975
7780; Toh-nih-yazzie, Edward; M; 17; Navajo; F; S; Son; 7791; Yes; Yes; 17976
7781; Toh-nih-yazzie, Tuly; M; 16; Navajo; F; S; Son; 7792; Yes; Yes; 17977

Census of the **Northern Navajo** reservation of the **Northern Navajo** jurisdiction, as of **April 1**, 19**31,** taken by **Ernest H. Hammond, District**, Superintendent. **in Charge**

**Key:** Number; NAME: Surname, Given; Sex; Birth Year (if given), Age At Last Birthday; Tribe; Degree of Blood; Marital Status; Relationship To Head of Family; Last Census Roll Number; At Jurisdiction Where Enrolled (Yes or No); At Another Jurisdiction; ELSEWHERE: Post office, County, State; Ward (Yes or No); Allotment, Annuity, and Identification Numbers.

7782;  Toh-nih-yazzie, Etta; F; 15; Navajo; F; S; Daughter; 7793; Yes; Yes; 17978
7783;  Hoska-yazzie; M; 6; Navajo; F; S; Son; 7794; Yes; Yes; 17979
7784;  Toh-nih-yazzie, Harry; M; 3; Navajo; F; S; Son; 7795; Yes; Yes; 17980

7785;  Top-ah-lonsoh, Eugene; M; 33; Navajo; F; M; Head; 7796; Yes; Yes; 21462
7786;  Louise; F; 25; Navajo; F; M; Wife; 7797; Yes; Yes; 21463
7787;  Eugene, Jr.; M; 4; Navajo; F; S; Son; 7798; Yes; Yes; 21464
7788;  Cody; M; 3; Navajo; F; S; Son; 7799; Yes; Yes; 21683

7789;  Toh-dih-cheeny-bega; M; 48; Navajo; F; M; Head; 7800; Yes; Yes; 21343
7790;  Hah-nah-gah-inh-bitsih[sic]; F; 44; Navajo; F; M; Wife; 7801; Yes; Yes; 21344
       [Name could be Hah-nah-gah-nih-bitsih]
7791;  Kee; M; 19; Navajo; F; S; Son; 7802; Yes; Yes; 21345
7792;  Nah-tah-yee-nih-hotzoh; M; 9; Navajo; F; S; Son; 7803; Yes; Yes; 21346
7793;  Awae-yazzie; F; 3; Navajo; F; S; Daughter; 7804; Yes; Yes; 21727

7794;  Toh-sonie-benally; M; 25; Navajo; F; M; Head; 7805; Yes; Yes; 21602
7795;  Soh-ah-tah-benally; F; 18; Navajo; F; M; Wife; 7806; Yes; Yes; 21603
7796;  Nah-tah-yil-deswudt; M; 3; Navajo; F; S; Son; 7807; Yes; Yes; 21604

7797;  Toh-dih-cheeny-bitsih; F; Unk; Navajo; F; Wd; Head; 7808; Yes; Yes; 21586
7798;  Nah-cheeny-benally; M; Unk; Navajo; F; S; Son; 7809; Yes; Yes; 21587
7799;  Jane; F; Unk; Navajo; F; S; Daughter; 7810; Yes; Yes; 21588
7800;  Nah-tah; M; Unk; Navajo; F; S; Son; 7811; Yes; Yes; 21589
7801;  Yee-hih-nas-bah; F; 17; Navajo; F; S; Daughter; 7812; Yes; Yes; 21590
7802;  Ida May; F; Unk; Navajo; F; S; Daughter; 7813; Yes; Yes; 21591
7803;  Hoska-yee-dal-wudt; M; Unk; Navajo; F; S; Grand-son; 7814; Yes; Yes;
21593

7804;  Toh-cih-cheeny-bega; M; 23; Navajo; F; M; Head; 7815; Yes; Yes; 20337
7805;  Chah-etseesih-bitsih; F; 23; Navajo; F; M; Wife; 7816; Yes; Yes; 20338
7806;  Chin-bah; F; 6; Navajo; F; S; Daughter; 7817; Yes; Yes; 20339
7807;  Yah-nez-bah; F; 1; Navajo; F; S; Daughter; 7818; Yes; Yes; 20445

7808;  Toh-ahk-cleenih-bitsih; F; 55; Navajo; F; Wd; Head; 7819; Yes; Yes; 23391
7809;  Yee-kah-naz-bah; F; 19; Navajo; F; S; Daughter; 7820; Yes; Yes; 23392
7810;  Zannie; F; 31; Navajo; F; Wd; Daughter; 7821; Yes; Yes; 23393
7811;  Glih-yil-nih-des-bah; F; 4; Navajo; F; S; Grand-Son[sic]; 7822; Yes; Yes;
23394                                           [Should be female]
7812;  Gleah-nes-bah; F; 1; Navajo; F; S; Daughter; 7823; Yes; Yes; 23969

7813;  Toh-nih-cheeny-bega; M; Unk; Navajo; F; M; Head; 7824; Yes; Yes; 23109

Census of the **Northern Navajo** reservation of the **Northern Navajo** jurisdiction, as of **April 1**, 19**31**, taken by **Ernest H. Hammond, District**, Superintendent. **in Charge**

Key: Number; NAME: Surname, Given; Sex; Birth Year (if given), Age At Last Birthday; Tribe; Degree of Blood; Marital Status; Relationship To Head of Family; Last Census Roll Number; At Jurisdiction Where Enrolled (Yes or No); At Another Jurisdiction; ELSEWHERE: Post office, County, State; Ward (Yes or No); Allotment, Annuity, and Identification Numbers.

7814; Binah[sic], Chicago; F; 55; Navajo; F; M; Wife; 7825; Yes; Yes; 23110
[Name should be Bimah, Chicago]
7815; Juan; M; 19; Navajo; F; S; Step-son; 7826; Yes; Yes; 23111
7816; Zih; M; 17; Navajo; F; S; Step-son; 7827; Yes; Yes; 23112
7817; Glih-haz-bah; F; 13; Navajo; F; S; Step-daughter; 7828; Yes; Yes; 23113
7818; Chee; M; 9; Navajo; F; S; Step-son; 7829; Yes; Yes; 23114

7819; Toh-nil-chonih-bitah; M; 43; Navajo; F; M; Head; 7830; Yes; Yes; 23376
7820; Natoni-alsosie-bitah; F; 40; Navajo; F; M; Wife; 7831; Yes; Yes; 23377
7821; Haska-bah-nih-gil-dil; M; 22; Navajo; F; S; Son; 7832; Yes; Yes; 23378
7822; Herbert; M; 11; Navajo; F; S; Son; 7833; Yes; Yes; 23380
7823; Doh-nah-des-bah; F; 9; Navajo; F; S; Daughter; 7834; Yes; Yes; 23381
7824; Ganh-has-bah; F; 7; Navajo; F; S; Daughter; 7835; Yes; Yes; 23382

7825; Top-ah-ah-sosie; M; Unk; Navajo; F; M; Head; 7836; Yes; Yes; 23349
7826; Glih-ee-bah; F; 41; Navajo; F; M; Wife; 7837; Yes; Yes; 23650
7827; Isobel; F; 14; Navajo; F; S; Daughter; 7838; Yes; Yes; 23651
7828; Keh-yil-nih-nih-bah; F; 11; Navajo; F; S; Daughter; 7839; Yes; Yes; 23652
7829; Keh-yil-hah-bah; F; 9; Navajo; F; S; Daughter; 7840; Yes; Yes; 23653
7830; Kee-yee-taz-bah; F; 4; Navajo; F; S; Daughter; 7841; Yes; Yes; 23654
7831; (Baby); F; 1; Navajo; F; S; Daughter; 7842; Yes; Yes; 23956

7832; Toh-ahk-gleenih-bega, John; M; Unk; Navajo; F; M; Head; 7843; Yes; Yes; 23568
7833; Adzan-l-suen; F; Unk; Navajo; F; M; Wife; 7844; Yes; Yes; 23569
7834; Bah-naz-nih-bah; F; Unk; Navajo; F; S; Daughter; 7845; Yes; Yes; 23570
7835; Bah-ne-dil-lih; M; 16; Navajo; F; S; Son; 7846; Yes; Yes; 23571
7836; Lily; F; 14; Navajo; F; S; Daughter; 7847; Yes; Yes; 23572

7837; Toh-ahk-gleeneh-bega[sic], Frank; M; 36; Navajo; F; M; Head; 7848; Yes; Yes; 23660    [Name could be Toh-ahk-gleenih-bega, Frank]
7838; Ah-hih-naz-bah; F; Unk; Navajo; F; M; Wife; 7849; Yes; Yes; 23661

7839; Toh-ahk-gleenah; M; 81; Navajo; F; M; Head; 7850; Yes; Yes; 23655
7840; Clah-yen-bitsih; F; 43; Navajo; F; M; Wife; 7851; Yes; Yes; 23656
7841; Margaret; F; 26; Navajo; F; S; Daughter; 7852; Yes; Yes; 23657
7842; Haska-yil-dah-yee-yah, Rob; M; 21; Navajo; F; S; Son; 7853; Yes; Yes; 23658
7843; Billy; M; 14; Navajo; F; S; Son; 7854; Yes; Yes; 23659

7844; Toh-lizin-bega; M; 41; Navajo; F; M; Head; 7855; Yes; Yes; 18601
7845; Toh-lizin-bega's wife; F; 30; Navajo; F; M; Wife; 7856; Yes; Yes; 18602
7846; Glinnih; F; 18; Navajo; F; S; Daughter; 7857; Yes; Yes; 18603
7847; Keh-cilth; M; 13; Navajo; F; S; Son; 7858; Yes; Yes; 18604

Census of the **Northern Navajo** reservation of the **Northern Navajo** jurisdiction, as of **April 1**, 1931, taken by **Ernest H. Hammond, District**, Superintendent. **in Charge**

**Key:** Number; NAME: Surname, Given; Sex; Birth Year (if given), Age At Last Birthday; Tribe; Degree of Blood; Marital Status; Relationship To Head of Family; Last Census Roll Number; At Jurisdiction Where Enrolled (Yes or No); At Another Jurisdiction; ELSEWHERE: Post office, County, State; Ward (Yes or No); Allotment, Annuity, and Identification Numbers.

7848; Toh-lizin, Blackwater, Gladys; F; 11; Navajo; F; S; Daughter; 7859; Yes; Yes; 18605

7849; Glih-hah-bah; F; 9; Navajo; F; S; Daughter; 7860; Yes; Yes; 18606

7850; Glih-yazzie; F; 7; Navajo; F; S; Daughter; 7861; Yes; Yes; 18607

7851; Toh-dih-lozie-bitah; M; 23; Navajo; F; M; Head; 7862; Yes; Yes; 17865

7852; Toh-dih-lozie-bitah's wife; F; 22; Navajo; F; M; Wife; 7863; Yes; Yes; 17866

7853; Toh-ahk-cleenih; M; 62; Navajo; F; M; Head; 7864; Yes; Yes; 20315

7854; Chah-dih-tlohi-bilah; F; 46; Navajo; F; M; Wife; 7865; Yes; Yes; 20316

7855; Toh-ahk-cleenih, Doris; F; 24; Navajo; F; S; Daughter; 7866; Yes; Yes; 20317

7856; Toh-ahk-cleenih, Elsie; F; 20; Navajo; F; S; Daughter; 7867; Yes; Yes; 20318

7857; Yazzie, Lizzie; F; 30; Navajo; F; Wd; Daughter; 7868; Yes; Yes; 20319

7858; Nal-wudt; M; 7; Navajo; F; S; Grand-son; 7869; Yes; Yes; 20320

7859; Adzan; F; 5; Navajo; F; S; Grand-daughter; 7870; Yes; Yes; 20321

7860; Nah-tah-yazzie; M; 4; Navajo; F; S; Grand-son; 7871; Yes; Yes; 20322

7861; Toh-ahk-cleenih's mother; F; 88; Navajo; F; Wd; Mother; 7872; Yes; Yes; 20323

7862; Toh-dih-cheeny-bega; M; 33; Navajo; F; M; Head; 7873; Yes; Yes; 17359

7863; Toh-dih-cheeny-bega's wife; F; 30; Navajo; F; M; Wife; 7874; Yes; Yes; 17360

7864; Toh-dih-cheeny, Herbert; M; 16; Navajo; F; S; Son; 7875; Yes; Yes; 17361

7865; Toh-dih-cheeny-wudt; M; 14; Navajo; F; S; Son; 7876; Yes; Yes; 17362

7866; Topahah-bitsees-chilli; M; 24; Navajo; F; S; Head; 7877; Yes; Yes; 17981

7867; Tohsonih-Nez; M; 34; Navajo; F; S; Head; 7878; Yes; Yes; 17384

7868; Todchi-cheeny-nez-bitsih; F; 30; Navajo; F; Wd; Head; 7879; Yes; Yes; 17128

7869; Haska-Jahih; M; 5; Navajo; F; S; Son; 7880; Yes; Yes; 17129

7870; Toh-nye-kadih-bega; M; Unk; Navajo; F; Wd; Head; 7881; Yes; Yes; 22344

7871; Biz-des-bah; F; 4; Navajo; F; S; Daughter; 7882; Yes; Yes; 22346

7872; Top-dih-kozie-soh; M; 62; Navajo; F; M; Head; 7883; Yes; Yes; 17389

7873; Descheeny-ahtcitty-bitsih; F; 43; Navajo; F; M; Wife; 7884; Yes; Yes; 17390

7874; McKeary, John; M; 35; Navajo; F; S; Son; 7885; Yes; Yes; 17391

7875; Ekee-pahih; M; 15; Navajo; F; S; Son; 7886; Yes; Yes; 17392

7876; Natoni-yazzie; M; 10; Navajo; F; S; Son; 7887; Yes; Yes; 17393

7877; Topahah-bega, Jake; M; 58; Navajo; F; M; Head; 7888; No; McElmo, Colo., San Juan, Utah; Yes; 19374

Census of the **Northern Navajo** reservation of the **Northern Navajo** jurisdiction, as of **April 1**, 1931, taken by **Ernest H. Hammond, District**, Superintendent. **in Charge**

**Key:** Number; NAME: Surname, Given; Sex; Birth Year (if given), Age At Last Birthday; Tribe; Degree of Blood; Marital Status; Relationship To Head of Family; Last Census Roll Number; At Jurisdiction Where Enrolled (Yes or No); At Another Jurisdiction; ELSEWHERE: Post office, County, State; Ward (Yes or No); Allotment, Annuity, and Identification Numbers.

7878; Nocki-deetsah-bitsah; F; 43; Navajo; F; M; Wife; 7889; No; McElmo, Colo., San Juan, Utah; Yes; 19375

7879; Topahah, Harriet; F; 22; Navajo; F; S; Daughter; 7890; No; McElmo, Colo., San Juan, Utah; Yes; 19376

7880; Topahah, Lansing, Elizabeth; F; 19; Navajo; F; S; Daughter; 7891; No; McElmo, Colo., San Juan, Utah; Yes; 19377

7881; Topahah, Francis; M; 17; Navajo; F; S; Son; 7892; No; McElmo, Colo., San Juan, Utah; Yes; 19378

7882; Topahah, Joe; M; 15; Navajo; F; S; Son; 7893; No; McElmo, Colo., San Juan, Utah; Yes; 19379

7883; Topahah, Blanche; F; 13; Navajo; F; S; Daughter; 7894; No; McElmo, Colo., San Juan, Utah; Yes; 19380

7884; Topahah, Jimmie; M; 9; Navajo; F; S; Son; 7895; No; McElmo, Colo., San Juan, Utah; Yes; 19381

7885; Yil-bah; F; 8; Navajo; F; S; Daughter; 7896; No; McElmo, Colo., San Juan, Utah; Yes; 19382

7886; Topahah, Lena; F; 6; Navajo; F; S; Daughter; 7897; No; McElmo, Colo., San Juan, Utah; Yes; 19383

7887; Toh-ahh-gleenih-bega; M; 29; Navajo; F; M; Head; 7898; Yes; Yes; 20276
7888; Senopas-yazzie-bitsih; F; 24; Navajo; F; M; Wife; 7899; Yes; Yes; 20277
7889; Haska-yil-nah-yah; M; 5; Navajo; F; S; Son; 7900; Yes; Yes; 20278
7890; Haska-yee-nas-wudt; M; 3; Navajo; F; S; Son; 7901; Yes; Yes; 20279

7891; Toh-dih-cheeny; M; 61; Navajo; F; M; Head; 7902; Yes; Yes; 17888
7892; Adzanih-Kin-lacheeny-nih; F; 46; Navajo; F; M; Wife; 7903; Yes; Yes; 17889
7893; Bah; F; 18; Navajo; F; S; Daughter; 7904; Yes; Yes; 17890
7894; Toh-dih-cheeny, Roy; M; 12; Navajo; F; S; Son; 7905; Yes; Yes; 17891
7895; Aht-citty; M; 9; Navajo; F; S; Son; 7906; Yes; Yes; 17892

7896; Tom Kee; M; 26; Navajo; F; M; Head; 7907; Yes; Yes; 22480
7897; Adzan-soh; F; 26; Navajo; F; M; Wife; 7908; Yes; Yes; 22481
7898; Haska-yil-yee-l-wudt; M; 9; Navajo; F; S; Son; 7909; Yes; Yes; 22482
7899; Nan-nih-bahih; F; 3; Navajo; F; S; Daughter; 7910; Yes; Yes; 22483

7900; Top-dih-cheeny-bega; M; 22; Navajo; F; M; Head; 7911; Yes; Yes; 17908
7901; Yah-nih-bah; F; 19; Navajo; F; M; Wife; 7912; Yes; Yes; 17909
7902; Thelma; F; 2; Navajo; F; S; Daughter; 7913; Yes; Yes; 18222

7903; Tah-nez-zanih-Nez; M; 62; Navajo; F; M; Head; 7915; Yes; Yes; 20099
7904; Senopas-sanih-bitsih; F; 40; Navajo; F; M; Wife; 7915; Yes; Yes; 20100
7905; Soh, Roy; M; 19; Navajo; F; S; Nephew; 7916; Yes; Yes; 20101
7906; Al-gih; M; 11; Navajo; F; S; Nephew; 7917; Yes; Yes; 20102

Census of the **Northern Navajo** reservation of the **Northern Navajo** jurisdiction, as of **April 1**, 19**31,** taken by **Ernest H. Hammond, District**, Superintendent. **in Charge**

**Key:** Number; NAME: Surname, Given; Sex; Birth Year (if given), Age At Last Birthday; Tribe; Degree of Blood; Marital Status; Relationship To Head of Family; Last Census Roll Number; At Jurisdiction Where Enrolled (Yes or No); At Another Jurisdiction; ELSEWHERE: Post office, County, State; Ward (Yes or No); Allotment, Annuity, and Identification Numbers.

7907; Toh-nih; M; 33; Navajo; F; M; Head; 7918; Yes; Yes; 17923
7908; Adzan-bye; F; 20; Navajo; F; M; Wife; 7919; Yes; Yes; 17924

7909; Toh-sonih-bega; M; 45; Navajo; F; M; Head; 7920; Yes; Yes; 20212
7910; Toh-sonih-bega's wife; F; 39; Navajo; F; M; Wife; 7921; Yes; Yes; 20213
7911; Shih-bah; F; 15; Navajo; F; S; Daughter; 7922; Yes; Yes; 20214
7912; Toh-sonih, Maud; F; 13; Navajo; F; S; Daughter; 7923; Yes; Yes; 20215
7913; Yil-nah-yah; M; 12; Navajo; F; S; Son; 7924; Yes; Yes; 20216
7914; Tah-ho-lel; M; 9; Navajo; F; S; Son; 7925; Yes; Yes; 20217
7915; Yee-nas-bah; F; 7; Navajo; F; S; Daughter; 7926; Yes; Yes; 20218
7916; Yah-nih-bah; F; 3; Navajo; F; S; Daughter; 7927; Yes; Yes; 20219
7917; Toh-dih-cheeny-yen-bitsih; F; 63; Navajo; F; Wd; Mother-in-law; 7928; Yes; Yes; 20220
7918; Nah-gee-bah; F; 32; Navajo; F; Wd; Sister-in-law; 7929; Yes; Yes; 20221

7919; Toh-dih-cheeny-Hosteen; M; 82; Navajo; F; M; Head; 7936; No; McElmo, Colo., San Juan, Utah; Yes; 19801
7920; Klizi-thani-hosteen-bitsih; F; 56; Navajo; F; M; Wife; 7937; No; McElmo, Colo., San Juan, Utah; Yes; 19802
7921; Hoska-yah-nah-sah; M; 22; Navajo; F; S; Son; 7938; No; McElmo, Colo., San Juan, Utah; Yes; 19803

7922; Toh-lizin-bega, Tuly; M; Unk; Navajo; F; M; Head; 7940; No; McElmo, Colo., San Juan, Utah; Yes; 18823
7923; Nocki-Dinay-Uienth-Nez-bitsih; F; 22; Navajo; F; M; 7941; Wife; No; McElmo, Colo., San Juan, Utah; Yes; 18824
7924; Bah-na-pah; F; 1; Navajo; F; S; Daughter; 7942; No; McElmo, Colo., San Juan, Utah; Yes; 18823[sic] [ID No. should be 18825]

7925; Top-ah-hah; M; 54; Navajo; F; M; Head; 7943; Yes; Yes; 21291
7926; Adzan-yazzie; F; 58; Navajo; F; M; Wife; 7944; Yes; Yes; 21292
7927; Adzan-top-ah-hah; F; 78; Navajo; F; Wd; Mother; 7945; Yes; Yes; 21293
7928; Yee-dis-bah; F; 15; Navajo; F; S; Niece; 7946; Yes; Yes; 21294

7929; Toh-sosie, Mark; M; 39; Navajo; F; M; Head; 7947; No; McElmo, Colo., San Juan, Utah; Yes; 18997
7930; Toh-sosie, Laura; F; 34; Navajo; F; M; Wife; 7948; No; McElmo, Colo., San Juan, Utah; Yes; 18998
7931; Toh-sosie, Irene; F; 15; Navajo; F; M[sic]; Daughter; 7949; No; McElmo, Colo., San Juan, Utah; Yes; 18999
7932; Toh-sosie, Francis; M; 7; Navajo; F; S; Daughter[sic]; 7950; No; McElmo, Colo., San Juan, Utah; Yes; 19000

Census of the **Northern Navajo** reservation of the **Northern Navajo** jurisdiction, as of **April 1**, 19**31**, taken by **Ernest H. Hammond, District**, Superintendent. **in Charge**

**Key:** Number; NAME: Surname, Given; Sex; Birth Year (if given), Age At Last Birthday; Tribe; Degree of Blood; Marital Status; Relationship To Head of Family; Last Census Roll Number; At Jurisdiction Where Enrolled (Yes or No); At Another Jurisdiction; ELSEWHERE: Post office, County, State; Ward (Yes or No); Allotment, Annuity, and Identification Numbers.

7933;  Toh-sosie, Harry; M; 4; Navajo; F; S; Son; 7951; No; McElmo, Colo., San Juan, Utah; Yes; 19001

7934;  Topah-Hosteen; M; 82; Navajo; F; M; Head; 7952; Yes; Yes; 29337
7935;  Topah-Hosteen's wife; F; 82; Navajo; F; M; Wife; 7953; Yes; Yes; 29338

7936;  Toh-dih-kozie-soh; M; 54; Navajo; F; M; Head; 7954; Yes; Yes; 29324
7937;  Toh-dih-kozie-soh's wife; F; 52; Navajo; F; M; Wife; 7955; Yes; Yes; 29325
7938;  Eskee-soh; M; 29; Navajo; F; S; Son; 7956; Yes; Yes; 29326
7939;  Eskee-seesih; M; 19; Navajo; F; S; Son; 7957; Yes; Yes; 29327
7940;  Frank; M; 16; Navajo; F; S; Son; 7958; Yes; Yes; 29328
7941;  Nah-bah; F; 13; Navajo; F; S; Daughter; 7959; Yes; Yes; 29329
7942;  Nah-tah-yil-nah-zinh; M; 5; Navajo; F; S; Son; 7960; Yes; Yes; 29330

7943;  Toh-bih-nah-kisih-bega; M; 24; Navajo; F; M; Head; 7961; Yes; Yes; 28387
7944;  Dohi-yen-bitsoih-bitsih; F; 20; Navajo; F; M; Wife; 7962; Yes; Yes; 28388
7945;  Bah-cheeih; F; 3; Navajo; F; S; Daughter; 7963; Yes; Yes; 28389
7946;  Silas; M; 16; Navajo; F; S; Brother-in-law; 7964; Yes; Yes; 28390
7947;  Adzan-yazzie; F; 11; Navajo; F; S; Sister-in-law; 7965; Yes; Yes; 28391

7948;  Topah-ah; M; 38; Navajo; F; M; Head; 7966; Yes; Yes; 28379
7949;  Batoni-bitsees-chilli-bitsih; F; 25; Navajo; F; M; Wife; 7967; Yes; Yes; 28380
7950;  Yazzie; F; 18; Navajo; F; S; Daughter; 7968; Yes; Yes; 28381
7951;  James; M; 17; Navajo; F; S; Son; 7969; Yes; Yes; 28382
7952;  Adzan-l-bahih; F; 11; Navajo; F; S; Daughter; 7970; Yes; Yes; 28383
7953;  Hosteen; M; 8; Navajo; F; S; Son; 7971; Yes; Yes; 28384
7954;  Nih-des-bah; F; 7; Navajo; F; S; Daughter; 7972; Yes; Yes; 28385
7955;  Al-chih-haz-bah; F; 5; Navajo; F; S; Daughter; 7973; Yes; Yes; 28386
7956;  Eskee; M; 2; Navajo; F; S; Son; 7974; Yes; Yes; 28550

7957;  Topah-hosteen-bega; M; 41; Navajo; F; M; Head; 7975; Yes; Yes; 29303
7958;  Boh-woh-atin-bitsih; F; 48; Navajo; F; M; Wife; 7976; Yes; Yes; 29304
7959;  Yil-deyah; M; 20; Navajo; F; S; Son; 7977; Yes; Yes; 29305
7960;  Woody; M; 19; Navajo; F; S; Son; 7978; Yes; Yes; 29306
7961;  Al-yazzie; M; 18; Navajo; F; S; Son; 7979; Yes; Yes; 29307
7962;  Thelma; M[sic]; 12; Navajo; F; S; Daughter; 7980; Yes; Yes; 29308
7963;  Bih-jih-kal; M[sic]; 10; Navajo; F; S; Daughter; 7981; Yes; Yes; 29309
7964;  Mell; M; 8; Navajo; F; S; Son; 7982; Yes; Yes; 29310
7965;  Awa-yazzie; F; 5; Navajo; F; S; Daughter; 7983; Yes; Yes; 29311

7966;  Toh-dih-kozie-yazzie; M; 35; Navajo; F; M; Head; 7984; Yes; Yes; 29286
7967;  Yil-kih-naz-bah; F; 26; Navajo; F; M; Wife; 7985; Yes; Yes; 29287
7968;  Toh-hah-bah; F; 10; Navajo; F; S; Daughter; 7986; Yes; Yes; 29288

Census of the **Northern Navajo** reservation of the **Northern Navajo** jurisdiction, as of **April 1**, 19**31,** taken by **Ernest H. Hammond, District**, Superintendent. **in Charge**

**Key:** Number; NAME: Surname, Given; Sex; Birth Year (if given), Age At Last Birthday; Tribe; Degree of Blood; Marital Status; Relationship To Head of Family; Last Census Roll Number; At Jurisdiction Where Enrolled (Yes or No); At Another Jurisdiction; ELSEWHERE: Post office, County, State; Ward (Yes or No); Allotment, Annuity, and Identification Numbers.

7969; Haska-yil-nil-wudt; M; 8; Navajo; F; S; Son; 7987; Yes; Yes; 29289
7970; Haska-yee-tah-des-wudt; M; 4; Navajo; F; S; Son; 7988; Yes; Yes; 29290
7971; Yee-nah-hoh-tahl; M; 22; Navajo; F; S; Cousin-in-law; 7989; Yes; Yes; 29291
7972; Rose; F; 2; Navajo; F; S; Daughter; 7990; Yes; Yes; 29410

7973; Toh-dih-kozie-, David; M; 34; Navajo; F; M; Head; 7991; Yes; Yes; 29214
7974; Zelma; F; 42; Navajo; F; M; Wife; 7992; Yes; Yes; 29215

7975; Toh-dih-lozie, Harry; M; 26; Navajo; F; M; Head; 7993; Yes; Yes; 29208
7976; Klizi-thlani-bitsih; F; 20; Navajo; F; M; Wife; 7994; Yes; Yes; 29209
7977; Chih-hah-nih-bah; F; 4; Navajo; F; S; Daughter; 7995; Yes; Yes; 29210

7978; Toh-nih-kozie-sosie; M; Unk; Navajo; F; M; Head; 7996; Yes; Yes; 29196
7979; Toh-dih-kozie-sosie's wife[sic]; F; 66; Navajo; F; M; Wife; 7997; Yes; Yes; 29197 [Name could be Toh-nih-kozie-sosie's wife]
7980; Lucy; F; 23; Navajo; F; S; Daughter; 7998; Yes; Yes; 29198
7981; Charles; M; 21; Navajo; F; S; Son; 7999; Yes; Yes; 29199
7982; Elizabeth; F; 20; Navajo; F; S; Daughter; 8000; Yes; Yes; 29200
7983; Lena; F; 20; Navajo; F; S; Daughter; 8001; Yes; Yes; 29201
7984; Shelly; M; 16; Navajo; F; S; Son; 8002; Yes; Yes; 29202
7985; Tom; M; 14; Navajo; F; S; Son; 8003; Yes; Yes; 29203
7986; Mary; F; 27; Navajo; F; S; Daughter; 8004; Yes; Yes; 29204
7987; Toh-dih-kozie-sosie, Cow boy; M; 22; Navajo; F; S; Son; 8005; Yes; Yes; 29373
7988; Yil-bah-ih; M; 9; Navajo; F; S; Grand-son; 8006; Yes; Yes; 29374
7989; Yil-hoh-lath; M; 2; Navajo; F; S; Son; 8007; Yes; Yes; 29375

7990; To-dih-kozih-Nez; M; 40; Navajo; F; M; Head; 8008; Yes; Yes; 29131
7991; Tom Farley's Bitsih; F; 32; Navajo; F; M; Wife; 8009; Yes; Yes; 29132
7992; Haska-yee-sil; M; 12; Navajo; F; S; Son; 8010; Yes; Yes; 29133
7993; Haska-yee-chih-has-wudt; M; 9; Navajo; F; S; Son; 8011; Yes; Yes; 29134
7994; Haska-yee-del-wudt; M; 7; Navajo; F; S; Son; 8012; Yes; Yes; 29135
7995; Chih-nih-bah; F; 4; Navajo; F; S; Daughter; 8013; Yes; Yes; 29137
7996; Haska-yil-wudt; M; 14; Navajo; F; S; Adopted son; 8014; Yes; Yes; 29138
7997; Tom Farley's son; M; 24; Navajo; F; S; Brother-in-law; 8015; Yes; Yes; 29139
7998; Sinn-sah-kadnih-benally; M; 25; Navajo; F; S; Cousin-in-law; 8016; Yes; Yes; 29140
7999; Pearl; F; 2; Navajo; F; S; Daughter; 8017; Yes; Yes; 29399

8000; Toh-ahk-gleenih-cheeny; M; Unk; Navajo; F; M; Head; 8018; Yes; Yes; 29950
8001; Dah-hal-tahih-bitsih; F; 48; Navajo; F; M; Wife; 8019; Yes; Yes; 29951
8002; Haska-yazzie; M; 24; Navajo; F; S; Son; 8020; Yes; Yes; 29952

Census of the **Northern Navajo** reservation of the **Northern Navajo** jurisdiction, as of **April 1**, 1931, taken by **Ernest H. Hammond, District**, Superintendent. **in Charge**

**Key:** Number; NAME: Surname, Given; Sex; Birth Year (if given), Age At Last Birthday; Tribe; Degree of Blood; Marital Status; Relationship To Head of Family; Last Census Roll Number; At Jurisdiction Where Enrolled (Yes or No); At Another Jurisdiction; ELSEWHERE: Post office, County, State; Ward (Yes or No); Allotment, Annuity, and Identification Numbers.

8003; Wudt; M; 21; Navajo; F; S; Son; 8021; Yes; Yes; 29953
8004; Ralph; M; 20; Navajo; F; S; Son; 8022; Yes; Yes; 29954
8005; Haska-yee-cah-yah; M; 10; Navajo; F; S; Son; 8023; Yes; Yes; 29955
8006; Dah-dee-bah; F; 7; Navajo; F; S; Daughter; 8024; Yes; Yes; 29956
8007; Yil-naz-bah; F; 4; Navajo; F; S; Daughter; 8025; Yes; Yes; 29957

8008; Toh-ahk-gleenih-cheeny-bega; M; 27; Navajo; F; M; Head; 8026; Yes; Yes; 29958
8009; Dinay-l-suen-benally; F; 25; Navajo; F; M; Wife; 8027; Yes; Yes; 29959
8010; Gah-lih; M; 7; Navajo; F; S; Son; 8028; Yes; Yes; 29960
8011; Tah-yil-nah-yah; M; 6; Navajo; F; S; Son; 8029; Yes; Yes; 29961
8012; Haska-yil-yee-deel; M; 3; Navajo; F; S; Son; 8030; Yes; Yes; 29962

8013; Topah-hah-soh; M; 64; Navajo; F; M; Head; 8031; Yes; Yes; 29927
8014; Uienth-nizzih-bitsih; F; 19; Navajo; F; M; Wife; 8032; Yes; Yes; 29928
8015; Topah-hah-soh-bega; M; 2; Navajo; F; S; Son; 8033; Yes; Yes; 29929

8016; Top-ahk-gleenih-soh-bih-adzan; F; 60; Navajo; F; Wd; Head; 8034; Yes; Yes; 29734
8017; Haska-yee-chih-nil-wudt; M; 18; Navajo; F; S; Son; 8035; Yes; Yes; 29735
8018; Haska-yil-nah-yah; M; 6; Navajo; F; S; Grand-son; 8036; Yes; Yes; 29736

8019; Toh-ahk-gleenih-soh-bega, Joe; M; 35; Navajo; F; M; Head; 8037; Yes; Yes; 29701
8020; Dah-bah; F; 26; Navajo; F; M; Wife; 8038; Yes; Yes; 29702
8021; Yil-ee-bah; F; 10; Navajo; F; S; Daughter; 8039; Yes; Yes; 29703
8022; Neh; M; 8; Navajo; F; S; Son; 8040; Yes; Yes; 29704
8023; Seesih; F; 6; Navajo; F; S; Daughter; [Blank] Yes; Yes; 29705

8024; Tuly-Soh; M; Unk; Navajo; F; M; Head; [Blank]; Yes; Yes; 22691
8025; Emma; F; 38; Navajo; F; M; Wife; [Blank]; Yes; Yes; 22692
8026; Mary Louise; F; 11; Navajo; F; S; Daughter; [Blank]; Yes; Yes; 22693
8027; Harold; M; 8; Navajo; F; S; Son; [Blank]; Yes; Yes; 22694
8028; Anna May; F; 6; Navajo; F; S; Daughter; [Blank]; Yes; Yes; 22695
8029; Esther Helen; F; 4; Navajo; F; S; Daughter; [Blank]; Yes; Yes; 22696
8030; Marjorie; F; Unk; Navajo; F; S; Daughter; [Blank]; Yes; Yes; 22749

8031; Toh-sonie, Bush Frank; M; 55; Navajo; F; M; Head; [Blank]; Yes; Yes; 32837
8032; Salou-sani-bitsih; F; 56; Navajo; F; M;; Wife; [Blank]; Yes; Yes; 32838

8033; Toh-zonnie-bega-bitsih; F; 35; Navajo; F; Wd; Head; 8041; Yes; Yes; 32839
8034; Nah-tah-tah-yah, Franklin; M; 19; Navajo; F; S; Son; 8042; Yes; Yes; 32840
8035; Nah-tah-yee-chih-yil-wohl; M; 13; Navajo; F; S; Son; 8043; Yes; Yes; 32841

Census of the **Northern Navajo** reservation of the **Northern Navajo** jurisdiction, as of **April 1**, 19**31**, taken by **Ernest H. Hammond, District**, Superintendent. **in Charge**

**Key:** Number; NAME: Surname, Given; Sex; Birth Year (if given), Age At Last Birthday; Tribe; Degree of Blood; Marital Status; Relationship To Head of Family; Last Census Roll Number; At Jurisdiction Where Enrolled (Yes or No); At Another Jurisdiction; ELSEWHERE: Post office, County, State; Ward (Yes or No); Allotment, Annuity, and Identification Numbers.

8036; Nah-tah-yee-chih-nil-yah; M; 8; Navajo; F; S; Son; 8044; Yes; Yes; 32842

8037; Tawk, Lilian; F; 33; Navajo; F; Div; Head; 8045; Yes; Yes; 32895
8038; Edith; F; 11; Navajo; F; S; Daughter; 8046; Yes; Yes; 32896
8039; Treva; F; 9; Navajo; F; S; Daughter; 8047; Yes; Yes; 32897

8040; Ton-ah-kady-bega; M; Unk; Navajo; F; Div; Head; 8048; Yes; Yes; 23932

8041; Toh-dih-cheeny-bitsih; F; 40; Navajo; F; Div; Head; 8049; Yes; Yes; 27706
8042; Sam; M; 19; Navajo; F; S; Son; 8050; Yes; Yes; 27707
8043; Keh-yee-taz-bah; F; 17; Navajo; F; S; Daughter; 8051; Yes; Yes; 27708
8044; Keh-yee-tah-nih-bah; F; 11; Navajo; F; S; Daughter; 8052; Yes; Yes; 27709
8045; Haska-yil-naw-wudt; M; 5; Navajo; F; S; Son; 8053; Yes; Yes; 27710

8046; Toh-dih-cheeny-l-chee-bega, Howard Thomas; M; 24; Navajo; F; S; Head; 8054; Yes; Yes; 25299

8047; Toh-dih-cheeny, Fred; M; 47; Navajo; F; M; Head; 8055; Yes; Yes; 19830
8048; Ashinh-clah-bitsih; F; 36; Navajo; F; M; Wife; 8056; Yes; Yes; 19831
8049; Donald; M; 17; Navajo; F; S; Son; 8057; Yes; Yes; 19832
8050; Al-soh-dez-bah; F; 10; Navajo; F; S; Daughter; 8058; Yes; Yes; 19833
8051; Haska-yee-tah-des-wudt; M; 8; Navajo; F; S; Son; 8059; Yes; Yes; 19834

8052; Toh-dih-cheeny, Mark; M; 35; Navajo; F; M; Head; 8061; Yes; Yes; 19826
8053; Ashnih-Clah-bitsih; F; 28; Navajo; F; M; Wife; 8062; Yes; Yes; 19827
8054; Willie; M; 4; Navajo; F; S; Son; 8063; Yes; Yes; 19828
8055; Hoover; M; 3; Navajo; F; S; Son; 8064; Yes; Yes; 19829

8056; Toh-dih-cheeny, Ben; M; 42; Navajo; F; S; Head; 8065; Yes; Yes; 19836
8057; Ashinh-Clah-bitsih; F; 20; Navajo; F; M; Wife; 8066; Yes; Yes; 19837
8058; Atate-l-chee; F; 3; Navajo; F; S; Daughter; 8067; Yes; Yes; 19838
8059; Nahn-nih-bah; F; 12; Navajo; F; S; Daughter; 8068; Yes; Yes; 19839
8060; Betty; F; 10; Navajo; F; S; Daughter; 8069; Yes; Yes; 19840

8061; Topah-ah-sosie-bitah; M; Unk; Navajo; F; M; Head; 8070; Yes; Yes; 23874
8062; Kee-ee-bah; F; 23; Navajo; F; M; Wife; 8071; Yes; Yes; 23875
8063; Chih-nih-nih-bah; F; 3; Navajo; F; S; Daughter; 8072; Yes; Yes; 23876
8064; Babay[sic]; M; 2; Navajo; F; S; Son; 8073; Yes; Yes; 23877
[Should be Baby]
8065; Wudt; M; 19; Navajo; F; S; Brother-in-law; 8074; Yes; Yes; 23878
8066; Chee-ih-soh; M; 13; Navajo; F; S; Brother-in-law; 8075; Yes; Yes; 23879

8067; Toh-sonie-Sani-bega; M; 45; Navajo; F; M; Head; 8076; Yes; Yes; 18215

Census of the **Northern Navajo** reservation of the **Northern Navajo** jurisdiction, as of **April 1** , 1931, taken by **Ernest H. Hammond, District**, Superintendent. **in Charge**

**Key:** Number; NAME: Surname, Given; Sex; Birth Year (if given), Age At Last Birthday; Tribe; Degree of Blood; Marital Status; Relationship To Head of Family; Last Census Roll Number; At Jurisdiction Where Enrolled (Yes or No); At Another Jurisdiction; ELSEWHERE: Post office, County, State; Ward (Yes or No); Allotment, Annuity, and Identification Numbers.

8068; Hosteen-en-clah-ih-bitsih; F; 59; Navajo; F; M; Wife; 8077; Yes; Yes; 18216
8069; Hosteen-yazzie-bitah; M; 18; Navajo; F; S; Step-son; 8078; Yes; Yes; 18217
8070; Hosteen-yazzie-j-k; F; 15; Navajo; F; S; Step-daughter; 8079; Yes; Yes; 18218
8071; Name-Unknown; F; 12; Navajo; F; S; Step-daughter; 8080; Yes; Yes; 18219
8072; Adzan-mazee; F; 5; Navajo; F; S; Step-grand-daughter; 8081; Yes; Yes; 18220

8073; Toh-sonie; M; 66; Navajo; F; Wd; Head; 8082; Yes; Yes; 18212
8074; Toh-sonie-bega (Crippled); M; 32; Navajo; F; S; Son; 8083; Yes; Yes; 18213
8075; Melvin; M; 20; Navajo; F; S; Son; 8084; Yes; Yes; 18214

8076; Toh-pah-sosie; M; Unk; Navajo; F; S; Head; 8085; Yes; Yes; 23998

8077; Toh-dih-koyie-soh-bidayih[sic]; M; 39; Navajo; F; Wd; Head; 8086; Yes; Yes;
17048    [Name should be Toh-dih-kozie-soh-bidayih]
8078; Glih-pah; F; 10; Navajo; F; S; Daughter; 8087; Yes; Yes; 17051
8079; Adyanih-bahik; F; 8; Navajo; F; S; Daughter; 8088; Yes; Yes; 17052
8080; Dina-yazzie; M; 4; Navajo; F; S; Son; 8089; Yes; Yes; 17053

8081; Toh-glena-tso; M; 48; Navajo; F; M; Head; 8090; Yes; Yes; 21641
8082; Ya-ni-da; F; 28; Navajo; F; M; Wife; 8091; Yes; Yes; 21642
8083; Carl; M; 20; Navajo; F; S; Son; 8092; Yes; Yes; 21643
8084; Hazel; F; 19; Navajo; F; S; Niece; 8093; Yes; Yes; 21647
8085; Lin-nas-bah; F; 11; Navajo; F; S; Niece; 8094; Yes; Yes; 21648
8086; Hosteen-chee; M; 9; Navajo; F; S; Son; 8095; Yes; Yes; 21644
8087; Yi-da-ni-do; F; 5; Navajo; F; S; Daughter; 8096; Yes; Yes; 21645
8088; Haskee-wudt; M; 2; Navajo; F; S; Son; 8097; Yes; Yes; 21646

8089; Toh-chol-badoni; M; Unk; Navajo; F; M; Head; 8098; Yes; Yes; 25401
8090; Bah; F; Unk; Navajo; F; M; Wife; 8099; Yes; Yes; 23972
8091; Henry, Harry; M; Unk; Navajo; F; S; Son; 8100; Yes; Yes; 23973
8092; Bal-nez-bah; F; Unk; Navajo; F; S; Daughter; 8101; Yes; Yes; 23974
8093; Johnny; M; Unk; Navajo; F; S; Son; 8102; Yes; Yes; 23975
8094; Al-kodez-bah; F; Unk; Navajo; F; S; Daughter; 8103; Yes; Yes; 23977
8095; Bul-nge-bah; F; Unk; Navajo; F; S; Daughter; 8104; Yes; Yes; 23976
8096; Al-chise-nez-bah; F; Unk; Navajo; F; S; Daughter; 8105; Yes; Yes; 23978

8097; Tom Jones Bega, Sam; M; 65; Navajo; F; M; Head; 8106; Yes; Yes; 29382
8098; Gonna-bylily-bitsih; F; 19; Navajo; F; M; Wife; 8107; Yes; Yes; 29383
8099; Haska-yee-che-yee-gath; M; 4; Navajo; F; S; Son; 8108; Yes; Yes; 29384
8100; Haska-yee-tah-yee-gath; M; 2; Navajo; F; S; Son; 8109; Yes; Yes; 29385

8101; Toechin, Albert; M; 31; Navajo; F; M; Head; 8110; Yes; Yes; 23990
8102; Albert Toechin's wife; F; 21; Navajo; F; M; Wife; 8111; Yes; Yes; 23992

255

Census of the **Northern Navajo** reservation of the **Northern Navajo** jurisdiction, as of **April 1**, 1931, taken by **Ernest H. Hammond, District**, Superintendent. **in Charge**

**Key:** Number; NAME: Surname, Given; Sex; Birth Year (if given), Age At Last Birthday; Tribe; Degree of Blood; Marital Status; Relationship To Head of Family; Last Census Roll Number; At Jurisdiction Where Enrolled (Yes or No); At Another Jurisdiction; ELSEWHERE: Post office, County, State; Ward (Yes or No); Allotment, Annuity, and Identification Numbers.

8103;  Haska-nah-gahl; M; 8; Navajo; F; S; Son; 8112; Yes; Yes; 23993
8104;  Kah-nah-bah; F; 3; Navajo; F; S; Daughter; 8113; Yes; Yes; 23991

8105;  Topah-ah-Hosteen-bitsih; F; 62; Navajo; F; Wd; Head; [Blank]; Yes; Yes; 29026
8106;  Agnes; F; 22; Navajo; F; S; Daughter; [Blank]; Yes; Yes; 29027
8107;  Nah-nih-bah; F; 21; Navajo; F; S; Daughter; [Blank]; Yes; Yes; 29028

8108;  Uienth-Nezzih; M; 49; Navajo; F; M; Head; 8124; Yes; Yes; 29074
8109;  Hosteen-soh-bitsih; F; 27; Navajo; F; M; Wife; 8125; Yes; Yes; 29075

8110;  Uienth-nezih, Tall Man; M; 29; Navajo; F; M; Head; 8126; Yes; Yes; 18154
8111;  Uienth-nezih's wife; F; 29; Navajo; F; M; Wife; 8127; Yes; Yes; 18155
8112;  Bah-yaz; F; 11; Navajo; F; S; Daughter; 8128; Yes; Yes; 18156
8113;  Uienth-nez, Paul; M; 9; Navajo; F; S; Son; 8129; Yes; Yes; 18157
8114;  Shay; F; 7; Navajo; F; S; Daughter; 8130; Yes; Yes; 18158
8115;  Tah-nih-bah; F; 4; Navajo; F; S; Daughter; 8131; Yes; Yes; 18159
8116;  Dah-yis-wudt; M; 2; Navajo; F; S; Son; 8132; Yes; Yes; 18238

8117;  Uintilli-bega; M; 29; Navajo; F; M; Head; 8133; Yes; Yes; 30604
8118;  Hah-tahly-bitsih; F; 22; Navajo; F; M; Wife; 8134; Yes; Yes; 30605
8119;  Al-nah-dez-bah; F; 5; Navajo; F; S; Daughter; 8135; Yes; Yes; 30606
8120;  Nah-tah-des-bah; F; 2; Navajo; F; S; Daughter; 8136; Yes; Yes; 30607

8121;  Uienth-Nez; M; 49; Navajo; F; M; Head; 8137; Yes; Yes; 21405
8122;  Uienth-Nez-bih-adzanih; F; 48; Navajo; F; M; Wife; 8138; Yes; Yes; 21406
8123;  Donald; M; 24; Navajo; F; S; Son; 8139;  Yes; Yes; 21407
8124;  Nah-tah-yil-nah-dalh; M; 22; Navajo; F; S; Son; 8140; Yes; Yes; 21408
8125;  Dorothy; F; 19; Navajo; F; S; Daughter; 8141; Yes; Yes; 21409
8126;  Baz-nih-bah; F; 17; Navajo; F; S; Daughter; 8142; Yes; Yes; 21410
8127;  Tahn-nih-des-hah; F; 15; Navajo; F; S; Daughter; 8143; Yes; Yes; 21411
8128;  Hoska-yah-deyah; M; 12; Navajo; F; S; Son; 8144; Yes; Yes; 21412
8129;  Hoska-tah-madzah; M; 8; Navajo; F; S; Son; 8145; Yes; Yes; 21413
8130;  Kay-hah-des-bah; F; 6; Navajo; F; S; Daughter; 8146; Yes; Yes; 21414
8131;  Zannie-bahih; F; 78; Navajo; F; Wd; Mother; 8147; Yes; Yes; 21415

8132;  Uienth-Nezih; M; Unk; Navajo; F; M; Head; 8148; Yes; Yes; 18190
8133;  Uienth-Nezih's wife; F; 43; Navajo; F; M; Wife; 8149; Yes; Yes; 18191
8134;  Yazzie; M; 9; Navajo; F; S; Son; 8150; Yes; Yes; 18192
8135;  Zannie-bah; F; 6; Navajo; F; S; Daughter; 8151; Yes; Yes; 18193

8136;  Uienth-Nezzi; M; 35; Navajo; F; M; Head; 8152; No; McElmo, Colo., San Juan, Utah; Yes; 19277

Census of the **Northern Navajo** reservation of the **Northern Navajo** jurisdiction, as of **April 1**, 19**31,** taken by **Ernest H. Hammond, District**, Superintendent. **in Charge**

**Key:** Number; NAME: Surname, Given; Sex; Birth Year (if given), Age At Last Birthday; Tribe; Degree of Blood; Marital Status; Relationship To Head of Family; Last Census Roll Number; At Jurisdiction Where Enrolled (Yes or No); At Another Jurisdiction; ELSEWHERE: Post office, County, State; Ward (Yes or No); Allotment, Annuity, and Identification Numbers.

8137; Nocki-chee-bitsih; F; 25; Navajo; F; M; Wife; 8153; No; McElmo, Colo., San Juan, Utah; Yes; 19278

8138; Ath-mah-gee-bah; F; 9; Navajo; F; S; Daughter; 8154; No; McElmo, Colo., San Juan, Utah; Yes; 19279

8139; Ath-nah-soe-bah; F; 7; Navajo; F; S; Daughter; 8155; No; McElmo, Colo., San Juan, Utah; Yes; 19280

8140; Nah-nas-bah; F; 3; Navajo; F; S; Daughter; 8156; No; McElmo, Colo., San Juan, Utah; Yes; 19281

8141; Uintilli-bega; M; 22; Navajo; F; M; Head; 8157; Yes; Yes; 25139

8142; Al-chih-hah-bah; F; 21; Navajo; F; M; Wife; 8158; Yes; Yes; 25140

8143; Nah-tah-yes-nas-wudt; M; 4; Navajo; F; S; Son; 8159; Yes; Yes; 25142

8144; Vicente; M; Unk; Navajo; F; M; Head; 8160; Yes; Yes; 30608

8145; Chih-chisih-benally; F; 31; Navajo; F; M; Wife; 8161; Yes; Yes; 30609

8146; Vicente-benally; M; Unk; Navajo; F; M; Head; 8162; Yes; Yes; 30494

8147; Vicente-benally-bih-adzan; F; 30; Navajo; F; M; Wife; 8163; Yes; Yes; 30495

8148; Kel-yil-nih-nih-bah; F; 7; Navajo; F; S; Daughter; 8164; Yes; Yes; 30496

8149; Haska-yee-nas-wudt; M; 13; Navajo; F; S; Nephew-in-law; 8165; Yes; Yes; 30499

8150; Warren, Dan; M; 24; Navajo; F; M; Head; 8166; Yes; Yes; 28309

8151; Nadine; F; 20; Navajo; F; M; Wife; 8167; Yes; Yes; 28310

8152; Luke's boy; M; 25; Navajo; F; S; Brother-in-law; 8168; Yes; Yes; 28311

8153; Nih-ziz-bah; F; 17; Navajo; F; S; Sister-in-law; 8169; Yes; Yes; 28312

8154; Tom Luke; M; 15; Navajo; F; S; Brother-in-law; 8170; Yes; Yes; 28313

8155; Fred Luke; M; 14; Navajo; F; S; Brother-in-law; 8171; Yes; Yes; 28314

8156; Sosie; M; 9; Navajo; F; S; Brother-in-law; 8172; Yes; Yes; 28315

8157; Warren, Benjamin; M; 1; Navajo; F; S; Son; 8173; Yes; Yes; 28544

8158; Waal-bitsih; M; 43; Navajo; F; Wd; Head; 8174; Yes; Yes; 17235

8159; Watchman, Lewis; M; 34; Navajo; F; M; Head; 8175; Yes; Yes; 25154

8160; Klizi-dal-cheeih-bega-bitsih; F; 28; Navajo; F; M; Wife; 8176; Yes; Yes; 25155

8161; Ben; M; 8; Navajo; F; S; Son; 8177; Yes; Yes; 25156

8162; Washburn Bega; M; 28; Navajo; F; M; Head; 8178; Yes; Yes; 23171

8163; Hosteen-ashihih-bitsih; F; 26; Navajo; F; M; Wife; 8179; Yes; Yes; 23172

8164; Washburn, Henry; M; 2; Navajo; F; S; Son; 8180; Yes; Yes; 23920

8165; Washburn- bega, Vernon; M; 29; Navajo; F; M; Head; 8181; Yes; Yes; 23596

Census of the **Northern Navajo** reservation of the **Northern Navajo** jurisdiction, as of **April 1**, 19**31,** taken by **Ernest H. Hammond, District**, Superintendent. **in Charge**

8166;  Washburn-bega's wife; F; Unk; Navajo; F; M; Wife; 8182; Yes; Yes; 23597
8167;  Navajo, John; M; Unk; Navajo; F; Wd; Father-in-law; 8183; Yes; Yes; 23598
8168;  Nora; F; 22; Navajo; F; S; Sister-in-law; 8184; Yes; Yes; 23921
8169;  Yazzie Brown; F; 20; Navajo; F; S; Sister-in-law; 8185; Yes; Yes; 23922


8170;  Washburn-bitsih; F; 18; Navajo; F; Wd; Head; 8186; Yes; Yes; 23165
8171;  Haska-yil-nih-nih-yah; F; 3; Navajo; F; S; Daughter; 8187; Yes; Yes; 23166


8172;  Washburn - bega; M; 35; Navajo; F; M; Head; 8188; Yes; Yes; 23395
8173;  Hosteen-ahtcitty-bitsih; F; 35; Navajo; F; M: Wife; 8189; Yes; Yes; 23396
8174;  Biz-nil-bah; F; 17; Navajo; F; S; Daughter; 8190;  Yes; Yes; 23397
8175;  Yee-naz-bah; F; 10; Navajo; F; S; Daughter; 8191; Yes; Yes; 23398
8176;  Yee-nah-gahl; M; 16; Navajo; F; S; Brother; 8192; Yes; Yes; 23399


8177;  Washburn; M; Unk; Navajo; F; M; Head; 8193; Yes; Yes; 23519
8178;  Nah-yil-mih-bah[sic]; F; 20; Navajo; F; M; Wife; 8194; Yes; Yes; 23520
       [Name should be Nah-yil-nih-bah]
8179;  Keh-yee-danih-bah; F; 3; Navajo; F; S; Daughter; 8195; Yes; Yes; 23521
8180;  Chih-hih-bah; F; 36; Navajo; F; S; Aunt-in-law; 8196; Yes; Yes; 23522


8181;  Washburn Bega; M; 29; Navajo; F; M; Head; 8197; Yes; Yes; 23485
8182;  Ah-keh-dee-bah; F; 23; Navajo; F; M; Wife; 8198; Yes; Yes; 23486
8183;  Haska-nah-tahl; M; 2; Navajo; F; S; Son; 8199; Yes; Yes; 23994


8184;  Washburn Bega; M; 26; Navajo; F; M; Head; 8200; Yes; Yes; 23400
8185;  Keh-yil-hah-bah; F; 20; Navajo; F; M; Wife; 8201; Yes; Yes; 23401


8186;  Washburn Bekis; M; Unk; Navajo; F; M; Head; 8202; Yes; Yes; 23167
8187;  Ah-hah-yee-bah; F; 48; Navajo; F; M; Wife; 8203; Yes; Yes; 23168
8188;  Haska-yee-a-zizih; M; 16; Navajo; F; S; Step-son; 8204; Yes; Yes; 23169
8189;  Haska-yil-nih-yah; M; 11; Navajo; F; S; Son; 8205; Yes; Yes; 23170


8190;  Washburn, Willis; M; 21; Navajo; F; M; Head; 8206; Yes; Yes; 30295
8191;  Al-naz-bah; F; 20; Navajo; F; M; Wife; 8207; Yes; Yes; 30296
8192;  Haska-yil-yil-wudt; M; 3; Navajo; F; S; Son; 8208; Yes; Yes; 30297


8193;  Wilson, Eldridge; M; Unk; Navajo; F; M; Head; 8209; Yes; Yes; 24706
8194;  Eldridge Wilson's wife; F; Unk; Navajo; F; M; Wife; 8210; Yes; Yes; 24707
8195;  Laura Lucy; F; 4; Navajo; F; S; Daughter; 8211; Yes; Yes; 24708
8196;  Dennison, Paul; M; Unk; Navajo; F; S; Step-son; 8212; Yes; Yes; 25297
8197;  Dennison, Esther; F; Unk; Navajo; F; S; Step-daughter; 8213; Yes; Yes; 25298


8198;  William, Frank; M; 26; Navajo; F; M; Head; 8214;  Yes; Yes; 29845

Census of the **Northern Navajo** reservation of the **Northern Navajo** jurisdiction, as of **April 1** , 19**31,** taken by **Ernest H. Hammond, District**, Superintendent. **in Charge**

**Key:** Number; NAME: Surname, Given; Sex; Birth Year (if given), Age At Last Birthday; Tribe; Degree of Blood; Marital Status; Relationship To Head of Family; Last Census Roll Number; At Jurisdiction Where Enrolled (Yes or No); At Another Jurisdiction; ELSEWHERE: Post office, County, State; Ward (Yes or No); Allotment, Annuity, and Identification Numbers.

8199; Esther; F; 18; Navajo; F; M; Wife; 8215; Yes; Yes; 29846

8200; Williams, Dudley; M; 57; Navajo; F; M; Head; 8216; Yes; Yes; 26396
8201; Nah-des-bah; F; 40; Navajo; F; M; Wife; 8217; Yes; Yes; 26397
8202; Williams, Laura; F; 11; Navajo; F; S; Daughter; 8218; Yes; Yes; 26398
8203; Yil-naz-bah; F; 10; Navajo; F; S; Daughter; 8219; Yes; Yes; 26401
8204; Haska-yee-nil-wudt; M; 6; Navajo; F; S; Son; 8220; Yes; Yes; 26402
8205; Paul; M; 4; Navajo; F; S; Son; 8221; Yes; Yes; 26403

8206; Wilson No-tah; M; 31; Navajo; F; M; Head; 8222; Yes; Yes; 26791

8207; Bah, Charles; F; 32; Navajo; F; M; Head; 8223; Yes; Yes; 26792
8208; John; M; 6; Navajo; F; S; Son; 8224; Yes; Yes; 26793
8209; Susie; F; 4; Navajo; F; S; Daughter; 8225; Yes; Yes; 26794
8210; Hosteen-skonihih-bih-adzan; F; 88; Navajo; F; Wd; Mother-in-law; 8226; Yes; Yes; 26796
8211; Nah-glih-yee-naz-bah; F; 9; Navajo; F; S; Daughter; 8227; Yes; Yes; 26795

8212; White, Lester; M; 29; Navajo; F; M; Head; 8228; Yes; Yes; 28053
8213; Bil-nih-ziz-bah; F; 21; Navajo; F; M; Wife; 8229; Yes; Yes; 28054
8214; Esther; F; 2; Navajo; F; S; Daughter; 8230; Yes; Yes; 28099

8215; Woodih; M; 54; Navajo; F; M; Head; 3231[sic]; Yes; Yes; 32384
              [Last Census Roll No. 8231]
8216; Dinay-chilli-bitsih; F; 50; Navajo; F; M; Wife; 3232[sic]; Yes; Yes; 32385
              [Last Census Roll No. 8232]
8217; Jane; F; 18; Navajo; F; S; Daughter; 8233; Yes; Yes; 32386
8218; Nah-bah; F; 14; Navajo; F; S; Daughter; 8234; Yes; Yes; 32387
8219; Nah-glih-yil-dez-bah; F; 10; Navajo; F; S; Daughter; 8235; Yes; Yes; 32388

8220; Woody, Charley; M; 33; Navajo; F; M; Head; 8236; Yes; Yes; 23468
8221; Yee-neh-bah; F; 29; Navajo; F; M; Wife; 8237; Yes; Yes; 23469
8222; Keh-hah-dez-bah; F; 10; Navajo; F; S; Daughter; 8238; Yes; Yes; 23470
8223; Naz-bah; F; Unk; Navajo; F; Wd; Mother-in-law; 8239; Yes; Yes; 23471
8224; Kee-chee; M; 13; Navajo; F; S; Brother-in-law; 8240; Yes; Yes; 23472

8225; Woody, Peter; M; 37; Navajo; F; M; Head; 8241; Yes; Yes; 30694
8226; Nita; F; 32; Navajo; F; M; Wife; 8242; Yes; Yes; 30695
8227; Tah-deyah; M; 32; Navajo; F; S; Brother; 8243; Yes; Yes; 30696
8228; Ben; M; 31; Navajo; F; S; Cousin; 8244; Yes; Yes; 30697
8229; Bessie; F; 10; Navajo; F; S; Niece; 8245; Yes; Yes; 17007

Census of the **Northern Navajo** reservation of the **Northern Navajo** jurisdiction, as of **April 1** , 1931, taken by **Ernest H. Hammond, District**, Superintendent. **in Charge**

Key: Number; NAME: Surname, Given; Sex; Birth Year (if given), Age At Last Birthday; Tribe; Degree of Blood; Marital Status; Relationship To Head of Family; Last Census Roll Number; At Jurisdiction Where Enrolled (Yes or No); At Another Jurisdiction; ELSEWHERE: Post office, County, State; Ward (Yes or No); Allotment, Annuity, and Identification Numbers.

8230; Yabeny[sic], Slim; M; 36; Navajo; F; M; Head; 8246; Yes; Yes; 28423
[Name should be Yabney, Slim]
8231; Uienth-nezzie-bih-dazih; F; 36; Navajo; F; M; Wife; 8247; Yes; Yes; 28424
8232; Helen; F; 22; Navajo; F; S; Step-daughter; 8248; Yes; Yes; 28425
8233; Seeih; M; 16; Navajo; F; S; Step-son; 8249; Yes; Yes; 28426
8234; Tah-zoaz-bah; F; 10; Navajo; F; S; Daughter; 8250; Yes; Yes; 28427
8235; Yah; M; 5; Navajo; F; S; Son; 8251; Yes; Yes; 28428
8236; Simon; M; 17; Navajo; F; S; Son; 8252; Yes; Yes; 28429

8237; Yabeny; M; Unk; Navajo; F; M; Head; 8253; Yes; Yes; 28445
[Name should be Yabney]
8238; Yabeny's wife; F; 64; Navajo; F; M; Wife; 8254; Yes; Yes; 28446
[Name should be Yabney's wife]
8239; Harriet; F; 20; Navajo; F; S; Grand-daughter; 8255; Yes; Yes; 28447
8240; Eva; F; 15; Navajo; F; S; Grand-daughter; 8256; Yes; Yes; 28448

8241; Yabeny-bega, Snoddy; M; Unk; Navajo; F; M; Head; 8257; Yes; Yes; 28449
[Name should be Yabney-bega, Snoddy]
8242; Yabeny-bega, Snoddy's wife; F; 35; Navajo; F; M; Wife; 8258; Yes; Yes;
28450 [Name should be Yabney-bega, Snoddy's wife]
8243; Atate-l-seesie; F; 9; Navajo; F; S; Daughter; 8259; Yes; Yes; 28451
8244; Neh; M; 7; Navajo; F; S; Son; 8260; Yes; Yes; 28452
8245; Bahih; M; 5; Navajo; F; S; Son; 8261; Yes; Yes; 28453
8246; Dez-bah; F; 2; Navajo; F; S; Daughter; 8262; Yes; Yes; 28454

8247; Yazzie, Franklin; M; 40; Navajo; F; M; Head; 8263; Yes; Yes; 26343
8248; Mamie; F; 39; Navajo; F; M; Wife; 8264; Yes; Yes; 26344
8249; James; M; 20; Navajo; F; S; Nephew; 8265; Yes; Yes; 26345
8250; Harry; M; 11; Navajo; F; S; Son; 8267; Yes; Yes; 26347
8251; Mary; F; 7; Navajo; F; S; Daughter; 8268; Yes; Yes; 26348
8252; Lucy; F; 4; Navajo; F; S; Daughter; 8269; Yes; Yes; 26349
8253; Frank; M; 3; Navajo; F; S; Son; 8270; Yes; Yes; 26350

8254; Yazzie, Ben; M; 44; Navajo; F; M; Head; 8271; Yes; Yes; 25982
8255; Bah; F; 31; Navajo; F; M; Wife; 8272; Yes; Yes; 25983
8256; Harley; M; 19; Navajo; F; S; Son; 8273; Yes; Yes; 25984
8257; Oh-dez-bah; F; 12; Navajo; F; S; Daughter; 8274; Yes; Yes; 25985
8258; Kee-soh; M; 7; Navajo; F; S; Son; 8275; Yes; Yes; 25986
8259; Yaz; M; 5; Navajo; F; S; Son; 8276; Yes; Yes; 25987
8260; Samuel; M; 3; Navajo; F; S; Son; 8277; Yes; Yes; 25988

8261; Yazzie, Harding H.; M; 24; Navajo; F; M; Head; 8278; Yes; Yes; 23543
8262; Elsie; F; Unk; Navajo; F; M; Wife; 8279; Yes; Yes; 23544

Census of the **Northern Navajo** reservation of the **Northern Navajo** jurisdiction, as of **April 1**, 19**31,** taken by **Ernest H. Hammond, District**, Superintendent. **in Charge**

**Key:** Number; NAME: Surname, Given; Sex; Birth Year (if given), Age At Last Birthday; Tribe; Degree of Blood; Marital Status; Relationship To Head of Family; Last Census Roll Number; At Jurisdiction Where Enrolled (Yes or No); At Another Jurisdiction; ELSEWHERE: Post office, County, State; Ward (Yes or No); Allotment, Annuity, and Identification Numbers.

8263; Yabury[sic], John; M; Unk; Navajo; F; Wd; Head; 8280; Yes; Yes; 29195 [Name is probably Yabney, John]

8264; Yazzie, Dinay; M; 60; Navajo; F; Wd; Head; 8281; Yes; Yes; 29171
8265; Yih-kih-das-wudt; M; 17; Navajo; F; S; Son; 8283; Yes; Yes; 29173
8266; Kih-doz-bah; F; 7; Navajo; F; S; Daughter; 8284; Yes; Yes; 29174
8267; Yah-he; M; 6; Navajo; F; S; Son; 8285; Yes; Yes; 29175

8268; Yazzie, David; M; Unk; Navajo; F; M; Head; 8286; Yes; Yes; 29145
8269; Hah-naz-bah; F; 18; Navajo; F; M; Wife; 8287; Yes; Yes; 29146

8270; Yabney-bitcilli-bega; M; 30; Navajo; F; M; Head; 8288; Yes; Yes; 29885
8271; Yah-hah-nih-bah; F; 27; Navajo; F; M; Wife; 8289; Yes; Yes; 29886
8272; Hah-ziz-bah; F; 10; Navajo; F; S; Daughter; 8290; Yes; Yes; 29887
8273; Glih-haz-bah; F; 8; Navajo; F; S; Daughter; 8291; Yes; Yes; 29888
8274; Nah-nih-bah; F; 6; Navajo; F; S; Daughter; 8292; Yes; Yes; 29889

8275; Yabeny-bitcilli-bega; M; 32; Navajo; F; M; Head; 8293; Yes; Yes; 29890 [Name is probably Yabney-bitcilli-bega]
8276; Hah-bah; F; 21; Navajo; F; M; Wife; 8294; Yes; Yes; 29891
8277; Yee-tah-nih-bah; F; 3; Navajo; F; S; Daughter; 8295; Yes; Yes; 29892
8278; Mamie; F; 17; Navajo; F; S; Sister; 8296; Yes; Yes; 29893
8279; Clyde; M; 14; Navajo; F; S; Brother; 8297; Yes; Yes; 29894
8280; Haska-yil-hah-wudt; M; 12; Navajo; F; S; Brother; 8298; Yes; Yes; 29895

8281; Yabney-bitcilli, bega, Roy; M; 34; Navajo; F; M; Head; 8299; Yes; Yes; 29896
8282; Baz-nih-bah; F; 26; Navajo; F; M; Wife; 8300; Yes; Yes; 29897
8283; Ah-hih-bah; F; 7; Navajo; F; S; Daughter; 8301; Yes; Yes; 29898
8284; Yil-naz-bah; F; 3; Navajo; F; S; Daughter; 8302; Yes; Yes; 29899

8285; Yah-hah-tahly-bitsih; F; 53; Navajo; F; Wd; Head; 8303; Yes; Yes; 21126
8286; Aht-citty; M; 30; Navajo; F; S; Son; Yes; Yes; 21127
8287; Dinay-ye-is-kinih, Fildin; M; 11; Navajo; F; S; Son; Yes; Yes; 21128
8288; Adzan-l-gaih-yazzie; F; 9; Navajo; F; S; Daughter; Yes; Yes; 21129
8289; Ah-kahn-bah; F; 17; Navajo; F; S; Daughter; Yes; Yes; 21130
8290; Hah-nah-bah; F; 2; Navajo; F; S; Grand-daughter; Yes; Yes; 21131

8291; Dinay-Chilly-bega, Pretty; Head of Family listed with 'd's". 6751
8292; Yee-kih-dez-bah[sic], Lydia; F; 11; Navajo; F; S; Daughter; 6752; Yes; Yes; 32458 [Name could be Kee-kih-dez-bah]
8293; Haska-yee-tah-nil-wudt; M; 9; Navajo; F; S; Son; 6753; Yes; Yes; 32459
8294; Dah-naz-bah; F; 7; Navajo; F; S; Daughter; 6754; Yes; Yes; 32460

Census of the **Northern Navajo** reservation of the **Northern Navajo** jurisdiction, as of **April 1**, 19**31,** taken by **Ernest H. Hammond, District**, Superintendent. **in Charge**

**Key:** Number; NAME: Surname, Given; Sex; Birth Year (if given), Age At Last Birthday; Tribe; Degree of Blood; Marital Status; Relationship To Head of Family; Last Census Roll Number; At Jurisdiction Where Enrolled (Yes or No); At Another Jurisdiction; ELSEWHERE: Post office, County, State; Ward (Yes or No); Allotment, Annuity, and Identification Numbers.

8295; Cheh-naz-bah; F; 4; Navajo; F; S; Daughter; 6755; Yes; Yes; 32461

8296; Yee-thlohi-bitcilli; M; 25; Navajo; F; M; Head; 8309; Yes; Yes; 28070
8297; Nah-glih-l-bahih; F; 20; Navajo; F; M; Wife; 8310; Yes; Yes; 28071
8298; Keh-hah-nih-bah; F; 4; Navajo; F; S; Daughter; 8311; Yes; Yes; 28072
8299; Baby; F; 2; Navajo; F; S; Daughter; 8312; Yes; Yes; 28073

8300; Yellow Hair Bega; M; 24; Navajo; F; M; Head; 8313; Yes; Yes; 31069
8301; Klizi-Thani-benally; F; 20; Navajo; F; M; Wife; 8314; Yes; Yes; 31070
8302; Nell; F; 2; Navajo; F; S; Daughter; 8315; Yes; Yes; 31251

8303; Yis-clehih-yen-bega; M; 58; Navajo; F; M; Head; 8316; Yes; Yes; 23352
8304; Bah; F; 41; Navajo; F; M; Wife; 8317; Yes; Yes; 23353
8305; Tahn-des-bah; F; 23; Navajo; F; S; Daughter; 8318; Yes; Yes; 23354
8306; Hah-tah-yee-chih-nil-wudt; M; 20; Navajo; F; S; Son; 8319; Yes; Yes; 23355
8307; Albert; M; 17; Navajo; F; S; Son; 8320; Yes; Yes; 23356
8308; Ambrose; M; 15; Navajo; F; S; Son; 8321; Yes; Yes; 23357
8309; Olive; F; 12; Navajo; F; S; Daughter; 8322; Yes; Yes; 23358
8310; Keh-hah-nih-bahih; F; 7; Navajo; F; S; Daughter; 8323; Yes; Yes; 23359
8311; Nah-tah-yee-chih-has-wudt; M; 6; Navajo; F; S; Son; 8324; Yes; Yes; 23360
8312; Alice; F; 25; Navajo; F; S; Niece; 8325; Yes; Yes; 23361

8313; Yis-clay-ih-benally; M; 28; Navajo; F; M; Head; 8326; Yes; Yes; 24798
8314; Kih-dez-bah; F; 24; Navajo; F; M; Wife; 8327; Yes; Yes; 24799

8315; Yis-clay-yen-benally; M; Unk; Navajo; F; M; Head; 8328; Yes; Yes; 23722
8316; Dinay-l-suen-bitsih; F; 43; Navajo; F; M; Wife; 8329; Yes; Yes; 23723
8317; Imogene; F; 22; Navajo; F; S; Step-daughter; 8330; Yes; Yes; 23724
8318; See-codih, Ella; F; 18; Navajo; F; S; Step-daughter; 8331; Yes; Yes; 23725
8319; Anita; F; 9; Navajo; F; S; Daughter; 8332; Yes; Yes; 23726
8320; Al-soh-naz-bah; F; 6; Navajo; F; S; Daughter; 8333; Yes; Yes; 23727
8321; Keh-yee-kid-dah-yis-bah; F; 2; Navajo; F; S; Daughter; 8334; Yes; Yes; 23728

8322; Yil-dez-bah; F; 19; Navajo; F; Wd; Head; 8335; Yes; Yes; 23508

8323; Yoh-hah-tahly, Tyler; M; 31; Navajo; F; M; Head; 8336; Yes; Yes; 23403
8324; Bih-zoh-nih-bitsih; F; 29; Navajo; F; M; Wife; 8337; Yes; Yes; 23404
8325; Nap-des-bah[sic]; F; 9; Navajo; F; S; Daughter; 8338; Yes; Yes; 23405
[Name could be Na-des-bah]
8326; Haska-yee-cha-nee-nih-yah; M; 6; Navajo; F; S; Son; 8339; Yes; Yes; 23406
8327; Haska-yee-cha-nil-wudt; M; 4; Navajo; F; S; Son; 8340; Yes; Yes; 23407
8328; Myrtle; F; 2; Navajo; F; S; Daughter; 8341; Yes; Yes; 23880
8329; Yah-hah-tahly, Tyler; F; 1; Navajo; F; S; Daughter; 8342; Yes; Yes; 23967

Census of the **Northern Navajo** reservation of the **Northern Navajo** jurisdiction, as of **April 1**, 19**31**, taken by **Ernest H. Hammond, District**, Superintendent. **in Charge**

**Key:** Number; NAME: Surname, Given; Sex; Birth Year (if given), Age At Last Birthday; Tribe; Degree of Blood; Marital Status; Relationship To Head of Family; Last Census Roll Number; At Jurisdiction Where Enrolled (Yes or No); At Another Jurisdiction; ELSEWHERE: Post office, County, State; Ward (Yes or No); Allotment, Annuity, and Identification Numbers.

8330; Yoh-hah-tahly-bega; M; 43; Navajo; F; S; Head; 8343; Yes; Yes; 23421

8331; Yoh-hah-tahly-bega; M; 22; Navajo; F; M; Head; 8344; Yes; Yes; 23408
8332; Biz-nih-bah; F; 20; Navajo; F; M; Wife; 8345; Yes; Yes; 23409
8333; Haska-yil-nih-dee-zah; F; 3; Navajo; F; S; Daughter; 8346; Yes; Yes; 23410

8334; Yoh-hah-tahly-bega; M; 33; Navajo; F; M; Head; 8347; Yes; Yes; 22434
8335; Nah-glih-yee-nas-bah; F; 27; Navajo; F; M; Wife; 8348; Yes; Yes; 22435
8336; Dah-dee-bah; F; 11; Navajo; F; S; Daughter; 8349; Yes; Yes; 22436
8337; Yohn-ni-nih-bah; F; 9; Navajo; F; S; Daughter; 8350; Yes; Yes; 22437
8338; Yee-kih-dah-yis-bah; F; 7; Navajo; F; S; Daughter; 8351; Yes; Yes; 22438
8339; Nah-tah-hah-deyah; M; 5; Navajo; F; S; Son; 8352; Yes; Yes; 22439

8340; Yoh-hoh-tahly-sosie-bih-adzan; F; 53; Navajo; F; Wd; Head; 8353; Yes; Yes; 22712
8341; Yoh-hah-tahly-sosie-bega; M; 36; Navajo; F; S; Son; 8354; Yes; Yes; 22713
8342; Haska-yil-nih-des-zah; M; 12; Navajo; F; S; Son; 8355; Yes; Yes; 22714
8343; Sam; M; 11; Navajo; F; S; Grand-son; 8356; Yes; Yes; 22715
8344; Ah-keh-dee-bah; F; 8; Navajo; F; S; Grand-daughter; 8357; Yes; Yes; 22716

8345; Yoh-hon-tohly; M; 43; Navajo; F; M; Head; 8114; Yes; Yes; 21649
8346; To-glena-bitsih; F; 36; Navajo; F; M; Wife; 8115; Yes; Yes; 21650
8347; Wi-na-no-ga; M; 12; Navajo; F; S; Son; 8116; Yes; Yes; 21651
8348; Yi-ned-ba; F; 10; Navajo; F; S; Daughter; 8117; Yes; Yes; 21652
8349; Ah-kee-bai; F; 8; Navajo; F; S; Daughter; 8118; Yes; Yes; 21653
8350; Yom-des-bah; F; 7; Navajo; F; S; Daughter; 8119; Yes; Yes; 21654
8351; Al-onba; F; 6; Navajo; F; S; Daughter; 8120; Yes; Yes; 21655
8352; Al-kin-bah; F; 5; Navajo; F; S; Daughter; 8121; Yes; Yes; 21656
8353; Toh-hoh-nal-bah; F; 2; Navajo; F; S; Daughter; 8122; Yes; Yes; 21657
8354; Ason-toh-de-chi-he; F; 76; Navajo; F; Wd; Grand- Mother-in-law; 8123; Yes; Yes; 21658

8355; Yoh-nil-chinnih-badoni; M; 59; Navajo; F; M; Head; 8358; Yes; Yes; 25210
8356; Yoh-yil-chinnih-bitsih; F; 52; Navajo; F; M; Wife; 8359; Yes; Yes; 25211
8357; Foster, Elsie; F; 29; Navajo; F; S; Daughter; 8360; Yes; Yes; 25212
8358; Foster, Donald; M; 28; Navajo; F; S; Son; 8361; Yes; Yes; 25213
8359; Foster, Opal; F; 26; Navajo; F; S; Daughter; 8362; Yes; Yes; 25214
8360; Foster, Ned; M; 24; Navajo; F; S; Daughter[sic]; 8363; Yes; Yes; 25215
8361; Foster, Bessie; F; 22; Navajo; F; S; Daughter; 8364; Yes; Yes; 25216
8362; Foster, Kenneth; M; 20; Navajo; F; S; Son; 8365; Yes; Yes; 25217
8363; Hahn-nih-bahih; F; 18; Navajo; F; S; Daughter; 8366; Yes; Yes; 25218
8364; Foster, Edward; M; 14; Navajo; F; S; Son; 8367; Yes; Yes; 25219
8365; Foster, Dick; M; 12; Navajo; F; S; Son; 8368; Yes; Yes; 25220

Census of the **Northern Navajo** reservation of the **Northern Navajo** jurisdiction, as of **April 1**, 19**31,** taken by **Ernest H. Hammond, District**, Superintendent. **in Charge**

Key: Number; NAME: Surname, Given; Sex; Birth Year (if given), Age At Last Birthday; Tribe; Degree of Blood; Marital Status; Relationship To Head of Family; Last Census Roll Number; At Jurisdiction Where Enrolled (Yes or No); At Another Jurisdiction; ELSEWHERE: Post office, County, State; Ward (Yes or No); Allotment, Annuity, and Identification Numbers.

8366; Foster, Lillian; F; 10; Navajo; F; S; Daughter; 8369; Yes; Yes; 25221
8367; Foster, Sadie; F; 8; Navajo; F; S; Daughter; 8370; Yes; Yes; 25222
8368; Glih-nih-bah; F; 6; Navajo; F; S; Daughter; 8371; Yes; Yes; 25223
8369; Hah-zoz-bah; F; 4; Navajo; F; S; Daughter; 8372; Yes; Yes; 25224

8370; Yoh-nil-chinnih-yen-bega; M; Unk; Navajo; F; M; Head; 8373; Yes; Yes; 25137
8371; Bil-kih-ziz-bah; F; 39; Navajo; F; M; Wife; 8374; Yes; Yes; 25138

8372; Yo-oh-sosie; M; 44; Navajo; F; M; Head; 7930; No; McElmo, Colo., San Juan, Utah; Yes; 18838
8373; Yo-oh-sosie's wife; F; 28; Navajo; F; M; Wife; 7931; No; McElmo, Colo., San Juan, Utah; Yes; 18839
8374; Whe-ah-kee; M; 10; Navajo; F; S; Son; 7932; No; McElmo, Colo., San Juan, Utah; Yes; 18840
8375; Natah-yee-nal-wolth; M; 7; Navajo; F; S; Son; 7933; No; McElmo, Colo., San Juan, Utah; Yes; 18841
8376; Glih-yilth-nih-bah; F; 6; Navajo; F; S; Daughter; 7934; No; McElmo, Colo., San Juan, Utah; Yes; 18842
8377; Natah-yee-chee-des-wudt; M; 3; Navajo; F; S; Son; 7935; No; McElmo, Colo., San Juan, Utah; Yes; 18843

8378; Yee-thlohi; M; 38; Navajo; F; M; Head; 8375; Yes; Yes; 18073
8379; Yee-thlohi's wife; F; 61; Navajo; F; M; Wife; 8376; Yes; Yes; 18074
8380; Yee-thlohi, Edith; F; 16; Navajo; F; S; Daughter; 8377; Yes; Yes; 18075
8381; Yee-thlohi, Jess; F[sic]; 14; Navajo; F; S; Nephew; 8378; Yes; Yes; 18076
8382; Adzan-ih-Chee; F; 13; Navajo; F; S; Niece; 8379; Yes; Yes; 18077
8383; Yee-thlohi, Otwell; M; 9; Navajo; F; S; Nephew; 8380; Yes; Yes; 18078

8384; Yoh-hah-tahly; M; 86; Navajo; F; M; Head; 8381; Yes; Yes; 21509
8385; Yoh-hah-tahly's wife; F; 64; Navajo; F; M; Wife; 8382; Yes; Yes; 21510

8386; Zil-tah-tah-hih; M; 62; Navajo; F; M; Head; 8383; Yes; Yes; 20159
8387; Adzan-la-bah; F; 28; Navajo; F; M; Wife; 8384; Yes; Yes; 20160
8388; Tah-deyah; M; 13; Navajo; F; S; Son; 8385; Yes; Yes; 20161
8389; Tahn-des-bah; F; 11; Navajo; F; S; Daughter; 8386; Yes; Yes; 20162
8390; Batoni; M; 8; Navajo; F; S; Son; 8387; Yes; Yes; 20163
8391; Bah-hih; M; 5; Navajo; F; S; Son; 8388; Yes; Yes; 20164
8392; Billy; M; 2; Navajo; F; S; Son; 8389; Yes; Yes; 20402

8393; Zah-nez-la-chee-bega-bih-adzan; F; 47; Navajo; F; Wd; Head; 8390; Yes; Yes; 32923
8394; Bowen, Charley; M; 30; Navajo; F; S; Son; 8391; Yes; Yes; 32924

Census of the __Northern Navajo__ reservation of the __Northern Navajo__ jurisdiction, as of __April 1__, 1931, taken by __Ernest H. Hammond, District__, Superintendent. **in Charge**

**Key:** Number; NAME: Surname, Given; Sex; Birth Year (if given), Age At Last Birthday; Tribe; Degree of Blood; Marital Status; Relationship To Head of Family; Last Census Roll Number; At Jurisdiction Where Enrolled (Yes or No); At Another Jurisdiction; ELSEWHERE: Post office, County, State; Ward (Yes or No); Allotment, Annuity, and Identification Numbers.

8395; Jim; M; 22; Navajo; F; S; Son; 8392; Yes; Yes; 32925
8396; Yil-nez-bah; F; 19; Navajo; F; S; Daughter; 8393; Yes; Yes; 32926
8397; Glih-hah-nih-bah; F; 15; Navajo; F; S; Daughter; 8394; Yes; Yes; 32927
8398; Glih-hah-bah; F; 13; Navajo; F; S; Daughter; 8395; Yes; Yes; 32928
8399; Haska-yil-hah-yah; M; 9; Navajo; F; S; Son; 8396; Yes; Yes; 32929
8400; Nah-tah-yee-chih-has-wudt; M; 17; Navajo; F; S; Son; 8397; Yes; Yes; 32930

8401; Zah-nez-bitsih-adzanih; F; 35; Navajo; F; Wd.; Head; 8398; Yes; Yes; 31126
8402; Yil-nih-bah; F; 5; Navajo; F; S; Daughter; 8399; Yes; Yes; 31127
8403; Yabury-bitcilli's wife[sic]; F; 32; Navajo; F; Wd; Sister; 8400; Yes; Yes; 31128
[Name is probably Yabney-bitcilli's wife]
8404; Woodrow Nelson; F[sic]; 29; Navajo; F; S; Brother; 8401; Yes; Yes; 31129
8405; Keh-yil-nih-bah; F; 26; Navajo; F; S; Sister; 8402; Yes; Yes; 31130
8406; Haska-yil-hah-deel; M; 24; Navajo; F; S; Son; 8404; Yes; Yes; 31131
8407; Dah-yil-wohl; M; 15; Navajo; F; S; Son; 8403; Yes; Yes; 31132
8408; Dah-hiz-bah; F; 13; Navajo; F; S; Daughter; 8405; Yes; Yes; 31133

8409; Zah-nez-badoni; M; Unk; Navajo; F; M; Head; 8406; Yes; Yes; 30746
8410; Zah-nez-bitsih; F; 47; Navajo; F; M; Wife; 8407; Yes; Yes; 30747
8411; Haska-yah-hah-zah; M; 14; Navajo; F; S; Son; 8408; Yes; Yes; 30748
8412; Naz-bah; F; 10; Navajo; F; S; Daughter; 8409; Yes; Yes; 30750
8413; Charley, Sarah; F; 19; Navajo; F; S; Daughter; 8410; Yes; Yes; 30752
8414; Charley, Stella; F; 12; Navajo; F; S; Daughter; 8411; Yes; Yes; 30753

# CENSUS OF THE

# NAVAJO

# NAVAJO RESERVATION

# NEW MEXICO

as of April 1, 1931,

Taken by Ernest H. Hammond, District Superintendent in Charge.

## "ADDITIONS"

Census of the __Navajo__ reservation of the __Northern Navajo__ jurisdiction, as of __April 1__, 1931, taken by __Ernest H. Hammond, District__, Superintendent. __"Additions"__ in Charge

**Key:** Number; NAME: Surname, Given; Sex; Age At Last Birthday; Tribe; Degree of Blood; Marital Status; Relationship To Head of Family; 1931 Census Roll Number; At Jurisdiction Where Enrolled (Yes or No); At Another Jurisdiction; ELSEWHERE: Post office, County, State; Ward (Yes or No); Allotment, Annuity, and Identification Numbers.

1; Binh-bih-tohnih-bega, Mary; F; 1; Navajo; F; S; Daughter; 1036; Yes; Yes; 28552

2; Denah Tuli; M; 13; Navajo; F; S; Son; 196; Yes; Yes; 17415

3; Kay-hahoz-bah; F; 1; Navajo; F; S; Daughter; 1981; Yes; Yes; 28559

4; Hosteen-yazzie-bega, Lee Joe; M; 25; Navajo; F; M; Head; 4142; Yes; Yes; 20175

5; Toh-ah-K-glin-nih-bitsih; F; 22; Navajo; F; M; Wife; 4143; Yes; Yes; 20176

6; Yazzie, Sarah; F; 4; Navajo; F; S; Daughter; 4144; Yes; Yes; 20177

7; Seesih; F; 6; Navajo; F; S; Daughter; 8023; Yes; Yes; 29705

8; Tuly-soh; M; Unk; Navajo; F; M; 8024; Yes; Yes; 22691

9; Emma; F; 38; Navajo; F; M; Wife; 8025; Yes; Yes; 22692

10; Mary Louise; F; 11; Navajo; F; S; Daughter; 8026; Yes; Yes; 22693

11; Harold; M; 8; Navajo; F; S; Son; 8027; Yes; Yes; 22694

12; Anna May; F; 6; Navajo; F; S; Daughter; 8028; Yes; Yes; 22695

13; Esther Helen; F; 4; Navajo; F; S; Daughter; 8029; Yes; Yes; 22696

14; Marjorie; F; Unk; Navajo; F; S; Daughter; 8030; Yes; Yes; 22749

15; Hoska-yil-des-wudt; M; 8; Navajo; F; S; Son; 3834; Yes; Yes; 30378

16; Scott, Ruth; F; 4; Navajo; F; S; Daughter; 6933; Yes; Yes; 25958

17; Topah-ah-hosteen bitsih; F; 61; Navajo; F; Wd; Head; 8105; Yes; Yes; 29026

18; Agnes; F; 22; Navajo; F; S; Son[sic]; 8106; Yes; Yes; 29027

19; Nah-nih-bah; F; 20; Navajo; F; S; Daughter; 8107; Yes; Yes; 29028

# CENSUS OF THE

# NAVAJO

# NAVAJO RESERVATION

# NEW MEXICO

as of April 1, 1931,

Taken by Ernest H. Hammond, District Superintendent in Charge.

## "BIRTHS"

Census of the___**Navajo**___reservation of the___**Northern Navajo**___jurisdiction, as of___**April 1**___, 19**31,** taken by___**Ernest H. Hammond, District**___, Superintendent.　　　　**"BIRTHS"**

**Key:** Number; NAME: Surname, Given; Sex; Age At Last Birthday; Tribe; Degree of Blood; Marital Status; Relationship To Head of Family; 1931 Census Roll Number; At Jurisdiction Where Enrolled (Yes or No); At Another Jurisdiction; ELSEWHERE: Post office, County, State; Ward (Yes or No); Allotment, Annuity, and Identification Numbers.

1;　Ahtcity-bega, Big Ezyraht; M; 1; Navajo; F; S; Son; 191; Yes; Yes; 17417

2;　Kits-Wood; F; 1; Navajo; F; S; Grand-daughter; 192; Yes; Yes; 17416

3;　Wezbah; F; 1; Navajo; F; S; Daughter; 1112; Yes; Yes; 17418

4;　Bah Taihe; F; 1; Navajo; F; S; Daughter; 1172; Yes; Yes; 18301

5;　Hoskey Logai; M; 2/12; Navajo; F; S; Son; 1373; Yes; Yes; 24011

6;　Deswoody; M; 1; Navajo; F; S; Son; 2054; Yes; Yes; 25344

7;　Patrick, Kenneth; M; 3/12; Navajo; F; S; Son; 6655; Yes; Yes; 31298

8;　Denet-clah, Marian; F; 7/12; Navajo; F; S; Daughter; 3203; Yes; Yes; 22796

9;　Askee Tully; M; 1; Navajo; F; S; Son; 4214; Yes; Yes; 17420

10;　Deel, Joe; M; 5/12; Navajo; F; S; Son; 4724; Yes; Yes; 25345

11;　Tsi-Tse; Unk; 1; Navajo; F; S; Unk; 5028; Yes; Yes; 17421

12;　Young, William Henry; M; 6/12; Navajo; 1/4; S; Son; 5264; Yes; Yes; 18616

13;　Johnson, Martha Rosie; F; 6/12; Navajo; F; S; Daughter; 5275; Yes; Yes; 25346

14;　Harvey, Ray; M; 6/12; Navajo; F; S; Grand son; 6324; Yes; Yes; 31295

15;　Sells, Vera Mae; F; 5/12; Navajo; F; S; Daughter; 6947; Yes; Yes; 31296

16;　Utso; Unk; 2; Navajo; F; S; Unk; 7641; Yes; Yes; 17422

17;　Ket Sosie; Unk; 1; Navajo; F; S; Unk; 7642; Yes; Yes; 17423

18;　Toh-dih-cheeny, Mary Francis; F; 6/12; Navajo; F; S; Daughter; 7672; Yes; Yes; 31297

# CENSUS OF THE

# NAVAJO

# NAVAJO RESERVATION

# NEW MEXICO

as of April 1, 1931,

Taken by Ernest H. Hammond, District Superintendent in Charge.

## "DEATHS"

Census of the __Navajo__ reservation of the __Northern Navajo__ jurisdiction, as of __April 1__, 19**31,** taken by __Ernest H. Hammond, District__, Superintendent. **DEATHS** in **Charge**

**Key:** Number; NAME: Surname, Given; Sex; Age At Last Birthday; Tribe; Degree of Blood; Marital Status; Relationship To Head of Family; Last Census Roll Number; At Jurisdiction Where Enrolled (Yes or No); At Another Jurisdiction; ELSEWHERE: Post office, County, State; Ward (Yes or No); Allotment, Annuity, and Identification Numbers.

1; Hah-gee-bah; F; 5; Navajo; F; S; Daughter; 276; Yes; Yes; 26029
2; Martha; F; 28; Navajo; F; M; Wife; 554; Yes; Yes; 30677
3; Ziz-bah; F; 4; Navajo; F; S; Daughter; 898; Yes; Yes; 20056
4; Haska-yil-nah-gah; M; 18; Navajo; F; S; Son; 1029; Yes; Yes; 27540
5; Bah-tohl; F; 87; Navajo; F; Wd; Mother-in-law; 1031; Yes; Yes; 27542
6; Bah-ahzonih-kin-lachee-nih; M; 13; Navajo; F; S; Son; 1118; Yes; Yes; 17217
7; Bitsee-lagaih-bega; M; 49; Navajo; F; M;; Head; 1194; Yes; Yes; 26404
8; Beleen-thlani-benally; M; Unk; Navajo; F; M; Head; 1251; Yes; Yes; 26977
9; Wilson; M; 2; Navajo; F; S; Son; 1593; Yes; Yes; 22779
10; Haska-yil-chil-wudt; M; 2; Navajo; F; S; 2261; Yes; Yes; 30980
11; Nelson Lewis; M; 24; Navajo; F; S; Son; 2939; Yes; Yes; 30355
12; Yil-nih-dez-bah; F; 5; Navajo; F; S; Daughter; 3130; Yes; Yes; 23438
13; Beleen-lizin-benally; F; 20; Navajo; F; M; Wife; 3132; Yes; Yes; 18249
14; Haska, Julian; M; 31; Navajo; F; S; Son; 3349; Yes; Yes; 28350
15; Nah-tah-yil-chin-yah; M; 10; Navajo; F; S; Son; 3758; Yes; Yes; 23781
16; Hoska-yee-seel; M; 24; Navajo; F; S; Son; 3767; Yes; Yes; 22407
17; Hosteen-ah-banih; M; 61; Navajo; F; M; Head; 3859; Yes; Yes; 30382
18; Hosteen Clitsoh-Bega-Atatl-pahih; F; 3; Navajo; F; S; Daughter; 4223; Yes; Yes; 17210
19; Yahn-nah-bah; F; 4; Navajo; F; S; Daughter; 4296; Yes; Yes; 23307
20; Haska-yil-yah; M; 9; Navajo; F; S; Son; 4579; Yes; Yes; 26876
21; Hosteen-bitsee-lagaih-bega; M; 36; Navajo; F; M; Head; 5032; Yes; Yes; 19910
22; Inky-tohsonih-bega; M; 32; Navajo; F; M; 5227; Yes; Yes; 17862
23; Johnson, Margaret; F; 1; Navajo; F; S; Daughter; 5306; Yes; Yes; 31030
24; Natae-Keswudt; M; 4/12; Navajo; F; S; Son; 5675; Yes; Yes; 20412
25; Haska-yil-ol-wudt; M; 4; Navajo; F; S; Son; 5858; Yes; Yes; 29316
26; Yil-hah-bah; F; 11; Navajo; F; S; Daughter; 5970; Yes; Yes; 21253
27; Nocki-yazzie; M; 54; Navajo; F; M; Head; 6331; Yes; Yes; 30326
28; Ath-kee-gee-bah; F; 4; Navajo; F; S; Daughter; 6436; Yes; Yes; 17994
29; Sandoval-benally; M; 26; Navajo; F; M; Head; 6796; Yes; Yes; 30489
30; Bimah, John; F; 40; Navajo; F; M; Wife; 7668; Yes; Yes; 25933
31; Adzan-l-bahih; F; 16; Navajo; F; S; Daughter; 7939; Yes; Yes; 19804
32; Yil-dez-bah; F; 2; Navajo; F; S; Daughter; 8060; Yes; Yes; 19835
33; Yazzie, Philip; M; 13; Navajo; F; S; Nephew; 8266; Yes; Yes; 26346
34; Dinay-yazzie's wife; F; 52; Navajo; F; M; Wife; 8282; Yes; Yes; 29172

# CENSUS OF THE

# NAVAJO

# NAVAJO RESERVATION

# NEW MEXICO

**1931 Census Recapitulation Sheet**

# UNITED STATES DEPARTMENT OF THE INTERIOR
## OFFICE OF INDIAN AFFAIRS

NORTHERN NAVAJO AGENCY
SHIPROCK, NEW MEXICO

### II. CENSUS RECAPITULATION SHEET

| AGE GROUP | MIXED BLOOD Total Male | Female | Total | FULL BLOOD (Degree of Blood) Total | Male | Female | TOTAL Total | Male | Female |
|---|---|---|---|---|---|---|---|---|---|
| Under one Year | | | | 117 | 49 | 68 | 117 | 49 | 68 |
| 1 to 5 yrs. | | | | 1126 | 481 | 645 | 1126 | 481 | 645 |
| 4 to 9 " | | | | 1587 | 851 | 736 | 1587 | 851 | 736 |
| 10 to 19 " | | | | 1895 | 920 | 975 | 1895 | 920 | 975 |
| 20 to 29 " | | | | 1297 | 702 | 595 | 1297 | 702 | 595 |
| 30 to 39 " | | | | 719 | 366 | 353 | 719 | 366 | 353 |
| 30 to 49 " | | | | 416 | 217 | 199 | 416 | 217 | 199 |
| 40 to 59 " | | | | 347 | 167 | 180 | 347 | 167 | 180 |
| 50 to 59 " | | | | 146 | 89 | 57 | 146 | 89 | 57 |
| 60 to 69 " | | | | 97 | 34 | 63 | 97 | 34 | 63 |
| 70 to 79 " | | | | 45 | 21 | 24 | 45 | 21 | 24 |
| 80 to 89 " | | | | 11 | 8 | 3 | 11 | 8 | 3 |
| 90 to Over | | | | | | | | | |
| Unknown | | | | 416 | 234 | 82 | 416 | 334 | 182 |
| TOTAL | | | | 8219 | 4239 | 3980 | 8219 | 4239 | 3980 |

# Research Books

Bailey, L. R., *The Long Walk A History of the Navajo Wars, 1846-68*, Westernlore Press, Copyright 1964.

Bailey, Lynn R., *Bosque Redondo The Navajo Internment at Fort Sumner, New Mexico, 1863-68*, Westernlore Press, Copyright 1998.

Denetdale, Jennifer, *The Long Walk The Forced Navajo Exile*, Chelsea House Publishers, Copyright 2008, 2008 by Infobase Publishing.

Dyk, Walter, *Son of Old Man Hat*, University of Nebraska Press, Copyright 1938, Renewal Copyright 1966, First Bison Book Printing 1967.

Dyk, Walter and Ruth, *Left Handed A Navajo Autobiography*, Columbia University Press, New York, Copyright 1980.

Iverson, Peter, *Dine A History of The Navajos*, University of New Mexico Press, Copyright 2002.

Kelly, Lawrence, *Navajo Roundup Selected Correspondence of Kit Carson's Expedition Against the Navajo 1863-1865*, The Pruett Publishing Company, Copyright 1970.

McPherson, Robert S., *The Northern Navajo Frontier, 1860-1900: Expansion Through Adversity*, Dissertation Presented to the Department of History Brigham Young University, April, 1987.

McPherson, Robert S., *Stories From The Land A Navajo Reader about Monument Valley*, Independently Published, Copyright 2021.

Magoffin, Susan Shelby, *The Diary of Susan Shelby Magoffin, 1846-1847 Down the Santa Fe Trail and into Mexico*, University of Nebraska Press, Copyright 1926, 1962 by Yale University Press, August, 1982 Bison Books.

Sabin, Edwin L., *Kit Carson Days 1809-1868 Volume 1*, Originally Published: New York: Press of the Pioneers, 1935, University of Nebraska Press, Copyright 1995, First Bison Books Printing 1995.

Sabin, Edwin L., *Kit Carson Days 1809-1868 Volume 2*, Originally Published: New York: Press of the Pioneers, 1935, First Bison Books Printing 1995.

Sides, Hampton, *Blood and Thunder The Epic Story of Kit Carson and the Conquest of the American West,* Anchor Books, Copyright 2006.

Simpson, Lieutenant James H., *Navajo Expedition Journal of a Military Reconnaissance From Santa Fe, New Mexico To The Navajo Country Made in 1849*, University of Oklahoma Press, Norman, Copyright 1964.

Thompson, Gerald, *The Army And The Navajo The Bosque Redondo Reservation Experiment 1863-1868*, University of Arizona Press, Copyright 1976, Second Printing 1982.

297